WOMEN AND POWER IN AMERICAN HISTORY

WOMEN AND POWER IN AMERICAN HISTORY

Third Edition

Kathryn Kish Sklar
State University of New York at Binghamton

Thomas Dublin
State University of New York at Binghamton

Prentice Hall
Upper Saddle River, New Jersey 07458

Library of Congress Cataloging-in-Publication Data

Women and power in American history / [edited by] Kathryn Kish Sklar, Thomas Dublin.—3rd ed.
    p. cm.
  Includes bibliographical references.
  ISBN-13: 978-0-205-64575-6 (alk. paper)
  ISBN-10: 0-205-64575-5 (alk. paper)
  1. Women—United States—History. 2. Women—United States—Social conditions.
I. Sklar, Kathryn Kish. II. Dublin, Thomas

HQ1410.W643 2009
305.420973—vdc22

2008024749

Publisher: Charlyce Jones Owen
Editorial Assistant: Maureen Diana
Media Project Manager: Brian Hyland
Marketing Manager: Sue Westmoreland
Production Manager: Kathleen Sleys
Cover Design: Bruce Kenselaar
Cover Illustration/Photo: Schlesinger Library, Radcliffe Institute, Harvard University
Manager, Rights and Permissions: Zina Arabia
Manager, Cover Visual Research & Permissions: Karen Sanatar
Composition/Full-Service Project Management: GGS Book Services PMG/Karpagam Jagadeesan
Printer/Binder: RR Donnelley & Sons Company / Harrisonburg

Credits and acknowledgments borrowed from other sources and reproduced, with permission, in this textbook appear on page 342.

Pearson Education LTD., London
Pearson Education Singapore, Pte. Ltd
Pearson Education, Canada, Inc.
Pearson Education–Japan
Pearson Education Australia PTY, Limited

Pearson Education North Asia, Ltd., Hong Kong
Pearson Educación de Mexico, S.A. de C.V.
Pearson Education Malaysia, Pte. Ltd.
Pearson Education, Upper Saddle River, New Jersey

Prentice Hall
is an imprint of

www.pearsonhighered.com

10 9 8 7 6 5 4 3 2 1
ISBN-13: 978-0-20-564575-6
ISBN-10:   0-20-564575-5

CONTENTS

PREFACE TO THE THIRD EDITION

When we completed the first edition of *Women and Power in American History* in 1991, we commented on the phenomenal growth of the field of U.S. women's history over the previous two decades. Now, seventeen years later, the continuing vitality of the field is even more visible. Two major journals, the *Journal of Women's History* and *Gender and History*, are now almost two decades old and the Organization of American Historians has awarded a dissertation prize in U.S. women's history, the Lerner-Scott Award, for sixteen years. These markers of the field's strength were joined in 2004 by the appearance of an online journal/database/website, *Women and Social Movements in the United States, 1600–2000*, which publishes new scholarly work and full-text, indexed groups of primary sources. The number of graduate programs in U.S. women's history has expanded as universities have responded to the growing demand for faculty in the field. While initially a department of history typically had a faculty member in U.S. women's history and perhaps another in European women's history, today it is increasingly common to find several faculty members with interests in each of these fields, as well as other colleagues studying women or gender in Asia, Africa, or Latin America.

The continuing growth and development of scholarship in U.S. women's history has prompted us to prepare this third edition. Our goal remains the same as in 1991: to bring together a coherent group of articles related to the unifying theme of power in women's lives over time. This focus helped us consider new selections as we sorted through voluminous recent additions to scholarship in American women's history. Seven of the twenty-seven articles that we employ in this edition are new to the reader, reflecting the changing perspectives that have emerged in the field as it has matured. In addition, we have revised and expanded the selected bibliography and the listing of related links of resource materials in U.S. women's history on the World Wide Web (WWW). The dramatic growth of the WWW has been one of the signal changes in the academic world since the appearance of our second edition, and in history as well as in other disciplines, it offers rich new possibilities for research and teaching. We encourage users of *Women and Power* to draw on the wealth of primary sources that the WWW now provides for teaching in U.S. women's history.

U.S. women's history emerged as a specialized field of historical study partly in response to the resurgence of feminism beginning in the 1960s. In the women's movement, women addressed gender inequalities in the broader society and struggled against barriers to women's full participation in American society. To us as scholars it seems particularly appropriate to focus our readings in U.S. women's history on questions of women and power in American history. A greater understanding of how power inequalities are organized along gender lines can help us work toward a more egalitarian and just society. Because the work of the women's movement is far from complete, the need for a fuller historical understanding of how women's lives have changed over time remains great. We hope this new reader will contribute to greater understanding of continuing change in women's and men's lives.

Our thanks to Professors Mari Jo Buhle, Jane Gerhard, and Teresa Murphy for their suggestions for new articles for this new edition, and to Lisa Louk, Aaron Shaughnessy, and Corinne Weible of the State University of New York at Binghamton for helpful support as this project evolved.

Kathryn Kish Sklar
Thomas Dublin

ABOUT THE EDITORS

Kathryn Kish Sklar is Distinguished Professor of History and Codirector of the Center for the Historical Study of Women and Gender at the State University of New York at Binghamton. In 2005–2006 she served as the Harmsworth Professor of American History at the University of Oxford. She is the author of *Florence Kelley and the Nation's Work: The Rise of Women's Political Culture, 1830–1900* (1995), and other books and articles on women and social movements. Her first book, *Catharine Beecher: A Study in American Domesticity* (1973), analyzed how women reshaped gender identities and gender relationships in the antebellum era. She is currently completing a study of women and social movements in the Progressive Era, 1900–1930.

Thomas Dublin is Professor of History and Codirector of the Center for the Historical Study of Women and Gender at the State University of New York at Binghamton. He is the author or editor of seven books including *Women at Work: The Transformation of Work and Community in Lowell, Massachusetts, 1826–1860* (1979), winner of the Bancroft Prize and the Merle Curti Award. His latest book, *The Face of Decline: The Pennsylvania Anthracite Region in the Twentieth Century,* coauthored with Walter Licht, received the 2006 Merle Curti Award for Social History and the Philip S. Klein Prize.

CONTRIBUTORS

Xiaolan Bao was associate professor of history at California State University, Long Beach, where she taught Chinese and women's history. She wrote *Holding Up More Than Half the Sky: A History of Chinese Women Garment Workers in New York City, 1948–1992* as well as a number of articles about Chinese and Chinese-American women.

Janet Farrell Brodie is professor of history at Claremont Graduate University and the author of *Contraception and Abortion in Nineteenth-Century America.* Her current research project, *Cultures of Secrecy in Cold War Los Angeles*, explores popular reactions to nuclear weapons and the institutionalization of national security culture in the 1940s and 1950s.

Kathleen M. Brown is associate professor of history at the University of Pennsylvania, where she teaches the history of women and gender and early American history. She is currently working on a history of cleanliness in the United States before the Civil War.

Sucheng Chan is professor emerita of Asian American studies and global studies at the University of California, Santa Barbara. She is the author of more than twenty books and monographs in Asian American history and studies.

Ruth Feldstein is associate professor in the Department of History and the Graduate Program in American Studies at Rutgers University-Newark. She is the author of *Motherhood in Black and White: Race and Sex in American Liberalism, 1930–1965,* and is currently working on *Do What You Gotta Do: Black Women Entertainers and the Civil Rights Movement.*

Estelle Freedman, Edgar E. Robinson Professor of United States History at Stanford University, is the author of *Their Sisters' Keepers: Women's Prison Reform in America, 1830–1930* and *Maternal Justice: Miriam Van Waters and the Female Reform Tradition,* and coauthor of *Intimate Matters: A History of Sexuality in America.*

Glenda Elizabeth Gilmore, the Peter V. and C. Vann Woodward Professor of History at Yale University, teaches in the history, African American studies, and American studies departments. She is the author of the prize-winning book, *Gender and Jim Crow: Women and the Politics of White Supremacy in North Carolina, 1896–1920* and *Defying Dixie: The Radical Roots of Civil Rights, 1919-1950.*

Linda Gordon is professor of history at New York University. Her most recent book is *Impounded: Dorothea Lange and Japanese Americans in World War II.*

Virginia Meacham Gould is the author of *Chained to the Rock of Adversity: To Be Free, Black, and Female in the Old South* and, with Charles E. Nolan, *No Cross, No Crown: Black Nuns in Nineteenth Century New Orleans.* Her forthcoming book, *Piety in a Slave Society: The Life and Times of Henriette Delille,* is a biography of a free woman of African descent who founded a congregation of black nuns that worked with abandoned slave women in New Orleans.

Cynthia Harrison is associate professor of history and of women's studies at George Washington University, where she teaches courses on women's history and women and public policy. Her current work deals with the impact of the women's movement on federal policy concerning poor women.

María de la Luz Ibarra is associate professor in the Chicana and Chicano studies department at San Diego State University. She is the author of many articles on domestic labor, some of which appear in *Frontiers, Aztlan, Human Organization,* and *Urban Anthropology.*

Julie Ingersoll is associate professor of religious studies at the University of North Florida in Jacksonville, Florida. Her research and teaching focus on the relationship between religion, especially conservative American Protestantism, and American culture, and she is currently working on a book on the religious right.

Allan Kulikoff is the Abraham Baldwin Professor of the Humanities at the University of Georgia. His current work concerns the development of the yeoman classes in early America and he is author of *From British Peasants to Colonial American Farmers*.

Carol Lasser is professor of history at Oberlin College. She works in nineteenth-century American history and is currently researching the interracial history of Oberlin, Ohio.

Ruth Milkman is professor of sociology at the University of California, Los Angeles, and director of the UC Institute for Labor and Employment. Her most recent book is *L.A. Story: Immigrant Workers and the Future of the U.S. Labor Movement*.

Kathy Peiss teaches history at the University of Pennsylvania. She is the author of *Hope in a Jar: The Making of America's Beauty Culture* and *Cheap Amusements: Working Women and Leisure in Turn-of-the-Century New York*.

Glenda Riley is the Alexander M. Bracken Professor of History Emerita at Ball State University and a past president of the Western History Association. Her latest books are *Confronting Race: Women and Indians on the Frontier, 1815–1915* and the fourth edition of her textbook, *Inventing the American Woman: An Inclusive History*.

Deborah A. Rosen is a professor of history at Lafayette College. She is the author of *American Indians and State Law: Sovereignty, Race, and Citizenship, 1790–1880* and *Courts and Commerce: Gender, Law, and the Market Economy in Colonial New York*.

Helene Silverberg is an attorney practicing antitrust and intellectual property litigation in the San Francisco office of Morrison & Foerster. She previously taught American politics and women's studies at Princeton University and the University of California, Santa Barbara.

Christina Simmons teaches U.S. women's history and the history of sexuality at the University of Windsor, Windsor, Ontario. She is the author of "Women's Power in Sex Radical Challenges to Marriage in the Early Twentieth-Century United States," *Feminist Studies*.

Barbara Clark Smith studies forms of political participation in her position as curator in the Division of Politics and Reform at the National Museum of American History, Smithsonian Institution. She is most interested in eighteenth-century political history "close to the ground"—focusing on ways that ordinary women and men made their ideas of what was fair and right felt in their society.

Rosalyn Terborg-Penn is professor of history at Morgan State University in Baltimore, where she has also served as the coordinator of the African/Afro-American Studies Program and director of the history Ph.D. program. She is the author of numerous works on black women's history, including *African American Women in the Struggle for the Vote, 1850–1920*.

Introduction: Power as a Theme in Women's History

One of the biggest challenges facing historians of American women is the task of identifying the causes and consequences of long-term changes in women's lives. That task looms large not only because it is central to the historian's chief calling—analyzing change over time—but also because the turning points of historical change for women differ from those that have mattered most for men. When history is seen from the perspective of women's experience, new categories of analysis are clearly needed, since wars and other political events that have marked the standard historical divisions have usually been less important in the lives of average women than changes in family relationships, social movements, or the organization of the paid labor force. Thus, during its almost forty years of existence as an academic discipline, the field of U.S. women's history has focused more attention on women's family lives, their working lives, and their community activism than on the themes of power that pervade male-centered treatments of American history.

Yet the need to analyze change over time in U.S. women's history has grown more urgent as the field itself has grown. Its abundant diversity, embracing women of all classes, ethnicities, races, religions, sexual orientations, and regions, poses serious challenges as to how this diversity can be meaningfully synthesized into a coherent whole. In their search for unifying themes, historians of American women have found new uses for the most fundamental category of analysis known in the discipline of history—the study of social power, its components, causes, and consequences.

Power is a very useful means of depicting change in women's lives over time. First, it is a theme capable of linking changes in the three fundamental dimensions of women's lives—family, work, and community experiences. We know that changes in these three arenas of women's experience overlap and influence one another, but to understand that process we need tools of analysis that cut across all three. Themes relating to power do that effectively because they embrace personal relations of the sort found in family life as well as collective identities located in community activities and the workplace.

Second, power is a valuable theme for connecting women's history with other dimensions of American history. The field's effectiveness as an illuminator of all American history hinges on its use of a Promethean new category of historical analysis: gender as a principle of social organization. Since women can never be studied totally in isolation from men, gender relations are central to women's history, bringing with them the experience of men and their relations with women. In this context, power is a key category of analysis because it illuminates the relationships between men and women.

Third, power is a helpful vehicle for understanding relations among women of different social groups. Most differences among women are socially constructed. Differences of class, race, ethnicity, religion, sexual orientation, or region are generated by social structures. Although they might appear to be natural, they are created by social values and social institutions that reinforce social hierarchies and distribute power unevenly. Women's history needs to take account of differences among women and how social disparities translate into differences of power.

For these and other reasons, historians of women are increasingly using power as a leading category of analysis. This collection of writings in American women's history focuses centrally on themes of power in women's lives. It seeks to convey the diverse perspectives from which this theme can fruitfully be viewed, as well as the wide variety of female experiences the theme can integrate.

What do historians of women mean by "power"? The newness of the term's application to women can be seen in historians' tendency to leave the term undefined. Many dictionaries define power as the "possession of control, authority, or influence over others,"* yet an important aspect of women's power has been expressed in their ability to exercise control over their own bodies, to limit men's access to their sexuality, and to control their own reproductive lives. Therefore, from the perspective of women's history, a more suitable definition of power is the ability to control the distribution of social resources. Women's power has often rested in their ability to control the distribution of things or services rather than persons. Put another way, the essence of women's power has historically rested in their control of goods or services through which they frequently, albeit indirectly, have controlled persons. Women's economic and social power, for instance, among Algonquian-speaking Indians in Virginia, stemmed from their control of "cultivating and processing corn, which provided up to seventy-five percent" of Indians' consumption, according to Kathleen M. Brown in chapter 1.

Short introductions to each article in this collection provide a guide to how each historian analyzes themes of power. Less evident are the ways that women's power has changed over time. It is useful to identify four principles of change that have operated across four centuries of historical development, first in the American colonies and then in the United States.

The first principle concerns the interconnectedness of the major arenas of women's activities—family, work, and community life. Changes in one of these dimensions have invariably been linked to changes in the others. Thus, for example, changes in the working lives of New England women who constituted the first industrial workforce at textile mills in Lowell, Massachusetts, in the 1830s, were closely related to changes in women's family lives, in which young women experienced a period of independence from family life while living together in boardinghouses in Lowell, and changes in community life, in which Lowell women formed peer communities that supported their decision to strike in protest against reduced wages. How the causal arrows point within the triad of family, work, and community life depends upon the circumstances at any given moment, but those connections have been central to women's experience of change over time.

Another important principle is that change in female experience is often excruciatingly slow. Perhaps because gender constitutes one of the most fundamental forms of social organization—one upon which others are often built—changes in gender relations involve a multitude of other categories of change, and these, in turn, require their own set of causes, many of which are long in the making. The best example of such slow processes is the "demographic transition" between 1800 and 1950 from high birth and death rates to low birth and death rates (see Figure 1). This long-term decline was caused by factors so complex and pervasive that they continue to elude definitive historical analysis today. Women in all races, classes, and regions in the United States experienced this dramatic decline in birth rates between 1800 and 1950, which reduced from seven to two, the average number of children born to women who survived to the age of 50. Two-thirds of this decline occurred before 1880, before widespread use of artificial contraceptive techniques. The proportion of women who never married rose between 1870 and 1910 to a level only equaled in the 1990s. Relying mostly on withdrawal and sexual abstinence to lengthen the intervals between births, couples were aided by Victorian sexual values, which discouraged the expression of sexual desire and granted women unprecedented control over their own bodies. These values also exaggerated the

*Merriam-Webster's Tenth Collegiate Dictionary, online edition, accessed December 2007.

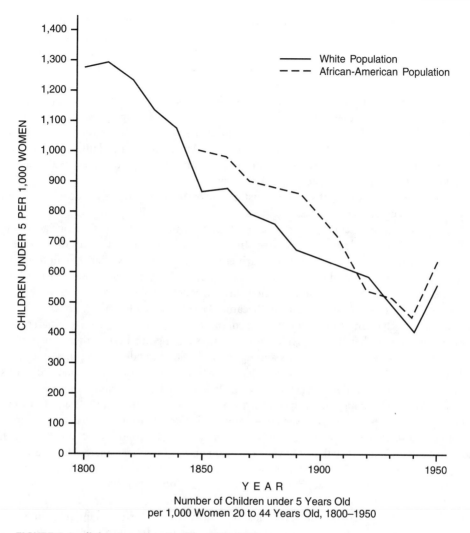

FIGURE 1 Declining American Fertility, 1800–1950

Source: Bureau of the Census, *Historical Statistics of the United States: Colonial Times to 1957* (Washington, D.C.: Government Printing Office, 1960), Series B37-68, p. 24.

differences between the sexes and treated women as morally superior to men. In this context, many women—married and unmarried—formed what historians have come to call "homosocial" relationships with other women.

Historians used to attribute the long-term decline in birth rates to industrialization and urbanization. However, recent research has shown that rural Americans accounted for most of that decline during its most intensive decades—the 1840s and 1850s. Historians also found that since birth rates began to decline before significant reduction in infant mortality (the chief contributor to high death rates), the decline in birth rates cannot be explained as due to declining death rates. Recently, historians have turned to even larger and more elusive causes, such as the growth of the market economy and its mirror image, the decline of subsistence agriculture. Historians now believe that the new valuation placed on each individual child was also important, along with religious beliefs that made human agency the cause of salvation. Since each of these and other components of fertility decline had its own chain of causes, fertility decline rested upon a pyramid of other historical changes. Taken together, they constituted an almost total transformation in American life, a transformation that took more than one hundred years to achieve.

Other, less complicated changes in women's lives also need to be measured by decades rather than years. For example, the women's rights movement—born during a speaking tour by Angelina and Sarah Grimké in Massachusetts in 1837, codified in Seneca Falls, New York, in 1848, and advocated by the National Woman Suffrage Association and American Woman Suffrage Association after 1869—took more than seventy years to achieve its goal of woman suffrage in 1920, making it the longest continuous social movement in U.S. history.

This does not mean that women's history lacks turning points or that it forms one long progression of achievement. Rather, it shows us that when turning points do occur, they usually involve multiple causes that have deep social roots and extend across more than one generation.

Another key principle of change over time in women's history involves differences among women. The social construction of dissimilarities among women may change, reflecting changing social, economic, or political structures. For example, the Virginia slave codes for the 1660s and 1670s created new inequalities among women when they defined slavery as a status derived from the mother: children of slave women thereby became slaves, while children of free women remained free. Conversely, changing social, political, or economic realities have also eroded differences among women. For example, heightened gender consciousness among northern white women in the early nineteenth century created new bonds among them that transcended differences of age, religious affiliation, and education. Differences and similarities among women are therefore constantly shifting, reflecting, and influencing changes in the larger society, polity, and economy.

Finally, and perhaps most importantly, women's agency—that is, their ability to influence changes in their lives and in their society—commands our attention as a crucial principle in the interpretation of change over time in women's history. No one proposition is more widely held in the field of women's history than the view that women have not been merely passive victims, but have played a part in shaping their historical destiny. No women were totally lacking in agency; even slave women made choices that enhanced their ability to control their life circumstances.

The extent to which women have been able to shape the circumstances of their lives has itself changed over time, offering us one of the most fruitful avenues of historical inquiry. For example, by comparing the activities of and expectations for Algonquian and English women in the first half of the seventeenth century with the reform activities of women in the antislavery movement in the 1830s and with the emergence of second-wave feminism in the 1960s, we are struck by the expansion of women's agency over the course of American history.

By viewing changes in women's agency over time we gain a clearer understanding of the other principles of change evident in women's history: the interrelationships among family, work, and community life; the tendency for changes in women's lives to reflect long-term, deeply rooted transformations; and the shifting relationships between different groups of women. For example, women's growing power in middle-class family life, as exemplified by Elizabeth Cady Stanton and Harriet Beecher Stowe, led many women to control the spacing of their pregnancies, which in turn facilitated their work as writers and leaders of social movements. As Stanton and Stowe show, the long-term change of fertility decline after 1800 empowered many women who chose abstinence in intimate negotiations with their husbands, especially in the decades before 1880, when fertility decline was most rapid. During those decades women also chose abortion as a means of controlling their reproductive lives, launching a debate that continued long after fertility decline was achieved (see Janet Farrell Brodie in chapter 11). Differences among women were dramatically visible on the frontier, where white women enhanced their ability to survive in the often hostile environment by befriending Indian women, turning those differences into an asset (see Glenda Riley in chapter 9).

The history of American women is a history of struggle. We can understand that struggle better by viewing the changing dimensions of power in women's lives.

*   *   *

These essays reveal dramatic changes in all areas of women's lives over more than four hundred years. Women's domestic lives and family experiences, their work beyond the immediate household, their expression of sexuality, and their political culture underwent profound transformation in the four centuries since the first permanent British settlement in North America. Affecting Native American, European-American, African-American, Asian-American, and Latino women in different ways, these changes dramatically altered women's experiences, their ability to control their life circumstances, and their access to social resources.

Relations between Native Americans and the first British settlers of North America were shaped by the differing domestic gender relations in each culture, as Kathleen M. Brown has shown in chapter 1 for colonial Virginia. Women in the Powhatan confederacy held greater responsibilities in Indian agriculture than was the case in English seventeenth-century society, and their economic importance was reflected in women's greater power through the matrilineal transmission of wealth and in community decision making. The English perception of Indian society as feminized contributed to their sense of superiority in relation to Native Americans, but Brown shows that they nevertheless incorporated elements of Indian gender systems in their own practices in the New World.

The Indian–European divide is only one of a number of bases for fruitful comparisons in thinking about women in North American colonial societies. In older historiography much has been made of Old World–New World differences in the status of women. In chapter 3, Deborah Rosen has gone a step further examining women's property rights in Spanish and British colonial cultures in an analysis that offers insight into the limitations of women's rights that stemmed from the British common law system.

Legal systems were typically conservative forces in social relations across gender lines, preserving older practices with the passage of time. In contrast, changing family relations contributed to significant change in the lives of European-American women over time. By the 1830s, alterations long under way in American family and economic life matured to produce a fundamental transformation in the power of white American women by assigning to mothers rather than fathers primary responsibility for shaping the character of children. This marked the beginning of the end of patriarchal family relations and a crucial turning point in the history of middle-class women. This shift contributed to the rise of women's Victorian domestic strategies, as Kathryn Kish Sklar has demonstrated in chapter 10. Other changes, such as those associated with evangelical religion and continental expansion, combined with these shifts in family relationships to redefine domestic life as the basis for women's claim to a voice in public affairs and their unprecedented participation in secular social movements. Thus, while women's domestic status could and did serve to limit their access to the larger world, it also launched them into that world and justified their assumption of special responsibilities in it.

Family life was just as critical to the historical experience of African-American women. Because tobacco, the chief commercial crop of the southern colonies before 1800, utilized the labor of women and children all year round, almost as many women as men were imported slaves. This produced a relatively equal "sex ratio"—the number of men per one hundred women—and, as Allan Kulikoff has shown in chapter 2, encouraged family formation in the decades immediately before and after 1700, but it placed a double burden on slave women. Since most plantations were relatively small, most slave marriages occurred across plantations, and mothers and children often did not live in the same household as their husbands and fathers. Thus, in addition to their work in tobacco, women carried the main responsibility for the welfare of their children. Nevertheless, slave families became a major source of resistance to the oppressions of slavery. Newspaper ads placed for runaway slaves before 1700 indicate that owners expected to find errant slaves in the woods; after 1700, runaways were thought to be harbored by family members on other plantations.

Chinese-American women reflected their community's difficulties in forging family ties during an era when the vast majority of Chinese immigrants were men who entered the country as contract laborers expecting to postpone family life until they returned to China. Federal policies discouraged the entry of Chinese women, as Sucheng Chan has shown in chapter 12, resulting in small numbers of Chinese women and a continuing high male–female ratio that limited family formation throughout the period of Chinese exclusion. In this context, prostitution remained a prominent form of female wage labor.

Differences among women across the span of American history were easily measured by differences in their working lives. The production of goods for market flourished among women in the northeast, where a diversified agricultural economy encouraged exchange at the local level. In the late eighteenth and early nineteenth centuries spinning and weaving were important aspects of northern women's household productivity. However, household production among southern white women was constricted by the dominance of tobacco as a cash crop. Tobacco profits discouraged female employment in the production of eggs, poultry, or butter, when their time could be more profitably employed in the production of tobacco. This created opportunities for African-American women, slave and free, who produced those and other goods for sale and exchange. After the Civil War and the abolition of slavery, African-American women spent less time in the fields working crops for commercial exchange and concentrated on gardening and other forms of household production. In urban areas, such as New Orleans, slave women were more frequently employed in domestic work and marketing than in field labor, as Virginia Meacham Gould has shown in chapter 7.

In the early nineteenth century, the emergence of factory employment for women in textiles and shoemaking in the New England and Middle Atlantic states opened up a major division among women of different social classes. Increasing numbers of rural women left the countryside for employment in Lowell and other mill towns, as Thomas Dublin has shown in chapter 5, where they were joined by recent immigrants and daughters of immigrants as the century progressed. Factory employment had a decidedly contradictory impact on working women in these decades. It offered greater social and economic independence to some young, single women, while binding others firmly within the limits of an emerging family wage economy.

The interconnections of the family, work, and community lives of women were nowhere so evident as in domestic service, the occupation that remained the single largest source of employment for women between 1800 and 1940. Offering ready employment to generations of urban immigrant women, but isolating them in individual homes where class differences between employer and employee were dramatically evident, domestic service was shunned by those whose class, race, or skills gave them access to other work. Still, as Carol Lasser has demonstrated in chapter 6, Irish domestic servants in Boston in the mid-nineteenth century had a measure of bargaining power in relation to their Yankee employers.

Between 1630 and 1870, community life tested the relative power of women and men. While men dominated in public activities in the daily operations of church and state, in periods of crisis, women made their presence felt. As Barbara Clark Smith has shown in chapter 4, women's responsibilities in food preparation made them active participants in the widespread food riots that accompanied the American Revolution. Other changes after the Revolution made women more significant players in the public sphere. With the separation of church and state after 1800 and the end of public support for ministerial salaries, religious revivals and new optimistic theologies reinvigorated the independent cultural power of churches and their laity. Since the majority of the laity were women, many ministers developed new respect for them, and encouraged women to seek greater social influence. Women's empowerment within revitalized Protestantism fueled their participation in two social movements— one directed against slavery (see chapter 9), one against prostitution—and fostered the birth of the woman suffrage movement at a conference held at Seneca Falls, New York, in 1848.

In the twentieth century, growing labor force participation served as the most important engine of change, bringing new forms of power into women's lives. Before 1900, the vast majority of women wage earners were young and unmarried. This meant that they faced enormous difficulties in engaging in collective action to improve their working conditions. Scholars like Ruth Milkman (included here in chapter 21) have analyzed the process by which women have become permanent wage workers, part of a shift from earlier practice in which working women were distinguished from working men by their youth and temporary status in the waged labor force. Accompanying these demographic and life-cycle changes among women in the paid labor force, during the Depression and World War II periods, women increasingly came to be represented by trade unions in the collective bargaining process.

Crowding is a key concept that historians and sociologists have used to describe women's waged work and the powerlessness that has persistently accompanied it. Despite many significant changes in women's labor force participation between 1870 and 2000, the crowding of most women workers into relatively few sex-segregated occupations has not changed. A majority of wage-earning women in 1990 worked in occupations that were more than 75 percent female. Crowding has meant that women strenuously competed against one another for the few jobs available to them. It has rendered their skills less meaningful and has kept their wages low.

The crowding of women into limited occupational categories has been exacerbated by the impact of ethnicity on employment opportunities. For many African-American women, sex-segregated work has also been race segregated. For example, although the proportion of women who worked as household servants declined dramatically between 1900 and 1940, the proportion of wage-earning black women who worked as servants actually increased because their exclusion from manufacturing jobs crowded them into domestic service. This pattern eased somewhat in the second half of the twentieth century, but largely by the displacement of African-American women from domestic service and hotel work by recent immigrant women, especially from Mexico and Central America. The Mexican domestic workers in Santa Barbara interviewed by Maria de la Luz Ibarra (and discussed in chapter 26) are good examples of the new service workers recruited from this steady migration stream. While the specific identities of low-paid women workers have changed, the historic gender and ethnic segregation of the nation's workforce has changed very little in the past half century (on this pattern in the post-World War II period in New York's Chinatown, see Xiaolan Bao in chapter 22).

While many issues related to women's exploitation in the paid labor force remain, there is no doubt about the single most visible change in women's labor force participation in the twentieth century: the considerable increase in the proportion of women who work for wages. World War II is often seen as a turning point in the history of women's waged labor, but as Ruth Milkman's essay in chapter 21 argues, women's work experience remained sex-segregated even under those unusual conditions. As Figure 2 demonstrates, the most important change in women's labor force participation in the twentieth century has been the increasing proportion of women working for wages regardless of their age or marital status.

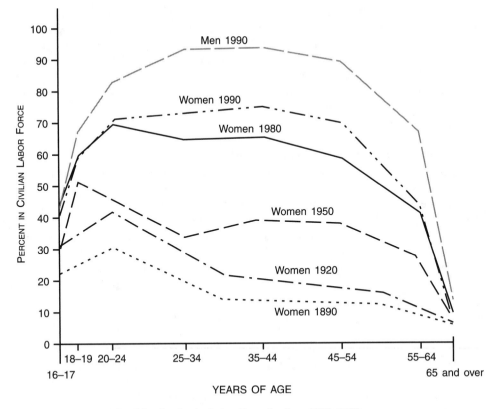

FIGURE 2 Women's Participation in the Labor Force by Age, 1890–1990

Sources: Historical Statistics of the United States: Colonial Times to 1970, Part 1. Bureau of the Census. U.S. Department of Commerce, 1975. "Employment and Earnings," Bureau of Labor Statistics, U.S. Department of Labor, January 1981. Adapted from Nancy Woloch, *Women and the American Experience*, 3rd ed. (Boston: McGraw-Hill, 2000), 609.

Have these increases in women's wage-earning activities significantly enhanced women's ability to control their life circumstances? For many women the answer to this question is no; wage-earning work has merely absorbed them into the same unrewarding routine that men have long known, the chief difference being that they now do two jobs: one at the workplace, one in the home. Nonetheless, women's increased earnings have laid the foundation for new sorts of power in their lives, flowing from their dramatically greater ability to contribute to their own and their family's support.

Important changes in women's family and sexual experience preceded this rapid rise in their labor force participation. While the 1960s and 1970s witnessed transforming changes in the proportion of women who worked outside the home, the 1920s introduced thoroughgoing and enduring changes into women's family and sexual lives. The first and most obvious of these might be called the "mandatory heterosexuality" associated with the final decades of the demographic transition. Whereas Victorian sexual practices relied on sexual abstinence to achieve dramatic reduction in birth rates between 1800 and 1920, after 1920 the widespread use of artificial contraceptive techniques, especially condoms, made abstinence seem old-fashioned. In chapter 20, Christina Simmons describes how the new sexual expressiveness of the 1920s pathologized the close affective ties among women that the Victorian era had encouraged, and promoted instead a new form of companionate marriage between men and women.

Kathy Peiss argues in chapter 16 that the heterosexual leisure culture of turn-of-the-century working-class women placed them in the vanguard of changing sexual mores. All that remained to make this change complete was the wider access to birth control techniques described in chapter 18 by Linda Gordon, who analyzes the strong support Margaret Sanger drew from middle-class women, who by the 1920s relied on artificial birth control techniques to limit their fertility. These three articles demonstrate the importance of women's actions in defining their own reproductive lives. They also illustrate some of the forces opposed to these actions. Ultimately, they show that this "personal" issue is also political.

Margaret Sanger was one of a multitude of women reformers who exemplified the power of women's political culture, which arose from women's separate institutions between 1870 and 1930, analyzed so thoughtfully by Estelle Freedman in chapter 13 of this collection. Launched in the ante-bellum era, women's political culture was energized through women's service in the Civil War. Many new institutions—the women's club movement, the Woman's Christian Temperance Union (see Glenda Elizabeth Gilmore in chapter 14), and the social settlement movement (see Kathryn Kish Sklar in chapter 15), to name only a few—emerged in the decades after 1870 to create the social space within which women attempted to bridge racial, class, and regional differences; train women leaders; and articulate women's issues. Forces promoting the extension of women's political culture embraced black as well as white women and extended into rural as well as urban areas. Nevertheless, the success of women's separate institutions can only partly be explained by women's triumphant mobilization in these decades. Equally important were the opportunities open to women in the U.S. political domain. Many of these opportunities were created by traditions of limited government that empowered the voluntary sector in which women played so important a part. For example, the U.S. Sanitary Commission during and after the Civil War empowered women in positions that in Europe were occupied by male bureaucrats. Under the Sanitary Commission, women held important positions in the administrations of hospital care and the awarding of widows' and other forms of war pensions.

Other gaps engendered by traditions of limited government became more apparent as American society underwent rapid industrialization and urbanization after 1880. In addition to its work for prohibition, the Woman's Christian Temperance Union offered shelter, food, and medical care to needy urban women, men, and children. Women on state charity boards urged more attention to the problems of the poor, and the social settlement movement found new ways to advocate the redistribution of social resources to meet the needs of working-class people. Not surprisingly in this context, the woman's suffrage movement justified its goals in social justice terms—women voters would end political corruption, reorient public policy, and eliminate social injustice.

While women's political culture depended upon coalition building, women's assumptions about gender-based solidarity were often disappointed by the persistence of class, ethnic, and racial distinctions within their political cultures. Viewed positively, these distinctions promoted women's collective action, thus efforts to unionize Jewish women garment workers expressed an ethnic view of social justice. Likewise, the political culture of African-American women was rooted in their distinctive experience of the social construction of race in the United States. Yet, as Rosalyn Terborg-Penn shows in chapter 17, white women's political culture often buttressed social distinctions that discriminated against black women. The Nineteenth Amendment did not bring suffrage to black women as readily as it did to white—especially in regions where black men did not vote. By accepting that outcome, the white-dominated suffrage movement reinforced the barriers between itself and black women's political culture. Not until the civil rights movement of the 1960s were those barriers significantly eroded, a process in which black women were central, even though they did not occupy the most visible leadership positions. As Ruth Feldstein's treatment of Nine Simone in chapter 23 demonstrates, women also participated in the reorientation of black activism with the emergence of black power out of the civil rights movement.

Just as a multitude of causes led to the empowerment of white women's political culture in the early nineteenth century, a confluence of many causes eroded its power in the 1920s. The dispute over whether to pursue strategies for women's advancement based on women's differences from men or on their similarities to men, dividing feminists in the debate over the Equal Rights Amendment (ERA) between the early 1920s and 1970, seriously debilitated the women's movement during the interwar years (see Kathryn Kish Sklar in chapter 19).

The reemergence of feminism in the 1960s built on four decades of growing equality between the sexes, as illustrated by women's labor force participation rates, their place in family life, and their sexual identity. As a result, the new feminists championed gender similarity rather than difference as the mode by which they advanced women's interests. A telling landmark in this shift was the endorsement of the ERA by women members of the United Automobile Workers and by the U.S. Women's Bureau in 1972, developments that extend the story told in chapter 24 by Cynthia Harrison.

The demands of the organized women's movement have been counterbalanced by traditions of limited government that have profoundly shaped public policy pertaining to women in the United States. During the half century of industrial transformation between 1880 and 1930, traditions of limited government generated unprecedented opportunities for women's voluntarism, which by 1920 meant that many social welfare and social justice policies that we take for granted today, such as the minimum wage, were initiated by women for women. In the early twenty-first century, traditions of limited government still shape the relationship between women and public policy in ways that often go unnoticed. In chapter 25, Helene Silverberg analyzes the effects of such traditions on American policy debates about women's access to abortion services, arguing that limited health care provision in the United States compared to European countries is one reason why that debate is so virulent in the United States and why women's access to abortion services is diminishing despite the legality of such services.

The abortion debate reflects as well a broader backlash that has accompanied the equal rights revolution since the emergence of second-wave feminism in the mid-1960s. The evangelical right has become, in the past thirty years, a strong factor in contemporary American politics and a counterweight to a resurgent feminism. Even while evangelicalism contested second-wave feminism, some women evangelicals sought biblical sources for their call for women's equality, as shown in chapter 27 by Julie Ingersoll, providing evidence of the influence of feminism in every corner of American society at the turn of the twenty-first century.

Viewed from the perspective of American history as a whole, these essays reveal the history of women as an integral part of the national story. They support the notion that women's power has evolved in a complex process of interaction within their families, their work, and their communities. They present us with different groups of women holding different degrees of power, differences that have played critical roles in the broader development of American history. Yet they also show that important aspects of women's experience resonate across the differences among them.

Chapter 1

The Anglo-Algonquian Gender Frontier

Kathleen M. Brown

Recent scholarship on first European contact and settlement in North America has illuminated the cultural differences between and mutual influences of European Americans and Native Americans. Offering a case study of English–Indian relations along the Chesapeake Bay in the seventeenth century, Kathleen M. Brown shows in this essay how gender differences were an important element in those early interactions. As Brown writes, "The gendering of Anglo–Indian relations in English writing was not without contest and contradiction . . . nor did it lead inevitably to easy conclusions of English dominance." Ultimately, she demonstrates the ways that the gender beliefs and structures of each group influenced their interaction and how, in turn, that interaction influenced each group's gender perspectives.

Recent scholarship has improved our understanding of the relationship between English settlers and Indians during the early seventeenth century. We know, for instance, that English expectations about American Indians were conditioned by Spanish conquest literature, their own contact with the Gaelic Irish, elite perceptions of the lower classes, and obligations to bring Christianity to those they believed to be in darkness.[1]

Largely unacknowledged by historians, gender roles and identities also played an important role in shaping English and Indian interactions. Accompanied by few English women, English male adventurers to Roanoake and Jamestown island confronted Indian men and women in their native land. In this cultural encounter, the gender ways, or what some feminist theorists might call the "performances," of Virginia Algonquians challenged English gentlemen's assumptions about the naturalness of their own gender identities. This interaction brought exchanges, new cultural forms, created sites of commonality, painful deceptions, bitter misunderstandings, and bloody conflicts.[2]

Identities as English or Indian were only partially formed at the beginning of this meeting of cultures; it required the daily presence of an "other" to crystalize self-conscious articulations of group identity. In contrast, maleness and femaleness within each culture provided explicit and deep-rooted foundations for individual identity and the organization of social relations. In both Indian and English societies, differences between men and women were critical to social order. Ethnic identities formed along this "gender frontier," the site of creative and destructive processes resulting from the confrontations of culturally-specific manhoods and womanhoods. In the emerging Anglo-Indian struggle, gender symbols and social relations signified claims to power. Never an absolute barrier, however, the gender frontier also produced sources for new identities and social practices.[3]

In this essay, I explore in two ways the gender frontier that evolved between English settlers and the indigenous peoples of Virginia's tidewater. First, I assess how differences in gender roles

Kathleen Brown, "The Anglo-Algonquian Gender Frontier," pp. 24–48 in *Negotiators of Change: Historical Perspectives on Native American Women,* ed. By Nancy Shoemaker (New York: Routledge, 1995).

shaped the perceptions and interactions of both groups. Second, I analyze the "gendering" of the emerging Anglo–Indian power struggle. While the English depicted themselves as warriors dominating a feminized native population, Indian women and men initially refused to acknowledge claims to military supremacy, treating the foreigners as they would subject peoples, cowards, or servants. When English warrior discourse became unavoidable, however, Indian women and men attempted to exploit what they saw as the warrior's obvious dependence upon others for the agricultural and reproductive services that ensured group survival.

The indigenous peoples who engaged in this struggle were residents of Virginia's coastal plain, a region of fields, forests, and winding rivers that extended from the shores of the Chesapeake Bay to the mountains and waterfalls near present-day Richmond. Many were affiliated with Powhatan, the *werowance* who had consolidated several distinct groups under his influence at the time of contact with the English.[4] . . . Although culturally diverse, tidewater inhabitants shared certain features of social organization, commonalities that may have become more pronounced with Powhatan's ambitious chiefdom-building and the arrival of the English.

*   *   *

Of the various relationships constituting social order in England, those between men and women were among the most contested at the time the English set sail for Virginia in 1607. Accompanied by few women before 1620, male settlers left behind a pamphlet debate about the nature of the sexes and a rising concern about the activities of disorderly women. The gender hierarchy the English viewed as "natural" and "God-given" was in fact fraying at the edges. Male pamphleteers argued vigorously for male dominance over women as crucial to maintaining orderly households and communities. . . . By the late sixteenth century, as English attempts to subdue Ireland became increasingly violent and as hopes for a profitable West African trade dimmed, gender figured increasingly in English colonial discourses.[5]

English gender differences manifested themselves in primary responsibilities and arenas of activity, relationships to property, ideals for conduct, and social identities. Using plow agriculture, rural Englishmen cultivated grain while women oversaw household production, including gardening, dairying, brewing, and spinning. Women also constituted a flexible reserve labor force, performing agricultural work when demand for labor was high, as at harvest time. While Englishmen's property ownership formed the basis of their political existence and identity, most women did not own property until they were no longer subject to a father or husband.[6]

By the early seventeenth century, advice-book authors enjoined English women to concern themselves with the conservation of estates rather than with production. Women were also advised to maintain a modest demeanor. Publicly punishing shrewish and sexually aggressive women, communities enforced this standard of wifely submission as ideal and of wifely domination as intolerable.[7] The sexual activity of poor and unmarried women proved particularly threatening to community order; these "nasty wenches" provided pamphleteers with a foil for the "good wives" female readers were urged to emulate.[8]

How did one know an English good wife when one saw one? Her body and head would be modestly covered. The tools of her work, such as the skimming ladle used in dairying, the distaff of the spinning wheel, and the butter churn reflected her domestic production. When affixed to a man, as in community-initiated shaming rituals, these gender symbols communicated his fall from "natural" dominance and his wife's unnatural authority over him.[9]

Advice-book authors described man's "natural" domain as one of authority derived from his primary economic role. A man's economic assertiveness, mirrored in his authority over wife, child and servant, was emblematized by the plow's penetration of the earth, the master craftsman's ability to shape his raw materials, and the rider's ability to subdue his horse. Although hunting and fishing supplemented the incomes of many Englishmen, formal group hunts—occasions in which associations with manual labor and economic gain had been carefully erased—remained the preserve of the aristocracy and upper gentry.

The divide between men's and women's activities described by sixteenth- and seventeenth-century authors did not capture the flexibility of gender relations in most English communities. Beliefs in male authority over women and in the primacy of men's economic activities sustained a perception of social order even as women marketed butter, cheese, and ale and cuckolded unlucky husbands.

*   *   *

Gender roles and identities were also important to the Algonquian speakers whom the English encountered along the three major tributaries of the Chesapeake Bay. Like indigenous peoples throughout the Americas, Virginia Algonquians invoked a divine division of labor to explain and justify differences between men's and women's roles on earth. A virile warrior god and a congenial female hostess provided divine examples for the work appropriate to human men and women.[10] Indian women's labor centered on cultivating and processing corn, which provided up to seventy-five percent of the calories consumed by residents of the coastal plain.[11] Women also grew squash, peas, and beans, fashioned bedding, baskets, and domestic tools, and turned animal skins into clothing and household items. They may even have built the houses of semi-permanent summer villages and itinerant winter camps. Bearing and raising children and mourning the dead rounded out the range of female duties. All were spiritually united by life-giving and its association with earth and agricultural production, sexuality and reproduction. Lineage wealth and political power passed through the female line, perhaps because of women's crucial role in producing and maintaining property. Among certain peoples, women may also have had the power to determine the fate of captives, the nugget of truth in the much-embellished tale of Pocahontas's intervention on behalf of Captain John Smith.[12]

Indian women were responsible not only for reproducing the traditional features of their culture, but for much of its adaptive capacity as well. As agriculturalists, women must have had great influence over decisions to move to new grounds, to leave old grounds fallow, and to initiate planting. As producers and consumers of vital household goods and implements, women may have been among the first to feel the impact of new technologies, commodities, and trade. And as accumulators of lineage property, Indian women may have been forced to change strategies as subsistence opportunities shifted.

Indian men assumed a range of responsibilities that complemented those of women. Men cleared new planting grounds by cutting trees and burning stumps. They fished and hunted for game, providing highly valued protein. After the last corn harvest, whole villages traveled with their hunters to provide support services throughout the winter. Men's pursuit of game shaped the rhythms of village life during these cold months, just as women's cultivation of crops determined feasts and the allocation of labor during the late spring and summer. By ritually separating themselves from women through sexual abstinence, hunters periodically became warriors, taking revenge for killings or initiating their own raids. This adult leave-taking rearticulated the *huskanaw*, the coming of age ritual in which young boys left their mothers' homes to become men.[13]

Men's hunting and fighting roles were associated with life-taking, with its ironic relationship to the life-sustaining acts of procreation, protection, and provision. Earth and corn symbolized women, but the weapons of the hunt, the trophies taken from the hunted, and the predators of the animal world represented men. The ritual use of *pocones,* a red dye, also reflected this gender division. Women anointed their bodies with *pocones* before sexual encounters and ceremonies celebrating the harvest, while men wore it during hunting, warfare, or at the ritual celebrations of successes in these endeavors.[14]

The exigencies of the winter hunt, the value placed on meat, and intermittent warfare among native peoples may have been the foundation of male dominance in politics and religious matters.

Women were not without their bases of power in Algonquian society, however; their important roles as agriculturalists, reproducers of Indian culture, and caretakers of lineage property kept gender relations in rough balance. . . . By no means equal to men, whose political and religious decisions directed village life, Indian women were perhaps more powerful in their subordination than English women.[15]

Even before the English sailed up the river they renamed the James, however, Indian women's power may have been waning, eroded by Powhatan's chiefdom-building tactics. During the last quarter of the sixteenth century, perhaps as a consequence of early Spanish forays into the region, he began to add to his inherited chiefdom, coercing and manipulating other coastal residents into economic and military alliances. . . . With the arrival of the English, the value of male warfare and the symbolism of corn as tribute only intensified, further strengthening the patriarchal tendencies of Powhatan's people.[16]

*   *   *

Almost every writer described the land west and south of Chesapeake Bay as an unspoiled "New World."[17] Small plots of cultivated land, burned forest undergrowth, and seasonal residence patterns often escaped the notice of English travelers habituated to landscapes shaped by plow agriculture and permanent settlement. . . .

Conquest seemed justifiable to many English because Native Americans had failed to tame the wilderness according to English standards. Writers claimed they found "only an idle, improvident, scattered people . . . careless of anything but from hand to mouth."[18] . . . The seasonal migration of native groups and the corresponding shift in diet indicated to the English a lack of mastery over the environment, reminding them of animals.

The English derision of Indian dependence on the environment and the comparison to animals . . . also contained implicit gender meanings. Women's bodies, for example, showed great alteration during pregnancy from fat to lean, strong to weak. English authors often compared female sexual appetites and insubordination to those of wild animals in need of taming. Implicit in all these commentaries was a critique of indigenous men for failing to fulfill the responsibility of economic provision with which the English believed all men to be charged. Lacking private property in the English sense, Indian men, like the Gaelic Irish before them, appeared to the English to be feminine and not yet civilized to manliness.[19]

For many English observers, natives' "failure" to develop an agricultural economy or dense population was rooted in their gender division of labor. Women's primary responsibility for agriculture merely confirmed the abdication by men of their proper role and explained the "inferiority" of native economies in a land of plenty. Smith commented that "the land is not populous, for the men be fewe; their far greater number is of women and children," a pattern he attributed to inadequate cultivation.[20] . . .

English commentators reacted with disapproval to seeing women perform work relegated to laboring men in England while Indian men pursued activities associated with the English aristocracy. Indian women, George Percy claimed, "doe all their drugerie. The men takes their pleasure in hunting and their warres, which they are in continually."[21] . . .

The English were both fascinated and disturbed by other aspects of Native American society through which gender identities were communicated, including hairstyle, dress and make-up. The native male fashion of going clean-shaven, for example, clashed with English associations of beards with male maturity, perhaps diminishing Indian men's claims to manhood in the eyes of the English. . . . It probably did not enhance English respect for Indian manhood that female barbers sheared men's facial hair.[22]

Most English writers found it difficult to distinguish between the sexual behavior of Chesapeake dwellers and what they viewed as sexual potency conveyed through dress and ritual. English male explorers were particularly fascinated by indigenous women's attire, which seemed scanty and immodest compared to English women's multiple layers and wraps. John Smith described an entertainment arranged for him in which "30 young women came naked out of the woods (only covered behind and before with a few greene leaves), their bodies al painted."[23] . . .

For most English writers, Indian manners and customs reinforced an impression of sexual passion. Hospitality that included sexual privileges, for instance, sending "a woman fresh painted red with *Pocones* and oile" to be the "bedfellow" of a guest, may have confirmed in the minds of English men the reading of Indian folkways as sexually provocative. Smith's experience with the thirty women, clad in leaves, body paint, and buck's horns and emitting, "hellish cries and shouts," undoubtedly strengthened the English association of Indian culture with unbridled passion. . . . These and other Indian gender ways left the English with a vivid impression of unconstrained sexuality that in their own culture could mean only promiscuity.

The stark contrast between Indian military techniques and formal European land stratagems reinforced English judgements that indigenous peoples were animalistic by nature.[24] George Percy's description of one skirmish invoked a comparison to the movement of animals: "At night, when we were going aboard, there came the Savages creeping upon all foure, from the Hills, like Beares, with their Bowes in their mouthes."[25] While writers regaled English readers with tales of Indian men in hasty retreat from English guns, thus reconfirming for the reader the female vulnerability of Indians and the superior weaponry of the English, they also recounted terrifying battle scenes such as the mock war staged for the entertainment of John Smith, which included "horrible shouts and screeches, as though so many infernall helhounds could not have made them more terrible."[26]

Although the dominant strand of English discourse about Indian men denounced them for being savage and failed providers, not all Englishmen shared these assessments of the meaning of cultural differences. Throughout the early years of settlement, male laborers deserted military compounds to escape puny rations, disease and harsh discipline, preferring to take their chances with local Indians whom they knew had food aplenty. . . . a lurking and disquieting suspicion that Indian men were like the English disrupted discourses about natural savagery and inferiority. John Smith often explained Indian complexions and resistance to the elements as a result of conditioning and daily practice rather than of nature.[27] Despite the flamboyant rhetoric about savage warriors lurking in the forests like animals, Smith soon had Englishmen learning to fight in the woods.[28] He clearly thought his manly English, many of whom could barely shoot a gun, had much to learn from their Indian opponents.

Most English did not dwell on these areas of similarity and exchange, however, but emphasized the "wild" and animalistic qualities of tidewater peoples. English claims to dominance and superiority rested upon constructions of Indian behavior as barbaric. . . . Through depictions of feminized male "naturalls," Englishmen reworked Anglo–Indian relations to fit the "natural" dominance of men in gender relations. In the process, they contributed to an emerging male colonial identity that was deeply rooted in English gender discourses.

The gendering of Anglo–Indian relations in English writing was not without contest and contradiction, however, nor did it lead inevitably to easy conclusions of English dominance. Englishmen incorporated Indian ways into their diets and military tactics, and Indian women into their sexual lives. Some formed close bonds with Indian companions, while others lived to father their own "naturall" progeny. As John Rolfe's anguish over his marriage to Pocahontas attested, colonial domination was a complex process involving sexual intimacy, cultural incorporation and self-scrutiny.[29]

* * *

The Englishmen who landed on the shores of Chesapeake Bay and the James River were not the first European men that Virginia Algonquians had seen. During the 1570s, Spanish Jesuits established a short-lived mission near the James River tributary that folded with the murder of the clerics.

The Spaniards who revenged the Jesuit deaths left an unfavorable impression upon local Chickahominy, Paspegh, and Kecoughtan Indians. . . .

The maleness of English explorers' parties and early settlements undoubtedly raised Indian suspicions of bellicose motives. Interrogating Smith at their first meeting about the purpose of the English voyage, Powhatan was apparently satisfied with Smith's answer that the English presence was temporary. Smith claimed his men sought passage to "the backe Sea," the ever-elusive water route to India which they believed lay beyond the falls of the Chesapeake river system. . . .

Frequent English military drills in the woods and the construction of a fort at Jamestown, however, may have aroused his suspicions that the English strangers planned a longer and more violent stay.[30]

Equipped with impressive blasting guns, the English may have found it easy to perpetuate the warrior image from afar; up close was a different matter, however. English men were pale, hairy, and awkward compared to Indian men. They also had the dirty habit of letting facial hair grow so that it obscured the bottom part of their faces where it collected food and other debris. Their clumsy stomping through the woods announced their presence to friends, enemies, and wildlife alike and they were forced, on at least one very public occasion, to ask for Indian assistance when their boats became mired in river ooze. Perhaps worst of all from the perspective of Indian people who valued a warrior's stoicism in the face of death, the Englishmen they captured and killed died screaming and whimpering. William Strachey recorded the mocking song sung by Indian men sometime in 1611, in which they ridiculed "what lamentation our people made when they kild him, namely saying how they [the Englishmen] would cry whe, whe."[31]

Indian assumptions about masculinity may have led Powhatan to overestimate the vulnerability of Smith's men. The gentlemen and artisans who were the first to arrive in Virginia proved to be dismal farmers, remaining wholly dependent upon native corn stores during their first three years and partially dependent thereafter. They tried, futilely, to persuade Indians to grow more corn to meet their needs, but their requests were greeted with scorn by Indian men who found no glory in the "woman-like exercise" of farming. . . .

When Powhatan and other Indian peoples reminded Smith of his dependence upon Indian food supplies, Smith reacted with anger. In his first account of Virginia, he recalled with bitterness the scorn of the Kecoughtan Indians for "a famished man": they "would in derision offer him a handfull of Corne, a peece of bread."[32] Such treatment signified both indigence and female vulnerability to the English, made worse by the fact that the crops they needed were grown by women. At Kecoughtan, Smith responded by "let[ting] fly his muskets" to provoke a Kecoughtan retreat and then killing several men at close range. . . . The English thus used their superior weaponry to transform themselves from scorned men into respected warriors and to recast the relationship: humble agriculturists became duty-bound to produce for those who spared their lives.[33]

Powhatan's interactions with Englishmen may also have been guided by his assessment of the gender imbalance among them. His provision of women to entertain English male guests was a political gesture whose message seems to have been misunderstood as sexual license by the English.[34] Smith, for example, believed the generosity stemmed from Powhatan's having "as many women as he will," and thereby growing occasionally "weary of his women."[35] By voluntarily sharing his wealth in women and thus communicating his benign intent, Powhatan invoked what he may have believed to be a transcendent male political bond, defined by men's common relationship to women.[36] Powhatan may also have believed that by encouraging English warriors' sexual activity, he might diminish their military potency. It was the fear of this loss of power, after all, that motivated Indian warriors' ritual abstinence before combat. Ultimately, Powhatan may have hoped that intimacy between native women and English men would lead to an integration of the foreigners and a diffusion of the threat they presented. Lacking women with whom to reciprocate and unfettered by matrilineage ties, the English, Powhatan may have reasoned, might be rapidly brought into alliance. Powhatan's gesture, however, only reinforced the English rationale for subjugating the "uncivilized" and offered English men an opportunity to express the Anglo–Indian power relationship sexually with native women.[37]

Indian women were often more successful than Powhatan in manipulating Englishmen's desires for sexual intimacy. At the James River village of Appocant in late 1607, the unfortunate George Cawson met his death when village women "enticed [him] up from the barge into their howses."[38] Oppossunoquonuske, a clever *werowansqua* of another village, similarly led fourteen Englishmen to their demise. Inviting the unwary men to come "up into her Towne, to feast and make Merry," she convinced them to "leave their Armes in their boat, because they said how their women would be afrayd ells of their pieces."[39]

Although both of these accounts are cautionary tales that represent Indians literally as feminine seducers capable of entrapping Englishmen in the web of their own sexual desires, the incidents suggest Indian women's canny assessment of the men who would be colonial conquerors. Exploiting Englishmen's hopes for colonial pleasures, Indian women dangled before them the opportunity for sexual intimacy, turning a female tradition of sexual hospitality into a weapon of war. . . .

Feigned sexual interest in Englishmen was not the only tactic available to Indian women. Some women clearly wanted nothing to do with the English strangers and avoided all contact with them. When John Smith traveled to Tappahannock in late 1607, for example, Indian women fled their homes in fear.[40] Other Indian women treated the English not as revered guests, to be gently wooed into Indian ways or seduced into fatal traps, but as lowly servants. . . .

In addition to violence and manipulations of economic dependence and sexual desire, Algonquians tried to maneuver the English into positions of political subordination. Smith's account of his captivity, near-execution, and rescue by Pocahontas was undoubtedly part of an adoption ritual in which Powhatan defined his relationship to Smith as one of patriarchal dominance. Smith became Powhatan's prisoner after warriors easily slew his English companions and then "missed" with nearly all of the twenty or thirty arrows they aimed at Smith himself. Clearly, Powhatan wanted Smith brought to him alive. Smith reported that during his captivity he was offered "life, libertie, land and women," prizes Powhatan must have believed to be very attractive to Englishmen, in exchange for information about how best to capture Jamestown.[41] After ceremonies and consultations with priests, Powhatan brought Smith before an assembly where, according to Smith, Pocahontas risked her own life to prevent him from being clubbed to death by executioners. It seems that Smith understood neither the ritual adoption taking place nor the significance of Powhatan's promise to make him a *werowance* and to "for ever esteeme him as [he did] his son Nantaquoud."[42]

*   *   *

Over the next weeks and months the two men wrangled over the construction of their short-lived alliance and the meaning of Powhatan's promises to supply the English with corn. . . . Smith and Powhatan continued to do a subtle two-step over the meaning of the corn. Was it tribute coerced by the militarily superior English? Or was it a sign of a father's compassion for a subordinate *werowance* and his hungry people? Powhatan made clear to Smith that he understood the extent of the English dependence upon his people for corn. . . . He also appreciated the degree to which the English could make him miserable if they did not get what they wanted. . . .

Ultimately, Powhatan attempted to represent his conflict with Smith as the clash of an older, wiser authority with a young upstart. "I knowe the difference of peace and warre, better then any in my Countrie," he reminded Smith, his paternal self-depiction contrasting sharply with what he labeled

Smith's youthful and "rash unadvisednesse." Displeased with this rendering of their relationship with its suggestion of childish inexperience, Smith reasserted the English warrior personae with a vengeance. He informed Powhatan that "for your sake only, wee have curbed our thirsting desire of revenge," reminding him that the "advantage we have by our armes" would have allowed the English easily to overpower Powhatan's men "had wee intended you anie hurt."[43]

*   *   *

Although we can never know with any certainty what the all-male band of English settlers signified to indigenous peoples, their own organization of gender roles seems to have shaped their responses to the English. Using sexual hospitality to "disarm" the strangers and exploiting English needs for food, Algonquians were drawn into a female role as suppliers of English sexual and subsistence needs. Although Indian women were occasionally successful in manipulating English desires for sexual intimacy and dominance, the English cast these triumphs as the consequence of female seduction, an interpretation that only reinforced discourses about feminized Algonquians. Dependence upon indigenous peoples for corn was potentially emasculating for the English; they thus redefined corn as tribute or booty resulting from English military dominance.

The encounter of English and Indian peoples wrought changes in the gender relations of both societies. Contact bred trade, political reshuffling, sexual intimacy and warfare. On both sides, male roles intensified in ways that appear to have reinforced the patriarchal tendencies of each culture. The very process of confrontation between two groups with male-dominated political and religious systems may initially have strengthened the value of patriarchy for each.

The rapid change in Indian life and culture had a particularly devastating impact upon women. Many women, whose office it was to bury and mourn the dead, may have been relegated to perpetual grieving. Corn was also uniquely the provenance of women; economically it was the source of female authority, and religiously and symbolically they were identified with it. The wanton burning and pillaging of corn supplies, through which the English transformed their dependence into domination, may have represented to tidewater residents an egregious violation of women. Maneuvering to retain patriarchal dominance over the English and invoking cultural roles in which women exercised power, Algonquian Indians may have presented their best defense against the "feminization" of their relationship to the English. But as in Indian society itself, warriors ultimately had the upper hand over agriculturists.[44]

English dominance in the region ultimately led to the decline of the native population and its way of life. As a consequence of war, nutritional deprivation, and disease, Virginia Indians were reduced in numbers from the approximately 14,000 inhabitants of the Chesapeake Bay and tidewater in 1607 to less than 3,000 by the early eighteenth century. White settlement forced tidewater dwellers further west, rupturing the connections between ritual activity, lineage, and geographic place. Priests lost credibility as traditional medicines failed to cure new diseases while confederacies such as Powhatan's declined and disappeared. Uprooted tidewater peoples also encountered opposition from piedmont inhabitants upon whose territory they encroached. The erosion of traditionally male-dominated Indian political institutions eventually created new opportunities for individual women to assume positions of leadership over tribal remnants.[45]

The English, meanwhile, emerged from these early years of settlement with gender roles more explicitly defined in English, Christian, and "middling order" terms. This core of English identity proved remarkably resilient, persisting through seventy years of wars with neighboring Indians and continuing to evolve as English settlers imported Africans to work the colony's tobacco fields. Initially serving to legitimate the destruction of traditional Indian ways of life, this concept of Englishness ultimately constituted one of the most powerful legacies of the Anglo–Indian gender frontier.

Notes

1. Spanish literature divided "barbaric" populations into two main categories: one of obedient and child-like laborers, and the other of evil, conniving and dangerous cannibals. The English similarly typed both Gaelic Irish and American Indians. See Anthony Pagden, *The Fall of Natural Man* (Cambridge: Cambridge University Press, 1986); Nicholas P. Canny, *The Elizabethan Conquest of Ireland: A Pattern Established 1565–76* (New York: Barnes and Noble, 1976), 160; Loren E. Pennington, "The Amerindian in English Promotional Literature 1575–1625" in *The Westward Enterprise: English Activities in Ireland, the Atlantic, and America, 1480–1650,* ed. K.R. Andrews, Nicholas P. Canny, and P.E.H. Hair (Detroit: Wayne State University Press, 1979), 184, 188; Anne Laurence, "The Cradle to the Grave: English Observation of Irish Social Customs in the Seventeenth Century," *The Seventeenth Century,* 3 (Spring 1988): 63–84; Nicholas P. Canny, "The Ideology of English Colonization: From Ireland to America," *William and Mary Quarterly,* 3rd ser., 30 (October 1973): 597 (hereafter cited as *WMQ*).

2. For a useful discussion of the performative nature of identity that is especially applicable to the early modern period and the encounter of cultures in the Americas, see Judith Butler, "Gender Trouble," in *Feminism/Postmodernism,* ed. Linda J. Nicholson (New York: Routledge, 1990), 336–339.

3. For the by-now classic account of gender as a means of communicating power, see Joan Scott, "Gender: A Useful Category of Historical Analysis," *American Historical Review,* 91 (December 1986): 1053–1075. For analyses of economic, linguistic, and religious "frontiers," see James Merrell, " 'The Customes of Our Country': Indians and Colonists in Early America," in *Strangers Within the Realm: Cultural Margins of the First British Empire,* ed. Bernard Bailyn and Phillip D. Morgan (Chapel Hill: University of North Carolina Press, 1991), 117–156. In no way separate or distinct, the gender frontier infiltrated other frontiers we usually describe as economic, social, or cultural; for further elaboration see Kathleen M. Brown, "Brave New Worlds: Women's and Gender History," *WMQ,* 3rd ser., 50 (April 1993): 311–328.

4. On Powhatan's influence over neighboring Algonquian-speaking peoples, see Nancy Lurie, "Indian Cultural Adjustment to European Civilization," in *Seventeenth-Century America,* ed. James Morton Smith (Westport, Ct.: Greenwood Press, 1980), 40–42. Lurie uses the term "Confederacy" to refer to these peoples, although she distinguishes between the "influence" Powhatan wielded and the "undisputed control" he never fully realized. Helen Rountree, *Pocahontas's People* (Norman, Ok.: University of Oklahoma Press, 1990), 3, argues that "Confederacy" is inaccurate, preferring to describe it as a "sophisticated government."

5. For examples of gendered discourses of difference in the Irish context, see Laurence, "Cradle to the Grave"; for a classic early English account of Africans, see Richard Jobson, *The Golden Trade* [London, 1623].

6. Among the most useful accounts of English agriculture are Joan Thirsk, ed., *The Agrarian History of England and Wales,* 6 vols. (Cambridge: Cambridge University Press, 1967) vol. 4; K.D.M. Snell, *Annals of the Laboring Poor: Social Change and Agrarian England, 1660–1900* (Cambridge: Cambridge University Press, 1985); D.E. Underdown, "Taming of the Scold: the Enforcement of Patriarchal Authority in Early Modern England," in Fletcher and Stevenson, *Order and Disorder in Early Modern England,* 116–136; Ann Kussmaul, *Servants in Husbandry in Early Modern England* (Cambridge: Cambridge University Press, 1981).

7. Cahn, *Industry of Devotion,* 80–90, 158; Amussen. *Ordered Society;* William Gouge, *Domesticall Duties* (London, 1622); Richard Brathwait, *The English Gentlewoman* (London, 1631); Gervase Markham, *Country Contentments or the English Housewife* (London, 1623).

8. For the terms "good wives" and "nasty wenches," see John Hammond, *Leah and Rachel, or the Two Fruitfull Sisters* (London, 1656).

9. Martin Ingram, "Ridings, Rough Music, and the 'Reform of Popular Culture,' in Early Modern England," *Past and Present,* 105 (November 1984): 79–113; Underdown. "The Taming of the Scold."

10. Ramon Gutierrez, *When Jesus Came the Corn Mothers Went Away* (Stanford, Ca.: Stanford University Press, 1991), 3–7; Hudson, *Southeastern Indians,* 148–159; Helen Rountree, *The Powhatan Indians of Virginia: Their Traditional Culture* (Norman, Ok: University of Oklahoma Press, 1989), 135–138; William Strachey; *The Historie of Travell into Virginia Britania* [London, 1612], 89, 103.

11. Edwin Randolph Turner, "An Archaeological and Ethnohistorical Study on the Evolution of Rank Societies in the Virginia Coastal Plain" (Ph.D. diss., The Pennsylvania State University, 1976), 182–187; Rountree, *Powhatan Indians,* 45, finds Turner's estimates perhaps too high.

12. Herndon, "Indian Agriculture in the Southern Colonies," 288, 292–296, especially the reference on 292 to "She-Corn." Hudson, *Southeastern Indians,* 151–156, 259–260; Wright, *Only Land They Knew,* 8–14; Silver, *New Face on the Countryside,* 39–41, 44–52; Colonel Henry Norwood, "A Voyage to Virginia" [London, 1649] in *Tracts and Other Papers, relating principally to the Origin, Settlement and Progress of the North American Colonies,* ed. Peter Force, 4 vols. (New York, 1836; rpt., Cambridge, Mass., Peter Smith, 1947), 3: 36–37. John Smith often rendered invisible or insignificant the work of women; see Kupperman, *John Smith,* 138–139. See also Kupperman, *John Smith,* 151, 156, for Smith's description of women's role as mourners and the passage of property and political power through women.

13. Wright, *Only Land They Knew,* 8–14; Hudson, *Southeastern Indians,* 148–156, 258–260; Kupperman, *John Smith,* 105, 144, 153; Henry Spelman, "Relation of Virginia," in *Travels and Works of Captain John Smith,* ed. Edward Arber and A. G. Bradley, 2 vols. (Edinburgh: John Grant, 1910), 1: cvi.

14. Hudson, *Southeastern Indians,* 259; Kupperman, *John Smith,* 61, 163.

15. Strachey, *Historie,* 83, 74.

16. For Powhatan's clever manipulation of gender customs and symbols of power, see Strachey, *Historie,* 40, 44, 62, 65–69, and Spelman, "Relation," cxiv.

17. For a survey of changing English attitudes toward Indians in the South, see Gary B. Nash, "The Image of the Indian in the Southern Colonial Mind," *WMQ,* 3rd ser., 29 (April 1972): 197–230. See also George Percy, "Observations by Master George Percy, 1607," [London, 1607], in Tyler, *Narratives,* 17–18, and Thomas Hariot, *A Briefe and True Report of the New Found Land of Virginia* (London, 1588; rpt. New York, 1903).

18. Smith, *Proceedings of the English Colonies,* in Tyler, *Narratives,* 178, John Smith, "Description of Virginia," [London, 1612], in Tyler, *Narratives,* 83; Pennington, "The Amerindians in English Promotional Literature," 189, for her summation of the argument in Robert Gray, *A Good Speed to Virginia* [London, 1609]. For Smith's recognition of native concepts of property, see Kupperman, *John Smith,* 140. Most early English commentators also noted the potential of New World abundance for exploitation by agriculturists and hunters: see, for example, Percy, "Observations" in Tyler, *Narratives,* 17–18; Hariot, *A Briefe and True Report.*

19. V.G. Kieman, "Private Property in History," in *Family and Inheritance: Rural Society in Western Europe, 1200–1800,* ed. Jack Goody, Joan Thirsk, and E. P. Thompson (Cambridge: Cambridge University Press, 1976), 361–398: see also E. P. Thompson, *Whigs and Hunters: The Origin of the Black Act* (New York: Random House, 1975). James Axtell, *The European and the Indian: Essays in the Ethnohistory of Colonial North America* (New York: Oxford University Press, 1981), discusses the English view of "civilizing" Indians as a process of making men out of children. Although most voyagers wrote critically of Indian men, others compared them favorably to English men whose overly cultured and effeminate ways had made them weak in character and resolve; Hariot, *A Briefe and True Report.* For a critique of English effeminacy, see *Haec Vir* [London, 1620] in Henderson and MacManus, *Half Humankind;* Richard Brathwait, *The English Gentleman* (London, 1631). Strachey, *Historie,* 18, 24, 25, equated civility with manliness.

20. Kupperman, *John Smith,* 158. Smith, "Description of Virginia," in Tyler, *Narratives,* 98–99.

21. Percy, "Observations," in Tyler, *Narratives,* 18. For an extended discussion of this theme for Virginia and elsewhere, see David D. Smits, "The Squaw Drudge: A Prime Index of Savagism," *Ethnohistory* 29 (1982): 281–306.

22. See Axtell, *The European and the Indian,* 45, 47–55, 57–60, for the deeper reverberations of different clothing and naming practices: Kupperman, *John Smith,* 100; Strachey, *Historie,* 73.

23. Smith, *Proceedings of the English Colonies,* in Tyler, *Narratives,* 153–154.

24. Hariot, *A Briefe and True Report.*

25. Percy, "Observations," in Tyler, *Narratives,* 10.

26. Smith, "Description," in Tyler, *Narratives,* 106. Percy, "Observations," in Tyler, *Narratives,* 6.

27. Smith, "Description," in Tyler, *Narratives,* 99; Strachey, *Historie,* 70.

28. Smith, *True Relation,* in Barbour, *Complete Works,* 1: 85.

29. "Letter of John Rolfe, 1614," in Tyler, *Narratives,* 241.

30. Smith, *True Relation,* in Barbour, *Complete Works,* 1: 39, 91.

31. Axtell, *Beyond 1492,* 101; Strachey, *Historie,* 85. See also *Ibid 66,* for an account of Warroskoyack Indians mocking the English when an Indian hostage escaped from an English ship.

32. Kupperman, *John Smith,* 174, for Powhatan's speech to Smith. For a Chickahominy orator's similar comments to Smith, see Kupperman, *John Smith,* 190. See also Kupperman, *John Smith,* 185, for Smith's admission of the English dependence on native corn supplies. For Smith's description of the engagement with the Kecoughtan, see Smith, *General Historie,* in Barbour, *Complete Works,* 2: 144.

33. Kupperman, *John Smith,* 175.

34. These sexual diplomats may well be the same women Smith claimed "were common whores by profession"; see Kupperman, *John Smith,* 156, 157.

35. Smith, "Description," in Tyler, *Narratives,* 114–115.

36. The provision of women to foreign men was a fairly common Indian diplomatic practice throughout the South as well as in Central and South America; see for example, Gutierrez, *Corn Mothers,* 16–20. This was a highly politicized form of sexual hospitality which stood in sharp contrast to the violent reaction when native women were kidnapped by foreign warriors: see Kupperman, *John Smith,* 100.

37. Axtell, *Beyond 1492,* 39, 45, 102; my interpretation is compatible with Axtell, *Beyond 1492,* 31–33, in which he claims that while Europeans stressed sharp distinctions between Europeans and non-Europeans. Indians stressed the similarities. William Strachey believed that assimilation was Powhatan's strategy for mediating English relations with other Indians outside the paramount chiefdom; see Strachey, *Historie,* 107.

38. Strachey, *Historie,* 60.

39. Strachey, *Historie,* 63; Smith, *True Relation,* in Barbour, *Complete Works,* 1: 71, for a similar tactic by Powhatan.

40. Smith, *True Relation,* in Barbour, *Complete Works,* 1:39.

41. Kupperman, *John Smith,* 62, 65.

42. J.A. Leo Lemay, *Did Pocahontas Save Captain John Smith?* (Athens, Ga.: University of Georgia Press, 1992) is the most recent interpretation of this event. An ardent believer in Smith's veracity, Lemay fails to explore the degree to which Smith may have misunderstood the meaning of the near-death ritual. For primary accounts of the events, see Smith, *True Relation,* in Barbour, *Complete Works,* 1: 45; Smith, *General Historie,* in Kupperman, *John Smith,* 64–65.

43. Kupperman, *John Smith,* 175.

44. Stephen R. Potter, "Early English Effects on Virginia Algonquian Exchange and Tribute," in Wood, *Powhatan's Mantle,* 151–172, especially 151, 160; Martha McCartney, "Cockacoeske, Queen of the Pamunkey: Diplomat and Suzeraine," in Wood, *Powhatan's Mantle,* 173–195; Merrell, "Customes of Our Country," 122–123; Robert Beverley, *The History and Present State of Virginia [1705],* ed. Louis V. Wright (Chapel Hill, 1947), 232–233.

45. For analyses of the devastation wrought by contact, see Hudson, *Southeastern Indians,* chap. 8; Silver, *New Face on the Countryside,* 74–83, 88, 102; Crosby, *Ecological Imperialism,* chap. 9; Merrell, "The Customes of Our Country," 122–126. Powhatan himself commented upon the devastation he had witnessed in the course of three generations; see Kupperman, *John Smith,* 174. See also Wright, *The Only Land They Knew,* 24–26; Peter Wood, "The Changing Population of the Colonial South: An Overview by Race and Region, 1685–1790," in Wood, *Powhatan's Mantle,* 38, 40–42; Silver, *New Face on the Countryside,* 72, 81, 87–88, 91; Potter, "Early English Effects on Virginia Algonquian Exchange and Tribute," Robert Steven Grumet, "Sunksquaws, Shamans, and Tradeswomen: Middle Atlantic Coastal Algonkian Women during the 17th and 18th Centuries" in *Women and Colonization: Anthropological Perspectives,* ed. Mona Etienne and Eleanor Leacock (New York: Praeger, 1980), 43–62.

Chapter 2

The Beginnings of the Afro-American Family in Maryland

Allan Kulikoff

The scarcity of surviving documents written by African-American women in the colonial period forces historians to employ indirect means to explore their experience. Allan Kulikoff relies upon a quantitative analysis of the black population in colonial Virginia and Maryland to explore change over time. His analysis charts the emergence of an African-American family and community between 1650 and 1750. Two findings stand out: first, the mother-- children group was central for the initial generation of African-born slaves. Second, over time an increasing share of slave parents lived together, but the small size of plantations and the frequent separation of family members meant that kinship and family bonds among slaves crossed plantation boundaries. Kulikoff presents evidence on the origins of patterns of slave family life in the nineteenth century, which are explored more fully in the article by Deborah G. White.

How did Afro-Americans organize their families in the Chesapeake colonies during the eighteenth century? Who lived in slave households? How many Afro-American fathers lived with their wives and children? What was the impact of arbitrary sale and transfer of slaves upon family life? How did an Afro-American's household and family relationships change through the life cycle?

This paper attempts to answer these questions.[1] While literary documents by or about slaves before 1800, such as runaway narratives, WPA freed-slave interviews, black autobiographies, or detailed travel accounts are very infrequently available to historians of colonial slave family life, they can gather age and family data from probate inventories, personal information from runaway advertisements, and depositions in court cases. These sources, together with several diaries and account books, kept by whites, provide a great deal of material about African and Afro-American family life in the Chesapeake region.

Almost all the blacks who lived in Maryland and Virginia before 1780 were slaves. Because their status precluded them from enjoying a legally secure family life, slave households often excluded important family members. Households, domestic groups, and families must therefore be clearly distinguished. A household, as used here, is a coresidence group that includes all who shared a "proximity of sleeping arrangements," or lived under the same roof. Domestic groups include kin and nonkin, living in the same or separate households, who share cooking, eating, childrearing, working, and other daily activities. Families are composed of people related by blood or marriage. Several distinctions are useful in defining the members of families. The immediate family includes husband and wife or parents and children. Near kin include the immediate family and all other kin,

Excerpted from "The Beginnings of the Afro-American Family in Maryland," by Allan Kulikoff, Chapter 8 in *Law, Society, and Politics in Early Maryland*, Aubrey Land, Lois Green Carr, and Edward C. Papenfuse, eds. (Baltimore: The Johns Hopkins University Press, 1977).

"The Old Plantation," c. 1790. Colonial Williamsburg Foundation, Williamsburg, Va.

such as adult brothers and sisters or cousins who share the same house or domestic tasks with the immediate family. Other kinfolk who do not function as family members on a regular basis are considered to be distant kin.[2]

The process of family formation can perhaps best be understood as an adaptive process. My ideas about this process owe much to a provocative essay by Sidney Mintz and Richard Price on Afro-American culture. Blacks learned to modify their environment, learned from each other how to retain family ties under very adverse conditions, and structured their expectations about family activities around what they knew the master would permit. If white masters determined the outward bounds of family activities, it was Africans, and especially their descendants, who gave meaning to the relationships between parents and children, among siblings, and with more distant kinfolk. As a result, black family structure on the eve of the Revolution differed from both African and white family systems.[3]

Africans who were forced to come to the Chesapeake region in the late seventeenth and early eighteenth centuries struggled to create viable families and households, but often failed. They suffered a great loss when they were herded into slave ships. Their family and friends, who had given meaning to their lives and structured their place in society, were left behind and they found themselves among strangers. They could never recreate their families and certainly not devise a West African kinship system in the Chesapeake. The differences between African communities were too great. Some Africans lived in clans and lineages, others did not; some traced their descent from women but others traced descent from men; mothers, fathers, and other kin played somewhat different roles in each community; initiation ceremonies and puberty rites, forbidden marriages, marriage customs, and household structures all varied from place to place.[4]

Though African immigrants did not bring a unified West African culture with them to the Chesapeake colonies, they did share important beliefs about the nature of kinship. Africans could modify these beliefs in America to legitimate the families they eventually formed. They saw kinship as the principal way of ordering relationships between individuals. Each person in the tribe was related to most others in the community. The male was father, son, and uncle; the female was mother, daughter, and aunt to many others. Because their kinship system was so extensive, Africans included kinfolk outside the immediate family in their daily activities. For example, adult brothers or sisters of the father or mother played an important role in childrearing and domestic activities in many African societies.[5]

Secondly, but far less certainly, African immigrants may have adapted some practices associated with polygyny, a common African marital custom. A few men on the Eastern Shore of Maryland in the 1740s, and perhaps others scattered elsewhere, lived with several women. However, far too few African women (in relation to the number of men) immigrated to make polygynous marriages common. Nevertheless, the close psychological relationship between mothers and children, and the great social distance between a husband and his various wives and children found in African polygynous societies might have been repeated in the Chesapeake colonies. In any event, African slave mothers played a more important role than fathers in teaching children about Africa and about how to get along in the slave system. Both African custom, and the physical separation of immigrant men and women played a role in this development.[6]

Africans faced a demographic environment hostile to most forms of family life. If Africans were to start families, they had to find spouses, and that task was difficult. Most blacks lived on small farms of less than 11 slaves; and the small black population was spread thinly over a vast territory. Roads were rudimentary. Even where concentrations of larger plantations were located, African men did not automatically find wives. Sex ratios in southern Maryland rose from 125 to 130 (men per 100 women) in the mid-seventeenth century to about 150 in the 1710s and 1720s, and to around 180 in the 1730s. In Surry County, Virginia, the slave sex ratio was about 145 in the 1670s and 1680s, but over 200 in the 1690s and 1700s. . . . The larger the plantation, the higher the sex ratio tended to be.[7]

African men had competition for the available black women. By the 1690s, some black women were natives, and they may have preferred Afro-American men. White men were also competitors. Indeed, during the seventeenth and early eighteenth centuries, white adult sex ratios were as high (or higher) than black adult sex ratios. At any period whites possessed a monopoly of power and some of them probably took slave women as their common-law wives. African men competed for the remaining black women, and probably some died before they could find a wife. In 1739 African men planned an uprising in Prince George's County partly because they could not find wives.[8] . . .

Unlike most African men, African women commonly lived with their children. Some African women may have been so alienated that they refused to have children, but the rest bore and raised several offspring, protected by the master's reluctance to separate very young children from their mothers. Since the children were reared by their mothers, and eventually joined them in the tobacco fields, these households were domestic groups, although incomplete as families.[9]

A greater proportion of African women than African men lived with both spouses and children. These opportunities usually arose on large plantations. There was such a surplus of men on large plantations that African women who lived on them could choose husbands from several African or Afro-American men. The sex ratio on large plantations in Prince George's during the 1730s, a period of heavy immigration, was 249. This shortage of women prevented most recently arrived African men from finding a wife on the plantation. For them the opportunity to live with a wife and children was rare. More Africans probably lived with their immediate families in the 1740s; immigration declined, large planters bought more African women, and the sex ratio on big plantations fell to 142.[10]

Because African spouses were usually separated, African mothers reared their Afro-American children with little help from their husbands. Even when the father was present, the extended kin so important in the lives of African children was missing. Mothers probably taught them the broad values they brought from Africa and related the family's history in Africa and the Chesapeake. When the children began working in the fields, they learned from their mothers how to survive a day's work and how to get along with master and overseer.

Each group of Africans repeated the experiences of previous immigrants. Eventually, more and more Afro-American children matured and began families of their own. The first large generation of Afro-Americans in Maryland probably came of age in the 1690s; by the 1720s, when the second large generation had matured, the black population finally began increasing naturally.[11]

The changing composition of the black population combined with other changes to restructure Afro-American households and families. Alterations in the adult sex ratio, the size of plantations, and black population density provided black people with opportunities to enjoy a more satisfying family life. The way masters transferred slaves from place to place limited the size and composition of black households, but Afro-American family members separated by masters managed to establish complex kinship networks over many plantations. Afro-Americans used these opportunities to create a kind of family life that differed from African and Anglo-American practices.

Demographic changes led to more complex households and families. As the number of adult Africans in the population decreased, the sex ratio in Maryland declined to between 100 and 110 by the 1750s. This decline gave most men an opportunity to marry by about age 30. The number of slaves who lived on plantations with more than 20 blacks increased; the density of the black population in tidewater Maryland and Virginia rose; the proportion of blacks in the total population of Prince George's County, in nearby areas of Maryland, and throughout tidewater Virginia rose to half or more by the end of the century; and many new roads were built. The number of friends and kinfolk whom typical Afro-Americans saw every day or visited with regularity increased, while their contact with whites declined because large areas of the Chesapeake became nearly black counties.[12]

How frequently masters transferred their Afro-American slaves, and where they sent them, affected black household composition. Surviving documents do not allow a systematic analysis of this point, but several conclusions seem clear. First, planters kept women and their small children together but did not keep husbands and teenage children with their immediate family. Slaveowner after slaveowner bequeathed women and their "increase" to sons or daughters. However, children of slaveowners tended to live near their parents; thus, even when members of slave families were so separated, they remained in the same neighborhood.[13] Secondly, Afro-Americans who lived on small farms were transferred more frequently than those on large plantations. At their deaths small slaveowners typically willed a slave or two to their widows and to each child. They also frequently mortgaged or sold slaves to gain capital. If a slaveowner died with many unpaid debts, his slaves had to be sold.[14] Finally, relatively few blacks were forced to move long distances. Far more blacks were affected by migrations of slaves from the Chesapeake region to the new Southwest in the nineteenth century than by long-distance movement in the region before the Revolution.[15] These points should not be misunderstood. Most Afro-Americans who lived in Maryland or Virginia during the eighteenth century experienced separations from members of their immediate families sometime in their lives. Most, however, were able to visit these family members occasionally.

These changes led to a new social reality for most slaves born in the 1750s, 1760s, and 1770s. If unrelated people and their progeny stay in a limited geographic area for several generations, the descendants of the original settlers must develop kin ties with many other people who live nearby. Once the proportion of adult Africans declined, this process began. African women married and had children; the children matured and married. If most of them remained near their first homes, each was bound to have siblings, children, spouses, uncles, aunts, and cousins living in the neighborhood. How these various kinspeople were organized into households, families, and domestic groups depended not only upon the whims of masters but also upon the meaning placed on kinship by the slaves themselves.

The process of household and family formation and dissolution was begun by each immigrant woman who lived long enough to have children. The story of Ann Joice, a black woman who was born in Barbados, taken to England as a servant, and then falsely sold into slavery in Maryland in the 1670s, may have been similar to that of other immigrant women once she became a slave. The Darnall family of Prince George's owned Ann Joice. She had seven children with several white men in the 1670s and 1680s; all remained slaves the rest of their lives. Three of her children stayed on the Darnall home plantation until their deaths. One was sold as a child to a planter who lived a few miles away; another was eventually sold to William Digges, who lived about five miles from the Darnall farm. Both the spatial spread and the local concentration of kinfolk continued in the next generation. Peter Harbard, born between 1715 and 1720, was the son of Francis Harbard, who was Ann Joice's child. Peter grew up on the Darnall farm, but in 1737 he was sold to George Gordon, who lived across the road from Darnall. As a child, Peter lived with or very near his grandmother Ann Joice, his father, and several paternal uncles and aunts. He probably knew his seven cousins (father's sister's children), children of his aunt Susan Harbard, who lived on William Digges's plantation. Other kinfolk lived in Annapolis but were too far away to visit easily.[16]

As Afro-American slaves were born and died, and as masters sold or bequeathed their slaves, black households were formed and reformed, broken and created. Several detailed examples can illustrate this process. For example, Daphne, the daughter of Nan, was born about 1736 on a large plantation in Prince George's owned by Robert Tyler, Sr. Until she was two, she lived with her mother, two brothers, and two sisters. In 1738, Tyler died and left his slaves to his wife, children, and grandchildren. All lived on or near Tyler's farms. Three of Daphne's siblings were bequeathed to grand-daughter Ruth Tyler, who later married Mordecai Jacob, her grandfather's next-door neighbor. Daphne continued to live on the Tyler plantation. From 1736 to 1787, she had six different masters, but she still lived where she was born. Daphne lived with her mother until her mother died, and with her ten children until 1779. Children were eventually born to Daphne's daughters; these infants lived with their mothers and near their maternal grandmother. When Robert Tyler III, Robert senior's grandson and Daphne's fifth master, died in 1779, his will divided Daphne's children and grandchildren between his son and daughter. Daphne was thus separated from younger children, born between 1760 and 1772. They were given to Millicent Beanes, Robert III's daughter, who lived several miles away. Daphne continued to live on the same plantation as her four older children and several grandchildren. An intricate extended family of grandmother, sons, daughters, grandchildren, aunts, uncles, nieces, nephews, and cousins resided in several households on the Tyler plantation in 1778, and other, more remote kinfolk could be found on the neighboring Jacob farm.[17]

Family separations might be more frequent on smaller plantations. Rachael was born in the late 1730s and bore ten children between 1758 and 1784. As a child she lived on the plantation of Alexander Magruder, a large slaveowner in Prince George's; before 1746, Alexander gave her to his son Hezekiah, who lived on an adjoining plantation. Hezekiah never owned more than ten slaves, and when he died in 1769, he owned only two—including one willed to his wife by her brother. Between 1755 and 1757, he mortgaged nine slaves, including Rachael, to two merchants. In 1757, Samuel Roundall (who lived about five miles from the Magruders) seized Rachael and six other slaves mortgaged to him. This and subsequent transfers can be seen on Figure 1. In 1760 Roundall sold Rachael and her eldest daughter to Samuel Lovejoy, who lived about nine miles from Roundall.

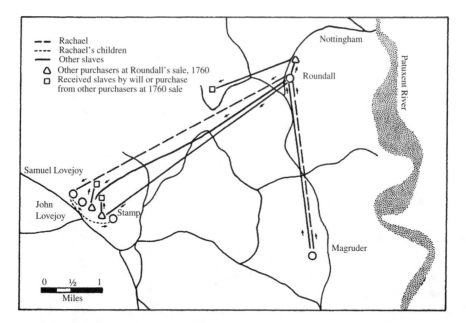

FIGURE 1 Sale and Later Transfer of Hezekiah Magruder's Slaves, 1755–1780.

At the same time, four other former Magruder slaves were sold: two to planters in Lovejoy's neighborhood, one to a Roundall neighbor, and one to a planter living at least fifteen miles away in Charles County. Rachael's separation from friends and family members continued. In 1761, her eldest child was sold at age three to George Stamp, a neighbor of Lovejoy. By the time Samuel Lovejoy died in 1762, she had two other children. She and her youngest child went to live with John Lovejoy, Samuel's nephew and near-neighbor, but her second child, about age two, stayed with Lovejoy's widow. Her third child was sold at age six, but Rachael and her next seven children lived with John Lovejoy until at least 1787.[18]

These three examples suggest how Afro-American households and families developed in the eighteenth century. Husbands and wives and parents and children were frequently separated by the master's transfers of family members. At the same time, as generation followed generation, households, or adjacent huts, became increasingly complex, and sometimes included grandparents, uncles, aunts, or cousins, as well as the immediate family. Since other kin lived on nearby or distant plantations, geographically concentrated (and dispersed) kinship networks that connected numbers of quarters emerged during the pre-Revolutionary era.

How typical were the experiences suggested by the examples? How were families organized into households and domestic groups on large and small quarters? Data from three large planters' inventories taken in 1759, 1773–74, and 1775, and from a Prince George's census of 1776 permit a test of the hypotheses concerning changes in household structure, differences between large and small units, and the spread of kinfolk across space. Table 1 details household structure on large quarters of over twenty and Table 2 shows the kinds of households on small farms. About half of all slaves probably lived on each plantation type.[19] This evidence provides a good test, because by the 1770s most Afro-Americans could trace a Chesapeake genealogy back to immigrant grandparents or great-grandparents.[20]

TABLE 1 Afro-American Household Structures on Three Large Plantations in Prince George's and Anne Arundel Counties, Maryland, 1759–1775

Household Type	Percentage in Household Type				Percentage of Total in Household Types
	Males 15+	Females 15+	Children 0–9	Children 10–14	
Husband–wife–children	40	43	55	44	47
Mother–children	2	17	22	10	14
Mother–children–other kin	4	14	8	13	9
Siblings	7	4	6	12	7
Husband–wife–children–other kin	2	2	2	2	2
Father–children	5	0	3	5	3
Husband–wife	2	2	0	0	1
Three generation	1	2	2	3	2
Unknown or mixed	36	16	3	12	15
Total percentage	99	100	101	101	100
Number of people	142	129	178	77	526

Sources: PG Inventories, GS No. 1, f. 73 (1759; James Wardrop's, 32 slaves); and GS No. 2, ff. 334–36 (1775; Addison's 3 plantations, 109 slaves) and Charles Carroll Account Book, Maryland Historical Society (rest of slaves). The three-generation households include grandparents and grandchildren, but not the generation in between. The unknown or mixed category includes all those apparently living away from all kinfolk, but perhaps living near them. Some of the slaves in this category probably belong in the others, but the sources (especially the Addison and Wardrop documents) do not permit location of them.

Kinfolk (immediate families and near kin) on large plantations were organized into three kinds of residence groups. Most of the slaves of some quarters were interrelated by blood or marriage. Domestic groups included kinfolk who lived on opposite sides of duplex slave huts and who shared a common yard and eating and cooking arrangements. Finally, most households included members of an immediate family.

The kinship structure of large plantations is illustrated by a household inventory taken in 1773–74 of 385 slaves owned by Charles Carroll of Carrollton on thirteen different quarters in Anne Arundel County. Because Carroll insisted that the inventory be "taken in Familys with their Ages," the document permits a detailed reconstruction of kinship networks.[21] Though the complexity and size of kinship groups on Carroll's quarters were probably greater than on other large plantations, the general pattern could easily have been repeated elsewhere.[22]

The ten men and three women who headed each list were probably leaders of their quarters. Five of the quarters were named for these individuals.[23] They tended to be old slaves who had been with the Carroll family for many years. While the mean age of all adults was 37 years, the mean age of the leaders was 49, and six of the thirteen were over 55.[24] The leader often lived with many kinfolk; he or she was closely related to about 36 to 38 percent of all the other slaves on the quarter. For example, Fanny, 69 years of age, was surrounded by at least 40 near kinfolk on the main plantation at Doohoregan, and Mayara James, 65 years of age, lived with 23 relatives on his quarter.[25]

TABLE 2 Afro-American Household Structures on Small Plantations (1–8 Slaves), Prince George's County, Maryland, 1776

Household Type	Percentage in Household Type				Percentage of Total in Household Type
	Males 15 +	Females 15 +	Children 0–9	Children 10–14	
Husband–wife–children	17	18	22	10	18
Mother–children	2	35	56	29	32
Father–children	2	*	4	1	2
Siblings	7	5	6	17	8
Mixed	72	42	12	43	41
Total percentage	100	100	100	100	101
Number of people	275	276	325	162	1038

Source: 1776 Census. The household types were assumed from black age structures on individual farms. Children and mothers were matched if a woman in the household could have been a mother to children in the same household (e.g., a woman 25 years old was assumed to be a mother of children aged 4, 2, and 1 years on the same plantation). Men and women were linked as husband and wife if a man and woman in the same household were close in age (e.g., a man of 35 linked with a woman of 25). Children and young adults (to c. 25) were assumed to be siblings if no parents were in the household, and the ages of the children were close. (Children aged 8, 10, 13 were linked as siblings when no adult in household could be their parent.) A man was assumed to be father to children who lived on the same farm if no other person who could be a parent was present (man aged 35 was father to children aged 12, 10, 8 when no woman was present in household to be wife). The mixed category included all others who could not be placed: these could include kinfolk like older siblings, or brothers or parents to women with children in the same household, or they could be unrelated. If more than one type was found on a farm, it was counted as two households despite the probability that the people lived in the same hut. The statistics must be treated as educated guesses. Since slave mothers and their children were usually kept together in slave sales and in wills of masters, it is fairly certain that all the children in the first two categories lived with their mothers. The other linkages must include many errors.

* = less than ½%.

The slave genealog[y] presented in Figure 2 provides a detailed example of the kinds of kinship networks that could develop on quarters after several generations of relative geographic stability. Because most slave quarters had between fifteen and thirty slaves, the network included just two or three households. The kin group shown in Figure 2 may have been typical. Thirteen of the seventeen slaves who lived at Annapolis Quarter in 1774 were descendants of Iron Works Lucy. Ten were children and grandchildren of Sall. One of Sall's sons-in-law and his brother also lived there. Peter and Charles, other descendants of Lucy, lived on the quarter but had families elsewhere.

Nearly half the slaves who resided on Riggs Quarter, Carroll's main plantation, were kinfolk (63/130). A network of this size could develop only on the home plantation of the largest Chesapeake planters.[26] Each of the members of the group was either a direct descendant or an affine (inlaw) of old Fanny. She was surrounded on her quarter by five children, nineteen grandchildren, nine great-grandchildren, four children-in-law, and three grandchildren's spouses. The network grew through the marriage of Fanny's children and grandchildren to children of other residents of the quarter. For example, Cooper Joe, his wife, and thirteen children and grandchildren were closely related to Fanny's family. By the early 1750s Cooper Joe had married Nanny of Kate, and about 1761 Fanny's son Bob married Frances Mitchell of Kate. Joe and Nanny's children were first cousins of the

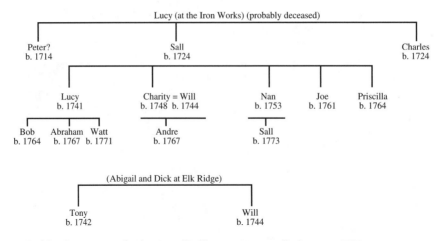

FIGURE 2 Kinship Ties Among Charles Carroll's Slaves at Annapolis Quarter, 1774.

Source: Charles Carroll Account Book, Maryland Historical Society.

Note: Will, son of Abigail and Dick and Charity's husband, appears twice. Peter may not be Lucy's son, but it seems probable. Mark (b. 1758) and Jem (b. 1754) apparently were not related to others on the quarter, but had relatives elsewhere on Carroll's plantation.

children of Bob and Frances, and thereby more remotely connected to all the rest of Fanny's descendants. The alliance of the two families was cemented in 1772, when Dinah, the daughter of Kate of Fanny, married Joe, the son of Cooper Joe.[27]

The intraquarter kinship network was also a work group. Fanny's and Lucy's adult and teenage kinfolk worked together in the fields. Masters separated their slaves by sex, age, and strength, and determined what each would do, but blacks judged each other in part by the reciprocal kinship obligation that bound them together. Afro-Americans worked at their own pace and frequently thwarted their master's desires for increased productivity. Part of this conflict can be explained by the Afro-American's preindustrial work discipline, but part may have been due to the desires of kinfolk to help and protect each other from the master's lash, the humid climate, and the malarial environment.[28] . . .

When Afro-Americans came home each night from the fields, they broke into smaller domestic groups. Their habitat set the scene for social intercourse. On large plantations "a Negro quarter is a Number of Huts or Hovels, built at some distance from the Mansion House; where the Negroes reside with their wives and families and cultivate at vacant times the little spots allow'd them."[29] Four early-nineteenth-century slave houses still standing in Southern Maryland suggest that slave families living on the same quarter were very close. Each house included two rooms of about sixteen-by-sixteen feet, separated by a thin wall. In three of the homes, the two huts shared the same roof but had separate doorways. Two had separate fireplaces, the residents of one duplex shared a fireplace, and one quarter (which was over a kitchen) did not have a fireplace.[30] Neither family had much privacy, and communication between them must have been commonplace. No activity could occur on one side of the hut without those on the other knowing about it. And the two halves of the hut shared a common yard, where residents could talk, eat, or celebrate.

On the quarters the smallest local residence unit to contain kinfolk was the household. Household members were not isolated from other kinfolk; they worked with their relatives in the fields, associated with neighbors in the common yard, and cooked meals or slept near those who lived on the other side of their duplex. Nevertheless, kinfolk who lived in the same household were spatially closer when at home than any other group of kin. Who lived in typical households on slave quarters? How many husbands lived with their wives and children? How many children were separated from their parents? Did kin other than the immediate family live in many households?

Nearly half of all the Afro-Americans who lived on the three large plantations described in Table 1 resided in households that included both parents and at least some of their children. Over half of the young children on all three plantations lived with both parents, but a far higher proportion of adults and children 10 to 14 years of age lived in two-parent households on the Carroll quarters than on the three Addison farms and Wardrop's plantation in Prince George's. While 49 percent of the women, 51 percent of the men, and 52 percent of children between ages 10 and 14 on Carroll's farms lived in two-parent households, only 28 percent of the women, 24 percent of the men, and 30 percent of those 10 to 14 year olds could be found in two-parent homes on the other farms. Almost all the other children lived with one parent, usually the mother; but over a quarter of those 10 to 14 years of age lived with siblings or with apparently unrelated people.

The differences between Carroll and the other two large slaveowners is striking. Carroll, unlike all but a few other Chesapeake gentlemen, was able to provide his people with spouses from his own plantations and chose to keep adolescent children with their parents. Over six-tenths of the men (62 percent) and 28 percent of the women on Addison's and Wardrop's plantations lived with siblings, were unmarried, or lived away from spouses and children. On Carroll's quarters only 27 percent of the men and 12 percent of the women were similarly separated from spouses and children.

Many blacks on these three large farms lived with or near kin other than their parents or children. About 7 percent were in the household of a brother or sister, and over a tenth (13 percent) of parents and children shared their homes with another kinsperson. There were several types of these extended households: seven included parent(s), children, and sibling(s) of the mother; two included a grandmother living with her children and grandchildren; in one household grandparents took care of two young grandchildren; and in one hut, an adult brother and sister lived with her children and one grandchild.

Far less can be learned about families on small plantations. On these farms, the slave quarter could be in an outbuilding or in a small hut.[31] All the slaves, whether kin or not, lived together, cooked together, reared children together, and slept in the same hut. Table 2 very roughly suggests the differences in household composition of large plantations and small farms. Only 18 percent of the blacks on small units lived in two-parent households. About a third resided in mother–child households, and that included over half the young children and three-tenths of those 10 to 14 years of age. Nearly three-quarters of the men and two-fifths of the women—some unmarried—lived with neither spouse nor children. Over two-fifths of the youths 10 to 14 years of age lived away from parents and siblings. . . .

On large plantations, mothers could call upon a wide variety of kin to help them raise their children: husbands, siblings, cousins, and uncles or aunts might be living in nearby huts. Peter Harbard learned from his grandmother, father, and paternal uncles how his grandmother's indentures were burned by Henry Darnall and how she was forced into bondage. He "frequently heard his grandmother Ann Joice say that if she had her just right that she ought to be free and all her children. He hath also heard his Uncles David Jones, John Wood, Thomas Crane, and also his father Francis Harbard declare as much." Peter's desire for freedom, learned from his kinfolk, never left him. In 1748, he ran away twice toward Philadelphia and freedom. He was recaptured, but later purchased his freedom.[32] . . .

As Afro-American slaves moved from plantation to plantation through the life cycle, they left behind many friends and kinfolk, and established relationships with slaves on other plantations.

And when young black men married off their quarter, they gained kinfolk on other plantations. Both of these patterns can be illustrated from the Carroll plantations. Sam and Sue, who lived on Sam's quarter at Doohoregan Manor, had seven children between 1729 and 1751. In 1774, six of them were spread over four different quarters at Doohoregan: one son lived with his father (his mother had died); a daughter lived with her family in a hut near her father's; a son and daughter lived at Frost's; one son headed Moses' quarter; and a son lived at Riggs. . . . Marriages increased the size and geographic spread of Fanny's relations. A third of the slaves (85/255) who lived away from Riggs Quarter (the main plantation) were kin to Fanny or her descendants. Two of Kate's children married into Fanny's family; Kate and one son lived at Frost's and another son lived at Jacob's. Cecilia, the daughter of Carpenter Harry and Sophia, married one of Fanny's grandchildren. Harry and Sophia lived with three of their children at Frost's, and two of their sons lived at Riggs, where they were learning to be wheelwrights with kinsperson Joe, son of Cooper Joe.[33]

Since husbands and wives, fathers and children, and friends and kinfolk were often physically separated, they had to devise ways of maintaining their close ties. At night and on Sundays and holidays, fathers and other kinfolk visited those family members who lived on other plantations. Fathers had regular visiting rights. Landon Carter's Guy, for instance, visited his wife (who lived on another quarter) every Monday evening.[34] Kinfolk, friends, and neighbors gathered in the yard around the slave cabins and talked, danced, sang, told stories, and drank rum through many an evening and special days on larger plantations.[35] These visits symbolized the solidarity of slave families and permitted kinfolk to renew their friendships, but did not allow nonresident fathers to participate in the daily rearing of their children.

The forced separation of Afro-American kinfolk by masters was not entirely destructive. Slave society was characterized by hundreds of interconnected and interlocking kinship and friendship networks that stretched from plantation to plantation and from county to county. A slave who wanted to run away would find kinfolk, friends of kinfolk, or kinfolk of friends along his route who willingly would harbor him for a while.[36] As Afro-American kinship and friendship networks grew ever larger, the proportion of runaways who were harbored for significant periods of time on slave quarters seemed to have increased in both Maryland and Virginia.[37]

There were three different reasons for slaves to use this underground. . . . In 1756, Kate, 30 years old, ran away from her master, who lived near Georgetown on the Potomac. She went to South River about thirty miles distant, where she had formerly lived. Friends concealed her there. Her master feared that since "she had been a great Rambler, and is well known in *Calvert* and *Anne Arundel* Counties, besides other parts of the Country," Kate would "indulge herself a little in visiting her old Acquaintances," but spend most of her time with her husband at West River.[38]

Indeed, 20 of 233 Maryland runaways (9 percent) left masters to join their spouses. Sue and her child Jem, 18 months old, went from Allen's Freshes to Port Tobacco, Charles County, a distance of about ten miles, "to go and see her husband." Sam, age 30, lived about thirty miles from his wife in Bryantown, Charles County, when he visited her in 1755. Will had to go over a hundred miles, from Charles to Frederick County, to visit his wife, because her master had taken her from Will's neighborhood to a distant quarter.[39]

This essay has pointed to the basic cultural and demographic cleavage between African and Afro-American families. African immigrants, like free and servant immigrants from Britain, remembered their native land but had to adjust to the new conditions of the Chesapeake. As free Africans they had lived among many kinfolk; in the Chesapeake, kin ties were established with difficulty. Because most immigrants were young adult males and because plantations were small, two-parent households were rare. Mothers by default became the major black influence upon Afro-American children.

After immigration from Africa slowed, the sex ratio declined, and plantation sizes increased. As generation followed generation, Afro-Americans in Maryland and Virginia created an extensive kinship system. More households, especially on large plantations, included two parents and their children. Although most households did not include kinfolk other than the immediate family, other relations lived in adjacent huts. Mothers and children worked in the tobacco fields with kinfolk, ate and celebrated with many relations, and invited kin who lived elsewhere to share in the festivities. Afro-Americans forcibly separated from relatives managed to maintain contact with them. And finally, slave resistance—whether expressed in the fields or by running away—was fostered and encouraged by kinfolk.

Notes

1. Pioneering essays by Russell Menard, "The Maryland Slave Population, 1658–1730: A Demographic Profile of Blacks in Four Counties," *William and Mary Quarterly,* 3d ser. 32 (1975):29–54, and Peter Wood, *Black Majority: Negroes in Colonial South Carolina through the Stono Rebellion* (New York, 1974), ch. 5, suggest some characteristics of colonial black families. Much more is known about slave families in the nineteenth century. Herbert G. Gutman, *The Black Family in Slavery and Freedom, 1750–1925* (New York, 1976) is the standard reference. Other studies include Eugene D. Genovese, *Roll, Jordan, Roll: The World the Slaves Made* (New York, 1974), pp. 443–524; E. Franklin Frazier, "The Negro Slave Family," *Journal of Negro History* 15 (1930):198–266; John Blassingame, *The Slave Community: Plantation Life in the Ante-Bellum South* (New York, 1972), ch. 3; George P. Rawick, *From Sundown to Sunup: The Making of the Black Community* (New York, 1972), ch. 5.
2. There are no standard definitions of household, domestic group, and family. I have borrowed my definitions of household and domestic group from Donald R. Bender, "A Refinement of the Concept of Household: Families, Co-residence, and Domestic Functions," *American Anthropologist* 69 (1967): 493–504, quote on p. 498. The use of "immediate family," "near kin," and "distant kin" were suggested to me by Herbert Gutman, and would be rejected by Bender.
3. Sidney W. Mintz and Richard Price, "The Study of Afro-American Culture History: Some Suggestions" (working paper presented to the Schouler Lecture Symposium, Creole Societies in the Americas and Africa, John Hopkins University, April 1973) cited with the permission of Mr. Mintz. This paper will be published in fall, 1976 by Ishi Publications, Philadelphia, as *An Anthropological Approach to the Afro-American Past: A Caribbean Perspective,* Occasional Papers in Social Change. A more systematic application of these hypotheses to the colonial Chesapeake will be found in Allan Kulikoff, "Tobacco and Slaves: Population, Economy, and Society in Eighteenth-Century Prince George's County, Maryland" (Ph.D. diss., Brandeis University, 1976), ch. 6.
4. It is difficult to be more precise because most data on African kinship systems comes from twentieth-century anthropological works. The following works suggest variations in African kinship patterns: A. R. Radcliffe-Brown, "Introduction" to *African Systems of Kinship and Marriage,* ed. Radcliffe-Brown and Daryll Ford (London, 1950), pp. 1–85; Meyer Fortes, "Kinship and Marriage among the Ashanti," ibid., pp. 252–84; Jack Goody, *Comparative Studies in Kinship* (Stanford, 1969), ch. 3; Robert Bain, *Bangwa Kinship and Marriage* (Cambridge, England, 1972); William J. Goode, *World Revolutions and Family Patterns* (New York, 1963), pp. 167–200.
5. Mintz and Price, "Afro-American Culture History," pp. 56–78 but esp. pp. 61–62; John S. Mbiti, *African Religions and Philosophy* (New York, 1969), pp. 104–9.
6. Goode, *World Revolutions,* pp. 167–68, 196; Mbiti, *African Religions,* pp. 142–45. Women in polygynous societies also nursed infants for three to four years and abstained from intercourse during part of that period. If this pattern was repeated in the Chesapeake, it was partially responsible for the low gross birth rate among blacks in seventeenth-century Maryland; see Kulikoff, "Tobacco and Slaves," ch. 4; Menard, "Maryland Slave Population," p. 41; Mbiti, *African Religions,* p. 111. For polygyny on the Eastern Shore,

see "Eighteenth-Century Maryland as Portrayed in the 'Itinerant Observations' of Edward Kimber," *Maryland Historical Magazine* 51 (1956):327.

7. For Maryland, see Kulikoff, "Tobacco and Slaves," ch. 4, table 4-3; Menard, "Maryland Slave Population," p. 32, for sex ratios; Kulikoff, "Tobaco and Slaves," ch. 6, for density. For Virginia, see Robert A. Wheeler, "Mobility of Laborers in Surry County, Virginia, 1674–1703 (paper presented at the Stony Brook, N.Y., Conference on Early Social History, June 1975), p. 6.

8. For the uprising of 1739 and some evidence concerning the competition of whites and Afro-American for African and Afro-American women, see Kulikoff, "Tobacco and Slaves," ch. 6.

9. White common-law husbands found open cohabitation with black women socially undesirable. When William Hardie of Prince George's accused Daniel Carroll of Upper Marlborough, a wealthy merchant of the same county, of buggery and of keeping mulattoes, since "he . . . could use them as he pleased," Carroll sued him for slander, finding both charges equally harmful; see Clinton Ashley Ellefson, "The County Courts and the Provincial Courts of Maryland, 1733–1764" (Ph.D. diss., University of Maryland, 1963), pp. 544–46.

10. PG Inventories, 1730–44.

11. Menard, "Maryland Slave Population," pp. 42–46; Kulikoff, "Tobacco and Slaves," ch. 4.

12. These points are fully developed in Kulikoff, "Tobacco and Slaves," ch. 6.

13. These statements are based upon PG Wills, 1730–69 and court cases discussed below.

14. PG Wills, 1730–69; mortgages in PG Land Records, libers T, Y, and PP, mss. Estate sales were sometimes advertised in the *Maryland Gazette*. Slaves could not be sold from an estate until all other moveable property had been used to pay debts. Elie Valette, *The Deputy Commissary's Guide within the Province of Maryland* (Annapolis, 1774), pp. 91, 134–35.

15. Eighteenth-century migrations of slaves are discussed in Kulikoff, "Tobacco and Slaves," ch. 4, and slave migrations in the nineteenth century are analyzed in Kulikoff, "Black Society and the Economics of Slavery," *Maryland Historical Magazine* 70 (1975):208–10.

16. Court of Appeals of the Western Shore, BW no. 10(1800–1801), ff. 456–83, but esp. ff. 459–60, mss.

17. Chancery Papers no. 5241 (1788) mss; PG Wills 1:280–5; PG Original Wills, box 7, folder 66, and box 13, folder 51, mss.; PG Inventories DD no. 1 ff. 22–24; DD no. 2, ff. 379–86; GS no. 1 ff. 246–48; and ST no. 1, ff. 96–100.

18. Chancery Records 16:298–304, ms.; PG Land Record PP (second part) 4; NN, f. 407; PG Original Wills, box 7, folder 3, and box 9, folder 52; PG Inventories DD no. 1, ff. 438–41, and GS no. 2, ff. 111–12.

19. About 40 percent of Prince George's slaves lived on large units from 1750 to 1779 (estimate based upon probate inventories), and 52 percent of the slaves in that county lived on big units in 1790 (federal census); see Kulikoff, "Tobacco and Slaves," table 6–1 for references.

20. Large in-migrations of Africans to the Chesapeake region occurred in the 1670s and 1690s (see Kulikoff, "Tobacco and Slaves," ch. 4, and references there). The great-grandmother of a man born in 1755 could have immigrated from Africa as a young woman in the 1690s.

21. "A List of Negroes on Dooheregan Manor taken in Familys with their Ages Decr 1 1773," and other lists of slaves at Popular Island, Annapolis Quarter, and Annapolis taken in February and July 1774, Carroll Account Book. There were ten quarters on the 10,500 acres of Doohoregan. I am greatly endebted to Edward Papenfuse for calling this list to my attention.

22. Only a handful of people in the Chesapeake colonies owned as many slaves as Carroll. He could therefore afford to keep most of his slave families together, an option not open even to the very large slaveowner with several children and 100 slaves. Nevertheless, two-thirds of Carroll's slaves lived on units with less than 40 people, and 57 percent of them on quarters with less than 30. Only the 130 slaves who lived at Riggs (the main plantation at Doohoregan) developed more extensive kinship networks on a single quarter than was possible for slaves who lived on other large Chesapeake quarters of 15 to 30 slaves.

23. See Menard, "Maryland Slave Population," pp. 35–36 for seventeenth-century examples of quarters named for slave residents.

24. There were 139 married adults (all ages) and single people 21 years and over in the group. While 46 percent of the leaders were over 55, only 11 percent (15/138) of all adults were over 55. The oldest member

of a quarter kin group did not necessarily head the list. For example, Carpenter Harry, 46, headed Frost's Quarter even though his mother, Battle Creek Nanny, 78, was also living there.

25. The statistics are means: 36 percent of all slaves counted together, 38 percent with each quarter counted separately (sum of means). The number of people related to leaders on each quarter was as follows:

Quarter	Leader	Age (Years)	No. of Kin Ties	No. on Quarter (Excluding Leader)
Riggs	Fanny	69	40	129
Sukey's	Sukey	69	9	21
Moses'	Moses	41	7	18*
Jacob's	Jacob	34	2	21*
Mayara James	Mayara James	65	23	27
Folly	Nacy	45	7	19*
Sam's	Sam	57	6	21
Frost's	Carpenter Henry	46	8	36
Sten's	Judith†	21	7	22
Capt. Field's	Phil	34	3	7*
House Servants at Annapolis	Johnny	30	4	12
Annapolis	Peter	60	13	16
Popular Island	James	73	3	25*

Note: The first ten quarters listed were all on Doohoregan. Because affines were unknown (except for Riggs, where they were eliminated for the sake of comparison), the figures are minimums.

*Only known relations were immediate family.

†Daughter of Long Grace, 47, on that quarter, who had lost the use of her feet.

26. Only a maximum of 6 percent of all the slaves in Prince George's, Anne Arundel, Charles, and St. Mary's Counties, Md., in 1790, lived on units of more than 100. (The 6 percent is a maximum number because the census taker sometimes put slaves from several of the same master's quarters in the same entry.) *Heads of Families at the First Census of the United States Taken in the Year 1790; Maryland* (Washington, 1907), pp. 9–16, 47–55, 92–98, 104–9.
27. Joe married his mother's sister's husband's mother's grandchild.
28. See Kulikoff, "Tobacco and Slaves," ch. 7.
29. Kimber, "Itinerant Observations," p. 327. See Kulikoff, "Tobacco and Slaves," ch. 6, for a fuller description of slave quarters.
30. Three of the structures are in St. Mary's; the other once stood in Prince George's. I am indebted to Cary Carson, coordinator of research, St. Mary's City Commission, for sharing the data on St. Mary's with me, and to Margaret Cook (a local historian, who lives in Oxon Hill, Md.) for her descriptions and slides of the Prince George's hut. These ideas will be expanded elsewhere.
31. On a small plantation a slave quarter located in a kitchen is described in Provincial Court Judgments, EI no. 4, ff. 110–12, ms.
32. Court of Appeals of the Western Shore, BW no. 10 (1800–1801), ff. 459–60; *Maryland Gazette*, 2 Nov. 1748.
33. Carroll Account Book.
34. Greene, *Diary of London Carter,* pp. 329, 348, 648, 845, 1109–10; *Maryland Gazette*, 11 July 1771.
35. See references cited in Kulikoff, "Tobacco and Slaves," ch. 6, note 44.

36. My work on slavery owes much to the pioneering book of Gerald Mullin, *Flight and Rebellion: Slave Resistance in Eighteenth-Century Virginia* (New York, 1972), but my perspective on runaways differs from the ones he presents in chapters 3 and 4 of his book. Mullin has, I believe, missed the significance of kin networks in helping most runaways.

37. See table 8.5; Kulikoff, "Tobacco and Slaves," table 6–4; Mullin, *Flight and Rebellion,* p. 129, shows that the proportion of visitors (as defined in table 8.5) increased from 29% before 1775 to 38% of all runaways whose destinations can be determined from 1776 to 1800. The major problem with this data and Mullin's is the large number of unknowns (52% in Maryland and 40% in Virginia).

38. Ibid., 4 Oct. 1749; 11 Nov. 1756; for other extensive visiting networks, see ibid., 11 Aug. 1751; 12 March 1772; 30 Jan. and 22 May 1777.

39. Ibid., 9 March 1758, 6 Feb. 1755, and 12 Aug. 1773; table 8.7. John Woolman claimed that husbands and wives were often separated, *The Journal of John Woolman* (Corinth ed., New York, 1961), p. 59.

Chapter 3

Women and Property across Colonial America: A Comparison of Legal Systems in New Mexico and New York

Deborah A. Rosen

In the past generation, historians have placed increasing emphasis on the diversity of colonial life in North America by expanding their view from an almost exclusive focus on British colonial rule to include the competing Spanish and French colonial systems. This development has opened up comparative perspectives that prove a valuable tool in illuminating women's power in colonial America. In the following article, Deborah Rosen offers very concrete evidence on issues of women and property by comparing legal codes and realities in colonial New Mexico and New York in the eighteenth century. Rosen argues that "women gained tangible benefits" under the Spanish civil law system in comparison to the rights enjoyed by women under British common law that prevailed in New York after 1664. These differences, of course, became particularly significant with the United States' annexation of the northern provinces of Mexico with the Treaty of Guadalupe Hidalgo in 1848.

Law was one of the main determinants of women's experiences in colonial America. Women throughout the colonies lived in patriarchal social systems that limited their autonomy and power. But the specific legal and cultural rules that set the boundaries in which women were supposed to live varied among different regions. It mattered if a woman lived in a colony controlled by a common law system (as in England) or a civil law system (such as that of Spain). When travelers from the United States later encountered Spanish-American law, they scornfully dismissed it as inferior to Anglo-American law. Yet civil law systems were far more protective of women's property than the common law system was. This may not seem to fit the common perception of Spanish law and culture as being particularly patriarchal; it may seem contrary to the assumption that Spanish men expected to exert authority over wives and continued to control children until marriage. And it may not seem consistent with the perception of English law as being more individualistic than Continental European legal systems. Nevertheless a comparison of women's lives under two different colonial legal regimes shows that women gained tangible benefits from civil law systems that they did not enjoy under common law. . . .

Since both Spain and England secured long-term control of their respective colonies during the last two decades of the seventeenth century, that is where this study begins. Comparing New

Mexico and New York allows us to explain the differences in laws governing women and property in those colonies and also to explore the practical effects of those laws on women.[1] In wills, probate inventories, deeds, and court records from the late seventeenth to the late eighteenth century, we can find evidence of how the different laws worked in practice and how the civil and common law regimes affected women's control over property and economic opportunities.[2]

Legal documents do not represent all segments of society equally. They may over-represent older and wealthier members, who may have been more likely to write wills, execute deeds, and initiate lawsuits and whose estates may have been more likely to be inventoried. In addition, people from nondominant racial groups were less likely to be parties to these kinds of legal proceedings. For both New Mexico and New York, that means little coverage of the Native American experience. For New York, it also means less attention to African Americans than their presence in the population warrants. The proportion of the population excluded because of age, wealth, or race may also differ from one jurisdiction to another. Together with the variable survival rate of colonial era documents, these circumstances mean that precise quantitative comparisons cannot justifiably be made between different jurisdictions. Despite these limitations, the documents provide useful information not available from other sources and contribute to our understanding of the comparative legal constraints on and resulting economic opportunities for women.

Spaniards in New Mexico tried to live in a way that maintained their Spanish culture, and they generally followed Spanish custom, law, and legal procedures in the colony.[3] The rules of Spanish law codified in *Las Siete Partidas* (1265) and the *Leyes de Toro* (1505) thus governed colonial New Mexico and determined the property rights of women.[4] Spanish law provided for women to inherit property from parents on an equal basis with their brothers.[5] Because parents traditionally provided their daughters with dowries when they got married, it was often the case that daughters received a large part of their inheritance before their parents died (and before their brothers received their own distribution from the parents' property). Although a woman's husband could administer and invest the dowry during the marriage, he was obligated to return the full value to the woman, her children, or her family of origin at the termination of the marriage by death or separation.

Customarily, at the time of marriage the husband also contributed to the dowry a sum of money known as the *arras* (up to 10 percent of the value of the man's assets). This contribution, which was also guaranteed to the woman or her heirs, further increased the woman's long-term financial security. During her marriage, the woman's own property (*bienes parafernales*) legally remained under her control and could not be sold by the husband. She had the right to dispose of this property by will without her husband's consent. When a man died, his widow continued to control the bienes parafernales; she also gained full control of the dowry and the arras as well as receiving half of the community property (*bienes gananciales*). During the marriage, the husband was free to manage or even sell the community property as he saw fit. But at his death, his widow received full control of half that property, and the other half was divided among the man's children.

Thus the combination of partible inheritance, a wife's legal control of her own property even after marriage, the special protection of the dowry and arras to guarantee the full value of that property to the woman and her heirs, and the distribution of half the community property to the widow all reinforced women's property rights and financial security in Spain and New Spain. Many of these same legal principles also governed colonies controlled by other civil law nations.[6]

What laws appear to mandate is often not the way they actually apply in practice. Yet an examination of a variety of legal documents in the Spanish Archives of New Mexico demonstrates that, women's property rights under the law were respected in practice; the application of the law was systematic and consistent. First, men's probate documents show that widows were left with both real and personal property. Whether men executed wills or died intestate, their widows received their personal belongings, dowry, property inherited from others, and one-half of the community property of the marriage. The various forms of property were carefully distinguished in the wills. Often other documents in the same archive file that holds a man's will or probate inventory provide evidence of careful investigation of the sources of various items of property in order to determine whether the wife or the husband had brought the property to the marriage or had inherited it or whether it was part of the property acquired jointly during the marriage. Surviving family members, including spouses, parents, siblings, and children, were often asked for their best recollection as to the origins of family property so that it might be properly distributed.

Second, men's and women's probate documents show that daughters' shares of their parents' estates tended to be equal to the shares inherited by sons. The main distinction that was made among siblings was between married daughters (who normally had already received a share of property as their dowry), on the one hand, and sons and unmarried daughters, on the other hand. Women were somewhat more likely to leave their personal belongings, such as clothes and jewelry, to daughters rather than to sons. In general, though, when a person died, his or her real and personal property was customarily divided equally among female and male children who had not yet received their share.

Because women inherited property from parents and had full ownership rights to community property of their marriages after their husbands died, they had property to sell during and after their marriages, they had property to litigate over, and they had property to bequeath to others when they died. Thus in colonial New Mexico both married and unmarried women wrote wills bequeathing their land and other property. For the period after the reconquest in 1693, more than one quarter of the wills in the Spanish Archives of New Mexico collection were written by women. The marital status of all but two of the testators is clear in the wills themselves, so we know that 55 percent of the women writing the wills were married; an even higher 63 percent of the female decedents with inventories whose marital status is known were married. Women's wills and probate inventories include land and houses as well as clothes, jewelry, and household goods among the property owned by the deceased. Ninety-two percent of the inventories and 97 percent of the wills specifically distinguish real estate as belonging to the woman. Even among the married women, 93 percent declared real estate as their own property.

In addition to writing wills independently, New Mexico women more frequently exercised a legal role as litigators and grantors than did New York women, though the difference is tempered by the fact that those women who were married did not typically carry out such roles entirely independently of their husbands. Nonetheless, it is clear that, unlike the English women of colonial New York, married and unmarried New Mexico women did litigate in court and did sell and buy land in their own names.

Surviving legal papers show that married women in New Mexico brought actions in their own names. Although the women frequently stated that they acted with their husband's consent or in their husband's absence, it is not clear whether such assurances were really required or were "merely courtesy," as Janet LeCompte found to be the case in the nineteenth century.[7]

Spanish colonial legal practice included several ways of protecting property on behalf of married women whose holdings were managed by their husbands. For example, in practice, the rules concerning alienation of community property were applied in reciprocal fashion. Women did not sell community property without their husbands' participation or permission, but there also appear to have been limits on men. Although the law did not require a husband to obtain his wife's permission before selling community property, a man making such a sale would declare that he represented both himself and "the person of his wife" or that he was selling the land "with the consent of his wife," and both parties would waive their community property rights in the land.[8] In this way, practice seems to have been more protective of women than the law actually required.

There were also formal requirements in Spanish law that tried to protect women from being coerced into selling land against their wishes. Those legal provisions are most often evident in two kinds of statements in New Mexico deeds: waivers of the benefits of certain specified laws protective of women and declarations that the female grantor was acting freely, not under coercion. Both assertions are included in a 1729 deed given by Nicolasa Montoya and her husband Bartolome Gutierres, who sold property inherited from Montoya's father. In addition to waiving any benefits from the laws regarding community property, she renounced "the laws of the Emperor Belellano Justiniano, *senatus consultos, toro y partida*, and the rest in favor of women." This deed also includes a statement that Montoya "has not been intimidated by her husband nor advised by any other person because it is her will to give consent to her said husband so that he may sell it."[9] Although similar testimony appears in almost every land transfer involving a female grantor, declarations of voluntary consent were less common. In 1723, when Maria Dominguez and her husband sold land that she had inherited from her father, the deed noted that she was relinquishing the land "of her own volition, without being forced by her said husband, she gives power and consent to him so that he may be able to make the sale."[10]

It was even possible for a woman to void a document on the ground that her husband had coerced her into executing it. In 1747, Rosalie Garcia took advantage of such protection: she argued that when she previously renounced further property from her paternal inheritance, she did so because "being threatened with so many injustices by my . . . husband that I found myself in fear, . . . I was forced to grant and declare everything that he wanted." "Interestingly, when Garcia later agreed to withdraw her petition for annulment of her renunciation, to terminate her lawsuit against her father's second wife, and to waive any right to additional property from her father's estate, her stated reasons for terminating the suit were "for the peace and tranquility of my estate, and containing the idea that it is unbecoming for married women to appear before tribunals in pursuit of lawsuits."[11]

Although women were protected against coercion and although in practice men in colonial New Mexico obtained their wives' consent before selling community property, in other ways husbands exerted more control in practice than the law technically mandated. For example, when a married woman inherited land from a parent, that property legally remained under her control. Yet husbands often joined their wives in selling such land to another. Although women sometimes appeared in land transfers as lone grantors, such women seem to have been widows, not married women (though the documents do not always specify marital status). We can see examples of the usual pattern of joint conveyances in eighteenth-century records: in 1736, Diego de Torres and Martin sold land that Martin had inherited from her father; in 1766, Domingo de Luna and his wife Maria Baca together sold land that Baca had inherited from her father.[12] Sometimes the husband appears to have conducted the sale by himself, without even a mention of the wife's involvement.[13] Furthermore, before selling land she had brought to a marriage, a woman often obtained the consent of her husband. In 1734, Juana de Sedillo sold a house and cultivated land that she had inherited from her first husband. At the time of the sale, she had remarried; the file documents include the notice that de Sedillo "has permission from her [second] husband to make this sale."[14]

Even when property law sounded gender neutral, men sometimes enjoyed advantages based on status. At the beginning of the eighteenth century, the *alcalde* (magistrate) Diego Arias de Quiros successfully fended off protests from several women that he had taken land that rightfully belonged to them. Two of the women were sisters whose father had owned land that Diego Arias claimed: the land had belonged to Juana and Maria Griego's father before the Pueblo Revolt, but Arias later obtained a royal grant to the land in appreciation of his role in reconquering New Mexico. The Griego sisters tried to argue against Arias receiving special privileges as a man. They argued that if Diego Arias "served his Majesty as a man, in the wars, we have served him, being poor women, in maintaining the Kingdom settling the same with our persons, and as it is customary to give to men titles and certificates of their services, if the same applied to women we could also present papers as to our services." Unpersuaded by this argument, the governor ruled in favor of Arias, deciding that the women had no right to the land in question. He expressed willingness to give them a grant only for the land that they had in Santa Fe, and, he pointed out, "as both of them are single women they will be much better off" in town than on their own on a ranch outside the city.[15]

Men were the primary public representatives of the family, and their status sometimes brought them greater clout in court. They managed most marital property, which meant that during marriage they often participated in lawsuits and deeds involving their wives' property. Laws protected women's ultimate rights to their own property, however, and those laws were applied in practice. Women's independent property was not sold without their permission, and married women had the right to dispose of their separate property and their share of the community property in their wills. It is likely that the laws protecting a woman's property were instituted to protect her biological family's interests, that is, to make sure the family property stayed with the woman's lineage. Nevertheless, the practical effect of the laws was to give women, including married women, considerable property ownership and freedom with regard to property.

English common law differed significantly from Spanish law in its provisions for inheritance and ownership of property.[16] Under English law a wife's or a daughter's inheritance depended on whether the husband/father died testate (with a will) or intestate (without a will); most men died intestate. Overall, Anglo-American law in the colonial period enforced the dependency of wives and widows. Under English common law, a married woman had no control over property and could not execute an enforceable contract, write a will, or initiate a legal action without her husband's consent or participation. While Spanish law allowed a married woman to continue to own and control her own property—her personal belongings along with inherited or donated property—and provided that her dowry automatically reverted to her on the death of her husband, in English America the husband owned and controlled all of the personal property that his wife brought to the marriage; he could sell that property or spend her money as he wished. He also gained the right to manage any real estate belonging to or inherited by his wife; though he could not sell it without her consent, he owned any income earned from the real property, just as he owned any property or money earned by the couple during marriage. A married woman could not sell or bequeath personal property without her husband's consent, and even with her husband's consent she could not sell or devise her real estate. Any dowry became merged with the family property managed by the husband and did not revert to the ownership and control of the woman on widowhood.

English common law guaranteed three kinds of property to a widow whether her husband died testate or intestate: her own paraphernalia (her clothes, jewelry, and other personal items), real estate she owned before marriage or inherited during the marriage, and her dower right. The dower right was the widow's life estate in one-third of the real property her husband owned at any point in the marriage. A man could, by will, devise more of the real property to his wife, but he could not leave her less than the fraction provided by law, nor could he sell property subject to her dower right during his lifetime without her consent. Holding the land as a life estate meant that the widow could not sell, mortgage, or devise the realty; she could use it to support herself during her lifetime, but when she died it passed to her husband's heirs. A husband's will did not have to leave his wife any personal property beyond her own paraphernalia. In the seventeenth century, if a man died intestate, his widow was granted full ownership of one-third of the household's personal property after payment of debts (one-half if the couple had no children).

Finally, English law contained presumptions that typically allowed sons to inherit more than daughters. If a man wrote a will in the eighteenth century, he was not required to leave any property to any of his children, though he was customarily expected to do so. If he died without a will, English law provided that his oldest son would inherit all of his real property and all of the children would share equally in the personal property. These basic principles were incorporated into New York's legal system by the end of the seventeenth century. In practice, although the great majority of New Yorkers legitimately circumvented primogeniture, they nevertheless favored sons over daughters, especially in the distribution of real property.

Even within the mandates of English law, individual New Yorkers enjoyed significant freedom in making family property arrangements, and many of them chose to follow a tradition other than that customary among the English. While English law clearly governed inheritance and property ownership throughout the colonial period in the New England and southern colonies, in New York, the situation was complicated by colonial New Yorkers' diverse ethnic backgrounds, and each group came to New York bearing a different tradition. Although the general trend was toward anglicization, many colonists from countries other than England retained at least some of their own customs throughout the entire colonial period.

*　*　*

How did these provisions of the law affect the extent of women's property ownership in colonial New York? Wills, probate inventories, lawsuits, and deeds from New York show that women's limited legal rights in the British colonies acted as a very real constraint on their legal and economic activities— and on their ability to accumulate property—in New York. As English inheritance law replaced Dutch law, widows were given less control over the property of their deceased husbands, and such property was instead placed under the control of sons.

In strict accordance with English law, married women in New York did not write wills independent of their husbands. David Narrett found that women wrote about 15 percent of the wills probated in colonial New York City and about 6 percent of the wills in rural Suffolk and Ulster Counties. Between 1664 and 1775, of the 254 female testators in New York City, 11 percent were married. Twenty-two married women left wills between 1664 and 1696, and twenty-one of those were mutual wills written with their husbands.[17] Only nine wives left wills between 1696 and 1775, and those wills also were not written independent of husbands: if they were not mutual wills, they normally noted the husband's consent at the time the will was drafted or in a previous antenuptial agreement.[18] Between 1664 and 1775, 77 percent of female testators were widows, and 11 percent were single.[19] Their wills more often bequeathed personal property—most commonly clothes, jewelry, special serving utensils, and beds—rather than land. Overall, in English colonial New York only about half of the female testators explicitly devised any real property. Few widows or single women had land to pass on to heirs because male New Yorkers customarily devised land to their sons rather than their daughters and widows were entitled only to a life estate in the family's (that is, the husband's) real property. The extent of women's control over property is closely correlated with the degree to which they inherited property from their husbands and fathers.

Narrett's study of colonial New York wills found that married male British testators who had at least one child rarely devised full title to land to their wives. Most British men restricted their widows' control over property; by the end of the colonial period, for example, only 6 percent of widows in New York City had the right to sell land that they received under their husbands' wills. A woman typically held property for her use during widowhood only; she did not have full control or ownership, nor did she have the right to say who would inherit the property after her own death. Even including land inherited on a limited and temporary basis, between 1664 and 1775, only one-third of British men in New York City who had at least one child left all or nearly all of their property to their wives.[20]

Differences between the wills of Dutch men and British men resulted in different patterns evident among Dutch women and British women. Because Dutch women were more likely to inherit full title to property that they could then pass on to their heirs (and also because Dutch women's husbands were more likely to support their writing wills even during marriage), Dutch women were more likely to write wills than were British women. In the first decade of the eighteenth century, for example, British men in New York constitute 50 percent of all men writing wills there and Dutch men, 38 percent. If British and Dutch women had written wills at the same rates as men of their national background did, the percentages would be the same for women. Instead, British women constituted only 19 percent of women writing wills and Dutch women 50 percent. Much of the difference was made up by resident French colonists, who tended to follow inheritance practices similar to Dutch practices; French men made up 9 percent of male testators and French women 25 percent of female testators.[21] The disparities among these groups decreased as inhabitants of all ethnicities became more anglicized over the course of the eighteenth century.

Women in New York were disadvantaged in inheriting from their fathers as well as from their spouses. Although Anglo-American families did not always apply the principle of primogeniture, they almost always favored sons over daughters, especially in rural areas. In particular, British farmers tended to leave their land to their sons exclusively, usually without leaving property or cash of comparable value to daughters. Daughters had no right to an equal portion of their parents' property, nor did they have any reason to expect that in practice they would receive a portion equal to that received by their brothers. As might be expected, given the different views of marital property in common law and civil law nations, daughters in British families of New York were less likely than those in Dutch households to receive shares equal to their brothers' shares. For some time after Dutch men in New York had begun restricting their wives' property rights during widowhood, they continued to adhere to the custom of dividing their land and other property equally among sons and daughters. Only in the mid-eighteenth century did Dutch men in New York adopt the practice of leaving real estate to their sons only; even then they provided their daughters compensation in cash, often to the extent of the market value of the realty given to sons.[22]

In any case, daughters rarely controlled their own inheritances, since married women's property came under the management and possession of their husbands. New York judges consistently ruled that on marriage the property of a woman passed to her husband and, with the exception of inheritances, property acquired during marriage also belonged to the husband.[23] Consistent with the rule that denied New York wives control over property and the right to convey real estate, deeds show that married women did not convey land. The absence of married women alienating land is evidenced, for example, in records of eighteenth-century deeds from two large tracts of land in Dutchess County: Rombout Precinct and Crum Elbow Precinct.[24] Deeds only bore a wife's name with that of her grantor-husband when the woman had to sign to show consent to her husband's conveyance of land subject to the dowry claim.[25] Mortgage records from those two precincts also show that married women did not use land as security for loans.

Nor did married women in New York initiate lawsuits without their husbands. A study of New York court records evidences the absence of cases involving married women suing or being sued alone. Even widows and single women did not litigate very often. A calculation of female plaintiffs' suing or being sued alone (excluding those suing as executors of their husbands' estates) in various New York courts illustrates the point. Out of 6,400 cases studied from the records of the Courts of Common Pleas of Dutchess, Orange, and Westchester Counties between 1721 and 1760, only about 1.5 percent (105 cases) had a sole female plaintiff, and less than 0.5 percent (23 cases) had a sole female defendant. That the frequency of sole female litigation declined over the course of the eighteenth century can be seen in a study of all civil cases in the Mayor's Court of New York City during three periods: the first decade of the eighteenth century (600 cases), the middle decade of the l740s (1,500 cases), and the last decade (15,000 cases). Non-executor women suing alone in that court composed 6 percent of plaintiffs in the first and second periods (48 and 113 cases, respectively), but only 3 percent (about 500) in the third period. They were an even smaller percentage of defendants: 4 percent, 2 percent, and 1 percent (37, 35, and 180 cases) respectively)[26] Although the vast majority of cases in colonial New York courts were debt cases, relatively few of the cases with female litigants involved disputes over property or money; rather, women were most likely to be involved in cases involving personal injury, such as slander, assault, and trespass. Thus the litigation patterns provide additional evidence that in practice women only rarely controlled property. In general, women's low litigation rate is correlated with their minimal property ownership and low level of independent participation in market activities.

Married women did not have control over the lawsuits that came out of their own property interests, economic activities, or tortious injuries suffered. Sometimes they were not even named in such suits. Johannis Snyder's suit against Henry Bartlet in the Dutchess County Court of Common Pleas provides an example. One of the claims in the lawsuit was for money owed for the work, labor, and attendance of Snyder's wife as a midwife for Bartlet's wife. Even though this case involved services supplied by one woman to another, neither woman was a party to the suit, and thus neither had any control over it.[27] A single woman, too, was sometimes excluded from litigation and even denied the right to decide whether or not to sue someone, if she was deemed to be still under her father's roof. When Frederick Williams brought an action in trespass against Charles Beekman, Jr., the "trespass" was getting Williams's daughter pregnant, which deprived Williams of her services and brought scandal on the family.[28]

As Mary Beth Norton's study of pre-1670 New England and Chesapeake cases revealed, colonial women had economic interests that were not adequately pursued in court by their husbands. Often the husband and wife had different priorities or even conflicting interests, but it was the husband's choices that prevailed under the common law. Furthermore, Norton observed, the low rate of single women's litigating shows that "men spoke on behalf of women in legal matters even when the law did not require them to do so." In sum, "inside the realm of the courts, all women, not just wives, were largely silenced."[29] Married women's inability to seek legal redress or to defend their own interests in court had serious adverse practical consequences.

For all of these reasons—because married women in colonial New York did not control the family property, because single women (especially those from British families) were unlikely to inherit adequate means of support from their fathers, because widows typically did not gain full ownership rights over income-producing land or other assets, and because married women could not protect their financial interests in court—female New Yorkers controlled little property in the colonial period. Overall between 1680 and 1770, probate inventories show that women owned less than 5 percent of inventoried personal property.[30] Tax records—which, unlike New York probate inventories, include assessments of real estate—also indicate a significant disparity between women's and men's control of property in eighteenth-century New York. In the mid-1730s, women owned only 6 percent of taxable wealth in Dutchess County and only 13 percent in New York City. No tax records are available for New York City for midcentury, but in Dutchess County by the mid-1750s women owned less than 2 percent of the taxable wealth. Women constituted a high percentage of poor people in the eighteenth century.[31] Because full ownership of property was not necessary in order to enjoy a comfortable standard of living or even to draw income from that property, not all women who had low tax assessments lived in poverty. Nevertheless, it is likely that even women who lived comfortably had little economic power or financial autonomy.

Thus in colonial New York, inheritance laws, men's preference for leaving property to sons rather than to wives or daughters, and other barriers to widows' ability to gain control over family property left rural and urban women alike living in significantly reduced financial circumstances

TABLE 1 Comparative Wealth of Husbands and Wives in Colonial New York

| Name | Dewsbury | | Youngs | | Pinckney | |
	John	Jane	Christopher	Elizabeth	William	Sarah
Date of death	1698	1703	1727	1748	1747	1747
Value of personal estate	£149	£11	£138	£11	£230	£76
Wealth ranking	middle third	lowest third	middle third	lowest third	middle third	lowest third

Source: Probate inventories of John Dewsbury (March 1698) and Jane Dewsbury (October 1703) of Oyster Bay, Queens County; of Christopher Youngs (September 1727) and Elizabeth Youngs (March 1748) of Southold, Suffolk County; and of William Pinckney, Jr. (January 1747) and Sarah Pinckney (September 1747) of Eastchester. Westchester County. New York Historical Society Collections.

after their husbands died. Comparing the values of several husbands' and wives' probate inventories illustrates this point. In each of the husband–wife pairs in Table I, the widow owned far less property than her husband had during his lifetime.

There has not yet been much research done on widows in Spanish America. It is likely that many of them also experienced reduced financial circumstances when their husbands died. If the couple was barely scraping by while the husband was alive, then the widow was likely to end up in poverty. After all, laws protecting women's property could only help women who lived in families with property. For those women in property-owning families, however, the laws made a difference in the financial security of the widows. One did not have to own very much property for the beneficial inheritance laws to make a difference; even among low-wealth families, inheritance by and from women was significant. Although the inheritance might not have been adequate to support profitable participation in the economy, it might have been enough to allow the heir to survive comfortably from day to day. Even inheriting a modest house with a small plot of land made a difference.

Since the New Mexico inventories did not systematically place a total value on the decedent's property, it is difficult to assess what percentage of all inventoried wealth belonged to women or to make exact comparisons between husbands' and wives' inventories. The lists of goods alone, however, suggest that there was not as large a gap in property ownership between women and men, and that New Mexico women had far more control over property than female New Yorkers did. The dramatic disparities seen in colonial New York seem less common in New Mexico during the same period, because wives and daughters of deceased men were more likely to inherit real and personal property. In general, women in colonial New York owned, controlled, and inherited far less property than did women in colonial New Mexico.

The legal provisions that allowed women more substantial property ownership in Spanish territories than in English areas resulted in greater opportunity for New Mexico women than for New York women to serve as creditors or to produce and sell goods in a market economy. Mortgage records show that the few widows who inherited large amounts of cash from their husbands were able to invest that capital profitably by lending money in exchange for mortgages, but the vast majority of New York widows were in no position to draw profits from credit relationships. Although half of the women's wills devised real property—typically a house and a small lot of land—only a minimal percentage of this property appears to have been large enough to produce significant income for the woman. Moreover, New York women's inventories and wills included only small amounts of personal property that could have been used to generate income. Only about 2 percent of the women's wills and 10 percent of the inventories mentioned even a single agricultural tool, and less than 1 percent of the wills and 7 percent of the inventories included one or more carpentry tools. These small numbers are no surprise, since in colonial New York, neither married women nor widows regularly contributed to the economy outside the home by growing staple crops or doing carpentry work.[32]

Nine percent of the women's wills and 20 percent of the inventories included animals, so ownership of livestock could have provided income for some women. Only a few owned enough animals to bring in significant income through breeding: although cows were the animal most commonly owned by women, for example, only 13 percent of all women's inventories listed five or more cows. Nor did the sale of eggs appear to be common; only one woman's inventory listed geese, and none listed any other kind of poultry. Some of the horses (owned by 10 percent of women) and oxen (by 3 percent) could have been used to pull plows, however, and bee hives (by 3 percent) produced potentially marketable honey. More significant, cows (owned by 20 percent) and sheep (by 10 percent) could also have been used by women to produce dairy products and textiles for sale to neighbors or local storekeepers. Milk, butter, cheese, and cloth were women's most significant contribution to the market economy in rural New York. Probate inventories of male and female rural decedents between the late seventeenth century and the late eighteenth century show that there was a rise in the percentage of households with spinning wheels, looms, and dairying equipment. Thirty-two percent of rural residents who died between 1680 and 1699 owned spinning wheels; by the period 1760–1775, 55 percent owned spinning wheels. During the same period, the percentage of inventories listing looms increased from 3 percent to 22 percent, and the percentage listing dairying equipment (such as butter churns, milk tubs, and cheese presses) grew from 24 percent to 60 percent. These increases are notable because they reflect women's increasing contribution to household and market production. Note, however, that even though women produced goods from this equipment, actual ownership of the implements usually lay with their husbands. Only 12 percent of women's inventories listed spinning wheels, and only 7 percent included dairying equipment. It was men, not women, who owned both the means of production and the income produced by women.

When men died, they tended to leave their income-producing property to sons rather than to wives or daughters. Examples can be found in the husband–wife pairs of inventories described in Table I. At the time of his death, John Dewsbury owned three weaver's looms and a variety of farming equipment with which to support himself and the family, yet his widow, Jane Dewsbury, owned none of those items when she died five years later. Similarly, at her death in 1748, Elizabeth Youngs no longer owned the farming equipment, livestock, weaver's looms, spinning wheels, and sides of leather that had been listed in her husband's inventory when he died.

Urban women, though less likely than rural dwellers to own equipment for producing crops or making cloth and butter, occasionally inherited whole businesses from their husbands, and some of those widows carried on their deceased husbands' businesses quite successfully.[33] The number of female merchants, shopkeepers, and artisans dropped over the course of the English colonial period, however. Particularly for Dutch women who had been born in New Netherland before the conquest and survived to live in the early decades of English rule, the erosion in women's legal rights had a substantial effect on their economic opportunities. As Carol Berkin has noted, while there were forty-six women traders in Albany in the decade before the English conquest, there were no female traders in the city in 1700. With regard to New York City, Berkin observes that "women disappeared from the ranks of tapsters, brewers, launderers, and bakers, as the number of female proprietors of businesses shrank from fifty in the pre-conquest decade in New Amsterdam to seventeen in the decade that followed."[34]

In sum, although many married women in rural areas of colonial New York were actively involved in producing products for the market, they did not own the means of production, and when their husbands died, the equipment, animals, land, and other property often passed out of their hands into their sons' families, leaving the widows with few resources. While a few urban widows inherited enough money or property from their husbands to serve as shopkeepers or creditors, the vast majority of them owned little property and depended on male relatives for support.

The legal situation for women in New Mexico was brighter. Women owned more property and had more opportunities to use that property to support themselves. Most important, women in colonial New Mexico owned land, which was the most crucial income-producing form of property in an agricultural society. In addition, among the items included in probate inventories of deceased women's property were a number of agriculture and craft tools that could have been used either to serve the household or to produce income. Included in Gertrudis Armijo's inventory (1776), for example, was a "blacksmith shop." Margarita Martin was a wealthy married woman when she died in 1744. Her inventory included basic tools for agriculture, carpentry, and sewing: a scythe, two hoes, a wheelbarrow, two carts, a grinding stone, an axe, a chisel, cloth, ribbon, lace, and knitting needles. Juanotilla, a married woman who was described as being of mixed Indian and Spanish parentage, was a resident of the Pueblo of Cochití who died in 1747. She, too, owned a number of agricultural and carpentry tools: in addition to land and livestock, she left for her children and grandchildren 7 axes, 2 hoes, 3 metal plowpoints, 1 wooden plowpoint, 3 digging sticks, an adze, and a chisel.[35] Overall, 42 percent of New Mexico women's inventories mentioned at least one agricultural tool, and the same percentage listed at least one carpentry tool. Other tools—including tools for spinning, weaving, and dairying, which were common activities of women in the northern, English colonies—were scarce in New Mexico women's inventories.

When studying colonial New Mexico, however, we need to look beyond tools to find other income-producing property. Most notably, animals were an important source of income in colonial New Mexico. Thirty-three percent of the women's inventories included at least 300 sheep or goats, and 58 percent contained at least five cows. Overall, 75 percent of the women's inventories included animals whose increase through breeding would bring significant profits to the owners (that is, 75 percent of the women owned at least 300 sheep or goats, five cows, or five mares and a stud horse). We can see the value the women themselves placed on their ownership of animals by the prominence of animals in their wills. In 74 percent of the wills, women declared ownership of specific animals.

Clearly these differences in women's ownership of economically productive property in New York and New Mexico affected their comparative degree of financial autonomy. Most likely, the differences between civil law and common law treatment of women also had an impact on other realms of women's experiences. Norton has suggested that women's legal dependency in the English colonies may have influenced their status in other aspects of their lives, such as their lack of independent religious identity[36] One way to test this hypothesis might be to do a comparative study. In general, comparative studies of different colonial legal regimes in the territory that later became the United States would help scholars answer many questions that cannot adequately be addressed using the common, geographically narrow approach that focuses on only one legal system or even on just one jurisdiction. Specifically, the impact of women's legal status on extralegal matters could be assessed by contrasting broader female life experiences in civil law and common law jurisdictions. Since civil law allowed women a more independent legal status with regard to property, differences between regions governed by the two legal systems could reveal ways in which single, married, and widowed women were affected by the substance of law. A complete study of the practical consequences of legal provisions relating to women in the United States would examine legal, economic, religious, and other arenas of women's experiences in all the different jurisdictions of the country, taking into account the diverse national systems that governed the early colonies. Conceivably, such a study would also consider colonies that remained under civil law powers. For example, comparing the status, experiences, and degree of autonomy of women in New Mexico with those of women in other countries in Latin America that continued to adhere to Spanish law in the nineteenth century might provide useful information about the effects of being subjected to Anglo-American law.

Like New York, New Mexico eventually experienced the displacement of its civil law system by Anglo-American laws and practices. Even though the displacement of Spanish law in New Mexico in the mid-nineteenth century was less thorough than the displacement of Dutch law in New York by the end of the colonial period, one can see a parallel effect on women's property rights when that displacement occurred. In both cases where civil law gave way to common-law, a degradation of women's property rights and economic status occurred. When Anglo-Americans arrived in the Southwest in the mid-nineteenth century, they regarded the Spanish-Mexican political system and legal tradition with disdain, viewing it as unenlightened, arbitrary, unpredictable, and irrational. They were so confident about their own legal system that they were oblivious to—or conveniently ignored—its adverse effects on women.

There were significant differences between Spanish and English legal practice, but not the differences that the American officials in the Southwest perceived. Given the greater benefits for women under Spanish-Mexican law, it is no surprise that women lost power after the United States conquest of New Mexico in 1846. Anglo-American legal principles did not completely supplant Spanish-Mexican laws relating to women and property, but the conquest nonetheless resulted in a decline in women's legal rights and a rise in women's poverty.[37]

This is not to suggest that Spanish-Mexican law treated men and women equally, or that women and men were equal partners in marriage or equal participants in public life. In addition to limitations on women's political rights, such as prohibitions on women voting and holding office, there were a number of limitations on women's ability to participate independently in economic activities in colonial New Mexico. Husbands often managed both the marital community property and their wives' own property. Consequently, married women were less likely than men to be independent actors in New Mexico's economy. Also, legal and customary limitations on married women's ability to make enforceable contracts without their husbands' participation often stifled their ability to make independent contractual arrangements. Yet inheritance laws that passed real and personal property to daughters and wives allowed many New Mexico women to acquire enough income-producing property to contribute to the community property during marriage and, perhaps more important, to sustain them in widowhood. Unlike widows in the English colonies, widows in colonial New Mexico routinely enjoyed the security of full title to land, houses, livestock, and personal property, and when New Mexico women died, whether as widows or as married women, their property went to their own heirs, not their husbands'. In these ways, the provisions of Spanish law that protected women's property rights were neither unpredictable nor uncertain, neither arbitrary nor capricious, and neither rude nor unenlightened. In fact, they had a significant positive impact on the lives of women living on the colonial frontier of New Mexico.

Notes

1. Mary Beth Norton, "'Either Married or to Bee Married': Women's Legal Inequality in Early America," in Carla Gardina Pestana and Sharon V. Salinger, eds., *Inequality in Early America* (Hanover, N. H., 1999), 25, observed that historians have not yet adequately explored the question of "what were the practical consequences for a woman whose identity was subsumed by law into her husband's identity." This article makes a start in addressing that question.
2. Colonial New York probate records (wills and inventories) are housed at the New York State Library and Archives, Albany, N. Y. Inventories for this article were drawn from all 10 counties of colonial New York,

with the largest concentrations from New York, Queens, Suffolk, and Westchester Counties. Of the 600 inventories analyzed in this study (1680–1775), 384 were stated to be from rural counties. Forty-two of the inventories listed property owned by women.

The New Mexico documents are all in the standard archival collection for colonial New Mexico, the Spanish Archives of New Mexico (SANM), manuscripts and microfilms at New Mexico State Records Center and Archives, Santa Fe. The SANM contains 31 wills written by women, 12 inventories of women's property, case files for 17 lawsuits and petitions involving female plaintiffs or defendants, and deeds for 20 sales of land with female grantors or grantees. The documents relate to property located throughout New Mexico, mostly in Santa Fe but also in the two other major jurisdictions, Albuquerque and Santa Cruz de la Cañada. The documents date from the time of the reconquest of New Mexico in the 1690s until the end of the eighteenth century. The vast majority of the documents involve women of full or part Spanish ancestry, but a few of the women are Pueblo Indians.

3. Weber, *Spanish Frontier*, 313–14.

4. For laws governing women and property in *Las Siete Partidas*, see esp. Part VI (Titles I, III, IV, XIII, XV) on wills and intestacy and Part IV (Title XI) on dowries. For laws relating to women and property in the *Leyes de Toro*, see laws LI through LXI.

5. Normal Spanish practice allowed a testator to dispose of 1/5 of his or her property as he or she wished before the equal division among the children. This did not, however, appear to be the practice in colonial New Mexico, or at least none of the women's wills mentioned disposition of the *quinto*. Couturier, "Women and the Family in Eighteenth-Century Mexico," 296–97, also found that most testators in 18th-century Mexico elected not to leave an extra fraction of the assets to one favored heir.

6. For example, French law that governed Louisiana and the Mississippi River Valley shared many characteristics of Spanish law. Consequently, it appears likely that women in those regions probably had more control over property than English colonial women did. Susan C. Boyle, "Did She Generally Decide? Women in Ste. Genevieve, 1750–1805." *William and Mary Quarterly*, 3d Ser., 44 (1987), 775–89, a fine study of Ste. Genevieve between 1750 and 1805, describes some of the benefits of French law for colonial women. She found that legal protection of brides' property, combined with equality of property distribution among children regardless of sex, resulted in French colonial women enjoying "appreciable economic independence."

7. LeCompte, "The Independent Women of Hispanic New Mexico, 1821–1846," *Western Historical Quarterly*, 12 (1981): 26

8. See, e.g., deed from Tomas Xiron de Texeda to Isabel Gonzales, Dec. 4, 1703, and deed from Diego Padilla to Diego Borrega, Jan. 7, 1734, SANM I, nos. 293, 178.

9. Deed from Bartolome Gutierres and Nicolasa Montoya to Maria Josepha Lopez, Feb. 15, 1729, SANM I, no. 443.

10. Deed from Dimas Xiron de Texada, who appeared with his wife, Maria Dominguez, to Sebastian Martin, his wife, children, and heirs, 1723, SANM I, no. 510.

11. Petition by Rosalie Garcia, Apr. 25, 1747, and compromise and agreement by Ramon Garcia Jurado and Rosalie Garcia, June 15, 1747, SANM I, no. 343.

12. Deed from Diego de Torres and Maria Martin to Nicolas Romero, 1736, SANM I, no. 752; deed from Domingo de Luna and Maria Baca to Miguel Tafoya, 1766, SANM I, no. 991. Other examples include deed from Lucas de Moya and Gertrude Gonzales to Manual Moya, 1766, SANM I, no. 575, and deed from Bartolome Gutierres and Nicolasa Montoya to Maria Josepha Lopez, Feb. 15, 1729, SANM I, no. 443.

13. See, e.g., deed from Thorivio Ortiz to Manuel Rodriguez, 1772, SANM I, no. 795.

14. Deed from Juana de Sedillo to Antonio de Sedillo, 1734, SANM I, no. 178.

15. Proceedings in lawsuit by Maria and Juana Griego against Diego Arias de Quiros Dec. 1703 SANM I, no. 294.

16. It is not clear exactly *why* there are such differences between common law systems and community property systems, but whatever the explanation it probably requires close examination of the thirteenth century, when the two systems appear to have diverged. See Charles Donahue, Jr., "What Causes Fundamental Legal Ideas? Marital property in England and France in the Thirteenth Century," *Michigan Law Review*, 78 (1979): 59–88, which analyzes 4 possible explanations for the differences in marital property law, including political, social, and anthropological explanations as well as a technical legal explanation.

17. David E. Narrett, *Inheritance and Family Life in Colonial New York City* (Ithaca, 1992), 238–43, and Narrett, "Men's Wills and Women's Property Rights in Colonial New York," in *Women in the Age of the American Revolution* ed. (Ronald Hoffman and Peter J. Albert, Charlottesville, 1989), 91–133. See especially p. 96. I have relied primarily on Narrett's excellent description and analysis in those two publications for overall patterns and statistical information from New York wills discussed in this article.

18. See wills of Elizabeth Goelet (dated Nov. 9, 1769; probated Sept. 12, 1771); Mary Miller (dated Oct. 15, 1770; probated Nov. 28, 1775); Elizabeth Sands (dated June 4, 1759; probated Jan. 15, 1760); Martiena and William Hogan (dated Sept. 18, 1732; probated Apr. 7, 1739); Maria and Jurian Hogan (dated May 4, 1764; probated May 27, 1766); Mary Horsmanden (dated Jan. 31, 1756; probated Dec. 16, 1763); and Margarite Van Beverhoudt Bayard (dated May 26, 1758; probated Oct. 29, 1770); Dorothy Tarpy (dated Oct. 20, 1712; probated Dec. 11, 1712); and Sarah Field (dated Nov. 26, 1732; probated Mar. 20, 1735).

19. Narrett, *Inheritance and Family Life in Colonial New York City*, 239.

20. Ibid., 94–106.

21. These data were calculated from wills probated between 1700 and 1710. A few of the testators were from other European groups—e.g., Germans, Jews—or were of undeterminable ancestry. There do not appear to be any wills written by Native Americans in colonial New York, and there was apparently only one black testator. . . .

22. On inheritance by daughters and sons in colonial New York, see Narrett, *Inheritance and Family Life in Colonial New York City*, 126–37, 144–46, 206–08, and "Men's Wills," 101, 119–33.

23. On married women's limited contractual and property rights, see *Jackson v. Vanderheyden*, 17 Johns: Rep. 167 (1819); *Whitbeck v. Cook et ux*, 15 Johns 483 (1818); *Rumsey v. Leek*, 5 Wend. 20 (1830); *Martin v. Dwelly et al*, 6 Wend. 9 (1830); *Hyde v. Stone*, 9 Cowen 230 (1828); *Minard v. Mead*, 7 Wend. 68 (1831); and *Mott v. Comstock*, 8 Wend. 544 (1832). No New York law reports recording judicial opinion on legal issues exist for the 17th or 18th centuries, but the rules of coverture did not change much between the 18th and the early 19th centuries.

24. Even if all deeds from colonial New York were still available (winch they are not), analysis of the documents would not provide accurate data for calculating what percentage of land was controlled by women because deeds record only a fraction of acquisitions of land. That is, deeds evidence sales or gifts of land but not inheritance of land. Some information about how much land women inherited may he gleaned from wills, but wills do not always specify how much land was in each bequest, much less the value of that land. More important, only about 20% of men wrote wills in colonial New York, and we do not have comparable information about land inherited by women through the operation of rules of intestacy. Tax lists are the best indicator we have of the extent of women's ownership of property in colonial New York, but unfortunately they do not specify how much of the property assessed was personal property and how much was real estate. Because of these limitations in the sources, it is difficult to assess how much real property women owned in colonial New York.

25. Because women could not convey land with or without their husbands in early New York, there was no need for any law protecting women against being coerced into signing such deeds. If a man tried to sell property in which his wife had a dower interest, however, some English colonial jurisdictions, including New York, required a private examination of the wife by a judge, to make sure that she understood and agreed to the conveyance.

26. The figures for the first and the middle decades of the century are based on total counts of all cases in the minute books, but the figures for the 1790s were extrapolated from a study of just two years, 1794 and 1795. For a more extensive discussion of women's litigation in colonial New York, see Deborah A. Rosen, *Courts and Commerce: Gender, Law, and the Market Economy in Colonial New York* (Columbus, Ohio, 1997), chap. 5. Cornelia Hughes Dayton, *Women before the Bar: Gender, Law, and Society in Connecticut, 1639–1789* (Chapel Hill, 1995), chap. 2, has found similar patterns of litigation among women in colonial Connecticut.

27. Plaintiff's declaration in *Johannis Snyder* v. *Henry Bartlet*, May 20, 1752, Dutchess County Court of Common Pleas. Ancient Documents, Document 3111, Dutchess County Clerk's Office, Poughkeepsie, N.Y.

28. Plaintiff's declaration in *Frederick Williams* v. *Charles Beekman, Jr.*, 1735, Joseph Murray, "Precedent Book" (1740–1741), 152, in Murray Collection, Columbia University Law Library, Special Collections, New York.

29. Norton, "Either Married or to Bee Married," 36. For Norton's broader study of gender and power relationships in colonial New England and Chesapeake between 1620 and 1670, see *Founding Mothers and Fathers: Gendered Power and the Forming of American Society* (New York, 1996).

30. New York probate inventories did not include real property, only sometimes enumerated debts owed to a decedent, and rarely indicated debts owed by decedents. Since women were less likely than men to borrow or lend money or to own land, women's inventories were more likely than men's to include all, or almost all, of the decedent's property. If real property, credits, and debts were also included in the calculations, the figures would show control of an even higher proportion of total property by men.

31. Of the 62 people mentioned on the New York City tax list of 1734 whose assessment was £0, 35 were widows or other single women. Christine H. Tompsett, "A Note on the Economic Status of Widows in Colonial New York," *New York History*, 55 (1974), 319–32, found a number of widows listed in the New York City poorhouse records whose names did not appear on the tax lists. . . .

32. For a fuller discussion of changes in New Yorkers' ownership of craft tools, agricultural equipment, transportation vehicles, and consumer goods over the course of the colonial period, see Rosen, *Courts and Commerce*, chap. 1. See chap. 2 for a discussion of mortgage lending, credit, and debt in colonial New York.

33. Jean P. Jordan, "Women Merchants in Colonial New York," *N. Y. Hist.*, 58 (1977), 412–39; Patricia Cleary, "'She Will Be in the Shop': Women's Sphere of Trade in Eighteenth-Century Philadelphia and New York," *PMHB*, 119 (1995), 181–202; Elisabeth Anthony Dexter, *Colonial Women of Affairs: A Study of Women in Business and the Professions in America before 1776* (New York, 1924).

34. Berkin, *First Generations: Women in Colonial America* (New York, 1996), 87. In her discussion of women in colonial New York, Berkin focuses especially on the experience of Margaret Hardenbroeck, a successful merchant in New Amsterdam who found her opportunities seriously circumscribed by English law in the late 17th century. Running a business did not always indicate ownership of significant amounts of property. . . .

35. Probate inventories of Gertrudis Armijo, Margarita Martin, and Juanotilla, in SANM I, nos. 48, 530, 185. Juanotilla was one of the rare Pueblo Indian women to appear in the wills, inventories, deeds, and lawsuits of 18th-century New Mexico.

36. Norton, "Either Married or to Bee Married," 37–41.

37. Deena J. González, *Refusing the Favor: The Spanish-Mexican Women of Santa Fe, 1820–1880* (New York, 1999).

Chapter 4

Food Rioters and the American Revolution

Barbara Clark Smith

Colonial women drew upon their responsibilities in everyday life in contributing to the emerging colonial conflict that led to the American Revolution. Women's support for the boycott of British imports such as tea and textiles to protest British duties on colonial trade is well known. Less visible to historical view has been women's participation in food riots that represented collective responses to the food shortages that accompanied the military struggle and the British blockade of ports as the Revolution proceeded. Barbara Clark Smith highlights this aspect of the class conflict that accompanied the broader colonial struggle and reveals its gendered dimension. Her analysis speaks to the difficulty of distinguishing between "private" and "public" spheres in Revolutionary America, a theme that emerges repeatedly in the study of American women's history.

On more than thirty occasions between 1776 and 1779, American men and women gathered in crowds to confront hoarding merchants, intimidate "unreasonable" storekeepers, and seize scarce commodities ranging from sugar to tea to bread. . . . Such food or price riots occurred in at least five northern states—New York, Pennsylvania, Massachusetts, Rhode Island, and Connecticut—as well as in Maryland and, according to one report, Virginia. Some towns, such as East Hartford, Connecticut, and Beverly, Massachusetts, seem to have witnessed only one incident; others, including Boston and Philadelphia, experienced deep, sustained conflict. A good-sized minority of the crowds we know about consisted largely of women; a few others may have included men and women alike. Whatever their composition, most crowds objected to "exorbitant" prices that shopkeepers demanded for their goods or to merchants' practice of withholding commodities from the market altogether. Each crowd voiced specific local grievances, but it is clear that their participants sometimes knew of actions elsewhere and viewed each episode as part of a wider drama.[1]

These riots took place at the intersection of several streams of historical experience. First, they represent one moment in the long-term development of capitalist social relationships in America, particularly in the northern colonies and states.[2] Promoting the availability of foodstuffs, pressing farmers and merchants to sell rather than withhold their wares, rioters acted on behalf of a plentiful market, although not, it must be stressed, on behalf of a free one.[3] Their actions map an immediate experience of economic distress and articulate popular ideas about economic exchange, its meaning, and the crucial issues of who might claim jurisdiction over it and through what political forms.

The forms themselves compose a second interpretive context, as elements of "the common people's politics" in England and American.[4] In the prominence of women, rioters' adoption of the symbols of authority, and their efforts to pay victims a "reasonable price," America's Revolutionary price riots followed Old World precedents. These riots, which were far more numerous than historians have realized, testify to colonists' access to the repertoire of the English plebeian public, to lines of information and identity that linked ordinary people on either side of the Atlantic. They therefore challenge interpretations that place eighteenth-century crowds solely in a vertical framework defined by elite ideology and accommodation. By contesting high prices and withholding, Americans of lower and middling status often stood against their better-off neighbors; in doing so they laid claim to the powers and rites of Englishmen.[5]

Third, women's prominence in many crowds of the 1770s illuminates aspects of the eighteenth century's construction of gender. Excluded from the vote, unqualified to serve as jurors at courts of law, free women—together with servants, slaves, children, and propertyless men—were politically disabled by their dependent status. Yet women conducted nearly one-third of the riots. Here, then, were possibilities for political action that resistance and revolution opened for women, not as republican wives or mothers but as social and economic actors within household, neighborhood, and marketplace. Food riots have a history in this context, too—in women's substantive, routine participation, not strictly "private" or "public" in nature, in the life of their communities.[6]

Finally, the Revolutionary War, with its dislocations of supply and redoubling of demand, reliance on depreciating paper currency, and rampant inflation, formed the necessary economic context for these riots' occurrence.[7] Beyond that, crowd members and newspaper writers who noted their activities expressed the conviction that a fundamental relationship existed between these incidents and the patriot cause. In a variety of ways, rioters and their allies claimed that confronting merchants in their shops was a patriotic action, much like facing redcoats on the battlefield. As a result, these riots offer a new and decidedly popular angle of vision on Americans' movement for independence from Great Britain and for liberty at home. This essay suggest a new reading of the resistance movement, tracing its relationship to the local world of exchange and marketplace ethics. Most important, it contends that some patriot men and women's resistance to Britain took shape as they negotiated experiences within local networks of exchange, on the one hand, and within the broad Atlantic market on the other. This account of popular participation in the war effort explores one context within which the ideas disseminated by patriot writers and spokesmen in pamphlets, sermons, and the like were received and interpreted.

*   *   *

Women's participation, above all else, marked price rioting as revolutionary and its suppression as counterrevolutionary. True, women had not been altogether absent from earlier eighteenth-century crowds. When Boston soldiers returned from defeat at Port Royal in 1707, women met them with jeers and soaked them with the contents of chamber pots in an act of public judgment. Women may have participated in Boston's 1747 anti-impressment riots, and evidence suggests that in rural areas women were among the "people" or "inhabitants" who defended community interests and enforced community morality.[8] For all that, however, women participated more fully in food riots than they had in earlier riots, as the comments of contemporaries make clear. Abigail Adams referred to a Boston's women's crowd as "a New Set of Mobility," during whose proceedings a number of men "stood amazd silent Spectators." The New Windsor store manager who reported that "the women! in this place" had formed a mob to seize tea clearly felt some surprise about it.[9]

Some people had a hard time accepting the political nature of women's actions. When Boston women who forced Thomas Boylston into a cart, confiscated his warehouse keys, and made away with his supply of coffee, they provoked revealing comments. Abigail Adams reported the rumor that Boylston had received "a Spanking" from the women and added, "this I believe was not true." Given Adams's sense of its unlikelihood, along with the absence of any report of spanking in other accounts of the incident, what seems interesting is the existence of the titillating rumor. Eighteenth-century people may have found it more plausible to characterize the women's effort to mete out punishment in terms of parental discipline, thus casting the action in terms proper to women's familial role, than to invoke metaphors of public hangings and public justice associated with male crowds that, in like manner, put their victims in a cart. John Adams was both condescending and moralistic toward the Boston women. "You have made me merry with the female Frolic," he wrote Abigail, and appended the pious hope that the women would overcome their love of coffee in the future.[10] The association between women and frivolous consumption apparently prevented John from considering other motivations for and implications of the crowd. Yet the Boston town meeting recognized that city dwellers needed coffee and other imported groceries not only for their own consumption but to exchange with farmers for produce and meat.[11]

Despite the mixed reactions to women's crowds, no one seems to have argued that women overstepped their bounds when they challenged hoarding merchants. The *Connecticut Courant* came close. In August 1777, about twenty women met at the Lyon Tavern and, "with a Flank Guard of three chosen Spirits of the male line," began an orderly one-mile march to "Mr. Pitkin's store" in East Hartford. There is no record of the confrontation with Pitkin or his clerk, but the newspaper reported that the women took 218 pounds of sugar that had been stored there for the army. There was a short scuffle with a man on horseback, whom the women took for the owner of the sugar but who quickly rode away. The *Courant* mocked "so unexampled a Spirit of Heroism" and suggested that the women form a battalion to range the countryside and live off of their "perquisites and plunder." Their standard, said the paper, could be decorated with "an elegant device of a lady inverted," a comment implying that the women had indeed stepped out of their place, turning the world upside down. Even here, however, the *Courant*'s real objection was that the sugar was earmarked for the army, not that the rioters were female. Victims of the Salem's women's crowd seem to have taken the women quite as seriously as if they had been men, for the victims entered a prosecution against the rioters for theft of goods. (The women—or someone else—responded in dead earnest by leaving burning coals at their prosecutors' doors.)[12]

Overall, the women acted seriously. The Kingston women who threatened that, without tea, they would prevent their sons and husbands from fighting for the cause drew on their power in the household. Elsewhere, women showed that they felt entitled to use conventions more proper to a public role. True, a number of women's crowds engaged at least a few men in their enterprises. The Fishkill women "entreated" male passersby for aid; the East Hartford crowd enlisted three men to raid Pitkin's store; in Beverly, women took along a few men with axes to chop down distillery gates; and the New York women who confronted Messier had three continental soldiers accompany them, thereby arming themselves with male authority in general and army authority in particular. Similarly, women's crowds invoked committees or the Continental Congress to justify or legitimate their actions.[13] But male presence was apparently unnecessary—some crowds involved no men at all—and even support from committees or other Revolutionary authorities was dispensable.[14]

Eighteenth-century women had little reason to doubt their competence at such matters as equitable pricing and neighborly dealing. In America, as in England and on the continent, women took part in marketing and buying for their households. Women were innkeepers, victualers, greenwomen (supplying urban markets), and storekeepers, like the one who presided over sales of the crowd's booty in Beverly. Female shopkeepers and innkeepers were accustomed to facing profit-seeking wholesalers. Rural and urban housewives participated with men in the exchanges of labor and goods that marked everyday life. Equally important, women were accustomed to responsibility for the welfare of their neighbors. "Charity" and mutual support in times of difficulty lay within women's as well as men's purview.[15] Neither housewives nor tradeswomen trespassed on male terrain when they worried about the equity of prices, for prices represented relationships between neighbors, a part of community life in which women had long been competent and involved. When the Boston women offered Boylston's tea to the impoverished North End, or when the Fishkill women doled out tea in small quantities, they acted in familiar roles if not strictly in familiar ways.[16]

Despite that, women in Boston, Beverly, East Hartford. New Windsor, Fishkill, and Salem established a public presence in ways that their mothers and grandmothers had not done. It was an extraordinary and radical leap for women to claim authority from the Continental Congress or local Revolutionary committees. When they modeled their actions on the activities of Revolutionary authorities, marched the streets as if in the army, or enacted the rituals of male crowds, these women cast themselves as competent actors in a political context from which they had largely been excluded.

Two conditions allowed that to happen. One was the willingness of patriot leaders to breach the line that had separated governmental affairs from everyday life. Beginning in 1765, members of the colonial elite made common cause with their social inferiors. The nonimportation, nonconsumption agreements central to the patriot movement embraced local networks of exchange and ideas about exchange that inhered in those networks. Moreover, pacts such as the Association linked abstract issues of imperial relations, normally the exclusive preoccupation of the elite, to the daily life of free Americans. Such mundane matters as tea drinking, thread spinning, and buying and selling became crucial political matters; their implications in local, provincial, and imperial patterns of power were laid bare. Not only did ordinary men and women join the elite to defend the rights of colonial assemblies, the elite joined ordinary men and women to endorse local ideals of equitable dealing and encourage popular cultural forms. With fervent injunctions to vigilance, patriot leaders authorized ordinary people, men and women alike, to enforce local notions of fairness and the common good.[17]

Equally important, women themselves brought into the resistance and war sources of legitimacy that were their own and that remained even when patriot leaders' commitment to those values wavered and crumbled. It made a difference that Americans knew that women figured prominently in food riots in England and Europe, and it made a difference that ideals of equity, neighborly dealing, and charity informed American women's daily lives in the colonial period. As a result, with or without price control laws on the books, and with or without the support of men, women acted. And what was starkly the case for women's crowds—that some sources for their legitimacy lay outside the control of the elites—was also the case for men's crowds. In responding to price control riots, patriot leaders had to contend with deep-seated and self-supported beliefs that held it legitimate for people outside the political nation, even women, to act to secure equitable dealings according to local standards for the same.

What is revealed by wartime food riots was the existence of a particular political role in the eighteenth century, the experience of a public formed outside the town meeting and open to participation by some who could not vote as well as by many who could.[18] . . . Price rioters exhibited the capacity for independent judgment; they assumed the right not to be convinced by elite ideas of justice; they asserted the ability to hold and express their own.

How are we to understand this form of politics and the political identity that it offered and required? What relationship did it bear to the more familiar institutions of citizenship that replaced it? In the first place, it was not a liberal form. In the liberal state, citizens offer their allegiance and the state engages to protect them from interference by others and from the state itself. Relationships among citizens may be economic, social, or cultural in nature, but not political, because the "public" is created preeminently by the individual ballot. Citizenship thus consists of vertical ties connecting each individual with the state.[19] By contrast, eighteenth-century Americans lived within and acknowledged horizontal linkages, notable for their multiplicity and intricacy, created by kinship, fellowship, neighboring, and local exchange, and eroded or at least challenged, on the one hand, by growth of a liberal bureaucratic state and, on the other, by increased engagement within the Atlantic market. Relationships within this public were not equal, but they were reciprocal and at one and the same time economic, social, cultural, and political. Women's participation clarifies and secures this conclusion: their political capacity bespoke an economic and social competence derived from neither the Atlantic market nor liberal theory.

Indeed, women's entitlement to riot was not, as John Bohstedt claims for the English case, a form of "proto-citizenship." Women's actions are less easily understood as a parent to the modes of participation available in the nineteenth and twentieth centuries than as a particular eighteenth-century form that was not encompassed in liberal "citizenship." Their political practices were possible because, as Jan Lewis notes, eighteenth-century thought located family and state on a single continuum of society, rather than separating them into public and private realms. Women's participation was possible, in other words, given a peculiar popular access to public time that nineteenth-century citizenship would not encompass and that liberalism would reformulate and, in some instances, actively counter.[20] . . .

Seen from this perspective, patriotism took shape at the intersection of elite and popular cultural streams, combining the political forms of governed and governor. It is crucial not only to bear in mind that both streams existed but also to imagine their separation or independence as partial and problematic. After all, the food riots of Revolutionary America reveal unity as well as disagreement between different classes of Americans. At the outset, members of the Continental Congress, Revolutionary state governments, and local committees agreed with rioters that economics transactions hand political significance, that price gougers were tories, and that the Revolution hinged on the creation of new (or recreation of old) standards of obligation among neighbors. We need to consider and investigate the degree to which elite as well as popular republicanism drew on experiences of local exchange and incorporated ideals of neighboring inherent in the collective social arrangements of much of northern colonial society.

The story of wartime food riots involves the gradual abandonment of price control policies by patriot governments and the gradual radicalization of rioters. There were many moments of significance: Bostonians followed John Winthrop in carting tories out of town, then repeated the action without elite direction. A Boston crowd named representatives to negotiate with elected committees over the disposition of expensive sugars. In Boston, those left in charge of sugar sales were "gentlemen" rather than crowd members, whereas a Salem mob left retail of confiscated goods in the hands of one of its own, establishing itself in this way as an ongoing institution. North Enders held their own mass meeting to discuss grievances and determine appropriate action. Crowds appropriated the forms of the patriot movement. . . .

For some years, popular sentiment proved powerful enough to hold the patriot movement to ideals of social and economic equity. As late as 1779, Massachusetts, Rhode Island, and New Hampshire merchants responded to that power; alarmed by Philadelphia events and fearing "a like conflict," these traders took up voluntary price limits again. Although those agreements prevailed for only a few months, they testify to the tenacity of the popular desire to keep local standards of economic fairness central to the Revolution.[21]

It seems unlikely that most price rioters or their sympathizers discarded their belief in fair dealing, not least because those ideals had become bound up in their sense of what the Revolution was about. Long after the Revolution, many Americans maintained the association of moral values and economic life. As their society underwent broad structural change, many citizens of the early republic persisted in viewing such matters as prices, wages, employment, and debt as social relationships, rightfully vulnerable to community values and oversight, amenable to the competence of ordinary intelligence, and proper to the realm of the commonality.[22]

What *was* lost was the social and political frame that made sense of the food or price riot as a political form. The elite drew back from its endorsement of popular politics in 1780; the Continental Congress discouraged crowds and courted the support of wealthy and conservative men. Of all the changes of the postwar years, several were crucial; the suppression of popular cultural forms; the increasing dissociation (however inaccurate for many) of women and production; the growing association of women with consumption and leisure; the growing articulation of social experience into realms either "public" or "private." These aspects of capitalist development critically delimited political practice.[23] The Revolution itself made an ironic difference in political possibility: the new American governments, after all, claimed the status of "We the People." That revolutionary fact provided a rationale for suppressing crowds, channeling participation into the process of the vote, and closing down available terrain outside that chosen form.

Notes

1. . . . The gender composition of crowds and reporters' frequent ambiguity about it appear in the text below . . . Newspaper accounts provided one source by which people learned about the actions of others. The pattern of events in some areas—for example, the timing of rioting in Salem, Marblehead, and Boston, Mass., in spring 1777—strongly suggests that some riots unfolded as word of mouth brought news of others.

2. These terms are controversial; nonetheless, even those who contend that "capitalism came in the first ships" acknowledge substantial development and change over the following centuries. Two valuable reviews of the literature on early American social and economic structures that also provide new directions are Christopher Clark, "Economics and Culture: Opening Up the Rural History of the Early American Northeast," *American Quarterly*, XLIII (1991), 279–301, and Allan Kulikoff, "The Transition to Capitalism in Rural America,*William and Mary Quarterly*, 3d Ser., XLVI (1989), 120–144.

3. This distinction merits emphasis in light of recent debates over whether English and European food riots were anticapitalist. John Bohstedt queries that characterization, stressing that rioters accepted many aspects of the market and took marker price, under conditions of plentiful supply, as the fair or just price they sought. In his view, food rioters opposed only abuses of the capitalist market; Bohstedt, "The Moral Economy and the Discipline of Historical Context," *Journal of Social History*, XXVI (1992), 265–284. To address the issues raised by Bohstedr lies outside the purview of this article, yet note that price rioters clearly did not equate the free (that is, unregulated) market with an invariable experience of plenty and the reasonable prices provided thereby. Moreover, to withhold goods and raise prices was not unambiguously an "abuse" of capitalism. In the 18th century, certainly, what appeared to some as violations or the social rules governing exchange might be defended by a crowd victim as "the ordinary course of . . . business" (as did Samuel Colton, in "The Merchant Samuel Colton Documents," *The Longmeadow Centennial: Proceedings at the Centennial Celebration of the Incorporation of the Town of Longmeadow, 1883* [Longmeadow, Mass., 1884], 216.)

4. The phrase is Bohstedt's in "The Myth of the Feminine Food Riot: Women as Proto-Citizens in English Community Politics, 1790–1810," Harriet B. Applewhite and Darline G. Levy, eds., *Women and Politics in the Age of the Democratic Revolution* (Ann Arbor, Mich., 1990), 21. The classic literature on the common people's politics in France and England includes George Rudé. *The Crowd in History: A Study of Popular Disturbances in France and England, 1730–1848* (New York, 1964), and E. P. Thompson, "The Moral Economy of the English Crowd in the Eighteenth Century," *Past and Present*. No. 50 (1971), 76–131. "Patrician Society, Plebeian Culture." *J. Soc. Hist.*, VII (1974), 382–405, and "Eighteenth-Century English Society: Class Struggle without Class?" *Social History*, III (1978) 133–165. More recent studies are cited in Bohstedt. "Moral Economy," and Thompson, "The Moral Economy Reviewed," in *Customs in Common: Studies in Traditional Popular Culture* (New York, 1991), 259–351.

5. Students of food riots and *taxation populaire* will note that American practices departed from European ones in a variety of ways. Nonetheless, there was no uniform Old World model: English and French riots differed according to region, time, and circumstance, too. I emphasize here continuities of form and belief—the availability of Old World popular culture as a resource. . . .

6. Ruth H. Bloch. "The Gendered Meanings of Virtue in Revolutionary America," *Signs*, XIII (1987), 39, notes that "conceptions of sexual difference . . . underlay some of the most basic premises of the Revolution."

Linda K. Kerber, *Women of the Republic: Intellect and Ideology in Revolutionary America* (Chapel Hill, N.C., 1980), chap I, 265–288, describes women's exclusion from politics and also the ideal of republican motherhood. See also Jan Lewis. "The Republican Wife: Virtue and Seduction in the Early Republic," *WMQ*, 3d Ser., XL1V (1987) 689–721; Mary Beth Norton, *Liberty's Daughters: The Revolutionary Experience of American Women. 1750–1800* (Boston, 1980); Joan Hoff-Wilson, "The Illusion of Change:. Women and the American Revolution," in Young *American Revolution,* 383–445; and Joan R Gundersen, "Independence, Citizenship, and the American Revolution," *Signs,* XIII (1987), 59–77. Joan W Scott, "Gender: A Useful Category of Analysis," *American Historical Review,* XC1 (1986) 1053–1075, suggests that exploring women's experience is valuable not only in its own right but also because it clarifies men's experience and the history of society as a whole. I contend below that this is the case regarding Revolutionary food riots.

7. Ralph V. Harlow. "Aspects of Revolutionary Finance," *AHR,* XXXV (1929) 46–68. E. James Ferguson, *The Power of the Purse* (Chapel Hill, N.C., 1961), recounts the history of government emissions, depreciation, inflation, and price controls. Anne Bezanson, *Prices and Inflation During the American Revolution: Pennsylvania, 1770–1790* (Philadelphia, 1951), provides a thorough account of the course of price inflation in that state. See also Harlow, "Economic Conditions in Massachusetts During the American Revolution," Colonial Society of Massachusetts, *Publications,* XX (1917–1919), 163–190.

8. Alfred F. Young. "The Women of Boston: 'Persons of Consequence' in the Making of the American Revolution, 1765–76," in Applewhite and Levy, *Women and Politics,* 181–226. Elizabeth Cometti, "Women in the American Revolution," *NEQ,* XX (1947), 329–346, recounts a variety of women's activities, including the crowd that besieged Pitkin's store in East Hartford in 1777. See also Norton, *Liberty's Daughters,* and Henry Bamford Parkes, "Morals and Law Enforcement in Colonial New England," *NEQ,* V (1932), 431–452.

9. Abigail Adams to John Adams, July 31, 1777, *Adams Correspondence,* II, 295; Countryman, *People in Revolution,* 183.

10. Abigail Adams to John Adams, July 31, 1777, *Adams Correspondence,* II, 295; John Adams to Abigail Adams, Aug. II, 1777, ibid., 305.

11. Boston Town Records, XVIII, 262.

12. *Conn. Courant,* Sept. 3, 1777; Oliver, ed., *Diary of William Pynchon,* 46.

13. The mobs against Peter Messier reportedly claimed that the local committee authorized their actions . . .

14. The small numbers and distressingly thin descriptions of most riots make generalization doubly hazardous. It seems that crowds composed of women were as likely to work against patriot committees, as likely to act without such committees, and as likely to inflict physical violence in the course of their action as crowds of men. Their activity would have us modify somewhat Linda K. Kerber's statement that American women, compared with European ones, lacked a collective tradition; Kerber, " 'I have Don . . . much to Carrey on the Warr': Women and the Shaping of Republican Ideology after the American Revolution," in Applewhite and Levy, *Women and Politics,* 227–257.

15. Frances May Manges, "Women Shopkeepers, Tavernkeepers, and Artisans in Colonial Philadelphia" (Ph.D. diss., University of Pennsylvania, 1958). On neighborly charity see Laurel Thatcher Ulrich, *Good Wives: Image and Reality in the Lives of Women in Northern New England, 1650–1750* (New York, 1982), chap. 3.

16. Cynthia A. Bouton, "Gendered Behavior in Subsistence Riots: The French Flour War of 1775," *J. Soc. Hist.,* XXIII (1990), 735–754, associates women's activity in food riots with their role in the household economy. Hans Medick, "Plebeian Culture in the Transition to Capitalism," in Raphael Samuel and Gareth Stedman Jones, eds., *Culture, Ideology and Politics* (London, 1982), 84–113, similarly argues that women's role in the preindustrial household, not very distinctive from men's, empowered them to act to protect the local welfare. My emphasis is less on the household than on its integration into the community through practices of neighboring as well as on other aspects of women's economic lives. See Bohstedt, "Myth of the Feminine Food Riot," and Thompson's remarks on same in "Moral Economy Reviewed." Also of interest on a later period is Louise Tilly, "Paths of Proletarianization: Organization of Production, Sexual Division of Labor, and Women's Collective Action," *Signs,* VII (1981), 400–417, which

argues that, in the early 20th century, women's collective action grew out of a division of labor that assigned a woman the role of purchasing enough for the household from her husband's wages. It is notable that economic hardship for soldiers' families took a similar form during the American Revolution: the family was dependent on a cash wage, paid in a depreciated medium. Yet 18th-century American food riots do not suggest that women considered such actions to fall within their province alone. See Temma Kaplan, "Female Consciousness and Collective Action: The Case of Barcelona, 1910–1918," *Signs,* VII (1982), 545–566.

17. Smith, "Social Visions of Resistance." See also Buel, "Committee Movement of 1779"

18. As should be clear, this public is not identical to that delineated by Jürgen Habermas in *The Structural Transformation of the Public Sphere: An Inquiry into a Category of Bourgeois Society* (Cambridge, Mass., 1989), who describes the emergence of a bourgeois public sphere as the opening of a critical terrain, a space for discourse and evaluation sited between state and civil society, within which citizens might freely discuss political matters. The development of that terrain in America, most notably in the institutions of the colonial press, was undoubtedly crucial to the Revolution and, as Michael Warner emphasizes in *The Letters of the Republic: Publication and the Public Sphere in Eighteenth-Century America* (Cambridge, Mass., 1990), to the articulation of republican ideas. At the same time, that "public" excluded most women and the illiterate, people who qualified as potential actors in food riots. By contrast, Revolutionary food rioters occupied a different political space, one that we must hesitate to assimilate to the sorts of citizenship described by Habermas. Food riots used forms proper to a plebeian public; as noted below, they arose out of a "society" that located state and family relations along a single continuum. Lewis, "Republican Wife," 693.

19. Michael Walzer, *Obligations: Essays on Disobedience, War, and Citizenship* (Cambridge, Mass., 1970), informs this definition of liberalism. See also Lance Banning, "Jeffersonian Ideology Revisited: Liberal and Classical Ideas in the New American Republic," *WMQ,* 3d Ser., XLIII (1986), 11–12, 18.

20. Bohstedt, "Myth of the Feminine Food Riot"; Lewis, "Republican Wife," 693.

21. Davis and Benson to Welcome Arnold, June 19, 1779. Arnold-Greene Correspondence, Box 1, Welcome-Arnold Papers, John Carter Brown Library, Providence, R. I; Welcome Arnold to John Wiley, Aug. 30, 1779. ibid. See also John Clarke to Timothy Pickering, Oct. 21, 1779. Timothy Pickering Papers, Mass. Hist. Soc. For renewed price control activity in New England in 1779 see Smith, "Politics of Price Controls," chap. 7, and Buel, "Committee Movement of 1779."

22. On social formulations of economic life in the new republic see Christopher Clark, *Roots of Rural Capitalism*; Bogin, "Petitioning and the New Moral Economy," 391–425; James A. Henretta, "The Transition to Capitalism in America," in Henretta, Kammen, and Katz, eds., *Transformation of Early American History,* 218–237; Merrill, "The Anticapitalist Origins of the United States," *Review—A Journal of the Fernand Braudel Center,* XIII (1990), 465–498; Countryman, "The Uses of Capital in Revolutionary America: The Case of the New York Loyalist Merchants," *WMQ,* 3d Ser., XLIX (1992), 3–28; Wilentz, *Chants Democratic: New York City and the Rise of the American Working Class, 1788–1850* (New York, 1984); Ronald Douglas Schultz, "Thoughts Among the People: Popular Thought, Radical Politics, and the Making of Philadelphia's Working Class, 1765–1828" (Ph.D. diss., University of California, Los Angeles, 1985); and Nash, "Artisans and Politics in Eighteenth-Century Philadelphia," in Jacob and Jacob, eds., *Origins of Radicalism,* 162–182.

23. Christine Stansell, *City of Women: Sex and Class in New York,* 1789–1860 (New York, 1986); Mary P. Ryan, *Women in Public: Between Banners and Ballots,* 1825–1880 (Baltimore, 1990).

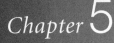
Women, Work, and Protest in the Early Lowell Mills: "The Oppressing Hand of Avarice Would Enslave Us"

Thomas Dublin

The emergence of factory employment between 1820 and 1850 had contradictory results. On the one hand, this new employment offered young, single women wages far in excess of anything else they could earn in teaching, sewing, or domestic service. On the other hand, it led to the first sustained collective labor protests by women workers.

Thomas Dublin attempts to explain this contradiction by exploring the nature of the female experience in the first cotton textile mills of Lowell, Massachusetts. He finds that worksharing in the mills and shared mill housing contributed to the growth of a close-knit community among mill workers, and that the sense of community coupled with republican egalitarian traditions lead women to be sensitive to declining wages and working conditions. Women workers responded collectively to wage cuts, speedups, and stretchouts, and challenged the power of mill employers. While the protests rarely succeeded, they reveal well the clash of values that accompanied the industrial revolution.

In the years before 1850 the textile mills of Lowell, Massachusetts, were a celebrated economic and cultural attraction. Foreign visitors invariably included them on their American tours. Interest was prompted by the massive scale of these mills, the astonishing productivity of the power-driven machinery, and the fact that women comprised most of the work force.

Lowell was, in fact, an impressive accomplishment. In 1820, there had been no city at all—only a dozen family farms along the Merrimack River in East Chelmsford. In 1821, however, a group of Boston capitalists purchased land and water rights along the river and a nearby canal, and began to build a major textile manufacturing center. Opening two years later, the first factory employed Yankee women recruited from the nearby countryside. By 1840, ten textile corporations with thirty-two mills valued at more than ten million dollars lined the banks of the river and nearby canals.[1] Adjacent to the mills were rows of company boarding houses and tenements which accommodated most of the eight thousand factory operatives.

As Lowell expanded and became the nation's largest textile manufacturing center, the experiences of women operatives changed as well. The increasing number of firms in Lowell and in the other mill towns brought the pressure of competition. Overproduction became a problem and the prices of finished cloth decreased. The high profits of the early years declined and so, too, did conditions

Adapted from "Women, Work, and Protest in the Early Lowell Mills: 'The Oppressing Hand of Avarice Would Enslave Us,'" by Thomas Dublin in *Labor History* 16 (1975): 99–116. Reprinted by permission of the publisher Taylor & Francis Ltd (http://www.tandf.co.uk).

Women weavers, c. 1860. American Textile History Museum. Lowell, Mass.

for the mill operatives. Wages were reduced and the pace of work within the mills was stepped up. Women operatives did not accept these changes without protest. In 1834 and 1836 they went on strike to protest wage cuts, and between 1843 and 1848 they mounted petition campaigns aimed at reducing the hours of labor in the mills.

These labor protests in early Lowell contribute to our understanding of the response of workers to the growth of industrial capitalism in the first half of the nineteenth century. They indicate the importance of values and attitudes dating back to an earlier period and also the transformation of these values in a new setting.

The preconditions for the labor unrest in Lowell before 1850 may be found in the study of the daily worklife of its operatives. In their everyday, relatively conflict-free lives, mill women created the mutual bonds which made possible united action in times of crisis. The existence of a tight-knit community among them was the most important element in determining the collective, as opposed to individual, nature of this response.

The mutual dependence among women in early Lowell was rooted in the structure of mill work itself. Newcomers to the mills were particularly dependent on their fellow operatives, but even experienced hands relied on one another for considerable support.

New operatives generally found their first experiences difficult, even harrowing, though they may have already done much handspinning and weaving in their own homes. The initiation of one of them is described in fiction in the *Lowell Offering*:

> The next morning she went into the Mill; and at first the sight of so many bands, and wheels, and springs in constant motion, was very frightful. She felt afraid to touch the loom, and she was almost sure she could never learn to weave . . . the shuttle flew out, and made a new bump on her head; and the first time she tried to spring the lathe, she broke out a quarter of the treads.[2]

While other accounts present a somewhat less difficult picture, most indicate that women only became proficient and felt satisfaction in their work after several months in the mills.[3]

The textile corporations made provisions to ease the adjustment of new operatives. Newcomers were not immediately expected to fit into the mill's regular work routine. They were at first assigned work as sparehands and were paid a daily wage independent of the quantity of work they turned out. As a sparehand, the newcomer worked with an experienced hand who instructed her in the intricacies of the job. The sparehand spelled her partner for short stretches of time and occasionally took the place of an absentee. After the passage of some weeks or months, when she could handle the normal complement of machinery—two looms for weavers during the 1830s—and when a regular operative departed, leaving an opening, the sparehand moved into a regular job.

Through this system of job training, the textile corporations contributed to the development of community among female operatives. During the most difficult period in an operative's career, the first months in the mill, she relied upon other women workers for training and support. And for every sparehand whose adjustment to mill work was aided in this process, there was an experienced operative whose work was also affected. Women were relating to one another during the work process and not simply tending their machinery. Given the high rate of turnover in the mill work-force, a large proportion of women operatives worked in pairs. At the Hamilton Company in July 1836, for example, more than a fifth of all females were sparehands.[4] Consequently, over 40 percent of the females employed there in this month worked with one another. Nor was this interaction sur-reptitious, carried out only when the overseer looked elsewhere; rather, it was formally organized and sanctioned by the textile corporations themselves.

In addition to the integration of sparehands, informal sharing of work often went on among regular operatives. A woman would occasionally take off a half or full day from work either to enjoy a brief vacation or to recover from illness, and fellow operatives would each take an extra loom or side of spindles so that she might continue to earn wages during her absence.[5] Women were gener-ally paid on a piece rate basis, their wages being determined by the total output of the machinery they tended during the payroll period. With friends helping out during her absence, making sure that her looms kept running, an operative could earn almost a full wage even though she was not physically present. Such informal work-sharing was another way in which mutual dependence developed among women operatives during their working hours.

Living conditions also contributed to the development of community among female operatives. Most women working in the Lowell mills of these years were housed in company boarding houses. In July 1836, for example, more than 73 percent of females employed by the Hamilton Company resided in company housing adjacent to the mills.[6] Almost three-fourths of them, therefore, lived and worked with each other. Furthermore, the work schedule was such that women had little opportunity to interact with those not living in company dwellings. They worked, in these years, an average of 73 hours a week. Their work day ended at 7:00 or 7:30 P.M., and in the hours between supper and the 10:00 curfew imposed by management on residents of company boarding houses there was little time to spend with friends living "off the corporation."

Women in the boarding houses lived in close quarters. A typical boarding house accommodated twenty-five young women, generally crowded four to eight in a bedroom.[7] There was little possibility of privacy within the dwelling, and pressure to conform to group standards was very strong. The community of operatives which developed in the mills carried over into life at home as well.

The boarding house became a central institution in the lives of Lowell's female operatives in those years, but it was particularly important in the initial integration of newcomers into urban industrial life. Upon first leaving her rural home for work in Lowell, a women entered a setting very different from anything she had previously known. One operative, writing in the *Offering,* described the feelings of a fictional character: ". . . the first entrance into a factory boarding house seemed something dreadful. The room looked strange and comfortless, and the women cold and heartless; and when she sat down to the supper table, where among more than twenty girls, all but one were strangers, she could not eat a mouthful."[8] In the boarding house, the newcomer took the first steps in the process which transformed her from an "outsider" into an accepted member of the community of women operatives.

Recruitment of newcomers into the mills and their initial hiring were mediated through the boarding house system. Women generally did not travel to Lowell for the first time entirely on their own. They usually came because they knew someone—an older sister, cousin, or friend—who had already worked in Lowell.[9] The scene described above was a lonely one—but the newcomer did know at least one boarder among the twenty seated around the supper table. The Hamilton Company Register Books indicate that numerous pairs of operatives, having the same surnames and coming from the same town in northern New England, lived in the same boarding houses.[10] Given the personal nature of recruitment in this period, therefore, newcomers usually had the company and support of a friend or relative in their first adjustment to Lowell.

Upon entering the boarding house, the newcomer came under pressure to conform with the standards of the community of operatives. Stories in the *Offering* indicate that newcomers at first stood out from the group in terms of their speech and dress. Over time they dropped the peculiar "twang" in their speech which so amused experienced hands. Similarly, they purchased clothing more in keeping with urban than rural styles. It was an unusual and strongwilled individual who could work and live among her fellow operatives and not conform, at least outwardly, to the customs and values of this larger community.[11]

Given the all-pervasiveness of this community, one would expect it to exert strong pressures on those who did not conform to group standards. Such appears to have been the case. The community influenced newcomers to adopt its patterns of speech and dress. In addition, it enforced an unwritten code of moral conduct. Henry Miles, a minister in Lowell, described the way in which the community pressured those who deviated from accepted moral conduct:

> A girl, suspected of immoralities, or serious improprieties, at once loses caste. Her fellow boarders will at once leave the house, if the keeper does not dismiss the offender. In self-protection, therefore, the patron is obliged to put the offender away. Nor will her former companions walk with her, or work with her; till at length, finding herself everywhere talked about, and pointed at, and shunned, she is obliged to relieve her fellow-operatives of a presence which they feel brings disgrace.[12]

One should not conclude, however, that women always enforced a moral code agreeable to Lowell's clergy, or to the mill agents and overseers for that matter. After all, the kind of peer pressure imposed on Hannah could be brought to bear on women in 1834 and 1836 who, on their own, would not have protested wage cuts. It was much harder to go to work when one's roommates were marching about town, attending rallies, or circulating strike petitions. Similarly, the ten-hour petitions of the 1840s were certainly aided by the fact of a tight-knit community of operatives living in a dense neighborhood of boarding houses. To the extent that women could not have completely private lives in the boarding houses, they probably had to conform to group norms, whether these involved speech, clothing, relations with men, or attitudes toward the ten-hour day. Group pressure to conform, so important to the community of women in early Lowell, played a significant role in the collective response of women to changing conditions in the mills.

In addition to the structure of work and housing in Lowell, a third factor, the homogeneity of the mill workforce, contributed to the development of community among female operatives. In this period, the mill work-force was homogeneous in terms of sex, nativity, and age. Payroll and other records of the Hamilton Company reveal that more than 85 percent of those employed in July, 1836, were women and that over 96 percent were native-born.[13] Furthermore, over 80 percent of the female workforce were between the ages of 15 and 30; and only 10 percent were under 14 or over 40.[14]

Workforce homogeneity takes on particular significance in the context of work structure and the nature of worker housing. Together these factors meant that women operatives had little daily interaction with men. Men and women did not perform the same work in the mills, and generally did not even labor in the same rooms. Men worked in the initial picking and carding processes, in the repair shop, and on the watchforce and filled all supervisory positions in the mills. Women held all sparehand and regular operative jobs in drawing, speeding, spinning, weaving and dressing. A typical room in the mill employed eighty women tending machinery, with two men overseeing the work and two boys assisting them. Women had little contact with men other than their supervisors in the course of the working day. After work, women returned to their boarding houses, where once again there were few men. Women, then, worked and lived in a predominantly female setting.

Ethnically the workforce was also homogeneous. Immigrants formed only 3.4 percent of those employed at Hamilton in July, 1836. In addition, they comprised only 3 percent of residents in Hamilton Company housing.[15] The community of women operatives was composed of women of New England stock drawn from the hill-country farms surrounding Lowell. Consequently, when experienced hands made fun of the speech and dress of newcomers, it was understood that they, too, had been "rusty" or "rustic" upon first coming to Lowell. This common background was another element shared by women workers in early Lowell.

The work structure, the workers' housing, and workforce homogeneity contributed to the growth of community among Lowell's women operatives. To understand the larger implications of community, it is necessary to examine the labor protests of this period. For in these struggles, the new values and attitudes which developed in the community of women operatives are most visible.

In February 1834, 800 of Lowell's women operatives "turned-out"—went on strike—to protest a proposed reduction in their wages. They marched to numerous mills in an effort to induce others to join them, and, at an outdoor rally, they petitioned others to "discontinue their labors until terms of reconciliation are made." Their petition concluded:

> Resolved, That we will not go back into the mills to work unless our wages are continued . . . as they have been.
>
> Resolved, That none of us will go back, unless they receive us all as one.
>
> Resolved, That if any have not money enough to carry them home, they shall be supplied.[16]

The strike proved to be brief and failed to reverse the proposed wage reductions. Turning-out on a Friday, the striking women received their back wages on Saturday, and by the middle of the next week had returned to work or left town. Within a week of the turn-out, the mills were running near capacity.[17]

This first strike in Lowell is important not because it failed or succeeded, but simply because it took place. In an era in which women had to overcome opposition simply to work in the mills, it is remarkable that they would further overstep the accepted middle-class bounds of female propriety by participating in a public protest. The agents of the textile mills certainly considered the turn-out unfeminine. William Austin, agent of the Lawrence Company, described the operatives' procession as an "amizonian [*sic*] display." He wrote further, in a letter to his company treasurer in Boston: "This afternoon we have paid off several of these Amazons & presume that they will leave town on Monday."[18] The turn-out was particularly offensive to the agents because of the relationship they thought they had with their operatives. Mill agents assumed an attitude of benevolent paternalism toward their female operatives, and found it particularly disturbing that the women paid such little heed to their advice. The strikers were not merely unfeminine, they were ungrateful as well.

Such attitudes notwithstanding, women chose to turn-out. They did so for two principal reasons. First, the wage cuts undermined their sense of dignity and social equality, which was an important element in their Yankee heritage. Second, these wage cuts were seen as an attack on their economic independence.

A prime motive for the strike was outrage at the social implications of the wage cuts. In a statement of principles which circulated among operatives, women expressed well the sense of themselves which prompted their protests:

UNION IS POWER

Our present object is to have union and exertion, and we remain in possession of our unquestionable rights. We circulate this paper wishing to obtain the names of all who imbibe the spirit of our Patriotic Ancestors, who preferred privation to bondage, and parted with all that renders life desirable—and even life itself—to procure independence for their children. The oppressing hand of avarice would enslave us, and to gain their object, they gravely tell us of the pressure of the time, this we are already sensible of, and deplore it. If any are in want of assistance, the Ladies will be compassionate and assist them; but we prefer to have the disposing of our charities in our own hands; and as we are free, we would remain in possession of what kind Providence has bestowed upon us; and remain daughters of freemen still.[19]

At several points in the proclamation the women drew on their Yankee heritage. Connecting their turn-out with the efforts of their "Patriotic Ancestors" to secure independence from England, they interpreted the wage cuts as an effort to "enslave" them—to deprive them of their independent status as "daughters of freemen."

Though very general and rhetorical, the statement of these women does suggest their sense of their own worth and dignity. Elsewhere, they expressed the conviction that they were the social equals of the overseers, indeed of the mill owners themselves.[20] The wage cuts, however, struck at this assertion of social equality. These reductions made it clear that the operatives were subordinate to their employers, rather than equal partners in a contract binding on both parties. By turning-out, the women emphatically denied that they were subordinates; but by returning to work the next week, they demonstrated that in economic terms they were no match for their corporate superiors.

In point of fact, these Yankee operatives were subordinate in early Lowell's social and economic order, but they never consciously accepted this status. Their refusal to do so became evident whenever the mill owners attempted to exercise the power they possessed. This fundamental contradiction between the objective status of operatives and their consciousness of it was at the root of the 1834 turn-out and of subsequent labor protests in Lowell before 1850. The corporations could build mills, create thousands of jobs, and recruit women to fill them. Nevertheless, they bought only the workers' labor power, and then only for as long as these workers chose to stay. Women could always return to their rural homes, and they had a sense of their own worth and dignity, factors limiting the actions of management.

Women operatives viewed the wage cuts as a threat to their economic independence. This independence had two related dimensions. First, the women were self-supporting while they worked in the mills and, consequently, were independent of their families back home. Second, they were able to save out of their monthly earnings and could then leave the mills for the old homestead whenever they so desired. In effect, they were not totally dependent upon mill work. Their independence was based largely on the high level of wages in the mills. They could support themselves and still save enough to return home periodically. The wage cuts threatened to deny them this outlet, substituting instead the prospect of total dependence on mill work. Small wonder, then, there was alarm that "the oppressing hand of avarice would enslave us." To be forced, out of economic necessity, to lifelong labor in the mills would have indeed seemed like slavery.[21] The Yankee operatives spoke directly to the fear of a dependency based on impoverishment when offering to assist any women workers who "have not money enough to carry them home." Wage reductions, however, offered only the *prospect* of a future dependence on mill employment. By striking, the women asserted their actual economic independence of the mills and their determination to remain "daughters of freemen still."

While the women's traditional conception of themselves as independent daughters of freemen played a major role in the turn-out, this factor acting alone would not necessarily have triggered the 1834 strike. It would have led women as individuals to quit work and return to their rural homes. But the turn-out was a collective protest. When the wage reductions were announced, women began to hold meetings in the mills during meal breaks in order to assess tactical possibilities. Their turn-out began at one mill when the agent discharged a woman who had presided at such a meeting. Their procession through the streets passed by other mills, expressing a conscious effort to enlist as much support as possible for their cause. At a mass meeting, the women drew up a resolution which insisted that none be discharged for their participation in the turn-out. This strike, then, was a collective response to the proposed wage cuts. The existence of a tight-knit community among women turned individual opposition to the wage cuts into a collective protest.

In October 1836, women again went on strike. This second turn-out was similar to the first in several respects. Its immediate cause was also a wage reduction; marches and a large outdoor rally were organized; again, like the earlier protest, the basic goal was not achieved: the corporations refused to restore wages and operatives either left Lowell or returned to work at the new rates.

Despite these surface similarities between the turn-outs, there were some real differences. One involved scale: over 1500 operatives turned out in 1836, compared to only 800 earlier.[22] Moreover, the second strike lasted much longer than the first. In 1834 operatives stayed out for only a few days; in 1836, the mills ran far below capacity for several months. Two weeks after the second turn-out began, a mill agent reported that only a fifth of the strikers had returned to work: "The rest manifest *good 'spunk'* as they call it."[23] Several days later he described the impact of the continuing strike on operations in his mills: "We must be feeble for months to come as probably not less than 250 of our former scanty supply of help have left town."[24] These lines read in sharp contrast to the optimistic reports of agents following the turn-out in February 1834.

Differences between the two turn-outs were not limited to scale and duration. Women displayed a much higher degree of organization in 1836 than earlier. To coordinate strike activities, they formed a Factory Girls' Association whose membership reached 2500 at its height.[25] The new organization among women was reflected in the tactics employed. Strikers, according to one mill agent, were able to halt production to a greater extent than numbers alone could explain; and, he complained that although some operatives were willing to work, "it has been impossible to give employment to many who remained." He attributed this difficulty to the strikers' tactics: "This was in many instances no doubt the result of calculation and contrivance. After the original turn-out they [the operatives] would assail a particular room—as for instance, all the warpers, or all the warp spinners, or all the speeder and stretcher girls, and this would close the mill as effectually as if all the girls in the mill had left."[26] Now giving more thought than they had in 1834 to the specific tactics of the turn-out, the women made a deliberate effort to shut down the mills in order to win their demands. They attempted to persuade less committed operatives, concentrating on those in crucial departments within the mill. Such tactics anticipated those of skilled mulespinners and loomfixers who went out on strike in the 1880s and 1890s.

In their organization of a Factory Girls' Association and in their efforts to shut down the mills, the female operatives revealed that they had been changed by their industrial experience. Increasingly, they acted not simply as "daughters of freemen" offended by the impositions of the textile corporations, but also as industrial workers intent on improving their position within the mills.

There was a decline in protest among women in the Lowell mills following these early strike defeats. During the 1837–1843 depression, textile corporations twice reduced wages without evoking a collective response from operatives. Because of the frequency of production cutbacks and layoffs in these years, workers probably accepted the mill agents' contention that they had to reduce wages or close entirely. But with the return of prosperity and the expansion of production in the mid-1840s, there were renewed labor protests among women.

In contrast to the protests of the previous decade, the struggles now were primarily political. Women did not turn out in the 1840s; rather, they mounted annual petition campaigns calling on the state legislature to limit the hours of labor within the mills. These campaigns reached their height in 1845 and 1846, when 2,000 and 5,000 operatives respectively signed petitions. Unable to curb the wage cuts or the speed-up and stretch-out imposed by mill owners, operatives sought to mitigate the consequences of these changes by reducing the length of the working day. Having been defeated earlier in economic struggles, they now sought to achieve their new goal through political action. The Ten Hour Movement, seen in these terms, was a logical outgrowth of the unsuccessful turn-outs of the previous decade. Like the earlier struggles, the Ten Hour Movement was an assertion of the dignity of operatives and an attempt to maintain that dignity under the changing conditions of industrial capitalism.

The growth of relatively permanent labor organizations and institutions among women was a distinguishing feature of the 1840s. The Lowell Female Labor Reform Association was organized in 1845 by women operatives. It became Lowell's leading labor organization over the next three years, organizing the city's female operatives and helping to set up branches in other mill towns. The Association was affiliated with the New England Workingmen's Association and sent delegates to its meetings. It acted in concert with similar male groups and yet maintained its own autonomy. Women elected their own officers, held their own meetings, testified before a state legislative committee, and published a series of "Factory Tracts" which exposed conditions within the mills and argued for the ten-hour day.[27]

An important educational and organizing tool of the Lowell Female Labor Reform Association was the *Voice of Industry,* a labor weekly published in Lowell between 1845 and 1848 by the New England Workingmen's Association. Female operatives were involved in every aspect of its publication and used the *Voice* to further the Ten Hour Movement among women. Their Association owned the press on which the *Voice* was printed. Sarah Bagley, the Association president, was a member of the three-person publishing committee of the *Voice* and for a time served as editor. Other women were employed by the paper as travelling editors. They wrote articles about the Ten Hour Movement in other mill towns, raised money for the *Voice* and increased its circulation by selling subscriptions to the paper in their travels about New England, and used the *Voice* to appeal directly to their fellow operatives. They edited a separate "Female Department," which published letters and articles by and about women in the mills.

Another aspect of the Ten Hour Movement which distinguished it from the earlier labor struggles in Lowell was that it involved both men and women. At the same time that women in Lowell formed the Female Labor Reform Association, a male mechanics' and laborers' association was also organized. Both groups worked to secure the passage of legislation setting ten hours as the length of the working day. Both groups circulated petitions to this end, and when the legislative committee came to Lowell to hear testimony, both men and women testified in favor of the ten-hour day.

The two groups, then, worked together, and each made an important contribution to the movement in Lowell. Women had the numbers, comprising as they did over 80 percent of the mill workforce. Men, on the other hand, had the votes, and since the Ten Hour Movement was a political struggle, they played a crucial part. After the State committee reported unfavorably on the ten-hour petitions, the Female Labor Reform Association denounced the committee chairman, a state representative from Lowell, as a corporation "tool," and successfully worked for his defeat at the polls. Women took a more prominent part in the Ten Hour Movement in Lowell than did men, but they obviously remained dependent on male voters and legislators for the ultimate success of their movement.

Although co-ordinating their efforts with those of working men, women operatives organized independently within the Ten Hour Movement. For instance, in 1845 two important petitions were sent from Lowell to the state legislature. Almost 90 percent of the signers of one petition were females, and more than two-thirds of the signers of the second were males.[28] Clearly the separation of men and women in their daily lives was reflected in the Ten Hour petitions of these years.

The way in which the Ten Hour Movement was carried from Lowell to other mill towns also illustrated the independent organizing of women within the larger movement. For example, at a spirited meeting in Manchester, New Hampshire, in December, 1845—one presided over by Lowell operatives—more than a thousand workers, two-thirds of them women, passed resolutions calling for the ten-hour day. Later, those in attendance divided along male-female lines, each group meeting separately to set up parallel organizations. Sixty women joined the Manchester Female Labor Reform Association that evening, and by the following summer it claimed over three hundred members. Female operatives met in company boarding houses to involve new women in the movement.

In their first year of organizing, Manchester workers obtained more than 4,000 signatures on ten-hour petitions.[29] While men and women were both active in the movement, they worked through separate institutional structures from the outset.

The women's Ten Hour Movement, like the earlier turn-outs, was based in part on the participants' sense of their own worth and dignity as daughters of freemen. At the same time, however, it indicated the growth of a new consciousness. It reflected a mounting feeling of community among women operatives and a realization that their interests and those of their employers were not identical, that they had to rely on themselves and not on corporate benevolence to achieve a reduction in the hours of labor. One woman, in an open letter to a state legislator, expressed this rejection of middle-class paternalism: "Bad as is the condition of so many women, it would be much worse if they had nothing but your boasted protection to rely upon; but they have at last learnt the lesson which a bitter experience teaches, that not to those who style themselves their 'natural protectors' are they to look for the needful help, but to the strong and resolute of their own sex."[30] Such an attitude, underlying the self-organizing of women in the ten-hour petition campaigns, was clearly the product of the industrial experience in Lowell.

Both the early turn-outs and the Ten Hour Movement were dependent upon the existence of a close-knit community of women operatives. Such a community was based on the work structure, the nature of worker housing, and workforce homogeneity. Women were drawn together by the initial job training of newcomers, by the informal work-sharing among experienced hands, by living in company boarding houses, and by sharing religious, educational, and social activities in their leisure hours. Working and living in a new and alien setting, they came to rely upon one another for friendship and support.

This evolving community as well as the common cultural traditions which Yankee women carried into Lowell were major elements that governed their response to changing mill conditions. The pre-industrial tradition of independence and self-respect made them particularly sensitive to management labor policies. The sense of community enabled them to transform their individual opposition to wage cuts and to the increasing pace of work into public protest. In these labor struggles women operatives expressed a new consciousness of their rights both as workers and as women. Such a consciousness, like the community of women itself, was one product of Lowell's industrial revolution.

The experiences of Lowell women before 1850 present a fascinating picture of the contradictory impact of industrial capitalism. Repeated labor protests reveal that female operatives felt the demands of mill employment to be oppressive. At the same time, however, the mills provided women with work outside the home and family, thereby offering them an unprecedented independence. That they came to challenge employer paternalism was a direct consequence of the increasing opportunities offered them in these years. The Lowell mills both exploited and liberated women in ways unknown to the pre-industrial political economy.

Notes

1. *Statistics of Lowell Manufacturers,* January 1, 1840. Broadside available in the Manuscripts Division, Baker Library, Harvard Business School.
2. *Lowell Offering* I, p. 169.
3. *Ibid.* IV, p. 145–148, 169–172, 237–240, 257–259.
4. These statistics are drawn from the author's dissertation, "Women at Work: The Transformation of Work and Community in Lowell, Mass., 1826–1860" (Columbia Univ. 1975).
5. Harriet Hanson Robinson, *Loom and Spindle, Or Life Among the Early Mill Girls* (New York, 1898), p. 91.

6. Dublin, "Women at Work," Chapter 4.

7. Dublin, "Women at Work," Chapter 5. Statistics based on analysis of federal manuscript census listings of Hamilton boarding houses in 1830 and 1840.

8. *Lowell Offering* I, p. 169.

9. *Ibid.* II, pp. 145–155; I, pp. 2–7, 74–78.

10. *Hamilton Manufacturing Company Records,* vol. 283, *passim.* This volume, along with all the other company records cited in this article, is located in the Manuscript Division of Baker Library, Harvard Business School.

11. *Ibid.* I, p. 5; IV, p. 148.

12. Henry A. Miles, *Lowell As It Was and As It Is* (Lowell, 1845), pp. 144–145.

13. These statistics are based on the linkage of payroll and register books of the Hamilton Company as were the data on residence presented above. See Chapter 4 and Appendices of Dublin, "Women at Work."

14. These data are based on an analysis of the age distribution of females residing in Hamilton Company boarding houses as recorded in the federal manuscript censuses of 1830 and 1840. See Dublin, "Women at Work," Chapter 4.

15. Federal Manuscript Census of Lowell, 1830.

16. Boston *Evening Transcript,* February 18, 1834.

17. *Lawrence Manufacturing Company Records,* Correspondence, Vol. MAB-1, March 4 and March 9, 1834.

18. *Ibid.,* February 15, 1834.

19. Boston *Evening Transcript,* February 18, 1834.

20. Robinson, *Loom and Spindle,* p. 72; *Lowell Offering,* February 1841, p. 45. For an interesting account of conflict between an operative and an overseer, see Robinson, p. 57.

21. The wage cuts, in still another way, might have been seen as threatening to "enslave." Such decreases would be enacted by reductions in the piece rates paid women. If women were to maintain their overall earnings, given the wage cuts, they would have to speed up their work or accept additional machinery, both of which would result in making them work harder for the same pay. Opposition to the speed-up and the stretch-out were strong during the Ten Hour Movement in the 1840s, and although I have found no direct evidence, such feeling may have played a part in the turn-outs of the 1830s as well.

22. Robinson, *Loom and Spindle,* p. 83; Boston *Evening Transcript,* October 4 and 6, 1836.

23. *Tremont-Suffolk Mills Records,* unbound letters, Vol. FN-1, October 14, 1836.

24. *Ibid.,* October 18, 1836.

25. Hannah Josephson, *The Golden Threads: New England's Mill Girls and Magnates* (New York, 1949), p. 238.

26. *Tremont-Suffolk Mills Records,* Unbound Letters, Vol. FN-1, October 10, 1836.

27. Massachusetts *House Document* No. 50, 1845. Quoted in John R. Commons et al., *A Documentary History of American Industrial Society* (Cleveland, 1910), Vol. 3, pp. 133–151.

28. Based on author's examination of Ten Hour Petitions at Massachusetts State Archives, 1845, 1587/8 and 1587/9.

29. *Voice of Industry,* December 5 and 19, 1845, July 24, 1846, October 30, 1846, December 4, 1846, January 8, 1847.

30. *Voice of Industry,* March 13, 1846.

Chapter 6

The Domestic Balance of Power: Relations Between Mistress and Maid in Nineteenth-Century New England

Carol Lasser

Much has been written about domestic service in Europe and the United States, but only in recent years have servants themselves received much attention. Carol Lasser places power relations between mistress and maid at the center of her study. She argues that what was viewed as "decline" by employers was simply evidence of an improving bargaining position for servants. Lasser documents the ways in which Yankee and Irish servants used their newfound bargaining power to secure improvements in the terms of their employment. Increasingly, mistresses had to accommodate to a free labor system in which servants staunchly defended what freedom they did possess. The nature of domestic service and discrimination in the broader labor market limited options for Irish servants at mid-century, but they did exercise a measure of agency, as Lasser emphasizes.

After a long period of neglect, the history of domestic service, particularly in its American context, has begun to receive the scholarly attention it deserves. Careful study of the development of service and servants has begun to reveal the intriguing and complex nature of relations between mistress and maid, relations that cross class but not gender boundaries, and connect women to each other as employer and employee in the private arena of the upper-and middle-class home, not the traditional public realm of exchange. Although much remains to be explored, a decade of research has made clear that the status of servants, and, with this, relations within American households, changed significantly in the first half of the 19th century. Especially in urbanizing areas, native born "help"—those farmers' daughters who traded youthful energy for training in housewifery (and perhaps a little extra cash)—were replaced by immigrant domestics; paralleling this shift, the service relation lost its reciprocal character and came to resemble more closely wage relations of the typical external workplace.[1]

Following the lead of 19th-century observers who lived through the change, historians have generally interpreted this shift as a "decline" in service; but the concept of "decline" explains only part of the story. Influenced by the relative abundance of sources reflecting the employers' point of view, scholars have too readily accepted at face value the nostalgic lamentations of mistresses longing for a lost age. For the diaries and letters of employers and the household manuals and advice books to which they turned can also reveal what the changes in the service relation meant "from the bottom up." A growing body of works in women's and labor history has demonstrated the ability of

Excerpted from "Domestic Balance of Power: Relations Between Mistress and Maid in Nineteenth-Century New England," by Carol Lasser in *Labor History* 28 (1987): 5–22. Reprinted by permission of the publisher Taylor & Francis Ltd (http://www.tandf.co.uk).

Domestic servants posing for photographer. Smithsonian Institution/Office of Imaging, Printing, and Photographic Services.

human beings working in oppressive and often despised conditions to create for themselves ways to maintain their dignity, and to exercise some power over their lives. Drawing upon this scholarship, the historian of domestic service should ask whether the loss of the personal, almost feudalistic tie between mistress and maid was an unmitigated and equal loss for both parties to the relationship.[2]

Once the question is posed from the servants' perspective, the traditional elite sources yield new insights. The lamentations of declension suggest employers' protests against their relative loss of power, and in particular, loss of their nonmonetary influence in an increasingly competitive market in labor.

Seen in this way, it is clear that the curtailment of what has been called "benevolent maternalism" paralleled the growth of a new set of more impersonal, market mediated labor relations, constituting for servants a kind of "bourgeois freedom" which they slowly learned to use to develop leverage and to bargain more openly, thus asserting a new kind of control over their conditions of employment. While domestic work remained a physically demanding and often demeaning employment, 19th century servants found ways to exercise some power in the houses in which they worked, and with this, to establish for themselves a limited but significant sense of their own autonomy and agency.[3]

Drawing largely on materials from southern New England, especially Boston, an area in the forefront of economic and social change in the 19th century, this essay suggests how some servants used the leverage of the market to free themselves from some of the most grating restraints of the personal bonds with their employers. First, it examines the potential female labor force and the limited market for women's wage labor in the opening years of the 19th century; then, it analyzes the attraction of service for immigrant women arriving in large numbers in the 1840s in the midst of the transition. Finally, it explores the rhetoric of mistresses' complaints, finding in it evidence of employers' growing awareness of the pressures the labor market placed upon them. What employers experienced as threats to their domestic comfort and maternal authority, servants understood as avenues for at least limited autonomy in an oppressive relationship.

*   *   *

Throughout the 19th century, the wage-earning options available to women were quite limited and domestic service remained the single most important source of women's paid employment. Yet amid this continuity, the larger meaning of wage work, as well as the character of the female labor force, changed substantially. In New England, young, native-born women working within the context of a rural family economy often spent time as "help" in the household of a neighbor. Such employment did not represent long-term commitment to, nor a serious dependence upon, wage work. Rather, the earning strategy was temporary, since even if women were expected to generate cash the choice was not so much between service and other forms of paid employment as it was between working for others and engaging in some sort of commodity production for market—dairy or poultry work, raising butter or eggs for sale, weaving, spinning, or making palm leaf hats.[4]

During the first few decades of the 19th century, increasingly marginalized farms were hard pressed to sustain a household economy based on commodity production, even with the regular contribution of women's labor. Wage-earning employment off the farm gained significance for both men and women. As family orientations shifted from the lineal to the conjugal unit, the out migration of marriageable young men increased, and the need for individual wage-earning strategies for young women intensified. Some joined Lucy Larcom in New England's first textile factories; others explored the region's cities, particularly Boston.[5]

The expanding urban economy did offer work for women, but the range of choices remained narrow, particularly for the unskilled. Sewing, an occupation which required no special training for women who had from childhood been taught the use of the needle, was, as a result, characterized by "low wages, underemployment, and overwork." Despite its position as the second most common employment for women, it held little attraction for those who sought to support themselves. Even married women who took in some sewing to supplement their husbands' earnings complained bitterly about the exploitive pay structure. But alternatives were few; even in Boston, only a handful of women found employment in such light manufacturing as paper, tobacco, and trusses. Moreover, at mid-century, none of these occupations was particularly well-paying.[6] Thus women migrating from the New England countryside regularly turned to domestic service.

In this situation, the typical young, native-born woman who took a place in an urban household in ante-bellum New England was probably not motivated by hopes of the protection and maternal benevolence of her employer. Nor was she likely to desire an apprenticeship in housewifery. Rather, the simple cash nexus was, increasingly, the likely inducement; she wanted money and the autonomy money could buy.[7]

Young women with such aims did not make the most docile of servants, and reactions to them were mixed. As Hezekiah Niles reported in his *Weekly Register:*

> Europeans . . . have a universal complaint to make about the "impertinence of servants," . . . These girls will not call the lady of the house *mistress* or drop a *curtsey* when honored with a command; and if they do not like the usage they receive, will be off in an instant. . . . They think that the employer is quite as much indebted to them as they are to the employer. . . .

But American mistresses accustomed to the peculiarities of "help" were less surprised by such behavior. Catharine Sedgwick found the paradox of the "republican independent dependent" salutary, for, she believed, it produced "the very best servant . . . for capability and virtue of a self-regulating and self-respecting agent." The independence of domestics, she noted with satisfaction, was indicative of the relative freedom enjoyed even by young women to contract their time for the best available wages, whether in service or in other employments. For them, work was a means to an end. As Sedgwick noted, such women "used their power; they had something better before them than domestic subordination and household service."[8]

By the 1830s and 1840s, the ability of native-born women to use the market for domestic service to their own advantage was strengthened by several additional factors. First, the economy of rural New England which had forced young women beyond the boundaries of the household economy began to stabilize as birth rates fell and out migration rose. Thus, it was less imperative for large numbers of young women to leave their parental homes; indeed, there were relatively fewer women to leave, and hence fewer native-born women seeking work as servants in the city. Second, women could choose from a growing number of alternative employments in the region, including school teaching, shoe work, and greater opportunities in the textile factories. Third, those who did migrate to cities in search of employment in service found a rapidly rising urban population, and with it, a fast growing market for domestic servants. Between 1820 and 1850, for example, Boston's population more than tripled; and, as wealth and inequality rose in tandem, a larger number of families undoubtedly sought servants to enable them to participate in the "cult of domesticity," which mandated higher standards of comfort, cleanliness and gentility. . . . Taken together, all these factors suggest that an increasing demand for servants among a growing urban population, combined with a relatively stable, or perhaps even declining, supply of native-born women, meant the market in domestic labor favored the laborer.[9]

Employers' diaries and letters of the 1830s complained constantly about their difficulty in finding and keeping servants. Desperate employers expressed their feelings as a sense of their own victimization by those who were supposed to serve them. When young Lucy Pierce married the Transcendentalist minister Frederic Henry Hedge, her mother in outlying Brookline searched the countryside as well as Boston itself for appropriate household help to send to her frantic daughter in Cambridge. Louisa Lee Waterhouse complained to her husband that in the past, she had been able to hire several able servants, but, in the late 1830s, could secure now only one and "I can't depend on her and had rather bear and forbear a while than change." Most telling, perhaps, was the letter Mehitable Mary Dawes Goddard wrote to her sister in 1830 expressing her gratitude for a downturn in the local economy, noting that it meant a momentary advantage for the mistress: "wages are lower, & of course there is a corresponding improvement in the behavior of this class of people—I do not wish them to suffer for suffering's sake, but I do fear nothing but absolute want will compel them to do their duty. . . ." Yet she admitted the change could be only temporary, for "the instant the pressure is over, they will be as topping as ever."[10]

The vast international migrations beginning in the late 1840s should have marked a turning point in the labor market balance by bringing to New England cities a large unskilled female labor force eager to take employment as domestic servants; and, in an economy based on simple supply and demand, mistresses should then have gained the upper hand. Certainly, there were more women available; Irish women were particularly attracted to service for the advantages it offered to them. Many had come to America alone and needed housing as well as employment; moreover, live-in service meant that most of a woman's earnings could be sent back to Ireland to support family members left behind, or perhaps finance their migration. In addition, service promised year-round employment, avoiding the periodic or seasonal layoffs that accompanied work in many industries, especially the needle trades. For all these reasons, immigrant Irish women found in domestic service an excellent opportunity. Yet the sheer availability of new laborers did not end the employers' perceptions of an ongoing crisis in service.[11]

For a time, prejudice seems to have played a role in imposing an artificial limit on what mistresses defined as the supply of appropriate workers thus exacerbating for some old school mistresses their sense of exasperation. While it maintained great strength, discrimination hindered the ability of willing immigrant workers to make the best of their situation. Yet slowly, even the most prestigious families accepted their dependence on Irish servants. Mary Gardner Lowell, brought up in one prominent New England family and married into another, noted in her 1849 diary that she had, for the first time, hired Irish women, to work as cook and chambermaid in her country home in Waltham for the summer. Louisa Crowninshield Bacon, a descendant of one of the great merchant families of Salem, noted that before 1850, the domestics in her house were "always American," but thereafter, "when no more American servants could be found, like everyone else we had Irish. In fact, they were the only ones available." . . . Yet the eventual acceptance of servants from so distinctly different a cultural background marked an important transition in the evolution of New England service toward a simple cash nexus.[12]

Once they entered the homes of the Yankee middle and upper classes, Irish domestics proved no more docile nor settled than their Yankee predecessors. Moreover, the immigrant servants soon found that they too could shop for the best situation. They learned to bargain—sometimes with their feet—for the highest wages, the most conducive working conditions, and the best locations. From the servants' point of view, the loss of the reciprocity of "benevolent maternalism" was balanced by two key acquisitions; first, they now had access to places for which they never would have been hired as "help"; and second, they could use their growing knowledge of the labor market for immediate, personal gain.

It was not that servants had never before bargained for higher wages and better conditions. . . . But employers and didactic writers were especially distressed by the attempts of Irish domestics to assert their own needs and to bargain for their own ends. Reacting with alarm, they charged that these recent immigrants were not yet ready to understand and enjoy the privileges of a republic, including the contractualism of its market system. As Catharine Beecher complained in 1869:

> . . . the Irish and German servants . . . became more or less infected with the spirit of democracy. They came to this country with vague notions of freedom and equality . . . they repudiated many of those habits of respect and courtesy which belonged to their former condition, and asserted their own will and way in the round unvarnished phrase which they supposed to be their right as republican citizens. Life became a sort of domestic wrangle and struggle between the employers, who secretly

confessed their weakness, but endeavored openly to assume the air and bearing of authority, and the employed, who knew their power and insisted on their privileges.

Yet Beecher recognized that the clock could not be turned back toward the older notions of domestic apprenticeship. Thus, to counteract what she saw as the excessive power enjoyed by servants, Beecher pointedly advised employers to take their best advantage of the freedom of contract:

> The more strictly and perfectly the business matters of the first engagement of domestics are conducted, the more likelihood there is of mutual quiet and satisfaction in the relation. . . . It is much better to regulate such affairs by cool contract in the outset than by warm altercations and protracted domestic battles.

So the struggle of servants to establish their economic rights, buying and selling their own labor power, clearly threatened Beecher and the women for whom she wrote. And Beecher's answer for employers rested on the abandonment of the notions of reciprocity and responsibility which, she asserted, immigrants were incapable of understanding. She sought for mistresses to recover not only some vague emotional satisfaction, but, more importantly, real power in the household relationship as well.[13]

Yet even when mistresses tried to reconcile themselves to the exigencies of the new relations, they charged that the transition of servants to the ethics of a marketplace economy was at best incomplete. Commentators and employers complained that domestics were annoyingly casual about the niceties of contracts, the touchstone of free labor engagements. Under the pen name "Gail Hamilton," New England author Mary Abigail Dodge charged that servants "lack a moral sense, a mental perception, or whatever the faculty is which makes one capable of contracting an engagement." Employers recounted with annoyance the myriad of incidents in which domestics verbally committed never arrived or left abruptly without giving the expected and customary notice. Few employers, however, understood the inconsistencies of their position, demanding feudal loyalty on the one hand, and free market contractualism on the other. One observer who placed this problem in its particular 19th century American context was E. L. Godkin, editor of the progressive periodical *The Nation*. As he noted, the behavior of household employees was simply an accurate assessment of their labor market position: "The only real restraint on laborers of any class among us nowadays, is the difficulty of finding another place." He admitted that it appeared a servant's "sense of the obligations of contracts is feeble," yet he reminded his readers:

> her spirit about contracts is really that of the entire community in which she lives. . . . Native mechanics and seamstresses are just as perfidious as Bridget, but incur less obloquy, because their faithlessness causes less annoyance. . . . What makes [her] so fond of change is that she lives in a singularly restless society, in which everybody is engaged in a continual struggle to "better himself"—her master, in nine cases out of ten, setting her an example of dislike to steady industry and slow gains.[14]

In short, the servant was learning from the surrounding society how to perform as a well-informed actor on the expanding urban labor market.

A rare piece of advice literature aimed directly at the immigrant domestic, not her mistress, dignified the servant's attempts to make the best of the market, urging even further that it was, at times, a duty. The "Nun of Kenmare," writing *Advice to Irish Girls in America,* counseled her readers not to change their places for transient reasons, but noted that "there is no harm in changing a place to better oneself. . . . If you have a father and mother or other relatives depending on you, whom you ought to support, or if you are engaged to be married, and want to lay by something for your future home, then you would be quite right" to leave when offered higher wages. "The Nun" expected and even encouraged servants to exercise their bargaining powers as free persons and free laborers.[15]

But critics proved reluctant to acknowledge fully the right of servants to use to their own advantage a market they had not created; and in their resistance, employers and their advisors often obscured the relationship of the domestic to her own labor power. Such mystification is apparent in the attacks of advice books on housekeepers who offered high wages to lure good servants away from the homes of friends and acquaintances. Eunice Beecher, the wife of Henry Ward Beecher and sister-in-law of Catharine Beecher, devoted an entire chapter in her 1875 work, *Motherly Talks with Young Housekeepers*, to the evil of "stealing" servants. According to her analysis,

> We object to no one's obtaining the full value for his [*sic*] work, but claim that there should be no meddling, no underhand work to buy servants or laborers from another, by private offer of larger wages. Advertising is open to all, and brings the needed help.

Beecher seemed reluctant to recognize that it was the employees themselves and not their employers who were selling their labor, and, moreover, that "full value" might be a larger amount than prevailing wage rates. Her conclusion that enticing servants to leave their positions represented an *employer's* violation of the golden rule overlooked the other parties in the relation to whom justice was also due. Another domestic handbook charged that offers of enticing raises were "a kind of larceny [that] should be punished." Yet what was theft from the employer's point of view was power to the employee.[16]

The intelligence office, or employment agency, incontrovertible proof of the growing market orientation of relations between housewife and hireling, became a favorite target for critics of the transformation of service; as "Gail Hamilton" commented acerbically, it "was the last place in the world to look for intelligence." Maternalistic mistresses blamed these employment agencies for undermining older notions of a reciprocal, benevolent relationship by turning the delicate matter of matching mistress and maid into a profit-oriented business. At intervals throughout the 19th century, wealthy women worked through orphan asylums, female moral reform societies and charitable agencies to provide institutional alternatives to these crassly commercial enterprises.[17]

By the second half of the 19th century, mistresses had no choice but to accept the commercial intelligence office as a necessary evil. Employers' diaries and letters chronicle the seemingly endless numbers of agencies on which they called in their search for servants, and record as well employers' resentment at being at the mercy of the market. In 1870, for example, Elizabeth Ellery Dana lamented that the cook her mother had just engaged decided not to come since she heard that the family work was too hard. "Lily" Dana then visited four intelligence offices in the morning, and her mother called upon a fifth. Less than two months later, the sudden flight of another new servant sent Dana to six intelligence offices one morning, and an additional four (not counting a charitable society) three days later. As Dana made clear, she took little pleasure in her task, but found no alternative. She resented, but could not resist, trading in the market for labor power.[18]

Dana well knew the relationship that had been lost between mistress and servant. As part of an old Boston Brahmin family, she had long observed the closeness between her imperious aunt Charlotte Dana, and Maria, her aunt's steadfast privileged domestic who enjoyed almost familial standing. Aunt Charlotte defended the prerogatives of her servant against the encroachments of less established newcomers; Maria's sleeping accommodations rivaled those of Dana's sisters, and the care taken of her health was comparable to that taken of family members, not other servants. In return, Aunt Charlotte was richly rewarded with the devotion and endurance of faithful Maria who remained with her hot-tempered mistress despite arbitrary and pre-emptive commands and general unpredictability. Indeed, the symbiosis of this mistress and maid contrasted sharply with the crassly materialistic ties which often failed to secure the service of other wage-labor employees in the various Dana households. Domestics hired at commercial agencies tested the limits of family patience and proved the buoyancy of the market. For Lily Dana, the result of the passing of benevolent maternalism was her frequent and frustrating visits to Boston intelligence offices to replenish the supply of household help.[19]

But the eloquent testimony to the transformation of employers' experiences in hiring servants left in the diaries and letters of the Dana family, and similar households, should not, however, blind historians to the other side of the story. If the Danas—and even Aunt Charlotte's Maria—mourned the growing distance between employer and employee, the passing of sponsored mobility, and the end of surrogate familial relationships, few 19th century domestics shared their longing for household harmony reconstructed on an earlier model. By the middle of the 19th century, domestics were increasingly different from their employers, in class and culture. For these servants, their work was primarily a way to earn cash and independence. They did not seek ersatz mothers or benevolent guardians.

These new servants were *not* loyal, docile employees; they *did* leave what employers viewed as essentially suitable situations to suit their own convenience, and they *did* often evaluate their satisfaction according to narrowly materialistic standards. From their perspective, benevolent maternalism represented anachronistic inequality in the marketplace. Kindness and reciprocity often cloaked the locus of power in the caretaker relationship; benevolent mistresses defined the care to be taken, imposing it upon the object of benevolence. In the name of charity and uplift, mistresses had waged unconscious and unintentional wars of "cultural imperialism" upon their maids, struggling to win the hearts and minds of their employees, assuming that both sides could establish a unity of interests. Early in the century, when class and culture of mistress and maid had been more similar, genuine collaboration was more likely; and sympathy and tradition served to soften the lines of power on either side. But the growing impersonality of urban market relations shifted the context in which employer and employee met and negotiated, and employers felt victimized. Unwilling to recognize the existence of a growing conflict of interests between the two sides in the marketplace, employers charged servants with at best ingratitude, at worst treason, to the family state.[20]

But servants declared independence from arbitrary rule and sought to exercise their limited but significant "freedom"—the power to sell their labor to the highest bidder. There were, of course, limits to this freedom. Domestics needed work, so their ability to exercise choice was never unlimited. And servants' separation from their employers could be only at best incomplete while domestics still lived in. . . . And, in addition, hard work and deplorable situations often characterized both the employment itself and the conditions which drove women to seek it. Nonetheless, mid-19th century domestics were beginning to learn to use the market relations on which service was increasingly based to their own advantage.

Domestics learned to bargain, but it is important to remember that the transformation of service was not wholly a revolution from the bottom up. Perhaps more than they realized, mistresses themselves were at least in part responsible for the deteriorating viability of benevolent materialism. The growth of cities, foreign immigration, and increasingly complex exchange relations in broader society are all important, but one suspects another factor as well.

Beginning in the 1840s, the authors of household manuals, cookbooks, and didactic literature noted the declension of housekeepers from the "noble matronage" who had helped their men secure the freedom of the land during the American revolution. In scathing indictments, they charged that academic and ornamental education had expanded at the cost of practical housekeeping instruction; mid-century middle-and upper-class girls, they asserted, lacked the experience that would have allowed them to teach their domestics what their surrogate daughters should know. In the years after the Civil War, advisors modified their expectations of young homemakers by suggesting that the ability to perform housework was not as important as the capacity to manage effectively; but many expressed their doubts that mistresses could operate even at this level.

Thus, neither benevolent mistresses nor competent managers, middle-class women trained to be merely decorative lacked practical skills and then lost their ability to exert competent authority. Enclosed within Victorian domesticity, these "ladies" confronted a sophisticated labor market of which they could make little sense despite dizzying dashes from domestic enclosure into the maze of intelligence offices in their efforts to hire other women to perform work that they could neither undertake, nor describe, nor direct.

The isolation of the mistress in her own "separate sphere" from the market further enlarged the growing chasm between employer and employee and contributed to their different interpretations of the shifting relations of service. As domestics learned to bring market pressures to bear—pressures their employers perceived as lack of faithfulness, unfair wage inflation, and instability—mistresses expressed resentment at the "power" of those who were supposed to be their servants. By the late 19th century, within the domestic service relation, "bourgeois woman" confined by patriarchal domesticity confronted "economic woman" forced to assert her bourgeois rights in the marketplace. "Economic woman" often suffered at the invisible hands of the market and, as a woman employed by a woman, found herself as the dependent of a dependent; but she nonetheless acted as an agent transforming the relationship of women to society, both within and outside the home. Mistresses might wistfully look back to an earlier age, but for servants, the decline of the surrogate familial relations of benevolent maternalism was not an unmitigated loss. The market offered, although it did not always provide, the opportunity for a new kind of economic independence, if not self-sufficiency. Servants learned to exercise new "power" while their mistresses perceived their own enslavement by the market.

Notes

1. The most important recent works on domestic service are: David M. Katzman, *Seven Days A Week: Women and Domestic Service in Industrializing America* (New York, 1978); and Faye E. Dudden, *Serving Women: Household Service in Nineteenth-Century America* (Middletown, 1983).

    Daniel E. Sutherland, *Americans and Their Servants: Domestic Service in the United States from 1800 to 1920* (Baton Rouge, 1981) disagrees with the idea of a major transformation in service. Hasia R. Diner, *Erin's Daughter in America: Irish Immigrant Women in the Nineteenth Century* (Baltimore, 1983) gave a particularly good account of Irish servants.

2. Among the best known 19th century authors who articulated notions of "decline" were Catharine Beecher, *Letters to Persons Who Are Engaged in Domestic Service* (New York, 1842); Lydia Maria Child, *History of the Condition of Women* (Boston, 1835); Sarah Josepha Hale, *Sketches of American Character* (Boston, 1831); [Elizabeth Stuart Phelps,] *The Sunny Side; Or, the Country Minister's Wife*. Writing in the tradition of "progressive history," Lucy Maynard Salmon in *Domestic Service* (New York, 1897) evaluated the 19th century trend as one of decline.

3. The term "bourgeois freedom" is used here in the sense that Karl Marx suggested it in "Manifesto of the Communist Party," *The Marx-Engels Reader*, Robert C. Tucker, ed. (New York, 1972), 348. Thomas Dublin argues that New England women in the 1830s and 1840s viewed their wages as their own, and saw them as a part of their "independence." See Thomas Dublin, "Introduction," *Farm to Factory: Women's*

Letters, 1830–1860 (New York, 1981), 23–25; and *Women at Work: The Transformation of Work and Community in Lowell, Massachusetts, 1826–1860* (New York, 1979), especially chapt. 3.

4. Michael Merrill, "Cash is Good to Eat: Self-Sufficiency and Exchange in the Rural Economy of the United States," *Radical History Review* 4(Fall 1976), 42–71 describes the flexibility of the early market economy; Dudden, *Serving Women,* 12–19 places domestic service in the context of the rural economy.

5. On the shift from the lineal to the conjugal family, see James A. Henretta, "Families and Farms: *Mentalité* in Pre-Industrial America," *William and Mary Quarterly* 3d ser., 35 (1978), 3–32.

6. The quotation characterizing sewing is from Christine Stansell, "The Origins of the Sweatshop: Women and Early Industrialization in New York City," in *Working-Class America: Essays on Labor, Community, and American Society,* Michael H. Frisch and Daniel J. Walkowitz, eds. (Urbana, IL, 1983), 78. For one view of the female labor market in Boston and the relationship of work to migration patterns, see Carol Lasser, "'The World's Dread Laugh': Singlehood and Service in Nineteenth-Century Boston," in *The New England Working Class and the New Labor History,* Donald H. Bell and Herbert C. Gutman, eds. (Urbana, IL, 1987).

   Wage rates for Boston women in industrial work in approximately 1830 ranged from 33 to 75 cents per day, out of which women had to pay for food, clothing and shelter; wage rates for servants were approximately $1.00 to 2.00 per week, and domestic servants received food and shelter, and often clothing as well.

7. Dublin, *Farm to Factory,* includes writings by Mary Paul, 97–99, and Mary Edwards, 83, both of whom undertook work as domestic servants for short periods of time. See also "Clarissa Packard" [Caroline Gilman], *Recollections of a Housekeeper* (New York, 1986), 32.

   Two well-known New England authors reiterated this theme later in the century. See Louisa May Alcott, *Work: A Story of Experience* (1873; reprint New York, 1977). Alcott herself worked in service for a short period of time when her parents' finances were especially bad; see Dudden, *Serving Women,* 87–89. Also Charlotte Perkins Gilman's heroine Diantha Bell in *What Diantha Did* quite explicitly sees service as a means to independence—in this case towards learning the skills she will need to open her own cleaning company. For an excerpt from the novel which makes clear the role of service in Diantha's quest for earning power, see "What Diantha Did," 123–140, *The Charlotte Perkins Gilman Reader,* Ann J. Lane, ed. (New York, 1980).

   Prevailing wage rates, described above, note 6, provided women who worked in service with a very modest, but nonetheless significant, amount of disposable cash.

8. *Niles Weekly Register,* 9 (Dec. 2, 1815), 238–239; Catharine Sedgwick, *Home* (Boston, 1839), 72; Catharine Sedgwick, *A New England Tale* (1852), 10–11; Mary E. Dewey, ed., *Life and Letters of Catharine M. Sedgwick* (New York, 1871), "Recollections of Childhood," 22.

9. J. Potter . . . concluded that the overall American birth rate declined between 1800 and 1860, particularly in New England: see "The Growth of Population in America, 1700–1860," in D. V. C. Glass and D. Eversley, *Population in History: Essays in Historical Demography* (Chicago, 1965), 672–673. More recently, Maris Vinovskis, *Fertility in Massachusetts from the Revolution to the Civil War* (New York, 1981), provides an analysis of declining birth rates including regional variations within the state; he concludes that, although urban fertility declined faster than rural fertility, the decline in rural fertility was, nonetheless, significant and a major factor in the overall decline of Massachusetts fertility in the years before 1860. See especially 100–101.

   On the new occupations available for women workers, see Richard M. Bernard and Maris A. Vinovskis, "The Female School Teacher in Ante-Bellum Massachusetts," *Journal of Social History* 10 (1977), 332–345, which analyzes the expansion in opportunities for school teaching; shoemaking is described by Alan Dawley, *Class and Community: The Industrial Revolution in Lynn* (Cambridge, MA, 1976); the expansion in the textile industry is detailed by Caroline Ware, *The New England Cotton Manufacture: A Study in Industrial Beginnings* (New York, 1931); and the expansion of Lowell in particular is chronicled in Thomas Dublin, *Women at Work.*

10. Lucy Tappan Pierce to Lucy Pierce Hedge, undated letter attributed to 1830–1832 period, Box 2, Folder 16, Poor Family Papers, Schlesinger Library; Louisa Lee Waterhouse, Journal entry, undated [1841],

Waterhouse Papers, Massachusetts Historical Society; Mehitable Mary Dawes Goddard to Lucretia Dawes, Boston, Feb. 21, 1830, May-Goddard papers, Schlesinger Library.

11. Dudden, *Serving Women*, 60–61; see also, for example, Oscar Handlin, *Boston's Immigrants: A Study in Acculturation*, rev. ed. (New York, 1971), 61–62; and Diner, *Erin's Daughters*, 93–94.

12. Mary Gardner Lowell, Diary Volume 81 (1849) May 5, 1849, Francis Cabot Lowell II Papers, Massachusetts Historical Society, Louisa Crowninshield Bacon, *Reminiscences* (Salem, 1922), 34–37.

13. Beecher and Stowe, *American Women's Home*, 320–321, 324.

14. "Gail Hamilton" [Mary Abigail Dodge,] *Woman's Worth and Worthlessness: The Complement to "A New Atmosphere"* (New York, 1872), 95–96. Edward Godkin, "Manners and Morals of the Kitchen," 63–64. *Reflections and Comments, 1867–1895* (New York, 1895); the piece originally appeared in the *Nation*, 16 (Jan 2, 1873), 6–7.

15. Sister Mary Francis Clare, *Advice to Irish Girls in America by the Nun of Kenmare* (New York, 1872), 28.

16. Eunice Beecher ("Mrs. Henry Ward Beecher"), *Motherly Talks with Young Housekeepers* (New York, 1875), 112–116; Mrs. Oakley, *From Attic to Cellar: A Book for Young Housekeepers* (New York, 1879), 26.

17. Dodge, *Woman's Worth*, 79; for one case study of orphan placement, see Carol Lasser, "'A Pleasingly Oppressive Burden': The Transformation of Domestic Service in Salem, 1800–1840," *Essex Institute Historical Collections*, 116 (1980), 156–175. Other Boston charitable agencies interested in placement included the Society for the Mutual Benefit of Female Domestics and Their Employers, the New England Female Moral Reform Association, and the Boston Society for the Prevention of Pauperism.

18. Elizabeth Ellery Dana, Diary for 1870, entries for Mar. 19, May 20, and May 23, Dana Family Papers, Schlesinger Library.

19. Elizabeth Ellery Dana, Diary for 1868, entries for Oct. 9, Nov. 5, for example. The whole family commented on Aunt Charlotte's temper, and Lily Dana noted her readiness for a walk-out of household servants if her aunt assumed the task of overseeing the home.

20. I am indebted to Diana Grossman Kahn for her astute observations on maternal benevolence and cultural imperialism, or, as she has also called it, internal "colonization." Too much of the current literature on "maternal thinking" and caretaking lacks this critical perspective. See especially Sarah Ruddick, "Maternal Thinking," *Feminist Studies*, 6(1980), 842–67.

Chapter 7

Gender and Slave Labor in Antebellum New Orleans

Virginia Meacham Gould

Plantation life and the experiences of male field hands have predominated in popular views of slavery before the Civil War, but urban slavery was an important element of the slave labor system in the antebellum decades, and in southern cities slave women did much to shape the "peculiar institution." Virginia Meacham Gould shows, for instance, that women consistently constituted the majority of slaves in New Orleans in the first half of the nineteenth century. While domestic work provided slave women's primary occupation, Gould demonstrates the importance of slave women's presence in the city's market activity. Moreover, slave women's economic activity and living arrangements in the city supported a degree of independence that gave women a significant place in the broader urban slave community.

The experiences of urban slave women have unfortunately been overlooked by historians who are interested in understanding the lives of slave women in the antebellum South. Indeed, the experiences of the slave women who lived in the towns and cities of the South have been virtually ignored. Failing to view slavery as an institution and a personal condition that by necessity changed over time and place, women's historians have not considered the various expressions that slavery took. And in so doing, they have ignored the influence that differing conditions of slavery had on the day-to-day lives of women. Instead, they have assumed that the identities of plantation slave women were applicable to other slave women in the South. Yet the conditions of slavery on the plantation must be understood as unique to the plantation and should not be transposed onto other forms of slavery. Nowhere is it more obvious that slavery could mean different things to different women than when comparing the day-to-day experiences of slave women living in antebellum New Orleans to those living on the plantations outside the city.

In fundamental ways, the lives of urban slave women throughout the Americas were circumscribed by a complex set of social relations. No matter whether they were enslaved in the city or on the plantation, slave women in the New World were encumbered with a double burden. As slaves, they were defined as property that could be bought and sold, as well as stripped of the product of their labor. As women, they were viewed as subordinate to men, both slave and free, and thus dominated by them. In short, slave women in the South's entrepôts, like those on the plantations, were exploited not only by race but also by gender. Yet, even though urban slave women were bound within the same exploitive system, the nature of that system, as redefined by the exigencies of the city, reshaped their lives.

In general, the day-to-day experiences of plantation women depended on the plantation's location, its size, and its crop. In the district around New Orleans, the crop was usually sugar cane and the work was done in gangs, with women working beside men, clearing the fields, planting them with cuts of cane, and finally cutting and grinding the cane. . . .

Frederick Law Olmsted described the fieldhands he saw returning from work on a sugar plantation near St. Francisville in 1854. "First came, led by an old driver carrying a whip, forty of the largest strongest women I ever saw together; they were all in a simple uniform dress of a bluish check stuff, the skirts reaching little below the knee; that legs and feet were bare; they carried themselves loftily, each having a hoe over the shoulder, and walking with a free, powerful swing. Behind them came the cavalry, thirty strong, mostly men, but a few of them women, two of whom rode astride on the plough mules."[1]

The organization of labor that Olmsted described on the sugar plantation in St. Francisville contrasts dramatically with that found in New Orleans. Slaveholders in the city certainly benefited from slave labor, as did those on the plantations and farms outside the city. But the benefits that planters and farmers expected from their slaves were different from those expected by urban slaveholders. Planters and farmers depended on the income their slaves could produce. Their financial status, or class, was determined by the capabilities, or production, of their slaves. Only a few urban slaveholders, however, depended on the income of their slaves. Instead, they generally relied on their slaves for production of goods and services for consumption within the household; many if not most of the city's slaves were domestics.

Slave women in the city, therefore, unlike those on the plantations, existed in a world in which their gender-specific, skills were highly desirable and, in many cases, preferable to those of men. It was only within that context, where the gender division of labor was informed by early modern European and African gender conventions, that women were prized for their capabilities. It was also only in the cities when women routinely capitalized on the gender division of labor to improve their economic conditions, without men. Yet, even though some of the conditions of urban labor could present slave women with social and economic advantages not commonly found in the plantation district, other conditions, in significant ways, rendered urban slavery an especially oppressive institution for slave women.

The absence of studies on urban slave women cannot be explained by a scarcity of resources. Slave women in the South's cities left clear traces of their lives. The records that include information about slaves in New Orleans, for instance, are extraordinary. The early Episcopal, Baptist, Methodist, Unitarian, and AME churches kept records of slave baptisms, marriages, and burials. The most inclusive sacramental records of urban slave women, however, are those of the Catholic Church. . . .

The Notarial Archives contain millions of property records of Orleans Parish. The records begin in the colonial period and continue nearly uninterrupted until today. The majority of the records are the wills, dowries, marriage contracts, and property sales—including those of slaves—on the local population. . . .

*   *   *

Despite such a wealth of available sources, as yet, few studies on slavery in Louisiana include specific information on the experiences and identities of slave women. Delores Labbé's dissertation, "Women in Early Nineteenth-Century Louisiana," includes a chapter on slave women and free women of color. Gwendolyn Midlo Hall's *Africans in Colonial Louisiana* also includes invaluable information for anyone attempting to understand the specific experiences of slave women in New Orleans. Ann Patton Malone does an excellent job of examining the forms and function of slaves on several of antebellum Louisiana's plantations in *Sweet Chariot*. In a more general work on New Orleans, John Blassingame touches on the experiences of slave women[2]. . .

Perhaps one reason so little attention has been paid to slave women in the urban South is that so little is known about most of the Old South's urban centers. The limited number of studies that focus on urban slavery is more than likely a reflection of the scarcity of urban centers in the antebellum

South. The South was overwhelmingly rural during its antebellum years. According to the 1860 census, only 7.1 percent of the South's population was urban while urban residents in the rest of the country comprised 19.8 percent of the population. Yet, even though the urban centers in the South were generally smaller and certainly fewer, they played a central role in the region's economy. Southern towns and cities like Richmond, Charleston, Savannah, Natchez, and New Orleans served as the region's entrepôts. They provided the facilities and labor for the exportation of the region's crops and the importation of the many necessary goods not produced in the South. The region's entrepôts also served as the centers for the importation and sale of slaves.[3]

Strategically located near the mouth of the Mississippi River, New Orleans was the fastest growing urban center in the South. A census taken in 1805, two years after the city was officially ceded to the United States, recorded its population at 8,222. Within five years, the number of inhabitants had grown to 17,242. Between 1820 and 1830, the city's population only increased from 27,176 to 29,737. But between 1830 and 1840, it boomed. The census of New Orleans in 1840 listed 102,193 inhabitants. The population had reached 116,375 by 1850 and 168,675 by 1860.

The growth of the city's population mirrored its commercial growth. By 1830, the port of New Orleans had begun to compete commercially with the older, more established ports of the United States. In fact, by 1830, New Orleans was second only to New York in commercial imports. By 1840, its exports had exceeded those of New York. Its inhabitants readily accepted its importance as a commercial center. To them, New Orleans had become "without exertion the metropolis of America, if not eventually of the world."[4]

The economy of the booming port provided the demand for the labor of tens of thousands of slaves. The 1805 census listed 3,105 slaves living in the city. Since the total population in that year, including slaves, free people of color, and whites, was approximately 8,222, the slave population represented 37.8 percent of the total population. By 1810, the number of slaves in the city had nearly doubled to 5,961, or 35 percent of the city's total population. In 1820, there were 7,355 slaves in the city. That number comprised nearly 27 percent of the population. By 1840, the city's slave population had grown to 23,448, a number that was approximately 23 percent of the total population. Thus, even though their raw numbers had grown, the percentage of slaves in the population had begun to shrink. When the 1850 census was taken, the percentage of slaves had not only declined but their raw numbers had decreased also. In that year, there were 17,011 slaves recorded in the city, a number that amounted to 14.6 percent of the entire population. The declining trend continued throughout the following decade. Therefore, by 1860 the city's slave population had decreased to 13,385, a number that amounted to only 7.9 percent of the population.[5]

The pattern of slaveholding in the city was a reflection of the nature of urban labor. Urban slaveholders generally held far fewer slaves than did plantation owners. The 1837 Tax Assessor's records for the First Municipality of New Orleans list 279 slaveholders (excluding businesses), who owned 785 slaves. Those numbers, consistent with data obtained from the slave schedules included in the U.S. Census Records, suggest that even though slaveholding was widespread, urban slaveholders owned fewer slaves. The majority of slaveholders (175) owned only one or two slaves. The rest (85) owned between three and five slaves. The pattern of slaveholding for the First Municipality in New Orleans was generally consistent for the other municipalities of New Orleans as well as other southern urban centers.[6]

Southern industry proved the only exception to this pattern. The 1837 Tax Assessor's Records for the First Municipality of New Orleans reported that nineteen companies owned thirty-nine slaves in that year. Most industrial slaves were men, but women and children also labored in the South's industries. For instance, of the thirty-nine slaves owned by companies reported in the 1837 tax records, ten were women and children. The S. W. Oakley and Co. owned four men (Octave. Roy, Pethien, and Lucien) and one woman (Ester).[7]

Gender also distinguished the general pattern of slaveholding in New Orleans from those of the plantations and farms that surrounded the city. The first census record that reports data for gender in New Orleans was the Spanish census of 1771. Of the 1,288 slaves in the city in that year, 568 were males and 720 were females. Those numbers constitute a sex ratio of 126.8, which means that there were 126.8 female slaves for every 100 male slaves. The census taken in New Orleans in 1805 reported that of the 3,105 slaves in the city that year, 1,343 were males and 1,762 were females. That year the sex ratio was 131.2. By 1850, the U.S. census lists more than 10,195 slave women living in the city, but only 6,818 slave men living there. Thus, in 1850, the sex ratio had reached 149.5[8] (Table 1).

Another difference in the pattern of urban slaveholding was especially significant for women. In particular, slaves were more likely to be owned by women in New Orleans than by those in its hinterlands. Of the 513 inhabitants in the First Municipality of New Orleans in 1837 who owned property (excluding companies), 107, or 21 percent, were women. Of those, 82 owned real estate, 25 owned real estate and slaves, and 43 owned slaves. Furthermore, according to the 1837 Tax Assessor's records, the 68 women who owned slaves in the First Municipality in that year owned a total of 154 slaves. In other words, the 21 percent of the slaveholding population who were women owned 20 percent of the slaves.

Female slaveholders in New Orleans demonstrated a strong preference for female slaves. Again, the 1837 Tax Assessor's records demonstrate the trend. Of the 154 slaves owned by women, 116 were females and only 38 were males. In short, 75 percent of the slaves owned by women were women and many owners were free women of color. In the First Municipality of the city in 1837, 62 free people of color were listed as property holders. Therein, 12 percent of the property holders listed were free people of color. Of those, 30 owned real estate only, 12 owned real estate and slaves, and 20 owned slaves only. A further analysis of the property records of free people of color demonstrates that the majority of the property holders, or 42 of 62, were women. The free women of color who were slaveholders owned a total of 40 slaves, 5 of whom were men and 35 of whom were women. For example, Pouponne Wiltz owned slave man, Jerry, and two women, both named Sally. Rosseline Topin owned a woman named Marie, and Angelique Ony owned Sophie, Marie, and Annette.[9]

The 1837 Tax Assessor's records for the First Municipality suggest the predominant patterns of slaveholding by free people of color. In that year, 245 white slaveholders owned 715 slaves. That number amounts to 2.92 slaves per slaveholder. In the same year, 32 free people of color owned 59 slaves. That number amounted to 1.84 slaves per owner. Of the women who owned slaves, 42 who were white owned 114 slaves, or each white slaveholding woman owned 2.71 slaves. Of the 32 free people of color who owned slaves, 26 were women who owned 40 slaves, or the women owned 1.54 slaves each. Interestingly, the data demonstrate that of the whites who held slaves 82.9 percent were men while the reverse was true for the free people of color. In that segment of the population, 81.2 percent of the slaveholders were women.

TABLE 1 Ratio of Female Slaves to Male Slaves in the Urban Centers of the South

	1830	1850
Baltimore	1.4849	2.1109
Charleston	1.2216	1.2630
New Orleans	1.5167	1.4950
Washington	1.2821	1.3827

Source: The Fifth Census or Examination of the Inhabitants of the United States, 1830; Statistical View of the United States. . . . Being a Compendium of the Seventh Census, 1850.

Occasionally free people of color owned family members. Sometimes they purchased members of their families of friends in order to free them. For instance, in February 1834 Marianne purchased her twenty-one-year-old daughter, Julie, for the sum of 400 piastres (dollars). She paid 200 piastres to Julie's owner and signed a mortgage for the rest. In February 1845 Louis Houlin, a *negre libre*, purchased an infant, Orpheline, and the four-year-old Marie Louise, from Euphrasie Barron, a *femme de couleur libre*. The condition of the sale was that Houlin would pay Barron 200 piastres for the children after which he would free them. Houlin had a personal stake: Orpheline and Marie Louise were his natural children with a deceased slave, Adeline. In that same month, Mr. Jeremiah, an *homme de couleur libre*, purchased Eliza from Mr. Alexander Periera for 350 piastres on the express condition that he would free her. A few slave women were fortunate enough to be purchased out of slavery by their relatives, but not all could depend on their kin to free them.[10]

Most slave or free men who were related or married to slave women could not afford to purchase their freedom. Therefore, a considerable number of slave women who were never legitimately freed went free or lived in de facto freedom. A few women slipped into freedom in the busy urban environment, passing either as free women of color or as white women. Those women had to depend on their free friends or relatives to ensure their de facto freedom and thus their safety, but even though that usually worked, it could also prove to be extremely risky. Euphemié Lemelle Moran left the details of her struggle for freedom when she had to fight her own sister-in-law in court to prove her freedom. Euphemié Lemelle was born in St. Landry Parish from the union of a free man of color and a slave woman. Even though she was legally defined as a slave, since her mother was a slave, Euphemié was raised as free by her free grandmother. Protected by her father's free family, she never knew the conditions of slavery and, indeed, she probably never would have if she had stayed with her birth family. Instead, she married Charles Moran, a free man of color. Unfortunately for Euphemié, even though she remained married to Charles Moran for many years and bore him seven children, he did not legitimately manumit her. Evidently, he, like her birth family, believed that he could protect her freedom. But Charles Moran did not, could not, protect her. He died, leaving her and their children as a part of his estate to be inherited by his sister, Juliette Moran, a free woman of color of New Orleans. Juliette's attitude toward Euphemié and her children did not reflect that of her brother. After convincing Euphemié to come to New Orleans with her children to "straighten out her free papers," Juliette had the sheriff arrest Euphemié and her children so that they could be sold into slavery. Euphemié sued, however, and after a lengthy court battle she satisfactorily proved to the court, with the help of her neighbors in New Orleans and St. Landry Parish, that she had lived as free for more than twenty years. Euphemié was legally declared free, and since the condition of her children followed her condition, they too were free.

Euphemié, however, was not the only woman who was threatened with reenslavement by her own family. Records in the city demonstrate that several women had to go to court to prove their freedom. Most won their cases and were declared legally free by the court. Those who could not prove their freedom were sold into slavery. After all, the labor of the women in question was becoming increasingly valuable.[11]

Although a few of the city's inhabitants owned their own relatives, most owned slaves for the benefit of their labor. The urban environment provided a variety of skilled and unskilled occupations traditionally defined as women's work, which is the primary reason that most urban slaves were women. The sexual division of labor that was less obvious on the sugar plantations was rarely ignored in the city. A few men worked as domestics. But most household chores were performed by women. Most of the city's slave women, the records suggest, worked at an endless round of domestic chores from before dawn until after sundown. A few very wealthy slaveholders who owned large numbers of domestic slaves assigned them individual tasks. In those households, slave women were assigned duties either as housekeepers, cooks or laundresses, or seamstresses or nurses. But many urban slave women lived in households where they were expected to perform a vast variety of domestic chores. Certainly, in the middle-class households of New Orleans, slave women performed all of the chores necessary for the operation of the household. They cleaned, cooked, nursed, washed, sewed, marketed, and gardened. It appears that slaveholders did as little of the work as possible.

But the city's slave women were not only to be found in private households. Many labored at domestic work in the city's hotels, inns, and boardinghouses. One slave woman who performed a variety of tasks belonged to Madame Tremoulet, an innkeeper in the city. When asked in 1818 about her favored slave by Benjamin Henry Latrobe, who later wrote extensively on the inhabitants of New Orleans, Tremoulet described her as "by far the best house servant of her sex that I know of, famous also as a seamstress and for her good temper." Besides waiting on boarders and making beds, Latrobe noted, the slave woman "made two shirts a day (and night) for the benefit of her mistresses purse." Indeed, she was of such value "that she could be sold for $2,000, and Tremoulet actually asks $3,000." Slave women who were especially skilled as seamstresses, laundresses, cooks, or merchants, Latrobe added, could produce enough income for a small white or free colored family to live on.[12]

Female slaves did not just perform their chores and duties in the presence of their owners. Their work often carried them into the bustling streets, alleyways, and markets of the city. The city's domestic slaves, whom Lyle Saxon described as "old negro women with bright stripped *tignons* on their heads and with baskets on their arms, wandered about buying a little of this and a little of that." They evidently purchased most if not all of the goods for the household. In fact, in 1835, one New Orleans resident wrote that the "only purchasers in the markets were Negroes and generally slaves."[13]

But slaves were more than just the buyers in the markets. The New Orleans resident who described the market's purchasers as mostly slaves also noted that the sellers were also often slaves. "Almost the whole of the purchasing and selling of edible articles for domestic consumption [is] transacted by colored persons." he wrote. "Our Butchers are Negroes; our fishmongers Negroes, our vendors of vegetables, fruits and flowers are all Negroes." Benjamin Henry Latrobe also described their domination of the trade in the 1830s when he wrote that in every street, during the whole day, women chiefly black women, are met carrying baskets upon their heads and calling at the doors of houses." The baskets, according to Latrobe, "contained an assortment of dry goods." The women sold rugs, shawls, fabrics, kerchiefs, and other dry goods. They also peddled fresh produce, coffee, baked goods, and confections. The women transformed the early morning streets and alleyways, shouting and singing, "*Belle fromage! Belle cala! Tout chaud!*" as they sought to entice city dwellers into making purchases from the baskets of food they carried on their hips or balanced gracefully on their heads. Some of the peddlers, Latrobe wrote, belonged to inhabitants who kept dry-goods stores. But others belonged to residents who were too poor to furnish a store with goods. The baskets, Latrobe noticed, were their shops.[14]

Ellen Call Long, another visitor to antebellum New Orleans, described the economic importance of the marketers. It was the slave women, she noted, dressed "in bright bandanas," who dominated the city's marketing trade as they "presided over tables." The slave women, according to Long, were "laughing and chatting, and apparently as free as the customer who ordered his omelet or fruit." Most of the women sold "beer, cakes and fruit at street comers, or with baskets of fancy goods which they carried to the houses of patrons; and a more free, rollicking set of creatures I never saw— slavery at least with them had little significance." Then directly contradicting her own statement, she noted that the same *marchandes*, or marketers, whom she had described as so carefree, worked for the livelihood of their owners. Their sales, she observed, often supported entire families.[15]

Marketing offered *marchandes* much more than an occupation or livelihood. The streets and alleyways, market stalls and levees, or the high earth embankments that edged the waterways around the city, provided the women with a public place in which they could freely communicate with each other and with the world. As Barbara Bush points out, "The public Sunday market was an important institution . . . from the very beginning of slavery." As Bush has observed as well, marketing activities gave slaves ample opportunity to disseminate information among themselves, since vigilance by their masters and mistresses was practically impossible. They created a community where none was expected, finding a measure of anonymity in the bustling marketplace.[16]

That the city's slave women dominated petty marketing was no accident. Slave women in the city, or their mothers or grandmothers, transported their knowledge of marketing with them from Africa to the New World. That transference is particularly obvious in Louisiana where the earliest African women from the region of Senegal also dominated the market trade. Moreover, the tradition of slave women as marketers in the urban centers of the New World was also reinforced by the traditions in early modern Europe where women also served as society's petty marketers.[17]

Yet it is no less important to recognize that slave women themselves carefully guarded the economic and political power they earned through their roles as petty marketers. Responding to a debate over closing the Sunday slave market, Benjamin Latrobe pointed out that the retail trade in dry goods had always been carried on by slave women "in this way before the United States got possession of the country." It had never been the "fashion for ladies to go shopping." Furthermore, according to Latrobe, there was a very practical reason that white New Orleanians encouraged the slave women to continue the practice. As he pointed out, there was so little land in or near the city for the cultivation of food that, were it not for the "vegetables and fowls and small marketing of all sorts, raised by the negro slaves, the city would starve." Slaves who raised produce on their allotted plots of ground or fished in their spare time, he noted, were allowed to keep some if not all of the money their labor produced. Moreover, Latrobe observed, despite the complaints of the slaveholders, they managed to live comfortably from the "labor of their slaves upon this traffic." And all the while, the peddlers were able to keep some control over their profitability.[18]

In fact, the dedication of slave women to peddling underscores their determination to retain as much power over their own lives as possible and the ways in which women in the city made opportunities for themselves. Slave women who peddled were left much to their own devices. Away from their master or mistress, the marketers were free to roam the port and even the countryside. After paying their masters or mistresses their fee, some could use the rest of their earnings to support themselves and their children. Moreover, some women were even able to save enough out of their earnings to purchase their de facto, if not legitimate, freedom. One such woman was Marie, the slave of Jean Baptiste Laporte. A contract drawn up between Laporte and Marie, who was described as about 40 years of age, documents that Laporte purchased Marie from Charles White on March 30, 1827, for the sum of 200 piastres. The contract stipulated, however, that Laporte owned Marie on the "express condition" that he free her when she had reimbursed the sum (200 piastres) plus interest at the rate of 10 percent.[19]

Fanny had also arranged to purchase her freedom from her owner. She agreed to pay Thomas McGovern $140, after which he would free her. But after receiving Fanny's money, McGovern broke the contract and refused to free her, claiming that she was a troublemaker, that she had run away and was living in another man's household. Denying McGovern's claims and refusing to remain in bondage, Fanny sued, claiming that she was free under the terms of the contract. Certainly, Fanny's court testimony demonstrates the day-to-day struggles of slave women in the city. It also shows that she did not reside with her owner. Louis Lamie testified that Fanny had rented a room from him in the yard and "paid me $5 for it." And, according to Lamie, Fanny "is very capable of gaining her living because she is a good washer & ironer." Fanny made her point and was allowed to go free.[20]

Since most of the city's slaves were household domestics or worked with their owners in commercial enterprises, their living arrangements usually resembled those of house servants on plantations. Most of Louisiana's planters normally housed their slaves in cabins arranged together some distance from the big house. The cabins served as basic shelter for the slaves, as their households, and, taken together, as quarters which usually represented a community. Slaveholders in New Orleans created living space for their slaves in the cramped conditions of the city where the residents were crowded together in every block. Slaves were sometimes housed in the main house, in a room at the back of the house, or in the attic. In 1842, Monsieur Isidore Löwenstern described the housing arrangements that he observed on his visit to New Orleans. Many of the houses in the American district of the city, he wrote, were very tall. with each floor having only two rooms. Slaveholders in that district economized on the upper floors where they housed the children and the servants. But, he added, slaveholders rarely resorted to that measure, since it was desirable for them to provide their slaves with a separate living space in order to enforce the distances between the races.[21]

Houses in New Orleans were usually constructed at the front of the lot with their front doors opening directly onto the street. Each house was adjoined to one of the houses next door and opened on the other side with an alleyway that led to the back yard, or courtyard. Most of the courtyards contained dependencies where slaves were housed. The dependencies inside the compounds were generally narrow two-story brick buildings, one room deep and two rooms wide. Verandas or balconies usually spanned the length of the building. Generally, the lower floor served as the kitchen for the entire household, with the upstairs serving as the slaves' living quarters.

The courtyards surrounded by the main house, walls of other houses, and other tall walls have been perceptively described by Richard Wade as compounds that served to constrain the movements of urban slaves in much the same way as the boundaries on plantations constrained slaves. There, urban slave women were not isolated by distance from others, but rather by the high walls that surrounded them. Urban slave women, therefore, spent as much time as possible outdoors, on the veranda, in the courtyard, or, if possible, abroad in the city.[22]

The dense living arrangements in New Orleans intensified relations between slave women and their owners. With living quarters in the house or within a few feet of it, staves, and especially domestic servants, could spend much of their time under the watchful eyes of their masters and mistresses. Such intimacy could lead to love and caring as well as to hate and cruelty. Benjamin Latrobe described one woman who maintained a close relationship with her mistress. "I know . . . an old, decrepit woman who is maintained entirely by an old slave whom she formerly emancipated, but who, on her mistress getting old and helpless, returned to her and devoted her labor to her support."[23]

Such physical intimacy could also lead to sexual liaisons between slave women and their masters or landlords. Some slave women participated in sexual liaisons with their masters or with other white men or free men of color for the relative or legitimate freedom or social mobility that such relationships could offer. Such relationships are difficult to prove, yet the patterns that suggest them appear regularly throughout the records. The freed slave woman Sarah Valentine had more than likely formed a liaison with her white master before he freed her. In her will in which Sarah Valentine left her master her house on Terpsicord Street and her slave, Harriet, she wrote, "This instrument is made of my own free will as all my prosperity is owing to the kindness of Mr. John Valentine."[24]

Notwithstanding Valentine's sentiments and those of other women like her, it seems that slave women were more likely to be victimized than supported by their masters. One example of a woman who was sexually victimized by her master and subsequently physically punished by her mistress was the slave Pauline. Ebenezer Davis recounted the tale in a letter he wrote home while visiting New Orleans during 1845. Davis noted Pauline's sexual victimization by her master, then described how her mistress had turned on her and how Pauline had struck her mistress for her cruelty. In Davis's words, when Pauline tried to repay "in some degree the scorn and abuse with which her mistress had made her painfully familiar," she was arrested. At her trial, Pauline was found guilty of assaulting her mistress and sentenced to be hanged. Her tragedy did not end there, however. Before she could be hanged, it was discovered that Pauline was "in a condition to become a mother." Remanded to her cell, Pauline was forced to await the birth of her child before she was "hanged by her neck until she died."[25]

The household compound in New Orleans, as in other southern cities, might have led to intimacy, for good and for bad, but it was the most practical and secure place in which to house slaves. By the antebellum period, however, the city had become so congested that many slaveholders did not have the space in which to house their slaves. Instead, they and other slaveholders who found it more profitable to allow their slaves to hire themselves out also allowed them to "live out" or make their own living arrangements. A comprehensive law was passed in New Orleans in 1817 that attempted to control the city's errant slave population. The law required slaves to live on the premises of their owners, their owners' representatives, or their employers. It ordered that those who occupied, resided, or slept outside the purview of an owner, an owner's representative, or a lessor were to have a "ticket." And finally, to further discourage the practice of slaves living away from their owners, the law made it illegal for anyone to rent to slaves, even with the permission of the master.[26]

Despite the laws that attempted to limit the practice of "living out," many slaves did. Richard Wade argues, in fact, that "living out" and "hiring out" were integrally related. As soon as slaves began to earn their own wages, he noted, they were also able to pay rent. And furthermore, owners whose slaves worked out were usually more lenient when a slave asked permission to sleep out. Therefore, slave women who obtained their owners' permission, and some who did not, could be found all over the city. Many women lived with the people who hired them, either in their households or in their dependencies. More fortunate women rented small rooms or spaces in hall ways, sheds, lean-tos. basements, and attics. Although most of the spaces were woefully inadequate, the women appear to have preferred their independence over the constant supervision and control of an owner or lessor.[27]

Slave women who could arrange to "live out" were better able to live with their families. But even then their living arrangements were tenuous, for slaveholders could relocate them back into their household or sell or rent them out to a distant location. A variety of sources suggest that urban slave women who lived within their owner's household and those who "lived out" had less opportunity to live with family members than did slaves on the plantation. Holdings were too small and housing too limited to allow slaves to live within more than just the simplest family form. The presumption that slave men and women were rarely able to cohabit is supported by the child–woman ratios of the population. Although child–woman ratios are not true measures of fertility, they are often used to demonstrate the gross fertility of the populations for which there are incomplete data. For New Orleans at this time, the data that allow for the best comparison of fertility rates are the census records and slave schedules that can be analyzed for child–woman ratios. Those records allow for the calculation of the percentage of children under the age of 15 years to women of childbearing age or, in this study, those between 15 and 49. According to comparative data, for every one thousand women between the ages of 15 and 45, slave women averaged less than one child per woman. Free women of color almost always had more than one child throughout the period of the study, and white women always had more than one child. Such information points to the destructive effects of urban slavery on the slave family with its concomitant effects on women. (See Table 2.)

The relative absence of slave children in the urban environment is so remarkable that it is more than likely explained by several factors. One reasonable explanation that actually has nothing to do with fertility is that many slave children, especially those over ten years of age, were sold away

TABLE 2 Child/Woman Ratio for Children under 15 and
Women between 15 and 49 in New Orleans

Status	Ratio		
	1791	1830	1850
Slave	0.781	0.934	0.639
FWC	1.260	1.532	0.934
White	1.683	1.823	1.060

Sources: Census of New Orleans, 6 November 1791, Louisiana Collection,
New Orleans Public Library: *The Fifth Census or Examination of the
Inhabitants of the Unites States, 1830; Statistical View of the United
States. . . . Being a Compendium of the Seventh Census, 1850.*

from their mothers, probably out of the city, and these would not show up in the data. This supposition is supported by Claudia Goldin's theory that urban slaves were increasingly pulled out of southern cities in the final decades before the war. Another explanation might well be that urban slave women who spent most of their time in the shadows of their owners and who substantially outnumbered slave men would have had fewer chances to become pregnant than plantation slave women, who usually lived on the plantation with their husbands. And, too, urban slave women who would have had difficulty caring for their children might have practiced a crude form of birth control, abortion, or even infanticide. Certainly the presence of children would have vastly complicated the life of Fanny, who lived in a room behind Louis Lamie's house and worked as a laundress in order to purchase her own freedom.[28]

Yet, even though it appears that the urban environment constrained the child–woman ratios of slave women and perhaps even their fertility, it is important to note that the same environment allowed urban slave women to formulate a cohesive community away from the supervision of their masters and mistresses. Slaves in New Orleans formulated their own churches and even their own neighborhoods. Indeed, an editor for *New Orleans Crescent* wrote that a traveler passing Baronne Street, between Perdido and Poydras Streets, on any Sunday afternoon could easily imagine him or herself in Africa. The area, he wrote, must have been some sort of slave exchange. There were "coloured churches, coloured ice-cream parlours, coloured restaurants, coloured coffee-houses, and a coloured barber-shop, which we have heard has a back communication with one of the groggeries, for the benefit of slaves."[29]

Fearing a revolt by the slaves who were constantly congregating around town, New Orleans officials did attempt to more closely monitor the slave population by passing increasingly stringent laws. Laws to prohibit slaves from assembling were passed throughout the colonial period, revised in 1817, and reinforced in subsequent years. Slaves were also required to carry passes or wear badges. An editorial in *New Orleans Crescent*, however, pointed out the inadequacies of the pass system. "Something must be done to regulate and prescribe the manner in which passes shall be given to slaves." The behavior of the slave population, the editor wrote, is deplorable because of the "indiscriminate license and indulgence extended them by masters, mistresses, and guardians, and to the practice of forging passes, which has now become a regular business in New Orleans." While the masters and mistresses of slaves were negligent in their policing, the editor noted, the greatest evil was a result of forged passes. "As things now stand, any negro can obtain a pass for four bits or a dollar, from miserable wretches who obtain a living by such infamous practices." The danger from the practice of forged passes, the editor pointed out, was that hundreds of slaves "spend their nights

drinking, carousing, gambling, and contracting the worst of habits, which not only make them use-
less to their owners, but dangerous pests to society."[30]

However, such laws proved impossible to enforce, and society's fears grew, leading to the increasing arrest of slaves, including women. Records reveal that nearly all of the women who were arrested
were those who were found out and about after the city's 8 P.M. curfew. A few, however, were runaways.
Pierre Lemoine's slave, Louise, was arrested at the house of Caroline McGary, ten days after running
away. Louise was punished for running away and Caroline McGary was punished for harboring a slave.
In another example, the slave Hannah and her child, both of whom belonged to Monsieur Avet &
Bros., were captured July 10, 1852. Yet, even though slave women ran away regularly, it appears that
they were still far less likely to try to escape from their owners than were men, perhaps because at least
some of the women would have had to take a child or children with them. In fact, a preliminary estimate suggests that less than 10 percent of New Orleans slaves who were official runaways were women.
Yet the records also show that a few of these women were so desperate to escape their circumstances
that they took their small children with them.[31]

Slave women who violated the city's restrictions were arrested and placed in the city's police
jail, an institution that was created specifically to incarcerate and punish slaves. The disciplinary
measures inflicted upon errant slave women depended upon the severity of their crimes and the
reactions of their owners. Most women were arrested for breaking curfew. Others were taken to the
police jail by their owners to be whipped. Still other women were taken to the jail by their owners for
safekeeping. On February 16, 1853, Mary was brought to the guardhouse at 10:45 A.M. by her master
for safekeeping. A few women even turned to the jail for help. For instance, Angel, the slave of
Mrs. Louis Garcia, gave herself up to the jailer at 7 P.M. on January 24, 1853, at the Watch House. She
told the guard that she was turning herself in because she was "ill-treated by her mistress."[32]

Most of the slaves incarcerated in the jail were men. Women rarely numbered more than
15 percent of the jail's population, and they infrequently remained for more than a few days.
For instance, J. B. Petrand's slaves, Martha and Jenie, were jailed on November 1, 1838, and released
on November 2. The slave of Monsieur Arceuil, Euphrasie, was also arrested on November 1 and
released two days later. The overwhelming number of slaves who found themselves in the police jail
were arrested for roaming about the city after curfew without a pass. That is more than likely why
Jane, Nancy, Mary, Rosalie, Clementine, Margarethe, Betty, Nancy, Matilde, and Anna were arrested
on December 31, 1838, and released January 3, 1839.[33]

Slave women who committed more serious crimes or who were remanded to the jail by their owners could be employed on the chain gang. Women who were picked up by the patrol and not claimed by
their owners within five days were assigned to the chain gang. Evidently not many owners felt compelled
to protect their slave women from the brutal conditions of the chain gang. In fact, since the jail paid a
daily fee to the slave's owner for time spent on the chain gang, owners had little to lose when their slaves
were "put to the chain." The *Rapport de la Geole de Police du 6 au 7 Janvier, 1830* reported 170 slaves in
custody. Of those, 71 were men who were assigned to work on the chain gang, and 25 were women.

Certainly, slavery in New Orleans was not necessarily any less abusive nor exploitive than that
on the plantation. The day-to-day lives of urban slave women, their routines of work, even the
organization, or disorganization, of their families, were ordered by the exigencies of the city. Yet,
even as the nature of housing in the city often isolated slave women from family and friends, the
nature of their work could carry them away from their owners' constant supervision. The wine
women who were locked up at night with their owners could be seen rambling about the streets during the day. Thus, even as the conditions of urban bondage could take away, they could give back. It
was within those contradictions, or tensions within the system, that slave women grasped as much
power over their lives as possible.

Notes

1. Frederick Law Olmsted, *The Cotton Kingdom*, ed. Arthur M. Schlesinger (New York: Modern Library, 1969), 407–8.
2. Dolores Labbé, "Women in Nineteenth Century Louisiana" (Ph.D. diss., University of Delaware, 1975); Gwendolyn Midlo Hall, *Africans in Colonial Louisiana* (Baton Rouge: Louisiana State University Press, 1992); Ann Patton Malone, *Sweet Chariot: State Family and Household Structure in Nineteenth-Century Louisiana* (Chapel Hill: University of North Carolina Press, 1992); John Blassingame, *Black New Orleans, 1860–1880* (Chicago: University of Chicago Press, 1973). For an excellent source that incidentally considers slave women in Spanish New Orleans, see Kimberly Hanger, "Personas de Varias Clases y Colores; Free People of Color in Spanish New Orleans, 1769–1803" (Ph.D. diss., Univeristy of Florida, 1991).
3. Robert S. Starobin's *Industrial Slavery in the Old South* (New York: Oxford University Press, 1970) includes some information on the slaves who labored in the industries in the southern city; as Wade points out, however, most of the South's industries were located in the hinterland. Richard Wade's *Slavery in the Cities: The South, 1820–1860* (New York: Oxford University Press, 1964) is also an excellent source for anyone considering slavery as an urban institution. In *Urban Slavery in the American South, 1820–1860* (Chicago: University of Chicago Press, 1976) Claudia Dale Goldin revisits the issue of the compatibility of slavery with the urban environment raised by Richard Wade. Goldin's book, too, is invaluable for anyone attempting to recover the experiences of urban slaves, as is that of Howard N. Rabinowitz, *Race Relations in the Urban South, 1865–1890* (New York: Oxford University Press, 1978); Michael P. Johnson and James L. Roark, *Black Masters: A Free Family of Color in the Old South* (New York: W. W. Norton, 1984); Loren Schweninger, *Black Property Owners in the South, 1790–1915* (Urbana: University of Illinois Press, 1990); and Barbara J. Fields, *Slavery and Freedom on the Middle Ground: Maryland during the Nineteenth Century* (New Haven: Yale University Press, 1985).
4. *New Orleans in 1805: A Directory and a Census Together with Resolutions Authorizing Same Now Printed for the First Time from the Original Manuscript* (New Orleans: Pelican, 1936); *Statistical View of the United States* (Washington, D.C.: A. O. P. Nicholson, 1854). The 1830 Census is compiled and analyzed in *The Fifth Census or Enumeration of the inhabitants of the United States, 1830* (Washington, D.C.: Duff Green, 1932). Statistics for the 1840 Census can be found in the *Compendium of the Sixth Census* (Washington, D.C.: Thomas Allen, 1841). Statistics for the 1850 Census can be found in *Statistical View of the United States* (Washington, D.C.: Beverly Tucker, 1854); Wade, *Slavery;* Goldin, *Urban Slavery;* Rabinowitz, *Race Relations;* Albert J. Pickett, *Eight Days in New Orleans* (n.p., 1847), 19.
5. *New Orleans in 1805; Statistical View of the United States.*
6. The 1837 Tax Assessor's records of the First Municipality of New Orleans are housed at the New Orleans Public Library, Louisiana Collection.
7. Starobin, *Industrial Slavery;* the 1837 Tax Assessor's records.
8. The 1771 Spanish Census of New Orleans, Lawrence Kinnaird, ed., "Spain in the Mississippi Valley, 1765–1794," *Annual Report of the American Historical Association for the Year 1945* (Washington, D.C.: Government Printing Office, 1946). *New Orleans in 1805: Statistical View of the United States.*
9. In *The Free Women of Petersburg* (New York: W. W. Norton, 1984) Suzanne Lebsock also states that slaveholding women in Petersburg preferred to own women.
10. Property records are found in the New Orleans Notarial Archives, Civil Court Building. L. T. Caire, notary, February 1834, a deed of sale to Marianne for the purchase of her daughter Julie; L. T. Caire, notary, February 4, 1845, a deed of sale from Barron to Houlin; L. T. Caire, notary, a deed of sale from Mr. Alexander Periera to Mr. Jeremiah.
11. See *Juliette Moran v Euphemié Lemella Moran*, Third District Court of New Orleans, January, 1859; *Tabé, FWC v Vidal*, First District Court of New Orleans, November, 1847; *Milky v Millandon*, Third District Court of New Orleans, 1847.
12. Benjamin Henry Latrobe, *The Journal of Latrobe* (New York: D. Appleton, 1905), 182– 83.
13. *New Orleans Bee*, 13 October 1835.

14. Latrobe, *Journal*, 203.

15. Ellen Call Long, *Florida Breezes, or Florida, New and Old* (1889; reprint, Gainesville: University of Florida Presses, 1962), 26–27.

16. Bush, *Slave Women*, 49. Bush explains that slave women were central to marketing in the Caribbean. Sidney Mintz and Douglas Hall suggest in "The Origins of the Internal Marketing Systems" in *Papers in Caribbean Anthropology*, ed. Sidney Mintz (New Haven: Human Relations Area Files Press, 1970) that it was through those activities that slave women contributed directly to the creolization of the population of the Islands. It appears that the same patterns of cultural transmission can be found on the Gulf Coast. Also see Sidney Mintz, "Caribbean Marketplaces and Caribbean History," *Radical History Review*, 27 (1985): 110–20. Morrissey, *Slave Women*, 53–54.

17. Barbara Bush, *Slave Women in the Caribbean, 1650–1838* (Bloomington: Indiana University Press, 1989); 49; Arlette Gautier, *Les Soeurs de Solitude: La Condition Feminine dans L'eslavage aux Antilles du XVIIe du XIXe Siède* (Paris: Editions Caribbiennes, 1985); David Barry Gaspar, *Bondmen and Rebels: A Case Study of Master–Slave Relations in Antigua, with Implications for Colonial British America* (Baltimore, Johns Hopkins University Press, 1985); Hall, *Africans*; Gwendolyn Midlo Hall, *Social Control in Slave Plantation Societies: A Comparison of St. Domingue and Cuba* (Baltimore: Johns Hopkins University Press, 1971), 80–92: Maria Rosa Cutrufelli, *Women in Africa: Roots of Oppression* (London: Zed Press, 1983).

18. Latrobe, *Journal*, 203.

19. Notarial records, L. T. Caire, 30 May 1827, 106.

20. *Fanny, FWC v. Thomas McGovern*, Third District Court of New Orleans, 1851, 37–38.

21. Isidore Löwenstern, *Les États-Unis et La Havane: Souvenirs d'un Voyageur* (Paris: Leipsick Press, 1842), 277.

22. Wade, *Slavery in the Cities*, 61.

23. Latrobe, *Jounral*, 204.

24. Succession of Sarah Valentine, Orleans Parish Succession Records, Court of Probates, Second District Court, No. 11, 194.

25. This account of the hanging of Pauline is recorded in Ebenezer Davis, *American Scenes and Christian Slavery: A Recent Tour of Four Thousand Miles in the United States* (London: John Snow, 1849), 20–21.

26. Ordinances of the Municipality of New Orleans, 1817, New Orleans Public Library, Louisiana Collection.

27. Wade, *Slavery in the Cities*, 55–79.

28. *Fanny, FWC v. Thomas McGovern*.

29. Olmsted, *Cotton Kingdom*, 234.

30. As quoted in Olmsted, *Cotton Kingdom*, 234–35.

31. *Rapport de la Geole de Police du Juillet 1845*.

32. *Rapport de la Geole de Police du Janvier et Fevrier, 1853*.

33. *Rapport de la Geole de Police du Novembre et Decembre, 1838 et Janvier 1839*.

Chapter 8

Women's Rights Emerges within the Anti-slavery Movement: Angelina and Sarah Grimké in 1837

Kathryn Kish Sklar

Women's rights emerged as a social force in American life in very specific circumstances in 1837. Kathryn Sklar examines the religious motivations and the antislavery impulse that combined to achieve this breakthrough. She draws on the lives and writings of Angelina and Sarah Grimké to show how their 1837 speaking tour against slavery required them to defend the rights of women to participate fully in the moral debates of their time. Their efforts laid a sturdy foundation on which Elizabeth Cady Stanton and Lucretia Mott built when they organized the historic women's rights convention held in Seneca Falls, New York, in July 1848.

In the summer of 1837, two sisters from South Carolina, Angelina and Sarah Grimké, age 32 and 45, respectively, began a speaking tour of New England that permanently altered American perceptions of the rights of women. What began as a tour to promote the abolition of slavery ended by introducing the new concept of women's rights into American public life. Between May and September, the Grimkés ignited a debate about the equality of the sexes that first enveloped the abolitionist movement and then extended into the lives of women who were active in other reforms, precipitating large changes in consciousness in a relatively short period of time.

The emergence of an autonomous women's rights movement from the struggle against slavery was not inevitable. Although women were also active in British antislavery circles, for example, their activism did not generate an equivalent women's rights movement in England. In the United States a movement arose out of the confluence of many causes in the 1830s, some rooted in the economic, social, and political significance of slavery in American society, some in the transformations occurring in American religious culture, and some arising from the growing power of white, middle-class women in American political culture. The movement began, however, with the unique position the Grimké sisters held, as exiles from South Carolina, within the campaign to end slavery.

Angelina and Sarah Grimké rose rapidly to occupy a powerful position in the antislavery movement between 1835 and 1837 because they were the daughters of an elite southern slaveholding family who left the South and became lecturers for the American Anti-Slavery Society. Their compelling descriptions of the horrors of slavery attracted audiences that otherwise might have remained

Adapted from the introduction to Kathryn Kish Sklar, *Women's Rights Emerges within the Antislavery Movement: A Short History with Documents, 1830–1870* (Boston: Bedford Books, St. Martin's Press, 2000).

Cover vignette from Lydia Maria Child, Authentic Anecdotes of American Slavery *(1838). Columbia University.*

indifferent to the topic, especially since a wide range of economic livelihoods in the North were closely intertwined with the system of racial slavery in the South. For example, the politically powerful class of northern merchants profited substantially by selling southern cotton to English manufacturers. And even New England textile workers depended on southern cotton for their earnings.[1]

Before 1830 the Grimké sisters seemed an unlikely pair to launch a revolution. Born to a prominent slave-owning family of Huguenot (French Protestant) descent in Charleston, South Carolina, Sarah was the sixth and Angelina the last of fourteen children. Their father was chief justice of the state's highest court; their mother's brother served as governor of North Carolina. The family's wealth derived from a distant plantation that they never visited, which was run by a hired overseer. Their substantial house in Charleston required the labor of many slaves, most of whom had relatives on the plantation.[2]

The seeds for the sisters' later abhorrence of slavery were sown by their privileged position within its embrace, when, during their childhood, they sympathized with the sufferings of slave children. For example, Angelina once witnessed the anguish of a young slave boy who had been so "dreadfully whipped that he could hardly walk." His "heartbroken countenance" moved her as much as his bloodied back.[3] Sarah and Angelina's mother, Mary Grimké, supervised her household with callous disregard for the well-being of the slaves who served her. Bondspeople slept on the floor without bed or bedding, ate from tin plates without a table, and had no lights in their quarters. Seamstresses were required to work after dark in winter by staircase lamps, so dim that they had to stand to see their work. "Mother," Angelina wrote in her diary in 1828, "rules slaves and children with a rod of fear."[4] After their father died in 1819, slave punishments became even more severe.

One important subtext of the cruelty within slave-owning households was, of course, the fact that slaves were held in bondage against their will. Charleston's 20,000 whites in 1820 were far outnumbered by the city's 60,000 slaves, a ratio that bred fears of slave revolts as well as brutal reprisals against potential uprisings. In Charleston in the summer of 1822, a free black carpenter, Denmark Vesey, secretly organized an extensive slave revolt that was discovered before it erupted. Vesey and thirty-six other black men were hanged.[5]

Yet like most southern critics of slavery, Angelina and Sarah Grimké would almost certainly have accepted their circumstances as beyond their ability to change had they not embarked on a search for a more meaningful religious faith than the comfortable Episcopalianism of their mother. Each in her own way came to reject slavery by first rejecting the religious alternatives available in Charleston and migrating to join the Quaker community in Philadelphia. There, each came to accept the Quaker view of slavery as sinful.[6]

Sarah, thirteen years older than Angelina, went first. Touched by the powerful forces of "the Second Great Awakening"—which transformed American Protestantism between 1800 and 1860 with the evangelical "good news" that individuals could will their own conversion from sin and achieve salvation—she had experienced religious conversion in Charleston under the guidance of a visiting Presbyterian minister in 1813. He preached that her soul would never be saved while she enjoyed fashionable Charleston society—dances, teas, house parties, and other frivolities.[7] In 1819, when Sarah traveled with her ailing father to consult Quaker physicians in Philadelphia and he died at a seaside resort they had recommended, she was befriended by Quakers. After his death she lingered two months under their calming influence, absorbing their spirituality, their belief in the unmediated relationship between God and the individual conscience, their plain style of dress, few servants, orderly habits, and their condemnation of slavery as ungodly.[8] Two years later she returned to Philadelphia and soon thereafter converted to Orthodox Quakerism.

In 1827, Sarah used religious arguments to convince Angelina to join her in Philadelphia. That year Sarah spent the winter in Charleston, reviving the close relationship she had forged with Angelina since the time of her younger sister's birth. Sarah had served as Angelina's godmother at the time of her baptism, and in many ways became a more meaningful parent than their mother. Angelina's letters to Sarah in Philadelphia addressed her as "dearest Mother" and Sarah's called her "my precious child."[9] In 1827, at the age of 22, Angelina led a vibrant social life, the center of which was her young Presbyterian minister. She led a "colored Sunday school," participated in religious societies, did charity work among the poor, and attended a "female prayer meeting" where Baptists, Methodists, Congregationalists, and Presbyterians met monthly to discuss their responsibilities as women. At home, Angelina had organized daily prayer meetings that were attended by her mother and sisters, the family slaves, and slaves from other households.[10]

A struggle for Angelina's soul ensued, with her "beloved" Presbyterian minister on one side and Sarah's Quakerism on the other. At issue was the question of whether Quakers or Presbyterians offered the more reliable route to religious salvation. Sarah won, but only after an intense battle. The older sister's victory was sealed when Angelina cut up her Walter Scott novels and stuffed a cushion with the laces, veils, and trimmings that had adorned her clothing. In July 1828, three months after Sarah returned to Philadelphia, Angelina joined her there.

Years of uncertain focus followed. Because the sisters' escape from Charleston had religious rather than antislavery motives, and because they joined the conservative Quaker community that had taken Sarah in when their father died, they had no contact with the antislavery movement that began to disrupt Philadelphia in 1831.[11] Their Quaker community valued silence and prohibited mingling with outsiders. Participation in "popular" causes—that is, those that were not exclusively Quaker—was strongly discouraged.[12] In 1827 a schism had split American Quakers into two groups. One, called "Hicksite" (after their leader Elias Hicks, a Long Island farmer), continued the traditional Quaker belief in the power of individual conscience over all other sources of authority, sacred or secular. The others called themselves "Orthodox" but actually were innovators who were adopting a creed that took precedence over individual conscience. For example, they began to require members to profess a belief in the divinity of Jesus. In the great social issues of the day, including slavery, Hicksite Quakers tended to promote radical reform and Orthodox Quakers shunned controversy.

Angelina and Sarah's friends were affiliated with the Arch Street Meeting House, seat of Orthodox Quaker conservatism. "We mingle almost entirely with a Society which appears to know but little of what is going on outside of its own immediate precincts," Angelina wrote in 1829. By 1836, she put it more strongly, "My spirit is oppressed and heavy laden, and shut up in prison."[13] Cut off from the city around her, Angelina Grimké withdrew into a five-year moratorium between late 1829 and early 1835, during which she never spoke in Quaker meetings. Having left the South but not really integrating herself into Northern culture, Angelina emerged from this moratorium as a person without regional loyalties who could challenge race and gender norms of both the North and the South.[14]

The sisters' inheritance from their father made it unnecessary for them to work for a living, and they lived comfortably in the home of a Quaker woman who had befriended Sarah in 1819. Both sisters became Quaker ministers. Quakers did not support a paid ministry; instead their ministers were itinerants for whom the "inner light" of their calling sufficed to qualify them as clergy. Unlike other Protestants, Quakers sanctioned women ministers, though they expected women to minister primarily to the needs of their own sex. Separate women's meetings gave the Grimkés and other Quaker women the opportunity to gain speaking and leadership skills. Quaker religious meetings consisted of silence broken only by those (women as well as men) who were inspired, however briefly, to share their thoughts.[15]

Sarah took both her religious quest and her ministerial calling quite seriously. Although her speaking style was halting and tentative, she spoke regularly in Sunday meetings and traveled to visit and speak to other Quaker groups, especially groups of women. Angelina, by contrast, never spoke in public. Searching for other avenues of usefulness, she explored the possibility of becoming a teacher, and visited Catharine Beecher's renowned female seminary in Hartford, Connecticut. Beecher, the daughter of prominent evangelical Congregational minister Lyman Beecher, was promoting the feminization of the teaching profession as an opportunity for women to become self-supporting.[16] But Angelina's Quaker mentors disapproved because such a move would take her out of the community. Permitted by the congregation to return to Charleston to care for her mother in 1829, Angelina spent nine anguished months viewing slavery for the first time through eyes that judged it a sin. Returning to Philadelphia, Angelina found no outlet for her growing conviction that something should be done to stop slavery in the South.

Meanwhile, Hicksite Quakers in Philadelphia were taking the lead in a radical new movement to end slavery. In 1831, Lucretia Mott, a Hicksite Quaker minister and the leading abolitionist in Philadelphia, befriended William Lloyd Garrison, an antislavery journalist who that year founded *The Liberator*, the nation's first newspaper to call for immediate and unconditional emancipation. Mott helped Garrison develop a more effective speaking and writing style. In 1833, she participated in the founding of Garrison's militant new organization, the American Anti-Slavery Society (AASS) and that year she also helped create one of the largest new Garrisonian women's organizations, the Philadelphia Female Anti-Slavery Society.[17]

The founding of the AASS in 1833 marked a turning point in American history because it fostered the growth of a social movement advocating the immediate, unconditional abolition of slavery and the racial equality that immediatism implied. Heretofore white northern and southern antislavery opinion had been dominated by gradualists in the American Colonization Society, who viewed blacks as inferior, had no immediate plans for emancipation, imagined emancipation would occur only after slave owners were compensated for the loss of their slave "property," and expected freed slaves eventually to settle in Africa. Colonization did not threaten the economic, political, and social status quo; Garrison's uncompromising call for immediate abolition did. By emphasizing the equality of blacks and whites, by attacking the racial basis of slavery, and by denouncing race prejudice in the North, the Garrisonian movement from Boston to Cincinnati was attacked by mobs that included "gentlemen of property and standing" when it first appeared in the 1830s.[18]

The power of Garrison's vision flowed from his contact with free blacks, who never accepted colonization as a strategy for ending slavery, from the radicalism of Hicksite Quakers, and from religious ideas about human perfectibility generated by the Second Great Awakening. A tiny minority in the 1830s, Garrisonians argued that slavery was a sin because it deprived human beings of the freedom they needed to choose their own salvation. Because all humans were moral beings, created free by God to determine their own salvation, no person could rightfully deprive others of the ability to make their own moral choices. To do so was a sinful abomination. The remedy? Immediate and unconditional abolition. In Garrison's movement the slave became a child of God, created equal in the eyes of God, and the abolition of slavery became the means by which the new nation could achieve a higher and purer form of God-given liberty.[19]

Garrisonians denounced the trend in northern states that had recently disfranchised free blacks—by 1840 over 90 percent of northern free blacks lived in states that denied them the right to vote.[20] In his 1832 book, *Thoughts on African Colonization*, Garrison scornfully asked those who believed that blacks and whites could never live together harmoniously: "are we pagans, are we savages, are we devils?" Quoting the Scripture, he declared: "In Christ Jesus, all are one: there is neither Jew nor Greek, there is neither bond nor free, there is neither male nor female."[21] This passage supported Garrison's commitment to racial equality; it also endorsed a related principle of sexual equality, which in 1837 the Grimké sisters would turn into a battle cry.

Large numbers of women responded to Garrison's new movement even before the Grimkés joined their ranks in 1835.[22] Three white women, three black men, and sixty white men were present at the founding of the AASS, a meeting that was not publicly announced because its organizers feared the mobs that had plagued Garrison's public appearances ever since he called for the unconditional abolition of slavery. Although women could join the AASS and its local branches, women also formed separate female organizations, like the Philadelphia Female Anti-Slavery Society, which included white and black women among its founders. Such public action was new for women. In the 1820s, women had begun to create maternal societies where they discussed the new meaning of motherhood in their culture, but before 1835, these groups usually met under religious auspices with ministerial leadership. Lucretia Mott, though a gifted speaker, did not feel capable of chairing the founding meeting of the Philadelphia Female Anti-Slavery Society. Yet she did not follow the common path and ask a white minister to preside; women who attended that meeting were led by "James McCrummel, a colored man."[23]

Although black women joined the Philadelphia and other female antislavery societies, they also formed their own groups. Indeed in Salem, Massachusetts, in 1832, when black women formed the Female Anti-Slavery Society of Salem, they created the nation's first women's antislavery group. Before Garrison began to reach African Americans through *The Liberator*, many free blacks were politicized by David Walker's *Appeal to the Colored Citizens of the World*, an 1829 pamphlet that predicted and urged armed rebellion in the South. An African-American merchant in Boston, Walker was a member of the Massachusetts General Colored Association, formed in 1826 to combat racial prejudice in the North and slavery in the South.

Most black women's organizations stressed racial betterment as well as the abolition of slavery. For example, the Afric-American Female Intelligence Society of America, founded in Boston in 1831, opposed slavery, but its constitution emphasized "the welfare of our friends."[24] While many white as well as black women abolitionists spoke out against racial prejudice, black women dedicated themselves to the improvement of African-American communities—a project that distinguished them from most though not all white abolitionist women. In the 1830s this emphasis within black women's organizations meant that racial justice became a higher priority for them than the advancement of women's rights. Although black women were prominent in the abolitionist movement, their voices were not generally heard on the question of women's rights until the 1850s.[25]

Angelina Grimké was jarred out of her moratorium and joined Garrisonian abolitionism in 1835, when she learned of the AASS's efforts to carry its militant new message into the South. Despite the disapproval of her Orthodox Quaker community, she attended a Garrisonian meeting in Philadelphia in March 1835, met with the Philadelphia Female Anti-Slavery Society, and began to read *The Liberator*, where she found thrilling accounts of the heroism and martyrdom of abolitionists threatened by angry mobs.

In the summer of 1835, in a step that unofficially severed her ties with her Quaker community, Angelina publicly joined the vilified abolitionist movement. She did so just after Garrisonians carried their message to Charleston. The AASS had launched a "postal campaign" that sent vast amounts of abolitionist literature through the mails that summer, 175,000 pieces through the New York City post office in July alone.[26] Mobs reacted by destroying these "inflammatory appeals" and attacking abolitionist meetings. In Charleston a mob broke into the post office, seized the AASS literature, and burned it beneath a hanged effigy of Garrison. With the bonfires in Charleston on her mind, in August Angelina sent a letter to Garrison that emphasized her profoundly personal commitment, saying, "it is my deep, solemn, deliberate conviction, that *this is a cause worth dying for*."[27] At the age of thirty, Angelina Grimké had found her voice.

When Angelina joined Garrison, Mott, and others in 1835 in the vanguard of her generation's concern for her nation's future as a land of freedom, three Americans who later played major parts in the national drama over slavery were relatively oblivious to its importance. Abraham Lincoln, twenty-six years old, was a freshman state legislator and law student in New Salem, Illinois. Jefferson Davis, twenty-six years old and later president of the Confederate States of America, had just moved with his bride and eleven slaves to begin a cotton plantation on rich Mississippi delta land. Harriet Beecher Stowe, twenty-four years old and future author of *Uncle Tom's Cabin* in 1852, was teaching school in Cincinnati. When Lincoln, Davis, and Stowe later became large public figures, they joined a discourse that had been shaped by the Grimké sisters and other Garrisonians.

At first, Sarah strongly disapproved of her sister's actions, writing in her diary, "The suffering which my precious sister has brought upon herself by her connection with the antislavery cause, which has been a sorrow of heart to me, is another proof how dangerous it is to slight the clear convictions of truth." Truth, for Sarah, lay in the Quaker admonition to be still and avoid conflict. Angelina wrote her, "I feel as though my character had sustained a deep injury in the opinion of those I love and value most—how justly, they will best know at a future day."[28]

Independently of her sister, Angelina moved ahead. She took refuge with a sympathetic friend in Shrewsbury, New Jersey, and spent the winter of 1836 writing *Appeal to the Christian Women of the South*. Writing as a southerner and a woman, she created a place for herself within the new Garrisonian movement. Promptly published and widely distributed by the AASS, her *Appeal* urged southern women to follow the example of northern women and mobilize against slavery. Rather than limiting their influence to their own domestic circle, Angelina argued, women should speak out and take public action. "Where *woman's* heart is bleeding," she insisted, "Shall woman's heart be hushed?" If championing the cause of the slave required them to break local laws, she called on her readers, in one of the nation's first expressions of civil disobedience, to follow higher laws.[29]

The exiled South Carolinian especially urged her readers to petition the national government to end slavery. The recent abolition of slavery in the British West Indies, she argued, was due to women's petitions. Sixty female antislavery societies in the North had already followed the British women's example, and she urged southern women to do the same. Petitions enlarged the public space that women occupied, and brought them into direct contact with their national government. At a time when the national government was a distant and somewhat ephemeral concept in the lives of most Americans, antislavery petitions made it a concrete reality. Women's antislavery petitions affirmed the potential power of the national government to redress grievances and restore "rights unjustly wrestled from the innocent and defenseless."[30]

Disfranchised individuals, like women and slaves, had petitioned the national government, particularly the U.S. House of Representatives, since the 1790s, drawing on the First Amendment to the Constitution, which guaranteed the right of "the people . . . to petition the government for a redress of grievances." What was new in the 1830s was the group petition with many signatures. Catharine Beecher organized the first national petition drive by women in the summer of 1829, opposing President Andrew Jackson's forced removal of Cherokee people from land they had historically occupied in Georgia.[31] In 1834, when the AASS organized petitions to end slavery in the District of Columbia, the Society printed a petition form especially designed for women.

The new Garrisonian women's antislavery societies dedicated themselves to gathering signatures, walking door to door, and driving wagons or carriages through their communities. Historians estimate that women contributed 70 percent of the signatures on antislavery petitions.[32] They collected three times as many signatures as those previously obtained by paid male AASS agents. By 1836 the petition campaign so disrupted the proceedings of the U.S. House of Representatives that a "gag rule" was passed to prevent congressmen from reading or otherwise presenting the petitions on the floor of the House. Passed with each Congress between 1836 and 1844, gag rules expanded support for the antislavery cause by linking it to free speech.[33]

Joining this insurgent movement in 1835, Angelina Grimké immediately attracted the attention of the AASS, which sent piles of her *Appeal* to Charleston. There, postmasters publicly burned the pamphlets. The city's mayor told Mrs. Grimké that her daughter would be arrested if she tried to enter the city.[34] Even before Angelina submitted her *Appeal* to the American Anti-Slavery Society, Elizur Wright, secretary of the society, invited her to come to New York and under the sponsorship of the AASS, meet with women in their homes and speak with them about slavery.

Sarah, meanwhile, was rebuked in the Arch Street Meeting House in a way that led her to leave Philadelphia. Although her speaking skills remained unimpressive, and her southern accent reminded her listeners that she remained an outsider in this elite Quaker community, Sarah often spoke in meetings. In July 1835, a presiding elder, probably expressing a consensus reached with other local leaders, rose and cut her off, saying: "I hope the Friend will now be satisfied." Silenced, Sarah sat down. His breach of Quaker discipline was clearly meant to silence her permanently in the meeting. For nine years she had struggled to develop ministerial speaking gifts, keenly aware of the cold indifference with which the elders viewed her efforts. That day she decided "that my dear Saviour designs to bring me out of this place." On learning the news, Angelina rejoiced, "I will break your bonds and set you free."[35] Within a few weeks Angelina had convinced Sarah of the righteousness of her Garrisonian views, and Sarah acknowledged her younger sister's leadership in setting their future course.

Renouncing the respectable comforts of northern as well as southern society, the sisters traveled to New York City in the autumn of 1836. There, for most of the month of November 1836, they joined a training workshop of about thirty men who were serving as the paid agents of the AASS. There they forged new identities as antislavery agitators. "We sit," Angelina wrote to a friend, "from 9 to 1, 3 to 5, and 7 to 9, and never feel weary at all," discussing biblical arguments against slavery and answering questions like "What is Slavery?"[36]

Although they declined to accept pay from the AASS, the sisters launched their new identity as the first women agents of the AASS on December 16, 1836, when they spoke in a Baptist meeting room, no home being large enough to hold the three hundred women who wanted to hear them. To speak in public they had to be willing to break the custom that prohibited respectable women from addressing large public gatherings, and oppose the Scriptural authority of Paul's admonition to the early Christians, "Let your women keep silence in the churches; for it is not permitted unto them to speak." Antislavery women had heretofore spoken to small groups of women, mostly neighbors, in their homes or churches. Angelina temporarily lost her nerve and feared it would be "unnatural" for her to proceed. Charismatic Theodore Weld, one of the leaders of their training group, whom Angelina would later marry, revived the sisters' courage by disparaging social norms that "bound up the energies of woman," and by reminding them of the high importance of their message.[37]

Public speaking was a form of performance in nineteenth-century culture that was strongly associated with the explicitly masculine virtues of virility, forcefulness, and endurance. Much of the vitality of the new nation's public life emanated from styles of oratory that began to emerge in the 1830s, first in the pulpit, then in politics. These new styles were part of the process by which the authority of the clergy and of traditional landed elites was being replaced in public life by the power of more popular groups, especially the broad middle class that ranged from artisans to professionals. The rise in public oratory placed great demands on both speaker and audience. Speakers were expected to engage their audiences' emotions in ways that entertained as well as enlightened, and they were not expected to be brief. Theirs was a culture in which "the word" carried great weight.[38]

Beyond the meetings of all-female societies, respectable women were permitted to enter this arena only as consumers, not as the producers of eloquence. The chief exceptions to this rule were itinerant women preachers, whose prophetic or visionary preaching was inspired by the new currents of expression within the Second Great Awakening. Yet the authority that these women claimed was spiritual, not social. One historian has called them "biblical feminists" because they asserted the spiritual but not the social equality of women. Women might have mystical powers but this did not translate into authority in society. Except among Quakers, female preachers were not ordained and worked outside the institutional religious authority of the clergy.[39] In 1836 and 1837, Angelina and Sarah Grimké would assert women's right to speak not only because women were the spiritual equals of men, but also because they were the moral and social equals of men. By so doing, they opened new channels to public life for women who were not visionaries or prophets.

Opponents tried to discredit women's public speaking by tainting it with the radicalism of Frances Wright, a British free thinker identified with the French Revolution, who spoke widely in the United States in the 1820s.[40] Even the term used to describe a mixed audience of men and women—promiscuous—conveyed the era's distrust of women moving freely in public space. Partly because public speaking was so central to the construction of contemporary civil society, the prohibition against respectable women's public speaking was a key ingredient in the practices that denied respectable women—that is, elite, white, middle-class, and artisan-class women—access to and equality within the new contours of public life. By speaking in public, the Grimké sisters precipitated a women's movement that rebelled against this exclusion. By breaking the prohibition against women's public speaking, they generated criticisms that denied their right to speak, which in turn prompted them to defend that right. This spiraling dynamic occurred because thousands of people wanted to hear the sisters speak more than they wanted to enforce customary strictures.[41]

Angelina's confidence in her public performances grew in the meetings that followed her first speaking date. Addressing a new audience each week, in January 1836, she wrote her Philadelphia friend, Jane Smith, "I love the work." By February she described her animated speaking style as yielding to "impulses of feeling." By then she was also beginning to defend women's "rights & duties" to speak and act on the topic of slavery.

The rapid growth of women's antislavery associations, and the stir that the Grimkés were making in their ranks, led to an unprecedented event in May 1837—a national convention of antislavery women. Organized by Angelina Grimké and other women abolitionist leaders, including Maria Weston Chapman of the Boston Female Anti-Slavery Society and Lucretia Mott and others in the Philadelphia Female Anti-Slavery Society, the convention was scheduled in conjunction with the annual meeting of the American Anti-Slavery Society. Planning for the meeting, Angelina urged Sarah Douglass, a black friend from Philadelphia, to attend it despite the prejudice she could expect to encounter there—from women abolitionists as well as the public at large. Accompanied by her mother, Sarah Douglass did attend. The three-day event attracted about two hundred women from nine states. About one in ten was African American.

The women's antislavery convention marked a new stage in the emergence of women's rights within the abolitionist movement. There Angelina presented her *Appeal to the Women of the Nominally Free States*, a lengthy pamphlet that defiantly defended women's right to speak and act. "The denial of our duty to act, is a bold denial of our right to act; and if we have no right to act, then may *we* well be termed 'the white slaves of the North'—for, like our brethren in bonds, we must seal our lips in silence and despair."[42]

At the convention, delegates adopted resolutions that urged women to circulate petitions that decried the indifference of American churches to the sin of slavery, that censured northerners who married southern slave holders, and that called for white women to associate with African-American women "as though the color of the skin was of no more consequence than that of the hair, or the eyes." Just as radically, the convention approved a resolution supporting women's rights. It declared that "certain rights and duties are common to all moral beings," and that it was the duty of woman "to do all that she can by her voice, and her pen, and her purse, and the influence of her example, to overthrow the horrible system of American slavery." Although most of the convention's resolutions were adopted without extensive discussion, this one "called forth an animated and interesting debate." Twelve delegates opposed the resolution so strongly that they had their names recorded in the minutes "as disapproving."[43]

Following the inaugural meeting of the Anti-Slavery Convention of American Women, the Grimkés launched their historic speaking tour of Massachusetts in the summer of 1837. Beginning in Boston, they felt that they pleaded "not the cause of the slave only" but "the cause of woman as a responsible moral being." In parlor meetings where they strategized with their supporters, men as well as women thought it was time their "fetters were broken." Many believed "that women could not perform their duties as moral beings, under the existing state of public sentiment." And very many thought "that a new order of things is very desirable in this respect." Angelina was stunned by this turn of events. "What an untrodden path we have entered upon," she wrote Jane Smith. "Sometimes I feel almost bewildered, amazed, confounded & wonder by what strange concatenation of events I came to be where I am and what I am."[44]

Reinforced by this support, Angelina declared before 300 members of the Female Moral Reform Society in Boston that they should see women's rights as a personal issue—"that this reform was to begin in ourselves." Women were "polluted" by the attitudes toward them, she said. For example, they felt "restraint and embarrassment" in the society of men. And the "solemn and sacred subject of marriage" was discussed in unseemly ways. Emphasizing the subjective, personal impact of gender inequalities, Angelina told her audience, "My heart is pained, my womanhood is insulted, my moral being is outraged continually."[45]

The sisters found support for this critique of male dominance when they left Boston to lecture in the surrounding countryside. Maria Weston Chapman, an elite leader of the Boston Female Anti-Slavery Society, sent a letter "to Female Anti-Slavery Societies throughout New England" supporting the Grimkés' discussion of "the condition of woman; her duties and her consequent rights." Disdaining those "who were grinding in the narrow mill of a corrupt publick opinion on this point," Chapman urged antislavery women to show the sisters "hospitality of the heart."[46]

In contrast to most British churchmen, who led public opinion in supporting abolition in the 1830s when Parliament ended slavery in the British West Indies, most American clergymen in the North did not support immediate abolition before the Civil War.[47] Thus most church doors were closed against them and ministers who invited the sisters to speak in their churches were exceptions to the rule.

People came to hear the sisters because they were curious about the phenomenon they now represented: southern women presenting in public their first-hand view of the horrors of slavery and defending their right to speak in public about those horrors. Their reception varied. "Great apathy" sometimes reigned in small outlying towns, but before large audiences in Boston and Lynn, Angelina found it "very easy to speak because there was great openness to hear." Men became an increasing part of their audiences. In Lynn on the evening of June 21, they addressed 500 women; a month later in that manufacturing town, they spoke to 1,500 men as well as women.[48] Seven months after their first speaking engagement they had successfully broken the customs against women speaking in public and against women speaking to mixed audiences.

The Grimkés maintained a grueling pace between June and November. Speaking every other day, sometimes twice a day, often for two hours at a time, they reached thousands. In June Angelina spoke seventeen times in ten towns, with over 8,000 attending. In July she gave nineteen lectures in fourteen towns, reaching nearly 12,000. In August, even though Angelina was ill for half the month, she gave eleven lectures in nine towns, with 6,000 present. In September, she spoke seventeen times in sixteen towns, with over 7,000 persons attending. In October she spoke fifteen times in fifteen towns, with 12,000 in her audiences. During these five months she lectured seventy-nine times to audiences totaling over 40,000 people.[49]

It does not seem that Sarah spoke independently of Angelina. Angelina was the one people came to hear. Her extraordinary oratory offered audiences the 1830s equivalent of an award-winning movie about slavery. "Never before or since have I seen an audience so held and so moved by any public speaker, man or woman," said a Massachusetts minister in whose pulpit she lectured.[50] Wendell Phillips, prominent Boston abolitionist, said that she "swept the cords of the human heart with a power that has never been surpassed, and rarely equalled." Phillips was impressed by "her serene indifference to the judgment of those about her. Self-poised, she seemed morally sufficient to herself." He thought her power derived from "the profound religious experience of one who had broken out of the charmed circle, and whose intense earnestness melted all opposition." Audiences felt that "she was opening some secret record of her own experience"; their "painful silence and breathless interest told the deep effect and lasting impression her words were making."[51]

Angelina's impact on her audiences issued partly from her mastery of an oratorical style that emphasized her feelings. Equally important, however, was her ability to use familiar language in new ways. She spoke in the religious discourse of her time, shaping it to fit her purposes. "Cast out the spirit of slavery from your own hearts," she said. "The great men of this country" and the "church" have become "worldly-wise, and therefore God in his wisdom, employs them not to carry on his plans of reformation and salvation." Instead, he has chosen "the weak to overcome the mighty." This use of familiar metaphors to convey new ideas had deep roots in Judeo-Christian traditions. Angelina stood in a long line of prophets who used that tradition to bring new concepts into their cultures. She equated herself to Isaiah and the Massachusetts clergy to old-testament Jewish priests. Like them, she was denounced by established religious authorities, who saw her as a defiant challenge to their leadership.[52]

Yet despite Angelina's greater oratorical gifts, the sisters' success was achieved jointly; neither could have done alone what they were able to accomplish together. Traveling among strangers, some of whom were friendly, some hostile, they could rely on one another as trusted family members and as dedicated colleagues with whom they shared the speaking platform. Neither had to bear all the burdens of their grueling schedule. Sarah was becoming a capable speaker on women's rights, and Angelina relied on her to elaborate that aspect of their message. "Sister Sarah does preach up woman's rights most nobly and fearlessly," Angelina wrote in July.[53]

One measure of the sisters' success was the exponential growth in membership of the American Anti-Slavery Society immediately after their speaking tour. Each meeting harvested new "subscribers" to the AASS. In 1837, the AASS claimed 1,000 auxiliaries and 100,000 members. A year later, their membership had more than doubled to 250,000, and the number of affiliated antislavery societies had increased by one third.[54]

A large number of these new members were women. Many women responded enthusiastically to the Grimkés' "breach in the wall of public opinion." Angelina wrote Jane Smith, "we find that many of our New England sisters are ready to receive these strange doctrines, feeling as they do, that our whole sex needs an emancipation from the thraldom of public opinion." In villages as well as cities, "the whole land seem[ed] roused to discussion on the *province of woman*."[55] While the sisters from South Carolina led the way, others willingly followed. Disciples attracted to their side—like Abby Kelley, a Quaker teacher in Lynn, Massachusetts—now embraced women's rights as well as Garrisonian abolition.

In June the Grimkés' campaign created a constituency for women's rights; in July their opponents emerged. Men within the Garrisonian movement, many of whom supported women's rights in the abstract, feared the issue would damage abolitionism by diffusing the movement's energies, and by linking antislavery with an even less popular idea. Sarah responded to this criticism in a letter to Amos Phelps, a Congregational minister who was an agent of the AASS. There was no going back on her right to speak to mixed assemblies, she said: "To close the doors *now* against our brethren wd. be a violation of our fundamental principle that man & woman are created equal, & have the same duties & the same responsibilities as moral beings. If, therefore, it is right for thee, my dear brother, to lecture to promiscuous assemblies, it is right for us to do the same."[56]

The sharpest criticism of the sisters came from a Pastoral Letter issued by the General Association of Massachusetts [Congregational] Churches, which in July condemned "those who encourage females to bear an obtrusive and ostentatious part in measures of reform, and countenance any of that sex who so far forget themselves as to itinerate in the character of public lecturers and teachers." The letter especially condemned the naming of "things which ought not to be named," as they delicately referred to the sisters' testimonials about the sexual exploitation of slave women. Indirectly the letter forbade clergymen to permit the sisters to speak in their churches.[57]

Clerical opposition to the Grimkés was fueled in part by ministers' desires to contain the power of the female laity in their own congregations. Historically excluded from leadership positions, except among Quakers, in the late 1830s women began to express views on a wide range of issues in their communities, including temperance and moral reform as well as abolition.[58] The growing power of women in the political culture of their communities on these and other issues threatened to undercut ministers' moral leadership. Reverend Albert Folsom of Hingham, Massachusetts, spoke for many clergymen when he sought to discredit women's participation in public life as "inappropriate and unlawful."[59] By August, Angelina felt that "a storm was gathering all around against our woman-hood," and feared that even more ministers would close church doors against them.[60]

Increasingly the defense of women's rights came to occupy the sisters' attention. They had not sought this controversy, Angelina emphasized. "We are placed very unexpectedly in a very trying situation, in the forefront of an entirely new contest—a contest for the rights of woman as a moral, intelligent & responsible being."[61] In the summer of 1837, Sarah began to publish a series of essays in defense of women's rights. Theodore Weld, the most charismatic of their male colleagues in the AASS, urged them both to cease such publications and stay focused on slavery. As "*southerners*," he argued, they could "do more at convincing the North than twenty northern females," an advantage that they lost by pursuing "*another* subject."[62] Standing her ground, Angelina explained to Weld why she and Sarah felt they now had to defend women's rights in their speaking and writing. "If we surrender the right to speak to the public this year, we must surrender the right to petition next year & the right to write the year after &c.," she wrote. "What *then* can *woman* do for the slave, when she herself is under the feet of man and shamed into *silence?*"[63]

The annual reports of many women's antislavery societies endorsed the Grimkés' fight for women's rights. At an October 1837 meeting, the Ladies Anti-Slavery Society in Providence, Rhode Island, resolved "that we act as moral agents"; and "that our rights are sacred and immutable, and founded on the liberty of the gospel, that great emancipation act for women." A majority of the nation's largest and most powerful women's abolitionist group, the Philadelphia Female Anti-Slavery Society, also voted their approval.[64]

In October 1837, the sisters settled into the home of friends in Brookline, Massachusetts. Both wrote essays in the form of letters that were later published as books, Sarah's as *Letters on the Equality of the Sexes and the Condition of Woman* (1838); Angelina's as *Letters to Catherine E. Beecher* (1838).[65] Their writings became the standard for women's rights thinking until a decade later, when the Seneca Falls Women's Rights Convention sparked another outpouring of commentary. Glowing with a white-hot radiance, Angelina and Sarah left an enduring legacy for women's rights advocates.

The sisters' writings on women's rights relied primarily on religious arguments. Yet because they buttressed these arguments with enlightenment notions about human equality and natural rights contained in the Declaration of Independence, their vision of female equality extended further than the "biblical feminism" of itinerant female preachers. In these "letters" they explored the implications of the ideas they had developed during their speaking tour. Insisting that all rights were grounded in "moral nature," they explored the personal aspects of moral identity and of rights. And they analyzed the social and political meaning of women's rights from a multitude of perspectives inside and outside the antislavery movement.

Angelina even argued that women should have equal rights in the secular social and political world. When she supported woman's "right to be consulted in all the laws and regulation by which she is to be governed, whether in Church or State," she was making a very large claim indeed. In a passage with closing words that must have thrilled some readers and shocked others, she further insisted "that woman has just as much right to sit in solemn counsel in Conventions, Conferences, Associations, and General Assemblies, as man—just as much right to sit upon the throne of England, or in the Presidential chair of the United States, as man." Sarah offered a new interpretation of the biblical admonition "wives, submit yourselves unto your own husbands." For nineteenth-century women, this biblical admonition often meant submitting to unwanted sexual intercourse, and, since intercourse often led to pregnancy, to unwanted pregnancy. The passage, Sarah wrote, merely recommended a Christian spirit of humility, not a literal rule of husbands over wives.[66] Aware of the radical implications of their arguments, Angelina wrote Sarah Douglass in February 1838, "We Abolition Women are turning the world upside down."[67]

That month, Theodore Weld declared his love and proposed marriage to Angelina Grimké. To gain her consent he wrote only one letter. There, he said that her 1835 letter to Garrison "formed an era in my feelings and a crisis in my history that drew my spirit toward yours." Reminded of her state of mind in 1835 when she wrote Garrison "under tremendous pressure of feelings bursting up with volcanic violence from the bottom of my soul . . . the first long breath of *liberty* which my imprisoned spirit dared to respire whilst it pined in hopeless bondage, panting after freedom to *think aloud*," she agreed to marry Weld.[68] She loved him as "a kindred mind, a congenial soul" with whom she "longed to hold communion."[69] They set the wedding for May. The "volcanic violence" of Angelina Grimké's commitment to Garrisonian abolitionism helped her break customary limits on women's participation in public life. By thinking aloud—fearlessly—she and her sister brought new words and new concepts into public life and created the basis for new relationships in marriage.

Perhaps reflecting the burdens of her pathbreaking three years, Angelina retired from public life after her marriage to Theodore Weld, and Sarah joined the couple in their rural New Jersey retreat. Theodore had lost his voice after one particularly exhausting lecture tour in 1836, and never fully recovered it. Although he continued to play a part in the antislavery movement, Theodore supported his growing family by becoming a teacher.

By autumn of 1837, a new era had taken shape in gender relations and gender ideology in the United States. Although limited geographically to New England and contained within a small social movement to end slavery, the ideas launched by Angelina and Sarah Grimké steadily gained authority through the 1840s, contributing substantially to the first women's rights convention at Seneca Falls, New York, in 1848, and that convention's historic "Declaration of Sentiments."[70] A series of women's rights conventions met during the 1850s, and, after an interregnum during the Civil War in the 1860s, led in 1869 to the founding of national and local woman suffrage organizations, and in 1920 to the adoption of woman suffrage in the Nineteenth Amendment to the U.S. Constitution.[71] The conversion of Angelina and Sarah Grimké to Garrisonian abolitionism and their 1837 speaking tour played a pivotal role in the emergence of this greatest of social movements in American history.

Notes

1. John Ashworth, *Slavery, Capitalism, and Politics in the Antebellum Republic*, vol. 1, *Commerce and Compromise, 1820–1850* (New York: Cambridge University Press, 1995), p. 365.
2. Brief biographies of Angelina and Sarah Grimké (hereafter AG and SG) and most other women mentioned in this essay can be found in Edward James, *et al.*, eds., *Notable American Women: A Biographical Dictionary* (Cambridge: Harvard University Press, 1971).
3. "Testimony of Angelina Grimké Weld," in Theodore D. Weld, ed., *American Slavery As It Is: Testimony of a Thousand Witnesses* (New York: American Anti-Slavery Society, 1839), pp. 54–55.
4. Large portions from AG's diary have been printed in Catherine H. Birney, *The Grimké Sisters: Sarah and Angelina Grimké: The First American Women Advocates of Abolition and Women's Rights* (Philadelphia: Lee and Shepard, 1885), pp. 55–93. The treatment of slaves in the Grimké household can be inferred from passages in "Testimony of Angelina Grimké Weld," and "Narrative and Testimony of Sarah M. Grimké," in *American Slavery As It Is*, pp. 52–57 and 22–24.
5. See John Lofton, *Denmark Vesey's Revolt: The Slave Plot that Lit a Fuse to Fort Sumter* (Kent, Ohio: Kent State University Press, 1983); and Edward A. Pearson, ed., *Designs Against Charleston: The Trial Record of*

the Denmark Vesey Slave Conspiracy of 1822 (Chapel Hill: University of North Carolina Press, 1999). The total slave population in the United States at this time was about two million.

6. This interpretation of the Grimké sisters draws on my research in primary materials. It builds on but is not the same as interpretations found in Birney, *The Grimké Sisters;* Larry Ceplair, ed., *The Public Years of Sarah and Angelina Grimké: Selected Writings, 1835–1839* (New York: Columbia University Press, 1989); Gerda Lerner, *The Grimké Sisters of South Carolina: Pioneers for Women's Rights and Abolitionism* (New York: Oxford University Press, 1967); Gerda Lerner, *The Feminist Thought of Sarah Grimké* (New York: Oxford University Press, 1998); and Katherine DePre Lumpkin, *The Emancipation of Angelina Grimké* (Chapel Hill: University of North Carolina Press, 1974).

7. For the feminist potential in the Second Great Awakening, see Nancy A. Hardesty, *Your Daughters Shall Prophesy: Revivalism and Feminism in the Age of Finney* (Brooklyn: Carlson, 1991). See also Nathan O. Hatch, *The Democratization of American Christianity* (New Haven: Yale University Press, 1989).

8. Quakers led the way in the abolition of slavery in the North. In 1758, the Philadelphia Yearly Meeting of the Society of Friends voted to exclude anyone who bought or sold slaves; in 1776, it excluded anyone who owned slaves. Between 1780 and 1800, most Northern states enacted statutes that abolished slavery, though this was usually accomplished gradually, as was the case in the Pennsylvania "Act for the Gradual Abolition of Slavery" of 1780, which immediately emancipated all children born after the passage of the act, but freed adults more gradually. See "Abolition Statutes," in Robert H. Bremner, et al., eds., *Children and Youth in America: A Documentary History*, Vol. I: 1600–1865 (Cambridge: Harvard University Press, 1970), pp. 324–26. In 1830, Negro slavery was still not totally abolished in the North; about 3,500 persons remained in bondage, mostly in New Jersey. See Leon F. Litwack, *North of Slavery: The Negro in the Free States, 1970–1860* (Chicago: University of Chicago Press, 1961), pp. 12–14.

9. Lumpkin, *The Emancipation of Angelina Grimké*, p. 20.

10. AG to Elizabeth Bascom, 23 July 1828; and AG to [her sister] Mrs. Anna Frost, 17 March 1828, both in Weld-Grimké Collection, William L. Clements Library, University of Michigan, Ann Arbor; Lerner, *The Grimké Sisters*, p. 54.

11. Although AG later claimed that antislavery motivations impelled her departure from South Carolina, the historical evidence supports a more gradual evolution of her antislavery views.

12. See Thomas D. Hamm, *The Transformation of American Quakerism: Orthodox Friends, 1800–1907* (Bloomington: Indiana University Press, 1988).

13. AG to Thomas Grimké [1829]; and AG to SG [1836], quoted in Birney, *The Grimké Sisters*, pp. 91, 137.

14. For another example of a young person who emerged from a moratorium to change his society, see Erik Erikson, *Young Man Luther* (New York: W. W. Norton, 1958).

15. For the endorsement of women's spiritual leadership within Quakerism, see Janis Calvo, "Quaker Women Ministers in Nineteenth Century America," *Quaker History* 63, no. 2 (1974): 75–93; and Margaret Hope Bacon, *Mothers of Feminism: The Story of Quaker Women in America* (New York: Harper, 1986).

16. See Kathryn Kish Sklar, *Catharine Beecher: A Study in American Domesticity* (New Haven: Yale University Press, 1973).

17. For Garrison and *The Liberator*, see William E. Cain, ed., *William Lloyd Garrison and the Fight Against Slavery: Selections from the Liberator* (Boston: Bedford Books, 1995). For Mott, see Margaret Hope Bacon, *Valiant Friend: The Life of Lucretia Mott* (New York: Walker, 1980); and Dana Greene, ed., *Lucretia Mott: Her Complete Speeches and Sermons* (New York: Mellen, 1980).

18. Paul Goodman, *Of One Blood: Abolitionism and the Origins of Racial Equality* (Berkeley: University of California Press, 1998); and Leonard L. Richards, *"Gentlemen of Property and Standing": Anti-Abolition Mobs in Jacksonian America* (New York: Oxford University Press, 1970).

19. Robert H. Abzug, *Cosmos Crumbling: American Reform and the Religious Imagination* (New York: Oxford University Press, 1994), pp. 129–62; and Caroline L. Shanks, "The Biblication Anti-Slavery Argument of the Decade, 1830–1840," *Journal of Negro History* XVI (April 1931).

20. Litwack, *North of Slavery*, p. 75.

21. William Lloyd Garrison, *Thoughts on African Colonization* (Boston, 1832), reprinted in George M. Fredrickson, ed., *William Lloyd Garrison* (Englewood Cliffs, N.J.: Prentice Hall, 1968), pp. 29–37; quote, p. 33.

22. For the growth of women's antislavery organizations in the 1830s, see Julie Roy Jeffrey, *The Great Silent Army of Abolitionism: Ordinary Women in the Antislavery Movement* (Chapel Hill: University of North Carolina Press, 1998), pp. 53–95.

23. Anna Davis Hallowell, *James and Lucretia Mott, Life and Letters* (Boston: Houghton Mifflin, 1884), p. 121, reprinted in Kathryn Kish Sklar, ed., *Women's Rights Emerges within the Antislavery Movement, 1830–1870: A Brief History with Documents* (Boston: Bedford/St. Martin's Press, 2000), p. 78.

24. *The Liberator*, Jan. 7, 1832, reprinted in Sklar, *Women's Rights Emerges*, p. 79.

25. See Shirley J. Yee, *Black Women Abolitionists: A Study in Activism, 1828-1860* (Knoxville: University of Tennessee Press, 1992), pp. 136–54.

26. Bertram Wyatt-Brown, "The Abolitionists' Postal Campaign of 1835," *Journal of Negro History* 50 (October 1963), 227–38.

27. AG to William Lloyd Garrison, August 30, 1835, printed in *The Liberator*, September 19, 1835, and reprinted in Ceplair, *The Public Years*, pp. 24–27, quote, p. 26. For AG's state of mind, see AG to SG, Sept. 27, 1835, quoted in Birney, *The Grimké Sisters*, p. 127.

28. Diary of SG, Sept. 25, 1835, and AG to SG, Sept. 27, 1835, both quoted in Birney, *The Grimké Sisters*, pp. 128–29.

29. For the visual images associated with this appeal to women, see Jean Fagan Yellin, *Women and Sisters: The Antislavery Feminists in American Culture* (New Haven: Yale University Press, 1989).

30. AASS petition form for women reprinted in Sklar, *Women's Rights Emerges*, p. 85.

31. Mary Hershberger, "Mobilizing Women, Anticipating Abolition: The Struggle against Indian Removal in the 1830s," *Journal of American History* 86 (1999); 15–40.

32. Gerda Lerner, "The Political Activities of Antislavery Women," in Lerner, *The Majority Finds Its Past: Placing Women in History* (New York: Oxford University Press, 1979), and Deborah Bingham Van Broekhoven, "'Let Your Names Be Enrolled': Method and Ideology in Women's Antislavery Petitioning," in Jean Fagan Yellin and John C. Van Horne, eds., *The Abolitionist Sisterhood: Women's Political Culture in Antebellum America* (Ithaca: Cornell University Press, 1994).

33. William W. Freehling, *The Road to Disunion, Vol. I, Secessionists at Bay, 1776–1854* (New York: Oxford University Press, 1990), pp. 308–36, 345–52.

34. AG to SG [Shrewsbury, summer 1836], quoted in Birney, *The Grimké Sisters*, p. 141. See also Stanley Harrold, *The Abolitionists and the South, 1831–1861* (Lexington: University Press of Kentucky, 1995).

35. Diary of Sarah Grimké, August 3, 1836; and AG to SG, n.d., both quoted in Birney, *The Grimké Sisters*, pp. 144–45.

36. AG to Jane Smith, Nov. 11, 1836, and AG to Jane Smith [November, 1836], both quoted in Birney, *The Grimké Sisters*, p. 159.

37. AG to Jane Smith, Dec. 17, 1836, reprinted in Sklar, *Women's Rights Emerges*, p. 89.

38. While literacy was universal in the North, the spoken word still had the authority that came in part from its identification with religious authority, as in "In the beginning was the Word, and the Word was with God, and the Word was God" (John 1:1).

39. Catherine Anne Brekus, *Strangers and Pilgrims: Female Preaching in America, 1740–1845* (Chapel Hill: University of North Carolina Press, 1998).

40. See A. J. G. Perkins and Theresa Wolfson, *Frances Wright, Free Enquirer: The Study of a Temperament* (New York: Harper & Bros., 1939).

41. For more on the Grimkés' oratory, see Stephen Howard Browne, *Angelina Grimké: Rhetoric, Identity, and the Radical Imagination* (East Lansing: Michigan State University, 1999); Lillian O'Connor, *Pioneer Women Orators: Rhetoric in the Ante-Bellum Reform Movement* (New York: Vantage Press, 1952); and Karlyn Kohrs Campbell, *Man Cannot Speak for Her: Volume I: A Critical Study of Early Feminist Rhetoric* (New York: Praeger, 1989). For an exploration of women's presence in public life, see Mary P. Ryan, *Women in Public: Between Banners and Ballots, 1825–1880* (Baltimore: Johns Hopkins University Press, 1990).

42. Angelina Grimké, *Appeal to the Women of the Nominally Free States* (New York: Dorr, 1837), reprinted in Sklar, *Women's Rights Emerges*, pp. 100–103.

43. The full proceedings of the convention have been published as *Turning the World Upside Down: The Anti-Slavery Convention of American Women, held in New York City, May 9–12, 1837* (New York: Feminist Press, 1987).

44. AG to Jane Smith, Boston, May 29, 1837, reprinted in Sklar, *Women's Rights Emerges*, pp. 110–12.

45. AG to Smith, May 29, 1837.

46. Maria Chapman, "To Female Anti-Slavery Societies throughout New England," Boston, June 7, 1837, reprinted in Sklar, *Women's Rights Emerges*, pp. 112–14. On Chapman and the Boston society, see Debra Gold Hansen, *Strained Sisterhood: Gender and Class in the Boston Female Anti-Slavery Society* (Amherst: University of Massachussetts, 1993); and Blanche Glassman Hersh, *The Slavery of Sex: Feminist-Abolitionists in America* (Urbana: University of Illinois Press, 1978).

47. See John R. McKivigan, *The War against Proslavery Religion: Abolitionism and the Northern Churches, 1830–1865* (Ithaca: Cornell University Press, 1984).

48. AG to Jane Smith, May 29, 1837; and AG to Jane Smith, Groton, Mass., Aug. 10, 1837, reprinted in Sklar, *Women's Rights Emerges*, pp. 122–24.

49. Lumkin, *The Emancipation of Angelina Grimké*, p. 128.

50. Birney, *The Grimké Sisters*, p. 190.

51. [Theodore D. Weld], *In Memory of Angelina Grimké Weld* (Boston: George Ellis, 1880).

52. For an example of AG's speaking style, see Sklar, *Women's Rights Emerges*, pp. 153–56, the only one of her lectures to be recorded by shorthand.

53. AG to Jane Smith, New Rowley, Mass., July 15, 1837, reprinted in Sklar, *Women's Rights Emerges*, p. 117.

54. Gilbert Hobbs Barnes, *The Antislavery Impulse, 1830–1844* (New York: Appleton-Century, 1933; reprint Smith, 1957), pp. 134–35; and Louis Filler, *The Crusade Against Slavery, 1830–1860* (New York: Harper, 1960), p. 67.

55. AG to Jane Smith, July 15, 1837.

56. Sarah and Angelina Grimké to Amos Phelps, Groton, Mass., August 3, 1837, reprinted in Sklar, *Women's Rights Emerges*, pp. 118–19.

57. "Pastoral Letter: The General Association of Massachusetts to Churches under Their Care," July 1837, reprinted in Sklar, *Women's Rights Emerges*, pp. 119–21.

58. For the temperance movement, see Ruth M. Alexander, "'We Are Engaged As a Band of Sisters': Class and Domesticity in the Washingtonian Temperance Movement, 1840–1850," *Journal of American History* 75 (1988): 763–85. For moral reform, see Carroll Smith-Rosenberg, "Beauty, the Beast, and the Militant Woman: A Case Study in Sex Roles and Social Stress in Jacksonian America," in this volume, and Daniel Wright, "What Was the Appeal of Moral Reform to Antebellum Northern Women?" on *Women and Social Movements in the United States, 1830–1930*, a website at http://womhist.binghamton.edu.

59. "Lecture by Albert Folsom, Pastor, Universalist Church, Hingham, Mass., August 27, 1837," reprinted in Sklar, *Women's Rights Emerges*, pp. 121–22.

60. AG to Jane Smith, Groton, Mass., August 10, 1837, reprinted in Sklar, *Women's Rights Emerges*, pp. 122–24.

61. AG to Theodore Weld, Groton, Mass., August 12, 1837, reprinted in Sklar, *Women's Rights Emerges*, pp. 124–27.

62. Theodore Weld to Sarah and Angelina Grimké, Hartford, Conn., May 22, 1837, in Gilbert H. Barnes and Dwight L. Dumond, *Letters of Theodore Dwight Weld, Angelina Grimké Weld and Sarah Grimké, 1822–1844*, 2 vols. (New York: Appleton-Century Crofts, 1934; reprinted Gloucester, Mass.: Smith, 1965), I, 389.

63. AG to Theodore Dwight Weld and John Greenleaf Whittier, Brookline, Mass., August 20, 1837, reprinted in Sklar, *Women's Rights Emerges*, pp. 130–34.

64. "Resolutions Adopted by the Providence, Rhode Island, Ladies' Anti-Slavery Society, October 21, 1837," and "Philadelphia Female Anti-Slavery Society Annual Report, 1837," reprinted in Sklar, *Women's Rights Emerges*, pp. 134–41.

65. Sarah M. Grimké, *Letters on the Equality of the Sexes, and the Condition of Woman, Addressed to Mary S. Parker, President of the Boston Female Anti-Slavery Society* (Boston: Knapp, 1838); and Angelina E. Grimké, *Letters to Catherine E. Beecher, in Reply to An Essay on Slavery and Abolitionism, Addressed to*

A. E. Grimké. Revised by the Author. (Boston: Isaac Knapp, 1838), portions reprinted in Sklar, *Women's Rights Emerges*, pp. 142–52.

66. Reprinted in Sklar, *Women's Rights Emerges*, pp. 145, 152.

67. AG to Sarah Douglass, Brookline [Mass.] Feb. 25 [1838], in Barnes and Dumond, *Weld-Grimké Letters*, I, p. 574.

68. Theodore Weld to AG, New York, Feb. 8, 1838, and AG to Theodore Weld, Brookline [Mass.] February 11, [1838], in Barnes and Dumond, *Weld-Grimké Letters*, II, pp. 533–34, 536–37.

69. Theodore Weld to AG, New York, Feb. 8, 1838, and AG to Theodore Weld, Brookline [Mass.] February 11, [1838], in Barnes and Dumond, *Weld-Grimké Letters*, I, pp. 533–34, and 536–37.

70. "Report of the Woman's Rights Convention, Seneca Falls, N.Y., July 19–20, 1848," reprinted in Sklar, *Women's Rights Emerges*, pp. 172–79.

71. For more on the emergence of the woman's suffrage movement, see Sklar, *Women's Rights Emerges*, pp. 179–204.

Chapter 9

Women and Indians on the Frontier

Glenda Riley

Interactions between white women and Native American men and women tell us a great deal about cultural patterns in both societies. In them we can see the distinctive quality of female culture within white society as well as the attractions Native American society held for white women. Glenda Riley shows us how white women enhanced their power in the new western territories by learning from and cooperating with Native Americans.

Because relations between whites and American Indians have not been examined in terms of gender, the assumption stands unchallenged that both white men and women played similar, if not identical, roles in their dealings with Indians. Once the issue of gender is introduced into the study of migration and settlement, however, it becomes apparent that men and women actually fulfilled different capacities in this and in almost every other facet of the westering experience. Both on the trail and in frontier settlements, men were charged with the care of the equipment and livestock, while women supervised the home and were responsible for children. Men who farmed produced the raw materials in their fields that their wives and daughters then converted into finished products in their houses or work places. Men who labored or managed businesses produced cash income instead of raw materials, yet they still depended upon women to function as domestic artisans.

Although men and women occasionally shared work or overlapping functions, the division of labor along the lines described was generally accepted. Applied to their associations with Indians, these labor assignments cast men into something of an adversary position with American Indians, while women played more of a collegial role. It was the men who were responsible for cutting paths into the Indians' domain. They pushed wagons, people, and stock over the trails; seized native hunting grounds; and fended off Indians who might choose to resist such incursions through pilferage or outright assault.

As a result, male migrants and settlers were wary of their opponents. They were constantly alert for any indication that their enemies were in the vicinity, and regular guards were mounted. It was primarily the men's responsibility to corral the wagons or to lie in the corners of fences to thwart attack. Moreover, men were committed to the success of these efforts because of their great desire to establish themselves in livelihoods in the West. They were also motivated by their firm belief in their own aggressive character and their equally firm convictions regarding the inferiority of their foes. . . .

Female migrants and settlers, on the other hand, did not share either the responsibilities or the bellicose way of thinking of their male counterparts. For one thing, in a large number of cases the decision to move westward was made by males. The enterprise itself was based on male desires and

Excerpted from Chapter 5 of *Women and Indians on the Frontier, 1825–1915*, by Glenda Riley (Albuquerque: University of New Mexico Press, 1984), pp. 167–84.

needs, with little thought for female wishes and concerns. A historian of western women, Lillian Schlissel, has argued that the westward move coincided perfectly with men's life cycles: it came at a time in their lives when they were "breaking away," that is, improving or bettering themselves. But for women the move was out of phase, for it usually disrupted their efforts to establish a home, produce children, and develop continuity for their families. Consequently, men's and women's accounts of the undertaking differed in predictable ways. Men focused on fighting, hunting, and conflict, while women concentrated upon family and domestic concerns, values, and other related matters.[1]

Whether as migrants or as settlers, women also differed from men in their primary responsibilities. In addition to child bearing and care, these duties centered around supplying food and clothing for their families. Therefore, women, like men, were dedicated to protecting themselves and their families from harm, but they were also constantly concerned with extracting vital resources for their families from the environment and its inhabitants.

Men too desired certain goods and services from American Indians. Grass, water, and route information were some of the commodities most commonly sought after, which men frequently attempted to wrest from the natives through cash payments, threats, or sheer pugnacity. In a typical action, the men of the Burrell party seized usage of an Indian-built bridge by brandishing their pistols at the American Indians who attempted to collect a modest toll.[2] But women, long taught to be soft and nurturing in their approach to problems and people, often derided their men for their aggressiveness. Women were usually dedicated to the success of their western venture because of their own involvement in it, the safety and survival of their families, or their own visions of frontier opportunity. Yet they did not necessarily support the means that men used to achieve that success. Steeped in the accepted female virtues of their era, these women frequently believed that "might" did not automatically make "right." . . . Thus, women tended to pursue a more gentle course than men in their dealings with native Americans.

As a consequence, women's sources portray American Indians as guides, assistants, and purveyors of provisions far more often than they describe them as enemies. According to Schlissel's study of 103 overland diaries, women, "having no special stake in asserting their bravery, having no special need to affirm their prowess . . . correct the historical record as they write of the daily exchanges by which the Indians were part of life of the road."[3] Women routinely bartered, traded, and entered into acts of mutual assistance. In other words, in their attempts to provide food, clothing, and other commodities for those people who depended upon them for succor, women often formed relationships for mutual support with Indians.

This is not meant to imply that women regularly allowed themselves to be pushed around or intimidated by intrusive Indians. On the contrary, numerous incidents involved newly confident women who resisted Indian demands that they deemed unreasonable. Women short-circuited native commands by actions that ranged from slapping their faces to brandishing empty pistols under their noses.[4] They also resorted to using a variety of threats. On one occasion, Susanna Ede evicted an Indian interloper from her kitchen by threatening to pour hot grease on him; in another incident, she raised a pot of boiling water to be thrown on the trespasser.[5] Still other women relied upon direct action. One woman simply tore her belongings out of the hands of trespassing American Indians.[6] Some of the truly assertive women depended on raw bravado to repel unwelcome requests. Lavinia Porter, for example, refused a demand for bread only to have bleeding scalps thrust at her to count and admire. When she refused to give ground, her would-be oppressor muttered "white squaw no fear" and departed.[7]

Some frontierswomen were even willing to engage in unfeminine, violent action when it was necessary to thwart natives. To protect stock from nearby Indians, Mary Burrell and Barsina French's mother took turns standing guard with the men.[8] An Arizona woman defended her family's horses and mules by spending a long night shooting at a band of Pima Indians from one end of the stable roof and then the other.[9] . . .

Apparently, some women were learning that their physical weakness was not as severe nor as debilitating as they had been led to believe. They also seemed quite willing to act in a martial fashion when they thought it was called for, even though they might decry such tactics as standard procedure.[10] These instances of aggressive action were, however, more often the exception than the rule. Women who recorded one or two such occurrences in their lives as migrants or settlers usually also noted many more occasions upon which they cooperated, traded, or had some other type of pleasant interaction with American Indians.[11]

Actually, the pattern that emerged in a great number of western women's accounts was one characterized by exchanges of goods and services between white women and native American men and women. Many frontierswomen overcame their anxiety to trade routinely items such as trinkets, clothing, and foodstuffs with Indians. Such trade occurred even during the years of intensified conflict during the 1860s and 1870s.[12] Both on the trail and in their new homes, women began to barter needles and thread, processed foods such as flour, articles of apparel, and trifles with natives, who usually offered fresh foods in return. Women's accounts frequently mentioned native American men and women bringing to them butter, eggs, potatoes, corn, pumpkins, melons, strawberries, blackberries, venison and other fresh meats, fish, and dried salmon.

The various types of food items supplied by Indians were often savored as a welcome relief from a diet of bread, bacon or salt pork, and beans. "We have so little change in our diet," Miriam Colt, a Kansas settler of the 1850s, wrote, "that almost anything is relished."[13] Similarly, California-bound Martha Moore considered some mountain trout that she purchased from an Indian to be "quite a treat." On another occasion, she was very pleased to have "procured a fine mess of fish."[14]

Many women also became interested in obtaining specialized Indian products and crafts for themselves. They grew skillful at bargaining for buffalo hides and robes, antelope and elk clothing, moccasins, baskets, and beadwork.[15] Army wife Cynthia Capron was particularly delighted with a watertight basket that she purchased for one dollar near Camp Wright in the 1860s.[16] Moccasins were probably the single most popular trade item, and some women even ordered them from native women.[17] Buffalo robes were also coveted, so much so that at least one woman agreed to surrender her shawl to obtain one.[18] Some of the other beautifully tanned skins, including beaver and otter, were carelessly used for rugs, a practice that women sometimes came to regret when these items were no longer widely available.[19] . . .

Women who engaged in trade with Indians soon learned, often to their amazement and occasionally to their dismay, that, in Catherine Haun's words, "the Indian is a financier of no mean ability." Bargains and good deals were not particularly easy to come by, for many natives had as strong a streak of Yankee cunning as the Yankees themselves. "Though you may, for the time congratulate yourself upon your own sagacity," Haun noted, "you'll be apt to realize a little later that you were not quite equal to the shrewd redman."[20] Katherine Dunlap, on her way to Montana in 1864, said that the Indians with whom she traded were so canny that they not only recognized the difference between "coin" and "greenbacks" but would only "take the latter at 50¢ on the dollar."[21]

Naturally, male migrants and settlers also traded with American Indians, but the types of goods involved were usually somewhat different from those purchased by women. Although men were also attracted by moccasins, buckskins, and buffalo hides, they generally spent more time on exchanges involving arms, ammunition, tobacco, horses, and other animals.[22] Men were generally judicious in distributing liquor or refused to do so at all.[23]

When they were part of an all-male expedition or settlement, many men found it necessary to purchase or swap food and clothing with the Indians. But when women were present they were not only primarily responsible for obtaining such items but commonly carried on the negotiations personally.[24] Apparently, as women's preconceptions concerning both themselves and American Indians began to dissipate they were able to enter into business dealings with their once-dreaded enemies. In so doing, they fulfilled their function as providers of domestic goods. They also demonstrated their ability to practice a relatively gentle style in their contact with American Indians.

In addition to trading with Indians, both male and female migrants and settlers began to hire native men, women and children to perform a myriad of services for them. Men frequently employed, or even kidnapped, Indians to serve as guides who would lead them to the best trails and to grass and water.[25] To help them ford swollen rivers safely, they paid Indians cash or, more often, items such as shirts and caps or ammunition.[26] Occasionally, men even entrusted their stock to an individual Indian hired to act as a herder.[27] It was also not uncommon for men to pay natives "rewards" for locating "lost" stock, but it is impossible to determine whether this was simply a variation of the age-old protection racket.[28]

There was a good deal of complaining about the amounts of money or quantities of goods charged by American Indians for these services.[29] So many men viewed the idea of employing Indian helpers as little more than extortion that they shunned native guides, pilots, herders, and other workers entirely. Due to their belligerent attitude, such men often left a sharp taste of bitterness in their wake. And because they shunned assistance they frequently met with disaster.[30]

Women also began to hire natives to perform chores for them. Californian Mary Ackley employed some Paiute men to shovel, cut wood, draw water, and even wash clothes.[31] Other women, evidently relieved of some of their former anxieties, began inviting Indians into their homes as domestic helpers. Native men, women, and children performed household chores, such as washing dishes and clothes. Their female employers frequently commented that they did a good job or that they were "a great help," and they were paid for their labors with such commodities as sugar, salt, and bread.[32]

The most significant capacity in which women employed both Indian men and women was as nursemaids to their children.[33] This practice seems almost unbelievable, given the widespread fear that American Indians were lying in wait to pounce upon white children and carry them away as adoptees or as captives. Yet many mothers grew to trust Indians so thoroughly that they brought them not only into their homes but into their nurseries.

Interestingly enough, many of the women who engaged American Indian nurses did not appear to object to them teaching the children native customs, dialects, food preferences, and games. Nannie Alderson seemed delighted that her baby's "good and faithful" nurse carried the child on her back like a "papoose." She was pleased that the nurse crooned native songs to the baby, taught her a "squaw dance," made her pretty beaded moccasins, and followed the Indian custom of never spanking her.[34]

In addition, deep affection often developed between the children and their native caretakers as well as between the parents and the nurses. In one case, a young Puget Sound woman, who was raised by an Indian nurse during the 1850s, acquired a fondness for native food and gained some proficiency with her nurse's language. She also expressed a love for the woman that was overshadowed only by her feelings for her mother.[35] When her male Indian nurse died, Caroline Phelps said that her entire family felt his loss very much; her children cried for him "as much as though he had been a relative."[36] . . .

Rachel Wright, a settler in the Upper Napa Valley, claimed that the key to such favorable working relations with American Indians rested with the migrants and settlers themselves. Indians could be "an advantage rather than otherwise," she argued, "as they were not only willing but glad to work if they were left free, well treated and properly paid for their labor."[37] It was in this same spirit of gentleness and fairness that many frontierswomen entered into various types of social affairs with American Indians. Women began to visit them in their homes and to attend their celebrations and ceremonies. They formed close friendships with Indians, particularly with native women. And they occasionally married native men.

These relations between women and Indians were often characterized by warmth and affection. They shared time together inside each other's homes, a stage seldom achieved by male migrants or settlers. Although men visited native camps and villages, they typically joined the "braves" and "chiefs" around the fire to smoke the pipe together, to talk about land and politics, and to negotiate trades. They were often treated to meals prepared by the women of the family, and sometimes they were expected to admire the children, but men were not welcomed into the bosom of the Indians' homes and families as women were. Moreover, men did not regularly form close friendships with Indian males, as women did with Indian females. Furthermore, when they married native women it was often done with an element of necessity or exploitation. Such marriages were almost never legalized or solemnized according to white terms, as with marriages between white females and native males. When a white man did marry a native woman according to white law, it was a matter for comment. In one such case, Alice Baldwin wrote that the man involved was "the soul of honor," who "had the decent courage to marry her legally."[38] . . .

Thus, although both men and women conducted trade with Indians and employed them along the trail and in their new homes, they did not achieve the same degree of closeness with Native Americans. Men's accounts generally lacked the fond references to American Indian friends and neighbors that filled many women's writings as the time they spent on the frontier lengthened. Rather, men tended to remain in their adversary position to the Indians, while women tended to develop and expand their collegial role.

Relationships between women and American Indians often began with group visits to Indian camps. Even the women who had been at first very apprehensive about Native Americans described pleasant social time spent with them. "We often visited Indian camps," Allene Dunham maintained. "They always treated us to a piece of dried buffalo, or venison, or some other kind of meat."[39] Another woman on the way to Salem, Oregon in 1851 claimed that "if there were Indians we would go visiting their lodges and go around among them."[40]

While such occasions nourished cordiality on both sides, it was usually the more personal visits between white women and native women that fostered warm feelings. One trail woman of the 1850s who visited some Sioux women came away favorably impressed by both their hospitality and their skill with a needle.[41] Another female migrant of the 1860s recorded frequent and very genial social calls between her friends and "the Cherokee Ladies."[42] A Mormon woman added that the Indian women whom she visited were "really friendly." She remarked that they had enjoyed "quite a dish of conversation" together.[43] An Iowa settler of the 1870s explained that she grew up with friendly feelings toward the Indians who roamed the woods and camped in the fields around her home. She attributed this to the fact that her Aunt Liza had regularly taken her and her sister to a nearby native village, where the women had given them beads that they "treasured greatly."[44]

Pleasant contacts between white and native women often blossomed into deeper associations. Once army wife Alice Baldwin had invested some time in crimping and waving native women's hair she discovered that "thereafter the Indian women were my firm friends, and rendered me various favors and kindnesses." She commented perceptively that they were brought together by "feminine vanity and tastes," which she felt were "much the same the world over, no matter what the race or color."[45] . . .

Many other white and native women also exchanged bits of female knowledge, lore, and folk medicine with each other. For instance, Mormon migrant Eliza Roxey Snow learned about the sego root from native women, and she claimed that it "proved to be a nutritious, substantial article of food, and not unpalatable."[46] An Oklahoma woman recalled that she had acquired an extensive knowledge of "palatable and very healthful" greens and roots by accompanying Indian women on their gathering and digging expeditions into nearby woods.[47] Others learned how to use herb remedies or how to treat a rattlesnake bite with raw turkey meat.[48] White women were assisted in childbirth by Indian midwives, and often they received thoughtful and sometimes ornate gifts for their new babies. One California woman raved about the "beautiful baskets and elaborate moccasins worked with beads and feathers" that Indian women brought to her mother upon the occasion of the birth of her baby, the first white child to be born in that part of the country. Another remembered the Native American woman who had brought her persimmon bread and a papoose board that was intricately worked with beading and fringe.[49]

A representative case of this congenial and helpful exchange between white and native women was Leola Lehman, an Oklahoma settler who befriended Indian women. In turn, they visited her, bringing small presents to her, and gathered around in admiration when she displayed her new baby. As Baldwin and other women mentioned, elements of female culture drew these women of different races into a close and easy bond. Lehman particularly liked one native woman who had come to see her because she thought that the transplanted white woman "might be lonesome." Lehman eventually came to "like and respect" this native woman and to regard her "as one of the best women she had ever known." She suggested that many such friendships between whites and natives were possible. However, whites must realize, she said, that American Indians were afraid of white people because they had heard terrifying stories about them. When she left the Indian region, Lehman wrote, "I was glad to be back among my own people but had learned to like the Indians. I was no longer afraid and understood that many of their ways that seemed strange to me were caused by fear of white people."[50] . . .

Women's friendships were . . . common . . . due to the crucial role played by female values in drawing together white and native women. They shared their interest in home, family, children, and domestic matters, and they were both committed to certain values, such as the ability to be open, nurturing, and supportive, which created a connection that was largely unavailable to the males of both cultures. It is unlikely, for example, that a native man would call upon a settler and tell him that he had come because he had thought the other might be lonely. An even more ridiculous picture emerges when one thinks of a settler partially disrobing to allow his new Indian friends to admire and assess his intimate apparel. Instead, males helped each other with weapons, stock, hunting, fighting, and similar activities that only infrequently resulted in the kind of mutuality and confidentiality that women so easily developed and shared.

It should be noted that frontierswomen almost never entered into close friendships with Indian males. They did, however, often find that their business and social relations with Indians generally, and with women particularly, fostered a sense of acceptance and admiration toward their male native acquaintances. As women overcame their anxieties and allowed themselves to know Indians, they soon realized that the natives were not as threatening as they had once appeared. Harriet Ward, for example, clearly contradicted her earlier negative attitudes when she wrote in her diary that her friends back home would "be surprised to see me writing so quietly in the wagon alone . . . with a great, wild looking Indian leaning his elbow on the wagon beside me, but I have not a single fear except that he may frighten the horses."[51] Women were often glad to see Indians arrive and sorry to see them leave. "We have parted with white folks that we did not regret so much," insisted one woman.[52] . . .

Most of these women, . . . were not reluctant to act upon their sentiments by actually visiting Indians and by attending native functions. Women did, for example, turn to Indian medical men for treatment for themselves or for other family members, and particularly for their children.[53] When her daughter's face was badly burned, Caroline Phelps called in a native doctor, who treated the child effectively.[54] In another case of Indian doctors treating settlers' ailments, a woman remarked that the Indians cared for her people "like a brother should treat a brother."[55] Women also aided Native Americans upon occasion. Nannie Alderson restored two "almost frozen" Indian men with a warm fire and a hearty meal.[56] . . .

When romantic love blossomed between a white woman and a native man, it often resulted in marriage. Since it is difficult for long-term affection to develop from occasional or superficial contact, it is not surprising that when intermarriage occurred it was usually the result of frequent contact based on mutual interests. In 1886, for example, a young New England woman of genteel family and demonstrated literary ability went to teach at the Great Sioux Reservation in the Dakota Territory. Here, Elaine Goodale came to see Indians as human beings, to respect their complex culture, and to like them as individuals. During her first five years among them, she wrote many articles and tracts about them and their problems. In 1891, she married a Sioux physician named Charles A. Eastman, with whom she shared a deep commitment toward helping the Sioux people adjust to a rapidly changing world. Together, the Eastmans wrote nine books, with Elaine continuing to write extensively about native American concerns.[57] That Elaine Goodale Eastman's decision to marry an American Indian was not unique among missionary women is supported by occasional and often passing references to other such instances in frontier accounts.[58]

Another situation that fostered marriages between white females and native males existed in Oklahoma during the 1880s, the 1890s, and the early 1900s. As large numbers of settlers took up land leases on Indian agencies, pushing into the region as "Sooners" in well-publicized land rushes, congenial associations often developed between whites and American Indians. These contacts, in turn, produced a large number of intermarriages. While reading through the hundreds of interviews with female settlers in Oklahoma during this era, one is struck by the recurrent references to intermarriages. A former Texas woman recalled, "I have two nieces who married Commanche Indians, one Clinton Red Elk, and one Buster Work-a-wam."[59] Other women mentioned that relatives, acquaintances, or they themselves had married native men.[60]

Oklahoma women chose a variety of Indian men as their mates. One woman explained that her husband was "a quarter-blood Choctaw Indian" who farmed near the Little Washita River.[61] Another woman said that she married a Cherokee who was a teacher trained at Tahlequah's male seminary.[62] Another chose as her husband "a full blood Chickasaw," an interpreter for the governor of the Chickasaw nation; she married him first under state law in 1892, and again under Indian law in 1897.[63]

Although the government fully recognized intermarriage by allowing the wives of native men to draw an allotment and payments made to blood Indians, there was some opposition to the idea from individual settlers.[64] Interviews with these Oklahoma women do not mention any objections being raised by other women, but they do call attention to male disapproval. One woman remembered that her father, a "one-half Cherokee," refused to prove a land claim because he thought it "a disgrace to be part Indian," and he would not publicly admit his background even to obtain a homestead.[65] Another woman spoke of her father's vehement objections to the possibility that any of his daughters would ever marry a Native American. Yet, in a curious twist of fate, after his sudden and tragic death, neighboring Indians were so kind to these women that, in the words of the interviewee, "my sister married a full blood and we have always been glad that she did."[66]

Unfortunately, current scholarship does not supply enough data or evidence to allow one to judge whether women and men were more, less, or equally accepting of the idea of marriages between white women and American Indian men. It might be hypothesized, however, that the female value system permitted relatively easy adjustment to the concept of intermarriage. Female values made it possible for women to enter into warm and comfortable situations with Indians in which intimate relationships could develop. In addition, because female ideals focused on home and family, women were not usually as dedicated as men to the eradication of Native Americans and the seizure of their property. Thus, it can be argued that it was at least possible that white women were more accepting of the idea of marriage between themselves and native men than were their white menfolk. . . .

. . . White women and white men developed quite dissimilar types of relationships between themselves and with American Indians. These differences in white female–American Indian and white male–native American contacts derived in large part from the roles and functions that women and men played in their dealings with Indians on the frontier. Because men were cast as aggressors and as land grabbers, they were pushed into an adversary role. Women, on the other hand, frequently had the opportunity—as procurers of food, clothing, and other domestic goods—to develop a collegial relationship with Indians in their mutual quest for survival.

Notes

1. Lillian Schlissel, *Women's Diaries of the Westward Journey* (New York: Schocken Books, 1982), 14.
2. Mary Burrell, "Diary of a Journey Overland from Council Bluffs to Green Valley, California, 1854," Beinecke Collection, Yale University Library, New Haven, Conn.
3. Schlissel, *Women's Diaries*, 15. See also Helen E. Clark, "Diary" (1860), and Cara Whitemore Bell, "Journal, 1872–1876," both in the Denver Public Library, Denver, Colo., and Carol Fairbanks and Sara Brooks Sundberg, *Farm Women on the Prairie Frontier: A Sourcebook for Canada and the United States* (Metuchen, N.J.: The Scarecrow Press, 1983), 47–48.
4. Laura Ingalls Wilder, *The First Four Years* (New York: Harper & Row, 1971), 33; Eliza Ann Egbert, "Diary" (1852), Bancroft Library, Berkeley, Calif.
5. Barbara B. Zimmerman and Vernon Carstensen, eds., "Pioneer Woman in Southwestern Washington Territory: The Recollections of Susanna Maria Slover McFarland Price Ede," *Pacific Northwest Quarterly* 66–67, no. 4 (1976), 143, 147.
6. Bessie L. Lyon, "Hungry Indians," *Palimpsest* 9 (October 1928), 366.
7. Lavinia H. Porter, *By Ox Team to California: A Narrative of Crossing the Plains in 1860* (Oakland, Calif.: Oakland Enquirer Publishing Company, 1910), 56.
8. Burrell, "Diary"; Barsina French, "Journal of a Wagon Trip" (1867), Huntington Library, San Marino, Calif.
9. Christiane Fischer, "A Profile of Women in Arizona in Frontier Days," *Journal of the West* 16, no. 3 (July 1977), 43.
10. Porter, *By Ox Team to California*, 67, 79.
11. Burrell, "Diary"; Porter, *By Ox Team to California*, 34, 67.
12. Schlissel, *Women's Diaries*, 154.
13. Miriam D. Colt, *Went to Kansas; Being a Thrilling Account of an Ill-Fated Expedition* (Watertown, N.Y.: L. Ingalls & Co., 1862), 125.
14. Martha M. Moore, "Journal of a Trip to California in 1860," Beinecke Collection, Yale University Library, New Haven, Conn.
15. Fleming Fraker, Jr., ed., "To Pike's Peak by Ox Wagon: The Harriet A. Smith Day-Book," *Annals of Iowa* 35, no. 2 (Fall 1959), 138; Martha M. Morgan, *A Trip across the Plains in the Year 1849* (San Francisco: Printed at Pioneer Press, 1864), 7, 12, 15–16; Ellen McGowen Biddle, *Reminiscences of a Soldier's Wife* (Philadelphia: J. B. Lippincott Company, 1907), 83; Mrs. Edward Dyer, "Diary" (1860), Barker Texas Center, University of Texas, Austin.
16. Cynthia J. Capron, "Life in the Army," *Journal of the Illinois State Historical Society* 13, no. 3 (October 1920), 369.
17. Egbert, "Diary."

18. Mrs. B. G. Ferris, *The Mormons at Home* (New York: Dix & Edwards, 1856), 63.

19. Mary A. Hodgson, "The Life of a Pioneer Family" (1922), California State Library, Sacramento; Biddle, *Reminiscences,* 83.

20. Catherine M. Haun, "A Woman's Trip across the Plains, from Clinton, Iowa, to Sacramento, California, by Way of Salt Lake City" (1849), Huntington Library, San Marino, Calif.

21. Katherine Dunlap, "Journal" (1864), Bancroft Library, Berkeley, Calif.

22. Frink, *Journal,* 68, 77; Guill, "Overland Diary"; Kate Roberts Pelissier, "Reminiscences of a Pioneer Mother," *North Dakota History* 24 (July 1957), 131; Morgan, *Trip across the Plains,* 15–16; Washburn, "Journal"; Hopping, "Incidents of Pioneer Life"; Edwin Bryant, *What I Saw in California* (Minneapolis: Ross & Holmes, 1967), 166; Raymond W. Settle, ed., *The March of the Mounted Riflemen* (Glendale, Calif.: Arthur H. Clark, 1940), 223. . . .

23. John D. Unruh, *The Plains Across: The Overland Emigrants and the Trans-Mississippi West, 1840–1860* (Urbana: University of Illinois Press, 1979), 166.

24. Schlissel, *Women's Diaries,* 53.

25. Helen Carpenter, "Diary" (1856), Bancroft Library, Berkeley, Calif.: Unruh, *Plains Across,* 157; Frink, *Journal,* 72; Bunyard, "Diary," 121; French, "Journal"; Mrs. Nicholas Harrison Karchner, "Diary" (1862), California State Library, Sacramento.

26. Maggie Hall, "The Story of Maggie Hall," Bancroft Library, Berkeley, Calif.; Elizabeth L. Lord, *Reminiscences of Eastern Oregon* (Portland, Oreg.: Irwin-Hodgson Company, 1903), 68–69; Charlotte Stearns Pengra, "Diary" (1853), Huntington Library, San Marino, Calif.; Unruh, *Plains Across,* 157.

27. Abby E. Fulkerth, "Diary of Overland Journey of William L. Fulkerth and Wife from Iowa to California in 1863," Bancroft Library, Berkeley, Calif.; Unruh, *Plains Across,* 159; Lord, *Reminiscences,* 86.

28. Leo M. Kaiser and Priscilla Knuth, eds., "From Ithaca to Clatsop Plains: Miss Ketcham's Journal of Travel," pt. 1, *Oregon Historical Quarterly* 62, no. 3 (1961), 255; Unruh, *Plains Across,* 163; Caroline D. Budlong, *Memories: Pioneer Days in Oregon and Washington Territory* (Eugene, Oreg.: Pictures Press Printers, 1949), 4; J. William Barrett, II, ed., *The Overland Journal of Amos Piatt Josselyn* (Baltimore: Gateway Press, 1978), 20.

29. Mary Fetter Hite Sandford, "A Trip across the Plains" (1853), California State Library, Sacramento; French, "Journal"; Unruh, *Plains Across,* 158.

30. Unruh, *Plains Across,* 158.

31. Mary E. Ackley, *Crossing the Plains and Early Days in California* (San Francisco: Privately printed, 1928), 66.

32. Budiong, *Memories,* 38; Nannie T. Alderson, *A Bride Goes West* (Lincoln: University of Nebraska Press, 1969), 186; Fraker, "To Pike's Peak," 137; Hodgson, "Life of a Pioneer Family"; Albert L. Hurtado, "'Hardly a Farmhouse—A Kitchen without Them': Indian and White Households on the California Borderland Frontier in 1860," *Western Historical Quarterly* 14, no. 3 (July 1982), 245–70.

33. Alderson, *Bride Goes West,* 131; Caroline Phelps, "Diary" (1830–1860), Iowa State Historical Society, Iowa City.

34. Alderson, *Bride Goes West,* 132, 136.

35. Sarah McAllister Hartman, "Reminiscences of Early Days on Puget Sound, the Friendliness of the Local Indians, and Experiences during the Indian War of 1855" (n.d.), Beinecke Collection, Yale University Library, New Haven, Conn.

36. Phelps, "Diary."

37. Rachel E. Wright, "The Early Upper Napa Valley" (1928), Bancroft Library, Berkeley, Calif.

38. Robert C. and Eleanor R. Carriker, eds., *An Army Wife on the Frontier: The Memoirs of Alice Blackwood Baldwin, 1867–1877* (Salt Lake City: Tanner Trust Fund, University of Utah Library, 1975), 108.

39. E. Allene Dunham, *Across the Plains in a Covered Wagon* (Milton, Iowa: n.p., ca. 1920s), 7.

40. Mrs. H. T. Clarke, "A Young Woman's Sights on the Emigrant's Trail" (1878), Bancroft Library, Berkeley, Calif.

41. Lodisa Frizzell, *Across the Plains to California in 1852* (New York: New York Public Library, 1915), 25.

42. Malvina V. Manning, "Diary" (1862), Bancroft Library, Berkeley, Calif.

43. Ferris, *Mormons at Home,* 24.

44. Louise S. Gellhorn Boylan, "My Life Story: Reminiscence of German Settlers in Hardin County, 1867–1883," Iowa State Historical Society, Iowa City.

45. Carriker, *Army Wife,* 79, 99–100.

46. Eliza R. Snow, "Sketch of My Life" (1885), Bancroft Library, Berkeley, Calif.

47. Mollie Beaver, interview 9409, vol. 6, Indian-Pioneer Papers, University of Oklahoma, Norman.

48. Belle M. Yates, interview 12817, vol. 101, Indian-Pioneer Papers, University of Oklahoma, Norman; Bertha Brewer Plummer, interview 4833, vol. 72, Indian-Pioneer Papers, University of Oklahoma, Norman; Fannie Birdwell, interview 8360, vol. 8, Indian-Pioneer Papers, University of Oklahoma, Norman; Dan McAllister, "Pioneer Woman," *New Mexico Historical Review* 34, no. 3 (July 1959), 162.

49. Jean Webster, "The Myth of Hardship on the Oregon Trail," *Reed College Bulletin* 24 (January 1946), 37; Hodgson, "Life of a Pioneer Family"; Lorene Millhollen, interview 8957, vol. 63, Indian-Pioneer Papers, University of Oklahoma, Norman.

50. Leola Lehman, "Life in the Territories," *Chronicles of Oklahoma* 41 (Fall 1963), 373–75.

51. Ward G. DeWitt and Florence S. DeWitt, *Prairie Schooner Lady: The Journal of Harriet Sherrill Ward, 1853* (Los Angeles: Westernlore Press, 1959), 78.

52. Hopping, "Incidents of Pioneer Life"; Egbert, "Diary."

53. Nancy C. Pruitt, interview 7855, vol. 73, Indian-Pioneer Papers, University of Oklahoma, Norman.

54. Phelps, "Diary."

55. Hartman, "Reminiscences."

56. Alderson, *Bride Goes West,* 91.

57. Kay Graber, ed., *Sister to the Sioux: The Memoirs of Elaine Goodale Eastman* (Lincoln: University of Nebraska Press, 1978), xi–xii, 172–75.

58. Emily McCowen Horton, *My Scrap-book* (Seattle, Wash.: n.p., 1927), 17.

59. Barnes, interview 9735.

60. Mrs. William N. Moore, interview 7365, vol. 64; Emma Jean Ross Overstreet, interview 7240, vol. 68; Sarah Scott Phillips, interview 6251, vol. 71; Mrs. J. B. Antles, interview 4163, vol. 2; Harriet Gibbons Oakes, interview 12028, vol. 68; all in Indian-Pioneer Papers, University of Oklahoma, Norman.

61. Mrs. Bill Moncrief, interview 4189, vol. 64, Indian-Pioneer Papers, University of Oklahoma, Norman.

62. Sallie Butler, interview 7244, vol. 14, Indian-Pioneer Papers, University of Oklahoma, Norman.

63. Alice Parker, interview 4021, vol. 69, Indian-Pioneer Papers, University of Oklahoma, Norman.

64. Mary Ellen Williams, interview 6877, vol. 98, Indian-Pioneer Papers, University of Oklahoma, Norman.

65. Mrs. B. M. Austin, interview 9189, vol. 3, Indian-Pioneer Papers, University of Oklahoma, Norman.

66. Beaver, interview 9409.

Chapter 10

Victorian Women and Domestic Life: Mary Todd Lincoln, Elizabeth Cady Stanton, and Harriet Beecher Stowe

Kathryn Kish Sklar

The most fundamental assertion of women's power in nineteenth-century America lay in the unprecedented control women exerted over their own bodies and the reproductive process. This article recounts how three women responded to the changes demographers call the "demographic transition." That transition from high birth and death rates to low birth and death rates, which began around 1800 and was not completed until after 1930, potentially empowered women as wives, as mothers, and as persons. But by encouraging women to view their children as irreplaceable individuals at a time when infant and childhood mortality still remained high, the demographic transition also made women feel the death of their children more keenly.

This essay explores themes in the private side of American life in the mid-nineteenth century. In particular it explores nineteenth-century family life from the female perspective, and studies the strategies women adopted in response to change in the domestic arena.

Historians have increasingly come to see the middle decades of the nineteenth century between 1830 and 1880 as sharing a common set of social and cultural assumptions called Victorianism. Daniel Howe has noted that not every American was a Victorian. "American Indians, recent arrivals from the peasant societies of Europe and Asia, and the Spanish-speaking inhabitants of lands taken from Mexico," had other cultural identities, as, to a significant degree, did Afro-Americans. The reign of American Victorianism extended primarily to white, English-speaking, Protestant members of the middle class—that entrepreneurially oriented, property-owning, and capital-investing group that emerged in the late eighteenth and early nineteenth centuries a little in advance of its modern companion, the industrial proletariat.[1]

Howe and other historians are interested in the Victorian period because it, more than any other, contains the social, economic, and cultural transformations that are referred to collectively as "modernization." Victorian culture, Howe concludes, may be thought of as the culture that characterized English-speaking Americans during the climactic era of modernization when changes that had been taking shape more slowly before 1830 entered a period of accelerated development.

Adapted from "Victorian Women and Domestic Life: Mary Todd Lincoln, Elizabeth Cady Stanton, and Harriet Beecher Stowe," by Kathryn Kish Sklar, Chapter 2 in *The Public and the Private Lincoln: Contemporary Perspectives*, Cullom Davis *et al.*, eds. (Carbondale and Edwardsville: Southern Illinois University Press, 1979). Courtesy of Cullom Davis and Sangamon State University.

"Joseph and Sarah Ann Emery," c. 1834. Fenimore Art Museum, Cooperstown, New York.

Profound changes in public life between 1830 and 1880 include the transportation and communication revolutions, the technologic culmination of the Industrial Revolution, and the abolition of slavery. Profound changes in family life include the widespread adoption of family limitation; the transfer of many domestic industries, such as spinning and weaving, from home to factory production; and the separation of public life and private life into two distinct spheres. Combined, these changes in family life constituted change in human history on the scale of the Neolithic Revolution.[2]

By the mid-nineteenth century when machine technology was recasting human work in unprecedented forms, human reproduction was already established on a new basis. This essay focuses on the first of these changes in Victorian families—the widespread adoption of family limitation. It illustrates how family limitation was integrated into the lives of three women who exemplify Victorian family planning and its various motivations: Harriet Beecher Stowe, Elizabeth Cady Stanton, and Mary Todd Lincoln. Each developed her own strategy toward, or response to, the conditions of mid-nineteenthcentury family life, and each typified a strategy commonly found among her contemporaries. Harriet Beecher Stowe's strategy could be called that of "female domestic control," Elizabeth Cady Stanton's strategy that of "feminist domestic reform," and Mary Todd Lincoln's strategy that of "total commitment to husband and children." These three strategies represent the options most often pursued by Victorian women, and the contexts within which much of Victorian domestic life reverberated.

Harriet Beecher Stowe left behind graphic historical evidence of her private life through an exchange of letters with her husband, which were quoted extensively in Edmund Wilson's *Patriotic Gore*.[3] The exchange began in the summer of 1844 when Harriet had been married for eight years, was thirty-three years old, and had borne five children, two of whom were twins. That summer, as in subsequent ones, Calvin Stowe left his Cincinnati home to raise funds in New England for Lane Theological Seminary where he taught biblical history and where his salary depended upon his summertime fund-raising efforts. Harriet and Calvin agreed to state their grievances openly to one another in their summer letters, a common practice in evangelical correspondence which usually included a good dose of mutual criticism.

Harriet's grievances began with the drudgery of nineteenth-century housework: "I am sick of the smell of sour milk and sour meat, and sour everything, and then the clothes *will* not dry, and no wet thing does, and everything smells mouldy; and altogether I feel as if I never [want] to eat again."[4] Calvin's grievances began with Harriet's aversion to the drudgery of nineteenth-century housework: "By the way there is one other thing I will mention because it has often vexed and irritated me intolerably. I must clean the stable, wash the carriage, grease the wheels, black my boots, etc. etc. but you scorn to sweep the carriage, you must always call your servant to do it and not stoop yourself to so menial an act. This makes me mad, for you are not too good to do in your line what I am everyday obliged to do in mine."[5]

Harriet's grievances included being solely responsible for running her household. Except for her, she said: "You know that . . . my unfortunate household has no mainspring, for nobody feels any kind of responsibility to do a thing in time, place, or manner, except as I oversee it."[6] On this score Calvin agreed: "You must manage all household matters in your own way—just as you would if I were dead, and you had never anything more to expect from me. Indeed, to all practical purposes I am dead for the present and know not when I shall live again."[7]

Harriet's grievances turned to the topic of her health: "As to my health, it gives me very little solicitude, although it is bad enough and daily growing worse. I feel no life, no energy, no appetite, or rather a growing distaste for food; in fact, I am becoming quite ethereal. . . . I suffer with sensible distress in the brain, as I have done more or less since my sickness last winter, a distress which some days takes from me all power of planning or executing anything."[8] While not challenging his wife's claims to the symptoms and prerogatives of an invalid, and while leaving his own symptoms unnamed, Calvin obscurely asserted that his own suffering had been greater than Harriet's: "I suffer amazingly every day. I hardly know what to make of it, unless it be the Lord's penance of our sin. You have suffered a great deal, but I doubt whether you have ever suffered as I have this summer."[9]

In addition to these everyday grievances, husband and wife discussed a larger problem in the summer of 1844—their sexual relationship. Calvin broached the topic by relating several recent instances of clerical disarray in the sexual arena, including the story of a fellow minister who "While half boozled [had] caught young ladies who were so unfortunate to meet him alone, and pawed them over in the most disgusting manner, and actually attempted to do them physical violence. This has been going on for years until it would be borne no longer, and now it all comes out against him, to the dishonor of religion, his own unspeakable shame and anguish, and the distress unutterable of his wife and children."[10] In connection with this "melancholy licentiousness" Calvin said he had "thought much of our domestic happiness," and in a paragraph packed with homesickness he drew both a parallel and a contrast between himself and his fallen colleagues.

Though I have, as you well know, a most enthusiastic admiration of fresh, youthful female beauty; yet it never comes anywhere near the kind of feeling I have for you. With you, every desire I have, mental and physical, is completely satisfied and filled up, and leaves me nothing more to ask for. My enjoyment with you is not weakened by time nor blunted with age, and every reunion after separation is just as much of a honeymoon as was the first month after the wedding. Is not your own experience and observation a proof of what I say? . . . No man can love and respect his wife more than I do mine. Yet we are not happy as we might be.

Let us look at the place the summer of 1844 occupied in the sequence of Harriet Beecher Stowe's childbearing to see if we can understand better why she and Calvin were "not as happy" as they might have been, in spite of Calvin's testimony to their sexual compatibility. For that summer was not a time when Harriet wanted to relive her honeymoon, but a time when she was looking forward to what she considered a well-earned relief from childbearing. Such relief had not been possible for her mother, since most women who were married before 1800 bore children, in sickness and in health, regularly every two years from the time they married to the end of their childbearing years, or until their death, whichever came first. But limitation of childbearing was an option for Harriet—one she had considered long before the summer of 1844.

Harriet Beecher married Calvin Stowe in 1836 at the age of twenty-six after she had nearly ten years' experience supporting herself as a teacher. Nine months after their marriage—almost to the day—Harriet gave birth to twins. Then, a few months later she was pregnant again. At this point she was visited by her reform-minded older sister, Catharine Beecher, who later described Harriet's plight in a letter to another married sister: "Harriet has one baby put out for the winter, the other at home, and number three will be here the middle of January. Poor thing, she bears up wonderfully well and I hope will live through this first tug of matrimonial warfare, and then she says she shall not have any more *children, she knows for certain* for one while. Though how she found this out I cannot say, but she seems quite confident about it."[11]

The outcome of matrimonial warfare in the Stowe family during the next five years was the addition of two more babies, the second born in the summer of 1843. This second baby was sickly and languished in Harriet's arms all fall and winter while she herself suffered through a prolonged illness related, apparently, to the birth. A year later, in the summer of 1844, Harriet replied to Calvin's amorous letter and to his descriptions of clerical licentiousness dramatically and emphatically. Taking up the implicit threat contained in Calvin's admission of his "most enthusiastic admiration of fresh, youthful female beauty," but assuming that sexual infidelity was unjustified on any grounds, Harriet dramatized her horror at the possibility of Calvin's infidelity, but she did not respond in kind to his suggestions that marital love was better than burning.

As I am gifted with a most horrible vivid imagination, in a moment I imagined—nay saw as in a vision all the distress and despair that would follow a fall on your part. I felt weak and sick—I took a book and lay down on the bed, but it pursued me like a nightmare—and something seemed to ask Is your husband any better seeming than so and so! I looked in the glass and my face which since spring has been something of the palest was so haggard that it frightened me. The illusion lasted a whole forenoon and then evaporated like a poisonous mist—but God knows how I pity those heart wrung women—wives worse than widows, who are called to lament that the grave has not covered their husband—the father of their children! Good and merciful God—why are such agonies reserved for the children of men![12]

Dwelling on the vividness, intensity, and even sublimity of her horror for a moment, Harriet continued: "I can conceive now of misery which in one night would change the hair to grey and shrivel the whole frame to premature decrepitude! misery to which all other agony is as a mocking sound!" Then, with a brief reference to Calvin's sex, Harriet launched into a discussion of their marital love from her point of view.

> What terrible temptations lie in the way of your sex—till now I never realised it—for tho I did love you with an almost *insane* love before I married you I never knew yet or felt the pulsation which showed me I could be tempted in that way—there never was a moment when I felt anything by which you could have drawn me astray—for I loved you as I now love God—and I can conceive of no higher love; and as I have no passion, I have no jealousy. The most beautiful woman in the world could not make me jealous so long as she only *dazzled the senses.*

Calvin might declare his love for Harriet as "mental and physical," but Harriet made it clear to him that it was not for his body that she loved him. She would admit to insanity before she would admit to sexual desire. In the spring of 1845 Harriet left Calvin at home to manage the household as best he could while she spent ten months at a Brattleboro, Vermont, water cure. Almost immediately upon her return home, Calvin departed for fifteen months of water cure himself.

From Brattleboro Harriet described to Calvin her analysis of their situation: "We have now come to a sort of crisis. If you and I do as we should for *five years* to come the character of our three oldest children will be established. This is why I am willing to spend so much time and make such efforts to have health. Oh, that God would give me these five years in full possession of mind and body, that I may train my children as they should be trained." Harriet may have related "full possession of mind and body" to the adoption of "system and order" in family life, for she immediately continued: "I am fully aware of the importance of system and order in a family. I know that nothing can be done without it; it is the keystone, the *sine qua non*, and in regard to my children I place it next to piety."[13]

For six years from 1843 to 1849, Harriet Beecher Stowe avoided pregnancy. After bearing children in a pattern that resembled her mother's up to the age of thirty-two, she enjoyed a long span of childlessness that was unknown to most women of her mother's generation, but quite common among Harriet's contemporaries. Her mother, Roxana Beecher, gave birth to nine children in seventeen years of marriage before she died at the age of thirty-seven. Harriet bore five children in the first seven years of marriage, none in the second six years of marriage, and two more at the end of her childbearing years, in 1849 and 1850, when she was thirty-eight and thirty-nine. She therefore omitted two to three children that her mother would not have omitted, and in this time before artificial contraceptive techniques, she must have relied largely on sexual abstinence.

How typical was the childbearing pattern of this distinguished nineteenth-century author who produced her most famous book the same year she birthed her last baby?

The timing of Elizabeth Cady Stanton's children was very similar to that of Harriet Beecher Stowe's. She had three in the first five years of marriage, then, like Harriet, went six years without bearing children. It was toward the end of this interval between 1845 and 1851 that she began her campaign for woman's rights. Then, during the eight years from 1851 to 1859, she gave birth to four more babies, the last when she was forty-four years old.[14]

Harriet Beecher Stowe, Elizabeth Cady Stanton, and, as we will see, Mary Todd Lincoln were all participating in Victorian family planning—a phenomenon that had begun before they were born, and that had, by the time they were married between 1835 and 1845, become (for reasons that still elude historical explanation) a much-accelerated national trend, most emphatically felt in middle-class families, but affecting all economic groups, both urban and rural. Victorian families were deeply involved in what is called the "demographic transition"—a shift from the high birth and high death rates characteristic of traditional populations, to the low birth and low death rates characteristic of our modern population. More people lived longer, so the population as a whole grew rapidly, but fewer babies were born to individual women. Whereas the average number of children born to women who survived to age forty was seven to eight in 1800, in 1900 it was less than half that number and still falling rapidly.[15]

Up until about ten years ago historians attributed this reduction in family size to industrialization and urbanization. Thanks to the statistical techniques developed by French demographer Louis Henry in the 1950s, and the application of these techniques to American data, we have learned that the origins of modern family limitation predate significant industrialization and urbanization—in France by almost a century; in the United States by at least a generation. Many questions remain to be answered about the connections between economic and demographic change in the first half of the nineteenth century. But since we now know that family limitation was widespread throughout Victorian society before 1850, when industrialization and urbanization had barely begun, these latter forces no longer explain the emergence of marital fertility control. Robert Wells argues in "Family History and Demographic Transition" that family limitation was the result of "modern attitudes"—the belief that "the world is knowable and controllable" and that it serves one's own interests to plan one's life.[16]

Harriet Beecher Stowe's matrimonial warfare would seem to fall in this category of thinking, as did her strategy of asserting female control in the sexual arena. Invalidism and Victorian sexuality were not the only means Stowe used to control her circumstances rather than be controlled by them. In a letter to a close friend shortly after Catharine's visit in 1838, she described the full scope of her domestic self-assertion: "I have about three hours per day in writing, and if you see my name coming out everywhere you may be sure of one thing, that I *do* it *for the pay*. I have determined not to be a mere domestic slave without even the leisure to excel in my duties. I mean to have money enough to have my house kept in the best manner and yet to have time for reflection and that preparation for the education of my children which every mother needs. I have every prospect of succeeding in this plan."[17]

Harriet Beecher Stowe was a unique and gifted woman whose novel dramatizing the effects of slavery on family life made her more famous than representative among her contemporaries, but the general circumstances of her domestic life were widely shared. Another young mother living five hundred miles away in western New York, Elizabeth Cady Stanton, approached her domestic responsibilities with the same modern effort to plan and control the outcome. As Stanton described her response to motherhood in 1842 in her autobiography: "Having gone through the ordeal of bearing a child, I was determined if possible to keep him, so I read everything I could find on the subject."[18] One of the manuals Stanton might have come across in her search for pediatric guidance was Catharine Beecher's *Treatise on Domestic Economy*, first published in 1841, reprinted every year until 1856, and distributed nationally by Harper and Brothers. For Beecher's *Treatise*, the most important fact in a woman's life was not whether she was pious or loving, but whether she controlled her own life, for "there is nothing, which so distinctly marks the difference between weak and strong minds, as the fact, whether they control circumstances, or circumstances control them."[19]

Not passive submission to their biological identity nor fetching dependence on their husbands, but active control of their immediate life circumstances was the model Harriet's sister held out to her readers. Adopting a typical Victorian perspective, Beecher viewed motherhood as a qualitative rather than a quantitative activity, useful to society for the kind of child rather than the numbers of children it produced. In a chapter entitled "The Peculiar Responsibilities of American Women," she wrote: "The success of democratic institutions, as is conceded by all, depends upon the intellectual and moral character of the mass of the people. If they are intelligent and virtuous, democracy is a blessing; but if they are ignorant and wicked, it is only a curse. It is equally conceded, that the formation of the moral and intellectual character of the young is committed mainly to the female hand."[20] Beecher's view of the relationship between childhood and society was an essentially modern one. Rather than viewing society as a traditional set of established controls, and early childhood as a time when the will must be broken to conform to those controls, she saw society as an uncontrolled growth, except as it was regulated by the internalized values of "character" developed during early childhood. Seeing it possible to exert in early childhood an influence of lifelong personal and social significance, Victorians were far more sensitive than their ancestors had been to the importance of the right kind of mothering.

Qualitative motherhood and the elevated status it brought Victorian women could be the basis for initiating improvements in other aspects of female life. For Beecher it justified an appeal for the advance of female education. As her *Treatise* stated: "Are not the most responsible of all duties committed to the charge of woman? Is it not her profession to take care of mind, body, and soul? and that, too, at the most critical of all periods of existence? And is it not as much a matter of public concern, that she should be properly qualified for her duties, as that ministers, lawyers, and physicians, should be prepared for theirs? And is it not as important, to endow institutions which shall make a superior education accessible to all classes—for females, as much as for the other sex?"[21]

But for some Victorian women, qualitative motherhood and the female control and assertion we have seen Harriet Beecher Stowe exercise and Catharine Beecher advocate for women in the domestic arena, did not go far enough. Basic inequalities of status between men and women still intruded sharply into domestic life. Married women could not, without special legal efforts, own property, and their earnings belonged to their husbands. Responding to these and other limitations of nineteenth-century domesticity, Elizabeth Cady Stanton decided to do something about it in 1848. As she described her state of mind prior to organizing the first Woman's Rights Convention:

> The general discontent I felt with woman's portion as wife, mother, housekeeper, physician, and spiritual guide, the chaotic conditions into which everything fell without her constant supervision, and the wearied, anxious look of the majority of women impressed me with a strong feeling that some active measure should be taken. My experience at the World's Anti-Slavery Convention, all I had read of the legal status of women, and the oppression I saw everywhere, swept across my soul intensified now by many personal experiences . . . I could not see what to do or where to begin—my only thought was a public meeting for protest and discussion.[22]

While the growth of female autonomy, power, and control within the home was an important component of Victorian domesticity, one of the central tenets of Victorian family life—its separation from the public sphere—prohibited women from exercising outside the domestic world the influence they held within it. Thus the family world of Victorian women was half full or half empty, depending on how one looked at it—half full in providing the potential for the assertion of control over one's life, or half empty in denying to women the legal, political, and economic rights that men enjoyed. For Harriet Beecher Stowe it was half full and she worked to fill it more completely through her writings. For Elizabeth Cady Stanton it was half empty and would only be adequately filled when women were recognized legally and politically as people, rather than the "female relatives of people."[23]

While Harriet Beecher Stowe represents one common female response to the changing conditions of domestic life in taking the initiative to control and plan her life, and Stanton represents a reform strategy in response to the same conditions, Mary Todd Lincoln represents a strategy of total commitment to husband and children.

In her we see a slightly different and even more modern pattern of childbearing than we have seen in Stowe or Stanton. Lincoln's wife, like Calvin Stowe's, bore her first baby a neat nine months after marriage.[24] Mary Todd Lincoln, however, subsequently maintained what seems to have been a more controlled and more even spacing of her children than either Stowe or Stanton and she ceased bearing children altogether at a much earlier age than Harriet or Elizabeth. After an interval of nearly three years between her first and second child, Mary was not pregnant again until four years later when her second child, Edward, died and her third, Willie, was immediately conceived. After another interval of three years between her third and fourth births, Mary Lincoln ceased bearing children altogether when she was only thirty-five years old.

With babies born in 1843, 1846, 1850, and 1853, Mary Todd Lincoln gave less of her own life cycle to the reproductive life of the species than either Harriet Beecher Stowe or Elizabeth Cady Stanton. Mary Todd's mother had given birth regularly every other year after her marriage until she died from causes related to the birth of her seventh when Mary was six years old. Mary's stepmother followed the same traditional pattern, bearing ten children in all, with shorter intervals between births and continuing childbearing well beyond her mid-thirties. But Mary's pattern of childbearing was quite different.

Whereas family limitation for Stowe and Stanton was an on-again, off-again activity, concentrated in a six-year interval in the middle of their childbearing years, Mary Lincoln's family limitation seems to have begun soon after her first child was born, and to have gained momentum in 1847, the year after her second child was born and the year when Lincoln was first elected to Congress. Over the course of the eleven years between 1847 and 1858 when Mrs. Lincoln was twenty-nine to forty years old, she conceived only two children, although her mother's pattern would have produced five children in that length of time.

The greater effectiveness and longevity of fertility control in the Lincoln family seems to suggest the cooperation of husband and wife in the effort. Mary and Abraham Lincoln may exemplify a different kind of family-limitation motivation than the female initiative we saw with Harriet and Calvin Stowe. In many Victorian families, probably including the Lincolns, we can assume that husbands as well as wives viewed their economic betterment or professional advancement as more important than the biblical imperative to "be fruitful and multiply."

We might, indeed, see the bias toward sexual abstinence that Victorian sexual ideology promoted in women as a kind of "fail-safe" protection against the victory of instinct over economic self-interest, and as positive reinforcement for what was, in any case, a necessity of everyday life. In many families husbands and wives may have been in complete agreement about their priorities and have placed the husband's advancement high among these. This certainly seems to have been the case with Mary and Abraham Lincoln.

Nineteenth-century "togetherness" was nowhere better exemplified than in the Lincoln family. All the basic components were there. In their devotion to their children, both Mary and Abraham were making up for unhappy childhoods, loving their sons in ways that compensated for their own maternal deprivation, both having lost their mothers before they were ten years old. The Lincolns indulged their children notoriously, but they had other ambitions that limited the number of children they could raise with such devotion. Until he was elected to the U.S. Congress in 1847, Lincoln's career ambitions in law and politics meant that he was away from home as frequently as he was present, and after his election the Lincoln's home life was even more disrupted. But Mary Lincoln endorsed her husband's career ambitions and gave them top priority in their mutual family life. In 1860 the Lincoln home was an important political meeting ground. As Mrs. Lincoln wrote a friend: "This summer we have had immense crowds of strangers visiting us, and have had no time to be occupied with home affairs."[25]

Perhaps even more important than the terms on which Lincoln family life proceeded were those under which the marriage had begun. In contrast to Harriet Beecher and Elizabeth Cady, Mary Todd married against her family's wishes. Whereas Harriet and Elizabeth both married protégés of their fathers, and both bore their first child in their parents' home, Mary encountered considerable opposition to her marriage from her sister and brother-in-law, Elizabeth Todd Edwards and Ninian Wirt Edwards, who were her de facto guardians in Springfield. The Edwards did not try to hide their disapproval of a marriage they thought was beneath Mary Todd's social standing, and their attitude may have contributed to Lincoln's decision to break off the engagement in 1841. Mary bore her first child in Springfield's Globe Tavern, assisted by her husband rather than her sister, even though her sister lived within walking distance. Marrying for love against the wishes of her family, enduring poverty in early marriage after a wealthy upbringing, but never losing faith in the promise of her husband's career, Mary Lincoln's marriage was in many ways the very model of a nineteenth-century romantic love success story.

But Mary Lincoln's commitment to her husband and children generated trauma as well as joy in her life. One might go as far as to say that her psychological "untogetherness" was reciprocally related to the modern "togetherness" in her family life. With so much love invested in her children, she was spiritually broken with the death of four-year-old Edward in 1850; and although she was pregnant a month after Edward's death and replaced the child numerically immediately, qualitatively the child was irreplaceable to her. It was after Edward's death, when she was thirty-two years old, that she began to lose control of her life. According to the editors of Mrs. Lincoln's letters: "The humor and control that had sustained her in the past became increasingly submerged in fearfulness, self-indulgence, and in sudden outbursts of rage." Meanwhile Abraham Lincoln emerged from the crisis with a new spiritual strength. "The man who was by nature melancholy, solitary, and self-doubting would from then on gain in assurance and magnetism."[26]

The death of her second son, twelve-year-old William in 1862, drove Mary Lincoln across the boundary between this world and the spirit world. She began to see visions of Willie and Edward standing at the foot of her bed, and, after an incomplete recovery, she launched on a compulsive and disastrous effort to make up for her loss by buying clothes, jewels, and household furnishings she could not afford, accumulating twenty thousand dollars in personal debts Lincoln did not know about at the time of his death.[27]

Whereas Harriet Beecher Stowe and Elizabeth Cady Stanton participated in the active and extensive female subculture contained within Victorian society, Stowe through her writing and Stanton through her reform activities, Mary Lincoln's activities outside the domestic arena tended to reinforce the centrality of her husband in her life.

For Mary Todd Lincoln the doctrine of separate spheres did not apply. Her unladylike participation in the political arena, in the name of defending or advancing her husband's interests, earned her many enemies while she occupied the White House; but, for her, family life, political life, and social life were a single unit organized around her husband. There was a great deal of truth to her description of him as "lover—husband—father & *all all to me*—truly my all."[28]

. . . Three years before her husband's assassination and nine years before the final blow of the death of eighteen-year-old Tad in 1871, Mary Lincoln wrote to a friend: "My question to myself is, 'Can life be endured?' "[29] In 1875 she was committed as a "lunatic" to a sanitarium for women in Batavia, Illinois, by her only living son, Robert.

Harriet Beecher Stowe, by contrast, after being very deeply shaken by the death of her eldest son at the age of nineteen in 1857, purged her despair and her fear for his afterlife in a novel set in the religious New England of her childhood, and through that novel moved from slavery to New England traditional life as the setting for her mature and best fiction. The interaction between Harriet's domestic life and her writing contained a built-in dynamic of growth, as through her writing she gained strength to endure family calamity, and through family loss she improved her writing.[30] Her 1858 novel, *The Minister's Wooing* (written after her son's sudden death), explored the similarities between Christ's love and a mother's love and concluded that her unconverted son could not be in hell because she (and therefore the Redeemer) loved him so much.

The contrast between Harriet Beecher Stowe and Mary Todd Lincoln is one between a Victorian woman who was able to build an autonomous self within the domestic arena and a woman who was not able to do so. The contrast between Stowe and Stanton is less marked, being between a Victorian wife and mother who was interested in portraying the private side of domestic life and therefore remained primarily a private person, and a Victorian wife and mother who wanted to portray and change the public policies governing domestic life and therefore grew into a public personage. Both women wrote at home, amid the play and interruptions of their children. Stanton, who after 1851 at the age of thirty-six began to spend a good deal of her life in public, bore four more children at the same time—two more than Harriet Stowe and four more than Mary Lincoln birthed after that age.

Stanton had help in sustaining this double commitment to family and public life. Indeed, one might say that after 1851 she lived in two marriages—one to Henry B. Stanton, one to Susan B. Anthony. Anthony came to visit Stanton often after they met in 1851, and their mutually supportive relationship formed the core of the woman's rights movement for almost fifty years. As Stanton described the relationship in her autobiography:

> We never met without issuing a pronunciamento on some question. In thought and sympathy we were one, and in the division of labor we exactly complemented each other. . . . We have indulged freely in criticism of each other when alone, and hotly contended whenever we have differed, but in our friendship of years there has never been the break of one hour. To the world we always seem to agree and uniformly reflect each other. Like husband and wife, each has the feeling that we must have no differences in public. Thus united at an early day we began to survey the state and nation, the future field of our labors.[31]

As Stanton described their equal division of domestic work: "We took turns on the domestic watchtowers, directing amusements, settling disputes, protecting the weak against the strong, and trying to secure equal rights to all in the home as well as the nation."

Scholars in American women's history have argued that "passionlessness" had positive effects on the lives of many Victorian women; that religion and female piety could serve as a basis for collective action in behalf of female interests; and that domesticity itself was not an empty set of prescriptions for idle women, but a vocation that complemented the career ambitions of nineteenth-century men.[32]

These three women have shown these modernizing trends in nineteenth-century family life. Each responded differently to the demands of qualitative motherhood, representing a common strategy found among her contemporaries. Stowe's strategy of female control in the domestic arena was a mainstream strategy shared by the "domestic feminism" of thousands, perhaps tens of thousands, of

New England and New York women who joined the American Female Moral Reform Society between 1840 and 1860—an organization founded in the 1830s with the sole purpose of eliminating prostitution and the double sexual standard on which it was based.

Stanton's strategy of feminist domestic reform was less widespread than Stowe's brand of domestic feminism, but more radical. The title of Stanton and Anthony's first newspaper, *Revolution,* revealed this, while at the same time it reflected their appreciation of the difficulties involved in achieving their goal of full citizenship for women and the legal equality of the sexes.

Mary Lincoln's strategy of fulfilling her own personal ambition vicariously through husband and children was another mainstream strategy—one that enjoys continued popularity in the last quarter of the twentieth century. Women married to men with political careers still find it especially difficult to pursue autonomous life goals.

Notes

1. Daniel Walker Howe, "American Victorianism as a Culture," *American Quarterly,* 27 (December 1975): 507–32.

2. The Neolithic Revolution, or the transition in the Near East from food gathering to food production, began after 9000 B.C. and was completed by 5500 B.C., when "farming and stock breeding were well established and the basic level of the effective village farming community had been achieved" (Carlo M. Cipolla, *The Economic History of World Population,* 6th ed. [Baltimore: Penguin Books, 1974] p. 19). Nineteenth-century family planning was a part of the second revolution in human population—the Demographic Transition, or the transition from relatively high birth and death rates to relatively low birth and death rates. Ansley J. Coale, "The History of the Human Population," *The Human Population* (New York: Scientific American Book, 1974), pp. 15–28.

3. Edmund Wilson, *Patriotic Gore: Studies in the Literature of the American Civil War* (New York: Oxford University Press, 1962), pp. 25–35. I am grateful to Louis Dabney for reminding me of these printed letters.

4. Annie Fields, ed., *Life and Letters of Harriet Beecher Stowe* (Cambridge, Mass.: Riverside Press; Boston, New York: Houghton Mifflin and Co., 1897), p. 110; Wilson, *Patriotic Gore,* p. 17, June 16, 1845.

5. Calvin Stowe to Harriet Beecher Stowe, September 30, 1844, Beecher-Stowe Collection, Schlesinger Library on the History of Women in America, Cambridge, Mass., folder 61.

6. Fields, *Life and Letters,* p. 110, June 16, 1845.

7. Wilson, *Patriotic Gore,* pp. 28–29, July 29, 1855. Summer correspondence between Harriet and Calvin Stowe continued for more than a decade to discuss the issues initially raised in 1844.

8. Fields, *Life and Letters,* p. 110, June 16, 1845.

9. Calvin Stowe to Harriet Beecher Stowe, September 30, 1844, Beecher-Stowe Collection, folder 61.

10. Calvin Stowe to Harriet Beecher Stowe, June 30, 1844, Beecher-Stowe Collection, folder 61.

11. Catharine Beecher to Mary Beecher Perkins, Fall 1837, Beecher-Stowe Collection, folder 17.

12. Harriet Beecher Stowe to Calvin Stowe, July 19, 1844, Beecher-Stowe Collection, folder 69.

13. Charles Edward Stowe, *Life of Harriet Beecher Stowe: Compiled from Her Letters and Journals* (Boston: Houghton, Mifflin & Co., 1889), p. 115. I am grateful to Rebecca Veach for pointing out this letter to me. Daniel Scott Smith, "Family Limitation, Sexual Control, and Domestic Feminism in Victorian America," *Feminist Studies* 1, nos. 3–4 (Winter–Spring 1973), discusses the extent to which family limitation fostered a new kind of personal autonomy among Victorian women.

14. Alma Lutz, "Elizabeth Cady Stanton," in Edward T. James et al., eds., *Notable American Women, 1607–1950: A Biographical Dictionary,* 3 vols. (Cambridge, Mass.: Harvard University Press, Belknap Press, 1971), 3:342–47.

15. Wilson H. Grabill, Clyde V. Kiser, and Pascal K. Whelpton, "A Long View," in Michael Gordon, ed., *The American Family in Social-Historical Perspective* (New York: St. Martin's Press, 1973), pp. 374–95, esp. 387.

16. Robert V. Wells, "Family History and Demographic Transition," *Journal of Social History* 9 (Fall 1975): 6.

17. Harriet Beecher Stowe to Mary Dutton, December 13, 1838, Mary Dutton-Beecher Letters, Bienecke Library, Yale University.
18. Elizabeth Cady Stanton, *Eighty Years and More: Reminiscences 1815–1897* (1898; reprint ed., New York: Shocken, 1971), p. 114.
19. Catharine Beecher. *A Treatise on Domestic Economy: For the Use of Young Ladies at Home and at School,* rev. ed. (Boston: Thomas H. Webb & Co., 1843), p. 160. See also Kathryn Kish Sklar, *Catharine Beecher: A Study in American Domesticity* (New Haven: Yale University Press, 1973), pp. 151–68.
20. Beecher, *A Treatise,* pp. 36–37.
21. Ibid., p. 52.
22. Stanton, *Eighty Years,* p. 148.
23. Aileen Kraditor, ed., *Up from the Pedestal: Selected Writings in the History of American Feminism* (New York: Quadrangle Books, 1968), Introduction, p. 8.
24. Justin G. Turner and Linda Levitt Turner, *Mary Todd Lincoln: Her Life and Letters* (New York: Alfred A. Knopf, 1972).
25. Ibid., p. 66.
26. Ibid., p. 41.
27. Turner and Turner, *Mary Todd Lincoln,* p. 237 and n., pp. 224–25, p. 355 and n.
28. Ibid., p. 534.
29. Turner and Turner, *Mary Todd Lincoln,* p. 128.
30. For a high critical estimate of Harriet Beecher Stowe's post-1857 fiction, see Alice Crozier, *The Novels of Harriet Beecher Stowe* (New York: Oxford University Press, 1969), pp. 85–151, and Henry F. May's "Introduction" to the John Harvard edition of *Oldtown Folks* (Cambridge, Mass.: Harvard University Press, 1966).
31. Stanton, *Eighty Years,* pp. 164, 166.
32. Carroll Smith-Rosenberg, "Beauty, the Beast and the Militant Woman: A Case Study in Sex Roles and Social Stress in Jacksonian America," *American Quarterly* 23 (1971): 562–84; Nancy F. Cott, *The Bonds of Womanhood: New England Women 1780–1820* (New Haven: Yale University Press, 1976).

Chapter 11

Reproductive Control and Conflict in the Nineteenth Century

Janet Farrell Brodie

In the following article, adapted from her book-length study, Contraception and Abortion in Nineteenth-Century America, *Janet Farrell Brodie considers the ways that nineteenth-century American women controlled reproduction and analyzes the writings of advocates and opponents of contraception and abortion. She shows how opponents of abortion mounted a "carefully orchestrated campaign" that criminalized contraception and abortion, driving their medical practitioners underground. Only with the Supreme Court decision,* Roe v. Wade, *in 1973, would women in the United States regain legal access to contraception and abortion.*

The ancient contraceptive practice of coitus interruptus took on new meaning in nineteenth-century America. It became increasingly well known and openly discussed, and it appears to have been widely practiced well into the twentieth century. Its growing public visibility can be seen in the number of synonyms it garnered, from the derogatory "conjugal onanism," "marital masturbation," and "coitus imperfecti," to the more benign "withdrawal," "the pullback," "the drawback," "the method of retraction," "incomplete coition," or simply "the way." Lecturing and writing on health, marriage, and sex in antebellum America, William Andrus Alcott expected audiences to understand his references to a reproductive control method that was "a species of selfdenial on the part of the husband, which though it should be in its essential form like that of Onan, would be without his particular form of guilt."[1] This was "withdrawal." In 1831, Robert Dale Owen, son of the founder of New Harmony in Indiana and a pioneer in publicizing reproductive control, described a Quaker couple who had been married for twenty years. They had six children and claimed that they would have had twelve if they had not practiced withdrawal.[2]

Couples in these case studies who discussed the need for spacing or preventing any further pregnancies whatsoever cited motivations that were primarily health concerns—a wife's or couple's fears about a wife's health, fears about a husband's overwork—and, secondarily, financial concerns. The late-eighteenth-century Quaker couple was greatly pleased to have only six children, but couples in the 1860s and 1870s found two children in four years or two children in seven years too many.

Coitus interruptus, for all its seeming simplicity, was not a uniform contraceptive technique. Historians have paid too little attention to the variations. Historians also disagree about whether withdrawal is one of those simple folk contraceptives that individuals can invent easily on their own or whether it needs special circumstances to be learned.[3] In Victorian America some said they had "invented" withdrawal, much like the young man who, after his marriage in the 1820s, wrote to Robert Dale Owen explaining that he had used withdrawal successfully for seven years to improve

MADAME RESTELL.

☞ FEMALE PHYSICIAN, is happy in complying with the solicitations of the numerous importunities of those who have tested the efficacy and success of her medicines, as being so especially adapted to female complaints.

Their known celebrity in the Female Hospitals of Vienna and Paris, where they have been altogether adopted as well as their adoption in this country, to the exclusion of the many and deleterious compounds heretofore palmed upon their notice, is ample evidence of the estimation in which they are held to make any lengthened advertisements superfluous: it is sufficient to say that her celebrated 'FEMALE MONTHLY PILLS,' now acknowledged by the medical fraternity to be the only safe, mild and efficient remedy to be depended upon in long standing cases of Suppression, Irregularity or stoppage of those functions of nature, the neglect of which is the source of such deplorable defects on the female frame, dizziness in the head, disturbed sleep, sallow complexion, and the innumerable frightful effects which sooner or later terminate in incurable consumption.

The married, it is desired necessary to state, must under some circumstances abstain from their use, for reasons contained in the full directions when and how to be used accompanying each box. Price $1.

Females laboring under weakness, debility, fluoral bas, often so destructive and undermining to the health, will obtain instant relief by the use of these Pills.

PREVENTIVE POWDERS, for married ladies in delicate health, the adoption of which has been the means of preserving many an affectionate wife and fond mother from an early and premature grave. Prices $5.00 a package. Their nature is most fully explained in a pamphlet entitled 'Suggestions to the Married.' which can be obtained free of expense, at the office, where ladies will find one of their own sex, conversant with their indisposition, in attendance.

FEMALE MEDICAL OFFICE, No. 7 Essex street, Boston. Office hours from 8 A.M. to 8 P. M.

Philadelphia Office, No 7 South Seventh street.

Principal Office, No 148 Greenwich street New York.

Abortifacient advertisement, Boston Daily Times, *Jan. 2, 1845.*

his economic circumstances and his health before having a family. He had learned about it, he claimed, when "withdrawal presented itself to my mind."[4] In the 1930s a white tenant farm woman in Appalachia told a WPA interviewer that withdrawal was easy to understand: "If you don't want butter, pull the dasher out in time."[5]

Others needed instruction. Owen described the visit to his New York newspaper office in the early 1830s of a man who lived "west of the mountains." He had used withdrawal successfully for nearly eight years after the birth of three children. Owen asked if his neighbors also found it effective, but his visitor had not thought it prudent "to speak with any but his own relations on the subject, one or two of whom, he knew had profited by his advice and afterwards expressed to him their gratitude for the important information."[6] Such reticence apparently did not bother an Upstate New York farm woman, Calista Hall, who wrote to her husband, Pliny, in 1849 to reassure him she was not pregnant, to commend him for using withdrawal so effectively, and to suggest that he instruct a friend or relative in its advantages: "The old maid came at the appointed time. . . . I do think you are a very *careful* man. You must take Mr. Stewart out one side and learn him."[7]

The publication in 1831 of Owen's pamphlet *Moral Physiology* made it easier to learn about withdrawal. It was concise and plainly written, without the many euphemisms and metaphors that cloaked so many discussions. . . . In its many editions and through its many imitators and competitors, Owen's tract put coitus interrupts in the culture. Almost all contraceptive advice literature from the 1830s through the 1880s gave explicit or tacit recognition to coitus interrupts. Much of it disparaged withdrawal because it competed with other methods such as douching, condoms, rhythm, or abortion, which they themselves were touting, but few ignored it.

Twentieth-century studies of the effectiveness of various contraceptive methods show that, under optimal conditions, coitus interruptus can be quite reliable but also that there is great variation in success rates.[8] It ranks in some studies as more effective than douching and nearly equal to spermicidal suppositories, contraceptive jelly, and condoms.[9] Its reliability depends on the care with which withdrawal is practiced—no sperm at all may be left in or near the vagina, even on the external labia, because sperm move quickly and can fertilize an ovum within minutes. Knowledge of sperm mobility grew only slowly in the last century.

Partial withdrawal, that is, ejaculation as far as possible from the cervix but possibly still in the vagina, appears to have been as widely known as complete withdrawal both in Europe and in America. Because it required less concentration from men, it may have been more widely practiced . . .

When people believed, as many did in earlier centuries, that conception occurred only if a woman experienced orgasm or if the sperm were thrown forcefully against the cervix, partial withdrawal appeared a logical method. But by the mid nineteenth century, new theories about how sperm reached the ovum (by their own motility, by absorbent vessels in the vaginal lining) convinced some that partial withdrawal could not work.[10] Yet wellestablished ideas and practices change slowly, and, apparently—or why were there so many continuing warnings against it?—at least some Americans continued to rely on partial withdrawal. . . .

Withdrawal of any degree fell into increasing disfavor as time went on, and medical professionals, promoters of reproductive control, and the middle class public began to raise doubts about it, or worse. Medical opponents claimed that withdrawal caused in men "general debility of brain and brawn," "tubercula foci" in the prostate and seminal vesicles, and symptoms like gonorrhea; and, in women, hysteria, degeneration of the womb, neuralgias, and a host of "local and constitutional disorders."[11]

Physicians frequently commented negatively on coitus interruptus. In 1876, Nicholas Francis Cooke, a physician and birth control critic, wrote *Satan in Society: A Plea for Social Purity. A Discussion of the True Rights of Woman, Marital and Social* chiefly "to stigmatize . . . conjugal onanism," which he deplored as a "deeply rooted vice . . . a national curse, a reason for the widespread moral degradation and a powerful reason for the decline of the native population."[12] . . .

Some physicians late in the century reported that withdrawal caused psychological disorders. A Philadelphia doctor who had advised a delicate female patient who was about to be married not to have children immediately and her husband-to-be to practice withdrawal, reported that the couple had no children for three years and the wife had become healthy and robust, but the husband "nervously affected" and "rendered delicate."[13] . . .

Yet the public may well have paid scant attention to the negative onslaught. The remark of a farmer in pre–World War I Germany (where withdrawal and postcoital douching were the most common forms of contraception among the working class) may be equally applicable to nineteenth-century Americans. Asked if he believed medical reports that withdrawal is harmful, the farmer replied no, "otherwise everybody would be sick."[14] Annie Besant wrote in her pamphlet *The Law of Population* in 1878 that although doctors said that withdrawal might be injurious to women, its universal practice by the French attested to its safety.[15]

Dislike of withdrawal became more openly expressed over the course of the century as other contraceptive and abortive options emerged in the commercialization of reproductive control. Men, in particular, began to express complaints about it more openly, centering on how difficult coitus interruptus was to practice and how much it lessened their sexual pleasure. . . .

When Gilbert Vale, Owen's fellow freethinker, published an edition of *Moral Physiology* in 1858, adding his own publisher's notes at the end, he said that withdrawal was difficult for any but mature men in "the decline of life." Younger men could not be expected to have sufficient control to practice withdrawal and so should use condoms or rely on partial withdrawal, followed by the wife's douching. The pirated edition of *Moral Physiology* put out in 1846 by the unknown "physician" Ralph Glover, too, played on the discontent, commenting, "How frequently do we hear the mothers say, I have all the family I want and am determined to have not more children if I can prevent it; but alas: she has not the power when the partner of her bosom loses the self-control of his passions.[16] . . .

Women had their own reasons for disliking withdrawal. A woman had to have great confidence in her sexual partner's reliability, self-control, good will, and judgment. This dependence was not satisfactory for many women. A man's reliance on coitus interruptus might actually have increased a woman's level of anxiety because a man who became more confident about his ability to "pull back" effectively may have become less willing to be abstinent or to be overruled in the timing and frequency of sexual intercourse. Still, family-limitation critic Nicholas Francis Cooke was lamenting in 1876 that a husband who practices coitus interruptus is "eulogized by his wife and applauded by her friends."[17] . . .

Unlike men, women did not leave a record of complaints about withdrawal's interference with their sexual pleasure, but it can hardly, one assumes, have had any other effect. And fears that the pullback would not be in time can only have increased their anxiety. Nevertheless, husbands and doctors occasionally blamed wives for making their husbands practice withdrawal. L. Bolton Bangs, a physician opposed to contraception, wrote in 1893 that his male patients felt anger and disgust toward their wives at the moment of withdrawal. Other historians have seen the practice of withdrawal as an example of the increasing power of women within marriage. Daniel Scott Smith's well-known article "Family Limitation, Sexual Control, and Domestic Feminism in Victorian America" argues that women in mid-nineteenth-century America gained considerable power within marriage to control the timing and frequency of sexual intercourse and thereby to control reproduction.[18] . . .

In what may be viewed as another variant of withdrawal in that it, too, involved a man's control of ejaculation during the sexual act, coitus reservatus was known and practiced by some in nineteenth-century America. Coitus reservatus (prolonged coition with no emission of semen and with gradual loss of the erection while the penis is still in the vagina) is an ancient sexual practice, but Americans believed that it was invented in the 1840s by John Humphrey Noyes, the leader of a New York communitarian group, the Oneida Perfectionists.[19] Noyes, who called the practice "male continence," explained that he invented it after his wife, Harriet, suffered six pregnancies but only one live birth in the eight years after they were married in 1838. He promised Harriet she would never again have to suffer the pain and anguish of childbirth even if they had to sleep apart. Worried by such a prospect, he "studied the subject of sexual intercourse in connection with my matrimonial experience and discovered the principle of male continence."[20] This then became the way conception was prevented at the Oneida Community, which from 1848 until the mid 1870s proved to be the longest-lasting, most publicized, and most financially successful of all the nineteenth-century American experiments in communal living. It apparently worked remarkably well, for there were only thirty-one accidental pregnancies from 1848 to 1869, although the community grew from some eighty-seven to 219 by 1874. To Noyes, for whom the method was as much a spiritual as a contraceptive practice, its advantages were manifold: it preserved men's health by preventing the loss of semen; it freed women from "the curses of involuntary and undesirable procreation," a freedom that, he believed, would promote happier relations between the sexes and happier maternity for women, who now regarded childbearing as a burden and a curse. Above all, it enabled both men and women to enjoy sexual intercourse.[21]

Male continence was probably never widely practiced in the United States except at Oneida, but it received considerable publicity and was far from unknown. Noyes first described it in a chapter of his book *The Bible Argument* in 1848.[22] In 1866 the Perfectionists decided that American society would benefit from a wider knowledge of male continence, so Noyes published as a four-page leaflet a letter he has written to a young medical student who requested detailed information on how the community controlled reproduction. They mailed the leaflet, *Male Continence; or, Self-Control in Sexual Intercourse. A Letter of Inquiry Answered by John Humphrey Noyes*, only in response to specific requests for information, but even so it went through four editions. In 1872 rather than issue a fifth edition, Noyes revised and enlarged the leaflet, adding twenty pages on the history of his discovery of male continence. This he published in 1877, and it was sold by general booksellers and agents. Ezra Heywood, who stood trial and served a jail term for breaking the laws against dispersing birth control information by selling his own book, *Cupid's Yokes*—an antimarriage tract—and Russell Thacher Trall's *Sexual Physiology*, sold *Male Continence* without any trouble.[23]

In some years over two hundred visitors a month passed through the Oneida Community, and all had access to freely given information about its beliefs and practices. The community's newspaper, the *Oneida Circular*, with a weekly circulation of two thousand in the 1860s, discussed male continence in its columns. Later birth control publicists included discussions of it in their books,[24] and critics of fertility intervention disparaged it. John Harvey Kellogg's *Plain Facts for Old and Young*, in 1880, labeled male continence "double masturbation" and warned readers that it was as destructive to health as withdrawal.[25] Members of the Boston Gynaecological Society in 1871 discussed "the pathological results of conjugal fraud as practiced in so disgusting a manner at the so-called Oneida Community."[26]

THE RIGHT TO DECIDE: EARLY SPOKESWOMEN

Before the 1860s there is little direct evidence that female lecturers disseminated contraceptive or abortive information. The most important of those who did do so was probably Mary Gove Nichols, whose public and private life, like that of Frances Wright, was full of sexual paradox. Mary Gove was intellectually curious and upwardly mobile, but at a young age married, unhappily, a dour Quaker, Hiram Gove. She secretly read medical textbooks and taught herself the rudiments of medicine and the water cure. Six years of increasing marital misery and five pregnancies later (all but one ending either in miscarriage or stillbirth), Mary and Hiram Gove left their New Hampshire farm and moved, in 1837, to Lynn, Massachusetts, where Mary supported the family by operating a boarding school run on the dietary principles of Sylvester Graham, supplementing this income by lectures on physiology and hygiene.[27] Her lectures, in turn, brought her to the attention of the American Physiological Society (founded in 1837 in Boston by William Andrus Alcott and Sylvester Graham).

Because some women attending the first lectures of the American Physiological Society were embarrassed to be in an audience with men, the society decided to hire separate speakers for men and women and create the Ladies Physiological Society. Mary Gove came to Boston in September 1837 and began to lecture on diet, dress, menstrual difficulties, and the dangers of female masturbation, sometimes to audiences of more than four hundred women.[28] So successful were these lectures that she continued throughout New England and as far south as Philadelphia and New York, speaking on "sanitary education," "the laws of life and health," the evils of wearing corsets, the problems of masturbation in girls' boarding schools, and, most radically of all, on the physical and emotional problems resulting from "indissoluble marriage." Desperately unhappy in her own marriage, she spent as much time away from her husband as possible, but he would not grant her a divorce. In 1842 she left him, but feared that he would never allow her to see their daughter and that he would continue to claim her financial earnings. Even though she was immersed in itinerant lecturing, consulting lawyers about her marital rights, and in poor health, she still found time in 1842 to publish some of her lectures as a book, *Lectures to Women on Anatomy and Physiology.*[29] If the book mirrored her lectures (as the title implies), then she did not speak on reproduction except to lament the prevailing ignorance among women on the subject of their bodies, but the book may have omitted such comments. Some of her lectures were given separately to married and unmarried women.[30] Her lectures scandalized some because of her comments on masturbation (the topic alone was shocking) and her references to her own (clothed) body to demonstrate anatomical points. She consulted a favorite cousin, the writer John Neal, whether he thought it proper to speak before men and women on the evils of "tight lacing," but added, "I think I have a *right* to speak on proper subjects in a proper manner before a mixed audience."[31] New York newspaper editor James Gordon Bennett denounced her, but the *Boston Medical and Surgical Reporter* commended her book and her lectures, noting that "useful knowledge becomes a woman, let it embrace whatever department it may," and adding that there is "nothing objectionable or indelicate for one woman to tell another those important facts . . . in a country where ladies have been too negligent of the laws of health, and sometimes apparently proud of being profoundly ignorant of the mechanism of themselves.[32]

Mary Gove supported herself (and her husband, though separated) as a water-cure physician in a series of hydropathic resorts, in Brattleboro, Vermont, Lebanon Springs, New York, and then at the establishment of Joel Shew in New York City, and finally in 1846 at her own water-cure boardinghouse on Tenth Street in Manhattan. In 1847 she met Thomas Low Nichols, a young itinerant novelist and journalist who had studied medicine at Dartmouth College and was absorbed in the theories of John Humphrey Noyes, Josiah Warren, and Charles Fourier. They married the following year when her husband, also wanting to remarry, finally granted a divorce.[33]

In the 1850s Mary and Thomas Gove Nichols became active New York water-cure practitioners and lecturers and writers on sexuality, marriage, and reproductive control. They operated a Reform Bookstore at 65 Walker Street in Manhattan, from which they sold their literature and advertised their services. Mary Gove Nichols probably influenced her new husband in these directions, for only after their marriage did he show any interest in many of the subjects they subsequently wrote about. Both lectured to large mixed audiences, but she specialized in intimate talks to small groups of women. They wrote and lectured on the benefits of the water cure, especially its aid in ameliorating the dangers and pains of pregnancy and childbirth,[34] and advocated easier divorce, women's property rights, and, above all, women's sexual rights. She had long believed that a woman had the right to determine if and when she would bear children and to choose who would father them. When Mary Gove Nichols and Thomas Low Nichols published such views they were branded "free lovers" by critics, although they emphasized the dangers of excessive sexuality, women's rights to *refuse* sex, and the legalized "prostitution" created by contemporary marriage laws.

The book *Esoteric Anthropology* appeared in 1853. Although Thomas Low Nichols is credited as its sole author, the wording of the text—especially the opinions about contraception and abortion—suggests that Mary Gove Nichols wrote parts.[35] In any case, both probably shared its views and may have expressed them in their lectures and, almost certainly, in their private consultations. *Esoteric Anthropology* boldly argued a position she had long held: "If a woman has any right in this world it is the right to herself; and if there is anything in this world she has a right to decide, it is who shall be the father of her children. She has an equal right to decide whether she will have children and to choose the time for having them."[36] . . .

Esoteric Anthropology suggested how women and men could achieve reproductive control, discussing a variety of methods, among them abstinence (it is "unhealthy and unnatural" but "easily done by most women and by many men"), and rhythm ("in ordinary cases . . . conception can only take place when connection is had a day or two before or ten, or for safety's sake, say sixteen days after menstruation"); complete withdrawal; use of a soft sponge "to cover the upper vagina over the mouth of the womb"; use of condoms or other "delicate coverings of the whole penis"; and "pressing upon the urethra to prevent emission of the semen," effectual but harmful. Above all, it advised an "immediate, very deep, thorough" douche—an "immediate injection of cold water by the vagina-syringe" to "kill and wash away zoosperms." Douching was, after all, an important part of the water cure. . . . *Esoteric Anthropology* included advice about the simplest and least dangerous abortion method, and warnings about the most dangerous techniques. The reformist physician Elizabeth Blackwell in 1853 noted with asperity in a letter to her sister Emily, who was studying medicine in Edinburgh, that "the Nichols set is spreading their detestable doctrines of abortion and prostitution under spiritual and scientific guise—they are placing agents with the advertisements of their books at the doors of the conventions now being held here, worded in the most specious and attractive manner." In her published autobiography, Blackwell changed the wording of these remarks slightly and referred not by name to the Nicholses but to "an active set of people," whose "detestable doctrines of abortion and prostitution" were now the "detestable doctrine of 'free love.'"[37]

Another lecturer, Paulina Kellogg Wright Davis, an antislavery and woman's rights activist in the 1830s, became active in health reform after her husband's death. From 1845 to 1849 she toured throughout the East and the Midwest speaking to audiences of women on health reform, anatomy, and physiology. Following the precedent established by Mary Gove Nichols, she used a manikin to illustrate her lectures; but unlikely Nichols, she did not publish them. . . .

Harriot K. Hunt, another antebellum lecturer, practiced medicine in Boston for more than forty years, trained by a husband-and-wife team of homeopathic physicians, though she was repeatedly denied entry to the Harvard Medical School. One of the best known and most outspoken of the first generation of women physicians and a fervent participant in the early woman's rights movement, Hunt had contact with an unusually wide range of women, from those in Charlestown, Massachusetts, who joined her "Ladies Physiological Society" in 1843 to those in a working class district in Boston before whom she gave free public lectures in 1849. . . . Earlier, in Lynn, she had boarded at Mary Gove's house "for a day or two every month," finding affinity with the water-cure practitioner: "Her deep interest in anatomy and physiology drew me to her."[38]

Hunt severely criticized doctors for conducting physical examinations of their female patients, calling them "skeptics who lived sensually and "contaminated their patients" with examinations "too often unnecessary."[39] She was obviously thinking about what she called "abuses of the marriage relation" and believed that women needed more control over a husband's sensuality. Investigating this complex issue, she visited a Shaker community in the late 1840s but found Shaker celibacy too extreme a response to the problems of fertility and sexuality.

* * *

General topics connected to reproductive control, such as the need for wives to have control of marital sexuality or to determine the timing and frequency of sexual intercourse, would, no doubt, have been easier than more explicit ones for women lecturers to raise. The rhythm method might well have been discussed without discomfort because of its seeming "naturalness." Withdrawal, on the other hand, might not have been, though it could have come up in connection with comments on menstruation or with recommendations for sexual abstinence. So, too, women lecturers may have found it relatively comfortable to refer to medicinal and hygienic douching or the use of vaginal suppositories or the vaginal sponge rather than measures men might take to avoid insemination of their wives. The freedom of women to speak publicly on sexual matters was greatly enhanced by the woman's rights movement that itself was stimulated by the war-time struggle for emancipation and racial equality.

* * *

ABORTION AS A BUSINESS

Folk remedies for abortion and superstitions about abortion survived essentially unchanged over many centuries. Older abortion methods continued to be available throughout the nineteenth century, but practices were changing. From the 1840s on, the selling of abortive products became a commercial business. Abortion was more openly discussed and increasingly available from sources that seemed scientific, modern, and professional.

Many women continued in the decades after 1840 to bring about abortion in their homes through use of the pills, fluid extracts, and medicinal oils that were nonpublicly marketed with such suggestive names as the "Female Regulator," "Periodical Drops," "Uterine Regulator," and "Woman's Friend." Ely Van de Warker, a Syracuse, New York, gynecologist who studied American abortion methods, noted that "every schoolgirl knows the meaning of these terms." Anyone who did not could have learned others from the printed labels on the drug containers. The label on Graves Pills for Amenorrhea was typical: "These pills have been approved by the Ecole de Medecine, fully sanctioned by the M.R.C.S. of London, Edinburgh, Dublin, as a never-failing remedy for producing the catamenial or monthly flow. Though perfectly harmless to the most delicate, yet ladies are earnestly requested not to mistake their condition [if pregnant] as MISCARRIAGE WOULD CERTAINLY ENSUE."[40] . . .

Most abortifacients were sold as pills or as fluid extracts in which one ingredient predominated, usually aloes or black hellebore. The pills often were combinations of aloes, hellebore, powdered savin, ergot, iron, and solid extracts of tansy and rue. The instructions on the pill bottles told women to supplement the doses by drinking tansy tea twice daily until the "obstruction" was removed. The fluid extracts were most commonly oils of savin, tansy, or rue dissolved in alcohol and improved in taste by wintergreen.[41] . . .

These medicines were often effective, though they also posed considerable risk and, at times, acute danger to a woman's life.[42] Ely Van de Warker concluded that "female pills" often worked as abortives because women took them in dangerously copious amounts without regard for their general health. He believed that the extensiveness of the trade in commercial abortion drugs and the relative rarity of publicized fatalities indicated a degree of effectiveness: "I know many married women who have gone years without the birth of mature children, who resort habitually to some one of the many advertised nostrums with as much confidence of 'coming around' as if they repaired to the shop of the professional abortionist."[43] . . .

In medical journals of the second half of the nineteenth century, physicians discussed the uses patients had made of catheters, speculua, and uterine sounds (a type of uterine probe).[44] The president of the Gynaecological Society of Boston said, in 1871, that "the populace seem to have the idea that Simpson's sound was designed to produce abortion," and in the 1890s a physician in the middle of a discussion with his medical peers about the dangers of coitus interruptus observed that he had advised a male patient who did not want additional children to stop using withdrawal because it was affecting his health; the patient managed to avoid an increase in his family because, the doctor implied, his wife was handy in the "occasional passing of a sound."[45]

Abortion instruments, like drugs, were readily available through the mails or from a variety of retail establishments, particularly drugstores, and wholesale druggists' catalogues carried a considerable variety of styles and models in uterine sounds and dilators. Newspapers regularly carried advertisements for abortion-inducing drugs.

In June 1870, Frank Leslie's *Day's Doings*, a racy New York newspaper carrying sensationalist articles and theatrical and sporting news, carried advertisements for seven medicines with language some women no doubt associated with abortion, including "Madame Van Buskirk's Regulating Medicine," "Dr. Richau's Female Remedy," and "Dr. Harrison's Female Antidote . . . certain to have the desired effect in twenty-four hours without any injurious results."[46] By mid century there was a growing number of "professional" abortionists, and not only in large cities, as W.M. Smith, a physician in the small farming town of Atkinson, Illinois (population 300), noted in 1874:

> I know three married women, respectable ones, who are notorious for giving instructions to their younger sisters as to the modus operandi of 'coming around.' After the failure of tansy, savin, ergot, cotton root, lifting, rough trotting horses, etc., a knitting needle is the stand by. One old doctor near here was so obliging as to furnish a wire with a handle, to one of his patients, which did the work for her, after which she passed it to one of her neighbors, who succeeded in destroying the foetus and nearly so herself.[47]

Smith estimated that his town had one abortion for every ten live births. He was opposed to abortion but expressed sympathy for women who needed some means of controlling reproduction, suggesting, ambiguously, that women use "bromide of potassium"—probably meaning a douche.

Urban women, in particular, and those with access to transportation to urban areas found highly desirable anonymity and the comfort of a supposedly safer, more modern abortion from the services of a newly visible entrepreneur: the "professional" abortionist.

The term "female physician" was frequently a euphemism for abortionist by mid century, a time when respectable women midwives found their role and power increasingly circumscribed by a medical profession intent on establishing its own professional identity. When Elizabeth Blackwell first tried to establish a medical practice in New York City in the 1850s she was denied rental at the first few boardinghouses she approached because landlords mistook her for an abortionist. This assumption was particularly galling to Blackwell, who abhorred abortion, and she described with scorn the flags midwives hung from their windows as wordless advertisements of their services.[48] . . .

In the cities of New England and of the Middle Atlantic states women could find a variety of offices, clinics, and boardinghouses offering lying-in services and illicit abortions. Although we do not know with any certainty who operated these establishments or even how many there were, contemporary observers believed that many were operated by women who had been trained as midwives in Europe.[49] . . .

Of all the nineteenth-century abortionists, Ann Trow Lohman (1812–1877) is the best documented. Better known as "Madame Restell," she ran a lucrative mail-order business and abortion service in New York City from the 1840s through the 1870s.[50] . . . Shortly after her marriage, Ann Trow Lohman adopted the alias "Madame Restell" and went into the abortion and contraceptives business, advertising her services and products in newspapers and hiring agents to distribute circulars along the eastern seaboard. Historian James C. Mohr notes that she had branch agencies in Boston and Philadelphia in the 1840s, and an 1846 article in the *Police Gazette* suggested that "Madame Costello," another female physician advertising abortifacient pills, was an agent of Restell's.[51] . . .

It did not take "Madame Restell" long to gain notoriety and a fortune. She appeared in the 1844 novel by Thomas Low Nichols, *The Lady in Black: A Story of New York Life, Morals, and Manners*, about the "tangled mass of vice and virtue" in New York City. . . . Lohman (Restell) was indicted and tried a number of times between 1841 and 1878, charged variously with performing abortions, manslaughter, and with running illegal adoption services for infants born in her establishment. One 1847 case tells a good deal about her practice: she was charged with second-degree manslaughter for producing an abortion on one Maria Bodine after quickening of the fetus. After a seventeen-day trial, reported in the sensationalist New York press. . . . Restell was convicted and sentenced to a year in prison on Blackwell's Island. The young woman obtaining the abortion was an unmarried servant who had been having regular sexual relations for two years with her employer, a widowed cotton manufacturer in Walden, New York. When she found herself pregnant in the spring of 1846, she took a boat down the Hudson to New York to stay with a married sister, and when she was nearly six months pregnant she called on Madame Restell. The price was five dollars for an examination, from one to five dollars for a box of pills, and one hundred dollars for "operating." Restell asked her whether her "beau" were employed and would help pay for the operation. When the girl returned several weeks later with seventy-five dollars from her lover, Restell induced an abortion by rupturing the amniotic sac and prescribing pills to cause uterine contractions. After several days in bed in a private room, the girl went home. Restell gave her money for the boat fare, told her how to alleviate her milk-swollen breasts, and advised her to come back for a private carriage if approached by the police. Although contemporary critics saw Restell as an avaricious quack, such details of her practice, ironically brought out at the trial by the prosecution, suggest compassion and competence as well as business shrewdness.

*   *   *

As reproductive control became commercialized after 1850, and as some women became increasingly able to assert a degree of independent control over their fertility through contraception and abortion, the deep ambivalences with which many Americans regarded such changes came increasingly into play. In the second half of the nineteenth century diverse groups emerged to try to restore American "social purity," and one of the issues they focused on was restricting sexual freedom and control of reproduction. Often historians have studied the campaigns against abortion and contraception as separate phenomena[52] but the two movements shared important similarities in the opponents' motivations, in the imagery and symbolism of their public campaigns, and in the consequences. Both crusades were led by energetic, driven men; both were backed by professional organizations of white, middle class, native-born men—and women, as well—who had assumed the role of custodians of the public good. All branches of government were their allies; their goals were won through enactments of federal and state legislation and sustained by judicial decisions that criminalized contraception and abortion, both of which had in earlier decades been legal.

AFTER TWO CENTURIES OF LEGALITY, REPRODUCTIVE CONTROL BECOMES A FELONY

In the second half of the nineteenth century, state laws altered two hundred years of American custom and public policy toward abortion. In some states it became illegal to obtain an abortion at any stage of pregnancy: abortionists began to face charges of second-degree homicide or manslaughter and women seeking abortions faced criminal prosecution.[53] Some but not all states made an exception if an official physician performed the abortion to save a woman's life.

For two centuries in America, abortion had been treated according to common law tradition in which abortions before "quickening"—fetal movement—were not punishable, and those procured later, after quickening, might be high misdemeanors if the woman died, but not felonies.[54] Some states began criminal code revisions in the 1830s and 1840s and included in those revisions statutes against abortion. The thrust of the new laws was twofold: to regulate those who could legally give abortions and to punish unlawful abortionists. In some states—Connecticut, Missouri, Illinois—abortion restrictions came in the form of tighter laws against the use of poisons. Only in New York was there a foretaste of the more stringent antiabortion laws to come. The New York law, passed in 1829, prohibited anyone, including a doctor, from attempting abortion at any period of pregnancy except to save a woman's life.

Between 1840 and 1860 the new statutory restrictions on abortion were challenged in nine state supreme courts, seven of which had upheld the common law tradition and ruled that an abortion before quickening was not a criminal offense.[55] Even after 1860 abortion cases were hard to prosecute: prosecutors found it difficult to obtain convictions, especially if there was any doubt about whether quickening of the fetus had occurred, or if common law traditions covering evidence and criminal defendants' rights appeared to have been violated by the prosecution or the police.[56] Juries continued to treat the prequickening distinction as significant, and of course it was difficult to prove that quickening had or had not occurred. . . .

From the 1860s through the 1880s, however, states passed a new wave of restrictive abortion legislation.[57] Hugh S. Pomeroy, a Boston physician opposed to reproductive control, compiled information in 1888 about state laws on the subject. He concluded that there was still considerable confusion over whether "destruction of the infant" before quickening was a common law offense, although he cited two states—Pennsylvania and North Carolina—which unambiguously declared it a misdemeanor, eight states—California, Connecticut, Indiana, New Hampshire, New York, Wisconsin, Wyoming, and the Dakota Territory—which made the abortion-seeking woman criminally liable, and five states—Kentucky, New Jersey, Oregon, South Carolina, Texas—and the District of Columbia which had not yet passed any law regulating abortion. Laws in eight states—California, Indiana, Kansas, Massachusetts, Michigan, Nebraska, New York, and Ohio—forbade the advertisement of abortion-inducing drugs, and Illinois, Indiana, and Michigan outlawed advertisements for medicines for women if the language was ambiguous, such as "caution to the married."[58] Loopholes in earlier laws were now gradually eliminated so that, for example, individuals charged with violating the law could no longer claim that the medicine would not have induced abortion.

The most general result of this welter of conflicting and confusing state statutes was to drive abortion underground, making it far more difficult, expensive, and dangerous to obtain—a criminalization that lasted until the 1960s, when sixteen states liberalized their laws, and until 1973, when the U.S. Supreme Court ruled in *Roe v. Wade* that a woman has a fundamental right to decide, without governmental interference, whether to have an abortion in the first three months. Even in the *Roe* decision, however, the Court upheld the right of the state to restrict abortion once fetal viability was determined, unless a woman's life was at stake.

In addition to the changing legal status of abortion, federal and state laws passed in the 1870s and 1880s made it a felony to mail any products or information about contraception or abortion. Between the 1860s and the 1880s activist opponents secured legislation that made contraceptive literature "obscene" and attempts to disseminate information about contraception felonies. In the closing days of its third session in March 1873, the fortysecond Congress, embattled and excoriated by the Credit Mobilier scandal (Union Pacific Railroad executives diverted funds into a separate company and bribed investigating congressmen and other politicians) passed what came to be called "the Comstock Law"—named for Anthony Comstock, a self-appointed vice hunter, a sponsor of the bill, and its zealous enforcer in the following decades. The stated purpose of the new law was to tighten loopholes in earlier legislation prohibiting the interstate trade in obscene literature and materials. But in one crucial departure from earlier laws, the long list of items prohibited from the mail, from private mail carriers, and from importation included "any article whatever for the prevention of conception, or for causing unlawful abortion." For the first time in U.S. history the federal government declared the dissemination of information about contraception and abortion to be illegal. State laws that followed went beyond the federal statute, punishing the receivers as well as the senders of information and in some cases making the actual practices of contraception and abortion illegal. Control of women's reproductive behavior now had the force of law. . . .

By 1885 twenty-four state legislatures had passed "little Comstock laws" modeled on the federal statute or on a more stringent New York obscenity law passed shortly after the federal statute. Because of the federal precedent, the existing obscenity laws of the other states had begun to be interpreted as prohibiting reproductive control itself.[59] Some state laws went considerably further than the federal law. Fourteen—Colorado, Indiana, Iowa, Massachusetts, Minnesota, Mississippi, Missouri, Montana, Nevada, New Jersey, New York, Pennsylvania, Washington, and Wyoming—sought to make even private conversations illegal by prohibiting the verbal transmission of information about contraception or abortion; eleven states—Colorado, Indiana, Iowa, Minnesota, Mississippi, New Jersey, New York, North Dakota, Ohio, Pennsylvania, and Wyoming—made it a criminal offense to possess instructions for the prevention of conception; the state of Colorado forbade anyone to bring contraceptive knowledge into the state; four states—Colorado, Idaho, Iowa, and Oklahoma—authorized the search for and seizure of contraceptive instructions. Connecticut—and only Connecticut—outlawed the act itself of controlling conception; this is why, in 1965, the Griswold case was brought in Connecticut: defense lawyers chose its law as the most extreme violation of women's sexual freedom.[60] . . .

The laws were upheld and even strengthened by court cases. In *U.S. v. Foote* in 1876 the court ruled that "a written slip of paper" giving prohibited information about contraception was a "notice" within the meaning of the law even if it had been sent in reply to a letter asking for information. In *U.S. v. Bott* in 1873 the defendant was found guilty of sending an advertisement even though the prohibited article was not at the designated place. In *Bates v. U.S.* in 1881 the defendant was guilty even though he had not actually deposited the pills in the mail himself and even though they "would not *alone* prevent conception or procure abortion."[61] Although in an 1892 case a Milwaukee judge chastized Comstock for his entrapment methods and in an 1897 case a judge ruled that a whole book and not just the passages deemed obscene had to be admitted as evidence, the Comstock laws were not mitigated by court decisions until the 1930s and were not overturned until a series of U.S. Supreme Court decisions in the 1960s and 1970s. . . .

The stronger antiabortion legislation of the second half of the nineteenth century was the result of a carefully orchestrated campaign organized and led by a few physicians in the nascent American Medical Association. Behind the obscenity laws were "social purity" reformers and their organizers. In the drives against both contraception and abortion, the determined will of zealous individuals gave focus and energy to large public crusades.

Notes

1. Alcott, *The Physiology of Marriage* (1866), p. 190.
2. Owen, *Moral Physiology* (1858), Appendix to 5th ed., p. 80.
3. Joan M. Jensen, *Loosening the Bonds: Mid-Atlantic Farm Women, 1750–1850* (New Haven: Yale University Press, 1986), p. 28, notes that historians are mystified by how withdrawal was learned and transmitted. She is incorrect, however, that this was the practice among the Oneida Perfectionists. Their method, "coitus reservatus," was different (requiring that a man never come to orgasm but gradually lose tumescence while inside a woman). For arguments that withdrawal was "close to being a self-evident method of contraception," see John T. Noonan, Jr., *Contraception: A History of Its Treatment by the Catholic Theologians and Canonists* (Cambridge: Harvard University Press, 1965), p. 10, while P. P. A. Biller, "Birth-Control in the West in the Thirteenth and Early Fourteenth Centuries," *Past and Present: A Journal of Historical Studies* 94 (1982): 5–7, argues that it was well understood in the medieval West from the twelfth century on. Orest Ranum and Patricia Ranum, eds., "Introduction," *Popular Attitudes toward Birth Control in Pre-Industrial France and England* (New York: Harper Torchbooks, Harper & Row, 1972), p. 6., argue that couples did not know withdrawal in the Middle Ages. M. K. Hopkins, "Contraception in the Roman Empire," *Comparative Studies in Society and History* 8 (1965–66): 124–51, argues that withdrawal needed to be learned.
4. Owen, *Moral Physiology* (1858), p. 78. Charles Knowlton, *Fruits of Philosophy* (Philadelphia, 1839), p. 8, made a similar comment about how easily people could think up withdrawal for themselves. Rebutting his critics who said that knowledge of "checks" would lead to illegitimate sex. Knowlton argued that if a couple had already become so "familiar" as to douche to prevent conception "they would practice the 'way' or drawback . . . [even] if no such book as this had ever been written."
5. Margaret Jarman Hagood, *Mothers of the South* (New York: Norton, c. 1939: rpt. ed. 1977), p. 123.
6. Owen, *Moral Physiology* (London, 1842), p. 38.
7. Quoted in Degler, *At Odds*, p. 211.
8. Studies of the effectiveness of individual birth control methods employ estimates of the number of pregnancies which would result if one hundred women used the method for one year. The base line is the estimate that with no birth control whatsoever eighty to ninety of the one hundred women would become pregnant in the first three to four months. In some contemporary studies, couples relying solely on withdrawal had only five to ten pregnancies per 100 woman years, while in others the failure rate was thirty-eight. Anna L. Southam, "Contraceptive Methods: Use, Safety, and Effectiveness," in *Family Planning and Population Programs: A Review of World Developments*, ed. Bernard Berelson (Chicago: University of Chicago Press, 1966).
9. See Robert W. Kistner, *Gynecology, Principles and Practice*, 2d ed. (Chicago: Year Book Medical Publishers, 1971), p. 676, and Christopher Tietze, "The Use-Effectiveness of Contraceptive Methods," in *Research in Family Planning*, ed. Clyde V. Kiser (Princeton: Princeton University Press, 1962), p. 362.
10. William Potts DeWees, *A Compendious System of Midwifery . . .* , 12th ed. (Philadelphia: Blanchard and Lea, 1853), p. 42. Nichols, *Esoteric Anthropology* (1853), pp. 171, 173, argued that pregnancy could result from semen left anywhere in the vagina; Soule, *Science of Reproduction and Reproductive Control* (1856), p. 64, noted that "withdrawal of the penis before emission" was a "sure prevention" as long as not even the smallest particle of semen got into the vagina.
11. Letter to the editor from "X.Y.Z.," [Philadelphia] *Medical and Surgical Reporter* 59 (1888): 600; W. R. D. Blackwood, letter to the editor, [Philadelphia] *Medical and Surgical Reporter* 59 (1888); 698; Thomas E. McArdle, "The Physical Evils Arising from the Prevention of Conception," *American Journal of Obstetrics and Diseases of Women and Children* 21 (1888): 934–37; S. G. Moses, "Marital Masturbation," [St. Louis] *Courier of Medicine* 8 (1882); 168–73.
12. Cooke, *Satan in Society* (1876), p. 146.
13. Letter to the editor from "X.Y.Z.": 600; Blount, *A Talk to Mothers*, no pagination.

14. Quoted in R. P. Neuman, "Working Class Birth Control in Wilhelmine Germany," *Comparative Studies in Society and History* 20 (1978): 419. Annie Besant, *The Law of Population: Its Consequences and Its Bearing Upon Human Conduct and Morals* (1878), p. 33, noted that although French doctors believed that withdrawal might be harmful to women, its universal practice in France attested otherwise.

15. Besant, *The Law of Population* (1878), p. 33.

16. [Glover], *Owen's Moral Physiology* (1846), p. 115.

17. Cooke, *Satan in Society* (1870), p. 146.

18. Bangs, "Some Effects of `Withdrawal,'" p. 119. Daniel Scott Smith, "Family Limitation, Sexual Control, and Domestic Feminism in Victorian America," in *Clio's Consciousness Raised: New Perspectives on the History of Women*, ed. Mary S. Hartman and Lois Banner (New York: Harper & Row, 1974), pp. 130–32.

19. References to coitus reservatus among twelfth- through fifteenth-century Catholic theologians are in Noonan, *Contraception*, pp. 296, 336–38, 447. The Oneida Community has been well studied. Maren Lockwood Carden, *Oneida: Utopian Community to Modern Corporation* (Baltimore: Johns Hopkins Press, 1969); Louis J. Kern, *An Ordered Love: Sex Roles and Sexuality in Victorian Utopias: The Shakers, the Mormons, and the Oneida Community* (Chapel Hill: University of North Carolina Press, 1981).

20. John Humphrey Noyes, *Male Continence* (1872), p. 10.

21. Noyes, *Male Continence*, p. 24.

22. John Humphrey Noyes, *The Bible Argument* (Oneida, N.Y.: The author, 1848). This had several editions but was out of print by 1872. Noyes reprinted all the essential points in the book except the chapter on male continence in his *Strange Cults and Utopias of Nineteenth Century America* (Philadelphia: J. B. Lippincott, 1870; rpt. ed., *History of American Socialisms*, New York: Dover, 1966).

23. See Sidney Ditzion, *Marriage, Morals, and Sex in America: A History of Ideas*, expanded ed. with a new chapter by the author (New York: W. W. Norton, 1953), p. 172.

24. See Foote, *Plain Home Talk* (1873), pp. 376–78, quoting Noyes, *Male Continence;* Alice Bunker Stockham, *Karezza: Ethics of Marriage* (1897), pp. 22–23, 120.

25. Kellogg, *Plain Facts for Old and Young*, chapter "Prevention of Conception."

26. Society Proceedings, *Journal of the Gynaecological Society of Boston* 4 (1871): 290.

27. Mary Sargeant Nichols [Mary Gove Nichols], *Mary Lyndon; or, Revelations of a Life: An Autobiography* (New York: Stringer and Townsend, 1855).

28. See Hebbel E. Hoff, "The Centenary of the First American Physiological Society Founded at Boston by William A. Alcott and Sylvester Graham," *Bulletin of the History of Medicine* 5 (1937): 687–734.

29. Mary S. Gove [Mary Gove Nichols], *Lectures to Women on Anatomy and Physiology with an Appendix on Water Cure* (New York: Harper, 1846). This is a reissue of an 1842 book with the appendix added.

30. See John B. Blake, "Mary G. Nichols, Prophetess of Health," *Proceedings* [of the American Philosophical Society] 106 (1962): 219–34.

31. Irving T. Richards, "Mary Gove Nichols and John Neal," *New England Quarterly* 7 (1934); 335–55. Blake, "Mary Gove Nichols," notes that she was denounced by some Quakers and by some newspapers that said that her lectures were obscene although Blake does not identify them.

32. No author, "Lectures to Ladies on Anatomy and Physiology," *Boston Medical and Surgical Journal* 26 (1842): 97–98. Grace Adams, *The Mad Forties* (New York: Harper, 1942), p. 20, cites Bennett's disapproval.

33. See Bertha-Monica Stearns, "Two Forgotten New England Reformers," *New England Quarterly* 6 (1933): 59–84. *The National Union Catalog of Pre-1956 Imprints* lists several of Nichols's novels from the 1840s: *The Lady in Black, Ellen Ramsay, Raffle for a Wife.*

34. Mary S. Gove Nichols, *Experience in Water-Cure* (New York: Fowlers & Wells, 1850), a twenty-five-cent pamphlet. There is information on their views in the short-lived *Nichols' Journal of Health, Water-Cure, and Human Progress* (1853–ca.1858).

35. Nichols, *Esoteric Anthropology* (1853), pp. 163–64, discusses female ovaries using the pronoun "we": "while zoosperms are formed by millions . . . we have but one or two, or in rare cases, three to five, ova perfected once a month."

36. Nichols, *Esoteric Anthropology* (1853), p. 151; page 192 noted that the "surgical" method of abortion was simplest and least dangerous.

37. Elizabeth Blackwell to Emily Blackwell, [August] 1853, in the Blackwell Family Papers, Library of Congress; Elizabeth Blackwell, *Pioneer Work* (1985), p. 162.

38. Hunt, *Glances and Glimpses*, pp. 139–140.

39. Quoted in Ann Douglas Wood, " 'The Fashionable Diseases': Women's Complaints and Their Treatment in Nineteenth-Century America," in *Women and Health in America*, ed. Leavitt, p. 231.

40. "Criminal Abortion," *Druggists Circular* 2 (1858): 139.

41. Van de Warker, "Abortion from Medication. Part II of The Detection of Criminal Abortion," *Journal of the Gynecological Society of Boston* 5 (1871): 229–45; pt. 1, vol. 4 (1871): 292–305; Van de Warker, "The Criminal Use of Proprietary or Advertised Nostrums," *New York Medical Journal* 17 (1873): 23–35.

42. Edward Shorter, *A Short History of Women's Bodies* (New York: Basic Books, 1982), pp. 184–88, discusses abortifacients.

43. Van de Warker, "The Criminal Use of Proprietary . . . Nostrums," p. 23.

44. See George W. Gay, "A Case of Criminal Abortion," *Boston Medical and Surgical Journal*, n.s. 9 (1872); 151–52; "The Causation of Sudden Death during the Induction of Criminal Abortion," *Journal of the Gynaecological Society of Boston* 2 (1870): 283–89; "Dr. Baxter," "Case of Abortion Procured by Violence," *American Medical Recorder* 8 (1825): 461–62.

45. Quoted in "The Liability of Physicians to a False Charge of Abortion," *Journal of the Gynaecological Society of Boston* 4 (1871): 348–49. See also L. Bolton Bangs, "Some of the Effects of 'Withdrawal'," *Transactions of the New York Academy of Medicine*, 2d ser. 9 (1893): 122.

46. *Day's Doings*, June 1870.

47. W. M. Smith, Letter to the editor, "The Prevalence of Abortion," *Medical and Surgical Reporter* 33 (1875): 259.

48. Elizabeth Blackwell to Emily Blackwell, 1851–56, Blackwell Family Papers; Ishbel Ross, *Child of Destiny* (New York: n.p., 1944), p. 87, attributes Blackwell's decision to become a doctor to her abhorrence of abortion.

49. James Dabney McCabe, *Lights and Shadows of New York Life* (Philadelphia: National Publishing Co., 1872; facsimile rpt., London: Deutsch, 1971), pp. 618–30, "Child Murder," discusses European-trained midwives operating lying-in institutes.

50. The sources differ on the details of Restell's life. Seymour Mandelbaum's entry on her in *Notable American Women* is the most authoritative to date. There is some information in [no author], *Wonderful Trial of Caroline Lohman, Alias Restell*, 3d ed. (New York: National Police Gazette [1847]), editorial. "Madame Restell and Some of Her Dupes," [New York] *Medical and Surgical Reporter* (1846), pp. 158–65, and James Dabney McCabe, *Lights and Shadows of New York Life* (London: Deutsch, 1971; facsimile of 1st ed., Philadelphia: National Publishing Co., 1872), pp. 618–30.

51. James C. Mohr, *Abortion in America: The Origins and Evolution of National Policy* (New York: Oxford University Press, 1978), p. 48. See also the article "Restell the Female Abortionist," *Police Gazette*, 21 February 1846.

52. Several studies see connections between the nineteenth-century opposition to abortion and contraception: Michael Grossberg, *Governing the Hearth: Law and the Family in NineteenthCentury America* (Chapel Hill: University of North Carolina Press, 1985), pp. 155–95; Linda Gordon, *Woman's Body, Woman's Right: A Social History of Birth Control in America* (New York: Grossman, 1976), chaps. 1, 3, 6; James Reed, *From Private Vice to Public Virtue: The Birth Control Movement and American Society since 1830* (New York: Basic Books, 1978), pp. 34–45. For extended analyses of one or the other oppositional impulse, see: James C. Mohr, *Abortion in America: The Origins and Evolution of National Policy, 1800–1900* (New York: Oxford University Press, 1978); John Paull Harper, " 'Be Fruitful and Multiply': The Reaction to Family Limitation in Nineteenth-Century America" (Ph.D. diss., Columbia University, 1975); David J. Pivar, *Purity Crusade, Sexual Morality, and Social Control, 1868–1900* (Westport, Conn.: Greenwood Press, 1973); Carroll Smith-Rosenberg, "The Abortion Movement and the AMA, 1850–1880," in her *Disorderly Conduct: Visions of Gender in Victorian America* (New York: A. Knopf, 1985).

53. The legal history of abortion is in Lawrence Lader, *Abortion* (New York: Bobbs-Merrill, 1966). Also Kristin Luker, *Abortion and the Politics of Motherhood* (Berkeley: University of California Press, 1984), p. 15.

54. See Harper, "'Be Fruitful and Multiply,'" chap. 2.

55. See Smith-Rosenberg, "The Abortion Movement," p. 219.

56. See Grossberg, *Governing the Hearth*, pp. 178–79.

57. Mohr, *Abortion in America*, identifies three phases to the antiabortion laws, the third, from the 1860s to the 1880s, the most stringent. Harper, "'Be Fruitful and Multiply,'" isolates the 1840s as the decade of hardening against abortion. Smith-Rosenberg, *Disorderly Conduct*, discusses the 1840s to 1880s as a single period.

58. See Hugh S. Pomeroy, *The Ethics of Marriage* (New York: Funk & Wagnalls, 1888), app.

59. See Mary Ware Dennett, *Birth Control Laws: Shall We Keep Them, Change Them, or Abolish Them?* (New York: Da Capo Press, 1970; Copyright 1926), pp. 10–15; C. Thomas Dienes, *Law, Politics, and Birth Control* (Urbana: University of Illinois Press, 1972), p. 40.

60. See Harriette M. Dilla, "Appendix No. 1," pp. 268–70, in Dennett, *Birth Control Laws*. Dennett, pp. 10–28, notes that in no other country was contraceptive information classified with "penalized indecency."

61. U.S. Code *Annotations*, 18, sec. 1461. Other cases summarized in this section include rulings that the public record does not have to record the exact language or titles of obscene works, that postmarks are presumptive proof of deposit in the U.S. mail, and that it is immaterial to show that obscene passages are common to other literature.

Chapter 12

The Exclusion of Chinese Women, 1870–1943

Sucheng Chan

Chinese immigration to the United States has commonly been viewed in terms of men's immigrant experience—with a focus on goldmining in the foothills of the Sierra Nevada mountains, construction of the transcontinental railroad, and building of flood control and irrigation systems in the West. Opposition to the economic competition of Chinese male laborers contributed to the passage of the Chinese Exclusion Act in 1882, but Sucheng Chan reminds us that Chinese women were also affected by exclusion. Between 1870 and 1940 the proportion of women and girls among Chinese immigrants in the United States grew from 7 to 30 percent. By virtue of their impact on female immigration and subsequent family formation, the "exclusion laws, judicial interpretations of them, and their administrative enforcement" became, in Sucheng Chan's words, "key factors in the social development of Chinese American communities after 1882."

One of the most noticeable characteristics of the Chinese population residing in the United States before World War II was a pronounced shortage of women. The United States censuses of population taken during the second half of the nineteenth century indicate that the number of Chinese females fluctuated between 3.6 percent (in 1890) and 7.2 percent (in 1870) of the total Chinese population. The percentage rose slowly during the twentieth century, but most of the increase was due to the birth of girls on American soil, not to immigration. In 1920, females comprised 12.6 percent of the U.S. Chinese population; by 1940, that figure stood at 30.0 percent. The history of other immigrant groups shows that a dearth of women in the first phase of their settlement in a new land is normal, so this shortage among the Chinese in the United States is a matter of degree rather than a difference in kind. Where the Chinese pattern deviates from the norm is that the imbalance in the sex ratio lasted for more than a century rather than for just a few decades.

Various explanations have been given for why so few Chinese women immigrated to the United States. Some scholars have claimed that because Chinese society was patriarchal, patrilineal, and patrilocal, the only acceptable roles for married women were bearing children and serving their husbands and parents-in-law. Given the central importance of filial piety in traditional Chinese culture, the moral duty of wives to remain in China to wait on their parents-in-law was greater than their obligation to accompany their husbands abroad. Consequently, only girls from poor families left their homes to earn a living elsewhere as prostitutes or as servants. These working women sent remittances home to help sustain their families and, by so doing, buttressed the very patriarchal order that relegated them to its lowest rung.[1]

Other writers have argued that since the majority of the Chinese who came to the United States were sojourners there was no reason to bring their wives with them. The main aim of sojourners

Chinese Prostitute in San Francisco, c. 1890. Photo by Arnold Genthe. Library of Congress.

being to earn money, it was cheaper to send savings home to sustain their families in China—where the cost of living was considerably lower—than to have them reside in America. Prostitutes were imported to take care of the sexual needs of the men.[2] A third reason offered is that restrictive immigration laws kept Chinese women out, but to date only one study has been published on the legal constraints on Chinese female immigration.[3]

There is no question that patriarchal cultural values, a sojourning mentality, differentials in the cost of living, and hazardous conditions in the American West—where thousands of Chinese men earned a living as migrant laborers and where intense anti-Chinese hostility existed during the latter half of the nineteenth century—all worked in tandem to limit the number of Chinese female immigrants during the early decades of the Chinese influx. But, as 1 shall argue, from the early 1870s onward, efforts by various levels of American government to restrict the immigration of Chinese women became the more significant factor. . . . I shall chronicle how different groups of Chinese women were denied entry. Contrary to the common belief that laborers were the target of the first exclusion act, the effort to bar another group of Chinese—prostitutes—preceded the prohibition against laborers. . . . To understand how state and national lawmakers, judges, local law-enforcement officers, and federal government officials fashioned an ever-tightening noose to constrict the volume of Chinese female immigration, it is necessary first to trace the history of persecution against Chinese women.

Hostility against Chinese women first surfaced in San Francisco. In August 1854, a municipal committee visited Chinatown and reported to the board of aldermen that most of the women found there were prostitutes.[4] This observation soon became a conviction, and it colored the public perception of, attitude toward, and action against all Chinese women for almost a century. During the gold rush and for several decades thereafter, prostitutes of many nationalities lived and worked in San Francisco. Municipal authorities tried sporadically to suppress prostitution and they singled out Chinese women for special attention from the beginning. Several months before the special committee's visit to Chinatown, the city fathers had passed Ordinance No. 546 "To Suppress Houses of Ill-Fame Within the City Limits.[5] But the effort to enforce it was desultory and racially selective: The police tried to close down mainly Mexican and Chinese brothels.[6] For the next dozen years, the city's police, board of health, and mayor all attempted to eradicate Chinese prostitution, but they managed only to reduce its visibility.

Discrimination against Chinese prostitutes was made explicit and statewide when the California legislature passed, on March 21, 1866, "An Act for the Suppression of Chinese Houses of Ill-Fame."[7] The statute . . . succeeded in confining Chinese prostitutes to limited geographic areas, [but] it did not end the traffic in Chinese women. The continuing arrival of the latter led the state legislature to pass "An Act to Prevent the Kidnapping and Importation of Mongolian, Chinese and Japanese Females, for Criminal or Demoralizing Purposes" on March 18, 1870, which made it illegal "to bring, or land from any ship, boat or vessel, into this State" any Asian women unless proof could be presented that they had come voluntarily and were "of correct habits and good character" . . . Another act passed in 1874 amended the 1866 statute, striking out the word "Chinese" in the first section, thereby making it applicable to alleged prostitutes of all national origins.[8]

Though the specific reference to the Chinese was removed in 1874, the law must have been enforced against them with enough rigor to cause them to challenge the rulings of the state commissioner of immigration in a test case that year. In late August, when the steamship *Japan* of the Pacific Mail Steamship Company brought eighty-nine Chinese women to San Francisco, the assistant state commissioner of immigration, E. B. Vreeland, acting on behalf of commissioner R. K. Pitrowski, boarded the vessel and questioned fifty to sixty of the women. He decided that twenty-two of them were coming for "immoral purposes." When the Pacific Mail Steamship Company refused to pay the $500 bond he demanded for each, he instructed Captain John H. Freeman to detain the twenty-two women on board.

Ah Lung, a Chinese in San Francisco who allegedly dealt in such women, immediately applied for writs of *habeas corpus* from the district court on behalf of the twenty-two women, on the grounds that they were being illegally deprived of their liberty. The case was heard by Judge Robert F. Morrison of the Fourth District Court, with all principals represented by counsel. Judge Leander Quint represented the Chinese, Cutler McAllister and T. I. Bergin appeared on behalf of the Pacific Mail Steamship Company, M. M. Estee and John H. Boalt represented the commissioner of immigration, and Thomas P. Ryan, the district attorney of San Francisco, represented the people. Quint argued that the women had a right to enter the country under the sixth article of the 1868 Burlingame Treaty between China and the United States. Bergin pointed out that there was no evidence that the women were lewd or debauched, the captain of the ship that brought them having testified that their behavior on board had been "as good as that of any of the other passengers." Estee, on the other hand, declared that the law under which the commissioner acted was constitutional, while Ryan stressed that the state had a right to protect itself and to exclude "pestilential immorality."[9]

During the trial, the Chinese women, contrary to expectations that they would be meek and mild, made it quite clear how they felt about their situation, even though they could not speak English. The reporter for the *Alta California* observed that Ah Fook, the petitioner, was very obstinate and saucy, and it was with a great deal of difficulty that she could be induced to answer the questions. She said she came here with good intentions, and wanted to know why so many questions were asked of her. At this point one of the women jumped to her feet and let out a most unearthly yell. Immediately the whole lot were jabbering and screaming at the top of their voices, and it was found impossible to quiet them until they were hustled from the Court-room.[10]

Later that day, when Chung Lee, a male passenger who had come on the same ship, identified those women whom he alleged were prostitutes,

> the women jumped to their feet and commenced yelling at the top of their voices. He [Chung Lee] said he was afraid that the women would attack him after he went out, but was reassured when Deputy Sheriff McNamara promised to protect him.[11]

Several missionaries, half a dozen Chinese merchants, and two Chinese male passengers gave contradictory opinions about whether it was possible to tell Chinese prostitutes apart from "moral" women by their looks and clothing. Meanwhile, Leander Quint, the counsel for the Chinese, pointed out that the women must first be *convicted* of prostitution (which they had not been) before they could be excluded from American territory. Despite the conflicting testimony and the important point that Quint made, Judge Morrison announced the following day to a packed courtroom that he thought, on balance, the evidence indicated that the women were indeed intended for immoral purposes and that the commissioner of immigration had acted legally. Accordingly, he remanded the women to the custody of Captain Freeman "to be returned to whence they came."[12]

Less than an hour before the *Japan* was scheduled to sail, however, Quint and the coroner of San Francisco, acting on behalf of the sheriff, boarded the vessel, served a writ of *habeas corpus* issued by Chief Justice William T. Wallace of the California State Supreme Court on Captain Freeman, and whisked the women away to the county jail.[13] Two weeks later, California Supreme Court Justice E. W. McKinstry upheld the decision of the lower court, after reviewing section 70 of the amendments to the Political Code, the 1868 Burlingame Treaty, and the fourteenth amendment. According to him, while the sixth article of the Burlingame Treaty allowed Chinese to enter the United States for instruction, curiosity, or a legitimate avocation, it could not prevent a state from keeping out criminals and paupers. As for the fourteenth amendment, he believed that so long as a person "is accorded every reasonable opportunity to defend his individual rights . . . a statute cannot be said to deprive a party of the benefits of due process of law."[14] One of his associates on the bench then compared the authority given the state commissioner of immigration to exclude the Chinese women to the power given a health officer, who could isolate

> those ill of contagious diseases, or those who have been in contact with such, or the power to prohibit the introduction of criminals or paupers. These powers are employed, not to punish for offenses committed without our borders, but to prevent the entrance of elements dangerous to the health and moral well-being of the community.[15]

In short, the court believed that allowing the alleged Chinese prostitutes to land would be akin to allowing persons with contagious diseases to enter; in both instances, the judges thought the state had a constitutional right to protect itself from danger.

The Chinese did not find this judgment acceptable and immediately applied for a third writ of *habeas corpus* to the U.S. Circuit Court, this time putting forward another woman, Ah Fong, as the petitioner. The circuit court that heard the case consisted of Justice Stephen J. Field (on circuit from the U.S. Supreme Court), Judge Ogden Hoffman of the U.S. District Court for the Northern District of California, and Judge Lorenzo Sawyer of the U. S. Circuit Court.

Justice Field reversed the decision of the California State Supreme Court and declared the 1870 California statute unconstitutional on three grounds. First, he thought that even though a state did have the right to exclude foreigners from its territory for reasons of self-defense, in his opinion the entry of some two dozen Chinese women hardly justified the extremes to which California had gone. Second, since the sixth article of the Burlingame Treaty guaranteed Chinese visitors and residents the same privileges, immunities, and exemptions with regard to travel or residence as those enjoyed by citizens or subjects of the most favored nation, Field believed no obstacles could be placed on the movement of any Chinese. Third, since the fourteenth amendment not only declared that no state may deprive a citizen of life, liberty, and property without due process of law, but also ensured that no *person* may be denied equal protection under the law, the efforts of the state commissioner of immigration to exclude the Chinese women in effect denied them the equal protection to which they were entitled. Equal protection, explained Field, meant not only equal access to the courts for the enforcement of rights and the redress of wrongs, but also equal exemption along with other members of the same class of persons from "all charges and burdens of every kind." He considered the $500 bond required by the California law an onerous charge.[16]

*   *   *

The victory won by the Chinese was a hollow one, however, for on March 3, 1875, Congress had already passed "An Act Supplementary to the Acts in Relation to Immigration"—commonly referred to as the Page Law after Congressman Horace F. Page of California—forbidding the entry of Chinese, Japanese, and "Mongolian" contract laborers, women for the purpose of prostitution, and felons. Those who violated this federal law could be jailed for as long as five years or fined a maximum of $2,000.[17] . . .

Historians have given different assessment of the effectiveness of the Page Law in limiting Chinese immigration. In her 1909 treatise, Coolidge claimed it did little good.[18] In his 1939 study, Sandmeyer alluded to its short-lived impact.[19] In her 1979 article, Cheng Hirata hedged that its effect was uncertain.[20] Finally, in a more recent study, Peffer, who analyzed the correspondence between three successive American consuls in Hong Kong and the US. State Department, argued that the law had a greater impact than has been hitherto assumed.[21]

There is some corroborating evidence that bolsters Peffer's contention that the Page Law was quite effective to restricting Chinese female immigration. The official in San Francisco charged with enforcing it—Giles H. Gray, surveyor of customs of the port of San Francisco—testified on May 27, 1876, before the Special Committee on Chinese Immigration of the California State Senate and offered the following details with regard to how the law was being implemented:

> When women come here, a letter is sent by the American Consul at Hongkong [*sic*], inclosing [*sic*] photographs of the women, and saying that he is satisfied that they do not come within the prohibited classes. . . . Before women are permitted to go on board ships, they must have photographs taken at their own expense, and must swear to a certain state of facts . . . [and] produce witnesses who must also swear to a similar state of affairs. If the Consul is satisfied that they are respectable women, tickets are sold them, and they come here. . . . Since last July there have arrived here not more

than two hundred and fifty women, but previous to that every steamer brought two hundred and fifty and upwards. . . . Very few prostitutes come now, the majority of the woman immigrants being family women. . . . I have no doubt but that the importation of women for lewd and immoral purposes has stopped. The adoption of the "certificate" system has had that effect. If the same rules and regulations were applied to the men, I think it would practically stop their coming also.[22] . . .

Tallies from the manuscript schedules of the 1870 and 1880 censuses of population corroborate the reduced numbers. In 1870 in San Francisco, there were 1,452 prostitutes out of a total Chinese female population of 2,022. Ten years later, there were only 444 prostitutes among 2,052 Chinese females. Statewide figures tell the same story: In California in 1870 there were 2,163 prostitutes and 405 probable prostitutes[23] out of a total Chinese female population of 3,797; in 1880, the figures were down to 786 and 268, respectively, out of 3,834 Chinese females.[24] . . .

Such evidence suggests that the Page Law in large measure did succeed in reducing the influx of Chinese women alleged to be prostitutes. The mechanisms for limiting their immigration were well in place before the first Chinese Exclusion Act was passed in 1882. The main impact of the exclusion laws, therefore, fell not on prostitutes but on other groups of Chinese women.

* * *

During the six decades(1882–1943) when the Chinese exclusion laws were in effect, the lower federal courts and the U.S. Supreme Court heard tens of thousands of cases related to the question of Chinese exclusion, in which Chinese appeared both as plaintiffs and as defendants. Of these more than a thousand were reported and published, and ninety-one of them involved Chinese women.[25] Over this span of time, the courts ruled on the status of six main categories of Chinese women: wives of laborers, wives of merchants, women claiming to be U.S.-born citizens, wives of U.S. citizens, daughters of U.S. citizens, and prostitutes.

* * *

Since the 1882 exclusion Law suspended the immigration of laborers, it is not surprising that the first case involving a Chinese woman heard in the lower federal courts and reported after 1882 concerned a woman who had married a Chinese laborer upon his return to China for a visit. Although no information is given about the husband in Judge Sawyer's opinion, delivered in the Circuit Court for the District of California on August 7, 1884, we can infer that he did possess the certificate stipulated under Section 4 of the 1882 act, obtainable from a collector of customs before a laborer's departure from the United States. Apparently on the basis of this document, the man was allowed to land, but his wife, Ah Quan, was not. Judge Sawyer declared that the wife of a laborer could not enter on the certificate issued to him alone In his view, a laborer's wife could land only if information about her had been entered into her husband's certificate or if she had an independent document of her own. Sawyer stated that the wife of a laborer, regardless of what occupation she herself might have followed before her marriage, acquired her husband's status upon marriage. Ah Quan's appeal was therefore denied and she was presumably returned to China.[26] . . . Other decisions also made it clear that no woman married to a Chinese laborer could come into the United States, unless she herself could prove prior residence here and she had obtained the same kind of certificate required of her husband. . . .

Like the wives of laborers, merchants' wives also had to go to court to clarify their right to enter the country. As it turned out, their status too was derivative: Since merchants were named as one of the "exempted classes" in each of the various exclusion laws, it followed that their wives were also "exempted." A question arose, nonetheless, with regard to what kind of documents merchants' wives must show upon arrival. The first reported case involving a merchant's wife in the federal courts was decided on May 23, 1890. Chung Toy Ho, the wife of Wong Ham, a well-known merchant in Portland, Oregon, returned with him to the United States after his visit to China. . . . Judge Matthew Deady of the Circuit Court for the District of Oregon, who heard the case, decided that "the petitioners are not within the purview of the exclusion act of 1888, which is confined to laborers," and that although they might conceivably be classed among the "Chinese persons other than laborers" specified in the act of 1884, he did not think they were the "persons" legislators were referring to when they wrote that act. He pointed out that Chinese women were not usually teachers, students, or merchants, so it was not possible for them to obtain "Section 6" certificates that allowed Chinese who were not laborers to be admitted. Moreover, the treaty of 1880 permitted Chinese merchants to bring their body and household servants with them, and if such persons could enter, surely the wives and minor children had an even greater right to do so. He therefore concluded that if merchants were entitled to come and dwell in the United States, so could their wives and children. . . .[27] The right of merchants' wives to enter without certificates was further affirmed in two cases involving Mrs. Gue Lim, whose husband was a domiciled merchant doing business in the state of Washington. . . . For the next quarter century, merchants' wives apparently had relatively little difficulty gaining admission into the country, since few court cases involving them were reported. . . .

Women of Chinese ancestry born in the United States (who by virtue of their birth were U.S. citizens) were the third group of women to receive judicial attention. Since the exclusion laws were not directed at American citizens of Chinese ancestry, they offered no clues on how such women were to be treated. Not surprisingly, judges interpreted the exclusion laws with regard to these women in an inconsistent manner. The opinions handed down in the earlier years tended to be more favorable than those rendered later.

The first reported case on American-born women of Chinese ancestry concerned Chin King, born in San Francisco in 1868, and her younger sister Chan San Hee, born in Portland in 1878. Their father, Chung Yip Gen, was a merchant who had done business in both cities. (Chin, Chan, and Chung are variant transliterations of the same last name.) In 1881, the two girls and their mother went to China for a visit; Chung told them they could "return when they pleased." But when Chin King and Chan San Hee sought readmission in 1888, the collector of customs at Portland refused them entry. (The reported opinion does not indicate the grounds on which the collector had based his decision.)

In considering their situation, Judge Matthew Deady, who heard the case in the Circuit Court for the District of Oregon, consulted several earlier rulings, including one involving the readmission of a male U.S. citizen of Chinese ancestry, *In re Look Tin Sing* (1884). In that instance, Justice Stephen J. Field had declared that "the inability of persons to become citizens under those laws [of naturalization] in no respect impairs the effect of their birth, or of the birth of their children, upon the status of either, as citizens of the United States."[28] As though to lend weight to his own desire to follow Justice Field's reasoning, Judge Deady noted that Judges Sawyer, Sabin, and Hoffman had all concurred in Field's opinion. Deady then proclaimed the collector's decision to deny Chin King and Chan San Hee entry "contrary to and in violation of the constitutional provision guarantying such right to every citizen" and ordered the two petitioners discharged from custody.[29] . . .

In later years and in other courts, Chinese women claiming American birth fared less well. It is difficult to estimate how many American female citizens of Chinese ancestry actually returned to

China and then sought readmission to the United States. Women allowed to enter without extensive questioning did not appear in the court records, so information is available mainly on those who were detained and denied landing. The latter were usually barred because of discrepancies found in the statements made by various witnesses during their hearings.[30]

Women married to American-born citizens of Chinese ancestry, the fourth group women to receive judicial notice, likewise were treated inconsistently. Some judges were quite favorably inclined toward them, while others were not at all sympathetic.[31] . . .

Many wives of American citizens were turned away. The two reasons immigration officials used most frequently to bar them were discrepancies in the testimonies given during their hearings and that medical examiners found some of them to be afflicted with "dangerous contagious diseases." To challenge this second reason, the lawyers hired by such Chinese women relied on Section 22 of the Act of February 5, 1917—the most comprehensive general immigration law passed by Congress to date. According to this law, the wife of a naturalized American citizen, if she married him after his naturalization, could enter the country without being detained for medical treatment even if she might have a "dangerous contagious disease." In a case that went all the way to the U.S. Supreme Court, Justice George Sutherland declared in 1923 that if the existing statute "unjustly discriminates against the native-born citizen, or is cruel and inhuman in its results, . . . the remedy lies with congress and not with the courts."[32]

*   *   *

A fifth group of females of Chinese ancestry that the courts dealt with were daughters born in China of Chinese American male citizens. According to Section 1993 of the U.S. Revised Statutes, the children of "native-born citizen fathers" (but not mothers) were considered derivative or statutory U.S. citizens. Chinese Americans discovered the utility of this provision in the early twentieth century. The first case involving the China-born son of an American citizen of Chinese ancestry appeared in the published court records in 1912.[33] As an increasing number of individuals claiming to be children of U.S. citizens sought admission into the United States, the tensions between the Bureau of Immigration and the Chinese themselves increased, because some of these children were so-called paper sons and paper daughters.

"Paper sons" were young men who bought documents from U.S. citizens of Chinese ancestry in an effort to enter the country as derivative citizens. As the exclusion laws were enforced in an increasingly stringent manner, one way the Chinese sought to replenish their numbers was for men who were U.S. citizens to return to China periodically to visit their families and to sire children. Upon their return to the United States, they would report the birth of such children. Some of the reports were true, while others were false. In any case, the reports created "slots" that the fathers could eventually sell to young men who were not their sons but who desperately wanted to come to the United States. By the 1920s, young men claiming to be the sons of U.S. citizens constituted the vast majority of the Chinese immigration cases published in the records of the federal courts.

*   *   *

Until research is done in all the unpublished records of the Bureau of Immigration, we shall not know how many Chinese women managed to get in as real or "paper" daughters before Congress rescinded the Chinese exclusion laws in 1943. What the reported court decisions show is that "paper daughters" were the main group of aspiring Chinese female immigrants to receive judicial review from the late 1920s through the early 1940s. During those years, the wives and daughters of merchants and female students were the only other categories of Chinese women to come into the country in numbers large enough to be counted.

*   *   *

Prostitutes (or, rather those alleged to be prostitutes) were the sixth kind of women the courts dealt with. Because of the widespread condemnation of prostitution in general, and of Chinese prostitution in particular, the Chinese women who gained entry into the country were still not safe: General immigration laws passed in 1903, 1907, and 1917, in particular, enabled immigration officials to launch a new campaign against Chinese prostitutes. Whereas the Page Law had been used to prevent alleged prostitutes from landing in the late nineteenth century, the new laws were used to deport them. Since the stereotypical view first formed in the 1850s that all Chinese women were prostitutes was still pervasive, it meant that no Chinese woman, regardless of her social standing, was safe from harassment.

In the late nineteenth century, immigration officials and judges who wished to deport prostitutes had to rely on the provisions of the Chinese exclusion laws: They got rid of women by classifying them as "manual laborers." The first reported case involving the deportation of a Chinese prostitute occurred in 1901. In April of that year, a commissioner arrested Lee Ah Ying for being a manual laborer without a certificate of registration and started deportation proceedings against her. The district court, where she took her case, affirmed the commissioner's ruling. Lee Ah Ying sued out a writ of *habeas corpus* and took her case in error to the Circuit Court of Appeals for the Ninth Circuit, where she argued she could not be deported because she had been born in the United States. According to the court, her testimony with regard to her American birth was "practically without contradiction." But unfortunately, she ran afoul of another fact—"she was, when arrested, with other girls in a house of ill fame, and . . . she stated to the officer making the arrest that she had been an inmate of the house for 'sometime.'"[34] The question before the court then became "whether a Chinese woman who is an inmate of a house of prostitution is a manual laborer." Circuit Judge Gilbert noted that his colleague, Circuit Judge Erskine M. Ross, had earlier ruled that Chinese gamblers and highbinders were laborers.[35] In Gilbert's view, prostitutes belonged to the same class of persons and thus could similarly be classified as manual laborers. He therefore upheld the lower court's opinion. Five months later in another case, Judge Thomas P. Hawley confirmed that Chinese prostitutes were indeed manual laborers deportable under the Chinese exclusion laws.[36]

*   *   *

While the courts were wrestling with the problem of how to deport prostitutes under the Chinese exclusion laws, Congress passed two general immigration laws in 1903 and 1907 designed to regulate the influx of a broad range of aliens. Prostitutes were listed among the various categories of persons with mental, physical, or social defects to be barred. . . . These general immigration laws provided a better basis for deporting Chinese prostitutes than did the Chinese exclusion laws, as immigration officials quickly realized. A reorganization of the Bureau of Immigration in 1903 also facilitated its efforts to step up the deportation of Chinese. Instead of relying on overworked collectors of customs to enforce the exclusion laws, officers of the bureau were now assigned to the task. The entire country was divided into districts, and a bureau officer vested with the authority to arrest "all unlawful Chinese residents" was put in charge of each district. The records of the collectors of customs were all transferred to Washington. D.C., for central processing.[37]

The first reported case in which the 1907 law was invoked involved Loue Shee, who had met and married Lew Chow, a Chinese laborer born in the United States, in Mexico City. When he returned to the United States, she accompanied him and was admitted. But he soon deserted her and she became a prostitute. In 1906 she was arrested by Immigration Commissioner Hart North in San Francisco and ordered deported. Her attorneys argued that North could not do so for three reasons. First, since past court decisions had ruled that a wife assumed her husband's status upon marriage, and since Lew Chow was an American citizen by birth, she had the right to stay. Second, since she had arrived in the United States before the 1907 act was passed, it did not apply to her. Third, even if the 1907 law applied to her, it could not be used against her because Section 43 of the law stated that "this Act shall not be construed to repeal, alter, or amend existing laws relating to the immigration or exclusion of Chinese persons or persons of Chinese descent."[38] Judge William M. Morrow of the Circuit Court of Appeals for the Ninth Circuit did not accept any of these arguments. He decided that the 1907 immigration law should be applied to "all aliens alike. To hold otherwise would be to favor the Chinese with respect to the admission of certain objectionable individuals." Therefore, despite having been admitted earlier as the wife of an American citizen, Loue Shee was now, by virtue of her profession, subject to deportation.[39]

*　*　*

The process by which Chinese women were excluded and deported from 1870 through 1943 shows that American public policy on this issue had moral, racial, and class dimensions. Until the mid 1870s, prostitutes among Chinese women were singled out for exclusion ostensibly for moral reasons. But within the expressions of morality there was hidden a racial—or, more accurately, racist—concern. Lawmakers and law-enforcement officers tried to keep out and control Chinese prostitutes not so much because they were prostitutes as such (since there were also many white prostitutes around plying their trade) but because—as Chinese—they allegedly brought in especially virulent strains of venereal diseases, introduced opium addiction, and enticed young white boys to a life of sin. In short, Chinese prostitutes were seen as potent instruments for the debasement of white manhood, health, morality, and family life. Thus, their continued presence was deemed a threat to white civilization. When the hostility against prostitutes became generalized, an exclusion campaign was launched against all Chinese women as an integral part of the larger anti-Chinese movement.

The exclusion laws further drew a fundamental distinction between laborers and merchants—that is, between working-class Chinese and the petite bourgeoisie—barring the former but keeping a crack open for the latter. Consequently, within the general racial antagonism there emerged differential degrees of discrimination according to class. There were several motives for treating the two classes of Chinese in such diametrically opposite ways. Quite apart from the fact that white workingmen had been among the most vociferous opponents of the Chinese presence—which made excluding Chinese laborers an expeditious means for politicians to win working-class votes—Americans simply found the higher-class Chinese more acceptable. Throughout the nineteenth century, newspaper reporters repeatedly praised the educated urbanity of Chinese merchants, often calling them gentlemen—in sharp contrast to the extremely derogatory manner in which they depicted Chinese laborers. Undergirding this class prejudice was the fact that one of the chief concerns of U.S. foreign policy during this period was expanding trade with China. Since Chinese merchants residing in the United States provided an important link in this trade, Congress made sure that they could continue to come in and that, once here, they were treated with a modicum of civility.

The solicitude toward merchants was especially apparent in the more favorable treatment accorded their wives. Even women who were themselves U.S. citizens or who were related to citizens did not fare as well as the wives and daughters of merchants at the hands of immigration officials and judges. The Justices of the U.S. Supreme Court felt compelled to defend the privilege enjoyed by merchants' wives because, they declared, to do so was a treaty obligation. What needs to be remembered, however, is that the treaties themselves were expressions of a strong class bias that favored members of the middle class and discriminated against the working class.

The exclusion laws, judicial interpretations of them, and their administrative enforcement, therefore, became key factors in the social development of Chinese American communities after

1882. By allowing merchants to have their wives with them, the laws made it possible for them to reproduce themselves biologically more readily than could other groups. That meant they could reproduce themselves socially as well, since the vast majority of the second-generation Chinese Americans were children of merchants who grew up in family settings with a petit bourgeois orientation. Thus, the Chinatowns that emerged during the early decades of the twentieth century were not so much the products of natural social forces as the distorted outgrowth of immigration and naturalization policies that discriminated against the Chinese as a people in general and against specific classes among them in particular.

The manner in which Chinese immigrant women were treated was part and parcel of this pattern of racial exclusion and externally imposed class differentiation within the Chinese American community. That being the case, a full understanding of Chinese American women's history can only be reached by examining how law and politics—institutions within the public sphere—interacted with the process of family formation, child rearing, and socialization in gender roles in the private sphere. The extraordinary impact that public policy had on the lives of Chinese women in America may well be one of the main differences between their historical experience and those of other groups of immigrant women.

Notes

1. Lucie Cheng Hirata, "Free, Indentured, Enslaved: Chinese Prostitutes in Nineteenth-Century America", *Signs* 5 (1979): 3–29.
2. Stanford M. Lyman, "Marriage and the Family among Chinese Immigrants to America, 1850–1960," *Phylon 24* (1968): 321–30, and *Chinese Americans* (New York: Random House, 1974), 86–105.
3. George Anthony Peffer, "Forbidden Families: Emigration Experiences of Chinese Women under the Page Law, 1875–1882," *Journal of American Ethnic History* 6 (1986): 28–46.
4. *Alta California*, August 22, 1854.
5. *Ordinances and Joint Resolutions of the City of San Francisco* (San Francisco: Mason and Valentine, Book and Job Printers, 1854).
6. Frank H. Soule et al., *The Annals of San Francisco and History of California* (1855; repr. Palo Alto, Calif.: Lewis Osborne, 1966), 550, as cited in Brenda E. Pillors, "The Criminalization of Prostitution in the United States: The Case of San Francisco, 1854–1919" (Ph.D. diss., University of California, Berkeley, 1982), 96.
7. Statutes of California (1865–1866), 81–82.
8. Statutes of California (1873–1874), 84.
9. *Alta California*, August 26 and 27, 1874.
10. Ibid., August 28, 1874.
11. Ibid.
12. Ibid., August 29 and 30, 1874.
13. Ibid., August 30, 1874.
14. *Ex parte Ah Fook*, 49 California Reports 402, at 406 (1874).
15. Ibid., at 406–7.
16. *In re Ah Fong*, I Federal Cases 213 (C.C.D.Cal. 1874)(No. 102).
17. Act of March 3, 1875, 18 United States Statutes at Large 477.
18. Mary Roberts Coolidge, *Chinese Immigration* (New York: Henry Holt, 1909), 419.
19. Elmer C. Sandmeyer, *The Anti-Chinese Movement in California* (1939; repr. Urbana: University of Illinois Press, 1973), 13.
20. Cheng Hirata, "Free, Indentured, Enslaved," 10.
21. George Anthony Peffer, *If They Don't Bring Their Women Here: Chinese Female Immigration Before Exclusion* (Urbana: University of Illinois Press, 1999).

22. California State Legislature, "Chinese Immigration: Its Social, Moral, and Political Effect," *Report to the California State Senate of Its Special Committee on Chinese Immigration* (Sacramento, Calif.: F. P. Thompson, Superintendent of State Printing, 1878), 154.

23. Women between the ages of fifteen and forty-five with no listed occupations or who were shown to be "keeping house" and living in all-female households—the vast majority of whom was single—were coded as "probable prostitutes" in my analysis of data from the manuscript schedules of the censuses of population.

24. My tallies from the manuscript schedules of the 1870 and 1880 censuses of population for California.

25. This count is based on my reading of the thousand-plus cases.

26. *In re Ah Quan,* 21 Federal Reporter 182 (C.C.D.Cal. 1884).

27. *In re Chung Toy Ho and Wong Choy Sin,* 42 Federal Reporter 398 (D.Ore. 1890).

28. *In re Look Tin Sing,* 21 Federal Reporter 905 (C.C.D.Cal. 1884).

29. *Ex parte Chin King. Ex parte Chan San Hee,* 35 Federal Reporter 354 (C.C.D.Ore. 1888).

30. *In re Ho: Quai Sin,* 84 Federal Reporter 310 (N.D.Cal. 1898); *Lee Sing Far v. United States,* 94 Federal Reporter 834 (9th Cir. 1899); *Woey Ho v. United States,* 109 Federal Reporter 888 (9th Cir. 1901); and *Yee N'goy v. United States,* 116 Federal Reporter 332 (9th Cir. 1902).

31. *Tsoi Sim v. United States,* 116 Federal Reporter 920 (9th Cir. 1902); *In re Tang Tun et ux. In re Gang Gong. In re Can Pon,* 161 Federal Reporter 618 (W. D. Wash. 1908); *Mah Shee v. White,* 242 Federal Reporter 868 (9th Cir. 1917); and *Halsey v. Ho Ah Keau,* 295 Federal Reporter 636 (9th Cir. 1924).

32. *Chung Fook v. White,* 264 United States Reports 443, at 446 (1924).

33. *United States v. Hom Young,* 198 Federal Reporter 577 (S.D.N.Y. 1912).

34. *Lee Ah Ying v. United States,* 116 Federal Reporter 614 (9th Cir. 1902), at 615.

35. *United States v. Ah Fawn,* 57 Federal Reporter 591 (S.D.Cal. 1893).

36. *Wang Ah Quie v. United States,* 118 Federal Reporter 1020 (9th Cir. 1902).

37. *Annual Report of the Commissioner of Immigration to the Secretary of Commerce and Labor for the Fiscal Year Ended June 30, 1904* (Washington, D.C.: Government Printing Office, 1905), 137 and 140.

38. Act of February 20, 1907, 34 United States Statutes at Large 898, at 911.

39. *Loue Shee v. North, 170* Federal Reporter 566 (9th Cir. 1909).

Chapter 13

Separatism as Strategy: Female Institution Building and American Feminism, 1870–1930

Estelle Freedman

For a variety of reasons, partly because of their exclusion from male organizations and partly because of cultural beliefs that emphasized differences between women and men, women's political culture flourished in separate institutions. Estelle Freedman analyzes some of the causes and effects of that separation. Accounting for much of the power of women's political culture before 1920, women's institutions declined thereafter, leading to an overall decline in women's social and cultural power. Not until women's institutions were again reconstructed on the new material basis of women's greatly expanded labor force participation in the 1960s, 1970s, and 1980s did women regain the political power they collectively wielded before 1920.

SCHOLARSHIP AND STRATEGIES

The feminist scholarship of the past decade has often been concerned, either explicitly or implicitly, with two central political questions: the search for the origins of women's oppression and the formulation of effective strategies for combating patriarchy. Analysis of the former question helps us to answer the latter; or as anthropologist Gayle Rubin has wryly explained:

> If innate male aggression and dominance are at the root of female oppression, then the feminist program would logically require either the extermination of the offending sex, or else a eugenics project to modify its character. If sexism is a by-product of capitalism's relentless appetite for profit, then sexism would wither away in the advent of a successful socialist revolution. If the world historical defeat of women occurred at the hands of an armed patriarchal revolt, then it is time for Amazon guerrillas to start training in the Adirondacks.[1]

Another anthropologist, Michelle Zimbalist Rosaldo, provided an influential exploration of the origins-strategy questions in her 1974 theoretical overview of women's status.[2] Rosaldo argued that "universal sexual assymmetry" (the lower value placed on women's tasks and roles in all cultures) has been determined largely by the sexually defined split between domestic and public spheres. To oversimplify her thesis: the greater the social distance between women in the home and men in the public sphere, the greater the devaluation of women. The implications for feminist

This article is reprinted from *FEMINIST STUDIES*, Volume 5, Number 3 (Fall 1979): 512–29, by permission of the publisher FEMINIST STUDIES, Inc., c/o Women's Studies Program, University of Maryland, College Park, MD 20742.

Woman suffrage demonstration. Library of Congress.

strategy become clear at the end of Rosaldo's essay in which she says that greater overlap between domestic and public spheres means higher status for women. Thus to achieve an egalitarian future, with less separation of female and male, we should strive not only for the entrance of women into the male-dominated public sphere, but also for men's entry into the female-dominated domestic world.

Rosaldo also discusses an alternative strategy for overcoming sexual asymmetry, namely, the creation of a separate women's public sphere; but she dismisses this model in favor of integrating domestic and public spheres. Nonetheless, the alternative strategy of "women's societies and African queens" deserves further attention.[3] Where female political leaders have power over their own jurisdiction (women), they also gain leverage in tribal policy. Such a separate sexual political hierarchy would presumably offer women more status and power than the extreme male-public/female-domestic split, but it would not require the entrance of each sex into the sphere dominated by the other sex. At certain historical periods, the creation of a public female sphere might be the only viable political strategy for women.

I would like to argue through historical analysis for the alternative strategy of creating a strong, public female sphere. A number of feminist historians have recently explored the value of the separate, though not necessarily public, female sphere for enriching women's historical experience. Carroll Smith-Rosenberg's research[4] has shown how close personal relationships enhanced the private lives of women in the nineteenth century. At the same time, private "sisterhoods," Nancy Cott has suggested, may have been a precondition for the emergence of feminist consciousness.[5] In the late nineteenth and early twentieth centuries, intimate friendships provided support systems for politically active women, as demonstrated by the work of both Blanche Cook and Nancy Sahli.[6] However, the women's culture of the past—personal networks, rituals, and relationships—did not automatically constitute a political strategy. As loving and supportive as women's networks may have been, they could keep women content with a status which was inferior to that of men.

I do not accept the argument that female networks and feminist politics were incompatible. Rather, in the following synthesis of recent scholarship in American women's history, I want to show how the women's movement in the late nineteenth and early twentieth centuries provides an example of the "women's societies and African queens" strategy that Rosaldo mentioned. The creation of a separate, public female sphere helped mobilize women and gained political leverage in the larger society. A separatist political strategy, which I refer to as "female institution building," emerged from the middle-class women's culture of the nineteenth century. Its history suggests that in our own time, as well, women's culture can be integral to feminist politics.[7]

WHAT HAPPENED TO FEMINISM?

My desire to restore historical consciousness about female separatism has both a personal and an intellectual motivation. As a feminist working within male-dominated academic institutions, I have realized that I could not survive without access to the feminist culture and politics that flourish outside of mixed institutions. How, I have wondered, could women in the past work for change within a men's world without having this alternative culture? This thought led me to the more academic questions. Perhaps they could not survive when those supports were not available; and perhaps this insight can help explain one of the most intriguing questions in American women's history: What happened to feminism after the suffrage victory in 1920?

Most explanations of the decline of women's political strength focus on either inherent weaknesses in suffragist ideology or on external pressures from a pervasively sexist society.[8] But when I survey the women's movement before suffrage passed, I am struck by the hypothesis that a major strength of American feminism prior to 1920 was the separate female community that helped sustain women's participation in both social reform and political activism. Although the women's movement of the late nineteenth century contributed to the transformation of women's social roles, it did not reject a separate, unique female identity. Most feminists did not adopt the radical demands for equal status with men that originated at the Seneca Falls Convention of 1848. Rather, they preferred to retain membership in a separate female sphere, one which they did not believe to be inferior to men's sphere and one in which women could be free to create their own forms of personal, social, and political relationships. The achievements of feminism at the turn of the century came less through gaining access to the male domains of politics and the professions than in the tangible form of building separate female institutions.

The self-consciously female community began to disintegrate in the 1920s just as "new women" were attempting to assimilate into male-dominated institutions. At work, in social life, and in politics, I will argue, middle-class women hoped to become equals by adopting men's values and integrating into their institutions. A younger generation of women learned to smoke, drink, and value heterosexual relationships over female friendships in their personal lives. At the same time, women's political activity epitomized the process of rejecting women's culture in favor of men's promises of equality. The gradual decline of female separatism in social and political life precluded the emergence of a strong women's political bloc which might have protected and expanded the gains made by the earlier women's movement. Thus the erosion of women's culture may help account for the decline of public feminism in the decades after 1920. Without a constituency a movement cannot survive. The old feminist leaders lost their following when a new generation opted for assimilation in the naive hope of becoming men's equals overnight.

To explore this hypothesis, I shall illustrate episodes of cultural and political separatism within American feminism in three periods: its historical roots prior to 1870; the institution building of the late nineteenth century; and the aftermath of suffrage in the 1920s.

HISTORICAL ROOTS OF SEPARATISM

In nineteenth-century America, commercial and industrial growth intensified the sexual division of labor, encouraging the separation of men's and women's spheres. While white males entered the public world of wage labor, business, the professions and politics, most white middle-class women remained at home where they provided the domestic, maternal, and spiritual care for their families and the nation. These women underwent intensive socialization into their roles as "true women." Combined with the restrictions on women which denied them access to the public sphere, this training gave American women an identity quite separate from men's. Women shared unique life experiences as daughters, wives, childbearers, childrearers, and moral guardians. They passed on their values and traditions to their female kin. They created what Smith-Rosenberg has called "The Female World of Love and Ritual," a world of homosocial networks that helped these women transcend the alienation of domestic life.[9]

The ideology of "true womanhood" was so deeply ingrained and so useful for preserving social stability in a time of flux that those few women who explicitly rejected its inequalities could find little support for their views. The feminists of the early women's rights movement were certainly justified in their grievances and demands for equal opportunity with men. The Seneca Falls Declaration of Sentiments of 1848, which called for access to education, property ownership, and political rights, has inspired many feminists since then, while the ridicule and denial of these demands have inspired our rage. But the equal rights arguments of the 1850s were apparently too radical for their own times.[10] Men would not accept women's entry into the public sphere, but more importantly, most women were not interested in rejecting their deeply rooted female identities. Both men and women feared the demise of the female sphere and the valuable functions it performed. The feminists, however, still hoped to reduce the limitations on women within their own sphere, as well as to gain the right of choice—of autonomy—for those women who opted for public rather than private roles.

Radical feminists such as Elizabeth Cady Stanton and Susan B. Anthony recognized the importance of maintaining the virtues of the female world while eliminating discrimination against women in public. As their political analysis developed at mid-century, they drew upon the concepts of female moral superiority and sisterhood, and they affirmed the separate nature of woman. At the same time, their disillusionment with even the more enlightened men of the times reinforced the belief that women had to create their own movement to achieve independence. The bitterness that resulted when most male abolitionists refused to support women's rights in the 1860s, and when they failed to include Woman Suffrage in the Fifteenth Amendment (as well as the inclusion of the term "male citizen" in the Fourteenth Amendment) alienated many women reformers. When Frederick Douglass proclaimed in defense that "This is the Negro's Hour," the more radical women's rights advocates followed Stanton and Anthony in withdrawing from the reform coalition and creating a separatist organization. Their National Woman Suffrage Association had women members and officers; supported a broad range of reforms, including changes in marriage and divorce laws; and published the short-lived journal, *The Revolution*. The radical path proved difficult, however, and the National Woman Suffrage Association merged in 1890 with the more moderate American Woman Suffrage Association.

FEMALE INSTITUTION BUILDING

The "transition period" that Stanton and Anthony invoked lasted from the 1870s to the 1920s. It was an era of separate female organization and institution building, the result on the one hand, of the negative push of discrimination in the public, male sphere, and on the other hand, of the positive attraction of the female world of close, personal relationships and domestic institutional structures. These dual origins characterized, for instance, one of the largest manifestations of "social feminism" in the late nineteenth century—the women's club movement.

The club movement illustrated the politicization of women's institutions as well as the limitations of their politics. The exclusion of women reporters from the New York Press Club in 1868 inspired the founding of the first women's club, Sorosis. The movement then blossomed in dozens and later hundreds of localities, until a General Federation of Women's Clubs formed in 1890. By 1910, it claimed over one million members. Although club social and literacy activities at first appealed to traditional women who simply wanted to gather with friends and neighbors, by the turn of the century women's clubs had launched civic reform programs. Their activities served to politicize traditional women by forcing them to define themselves as citizens, not simply as wives and mothers. The clubs reflected the societal racism of the time, however, and the black women who founded the National Association of Colored Women in 1896 turned their attention to the social and legal problems that confronted both black women and men.[11]

The Woman's Christian Temperance Union had roots in the social feminist tradition of separate institution building. As Ellen DuBois has argued, the WCTU appealed to late nineteenth-century women because it was grounded in the private sphere—the home—and attempted to correct the private abuses against women, namely, intemperance and the sexual double standard.[12] Significantly, though, the WCTU, under Frances Willard's leadership, became a strong prosuffrage organization, committed to righting all wrongs against women, through any means, including the vote.

The women's colleges that opened in these same decades further attest to the importance of separate female institutions during this "transition period." Originally conceived as training grounds of piety, purity, and domesticity, the antebellum women's seminaries, such as Mary Lyon's Mt. Holyoke and Emma Willard's Troy Female Academy, laid the groundwork for the new collegiate institutions of the postwar era. When elite male institutions refused to educate women, the sister colleges of the East, like their counterparts elsewhere, took on the task themselves. . . . At the same time, liberal arts and science training provided tools for women's further development, and by their examples, female teachers inspired students to use their skills creatively. As Barbara Welter noted when she first described the "Cult of True Woman-hood,"[13] submissiveness was always its weakest link. Like other women's institutions, the colleges could help subvert that element of the Cult by encouraging independence in their students.

The most famous example of the impact of women's colleges may be Jane Addams's description of her experience at Rockford Seminary where she and other students were imbued with the mission of bringing their female values to bear on the entire society. While Addams later questioned the usefulness of her intellectual training in meeting the challenges of the real world, other women did build upon academic foundations when increasingly, as reformers, teachers, doctors, social workers, and in other capacities they left the home to enter public or quasi-public work. Between 1890 and 1920, the number of professional degrees granted to women increased 226 percent, at three times the rate of increase for men. Some of these professionals had attended separate female institutions such as the women's medical colleges in Philadelphia, New York, and Boston. The new female professionals often served women and children clients, in part because of the discrimination against their encroachment on men's domains, but also because they sincerely wanted to work with the traditional objects of their concern. As their skills and roles expanded, these women would demand the right to choose for themselves where and with whom they could work. This first generation of educated professional women became supporters of the suffrage movement in the early twentieth century, calling for full citizenship for women.

The process of redefining womanhood by the extension, rather than by the rejection, of the female sphere may be best illustrated by the settlement house movement. Although both men and women resided in and supported these quasi-public institutions, the high proportion of female participants and leaders (approximately three-fifths of the total), as well as the domestic structure and emphasis on service to women and children, qualify the settlements as female institutions. . . . Thus did Jane Addams learn the techniques of the political world through her efforts to keep the neighborhood clean. So too did Florence Kelley of Hull House welcome appointment as chief factory inspector of Illinois, to protect women and children workers; and Julia Lathrop, another Hull House resident, entered the public sphere as director of the United States Children's Bureau; while one-time settlement resident Katherine Bement Davis moved from the superintendency of the Bedford Hills reformatory for women to become in 1914 the first female commissioner of corrections in New York City. Each of these women, and other settlement workers who moved on to professional and public office, eventually joined and often led branches of the National American Woman Suffrage Association.[14] They drew upon the networks of personal friends and professional allies that grew within separate female institutions when they waged their campaigns for social reform and for suffrage.

Separate female organizations were not limited to middle-class women. Recent histories have shown that groups hoping to bridge class lines between women existed within working-class or radical movements. In both the Women's Trade Union League and the National Consumers League, middle-class reformers strived for cooperation, rather than condescension, in their relationships with working women. Although in neither organization were they entirely successful, the Women's Trade Union League did provide valuable services in organizing women workers, many of whom were significant in its leadership. The efforts of the Consumers League, led by Florence Kelly, to improve working conditions through the use of middle-class women's buying power was probably less effective, but efforts to enact protective legislation for women workers did succeed. Members of both organizations turned to suffrage as one solution to the problems workers faced. Meanwhile, both in leftist organizations and in unions, women formed separate female organizations. Feminists within the Socialist Party met in women's groups in the early twentieth century, while within the clothing trades, women workers formed separate local unions which survived until the mid-1920s.[15]

As a final example of female institution building, I want to compare two actual buildings—the Woman's Pavillion at the 1876 Centennial Exposition in Philadelphia, analyzed recently by Judith Paine, and the Woman's Building at the 1893 World Columbian Exposition in Chicago. I think that the origins and functions of each illustrate some of the changes that occurred in the women's movement in the time interval between those two celebrations.

Originally, the managers of the 1876 Centennial had promised "a sphere for woman's action and space for her work" within the main display areas. In return women raised over $100,000 for the fair, at which point the management informed the Women's Centennial Executive Committee that there would not be any space for them in the main building. The women's response surprised the men: they raised money for a separate building, and although they hoped to find a woman architect to design it, there was no such professional at the time. From May through October, 1876, the Woman's Pavillion displayed achievements in journalism, medicine, science, art, literature, invention, teaching, business, and social work. It included a library of books by women; an office that published a newspaper for women; and an innovative kindergarten annex, the first such day school in the country. Some radical feminists, however, boycotted the building. Elizabeth Cady Stanton claimed that the pavillion "was no true exhibit of woman's art" because it did not represent the product of industrial labor or protest the inequalities of "political slavery."[16]

By 1893, there was less hesitation about the need for a woman's building and somewhat less conflict about its functions. Congress authorized the creation of a Board of Lady Managers for the

Columbian Commission, and the women quickly decided on a separate Woman's Building, to be designed by a woman architect chosen by nationwide competition. Contests were also held to locate the best women sculptors, painters, and other artists to complete the designs of the building. The Lady Managers also planned and provided a Children's Building that offered nursery care for over ten thousand young visitors to the fair. At this exposition, not only were women's artistic and professional achievements heralded, but industrial organizations were "especially invited to make themselves known," and women's industrial work, as well as the conditions and wages for which they worked, were displayed. Feminists found this exhibit more agreeable; Antoinette Brown Blackwell, Julia Ward Howe, and Susan B. Anthony all attended, and Anthony read a paper written by Elizabeth Cady Stanton at one of the women's symposia. The Board of Lady Managers fought long and hard to combine their separate enterprise with participation in the rest of the fair. They demanded equal representation of women judges for the exhibitions and equal consideration of women's enterprises in all contests.[17] While they had to compromise on some goals, their efforts are noteworthy as an indication of a dual commitment to separate female institutions, but only if they had equal status within the society at large.

THE POLITICAL LEGACY

The separate institution building of the late nineteenth century rested on a belief in women's unique identity which had roots in the private female sphere of the early nineteenth century. Increasingly, however, as its participants entered a public female world, they adopted the more radical stance of feminists such as Stanton and Anthony who had long called for an end to political discrimination against women.

The generation that achieved suffrage, then, stood on the border of two worlds, each of which contributed to its ideology and politics. Suffragists argued that women needed the vote to perform their traditional tasks—to protect themselves as mothers and to exert their moral force on society. Yet they also argued for full citizenship and waged a successful, female-controlled political campaign to achieve it.

The suffrage movement succeeded by appealing to a broad constituency—mothers, workers, professions, reformers—with the vision of the common concerns of womanhood. The movement failed, however, by not extending fully the political strengths of woman bonding. For one thing, the leadership allowed some members to exploit popular racist and nativist sentiments in their prosuffrage arguments, thus excluding most black and immigrant women from a potential feminist coalition. They also failed to recognize that the bonds that held the constituency together were not "natural," but social and political. The belief that women would automatically use the vote to the advantage of their sex overlooked both the class and racial lines that separated women. It underestimated the need for continued political organization so that their interests might be united and realized.

Unfortunately, the rhetoric of equality that became popular among men and women (with the exception of the National Woman's Party) just after the passage of the Suffrage Amendment in 1920 subverted the women's movement by denying the need for continued feminist organization. Of course, external factors significantly affected the movement's future, including the new Freudian views of women; the growth of a consumer economy that increasingly exploited women's sexuality; and the repression of radicalism and reform in general after World War I.[18] But at the same time, many women, seemingly oblivious that these pressures necessitated further separate organizing, insisted on striving for integration into a male world—sexually, professionally, and politically.

Examples of this integrationist approach can be found in the universities, the workplace, and politics. In contrast to an earlier generation, the women who participated in the New York World's

Fair of 1937 had no separate building. Woman, the Fair Bulletin explained, "will not sit upon a pedestal, not be segregated, isolated; she will fit into the life of the Exposition as she does into life itself—never apart, always a part." The part in this World's Fair, however, consisted primarily of fashion, food, and vanity fair.[19] In the universities, the success of the first generation of female academics did not survive past the 1920s, not only because of men's resistance, but, as Rosalind Rosenberg has explained, "Success isolated women from their culture of origin and placed them in an alien and often hostile community." Many academics who cut off their ties to other women "lost their old feminine supports but had no other supports to replace them."[20]

The lessons of women's politics in the 1920s are illustrated by the life of one woman, Emily Newell Blair, who learned first hand the pitfalls of rejecting a separatist basis for feminism.[21] Blair's life exemplified the transformation of women's roles at the turn of the century. Educated at a woman's college, Goucher, this Missouri-born, middle-class woman returned to her hometown to help support her family until she married and created her own home. Between 1900 and 1910 she bore two children, supported her husband's career, and joined in local women's club activities. In her spare time, Blair began writing short stories for ladies' magazines. Because she found the work, and particularly the income, satisfying, she became a free-lance writer. At this point, the suffrage movement revived in Missouri, and Blair took over state publicity, editing the magazine *Missouri Woman* and doing public relations. Then, in World War I, she expanded her professional activities further by serving on the Women's Council of the U.S. Council of National Defense. These years of training in writing, feminist organizing, and public speaking served Blair well when suffrage passed and she entered politics.

In 1920, women faced three major political choices: they could become a separate feminist political force through the National Woman's Party, which few did; they could follow the moderates of the NAWSA into the newly formed, nonpartisan League of Women Voters, concentrating on citizen education and good government; or they could join the mainstream political parties. Emily Newell Blair chose the last, and rose through the Democratic Party organization to become national vice-chairman of the party in the 1920s.

Blair built her political life and her following on the belief that the vote had made women the political equals of men. Thus, the surest path to furthering women's goals was through participation in the party structure. Having helped to found the League of Women Voters, Blair then rejected nonpartisanship, while she urged women not to vote as women but as citizens. In a 1922 lecture on "What Women May Do with the Ballot," Blair argued that "reactions to political issues are not decided by sex but by intellect and emotion. . . ." Although she believed that lack of political experience and social training made women differ from men temporarily, she expected those differences to be eliminated after a few years of political activity. To hasten women's integration into the mainstream of party politics, Blair set up thirty "schools of democracy" to train the new voters during the early twenties, as well as over one thousand women's clubs. Her philosophy, she claimed, was one of "Boring from Within." Blair rejected the "sex conscious feminists" of the Woman's Party and those who wanted "woman cohesiveness." Although she favored the election of women, she wanted them to be chosen not as women but as politicians. "Give women time," she often repeated, and they would become the equals of men in politics.

By the late 1920s, however, women had not gained acceptance as men's political equals, and Blair's views changed significantly. Once she had claimed that the parties did not discriminate against women, as shown by her own powerful position. After she retired from party office in 1928, however, Blair acknowledged that the treatment of women by the parties had deteriorated since the years immediately after suffrage passed. As soon as male politicians realized that there was no strong female voting bloc or political organization, they refused to appoint or elect powerful women, and a "strong masculine prejudice against women in politics" surfaced. Now they chose women for party office who seemed easiest to manage or who were the wives of male officeholders.

By 1931, Blair's former optimism had turned to disillusionment. She felt herself "ineffective in politics as a feminist," a term that she began to use positively. Blair realized that women could not command political power and the respect of their male colleagues unless, like the suffrage leaders, they had a visible, vocal following. "Unfortunately for feminism," she confessed, "it was agreed to drop the sex line in politics. And it was dropped by the women." In the pages of the *Woman's Journal*, Blair called for a revival of feminism in the form of a new politics that would seek to put more women into office. Reversing her former stance, she claimed that *women* voters should back *women* candidates, and use a *women's* organization to do so. They could remain in the parties, but should form "a new organization of feminists devoted to the task of getting women into politics."

The development of Emily Newell Blair's feminist consciousness may have been unique for her time, but it is a familiar process among educated and professional women today. Having gained access to formerly male institutions, but still committed to furthering women's struggles, today's "new women" are faced with political choices not dissimilar to the generation that achieved suffrage. The bitterness of Stanton and Anthony in their advice to the younger generation in 1881, and the strategy that Emily Newell Blair presented in 1931, may serve as lessons for the present.

THE LESSONS OF SEPARATISM

The strength of female institutions in the late nineteenth century and the weaknesses of women's politics after the passage of the Suffrage Amendment suggest to me that the decline of feminism in the 1920s can be attributed in part to the devaluation of women's culture in general and of separate female institutions in particular. When women tried to assimilate into male-dominated institutions, without securing feminist social, economic, or political bases, they lost the momentum and the networks which had made the suffrage movement possible. Women gave up many of the strengths of the female sphere without gaining equally from the man's world they entered.

This historical record has important implications for the women's movement today. It becomes clearer, I think, why the separate, small women's group, organized either for consciousness raising or political study and action, has been effective in building a grass-roots movement over the past ten years. The groups helped to reestablish common bonds long veiled by the retreat from women's institutions into privatized families or sexually integrated, but male-dominated, institutions. The groups encouraged the reemergence of female networks and a new women's culture which in turn have given rise to female institution building. . . .

The history of separatism also helps explain why the politics of lesbian feminism have been so important in the revival of the women's movement. Lesbian feminism, by affirming the primacy of women's relationships with each other and by providing an alternative feminist culture, forced many nonlesbians to reevaluate their relationships with men, male institutions, and male values. In the process, feminists have put to rest the myth of female dependence on men and rediscovered the significance of woman bonding. . . .[22]

I find two kinds of political lessons in the history of the separatist trend. In the past, one of the limitations of separate female institutions was that they were often the only places for women to pursue professional or political activities, while men's institutions retained the power over most of the society. Today it is crucial to press for feminist presence both outside and within the bastions of male dominance, such as politics, the universities, the professions, and the unions. But it is equally important for the women within mixed institutions to create female interest groups and support systems. Otherwise, token women may be coopted into either traditionally deferential roles, or they will assimilate through identification with the powers that be. In the process, these women will lose touch with their feminist values and constituencies, as well as suffer the personal costs of tokenism. . . .

I argue for a continuation of separatism not because the values, culture, and politics of the two sexes are biologically, irreversibly distinct, but rather because the historical and contemporary experiences that have created a unique female culture remain both salient for and compatible with the goal of sexual equality. Our common identities and heritage as women can provide enormous personal and political strength as long as we claim the power to define what women can be and what female institutions can achieve. I argue for renewed female institution building at this point in the contemporary women's movement because I fear that many feminists—faced with the isolation of personal success or dismayed by political backlash—may turn away from the separate women's politics that have achieved most of our gains in the past decade. And I argue as well for both greater respect for women's culture among political feminists and greater political engagement on the part of cultural feminists because we now face both external resistance and internal contradictions that threaten to divide our movement.

Notes

1. Gayle Rubin, "The Traffic in Women: Notes on the 'Political Economy' of Sex," in *Toward an Anthropology of Women,* ed. Rayna R. Reiter (New York and London: Monthly Review Press, 1975), pp. 157–58.
2. Michelle Zimbalist Rosaldo, "Woman, Culture, and Society: A Theoretical Overview," in *Woman, Culture and Society,* eds. Michelle Zimbalist Rosaldo and Louise Lamphere (Stanford, Calif.: Stanford University Press, 1974), pp. 17–42.
3. *Ibid.,* pp. 37–38. Rosaldo lists women's trading societies, church clubs, "or even political organizations" and cites both the Iroquois and West African societies in which "women have created fully articulated social hierarchies of their own."
4. Carroll Smith-Rosenberg, "The Female World of Love and Ritual: Relationships between Women in Nineteenth-Century America," *Signs* 1, no. 1 (Autumn 1975): 1–29.
5. Nancy F. Cott, *The Bonds of Womanhood: "Women's Sphere" in New England, 1780–1835* (New Haven: Yale University Press, 1977).
6. Blanche Wiesen Cook, "Female Support Networks and Political Activism: Lillian Wald, Crystal Eastman, Emma Goldman," *Chrysalis,* no. 3 (1977): 43–61; and Nancy Sahli, "Smashing: Women's Relationships Before the Fall," *Chrysalis,* no. 8 (Summer 1979): 17–27.
7. Feminist historians need clear definitions of women's culture and women's politics to avoid such divisions between the personal and political. Women's culture can exist at both private and public levels. Women's politics, too, can be personal (intrafamilial, through friendship and love, for example) as well as public (the traditional definition of politics). The question of when women's culture and politics are *feminist* has yet to be fully explored. At this time, I would suggest that any female-dominated activity that places a positive value on women's social contributions, provides personal support, and is not controlled by antifeminist leadership has feminist political potential.
8. These theories are surveyed in Estelle B. Freedman, "The New Woman: Changing Views of Women in the 1920s," *Journal of American History* 61 (September 1974): 372–93.
9. Smith-Rosenberg, "The Female World of Love and Ritual."
10. See Ellen DuBois, "The Radicalism of the Woman Suffrage Movement: Notes Toward the Reconstruction of Nineteenth-Century Feminism," *Feminist Studies* 3 (Fall 1975): 63–71. On opposition to women's rights from a "traditional" woman, see Kathryn Kish Sklar, *Catharine Beecher: A Study in American Domesticity* (New Haven: Yale University Press), pp. 266–67.
11. William O'Neill, ed., *The Woman Movement: Feminism in the United States and England* (Chicago: Quadrangle Books, 1969), pp. 47–54; and Gerda Lerner, ed., *Black Women in White America* (New York: Vintage, 1972), chap. 8.

12. DuBois, "Radicalism," p. 69.

13. Barbara Welter, "The Cult of True Womanhood, 1820–1860," *American Quarterly* 18 (Summer 1966): 150–74.

14. For biographical data on these and other reformers, see the entries in *Notable American Women, 1607–1950,* eds. Edward T. James, Janet Wilson James, and Paul S. Boyer (Cambridge, Mass.: Harvard University Press, 1971).

15. On women in labor and radical movements, see: Nancy Schrom Dye, "Feminism or Unionism? The New York Women's Trade Union League and the Labor Movement," and Robin Miller Jacoby, "The Women's Trade Union League and American Feminism," in *Feminist Studies* 3, no. 1–2 (Fall 1975): 111–40; Allis Rosenberg Wolfe, "Women, Consumerism, and the National Consumers League in the Progressive Era, 1900–1923," *Labor History* 16 (Summer 1975): 378–92; Mary Jo Buhle, "Women and the Socialist Party, 1901–1914," *Radical America* 4, no. 2 (February 1970): 36–55. . . .

16. Judith Paine, "The Women's Pavillion of 1876," *Feminist Art Journal* 4, no. 4 (Winter 1975–76): 5–12; and *The Woman's Building, Chicago, 1893/The Woman's Building, Los Angeles, 1973* (Los Angeles, 1975).

17. Bertha Honoré Palmer, "The Growth of the Woman's Building," in *Art and Handicraft in the Woman's Building of the World's Columbian Exposition,* ed. Maud Howe Elliott (New York, 1893), pp. 11–12.

18. See Ryan, *Womanhood in America,* for an exploration of these trends.

19. The New York World's Fair Bulletin 1, no. 8 (December 1937): 20–21; the *New York City World's Fair Information Manual,* 1939, index. Amy Swerdlow kindly shared these references and quotations about the 1937 fair from her own research on women in the World's Fairs.

20. Rosalind Rosenberg, "The Academic Prism: The New View of American Women," in *Woman of America: A History,* eds. Carol Ruth Berkin and Mary Beth Norton (Boston: Houghton Mifflin, 1979), pp. 318–38.

21. The following account of Blair is drawn from research for a biographical essay that appeared in *The Dictionary of American Biography* suppl., vol. 5 (New York: Charles Scribner, 1977), pp. 61–63. For examples of her writings, see "What Women May Do with the Ballot" (Philadelphia, 1922); "Boring from Within," *Women Citizen* 12 (July 1927): 49–50; "Why I am Discouraged About Women in Politics," *Woman's Journal* 6 (January 1931): 20–22.

22. Radicalesbians, "The Woman-Identified Woman," *Notes from the Third Year: Women's Liberation* (reprinted in *Radical Feminism,* ed. Anne Koedt, Ellen Levine and Anita Rapone [New York: Quadrangle, 1973] pp. 240–45); Lucia Valeska, "The Future of Female Separatism," *Quest* 2, no. 2 (Fall 1975): 2–16; Charlotte Bunch, "Learning from Lesbian Separatism," in *Lavender Culture,* eds. Karla Jay and Allen Young (New York: Jove Books, 1978), pp. 433–44.

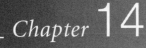

Race and Womanhood: The Woman's Christian Temperance Union and African-American Women in North Carolina, 1880–1900

Glenda Elizabeth Gilmore

Scholars have outlined the radical implications of the Woman's Christian Temperance Union's "Do Everything" policy; in the following article Glenda Gilmore examines the impact of that policy among African Americans in North Carolina. Although organized in segregated locals, the WCTU nonetheless provided an opportunity for middle-class African American women to advance their communities' goals. At a time when race relations were at their nadir, the WCTU promoted interracial cooperation and placed the resources of a national organization behind the efforts of local black unions. However, the legal exclusion of black voters at the end of the 1890s brought an end to these interracial efforts and cut one of the few lines of communication that had linked black and white women reformers.

The Woman's Christian Temperance Union joined women of both races who sought to impose new values on southern life. Drawing heavily from the ranks of Methodists and Baptists, the WCTU at last gave evangelical women an outlet to act on the ideals their mothers had embraced during the Second Great Awakening of the 1830s and 1840s. At that time, the southern slave system had worked against social reform, although some manifestations of new sensibilities had appeared in North Carolina. Interracial temperance societies sprang up across the state in the 1830s, temperance groups held mixed male/female meetings, and Wesleyan and Quaker ministers traveled across the state preaching abolition at the risk of losing their lives.[1] After the war, the WCTU tapped those evangelical values.

The roots of the organized African American temperance movement in the state went back to Reconstruction, when several black temperance clubs joined the Independent Order of Good Templars (IOGT), an international organization for both men and women. Headquartered in Great Britain, the IOGT already had active white chapters in North Carolina. When the newly formed black chapters petitioned the state organization for official recognition, however, the white members refused to grant them a charter and would not even divulge the secret Templar password. Stung by

Frances E. W. Harper

Sarah Early, The New York
Public Library

Lucy Thurman, National
Association of Colored
Women's Clubs

Early Superintendents of the Colored Department, Woman's Christian Temperance Union; Schomburg
Center for Research in Black Culture; National Association of Colored Women's Clubs

this exclusion, the black Templars forged ahead and formed lasting ties with other white and black chapters throughout the world.[2] Black men and women joined the Templars in great numbers; the Raleigh chapter boasted 200 members.[3] In 1873, Sarah Dudley Pettey's father, Edward, presided over the statewide organization, and her mother, Caroline, joined the New Bern chapter.[4] The African American Templars recruited women as full members, elected them to office, and applauded their speeches at meetings. At a black IOGT meeting in Fayetteville in 1875, the keynote speaker recognized "the power of the females, and their duty in exercising it" within the organization.[5] Black women gained experience and self-confidence through their work in the Templars, and men came to admire their forcefulness and courage. When Sarah McLaurin gave a rousing speech to the Cape Fear lodge on New Year's Day in 1888, a male listener reported that "she addressed the house with as much bravery as did some of our modern heroes."[6]

While black men and women worked together as Templars, the monumental statewide prohibition referendum of 1881 set the stage for the WCTU's entry into the state.[7] In the midst of the 1881 prohibition campaign, Frances Willard visited Wilmington to mobilize women and encourage them to join the WCTU.[8] Willard worried about how southern white women would receive a northern woman, but her nervousness did not prevent her from advocating temperance work among African Americans. To Willard's surprise, southern white women embraced her suggestion with enthusiasm.[9] She observed: "Everywhere the Southern white people desired me to speak to the colored."[10] Willard was not the only white woman reaching out to black women; for example, when a "ladies' prohibition club" met at the Methodist church in Concord, the white women reported that "the galleries of the church were set apart for our colored friends."[11] Black men's votes and black women's political influence mattered in the temperance election.

Statewide prohibition failed in North Carolina in 1881, and many whites blamed blacks, despite the nearly unanimous endorsement of prohibition by the black press. Reports from across the state declared that African Americans had voted overwhelmingly in favor of whiskey, probably because many blacks kept small shops in which liquor sold briskly.[12] White prohibitionists, mostly Democrats, charged that liquor interests bought black votes to tip the election.[13] After 1881, temperance strategy centered on local-option elections, and the WCTU attempted to win prohibition town by town, county by county.[14] To that end, the white women began to organize and support black WCTU chapters throughout the state that reported to the white statewide officers.

The Woman's Christian Temperance Union mattered so much to southern black women reformers of the late nineteenth century because it promoted a working model of finer womanhood that meshed with their own ideals.[15] The union joined black women's religious and class values to their activism, even as it provided a safe forum for agitation. Black women welcomed its legitimation of a public role for women, a role they knew would be necessary for racial uplift. Through the telescope of the WCTU, southern African Americans could gaze upward past vacuous white southern belles to solid white women such as Frances Willard, WCTU national president. For example, a black man who cited Sarah Dudley Pettey as an example of "womanly womanhood," capable of galvanizing mixed male and female audiences with her suffrage speeches, seized upon this comparison: "Mrs. Dudley Pettey is a brilliant Frances E. Willard."[16]

For black women and a growing number of educated white women from poor families, class identity was a lesson to be learned and one they bore a responsibility to teach, and the WCTU facilitated that task. Black women reformers tried to impose upon uneducated women and men sobriety, thrift, purity, and a love for learning; if a woman embraced those values, they embraced her, regardless of the trappings of her life or her origins. . . . Teaching and learning "finer womanhood" became a strategy black women deployed to counter white supremacy.

On the other hand, many southern white women initially found the WCTU's public duties a challenge to their sense of propriety. The WCTU asked its members to step beyond the pale of southern white ladyhood. It encouraged them not only to visit jails but to break bread with the prisoners, black and white; to spend Thanksgiving at the county poor farm with its biracial conglomeration of demented alcoholics, lice-ridden wayward girls, and toothless, tobacco-spitting old women; to throw up a beribboned gauntlet at that most raucous of masculine preserves, the polling place, buttonhole voters who tried to elbow past, and glare at them while they voted.[17] Once white women overcame their fears, WCTU work probably changed their lives a great deal more than they changed the lives of the recipients of their beneficence. One reflected on her lunch with two white and six black men in the Winston-Salem jail: "The power of the Holy Spirit rested upon all. . . . It was a melting time."[18]

In the 1880s and 1890s, the North Carolina WCTU undertook a novel experiment in interracial contact. Black women hoped to find common ground with white women in the WCTU to construct a cooperative venture joined by class and gender ties, one capable of withstanding the winds of white supremacist rhetoric. For several years in the 1880s, women worked as members of separate black and white chapters within a single statewide structure, the first postbellum statewide biracial voluntary organization in North Carolina.[19] Under the heat of temperance fever, racial boundaries softened ever so slightly.

Historians have argued that the WCTU's chief attraction for women was its critique of the drunken father and husband and that its activism sprang from belief in "feminine moral superiority."[20] White female temperance activists linked drinking with male profligacy, domestic physical abuse, and women's economic dependence. They drew on the doctrine of separate spheres to confer on women moral authority in family matters, even if the exercise of that power necessitated a temporary foray into the public sphere. Thus, among whites, temperance became increasingly a woman's issue, an expression of "female consciousness."[21] Black women's participation in the WCTU, however, meant something more than "home protection." Although domestic issues certainly mattered to southern African American women, participation in the WCTU also folded into the cause of racial uplift.[22]

To counteract whites' blindness to the realities of middle-class black life, African American women used the WCTU to point up black dignity, industriousness, and good citizenship. Since many whites predicted that the absence of the "civilizing" influence of slavery would result in the extinction of African Americans, occasions of black drunkenness generated self-satisfied notice among whites. When white southern tobacco farmers came to town to tie one on, no one suggested that their drinking sprees foretold the racial degeneracy of the Anglo-Saxon "race."[23] But a drunken black man staggering home from a saloon might inspire an "I-told-you-so" editorial in the local white newspaper replete with Darwinistic predictions of the extinction of the black race in a single generation.[24] Thus, black women temperance activists worried not just about the pernicious effects of alcohol on the family but also about the progress of the entire race, and temperance activities bolstered African Americans' contested claims to full membership in the polity.

Moreover, black women saw in the WCTU a chance to build a Christian community that could serve as a model of interracial cooperation on other fronts. If, through white women's recognition of common womanhood and shared class goals, black women could forge a structure that encouraged racial interaction, they might later build on that structure. The WCTU represented a place where women might see past skin color to recognize each other's humanity. One source of black women's optimism sprang from Frances Willard's family background. As a child, her abolitionist parents opened their home as a stop on the Underground Railway, and her father was a Free-Soiler. Willard had the confidence of Frederick Douglass and William Lloyd Garrison, both members of an older generation of abolitionists.[25]

White women, however, envisioned interracial cooperation as a partnership in which the women they referred to as "our sisters in black" were junior partners, participating in a segregated structure that reported to white women. They believed the power relations of a biracial WCTU should mirror the racial hierarchy of society at large. Nonetheless, founding a biracial organization, even one separated internally, required courage and a vision of the future that differed from the white male perspective. By organizing black WCTU chapters, white women recognized gender and class as binding forces that mitigated racial differences.

In the late nineteenth century, African Americans and whites used the term "interracial cooperation" to signify working across racial lines to solve common problems. Black women undertook interracial cooperation without illusions of sisterhood because they believed racial progress depended on it as long as whites controlled southern institutions. Nothing about the term implied a common commitment to civil rights, to racial equality, to working together cheerfully, or even to working together with civility. There was never a point in the two decades of interracial cooperation within the WCTU when white women could not be characterized according to today's standards as "racist." Yet such a characterization reveals little about actual practice and obscures a more important truth: racism is never a static phenomenon. It waxes and wanes in response to a larger social context, sometimes perniciously defining the contours of daily life, sometimes receding as behavior and speech challenge the boundaries of racial constructs.[26]

It was black political power that convinced white women to work with African American women, whose support they needed in local-option campaigns. In 1883, Frances Willard returned to North Carolina, where she spoke again to black audiences, including one at Livingstone College, and brought the existing WCTU chapters into a statewide organization.[27] Within the state structure, "Work amongst the Colored People" became one of six departments, and all black chapters were subordinated to the white female department head.[28] Despite the separate chapters and the reporting structure, the biracial WCTU was a dramatic departure from the past. For a brief period, black and white women in the WCTU circumvented the racial conventions of their time.

Most of the white women who volunteered to organize black WCTU chapters were already involved in interracial educational or religious work. Rosa Steele, the wife of Wilbur Steele, the white president of Bennett College, an institution for African Americans, headed the statewide "Work amongst the Colored People" department. Steele bridged two worlds, and she had already earned a reputation among blacks as a "zealous" woman.[29] . . .

White women like Steele saw temperance work among African Americans as missionary labor, uplifting for the white women as well as the black women. Clearly Steele used the WCTU to promote her own agenda: "uplifting" the black race under white direction. The fact that black women continued to work for temperance without the supervision of white women worried her. "They have many workers of their own and many teachers doing this temperance work among them," Steele noted, but she added that white women must take the lead by supervising chapters. She advised white women to attend "each meeting to keep the organization on its proper line of work."[30] Although her belief in the superiority of white leadership indicated the distance she perceived between herself and blacks, Steele's racial attitudes represented those of the most liberal white women in the South. Southern white communities generally ostracized white women who promoted black education, but the WCTU accepted and used their talents in order to achieve its goals.[31]

African American women drew upon their long experience in temperance, and they chafed at the patronizing missionary approach of whites. . . . The black women were understandably resentful, and the gap between them loomed large. To make matters worse, most white women approached black women only during local-option elections neglecting the work the rest of the time. Steele admonished white women not to view African Americans opportunistically or to cultivate them just for political purposes. Temperance would succeed only if whites showed a "real live interest in the colored man, not born of a disire [*sic*] to win his vote at election time," she argued.[32]

In many cities and towns, however, no white women came forward to head the "Work amongst the Colored People," and black women organized their own WCTU chapters. The experience of Mary Lynch and the Charlotte chapter illustrates how African American women came to the temperance cause and built their own statewide organization. A student at Scotia Seminary in Concord during the prohibition campaign of 1881 Lynch was caught up in the fever of the biracial ladies' temperance meetings and influenced by her teachers' participation in the WCTU.[33] Upon graduation, she moved to Charlotte to teach in the graded school, where she joined a sixty-member black WCTU chapter that formed in 1886.[34] That year, the Charlotte chapter sent delegates to the state convention who addressed the assembled white women.[35]

Once a town had black and white chapters, WCTU women occasionally launched joint ventures in community welfare that proved the WCTU cooperative potential. For example, in the final months of 1886, white and black women united to build a hospital for African Americans in Charlotte. . . . Despite everyone's good intentions, funds ran out quickly, and both chapters struggled to support the hospital.[36] Ultimately, the cooperative hospital failed, and a separate group of white women, with funding from the Northern Episcopal Church, opened a larger facility for blacks under white women's management.[37]

In 1888, after five years of appealing to white women to organize black temperance chapters, Rosa Steele tried a new tactic that produced extraordinary results: she invited Sarah Jane Woodson Early, the African American superintendent of "Colored Work for the South" for the national WCTU, to North Carolina. Early spent five weeks in the state.[38] She entered the local prohibition battles raging in Raleigh and Concord and encouraged African American women to join the campaign.[3] . . . Early's African American audiences financed her trip, and by the time she left the state, fourteen black WCTU chapters stood on solid ground.[40]

The next year, building on Early's organizing campaign, African American WCTU leaders seceded from the state organization. Ultimately, black women found the racial hierarchy embedded in the WCTU structure contradictory on its face. If all WCTU members were temperance women, they must be equally worthy, sisters in the family of God. Because their temperance work involved multiple goals, African American women refused to trade equality for interaction. With secession, they rejected their status as a subordinate department under white direction. The black women made this clear when they named their organization the WCTU No. 2 and announced, "We cautiously avoided using the word colored . . . for we believe all men equal."[41] The white "Colored Work" committee women reported to their organization that the African Americans "desire to attain their full development and think this can best be done in an independent organization . . . with the department work under their own control." The new African American WCTU reported directly to the national WCTU and achieved organizational status equal to the white group, holding separate statewide conventions in 1890 and 1891.[42]

As North Carolina's black women organized the WCTU No. 2, black women across the South replicated their experience. Prior to the organization of the National Association of Colored Women's Clubs in 1896, the WCTU represented the principal interdenominational voluntary association among black women. Black WCTU organizations flourished in the North and the West, and black women in five southern states managed statewide unions. Southern African American women traveled to national and international temperance conferences, published newspapers, and learned skills of self-presentation that they took back to their churches and women's clubs.[43]

Throughout the 1890s in North Carolina, the WCTU No. 2 continued under the direction of African American women. In 1891, when Mary Lynch became a professor at Livingstone College, she found the campus branch of the Young Woman's Christian Temperance Union (YWCTU) languishing. Lynch immediately revitalized it and invited Anna Julia Haywood Cooper to speak to the group.[44] From her post at Livingstone, Lynch threw herself into temperance work; within five years, she formed connections with the nation's leading African American women and became president of the WCTU No. 2. . . . [Lynch's student Annie] Kimball brought both racial and female consciousness to temperance work. She argued eloquently that where whites found black degeneracy, she found hope. On a May day in 1894, Annie Kimball graduated as salutatorian of her class, gave the commencement address in Latin, and, that afternoon, married an AME Zion minister, George Clinton, whom Charles Pettey had taught thirty years earlier. . . . The Clintons made their home in Charlotte, where she became state president of the YWCTU.[45]

After Annie Kimball Clinton moved to Charlotte, she joined a statewide network of African American women who had been active in the cause for over a decade. She could have attended any of several small WCTU group meetings in the city each week. In a single week in September 1897, one group met at the Congregational church, another at the Seventh Street Presbyterian Church, and the chapter at the Grace AME Zion Church kicked off its annual oratorical contest.[46] A "bicycle entertainment" raised almost $100 for "caring for the sick and needy and burying the dead."[47] To coordinate the separate groups, the citywide officers of the union met every Monday afternoon at a private home. . . .

When the WCTU No. 2 seceded, the white organization initially realized they should replace their outreach to African Americans with cooperation with the African American chapters. They appointed a committee to work with the black leaders, whom they called "genuine W.C.T.U. women."[48] But after a year, the whites again formed a committee on "Colored Work" that haltingly described its mission as "continu[ing] to work to assist in completing the work of organizing" African Americans. Two years later, the white superintendent entitled her report, "Home and Foreign Missionary Work among and through Afro-Americans." Did the switch to "Afro-Americans" indicate increased sensitivity, or was it a marketing ploy white organizers used to compete with the WCTU No. 2? Had "among and through" resulted from some sort of committee fight over whether to recognize black leaders by working "through" them? Whatever promise the new name held, "through" and "Afro-American" soon disappeared, and the white women returned to their work "amongst" the "colored people."[49]

White women knew about black women's activities, but apparently they refused to recognize black women's authority and competed with them to organize new African American WCTU chapters under local white control.[50] White women cryptically reported in 1895 that the "'sisters in black' have an Independent Union in Charlotte, well officered and doing good work."[51] The new white state superintendent noted, "Naturally we look for co-operation among the colored women under auspices of Unions controlled by them and this gives us an open door of helpfulness in many ways."[52] Black women must have resented white women who sought "cooperation" while assuming they knew best. The white women's efforts found some success among African American youth, in schools or prisons, all captive audiences, but only rarely did they form an organization of adult black women under white control after secession.[53]

Why did white women continue to try to establish black chapters even as they acknowledged the autonomy of the WCTU No. 2? There are at least two reasons. Except for a few leaders like Rosa Steele, most white women knew very little about, and discounted the abilities of, educated black women. Hence, they presumed that a black union would do better work under white leadership. Most importantly, however, the white women wanted very much to control the politics of the black temperance workers. They were not altogether sure that African Americans, because of their political allegiance to the Republican Party, could be trusted to vote for prohibition. Moreover, they believed that blacks proved easy prey for corrupt politicians and sinister forces. For example, after the formation of the WCTU No. 2, a white temperance worker announced an imminent Catholic peril among African Americans. . . . White women reasoned that, left on their own, black women might not serve as political allies in local prohibition elections. Indeed, a primary duty of the white superintendents after secession was to distribute white ribbons signifying prohibition support to black women when a local-option election seemed threatening.[54]

[Throughout the decade,] flawed but significant interracial contacts continued between black and white WCTU women in North Carolina. As a result of Wells-Barnett's antilynching crusade, North Carolina's white WCTU convention condemned lynching in 1896, a symbolic but nonetheless important gesture, particularly considering that more than twenty years would elapse before southern white women moved again in an organized way against lynching.[55] Delegate exchanges continued between the black and white WCTUs as well. For example, when the black women met in statewide convention in Salisbury in 1896, white WCTU delegates attended a session. That year, black women renamed their union the Lucy Thurman WCTU, honoring the black national organizer, and elected Mary Lynch state president. In 1897, Lynch presided over thirteen unions, attended the white state convention, and spoke at the national meeting, following Anthony Comstock and Anna Shaw.[56] The next year, she gave the opening prayer at the national WCTU convention marking the organization's twenty-fifth anniversary.[57]

In 1896, a black-supported coalition of Republicans and Populists won control of state government, giving African Americans their greatest political voice since Reconstruction and reordering the politics of temperance work. That year, Belle Kearney, a white Mississippian with North Carolina roots, delivered an address to the North Carolina white WCTU convention, the same one that condemned lynching, entitled, "Why the Wheels Are Clogged." Mary Lynch sat in the audience as a delegate from the Lucy Thurman WCTU and listened to Kearney tell the delegates that prohibition would never pass while 250,000 blacks voted in the South.[58] Quickly white women's local temperance strategies shifted to complement the Democratic Party's white supremacist platform. WCTU women helped organize mock elections limited to whites to demonstrate that prohibition would pass if blacks could not vote in temperance elections.[59] In 1898, the white WCTU ceased its work among African Americans forever, and delegate exchanges between the two WCTUs ended abruptly.[60] For the next few years, temperance, which had once held such promise for interracial understanding, would serve white supremacy.

It was a force beyond the control of women—party politics—that obliterated interracial contact within North Carolina's WCTU. Temperance was above all a political issue, and the WCTU solicited prohibition votes. As Democrats began to seek to exclude African Americans from the electoral process, white women were no longer concerned with black temperance and readily recast their former allies as part of the "Negro problem." Although the experience of the WCTU points up the difficulty of transcending difference, it also shows that as long as African Americans had political rights, women's interaction continued because black votes mattered. Electoral politics, then, had a powerful impact upon the lives of those normally cast as the group with the least direct involvement in the process—women. By the end of the decade, the political winds gathered strength until they swept through every corner of black women's lives, leaving few spaces untouched.

Notes

1. Whitener, *Prohibition in North Carolina*, pp. 27–28; Ida C. Hinshaw, "Pleasant Hill Temperance Society" (1931), unpublished paper, uncataloged, Frances E. Willard Memorial Library for Alcohol Research, Evanston, Ill; hereafter cited as FWML.
2. Templars material, file 1818–85, box 1, Hunter Collection, Manuscript Department, Perkins Library, Duke University, Durham, N.C.; hereafter cited as DU. For a discussion of the Good Templars and prohibition during this period, see Whitener, *Prohibition in North Carolina*, 56. For the IOGT and race, see Haley, *Charles N. Hunter*, 27–30. For a similar situation in Alabama in which whites seceded from the international IOGT organization, see Sellers, *Prohibition Movement in Alabama*, 45–47. . . .
3. Clipping from *Banner of Temperance*, n.d., file 1833–79, box 13, and "Temperance," n.p., 20 Nov. 1871, scrapbooks (xerox copies), file 1833–1902, box 13, Hunter Collection, DU.
4. Clipping from *New Bern Daily Times*, 12 June 1873, scrapbooks, file 1833–79, box 13, and "Fifth Anniversary of the Victor Fire Company," n.p., [1870], scrapbooks, file Mainly News and Editorials, box 16, both in Hunter Collection, DU.
5. *Educator*, 5 Feb. 1875. William A. Link finds the situation quite different within white male temperance societies, in which white men created a world "infused with the traditions of nineteenth-century male culture" (*Paradox of Southern Progressivism*, 35–36).
6. *Messenger*, 7 Jan. 1888; Fahey, *Collected Writings of Jessie Forsyth*.
7. Whitener, *Prohibition in North Carolina*, 60–80. On the racial politics of the 1881 election, see Helen Chesnutt, *Charles Waddell Chesnutt*, 29; Brodhead, *Journals of Charles W. Chesnutt*, 168–69; and Eric Anderson, *Race and Politics*, 96–98. On the election in Charlotte, see Greenwood, *Bittersweet Legacy*, 79–97, and clipping from *Daily Record*, 28 Apr. 1881, file 1880–86, box 13, Hunter Collection, DU.
8. Frances E. Willard Diary, 11, 12, 13, 14 Mar. 1881, and clippings from *Wilmington Morning Star*, 12 Mar. 1881, *News and Courier* (Charleston, S.C.), 15 Mar. 1881, and *Our Union*, May 1881, 10, all in Frances Willard Scrapbook, FWML; Ellen J. Y. Preyer to Mrs. Little, 11 Sept. 1939, in "Miss Frances Willard in North Carolina," uncataloged, FWML. My thanks to Alfred Epstein, librarian at the Frances E. Willard Memorial Library, for his invaluable assistance. See also Rogers, "W.C.T.U. in North Carolina."
9. On Willard's first southern trip, see Bordin, *Woman and Temperance*, 76–78; Frances E. Willard, *Glimpses of Fifty Years*, 373–74; and Slagell, "Good Woman Speaking Well," 292–314. On her visit to Georgia, see Ansley, *History of the Georgia Woman's Christian Temperance Union*.
10. Frances E. Willard, *Glimpses of Fifty Years*, 373.

11. *Temperance Herald,* 16 June 1881.
12. Every African American newspaper in the state, except for one, endorsed prohibition, according to the *Temperance Herald,* 16 June 1881. One-fourth of the liquor dealers attending a convention called to fight the referendum were African American, according to Whitener, *Prohibition in North Carolina,* 70. Municipal prohibition passed in Charlotte in 1881, and whites gave part of the credit to black allies, according to Greenwood, *Bittersweet Legacy,* 96. For an overview of why temperance was so important to white men and women, see William A. Link, *Paradox of Southern Progressivism,* 42–48.
13. Whitener, *Prohibition in North Carolina,* 58, 61–80. For similar situations in nearby states, see Moore, "The Negro and Prohibition in Atlanta," and Pearson and Hendricks, *Liquor and Anti-Liquor,* 212–13, 217. Blacks in Alabama voted for prohibition, according to Sellers, *Prohibition Movement in Alabama,* 259.
14. Whitener, *Prohibition in North Carolina,* 81–101.
15. There has been little mention of black women's participation in the WCTU. An exception is Anne Firor Scott, *Natural Allies,* 99–103. Scattered references include the following: Jean E. Friedman, *Enclosed Garden,* 124; Salem, *To Better Our World,* 36–37; Neverdon-Morton, *Afro-American Women of the South,* 206–7; Guy-Sheftall, *"Daughters of Sorrow,"* 22; Mossell, *Work of the Afro-American Woman,* 177–78; and Wedell, *Elite Women,* 67–68, 92–93. Thanks to Leslie Dunlap of Northwestern University for graciously sharing her research and ideas with me at a critical stage in my writing.
16. *Star of Zion,* 23 July 1896.
17. Wolfe, *Look Homeward, Angel,* 255–57, describes this sort of temperance assault on the polls in Asheville. As white Baptist women and their children surrounded voters, the children "sang with piping empty violence: 'Think of sisters, wives, and mothers; Of helpless babes in some low slum; Think not of yourself, but others; Vote against Demon Rum.'" For a visit to a county almshouse, see *North Carolina White Ribbon* 4 (Nov. 1899): 5.
18. *Anchor* 2, no. 4 (July 1886): 5.
19. After the Civil War, no male or female voluntary organizations in North Carolina admitted blacks or held regular biracial conventions prior to the WCTU. The IOGT accepted separate black chapters in 1886, after the WCTU came to the state. The only organization of any type that held biracial conventions prior to the WCTU may have been the Knights of Labor, which had black members (male and female) in separate chapters, but it was not a voluntary organization. See Whitener, *Prohibition in North Carolina,* 55–56. On the context of temperance reform in the United States, see Blocker, *American Temperance Movements,* and Epstein, *Politics of Domesticity.* On women in early postbellum temperance movements, see Blocker, *"Give to the Winds Thy Fears."*
20. Sims, " 'Sword of the Spirit,' " 394. Epstein builds on female consciousness in *Politics of Domesticity.* See also Anne Firor Scott, *Natural Allies,* 94–96.
21. Black women in the WCTU acted from female and communal consciousness. See Cott, "What's in a Name?," 826–27.
22. The term "uplift" represents the class presumptions inherent in educated black women's approach to community work. Black WCTU members used the term without question. See Higginbotham, "African-American Women's History," 271.
23. Sims, " 'Sword of the Spirit.' " For discussions of the WCTU ideology, see Bordin, *Woman and Temperance* and *Frances Willard;* Frances E. Willard, *Glimpses of Fifty Years;* and Ansley, *History of the Georgia Woman's Christian Temperance Union.*
24. Woodward, *Origins of the New South,* 352; Williamson, *Crucible of Race,* 115–16, 120. Williamson fixes 1915 as the year by which whites became convinced that blacks were not dying out but actually increasing in numbers (*ibid.,* 461). The progressive reformer Alexander McKelway of North Carolina insisted that alcohol had "annihilated other inferior races" and was doing the same to African Americans (quoted in William A. Link, *Paradox of Southern Progressivism,* 70–71).
25. "The Position of the National Woman's Christian Temperance Union of the United States in Relation to the Colored People," 6 Feb. 1895, uncataloged, FWML.
26. Simply calling white women "racist" does not help us, in David Roediger's words, "understand how historicized racial identities dramatically shaped what workers [or women] could do and dream in their

lifetimes and how better deeds and dreams can be made possible in ours" (*Towards the Abolition of Whiteness,* 77). My analysis of the relationship among electoral politics, social practice, and the changing construct of "racism" was strengthened by Goodwyn, "Populist Dreams and Negro Rights"; Horton, "Testing the Limits of Class Politics"; and Jacquelyn Hall's reading of this section.

27. Sims, " 'Sword of the Spirit' "; Bordin, *Woman and Temperance,* 78; Walls, *Joseph Charles Price,* 284.

28. Rogers, "W.C.T.U. in North Carolina," 22–23; Sims, " 'Sword of the Spirit,' " 398.

29. *Messenger,* 24 June 1887. When the African American editor of the *Messenger* visited his daughter at Bennett College, he and his wife had dinner with Rosa and Wilbur Steele. Apparently Rosa Steele preached and prayed during the dinner, and he left very impressed with her piety and enthusiasm.

30. *Minutes of the . . . [Third] Annual Meeting,* 29–30; *Minutes of the Fifth Annual Convention,* 12.

31. *[Minutes of the] First Convention,* 14; *Anchor* 2, no. 4 (July 1886): 2. The first superintendent of "Colored Work" was Mrs. L. P. Rothwell of Wilmington. To understand the advances made in "interracial cooperation" in a few short years, consider that Emma A. Unthank was one of the young girls in the Band of Hope organized by Steele in Greensboro. Unthank's father was the model for one of the black characters in Tourgee, *Fool's Errand.* See *Minutes of the Fourth Annual Convention,* 64.

32. *Anchor* 2, no. 2 (May 1886): 6.

33. *Messenger,* 17 June 1882, 8 Apr. 1883. Frances Willard's assistant, Anna A. Gordon, listed "Miss Ainsworth, Teacher of Colored School" (Scotia Seminary) in Concord as a contact in North Carolina in 1881. Ainsworth possibly taught Mary Lynch and introduced her to the WCTU. See Anna A. Gordon, "Directory of Southern Addresses," uncataloged, FWML.

34. *Minutes of the Fifth Annual Convention,* 29; *Messenger,* 7, 14 Aug. 1886.

35. *Anchor* 2, no. 5 (Aug. 1886): 2; *Minutes of the Fourth Annual Convention,* 37, 63.

36. *Ibid.,* 7, 28 Apr. 1888.

37. *Ibid.,* 19 May 1888; Greenwood, *Bittersweet Legacy,* 111–12. Jane Wilkes's papers and the annual reports of the hospital reveal that black women could not even form an auxiliary to support the hospital and that white women dictated all policies and hired all employees. See Wilkes Papers, CPL, and *Fifth Annual Report of the Good Samaritan Hospital for Colored People,* box 1, Good Samaritan Hospital Collection, North Carolina Division of Archives and History, Raleigh, N.C.; hereafter cited as NCDAH.

38. *Minutes of the Sixth Annual Convention,* 41. On Early, see Scruggs, *Women of Distinction,* 71–74, and Lawson, "Sarah Woodson Early."

39. *Minutes of the Sixth Annual Convention,* 41.

40. *Minutes of the Sixth Annual Convention,* 40.

41. *Union Signal,* 27 Nov. 1890, quoted in Sims, " 'Sword of the Spirit,' " 398.

42. *Minutes of the Seventh Annual Convention,* 17; *Minutes of the Ninth Annual Convention,* 17.

43. In 1898, black women organized southern unions in Georgia, North Carolina, Tennessee, Arkansas, and Texas. Unions in other states were organized at various times: Maryland in 1896; Washington, D.C., in 1897; Alabama (at least Tuskegee) in 1902; and Louisiana. See *Union Signal,* 24 Mar. 1898, 3; 3 Dec. 1896, 17; 25 Nov. 1897, 2; 25 Dec. 1902, 3; and Rowland, "Frances Joseph Gaudet."

44. *Living-Stone* 8, no. 3 (Sept. 1891): 44; no. 4 (Oct. 1891): 63; no. 6 (Dec. 1891); no. 7 (Jan. 1892): 145; Fonvielle, *Some Reminiscences,* 119. *Minutes of the Eighth Annual Convention,* 41, refers to the Charlotte WCTU No. 2.

45. *Star of Zion,* 15 June 1899, I. Annie Kimball Clinton died six years after her marriage, and her husband became a bishop in the church.

46. *Ibid.,* 9 Sept. 1897. The meetings at churches were not exclusively for church members and announcements stated, "Everyone Invited" or "Public Invited."

47. *Ibid.,* 14 Apr. 1898, 26 Aug., 2, 23 Sept., 7, 21 Oct. 1897.

48. *Minutes of the Seventh Annual Convention,* 17, 37.

49. In 1892, the national WCTU abolished the "Work amongst the Colored People" department and gave the black WCTU chapters equal organizational status. Mrs. J. E. Ray, the director of "Home and Foreign Missionary Work among and through Afro-Americans" for North Carolina, asked that the state's white WCTU retain this department as a "trial to local needs." Ray replaced Steele after she moved with her

husband to Denver. Elizabeth Putnam Gordon, *Women Torch-Bearers,* 252, lists Mrs. J. E. Ray as the superintendent of "Work amongst the Colored People" for the entire nation, among black women like Frances E. Harper and Lucy Thurman. This seems unlikely. See "Continue to Assist," in *Minutes of the Eighth Annual Convention,* 21; *Minutes of the Tenth Annual Convention,* 4; *Minutes of the Eleventh Annual Convention,* 68–74; and *Minutes of the Twelfth Annual Convention,* 4.

50. *Minutes of the Eleventh Annual Convention,* 68; *Minutes of the Tenth Annual Convention,* 4.

51. *Minutes of the Thirteenth Annual Convention,* 71.

52. *Minutes of the Eleventh Annual Convention,* 71.

53. *Minutes of the Thirteenth Annual Convention,* 70–72.

54. *Minutes of the Eleventh Annual Convention,* 69, 73.

55. *Minutes of the Fourteenth Annual Convention,* 15–16; Hall, *Revolt against Chinalry.*

56. *Star of Zion,* 6 Aug. 1896; *Minutes of the Fourteenth Annual Convention,* 20; *Minutes of the Fifteenth Annual Convention,* 8; *Charlotte Daily News,* 28 Nov. 1897, 12. Lynch served until 1917, and at some later date, the Lucy Thurman WCTU changed its name to the Sojourner Truth WCTU, according to Tyler, *Where Prayer and Purpose Meet,* 208, 275. The WCTU No. 2 did not hold a statewide convention from 1891 to 1896 and was restructured under Lynch's leadership in 1896. See *Union Signal,* 6 Aug. 1896, 1; 3 Dec. 1896, 9, 17.

57. *Star of Zion,* 7 Sept. 1899, 5; *A.M.E. Zion Quarterly Review,* nos. 1–2 (1899): 100; *Minutes of the Ninth Annual Convention,* 17. On the location of the WCTU convention, see Elizabeth Putnam Gordon, *Women Torch-Bearers,* 253. On Lynch's prayer, see *Union Signal,* 3 Dec. 1898, 4.

58. *North Carolina White Ribbon* 6, no. 1 (1 July 1896).

59. Whitener, *Prohibition in North Carolina,* 121. Walton, "Another Force for Disfranchisement," makes a similar argument for Tennessee. After disfranchisement, whites attributed passage of local-option prohibition laws to the absence of black voters. See Timberlake, *Prohibition and the Progressive Movement,* 155.

60. The last listing of "Work amongst the Colored People" is *Minutes of the Fifteenth Annual Convention,* 24.

Chapter 15

Hull House in the 1890s: A Community of Women Reformers

Kathryn Kish Sklar

In the movement for woman suffrage and in myriad reform movements at the turn of the twentieth century, women reformers exercised a degree of political power previously (some might add, subsequently) unknown in American society. Foremost among these women reformers was a generation of women active in the social settlement movement. Hull House, founded by Jane Addams in Chicago in 1889, was the leading institution in that movement. Through a case study of women reformers at Hull House, Kathryn Kish Sklar offers a window into the experiences that motivated and empowered this remarkable generation of reformers. She shows how our understanding of their substantial exercise of power within the broader social, economic, and political life of the nation can be illuminated through an appreciation of the community they constructed among themselves.

What were the sources of women's political power in the United States in the decades before they could vote? How did women use the political power they were able to muster? This essay attempts to answer these questions by examining one of the most politically effective groups of women reformers in U.S. history—those who assembled in Chicago in the early 1890s at Hull House, one of the nation's first social settlements, founded in 1889 by Jane Addams and Ellen Gates Starr. Within that group, this study focuses on the reformer Florence Kelley (1859–1932). Kelley joined Hull House in 1891 and remained until 1899, when she moved to Lillian Wald's Henry Street Settlement on the Lower East Side of New York, where she lived for the next twenty-seven years. According to Felix Frankfurter, Kelley "had probably the largest single share in shaping the social history of the United States during the first thirty years of this century," for she played "a powerful if not decisive role in securing legislation for the removal of the most glaring abuses of our hectic industrialization following the Civil War."[1] It was in the 1890s that Kelley and her colleagues at Hull House developed the patterns of living and thinking that guided them throughout their lives of reform, leaving an indelible imprint on U.S. politics.[2] This essay attempts to determine the extent to which their political power and activities flowed from their collective life as coresidents and friends and the degree to which this power was attributable to their close affiliation with male reformers and male institutions.

The effects of both factors can be seen in one of the first political campaigns conducted by Hull House residents—the 1893 passage and the subsequent enforcement of pathbreaking anti-sweatshop legislation mandating an eight-hour day for women and children employed in Illinois manufacturing. This important episode reveals a great deal about the sources of this group's political power, including their own collective initiative, the support of other women's groups, and the

Excerpted from "Hull House in the 1890s: A Community of Women Reformers," in *SIGNS* 10 (1985): 658–77. By permission of the University of Chicago Press.

Jane Addams, c. 1890. Sophia Smith Collection, Smith College

support of men and men's groups. Finally, it shows how women reformers and gender-specific issues they championed helped advance class-specific issues during a time of fundamental social, economic, and political transition.

One of the most important questions asked by historians of American women today is, To what degree has women's social power been based on separate female institutions, culture, and consciousness, and to what degree has it grown out of their access to male spheres of influence, such as higher education, labor organization, and politics.[3] This essay advances the commonsense notion that women's social power in the late nineteenth century depended on both sources of support. Women's institutions allowed them to enter realms of reality dominated by men, where, for better or for worse, they competed with men for control over the distribution of social resources. Thus although their own communities were essential to their social strength, women were able to realize the full potential of their collective power only by reaching outside those boundaries.

*   *   *

The community of women at Hull House made it possible for Florence Kelley to step from the apprenticeship to the journeyman stage in her reform career. A study of the 1893 antisweatshop campaign shows that the community provided four fundamental sources of support for her growth as a reformer. First, it supplied an emotional and economic substitute for traditional family life, linking her with other talented women of her own class and educational and political background and thereby greatly increasing her political and social power. Second, the community at Hull House provided Kelley with effective ties to other women's organizations. Third, it enabled cooperation with men reformers and their organizations, allowing her to draw on their support without submitting to their control. Finally, it provided a creative setting for her to pursue and develop a reform strategy she had already initiated in New York—the advancement of the rights and interests of working people in general by strengthening the rights and interests of working women and children.

As a community of women, Hull House provided its members with a lifelong substitute for family life. In that sense it resembled a religious order, supplying women with a radical degree of independence from the claims of family life and inviting them to commit their energies elsewhere. When she first crossed the snowy threshold of Hull House "sometime between Christmas and New Year's," 1891, Florence Kelley Wischnewetzky was fleeing from her husband and seeking refuge for herself and her three children, ages six, five, and four. "We were welcomed as though we had been invited," she wrote thirty-five years later in her memoirs.[4] The way in which Kelley's family dilemma was solved reveals a great deal about the sources of support for the political activity of women reformers in the progressive era: help came first and foremost from women's institutions but also from the recruited support of powerful men reformers. Jane Addams supplied Kelley with room, board, and employment and soon after she arrived introduced her to Henry Demarest Lloyd, a leading critic of American labor policies who lived with his wife Jessie and their young children in nearby Winnetka. The Lloyds readily agreed to add Kelley's children to their large nursery, an arrangement that began a lifelong relationship between the two families.[5] A sign of the extent to which responsibility for Kelley's children was later assumed by members of the Hull House community, even after her departure, was the fact that Jane Addams's closest personal friend, Mary Rozet Smith, regularly and quietly helped Kelley pay for their school and college tuition.[6]

A bit stunned by her good fortune, the young mother wrote her own mother a summary of her circumstances a few weeks after reaching Hull House: "We are all well, and the chicks are happy. I have fifty dollars a month and my board and shall have more soon as I can collect my wits enough to write. I have charge of the Bureau of Labor of Hull House here and am working in the lines which I have always loved. I do not know what more to tell you except this, that in the few weeks of my stay here I have won for the children and myself many and dear friends whose generous hospitality astonishes me."[7] This combination of loving friendship and economic support served as a substitute for the family life from which she had just departed. "It is understood that I am to resume the maiden name," she continued to her mother, "and that the children are to have it." It did not take Kelley long to decide to join this supportive community of women. As she wrote Friedrich Engels in April 1892, "I have cast in my lot with Misses Addams and Starr for as long as they will have me."[8] To her mother she emphasized the personal gains Hull House brought her, writing, "I am better off than I have been since I landed in New York since I am now responsible *myself* for what I do." Gained at great personal cost, Kelley's independence was her most basic measure of well-being. Somewhat paradoxically, perhaps, her autonomy was the product of her affiliation with a community.

One significant feature of Hull House life was the respect that residents expressed for one another's autonomy. Although each had a "room of her own," in Kelley's case this room was sometimes shared with other residents, and the collective space was far more important than their small private chambers.[9] Nevertheless, this intimate proximity was accompanied by a strong expression of personal individuation, reflected in the formality of address used at Hull House. By the world at large Kelley was called Mrs. Kelley, but to her close colleagues she was "Sister Kelley," or "Dearest F. K.," never Florence. Miss Addams and Miss Lathrop were never called Jane or Julia, even by their close friends, although Kelley occasionally took the liberty of calling Addams "gentle Jane." It was not that Hull House was bleak and business-like, as one resident once described male settlements in New York, but rather that the colleagues recognized and appreciated one another's individuality. These were superb conditions for social innovation since the residents could draw on mutual support at the same time that they were encouraged to pursue their own distinct goals.

This respect for individuality did not prevent early Hull House residents from expressing their love for one another. Kelley's letters to Jane Addams often began "Beloved Lady," and she frequently addressed Mary Rozet Smith as "Dearly Beloved," referring perhaps to Smith's special status in Addams's life. Kelley's regard for Addams and Addams's for her were revealed in their correspondence after Kelley left in 1899. Addams wrote her, "I have had blows before in connection with Hull House but nothing like this"; and Mary Rozet Smith added, "I have had many pangs for the dear presiding lady." Later that year Addams wrote, "Hull House sometimes seems a howling wilderness without you." Kelley seems to have found the separation difficult since she protested when her name was removed from the list of residents in the *Hull House Bulletin*. Addams replied, "You overestimate the importance of the humble Bulletin," but she promised to restore Kelley's name, explaining that it was only removed to "stop people asking for her." Fourteen years later in 1913 Addams wrote "Sister Kelley," "It is curious that I have never gotten used to you being away from [Hull House], even after all these years!"[10]

One source of the basic trust established among the three major reformers at Hull House in the 1890s—Jane Addams, Julia Lathrop, and Florence Kelley—was similarity of family background. Not only were they all of the upper middle class, but their fathers were politically active men who helped Abraham Lincoln found and develop the Republican Party in the 1860s. John Addams served eight terms as a state senator in Illinois, William Lathrop served in Congress as well as in the Illinois legislature, and William Kelley served fifteen consecutive terms in Congress. All were vigorous abolitionists, and all encouraged their daughters' interests in public affairs. As Judge Alexander Bruce remarked at the joint memorial services held for Julia Lathrop and Florence Kelley after their deaths in 1932, "Both of them had the inspiration of great and cultured mothers and both had great souled fathers who, to use the beautiful language of Jane Addams in speaking of her own lineage, 'Wrapped their little daughters in the large men's doublets, careless did they fit or no.' "[11]

These three remarkable women were participating in a political tradition that their fathers had helped create. While they were growing up in the 1860s and 1870s, they gained awareness through their fathers' experience of the mainstream of American political processes, thereby learning a great deal about its currents—particularly that its power could be harnessed to fulfill the purposes of well-organized interest groups.

Although Hull House residents have generally been interpreted as reformers with a religious motivation, it now seems clear that they were more strongly motivated by political goals. In that regard they resembled a large proportion of other women social settlement leaders, including those associated with Hull House after 1900, such as Grace and Edith Abbott, whose father was Nebraska's first lieutenant governor, or Sophonisba Breckinridge, daughter of a Kentucky congressman.[12] Women leaders in the social settlement movement seem to have differed in this respect from their male counterparts, who were seeking alternatives to more orthodox religious, rather than political, careers. In, but not of, the Social Gospel movement, the women at Hull House were a political boat on a religious stream, advancing political solutions to social problems that were fundamentally ethical or moral, such as the right of workers to a fair return for their labor or the right of children to schooling.

Another source of the immediate solidarity among Addams, Lathrop, and Kelley was their shared experience of higher education. Among the first generation of American college women, they graduated from Rockford College, Vassar College, and Cornell University, respectively, in the early 1880s and then spent the rest of the decade searching for work and for a social identity commensurate with their talents. Addams tried medical school; Lathrop worked in her father's law office; Kelley, after being denied admission to graduate study at the University of Pennsylvania, studied law and government at the University of Zurich, where she received a much more radical education than she would have had she remained in Philadelphia. In the late 1880s and early 1890s, the social settlement movement was the right movement at the right time for this first generation of college-educated women, who were able to gain only limited entry to the male-dominated professions of law, politics, or academics.[13]

While talented college women of religious backgrounds and inclinations were energetically recruited into the missionary empires of American churches, those seeking secular outlets for their talents chose a path that could be as daunting as that of a missionary outpost. Except for the field of medicine, where women's institutions served the needs of women physicians and students, talented women were blocked from entering legal, political, and academic professions by male-dominated institutions and networks. In the 1890s the social settlement movement supplied a perfect structure for women seeking secular means of influencing society because it collectivized their talents, it placed and protected them among the working-class immigrants whose lives demanded amelioration, and it provided them with access to the male political arena while preserving their independence from male-dominated institutions.

Since Hull House drew on local sources of funding, often family funds supplied by wealthy women,[14] Jane Addams found it possible to finance the settlement's activities without the assistance or control of established religious or educational institutions. In 1895 she wrote that Hull House was modeled after Toynbee Hall in London, where "a group of University men . . . reside in the poorer quarter of London for the sake of influencing the people there toward better local government and wider social and intellectual life." Substituting "college-trained women" for "University men," Hull House also placed a greater emphasis on economic factors. As Addams continued, "The original residents came to Hull House with a conviction that social intercourse could best express the growing sense of the economic unity of society." She also emphasized their political autonomy, writing that the first residents "wished the social spirit to be the undercurrent of the life of Hull-House, whatever direction the stream might take."[15] Under Kelley's influence in 1892, the social spirit at Hull House turned decisively toward social reform, bringing the community's formidable energy and talents to bear on a historic campaign on behalf of labor legislation for women and children.[16]

Meredith Tax's *Rising of the Women* contains the most complete account of this campaign, which culminated in the passage of landmark state legislation in 1893. There Tax justly reproves Jane Addams for assigning Hull House more than its share of the credit for the campaign. The settlement did play a critical leadership role in this venture, but it was never alone. Indeed it was part of a complex network of women's associations in Chicago in the 1890s.[17] About thirty women's organizations combined forces and entered into local politics in 1888 through the Illinois Women's Alliance, organized that year by Elizabeth Morgan and other members of the Ladies Federal Union no. 2073 in response to a crusading woman journalist's stories in the *Chicago Times* about "City Slave Girls" in the garment industry.[18] The alliance's political goals were clearly stated in their constitution: "The objects of the Alliance are to agitate for the enforcement of all existing laws and ordinances that have been enacted for the protection of women and children—as the factory ordinances and the compulsory education law. To secure the enactment of such laws as shall be found necessary. To investigate all business establishments and factories where women and children are employed and public institutions where women and children are maintained. To procure the appointment of women, as inspectors and as members of boards of education, and to serve on boards of management of public institutions."[19] Adopting the motto "Justice to Children, Loyalty to Women," the alliance acted as a vanguard for the entrance of women's interests into municipal and state politics, focusing chiefly on the passage and enforcement of compulsory education laws. One of its main accomplishments was the agreement of the city council in 1889 "to appoint five lady inspectors" to enforce city health codes.[20]

The diversity of politically active women's associations in Chicago in the late 1880s was reflected in a list of organizations associated with the alliance.[21] Eight bore names indicating a religious or ethical affiliation, such as the Woodlawn branch of the Woman's Christian Temperance Union and the Ladies Union of the Ethical Society. Five were affiliated with working women or were trade unions, such as the Working Women's Protective Association, the Ladies Federal Union no. 2703, and (the only predominantly male organization on the list) the Chicago Trades and Labor Assembly. Another five had an intellectual or cultural focus, such as the Hopkins Metaphysical Association or the Vincent Chatauqua Association. Three were women's professional groups, including the Women's Press Association and the Women's Homeopathic Medical Society. Another three were female auxiliaries of male social organizations, such as the Lady Washington Masonic Chapter and the Ladies of the Grand Army of the Republic. Two were suffrage associations, including the Cook County Suffrage Association; another two were clubs interested in general economic reform, the Single Tax Club and the Land Labor Club no. 1; and one was educational, the Drexel Kindergarten Association.

Florence Kelley's 1892 entrance into this lively political scene was eased by her previous knowledge of and appreciation for the work of the alliance. Soon after its founding she had written the leaders a letter that was quoted extensively in a newspaper account of an alliance meeting, declaring, "The child labor question can be solved by legislation, backed by solid organization, and by women cooperating with the labor organizations, which have done all that has thus far been done for the protection of working children."[22] In Chicago Kelley was perceived as a friend of the alliance because in 1889 and 1890 she had helped organize the New York Working Women's Society's campaign "to add women as officials in the office for factory inspection." According to Kelley, the Society, "a small group of women from both the wealthy and influential class and the working class, . . . circulated petitions, composed resolutions, and was supported finally in the years 1889 and 1890 in bringing their proposal concerning the naming of women to factory inspectorships to the legislature, philanthropic groups and unions."[23] As a result in 1890 the New York legislature passed laws creating eight new positions for women as state factory inspectors. This was quite an innovation since no woman factory inspector had yet been appointed in Great Britian or Germany, where factory inspection began, and the only four previously appointed in the United States had been named within the last two years in Pennsylvania.[24] Writing in 1897 about this event, Kelley emphasized the political autonomy of the New York Working Women's Society: "Their proposal to add women as officials in the office for factory inspection was made for humanitarian reasons; in no way did it belong to the goals of the general workers' movement, although it found support among the unions."[25] Thus when Kelley arrived at Hull House, she had already been affiliated with women's associations that were independent of trade unions even though cooperating with them.

For Kelley on that chilly December morning the question was not whether she would pursue a career in social reform but how, not whether she would champion what she saw as the rights and interests of working women and children but how she would do that. The question of means was critical in 1891 since her husband was unable to establish a stable medical practice, even though she had spent the small legacy inherited on her father's death the year before on new equipment for his practice. Indeed so acute were Kelley's financial worries that, when she decided to flee with her children to Chicago, she borrowed train fare from an English governess, Mary Forster, whom she had probably befriended at a neighborhood park.[26] Chicago was a natural choice for Kelley since Illinois divorce laws were more equitable, and within its large population of reform-minded and politically active women she doubtlessly hoped to find employment that would allow her to support herself and her children. Although the historical record is incomplete, it seems likely that she headed first to a different community of women—that at the national headquarters of the Woman's Christian Temperance Union (WCTU).[27] She had been well paid for articles written for their national newspaper, the *Union Signal*—the largest women's newspaper in the world, with a circulation in 1890 of almost 100,000—and the WCTU was at the height of its institutional development in Chicago at that time, sponsoring "two day nurseries, two Sunday schools, an industrial school, a mission that sheltered four thousand homeless or destitute women in a twelve-month period, a free medical dispensary that treated over sixteen hundred patients a year, a lodging house for men that had . . . provided temporary housing for over fifty thousand men, and a low-cost restaurant."[28] Just after Kelley arrived, the WCTU opened its Women's Temple, a twelve-story office building and hotel. Very likely it was someone there who told Kelley about Hull House.

The close relationship between Hull House and other groups of women in Chicago was exemplified in Kelley's interaction with the Chicago Women's Club. The minutes of the club's first meeting after Kelley's arrival in Chicago show that on January 25, 1892, she spoke under the sponsorship of Jane Addams on the sweating system and urged that a committee be created on the problem.[29] Although a Reform Department was not created until 1894, minutes of March 23, 1892, show that the club's Home Department "decided upon cooperating with Mrs. Kelly [*sic*] of Hull House in establishing a Bureau of Women's Labor." Thus the club took over part of the funding and the responsibility for the counseling service Kelley had been providing at Hull House since February. (Initially Kelley's salary for this service was funded by the settlement, possibly with emergency monies given by Mary Rozet Smith.) In this way middle- and upper-middle-class clubwomen were drawn into the settlement's activities. In 1893 Jane Addams successfully solicited the support of wealthy clubwomen to lobby for the antisweatshop legislation: "We insisted that well-known Chicago women should accompany this first little group of Settlement folk who with trade-unionists moved upon the state capitol in behalf of factory legislation." Addams also described the lobbying Hull House residents conducted with other voluntary associations: "Before the passage of the law could be secured, it was necessary to appeal to all elements of the community, and a little group of us addressed the open meetings of trades-unions and of benefit societies, church organizations, and social clubs literally every evening for three months."[30] Thus Hull House was part of a larger social universe of voluntary organizations, and one important feature of its political effectiveness was its ability to gain the support of middle-class and working-class women.

In 1893 the cross-class coalition of the Illinois Women's Alliance began to dissolve under the pressure of the economic depression of that year, and in 1894 its leaders disbanded the group. Hull House reformers inherited the fruits of the alliance's five years of agitation, and they continued its example of combining working-class and middle-class forces. In 1891 Mary Kenney, a self-supporting typesetter who later became the first woman organizer to be employed by the American Federation of Labor, established the Jane Club adjacent to the settlement, a cooperative boardinghouse for young working women. In the early 1890s Kenney was a key figure in the settlement's efforts to promote union organizing among working women, especially bookbinders.[31] Thus the combination of middle-class and working-class women at Hull House in 1892–93 was an elite version of the type of cross-class association represented by the Illinois Women's Alliance of the late 1880s—elite because it was smaller and because its middle-class members had greater social resources, familiarity with American political processes, and exposure to higher than average levels of education, while its working-class members (Mary Kenney and Alzina Stevens) were members of occupational and organizational elites.[32]

By collectivizing talents and energies, this community made possible the exercise of greater and more effective political power by its members. A comparison of Florence Kelley's antisweatshop legislation, submitted to the Illinois investigate committee in February 1893, with that presented by Elizabeth Morgan dramatically illustrates this political advantage. The obvious differences in approach indicate that the chief energy for campaigning on behalf of working women and children had passed from working-class to middle-class social reformers.[33] Both legislative drafts prohibited work in tenement dwellings. Morgan's prohibiting all manufacturing, Kelley's all garment making. Both prohibited the labor of children under fourteen and regulated the labor of children aged fourteen to sixteen. Kelley's went beyond Morgan's in two essential respects, however. Hers mandated an eight-hour day for women in manufacturing, and it provided for enforcement by calling for a state factory inspector with a staff of twelve, five whom were to be women. The reasons for Kelley's greater success as an innovator are far from clear, but one important advantage in addition to her greater education and familiarity with the American political system was the larger community on which she could rely for the law's passage and enforcement.

Although Elizabeth Morgan could draw on her experience as her husband's assistant in his work as an attorney and on the support of women unionists, both resources were problematic. Thomas Morgan was erratic and self-centered, and Elizabeth Morgan's relationship with organized women workers was marred by sectarian disputes originating within the male power structure of the Chicago Trades and Labor Assembly. For example, in January 1892, when she accused members of the Shirtwaist Union of being controlled by her husband's opposition within the assembly, "a half dozen women surrounded [her] seat in the meeting and demanded an explanation. She refused to give any and notice was served that charges would be preferred against her at the next meeting of the Ladies' Federation of Labor."[34] Perhaps Morgan's inability to count on a supportive community explains her failure to provide for adequate enforcement and to include measures for workers over the age of sixteen in her legislative draft. Compared to Kelley's, Morgan's bill was politically impotent. It could not enforce what it endorsed, and it did not affect adults.

Kelley's draft was passed by the Illinois legislature in June 1893, providing for a new office of enforcement and for an eight-hour day for women workers of all ages. After Henry Demarest Lloyd declined an invitation to serve as the state's first factory inspector, reform governor John Peter Altgeld followed Lloyd's recommendations and appointed Kelley. Thus eighteen months after her arrival in Chicago, she found herself in charge of a dedicated and well-paid staff of twelve mandated to see that prohibitions against tenement workshops and child labor were observed and to enforce a pathbreaking article restricting the working hours of women and children.

Hull House provided Kelley and other women reformers with a social vehicle for independent political action and a means of bypassing the control of male associations and institutions, such as labor unions and political parties; at the same time they had a strong institutional framework in which they could meet with other reformers, both men and women. The drafting of the antisweat-shop legislation revealed how this process worked. In his autobiography, Abraham Bisno, pioneer organizer in the garment industry in Chicago and New York, described how he became a regular participant in public discussions of contemporary social issues at Hull House. He joined "a group . . . composed of Henry D. Lloyd, a prominent physician named Bayard Holmes, Florence Kelley, and Ellen G. [Starr] to engage in a campaign for legislation to abolish sweatshops, and to have a law passed prohibiting the employment of women more than eight hours a day."[35] Answering a question about the author of the bill he endorsed at the 1893 hearings, Bisno said, "Mrs. Florence Kelly [*sic*] wrote that up with the advice of myself, Henry Lloyd, and a number of prominent attorneys in Chicago."[36] Thus as the chief author of the legislation, Florence Kelley drew on the expertise of Bisno, one of the most dedicated and talented union organizers; of Lloyd, one of the most able elite reformers in the United States; and, surely among the "prominent attorneys," of Clarence Darrow, one of the country's most able reform lawyers. It is difficult to imagine this cooperative effort between Bisno, Kelley, and Lloyd without the existence of the larger Hull House group of which they were a part. Their effective collaboration exemplified the process by which members of this remarkable community of women reformers moved into the vanguard of contemporary reform activity, for they did so in alliance with other groups and individuals.

What part did the Hull House community, essential to the drafting and passage of the act, have in the statute's enforcement? Who benefited and who lost from the law's enforcement? Answers to these questions help us view the community more completely in the context of its time.

During the four years that Kelley served as chief factory inspector of Illinois, her office and Hull House were institutionally so close as to be almost undistinguishable. Kelley rented rooms for her office across the street from the settlement, with which she and her three most able deputies were closely affiliated. Alzina Stevens moved into Hull House soon after Altgeld appointed her as Kelley's chief assistant. Mary Kenney lived at the Jane Club, and Abraham Bisno was a familiar figure at Hull House evening gatherings. Jane Addams described the protection that the settlement gave to the first factory inspection office in Illinois, the only such office headed by a woman in her lifetime: "The inception of the law had already become associated with Hull House, and when its ministration was also centered there, we inevitably received all the odium which these first efforts entailed. . . . Both Mrs. Kelley and her assistant, Mrs. Stevens, lived at Hull-House; . . . and one of the most vigorous deputies was the President of the Jane Club. In addition, one of the early men residents, since dean of a state law school, acted as prosecutor in the cases brought against the violators of the law."[37] Thus the law's enforcement was just as collective an undertaking as was its drafting and passage. Florence Kelley and Alzina Stevens were usually the first customers at the Hull House Coffee Shop, arriving at 7:30 for a breakfast conference to plan their strategy for the day ahead. Doubtlessly these discussions continued at the end of the day in the settlement's dining hall.

One important aspect of the collective strength of Kelley's staff was the socialist beliefs shared by its most dedicated members. As Kelley wrote to Engels in November 1893, "I find my work as inspector most interesting; and as Governor Altgeld places no restrictions whatever upon our freedom of speech, and the English etiquette of silence while in the civil service is unknown here, we are not hampered by our position and three of my deputies and my assistant are outspoken Socialists and active in agitation."[38] In his autobiography Bisno described the "fanatical" commitment that he, Florence Kelley, and most of the "radical group" brought to their work as factory inspectors. For him it was the perfect job since his salary allowed him for the first time to support his wife and children and his work involved direct action against unfair competition within his trade. "In those years labor legislation was looked on as a joke; few took it seriously," he later wrote. "Inspectors normally . . . were appointed from the viewpoint of political interest. . . . There were very few, almost no, court cases heard of, and it was left to our department to set the example of rigid enforcement of labor laws."[39] Although they were replaced with "political interests" after the election of 1896, this group of inspectors shows what could be accomplished by the enactment of reform legislation and its vigorous enforcement. They demonstrated that women could use the power of the state to achieve social and economic goals.

What conclusions can be drawn about the Hull House community from this review of their activities on behalf of antisweatshop legislation? First, and foremost, it attests to the capacity of women to sustain their own institutions. Second, it shows that this community's internal dynamics promoted a creative mixture of mutual support and individual expression. Third, these talented women reformers used their institutions as a means of allying with male reformers and entering the mainstream of the American political process. In the tradition of earlier women's associations in the United States, they focused on the concerns of women and children, but these concerns were never divorced from those of men and of the society as a whole. Under the leadership of Florence Kelley, they pursued gender-specific reforms that served class-specific goals.

In many respects the Hull House community serves as a paradigm for women's participation in Progressive reform. Strengthened by the support of women's separate institutions, women reformers were able to develop their capacity for political leadership free from many if not all of the constraints that otherwise might have been imposed on their power by the maledominated parties or groups with which they cooperated. Building on one of the strengths of the nineteenth-century notion of "women's sphere"—its social activism on behalf of the rights and interests of women and children—they represented those rights and interests innovatively and effectively. Ultimately, however, their power encountered limits imposed by the male-dominated political system, limits created more in response to their class-specific than to their gender-specific reform efforts.

Notes

1. Quoted in the foreword, Josephine Goldmark, *Impatient Crusader* (Urbana: University of Illinois Press, 1953), p. 5.
2. The best brief source on Jane Addams is Anne Firor Scott's entry in Edward James, Janet Wilson James, and Paul Boyer, eds., *Notable American Women, 1607–1950,* 3 vols. (Cambridge, Mass.: Harvard University Press, 1971), 1:16–22. For biographical information about Florence Kelley, see Louise C. Wade's entry in *ibid.,* 2:316–19; Goldmark; and Dorothy Rose Blumberg, *Florence Kelley: The Making of a Social Pioneer* (New York: Augustus M. Kelley, 1966).
3. See esp. Estelle Freedman, "Separatism as Strategy: Female Institution Building and American Feminism, 1870–1930," *Feminist Studies* 5, no. 3 (Fall 1979): 512–29; and Rosalind Rosenberg, "Defining Our Terms: Separate Spheres" (paper presented at the Organization of American Historians, Los Angeles, April 1984).
4. Florence Kelley, "I Go to Work," *Survey* 58, no. 5 (June 1, 1927): 271–77, esp. 271.
5. Nicholas Kelley, "Early Days at Hull House," *Social Service Review* 28, no. 4 (December 1954): 424–29.
6. Mary Rozet Smith sent money to Kelley on many occasions. See Mary Rozet Smith to Florence Kelley, October 6, 1899, Jane Addams Papers, University of Illinois at Chicago; Florence Kelley to Dearly Beloved [Mary Rozet Smith], February 4, 1899, Swarthmore College Peace Collection, Jane Addams Papers; Mary Rozet Smith to Florence Kelley, July 12, 1900, Addams Collection, University of Illinois at Chicago.
7. Florence Kelley to Caroline Kelley, Hull House, February 24, 1892, Nicholas Kelley Papers, New York Public Library (hereafter cited as NK Papers).
8. Florence Kelley to Friedrich Engels, Hull House, December 29, 1887, Archiv, Institute of Marxism-Leninism, Moscow, fund I, schedule 5. I am grateful to Dorothy Rose Blumberg for the use of her microfilm copy of these letters, some of which have been printed in her "'Dear Mr. Engels': Unpublished Letters, 1884–1894, of Florence Kelley (-Wischnewetsky) to Friedrich Engels," *Labor History* 5, no. 2

(Spring 1964): 103–33. Kelley's correspondence with Engels began in 1884, when she decided to translate his *Condition of the English Working Class in 1844* (New York: J. W. Lovell Co., 1887). Until 1958 hers was the only English translation of this classic work.

9. See Dolores Hayden, *The Grand Domestic Revolution: A History of Feminist Designs for American Homes, Neighborhoods, and Cities* (Cambridge, Mass.: MIT Press, 1981). pp. 162–74.

10. Jane Addams to Florence Kelley, [June 1899], NK Papers; Mary Rozet Smith to Florence Kelley, September 14, 1899, Addams Papers; and Jane Addams to Florence Kelley, November 8, 1899, NK Papers. Also Jane Addams to Florence Kelley, November 22, 1899, NK Papers; and Jane Addams to Florence Kelley, July 5, 1913, Special Collections, Columbia University.

11. See the biographies of Addams, Lathrop, and Kelly in James et al., eds. (n. 2 above); and Rebecca Sherrick, "Private Visions, Public Lives: The Hull-House Women in the Progressive Era" (Ph.D. diss., Northwestern University, 1980). Judge Bruce's remarks are in the transcription "Memorial Services for Mrs. Florence Kelley, Miss Julia C. Lathrop, Hull House, Chicago, May 6, 1932," Anita McCormick Blaine Papers, State Historical Society of Wisconsin, Madison (typescript, 1932), pp. 20–21. In this description of her lineage, Addams adapted lines from Elizabeth Browning's *Aurora Leigh*.

12. The political and secular backgrounds of women social settlement leaders can be seen in the biographies of the twenty-six listed as settlement leaders in the classified index of James et al., eds. (n. 2 above), vol. 3. More than a third had fathers who were attorneys or judges or held elected office. Only one was the daughter of a minister—Vida Scudder, whose father died when she was an infant.

13. For the most complete study of the settlements, see Allen F. Davis, *Spearheads for Reform: The Social Settlements and the Progressive Movement, 1890–1914* (New York: Oxford University Press, 1967).

14. Jane Addams, "Hull-House: A Social Settlement," in *Hull House Maps and Papers* (Boston: Thomas Crowell & Co., 1895), pp. 207–30, esp. p. 230.

15. *Ibid.*, pp. vii, 207–8.

16. For Kelley's singular influence on Addams's shift from philanthropist to reformer in 1892, see Allen F. Davis, *American Heroine: The Life and Legend of Jane Addams* (New York: Oxford University Press, 1973), p. 77.

17. Meredith Tax, *The Rising of the Women: Feminist Solidarity and Class Conflict, 1880–1917* (New York: Monthly Review Press, 1979), pp. 23–89, 302, n. 40. The number and variety of women's organizations in Chicago in the 1890s can be seen in the multitude whose remaining records are listed in Andrea Hinding, Ames Sheldon Bower, and Clark A. Chambers, eds., *Women's History Sources: A Guide to Archives and Manuscript Collections in the United States,* vol. 1, *Collections* (New York: R. R. Bowker Co., 1979), pp. 228–57.

18. See Ralph Scharnau, "Elizabeth Morgan, Crusader for Labor Reform," *Labor History* 14, no. 3 (Summer 1973): 340–51.

19. Newspaper clipping, [November] 1888, Thomas J. Morgan Papers, University of Illinois at Urbana-Champaign, box 4, vol. 2.

20. Alliance motto in the *Chicago Daily Interocean* (November 2, 1889), Morgan Papers; women inspectors are mentioned in the *Chicago Tribune* (July 26, 1889).

21. The list is reprinted in Tax, *Rising of the Women*, p. 301.

22. Newspaper clipping, November 1888, Morgan Papers, box 4, vol. 2.

23. Florence Kelley, "Die Weibliche Fabrikinspektion in den Vereinigten Staaten," in *Archiv für soziale Gesetzgebung und Statistik,* ed. H. Braun (Tübingen: Edgar Jaffe, 1897), 11:128–42, 130, translated by J. Donovan Penrose as "Women as Inspectors of Factories in the United States" (typescript).

24. *Ibid.*

25. *Ibid.*

26. Florence Kelley to Caroline Kelley, February 24, 1892, NK Papers.

27. In "Early Days at Hull House" (n. 5 above), Nicholas Kelley wrote that his mother "became a resident at Hull House almost at once after we came to Chicago" (p. 427).

28. Ruth Bordin, *Woman and Temperance: The Quest for Power and Liberty, 1873–1900* (Philadelphia: Temple University Press, 1981), pp. 90, 98, 142.

29. Minutes of board meeting, March 23, 1892, Chicago Women's Club Papers, Chicago Historical Society. See also Henriette Greenbaum Frank and Amalie Hofer Jerome, comps., *Annuals of the Chicago Women's Club*

for the First Forty Years of Its Organization, 1876–1916 (Chicago: Chicago Women's Club, 1916), p. 120. Kelley defined "sweating" as "the farming out by competing manufacturers to competing contractors the material for garments, which, in turn, is distributed among competing men and women to be made up. The middle-man, or contractor, is the sweater (though he also may be himself subjected to pressure from above), and his employees are the sweated or oppressed" ("Sweating System in Chicago," *Seventh Biennial Report of the Bureau of Labor Statistics of Illinois, 1892* [Springfield, Ill.: State Printer, 1893]).

30. Jane Addams, *Twenty Years at Hull-House* (New York: Macmillan Publishing Co., 1912), pp. 202, 201.

31. See Eleanor Flexner and Janet Wilson James's entry for Mary Kenney O'Sullivan in James *et al.,* eds. (n. 2 above), 2:655–56.

32. A typesetter and leading labor organizer, Alzina Parsons Stevens became Kelley's chief deputy in 1893, moving into Hull House that year. See Allen F. Davis's entry for Stevens in James *et al.,* eds. (n. 2 above), 3:368–69.

33. Testimony of Florence Kelley and Elizabeth Morgan, *Report and Findings of the Joint Committee to Investigate the "Sweat Shop" System, together with a Transcript of the Testimony Taken by the Committee* (Springfield, Ill.: State Printer, 1893), pp. 144–50, 135–40, respectively.

34. Newspaper clipping, Morgan Papers, box 4, vol. 6.

35. Abraham Bisno, *Abraham Bisno, Union Pioneer: An Autobiographical Account of Bisno's Early Life and the Beginnings of Unionism in the Women's Garment Industry* (Madison: University of Wisconsin Press, 1967), pp. 202–3.

36. *Report and Findings . . .* , p. 239.

37. Addams, *Twenty Years at Hull-House,* p. 207.

38. Florence Kelley to Friedrich Engels, November 21, 1893, Archiv, Institute of Marxism-Leninism.

39. Bisno, pp. 148–49.

Chapter 16

"Charity Girls" and City Pleasures: Historical Notes on Working-Class Sexuality, 1880–1920

Kathy Peiss

The emergence of heterosocial public culture and a more open sexuality are two of the major features that distinguish modern American culture from its nineteenth-century Victorian predecessor. In her research on the leisure world of working women in New York City, Kathy Peiss has uncovered evidence of the independent development of working-class sexuality. In the commercial dance halls, amusement parks, and movie theaters of turn-of-the-century New York, young, single working women affirmed a new expressive sexuality that disturbed many middle-class observers. In a world that subordinated women at work and within the family, leisure offered young women an unusual degree of power and social freedom. Peiss shows both the possibilities and the limitations of their new leisure world.

Uncovering the history of working-class sexuality has been a particularly intractable task for recent scholars. Diaries, letters, and memoirs, while a rich source for studies of bourgeois sexuality, offer few glimpses into working-class intimate life. We have had to turn to middle-class commentary and observations of working people, but these accounts often seem hopelessly moralistic and biased. The difficulty with such sources is not simply a question of tone or selectivity, but involves the very categories of analysis they employ. Reformers, social workers, and journalists viewed working-class women's sexuality through middle-class lenses, invoking sexual standards that set "respectability" against "promiscuity." When applied to unmarried women, these categories were constructed foremost around the biological fact of premarital virginity, and secondarily by such cultural indicators as manners, language, dress, and public interaction. Chastity was the measure of young women's respectability, and those who engaged in premarital intercourse, or, more importantly, dressed and acted as though they had, were classed as promiscuous women or prostitutes. Thus labor investigations of the late nineteenth century not only surveyed women's wages and working conditions, but delved into the issue of their sexual virtue, hoping to resolve scientifically the question of working women's respectability.[1]

Nevertheless, some middle-class observers in city missions and settlements recognized that their standards did not always reflect those of working-class youth. As one University Settlement worker argued, "Many of the liberties which are taken by tenement boys and girls with one another, and which seem quite improper to the 'up-towner,' are, in fact, practically harmless."[2] Working women's public behavior often seemed to fall between the traditional middle-class poles: they were not truly promiscuous in their actions, but neither were they models of decorum. A boarding-house

A young wage-earner and her gentleman friend meeting during a lunch break. Lewis Hine Collection, United States History, Local History & Genealogy Division, The New York Public Library, Aston, Lenox, and Tilden Foundations.

matron, for example, puzzled over the behavior of Mary, a "good girl": "The other night she flirted with a man across the street," she explained. "It is true she dropped him when he offered to take her into a saloon. But she does go to picture shows and dance halls with 'pick up' men and boys."[3] Similarly, a city missionary noted that tenement dwellers followed different rules of etiquette, with the observation: "Young women sometimes allow young men to address them and caress them in a manner which would offend well-bred people, and yet those girls would indignantly resent any liberties which they consider dishonoring."[4] These examples suggest that we must reach beyond the dichotomized analysis of many middle-class observers and draw out the cultural categories created and acted on by working women themselves. How was sexuality "handled" culturally? What manners, etiquette, and sexual style met with general approval? What constituted sexual respectability? Does the polarized framework of the middle class reflect the realities of working-class culture?

Embedded within the reports and surveys lie small pieces of information that illuminate the social and cultural construction of sexuality among a number of working-class women. My discussion focuses on one set of young, white working women in New York City in the years 1880 to 1920. Most of these women were single wage earners who toiled in the city's factories, shops, and department stores, while devoting their evenings to the lively entertainment of the streets, public dance halls, and other popular amusements. Born or educated in the United States, many adopted a cultural style meant to distance themselves from their immigrant roots and familial traditions. Such women dressed in the latest finery, negotiated city life with ease, and sought intrigue and adventure with male companions. For this group of working women, sexuality became a central dimension of their emergent culture, a dimension that is revealed in their daily life of work and leisure.[5]

These New York working women frequented amusements in which familiarity and intermingling among strangers, not decorum, defined normal public behavior between the sexes. At movies and cheap theaters, crowds mingled during intermissions, shared picnic lunches, and commented volubly on performances. Strangers at Coney Island's amusement parks often involved each other in practical jokes and humorous escapades, while dance halls permitted close interaction between unfamiliar men and women. At one respectable Turnverein ball, for example, a vice investigator described closely the chaotic activity in the barroom between dances:

> Most of the younger couples were hugging and kissing, there was a general mingling of men and women at the different tables, almost everyone seemed to know one another and spoke to each other across the tables and joined couples at different tables, they were all singing and carrying on, they kept running around the room and acted like a mob of lunatics let lo[o]se.[6]

As this observer suggests, an important aspect of social familiarity was the ease of sexual expression in language and behavior. Dances were advertised, for example, through the distribution of "pluggers," small printed cards announcing the particulars of the ball, along with snatches of popular songs or verse; the lyrics and pictures, noted one offended reformer, were often, "so suggestive that they are absolutely indecent."[7]

The heightened sexual awareness permeating many popular amusements may also be seen in working-class dancing styles. While waltzes and two-steps were common, working women's repertoire included "pivoting" and "tough dances." While pivoting was a wild, spinning dance that promoted a charged atmosphere of physical excitement, tough dances ranged from a slow shimmy, or shaking of the hips and shoulders, to boisterous animal imitations. Such tough dances as the grizzly bear, Charlie Chaplin wiggle, and the dip emphasized bodily contact and the suggestion of sexual intercourse. As one dance investigator commented, "What particularly distinguishes this dance is the motion of the pelvic portions of the body."[8] In contrast, middle-class pleasure-goers accepted the animal dances only after the blatant sexuality had been tamed into refined movement. While cabaret owners enforced strict rules to discourage contact between strangers, managers of working-class dance halls usually winked at spieling, tough dancing and unrestrained behavior.[9]

Other forms of recreation frequented by working-class youth incorporated a free and easy sexuality into their attractions. Many social clubs and amusement societies permitted flirting, touching, and kissing games at their meetings. One East Side youth reported that "they have kissing all through pleasure time, and use slang language, while in some they don't behave nice between [sic] young ladies."[10] Music halls and cheap vaudeville regularly worked sexual themes and suggestive humor into comedy routines and songs. At a Yiddish music hall popular with both men and women, one reformer found that "the songs are suggestive of everything but what is proper, the choruses are full of double meanings, and the jokes have broad and unmistakable hints of things indecent."[11] Similarly, Coney Island's Steeplechase amusement park, favored by working-class excursionists, carefully marketed sexual titillation and romance in attractions that threw patrons into each other, sent skirts flying, and evoked instant intimacy among strangers.[12]

In attending dance halls, social club entertainments, and amusement resorts, young women took part in a cultural milieu that expressed and affirmed heterosocial interactions. As reformer Belle Israels observed, "No amusement is complete in which 'he' is not a factor."[13] A common custom involved "picking up" unknown men or women in amusement resorts or on the streets, an accepted means of gaining companionship for an evening's entertainment. Indeed, some amusement societies existed for this very purpose. One vice investigator, in his search for "loose" women, was advised by a waiter to "go first on a Sunday night to 'Hans'l & Gret'l Amusement Society' at the Lyceum 86th Str & III Ave, there the girls come and men pick them up."[14] The waiter carefully stressed that these were respectable working women, not prostitutes. Nor was the pickup purely a male prerogative. "With the men they 'pick up,'" writer Hutchins Hapgood observed of East Side shop girls, "they will go to the theater, to late suppers, will be as jolly as they like."[15]

The heterosocial orientation of these amusements made popularity a goal to be pursued through dancing ability, willingess to drink, and eye-catching finery. Women who would not drink at balls and social entertainments were often ostracized by men, while cocktails and ingenious mixtures replaced the five-cent beer and helped to make drinking an acceptable female activity. Many women used clothing as a means of drawing attention to themselves, wearing high-heeled shoes, fancy dresses, costume jewelry, elaborate pompadours, and cosmetics. As one working woman sharply explained, "If you want to get any notion took of you, you gotta have some style about you."[16] The clothing that such women wore no longer served as an emblem of respectability. "The way women dress today they all look like prostitutes," reported one rueful waiter to a dance hall investigator, "and the waiter can some times get in bad by going over and trying to put some one next to them, they may be respectable women and would jump on the waiter."[17]

Underlying the relaxed sexual style and heterosocial interaction was the custom of "treating." Men often treated their female companions to drinks and refreshments, theater tickets, and other incidentals. Women might pay a dance hall's entrance fee or carfare out to an amusement park, but they relied on men's treats to see them through the evening's entertainment. Such treats were highly prized by young working women; as Belle Israels remarked, the announcement that "he treated" was "the acme of achievement in retailing experiences with the other sex."[18]

Treating was not a one-way proposition, however, but entailed an exchange relationship. Financially unable to reciprocate in kind, women offered sexual favors of varying degrees, ranging from flirtatious companionship to sexual intercourse, in exchange for men's treats. "Pleasures don't cost girls so much as they do young men," asserted one saleswoman. "If they are agreeable they are invited out a good deal, and they are not allowed to pay anything." Reformer Lillian Betts concurred, observing that the working woman held herself responsible for failing to wangle men's invitations and believed that "it is not only her misfortune, but her fault; she should be more attractive."[19] Gaining men's treats placed a high premium on allure and personality, and sometimes involved aggressive and frank "overtures to men whom they desire to attract," often with implicit sexual proposals. One investigator, commenting on women's dependency on men in their leisure time, aptly observed that "those who are unattractive, and those who have puritanic notions, fare but ill in the matter of enjoyments. On the other hand those who do become popular have to compromise with the best conventional usage."[20]

Many of the sexual patterns acceptable in the world of leisure activity were mirrored in the workplace. Sexual harassment by employers, foremen, and fellow workers was a widespread practice in this period, and its form often paralleled the relationship of treating, particularly in service and sales jobs. Department store managers, for example, advised employees to round out their meager salaries by finding a "gentlemen friend" to purchase clothing and pleasures. An angry saleswoman testified, for example, that "one of the employers has told me, on a $6.50 wage, he don't care where I get my clothes from as long as I have them, to be dressed to suit him."[21] Waitresses knew that accepting the advances of male customers often brought good tips, and some used their opportunities to enter an active social life with men. "Most of the girls quite frankly admit making 'dates' with strange men," one investigator found. "These 'dates' are made with no thought on the part of the girl beyond getting the good time which she cannot afford herself."[22]

In factories where men and women worked together, the sexual style that we have seen on the dance floor was often reproduced on the shop floor. Many factories lacked privacy in dressing facilities, and workers tolerated a degree of familiarity and roughhousing between men and women. One cigar maker observed that his workplace socialized the young into sexual behavior unrestrained by parental and community control. Another decried the tendency of young boys "of thirteen or fourteen casing an eye upon a 'mash.' " Even worse, he testified, were the

> many men who are respected—when I say respected and respectable, I mean who walk the streets and are respected as working men, and who would not under any circumstances offer the slightest insult or disrespectful remark or glance to a female in the streets, but who, in the shops, will whoop and give expressions to "cat calls" and a peculiar noise made with their lips, which is supposed to be an endearing salutation.[23]

In sexually segregated workplaces, sexual knowledge was probably transmitted among working women. A YWCA report in 1913 luridly asserted that "no girl is more 'knowing' than the wage-earner, for the 'older hands' initiate her early through the unwholesome story or innuendo."[24] Evidence from factories, department stores, laundries, and restaurants substantiates the sexual consciousness of female workers. Women brought to the workplace tales of their evening adventures and gossip about dates and eligible men, recounting to their co-workers the triumphs of the latest ball or outing. Women's socialization into a new shop might involve a ritualist exchange about "gentlemen friends." In one laundry, for example, an investigator repeatedly heard this conversation:

> "Say, you got a feller?"
> "Sure, Ain't you got one?"
> "Sure."[25]

Through the use of slang and "vulgar" language, heterosexual romance was expressed in a sexually explicit context. Among waitresses, for example, frank discussion of lovers and husbands during breaks was an integral part of the work day. One investigator found that "there was never any open violation of the proprieties but always the suggestive talk and behavior." Laundries, too, witnessed "a great deal of swearing among the women." A 1914 study of department store clerks found a similar style and content in everyday conversation:

> While it is true that the general attitude toward men and sex relations was normal, all the investigators admitted a freedom of speech frequently verging upon the vulgar, but since there was very little evidence of any actual immorality, this can probably be likened to the same spirit which prompts the telling of risqué stories in other circles.[26]

In their workplaces and leisure activities, many working women discovered a milieu that tolerated, and at times encouraged, physical and verbal familiarity between men and women, and stressed the exchange of sexual favors for social and economic advantages. Such women probably received conflicting messages about the virtues of virginity, and necessarily mediated the parental, religious, and educational injunctions concerning chastity, and the "lessons" of urban life and labor. The choice made by some women to engage in a relaxed sexual style needs to be understood in terms of the larger relations of class and gender that structured their sexual culture.

Most single working-class women were wage-earners for a few years before marriage, contributing to the household income or supporting themselves. Sexual segmentation of the labor market placed women in semi-skilled, seasonal employment with high rates of turnover. Few women earned a "living wage," estimated to be $9.00 or $10.00 a week in 1910, and the wage differential between men and women was vast. Those who lived alone in furnished rooms or boarding houses consumed their earnings in rent, meals, and clothing. Many self-supporting women were forced to sacrifice an essential item in their weekly budgets, particularly food, in order to pay for amusements. Under such circumstances, treating became a viable option. "If my boy friend didn't take me out," asked one working woman, "how could I ever go out?"[27] While many women accepted treats from "steadies," others had no qualms about receiving them from acquaintances or men they picked up at amusement places. As one investigator concluded, "The acceptance on the part of the girl of almost any invitation needs little explanation when one realizes that she often goes pleasureless unless she does accept 'free treats.' "[28] Financial resources were little better for the vast majority of women living with families and relatives. Most of them contributed all of their earnings to the family, receiving only small amounts of spending money, usually 25¢ to 50¢ a week, in return. This sum covered the costs of simple entertainments, but could not purchase higher priced amusements.[29]

Moreover, the social and physical space of the tenement home and boarding house contributed to freer social and sexual practices. Working women living alone ran the gauntlet between landladies' suspicious stares and the knowing glances of male boarders. One furnished-room dweller attested to the pressure placed on young, single women: "Time and again when a male lodger meets a girl on the landing, his salutation usually ends with something like this: 'Won't you step into my place and have a glass of beer with me?' "[30]

The tenement home too, presented a problem to parents who wished to maintain control over their daughters' sexuality. Typical tenement apartments offered limited opportunities for family activities or chaperoned socializing. Courtship proved difficult in homes where families and boarders crowded into a few small rooms, and the "parlor" served as kitchen, dining room, and bedroom. Instead, many working-class daughters socialized on streetcorners, rendezvoused in cafes, and courted on trolley cars. As one settlement worker observed, "Boys and girls and young men and women of respectable families are almost obliged to carry on many of their friendships, and perhaps their lovemaking, on tenement stoops or on street corners."[31] Another reformer found that girls whose parents forbade men's visits to the home managed to escape into the streets and dance halls to meet them. Such young women demanded greater independence in the realm of "personal life" in exchange for their financial contribution to the family. For some, this new freedom spilled over into their sexual practices.[32]

The extent of the sexual culture described here is particularly difficult to establish, since the evidence is too meager to permit conclusions about specific groups of working women, their beliefs about sexuality, and their behavior. Scattered evidence does suggest a range of possible responses, the parameters within which most women would choose to act and define their behavior as socially acceptable. Within this range, there existed a subculture of working women who fully bought into the system of treating and sexual exchange, by trading sexual favors of varying degrees for gifts, treats, and a good time. These women were known in underworld slang as "charity girls," a term that differentiated them from prostitutes because they did not accept money in their sexual encounters with men. As vice reformer George Kneeland found, they "offer themselves to strangers, not for money, but for presents, attention, and pleasure, and most important, a yielding to sex desire."[33] Only a thin line divided these women and "occasional prostitutes," women who slipped in and out of prostitution when unemployed or in need of extra income. Such behavior did not result in the stigma of the "fallen woman." Many working women apparently acted like Dottie: "When she needed a pair of shoes she had found it easy to 'earn' them in the way that other girls did." Dottie, the investigator reported, was now known as a respectable married woman.[34]

Such women were frequent patrons of the city's dance halls. Vice investigators note a preponderant number of women at dances who clearly were not prostitutes, but were "game" and "lively"; these charity girls often comprised half or more of the dancers in a hall. One dance hall investigator distinguished them with the observation, "Some of the women . . . are out for the coin, but there is a lot that come in here that are charity."[35] One waiter at La Kuenstler Klause, a restaurant with music and dancing, noted that "girls could be gotten here, but they don't go with men for money, only for good time." The investigator continued in his report, "Most of the girls are working girls, not prostitutes, they smoke cigarettes, drink liquers and dance dis.[orderly] dances, stay out late and stay with any man, that pick them up first."[36] Meeting two women at a bar, another investigator remarked, "They are both supposed to be working girls but go out for a good time and go the limit."[37]

Some women obviously relished the game of extracting treats from men. One vice investigator offered to take a Kitty Graham, who apparently worked both as a department store clerk and occasional prostitute, to the Central Opera House at 3 A.M.; he noted that "she was willing to go if I'd take a taxi; I finally coaxed her to come with me in a street car."[38] Similarly, Frances Donovan observed waitresses "talking about their engagements which they had for the evening or for the night and quite frankly saying what they expected to get from this or that fellow in the line of money, amusement, or clothes."[39] Working women's manipulation of treating is also suggested by this unguarded conversation overheard by a journalist at Coney Island:

"What sort of a time did you have?"
"Great. He blew in $5 on the blow-out."
"You beat me again. My chump only spent $2.50."[40]

These women had clearly accepted the full implications of the system of treating and the sexual culture surrounding it.

While this evidence points to the existence of charity girls—working women defined as respectable, but who engaged in sexual activity—it tells us little about their numbers, social background, working lives, or relationships to family and community. The vice reports indicate that they were generally young women, many of whom lived at home with their families. One man in a dance hall remarked, for example, that "he sometimes takes them to the hotels, but sometimes the girls won't go to [a] hotel to stay for the night, they are afraid of their mothers, so he gets away with it in the hallway."[41] While community sanctions may have prevented such activity within the neighborhood, the growth of large public dance halls, cabarets, and metropolitan amusement resorts provided an anonymous space in which the subculture of treating could flourish.

The charity girl's activities form only one response in a wide spectrum of social and sexual behavior. Many young women defined themselves sharply against the freer sexuality of their pleasure-seeking sisters, associating "respectability" firmly with premarital chastity and circumspect behavior. One working woman carefully explained her adherence to propriety: "I never go out in the evenings except to my relatives because if I did, I should lose my reputation and that is all I have left." Similarly, shop girls guarded against sexual advances from co-workers and male customers by spurning the temptations of popular amusements. "I keep myself to myself," said one saleswoman. "I don't make friends in the stores very easily because you can't be sure what any one is like."[42] Settlement workers also noted that women who freely attended "dubious resorts" or bore illegitimate children were often stigmatized by neighbors and workmates. Lillian Betts, for example, cites the case of working women who refused to labor until their employer dismissed a co-worker who had born a baby out of wedlock. To Betts, however, their adherence to the standard of virginity seemed instrumental, and not a reflection of moral absolutism: "The hardness with which even the suggestion of looseness is treated in any group of working girls is simply an expression of selfpreservation."[43]

Other observers noted an ambivalence in the attitudes of young working women toward sexual relations. Social workers reported that the critical stance toward premarital pregnancy was "not always unmixed with a certain degree of admiration for the success with the other sex which the difficulty implies." According to this study, many women increasingly found premarital intercourse acceptable in particular situations: " 'A girl can have many friends,' explained one of them, 'but when she gets a "steady," there's only one way to have him and to keep him; I mean to keep him long.' "[44] Such women shared with charity girls the assumption that respectability was not predicated solely on chastity.

Perhaps few women were charity girls or occasional prostitutes, but many more must have been conscious of the need to negotiate sexual encounters in the workplace or in their leisure time. Women would have had to weigh their desire for social participation against traditional sanctions regarding sexual behavior, and charity girls offered to some a model for resolving this conflict. This process is exemplified in Clara Laughlin's report of an attractive but "proper" working woman who could not understand why men friends dropped her after a few dates. Finally she receives the worldly advice of a co-worker that social participation involves an exchange relationship: "Don't yeh know there ain't no feller goin' t'spend coin on yeh fer nothin'? Yeh gotta be a good Indian, Kid—we all gotta!"[45]

For others, charity girls represented a yardstick against which they might measure their own ideas of respectability. The nuances of that measurement were expressed, for example, in a dialogue between a vice investigator and the hat girl at Semprini's dance hall. Answering his proposal for a date, the investigator noted, she "said she'd be glad to go out with me but told me there was nothing doing [i.e., sexually]. Said she didn't like to see a man spend money on her and then get disappointed." Commenting on the charity girls that frequented the dance hall, she remarked that "these women get her sick, she can't see why a woman should lay down for a man the first time they take her out. She said it wouldn't be so bad if they went out with the men 3 or 4 times and then went to bed with them but not the first time."[46]

For this hat girl and other young working women, respectability was not defined by the strict measurement of chastity employed by many middle-class observers and reformers. Instead, they adopted a more instrumental and flexible approach to sexual behavior. Premarital sex *could* be labeled respectable in particular social contexts. Thus charity girls distinguished their sexual activity from prostitution, a less acceptable practice, because they did not receive money from men. Other women, who might view charity girls as promiscuous, were untroubled by premarital intimacy with a steady boyfriend.

This fluid definition of sexual respectability was embedded within the social relation of class and gender, as experienced by women in their daily round of work, leisure, and family life. Women's wage labor and the demands of the working-class household offered daughters few resources for entertainment. At the same time, new commercial amusements offered a tempting world of pleasure and companionship beyond parental control. Within this context, some young women sought to exchange sexual goods for access to that world and its seeming independence, choosing not to defer sexual relations until marriage. Their notions of legitimate premarital behavior contrast markedly with the dominant middle-class view, which placed female sexuality within a dichotomous and rigid framework. Whether a hazard at work, fun and adventure at night, or an opportunity to be exploited, sexual expression and intimacy comprised an integral part of these working women's lives.

Notes

1. See, for example, Carroll D. Wright, *The Working Girls of Boston* (1889; New York: Arno Press, 1969).
2. "Influences in Street Life," University Settlement Society *Report* (1900), p. 30.
3. Marie S. Orenstein, "How the Working Girl of New York Lives," New York State, Factory Investigating Commission, *Fourth Report Transmitted to Legislature*, February 15, 1915, Senate Doc. 43, vol. 4, app. 2 (Albany: J. B. Lyon Co., 1915), p. 1697.
4. William T. Elsing, "Life in New York Tenement-Houses as Seen by a City Missionary," *Scribner's* 11 (June 1892): 716.
5. For a more detailed discussion of these women, and further documentation of their social relations and leisure activities, see my dissertation, "Cheap Amusements: Gender Relations and the Use of Leisure Time in New York City, 1880 to 1920," Ph.D. diss., Brown University, 1982.
6. Investigator's Report, Remey's, 917 Eighth Ave., February 11, 1917, Committee of Fourteen Papers, New York Public Library Manuscript Division, New York.
7. George Kneeland, *Commercialized Prostitution in New York City* (New York: The Century Co., 1913), p. 68; Louise de Koven Bowen, "Dance Halls," *Survey* 26 (3 July 1911): 384.
8. Committee on Amusements and Vacation Resources of Working Girls, two-page circular, in Box 28, "Parks and Playgrounds Correspondence," Lillian Wald Collection, Rare Book and Manuscripts Library, Columbia University, New York.
9. See, for example, Investigator's Report, Princess Cafe, 1206 Broadway, January 1, 1917; and Excelsior Cafe, 306 Eighth Ave., December 21, 1916, Committee of Fourteen Papers.
10. "Social Life in the Streets," University Settlement Society *Report* (1899), p. 32.
11. Paul Klapper, "The Yiddish Music Hall," *University Settlement Studies* 2, no. 4 (1905): 22.
12. For a description of Coney Island amusements, see Edo McCullough, *Good Old Coney Island: A Sentimental Journey into the Past* (New York: Charles Scribner's Sons, 1957), pp. 309–13; and Oliver Pilot and Jo Ransom, *Sodom by the Sea: An Affectionate History of Coney Island* (Garden City, N.J.: Doubleday, 1941).
13. Belle Lindner Israels, "The Way of the Girl," *Survey* 22 (3 July 1909): 486.
14. Investigator's Report, La Kuenstler Klause, 1490 Third Ave., January 19, 1917, Committee of Fourteen Papers.
15. Hutchins Hapgood, *Types from City Streets* (New York: Funk and Wagnalls, 1910), p. 131.
16. Clara Laughlin, *The Work-A-Day Girl: A Study of Some Present Conditions* (1913; New York: Arno Press, 1974), pp. 47, 145. On working women's clothing, see Helen Campbell, *Prisoners of Poverty: Women Wage Earners, Their Trades and Their Lives* (1887; Westport, Conn.: Greenwood Press, 1970), p. 175; "What It Means to Be a Department Store Girl as Told by the Girl Herself," *Ladies Home Journal* 30 (June 1913): 8; "A Salesgirl's Story," *Independent* 54 (July 1902): 1821. Drinking is discussed in Kneeland, *Commercialized Prostitution*, p. 70; and Belle Israels, "Diverting a Pastime," *Leslie's Weekly* 113 (27 July 1911): 100.
17. Investigator's Report, Weimann's, 1422 St. Nicholas Ave., February 11, 1917, Committee of Fourteen Papers.
18. Israels, "Way of the Girl," pp. 489; Ruth True, *The Neglected Girl* (New York: Russell Sage Foundation, 1914), p. 59.
19. "A Salesgirl's Story," p. 1821; Lillian Betts, *Leaven in a Great City* (New York: Dodd, Mead, 1902), pp. 251–52.
20. New York State, Factory Investigating Commission, *Fourth Report*, vol. 4 pp. 1585–86; Robert Woods and Albert Kennedy, *Young Working-Girls: A Summary of Evidence from Two Thousand Social Workers* (Boston: Houghton Mifflin, 1913), p. 105.
21. New York State, Factory Investigating Commission, *Fourth Report*, vol. 5, p. 2809; see also Sue Ainslie Clark and Edith Wyatt, *Making Both Ends Meet: The Income and Outlay of New York Working Girls* (New York: Macmillan, 1911), p. 28.
22. Consumers' League of New York, *Behind the Scenes in a Restaurant: A Study of 1017 Women Restaurant Employees* (n.p., 1916), p. 24; Frances Donovan, *The Woman Who Waits* (1920; New York: Arno Press, 1974), p. 42.

23. New York Bureau of Labor Statistics, *Second Annual Report* (1884), pp. 153, 158; *Third Annual Report* (1885), pp. 150–51.

24. Report of Commission on Social Morality from the Christian Standpoint, Made to the 4th Biennial Convention of the Young Women's Christian Associations of the U.S.A., 1913, Records File Collection, Archives of the National Board of the YWCA of the United States of America, New York, N.Y.

25. Clark and Wyatt, *Making Both Ends Meet*, pp. 187–88; see also Dorothy Richardson, *The Long Day*, in *Women at Work*, ed. William L. O'Neill (New York: Quadrangle, 1972); Amy E. Tanner, "Glimpses at the Mind of a Waitress," *American Journal of Sociology* 13 (July 1907): 52.

26. Committee of Fourteen in New York City, *Annual Report for 1914*, p. 40; Clark and Wyatt, *Making Both Ends Meet*, p. 188; Donovan, *The Woman Who Waits*, pp. 26, 80–81.

27. Esther Packard, "Living on Six Dollars a Week," New York State, Factory Investigating Commission *Fourth Report*, vol. 4, pp. 1677–78. For a discussion of women's wages in New York, see *ibid.,* vol. 1, p. 35; and vol. 4, pp. 1081, 1509.

28. Packard, "Living on Six Dollars a Week," p. 1685.

29. New York State, Factory Investigating Commission, *Fourth Report*, vol. 4, pp. 1512–13, 1581–83; True, *Neglected Girl*, p. 59.

30. Marie Orenstein, "How the Working Girl of New York Lives," p. 1702. See also Esther Packard, *A Study of Living Conditions of Self-Supporting Women in New York City* (New York: Metropolitan Board of the YWCA, 1915).

31. "Influences in Street Life," p. 30; see also Samuel Chotzinoff, *A Last Paradise* (New York: Knopf, 1955), p. 81.

32. On the rejection of parental controls by young women, see Leslie Woodcock Tentler, *Wage-Earning Women: Industrial Work and Family Life in the United States, 1900–1930* (New York: Oxford University Press, 1979), pp. 110–13. For contemporary accounts, see True, *Neglected Girl*, pp. 54–55, 62–63, 162–63; Lillian Betts, "Tenement House Life and Recreation," *Outlook* (11 February 1899): 365.

33. "Memoranda on Vice Problem: IV. Statement of George J. Kneeland," New York State, Factory Investigating Commission, *Fourth Report*, v.1, p. 403. See also Committee of Fourteen, *Annual Report* (1917), p. 15, and *Annual Report* (1918), p. 32; Woods and Kennedy, *Young Working Girls*, p. 85.

34. Donovan, *The Woman Who Waits*, p. 71; on occasional prostitution, see U.S. Senate, *Report on the Condition of Women and Child Wage-Earners in the United States*, U.S. Sen. Doc. 645, 61st Cong., 2nd Sess. (Washington, D.C.: GPO), vol. 15, p. 83; Laughlin, *The Work-A-Day Girl*, pp. 51–52.

35. Investigator's Report, 2150 Eighth Ave., January 12, 1917, Committee of Fourteen Papers.

36. Investigator's Report, La Kuenstler Klause, 1490 Third Ave., January 19, 1917, Committee of Fourteen Papers.

37. Investigator's Report, Bobby More's, 252 W. 31 Street, February 3, 1917, Committee of Fourteen Papers.

38. Investigator's Report, Remey's, 917 Eighth Ave., December 23, 1916, Committee of Fourteen Papers.

39. Donovan, *The Woman Who Waits*, p. 55.

40. Edwin Slosson, "The Amusement Business," *Independent* 57 (21 July 1904): 139.

41. Investigator's Report, Clare Hotel and Palm Gardens/McNamara's, 2150 Eighth Ave., January 12, 1917, Committee of Fourteen Papers.

42. Marie Orenstein, "How the Working Girl of New York Lives," p. 1703; Clark and Wyatt, *Making Both Ends Meet*, pp. 28–29.

43. Betts, *Leaven in a Great City*, pp. 81, 219.

44. Woods and Kennedy, *Young Working-Girls*, pp. 87, 85.

45. Laughlin, *The Work-A-Day Girl*, p. 50.

46. Investigator's Report, Semprini's, 145 W. 50 Street, October 5, 1918, Committee of Fourteen Papers.

Chapter 17

Discontented Black Feminists: Prelude and Postscript to the Passage of the Nineteenth Amendment

Rosalyn Terborg-Penn

Although numerous black leaders and organizations were counted among the supporters of woman suffrage, Rosalyn Terborg-Penn describes widespread discontent among black feminists at the suffrage movement's accommodation to racism among white voters. With the achievement of suffrage, black women found their right to vote frequently denied in southern states with little response on the part of white suffragists. As a result of continuing racial discrimination, black feminists increasingly focused on race issues in the 1920s and after. A predominantly white feminist movement that turned a blind eye to racial discrimination had little appeal for black feminists. These women organized primarily on behalf of their race, a stance that reflected a reasonable appraisal of the realities of power in the United States in the interwar years.

A significant number of black women and black women's organizations not only supported woman suffrage on the eve of the passage of the Nineteenth Amendment but attempted to exercise their rights to vote immediately after the amendment's passage in 1920. Unfortunately for them, black women confronted racial discrimination in their efforts to support the amendment and to win the vote. Consequently, discontented black feminists anticipated the disillusionment that their white counterparts encountered after 1920. An examination of the problems black women faced on the eve of the passage of the woman suffrage amendment and the hostility black women voters endured after the amendment passed serves as a preview of their political status from 1920 to 1945.

The way in which black women leaders dealt with these problems reveals the unique nature of feminism among Afro-American women. Black feminists could not overlook the reality of racism and class conflict as determining factors in the lives of women of their race. Hence, black feminists of the post-World War I era exhibited characteristics similar to those of black feminists of the woman suffrage era and of the late nineteenth-century black women's club movement. During each era, these feminists could not afford to dismiss class or race in favor of sex as the major cause of oppression among black women.

This material originally appeared in *Decades of Discontent: The Women's Movement, 1920–1940*, Lois Scharf and Joan M. Jensen, eds. (Contributions in Women's Studies, No. 28, Greenwood Press, Westport, CT, 1983), pp. 261–78. Copyright © 1983 by Lois Scharf & Joan M. Jensen. Abridged and reprinted with permission.

PRELUDE TO PASSAGE OF THE NINETEENTH AMENDMENT

On the eve of the passage of the Nineteenth Amendment, black women leaders could be counted among other groups of women who had worked diligently for woman suffrage. At least ninety black women leaders endorsed woman suffrage, with two-thirds of these women giving support during the decade immediately before passage of the amendment. Afro-American women organized suffrage clubs, participated in rallies and demonstrations, spoke on behalf of the amendment, and wrote essays in support of the cause. These things they had done since the inception of the nineteenth-century woman's rights movement. However, the largest woman suffrage effort among black women's groups occurred during the second decade of the twentieth century. Organizations such as the National Federation of Afro-American Women, the National Association of Colored Women (NACW), the Northeastern Federation of Colored Women's Clubs, the Alpha Kappa Alpha Sorority, and the Delta Sigma Theta Sorority actively supported woman suffrage. These organizations were national or regional in scope and represented thousands of Afro-American women. Some of the women were from the working class, but most of them were of middle-class status. Across the nation, at least twenty black women suffrage organizations or groups that strongly endorsed woman suffrage existed during the period.[1] . . .

The enthusiastic responses of black women to woman suffrage may seem astonishing when one realizes that woman suffrage was a predominantly middle-class movement among native born white women and that the black middle class was very small during the early twentieth century. Furthermore, the heyday of the woman suffrage movement embraced an era that historian Rayford Logan called "the nadir" in Afro-American history, characterized by racial segregation, defamation of the character of black women, and lynching of black Americans, both men and women. It is a wonder that Afro-American women dared to dream a white man's dream—the right to enfranchisement—especially at a time when white women attempted to exclude them from that dream.[2] . . .

The existence of a double standard for black and white women among white woman suffragists was apparent to black women on the eve of Nineteenth Amendment passage. Apprehensions from discontented black leaders about the inclusion of black women as voters, especially in the South, were evident throughout the second decade of the twentieth century. During the early years of the decade, black suffragists such as Adella Hunt Logan, a club leader and suffragist from Tuskegee, Alabama; Mary B. Talbert, president of the National Association of Colored Women; and Josephine St. Pierre Ruffin, a suffragist since the 1880s from Boston and the editor of the *Woman's Era*, a black women's newspaper, complained about the double standard in the woman suffrage movement and insisted that white suffragists set aside their prejudices to allow black women, burdened by both sexism and racism, to gain political equality.[3]

Unfortunately, with little influence among white women, the black suffragists were powerless and their words went unheeded. By 1916 Carrie Catt, president of the NAWSA, concluded that the South had to be conciliated if woman suffrage was to become a reality. Thus, in order to avoid antagonizing southern white women who resented participating in the association with black women, she urged southern white delegates not to attend the NAWSA convention in Chicago that year because the Chicago delegation would be mostly black.[4]

The trend to discriminate against black women as voters continued, and in 1917 the *Crisis*, the official organ of the National Association for the Advancement of Colored People (NAACP), noted that blacks feared white female voters because of their antiblack woman suffrage and antiblack male sentiments. Afro-American fears went beyond misgivings about white women. In 1918 the editors of the *Houston Observer* responded to black disillusionment when they called upon the men and women of the race to register to vote in spite of the poll tax, which was designed especially to exclude black voters.[5]

Skepticism about equality of woman suffrage among blacks continued. Mrs. A. W. Blackwell, an African Methodist Episcopal Church leader in Atlanta, estimated that about 3 million black women were of voting age. She warned, however, that a "grandmother clause" would be introduced after passage of a suffrage amendment to prevent black women, 90 percent of whom lived in the South, from voting.[6]

Disillusionment among black suffrists became so apparent that several national suffrage leaders attempted to appease them with reassurances about their commitment to black woman suffrage. In 1917 Carrie Catt and Anna Shaw wooed black female support through the pages of the *Crisis*. In the District of Columbia, the same year, Congresswoman Jeanette Rankin of Montana addressed an enthusiastic group of Alpha Kappa Alpha Sorority women at Howard University. There she assured the group that she wanted all women to be given the ballot regardless of race.[7]

However, in 1917 while the New York state woman suffrage referendum was pending in the legislature, black suffrists in the state complained of discrimination against their organizations by white suffrists during the statewide woman suffrage convention at Saratoga. White leaders assured black women that they were welcomed in the movement. Although the majority of the black delegates were conciliated, a vocal minority remained disillusioned.[8]

By 1919, the year before the Nineteenth Amendment was adopted by Congress, antiblack woman suffrage sentiments continued to plague the movement. Shortly before the amendment was adopted, several incidents occurred to further disillusion black feminists. Mary Church Terrell, a Washington, D.C., educator and national leader among black club women, reported that white suffrists in Florida discriminated against black women in their attempts to recruit support for the campaign. In addition, the NAACP, whose policy officially endorsed woman suffrage, clashed with Alice Paul, president of the NWP because she allegedly said "that all this talk of Negro women voting in South Carolina was nonsense."[9] Later, Walter White, the NAACP's assistant to the executive secretary, complained to Mary Church Terrell about Alice Paul and agreed with Terrell that white suffrage leaders would be willing to accept the suffrage amendment even if it did not enfranchise black women.[10]

Within a week after receiving Walter White's letter, Mary Church Terrell received a letter from Ida Husted Harper, a leader in the suffrage movement and the editor of the last two volumes of the *History of Woman Suffrage*, asking Terrell to use her influence to persuade the Northeastern Federation of Colored Women's Clubs to withdraw their application seeking cooperative membership in the NAWSA. Echoing sentiments expressed earlier by NAWSA president Carrie Catt, Harper explained that accepting the membership of a black organization was inexpedient for NAWSA at a time when white suffrists sought the cooperation of white southern women. Harper noted that the major obstacle to the amendment in the South was fear among whites of the black woman's vote. She therefore asked federation president Elizabeth Carter to resubmit the membership application after the passage of the Nineteenth Amendment.[11] . . .

During the last months before the passage of the Susan B. Anthony amendment, black suffrists had been rebuffed by both the conservative wing of the suffrage movement, the NAWSA, and by the more radical wing, the NWP. Why then did Afro-American women continue to push for woman suffrage? Since the 1880s, most black women who supported woman suffrage did so because they believed that political equality among the races would raise the status of blacks, both male and female. Increasing the black electorate, they felt, would not only uplift the women of the race, but help the children and the men as well. The majority of the black suffrists were not radical feminists. They were reformers, or what William H. Chafe calls social feminists, who believed that the system could be amended to work for them. Like their white counterparts, these black suffrists assumed that the enfranchised held the key to ameliorating social ills. But unlike white social feminists, many black suffragists called for social and political measures that were specifically tied to race issues. Among these issues were anti-miscegenation legislation, Jim Crow legislation, and "lynch law." Prominent black feminists combined the fight against sexism with the fight against racism by continuously calling the public's attention to these issues.[12] . . .

Blacks understood the potential political influence, if not political power, that they could harness with woman suffrage, especially in the South. White supremacists realized it too. Although there were several reasons for southern opposition to the Nineteenth Amendment, the one common to all states was fear of black female suffrage. This fear had been stimulated by the way in which Afro-American women responded to suffrage in states that had achieved woman suffrage before the passage of the federal amendment. In northern states with large black populations, such as Illinois and New York, the black female electorate was significant. Chicago elected its first black alderman, Oscar De Priest, in 1915, the year after women won the right to vote. In 1917, the year the woman suffrage referendum passed the New York state legislature, New York City elected its first black state assemblyperson, Edward A. Jonson. In both cities the black female vote was decisive in the election. In the South, Texas Afro-American women mobilized in 1918 to effectively educate the women of their race in order to combat white opposition to their voting.[13]

By 1920 white southern apprehensions of a viable black female electorate were not illusionary. "Colored women voters' leagues" were growing throughout the South, where the task of the leagues was to give black women seeking to qualify to vote instructions for countering white opposition. Leagues could be found in Alabama, Georgia, Tennessee, and Texas. These groups were feared also by white supremacists because the women sought to qualify black men as voters as well.[14]

Whites widely believed that black women wanted the ballot more than white women in the South. Black women were expected to register and to vote in larger numbers than white women. If this happened, the ballot would soon be returned to black men. Black suffrage, it was believed, would also result in the return of the two-party system in the South, because blacks would consistently vote Republican. These apprehensions were realized in Florida after the passage of the Nineteenth Amendment. Black women in Jacksonville registered in greater numbers than white women. In reaction, the Woman Suffrage League of Jacksonville was reorganized into the Duval County League of Democratic Women Voters. The members were dedicated to maintain white supremacy and pledged to register white women voters.[15]

In Texas, where women could vote before the passage of the Nineteenth Amendment, black women, nevertheless, were discriminated against. In 1918 six black women had been refused the right to register at Fort Worth on the ground that the primaries were open to white Democrats only. Efforts to disfranchise black women in Houston failed, however, when the women took legal action against the registrars who attempted to apply the Texas woman suffrage law to white women only. A similar attempt to disqualify Afro-American women in Waxahachie, Texas, failed also.[16]

Subterfuge and trickery such as the kind used in Texas was being used throughout the South by 1920. In North Carolina, the predictions of Mrs. A. W. Blackwell came true when the state legislature introduced a bill known as the "grandmother clause" for women voters. The bill attempted to protect illiterate white women from disfranchisement, but the legislators had not taken into account that "grandfather clauses" had been nullified by the Supreme Court. Nonetheless, black leaders called to the women of the race to stand up and fight. This they did.[17]

In 1920 black women registered in large numbers throughout the South, especially in Georgia and Louisiana, despite major obstacles placed against them by the white supremacists. In defense, Afro-American women often turned to the NAACP for assistance. Field Secretary William Pickens was sent to investigate the numerous charges and recorded several incidents which he either witnessed personally or about which he received reports. In Columbia, South Carolina, during the first day of registration black women apparently took the registrars by surprise. No plan to disqualify them had been put into effect. Many black women reported to the office and had to wait for hours while the white women were registered first. Some women waited up to twelve hours to register. The next day, a $300 tax requirement was made mandatory for black women. If they passed that test, the women were required to read from and to interpret the state or the federal constitutions. No such tests were required of white women. In addition, white lawyers were on hand to quiz and harass black women. Although the *Columbia State*, a local newspaper, reported disinterest in registering among black women, Pickens testified to the contrary. By the end of the registration period, twenty Columbia black women had signed an affidavit against the registrars who had disqualified them. In the surrounding Richland County, Afro-American women were disqualified when they attempted to register to vote. As a result, several of them made plans to appeal the ruling.[18]

Similar reports came from Richmond, Virginia, where registrars attempted to deny or successfully denied black women the right to register. A black woman of Newburn, North Carolina, signed an affidavit testifying to the difficulty she had in attempting to register. First she was asked to read and to write the entire state constitution. After successfully reading the document, she was informed that no matter what else she did, the registrar would disqualify her because she was black. Many cases like this one were handled by the NAACP, and after the registration periods ended in the South, its board of directors presented the evidence to Congress. NAACP officials and others testified at a congressional hearing in support of the proposed enactment of the Tinkham Bill to reduce representation in Congress from states where there was restriction of woman suffrage. White supremacy prevailed, however, as southern congressmen successfully claimed that blacks were not disfranchised, just disinterested in voting. Hence, despite the massive evidence produced by the NAACP, the Tinkham Bill failed to pass.[19]

The inability of the NAACP to protect the rights of black women voters led the women to seek help from national woman suffrage leaders. However, these attempts failed also. The NWP leadership felt that since black women were discriminated against in the same ways as black men, their problems were not woman's rights issues, but race issues. Therefore, the woman's party felt no obligation to defend the rights of black women.[20]

That they would be abandoned by white female suffragists in 1920 came as no surprise to most black women leaders. The preceding decade of woman suffrage politics had reminded them of the assertions of black woman suffrage supporters of the past. Frederick Douglass declared in 1868 that black women were victimized mainly because they were blacks, not because they were women. Frances Ellen Watkins Harper answered in 1869 that for white women the priorities in the struggle for human rights were sex, not race. By 1920 the situation had changed very little, and many black suffragists had been thoroughly disillusioned by the machinations of the white feminists they had encountered.[21]

POSTSCRIPT—BLACK FEMINISTS, 1920–1945

Afro-American women continued to be involved in local and national politics during the post-World War I years. However, few organized feminist activities were apparent among the disillusioned black feminists of the period. Afro-American women leaders and their organizations began to focus on issues that continued to plague both the men and women of the race, rather than upon issues that concerned white feminists. The economic plight of black women kept most of them in poverty and among the lowest of the working classes. Middle-class black women were still relatively few in number. They were more concerned about uplifting the downtrodden of the race or in representing people of color throughout the world than in issues that were limited to middle-class feminists. Hence, during the 1920s there was little concern among black women over the Equal Rights Amendment debate between the more conservative League of Women Voters (LWV) and the more radical NWP. Although the economic roles of many white American women were expanding, the status of black women remained basically static between the wars. As a result, black feminists identified more with the plight of third world people who found themselves in similar oppressed situations. Former black suffragists were more likely to participate in the Women's International League for Peace and Freedom (WILPF) or the International Council of Women of the Darker Races than in the LWV or the NWP.

A look at the 1920s reveals that most of the black women's organizations that were prominent during the woman suffrage era remained so. Nonetheless, new groups were organized as well. Elizabeth Carter remained president of the Northeastern Federation of Colored Women's Clubs, which celebrated its twenty-fifth anniversary in 1921. The leadership of the NACW was in transition during the 1920s. Mary B. Talbert retired as president and was succeeded by a former suffragist, Hallie Q. Brown, in 1922. In the middle of the decade Mary McLeod Bethune assumed the presidency. In 1922 several NACW leaders organized the International Council of Women of the Darker Races. Margaret Murray Washington, the wife of the late Booker T. Washington and the first president of the National Federation of Afro-American Women, was elected president.[22]

In addition to these established black women's organizations, there was the women's arm of Marcus Garvey's United Negro Improvement Association (UNIA). At its peak, in 1925, the UNIA had an estimated membership of 2 million and can be considered the first mass movement among working-class black people in the nation. Amy Jacques Garvey, Marcus Garvey's wife, was the articulate leader of the women's division and the editor of the women's department of the UNIA official newspaper, *Negro World*. A feminist in the international sense, Amy Jacques Garvey's feminist views embraced the class struggle as well as the problems of Third World women. . . . Garvey called for black women's dedication to social justice and to national liberation, abroad as well as at home.[23]

Garvey was a radical who happened to be a feminist as well. Her views were ahead of her time; thus, she would have fit in well with the midtwentieth century radical feminists. However, the demise of the UNIA and the deportation of Marcus Garvey in 1927 shattered much of Amy Jacques Garvey's influence in the United States and she returned to Jamaica. In the meantime, the majority of black feminists of the 1920s either joined the white social feminists, such as Jane Addams and the WILPF, or bypassed the feminists altogether to deal with race issues within black organizations.

The leadership of the WILPF was old-line and can be characterized as former progressives, woman suffragists, and social feminists. Jane Addams presided over the organization before U.S. entry into World War I and brought black women such as Mary Church Terrell, Mary B. Talbert, Charlotte Atwood, Mary F. Waring, and Addie W. Hunton into the fold. Terrell had been a member of the executive committee since 1915. As a league representative, she was elected a delegate to the International Congress of Women held in Paris in 1919. Upon her arrival, Terrell was impressed with the conference delegates but noticed that there were none from non-western countries and that she was the only delegate of color in the group. As a result, she felt obliged to represent the women of all the nonwhite countries in the world, and this she attempted to do. . . . Terrell's position and thinking were in keeping with the growing awareness among black women leaders in the United States that Third World people needed to fight oppression together.[24]

Although Mary Church Terrell remained an active social feminist, her public as well as her private views reflected the disillusionment of black feminists of the woman suffrage era. In 1921 she was asked by members of the WILFP executive committee to sign a petition requesting the removal of black troops from occupied German territory, where they were alleged to be violating German women. Terrell refused to sign the petition because she felt the motives behind it were racist. In a long letter to Jane Addams, the executive committee chairman, Terrell explained why she would not sign the petition. She noted that Carrie Catt had investigated the charges against the black troops and found them to be unfounded. The troops, from French colonies in Africa, were victims, Terrell contended, of American propaganda against black people. Making a dramatic choice between the feminist organization position and her own loyalty to her race, Terrell offered to resign from the executive committee. Addams wrote her back, agreeing with Terrell's position and asking her not to resign.[25] In this case, when given the choice between the politics of feminism and race pride, Terrell felt that her energies were needed most to combat racism, and she chose to take a nationalist position in the controversy. . . .

[In the 1920s] most black women's organizations had turned from attempts to establish coalitions with white women's groups to concentrate upon pressing race problems. Lynching was one of the major American problems, and black women organized to fight it. On the national front, black women's groups used political strategies and concentrated their efforts toward passage of the Dyer Anti-Lynching Bill. In 1922 the Northeastern Federation of Colored Women's Clubs appointed a delegation to call on Senator Lodge of Massachusetts to urge passage of the Dyer bill. In addition, the Alpha Kappa Alpha Sorority held its national convention in Indianapolis and sent a telegram to President Warren Harding urging the support of his administration in the passage of the bill. Also that year, the NACW met in Richmond and appointed an antilynching delegation to make contact with key states needed for the passage of the Dyer bill in Congress. In addition, the delegation was authorized to meet with President Harding. Among the black women in the delegation were veteran antilynching crusader Ida B. WellsBarnett, NACW president Hallie Q. Brown, and Rhode Island suffragist Mary B. Jackson.[26]

Perhaps the most renowned antilynching crusader of the 1920s was Spingarn Medal winner Mary B. Talbert. In 1922 she organized an executive committee of 15 black women, who supervised over 700 state workers across the nation in what Talbert called the Anti-Lynching Crusade. Her aim was to "unite a million women to stop lynching," by arousing the consciences of both black and white women. One of Talbert's strategies was to provide statistics that showed that victims of lynching were not what propagandists called sex-hungry black men who preyed upon innocent white women. The crusaders revealed that eighty-three women had been lynched in the United States since Ida B. Wells-Barnett had compiled the first comprehensive annual report in 1892. The Anti-Lynching Crusade was truly an example of woman power, for the crusaders believed that they could not wait for the men of America to stop the problem. It was perhaps the most influential link in the drive for interracial cooperation among women's groups. As a result of its efforts, the 1922 National Council of Women, representing 13 million American women, resolved to "endorse the Anti-Lynching Crusade recently launched by colored women of this country."[27]

Although the Dyer bill was defeated, it was revised by the NAACP and introduced again in the House of Representatives by Congressman Leonidas C. Dyer of Missouri and in the Senate by William B. McKinley of Illinois in 1926. That year the bill failed again, as did similar bills in 1935, 1940, and 1942. However, it was the effort of blacks and white women organized against lynching that pressed for legislation throughout the period. Without a doubt, it was the leadership of black women, many of whom had been active in the late nineteenth-century women's club movement and in the woman suffrage movement, who motivated white women in 1930 to organize the Association of Southern Women for the Prevention of Lynching. Although a federal antilynching bill never passed the Congress, by the end of the 1940s public opinion had been sufficiently convinced by the efforts of various women's groups that lynching was barbarous and criminal. Recorded incidents of lynching ceased by 1950.

Even though interracial cooperation in the antilynching campaign was a positive factor among black and white women, discrimination against black women by white women continued to plague feminists. In 1925, for example, the Quinquennial of the International Council of Women met at the Washington Auditorium in the District of Columbia. The council sought the cooperation of NACW president Mary McLeod Bethune and arrangements were made to have a mass choir of black women perform. The night of the concert, black guests were placed in a segregated section of the auditorium. Mary Church Terrell reported that when the singers learned of what was happening, they refused to perform.[28]. . .

National recognition of black women did not really come until 1936, when Mary McLeod Bethune was appointed director of the Division of Negro Affairs, National Youth Administration, under the Franklin D. Roosevelt administration. The founder of Bethune-Cookman Institute in Daytona, Florida, Bethune had been a leader in the black women's club movement since the early 1920s. NACW president from 1924 to 1928, she founded the National Council of Negro Women (NCNW) in 1935. What feminist consciousness Bethune acquired was thrust upon her in the mid-1930s because for the first time, a black woman had the ear of the president of the United States and the cooperation of the first lady, who was concerned not only about women's issues, but about black issues. In 1936 Bethune took advantage of her new status and presented the concerns of the NCNW to Eleanor Roosevelt. As a result, sixty-five black women leaders attended a meeting with Eleanor Roosevelt to argue the case for their greater representation and appointments to federal bureaus. They called for appointments of professional black women to the Children's Bureau, the Women's Bureau, and each department of the Bureau of Education that dealt with the welfare of women and children. The NCNW also wanted the appointment of black women to administrative positions in the Federal Housing Administration and Social Security Board. In addition, they called for enlarging the black staff of the Bureau of Public Health and for President Roosevelt to suggest to the American Red Cross that they hire a black administrator.[29]

The NCNW requests reflect two trends among middle-class women in the mid-1930s. First, they were calling for positions that black women had never held, nor would achieve until a generation later; consequently, their ideas were revolutionary ones in terms of federal policies. Second, they were calling for policies to benefit not only their sex, but their race; hence, the NCNW reflected the position established by black feminists a generation before.

Middle-class black women clearly reflected their dedication to uplifting the race at a time when most Afro-Americans were thwarted not only by race prejudice but also by economic depression. Although activities that involved race uplift were not feminist in orientation, many black feminists took an active role in them. In an interview with Mary McLeod Bethune in 1939, Lillian B. Huff of the *New Jersey Herald News* asked her about the role of black women leaders and how Bethune related to her leadership position. Bethune, who had come from humble origins, felt that black women had room in their lives to be wives and mothers as well as to have careers. But most importantly, she thought, black women should think of their duty to the race.[30]

Bethune's feelings were not unique to black women, for most black feminists and leaders had been wives and mothers who worked yet found time not only to struggle for the good of their sex, but for their race. Until the 1970s, however, this threefold commitment—to family and to career and to one or more social movements—was not common among white women. The key to the uniqueness among black feminists of this period appears to be their link with the past. The generation of the woman suffrage era had learned from their late nineteenth-century foremothers in the black women's club movement, just as the generation of the post-World War I era had learned and accepted the experiences of the preceding generation. Theirs was a sense of continuity, a sense of group consciousness that transcended class. Racial uplift, fighting segregation and mob violence, contending with poverty, as well as demanding rights for black women were long-standing issues of concern to black feminists. . . .

By 1940 Mary Church Terrell had written her autobiography. At the age of seventy-seven, she was one of the few living links with three generations of black feminists. In her introduction, Terrell established her own interpretation of her life story, which in many ways reflected the lives of other black feminists. "This is the story of a colored woman living in a white world. It cannot possibly be like a story written by a white woman. A white woman has only one handicap to overcome—that of sex. I have two—both sex and race. I belong to the only group in this country which has two such huge obstacles to surmount. Colored men have only one—that of race."[31]

Terrell's reference to her status as an Afro-American woman applied throughout United States history to most black women, regardless of class. In view of this, it is not surprising that black women struggled, often in vain, to keep the right to vote from 1920 to 1940. A brief reference to this struggle, a story in itself, reveals that they fought to keep the little influence they had although black feminists anticipated that many of them would lose. Nonetheless, black female enthusiasm was great immediately following passage of the Nineteenth Amendment. In Baltimore alone, the black electorate increased from 16,800 to over 37,400 in 1921, indicating that the number of black women voters surpassed the number of black men registered to vote. By 1922, however, attempts to thwart the influence of black women voters were spreading across the South. As a result, the NACW recommended that all of its clubs lobby for the enforcement of the Nineteenth Amendment.[32]

By 1924 feminist Nannie Burroughs had assessed the status of black women of voting age and their relationship to white feminists. Burroughs noted that white women continued to overlook or to undervalue the worth of black women as a political force in the nation. She warned white female politicians to tap the potential black female electorate before white men exploited it.[33] With the exception of Ruth Hanna McCormick, who recruited Mary Church Terrell to head her 1929 Illinois campaign for the United States Senate, warnings such as Burroughs's did not seem to influence white female leaders. For example, disillusioned members of the Republican Colored Women State Committee of Wilmington, Delaware, protested unsuccessfully when they lost their representation on the state Republican committee. A merger of the Women's Advisory Committee, a white group, with the State Central Committee had caused the elimination of black women representatives. The decline in black women's participation in Republican party politics was evident by 1928, when only 8 out of 104 black delegates to the Republican National Convention were women. The same year, the NACW program did not even bother to include suffrage among its priorities for women of the race.[34]

Although President Roosevelt made good his promise to Mary McLeod Bethune, so that by 1945 four black women had received outstanding federal appointments, the political viability of black women in the early 1940s was bleak. The list of black elected officials from 1940 to 1946 included no women.[35] Agents of white supremacy continued to subvert what vestiges of political influence blacks held. For example, in 1942 Congressman Martin Dies, chairman of the congressional committee investigating un-American activities, attempted to link several national black leaders to the Communist party. Among the group was Mary McLeod Bethune, who remained the only black woman prominent in national politics.[36]

Hence, over twenty years after the passage of the Nineteenth Amendment racial discrimination festered in most areas of American life, even among feminists and women in political life. Prejudice did not distinguish between middle-class and working-class black women, nor between feminists and nonfeminists who were black. Although black women continued to use what political rights they maintained, the small number of those politically viable made little impact upon public policies.

Notes

1. See Rosalyn Terborg-Penn, "Nineteenth Century Black Women and Woman Suffrage," *Potomac Review* 7 (Spring-Summer 1977): 13–24; and Rosalyn M. Terborg-Penn, "Afro-Americans in the Struggle for Woman Suffrage" (Ph.D. dissertation, Howard University, 1977), pp. 180–85.
2. See Rayford W. Logan, *The Negro in the United States* (Princeton, N.J.: Van Nostrand, 1957); and Terborg-Penn, "Discrimination Against Afro-American Women," pp. 17–27.

3. Terborg-Penn, "Afro Americans in the Struggle for Woman Suffrage," chapter 4.

4. David Morgan, *Suffragists and Democrats: The Politics of Woman Suffrage in America* (East Lansing, Mich.: Michigan State University Press, 1972), pp. 106–07.

5. *Crisis* 15 (November 1917): 18; *Negro Year Book, 1918–1919*, p. 60.

6. Mrs. A. W. Blackwell, *The Responsibility and Opportunity of the Twentieth Century Woman* (n.p., n.d.), pp. 1–5. This pamphlet is housed in the Trevor Arnett Library, Atlanta University.

7. *The Crisis* 15 (November 1917): 19–20; *New York Age*, 10 May 1917.

8. *New York Age*, September 20, 1917.

9. Walter White to Mary Church Terrell, 14 March 1919, Mary Church Terrell Papers, Box no. 3, Library of Congress, Washington, D.C. (hereafter cited as MCT Papers); Charles Flint Kellogg, *NAACP: A History of the National Association for the Advancement of Colored People, 1909–1920* (Baltimore: Johns Hopkins University Press, 1967), p. 208.

10. Walter White to Mary Church Terrell, 14 March 1919, MCT Papers, Box no. 3.

11. Ida Husted Harper to Mary Church Terrell, 18 March 1919, and Ida Harper to Elizabeth Carter, 18 March 1919, MCT Papers, Box no. 3.

12. Terborg-Penn, "Afro-Americans in the Struggle for Woman Suffrage," chapters 4 and 5.

13. *Ibid.*, pp. 207, 217–18, 225.

14. *Crisis* 19 (November 1920): 23–25; *Negro Year Book, 1921*, p. 40.

15. Kenneth R. Johnson, "White Racial Attitudes as a Factor in the Arguments Against the Nineteenth Amendment," *Phylon* 31 (Spring 1970): 31–32, 35–37.

16. Terborg-Penn, "Afro-Americans in the Struggle for Woman Suffrage," pp. 301–02.

17. *Ibid.*, pp. 303–04.

18. William Pickens, "The Woman Voter Hits the Color Line," *Nation* 3 (October 6, 1920): 372–73.

19. *Ibid.*, p. 373; NAACP, *Eleventh Annual Report of the NAACP for the Year 1920* (New York: NAACP, 1921), pp. 15, 25–30.

20. William L. O'Neill, *Everybody Was Brave* (Chicago: Quadrangle Press, 1969), p. 275.

21. Terborg-Penn, "Afro-Americans in the Struggle for Woman Suffrage," p. 311.

22. *Negro Year Book, 1922–24*, p. 37.

23. *The Negro World*, 24 October 1925, 5 March 1927. See Mark D. Matthews, "'Our Women and What They Think,' Amy Jacques Garvey and *The Negro World*," *Black Scholar* 10 (May–June 1979); 2–13.

24. Mary Church Terrell, *A Colored Woman in a White World* (Washington, D.C.; Randsdell, Inc., 1940), pp. 330–33.

25. *Ibid.*, pp. 360–64.

26. *Ibid.*, pp. 37–38; *Crisis* 23 (March 1922): 218; *Crisis* 24 (October 1922): 260.

27. *Crisis* 24 (November 1922): 8.

28. Terrell, *A Colored Woman in a White World*, pp. 370–71.

29. Mary McLeod Bethune, Vertical File, Howard University, Washington, D. C., Clippings Folder, 1930, *Black Dispatch*, 16 April 1936 (hereafter cited as Bethune Vertical File and the source).

30. Bethune Vertical File, *New Jersey Herald News*, 14 October 1939.

31. Terrell, *A Colored Woman in a White World*, first page of the introduction.

32. *Crisis* 23 (December 1921): 83; *Negro Year Book, 1922–24*, p. 37.

33. *Negro Year Book, 1922–24*, p. 70.

34. Terrell, *A Colored Woman in a White World*, pp. 355–56; *Negro Year Book, 1922–24*, p. 70; *Negro Year Book, 1931–32*, pp. 13, 92–93. Blacks did not vote the Democratic party on a large scale until the second Franklin D. Roosevelt administration.

35. *Negro Year Book, 1947*, pp. 286–87, 289–91.

36. Bethune Vertical File, *Black Dispatch*, 10 October 1942.

Chapter 18

The Professionalization of Birth Control

Linda Gordon

Reproductive rights have emerged as one of the most contested arenas of twentieth-century political activity. Linda Gordon's account of Margaret Sanger's place in that struggle between 1914 and 1940 helps us understand the origin of many features of women's reproductive struggles in the 1990s. Chief among these is the difficulty of advocating change through cross-class alliances. In this chapter Gordon shows us how, through Sanger's support of the "Doctors-Only Bill" in 1926, the medical profession gained the power it enjoys today in shaping the nation's reproductive policies. Sanger's alliance with physicians and the medical profession's definition of reproductive rights as the right to privacy set the stage for today's debate. In that debate the rights of middle-class women to the privacy of their personal choice are rarely linked with the rights of poor women to publicly funded reproductive choice.

The socialists and sex radicals who began the birth-control movement before the First World War were amateurs. With few exceptions, mostly men, they had no professional or socially recognized expertise in sexology, public health, demography, or any related fields. (If they were professionals at anything, it was radical agitation!) They fought for birth control because it was self-evidently in their own interest as women. The intellectual work that had influenced them most in their birth-control views was philosophy, radical ethics sometimes grounded in political appraisals of social problems. Birth control was, for them, pre-eminently a political and moral issue.

But after the war, the birth-control movement changed. The local birth-control leagues with radical and socialist leadership lost their momentum. Birth control became an increasingly centralized cause, dominated from New York City by Sanger's American Birth Control League and Dennett's Voluntary Parenthood League. The strategies that dominated—opening clinics and lobbying for legislation—required large sums of money, and the power of the wealthy in the organizations increased accordingly. People accustomed to working in respectable, even elegant, charity organizations joined the movement. Birth-control leagues began to sponsor balls and expensive white-tie dinners. Simultaneously the weakening of the organized Left deprived the birth-control movement of leadership that might have created alternative tactics and strategies. Respectable legal tactics produced different results from militant law-defying ones. The latter attracted radicals and angry, poor people; the former attracted more prosperous people, those eager for reform but not desperately in need of fundamental social change. It was not always possible for more conservative reformers to forgive birth control's early associations with bohemianism, radicalism, and illegality. In efforts to break those associations, birth-control organizers in the 1920s often condemned and publicly disassociated themselves from radicals.

Excerpted from Chapter 10 of *Woman's Body, Woman's Right: A Social History of Birth Control in America* (New York: Grossman Publishers, 1976). Reprinted by permission of the author. Notes have been renumbered.

Margaret Sanger awaiting trial, 1916. Sophia Smith Collection, Smith College.

The main factor behind this new conservatism of the birth-control movement was the entrance of professionals into the cause on a large scale. Professionalization was not the only important development in the birthcontrol cause in the 1920s, but it was the single most influential one. The professionals took over birth-control groups less often by driving out the radicals (though this did happen in a few places), than by joining a cause that radicals had deserted. For most socialists, the war itself, then the Russian Revolution and the defense of the American Left against repression seemed more pressing issues from 1918 on. . . .

The leadership of Margaret Sanger was an important factor in facilitating, even encouraging, the professionalization of the birth-control movement. Despite a tactical radicalism, which she learned from and shared with other socialists, Sanger's approach to birth control was distinguished by her willingness to make it her full-time, single cause. From her return from Europe to face trial for *The Woman Rebel* in 1915, until her trial for the illegal Brownsville clinic in 1917, an ambivalent political posture helped her to retain the support of many disparate political groups. She simultaneously pursued direct action and defiance of the law and, with a "low profile" on her radical ideas, organized financial and public-relations support from conservative and wealthy reformers. At the same time Sanger was preparing an organizational structure to give her ongoing power.

In the fall of 1916—even while she had been working on the Brownsville clinic—she founded the *Birth Control Review*. She recruited Frederick Blossom, a professional charity fund-raiser from Cleveland, to come to New York as its paid editor and manager.[1] In December she founded the New York Birth Control League (NYBCL) as an alternative to the National Birth Control League (NBCL), organized by Mary Ware Dennett, and Blossom also worked for Sanger's organization. An ugly disagreement and then split between Sanger and Blossom exploded in 1917. Whoever was in the right—and it seems likely both of them acted badly—the quarrel demonstrated Sanger's rigid need for personal control and separated her still further from the radical movement. Blossom quit when he could not have his way and took the records and small bank account of the *Review*. Sanger brought formal charges against him. Blossom had been a member of the Socialist party, and other socialists in the NYBCL were infuriated at Sanger's turning to the capitalist state to solve her quarrel; they formed an investigation committee which condemned Sanger and exonerated Blossom. Ironically, Blossom's subsequent behavior led the IWW to conduct another investigation in 1922 which condemned him for the break with Sanger.[2]

Whatever the actual issues involved, Sanger did not quail before the disapproval of her former socialist comrades. Ironically, some of them had defended Sanger's need for personal control on the grounds that she was trying to create a movement with radical politics. Dennett's NBCL had always excluded people identified with the far Left and avoided radical tactics like civil disobedience, and Sanger's radical reputation had arisen partly in being distinguished from Dennett. But even before the break with Blossom and his socialist supporters, Sanger had begun to move in another equally conservative direction, though it was not widely perceived as such at the time.

From the beginning of planning for her Brownsville clinic she had sought a doctor to prescribe and fit contraceptives. New York state law at the time would have permitted her to legalize the clinic by putting it under a physician's supervision, and this was an important part of her motivation. Section 1142 of the New York State Penal Code made it a misdemeanor to give out any contraceptive information, but section 1145 allowed lawfully practicing physicians to prescribe devices for the cure and prevention of disease. Sanger believed that this provision intended to allow only the prescription of prophylactic measures against venereal disease, and wanted to challenge and broaden its interpretation. But Sanger's conviction that contraception required the attendance of a physician was based on a belief deeper then mere legal tactics. Since she was a nurse herself, it seems odd that she should have doubted that a nurse could fit a diaphragm as well as a doctor. Her earliest medical tutor, Dr. Johannes Rutgers of Holland, had taught her to fit a diaphragm; she herself fitted some of his patients while in The Hague. While she was there, Rutgers was training midwives in contraceptive technique so that they could start birth-control clinics elsewhere.[3] Nevertheless, Sanger argued to the end of her career—even after laws no longer stood in her way—that every applicant for birth control should see a doctor. After the forcible closure of the clinic, Sanger quickly returned to the search for medical support for her work. As early as January 11, 1917, a year before Sanger was brought to trial for the Brownsville Clinic, her New York Birth Control League was urging modification of the laws to permit physicians only to give out birth-control information.[4] Dennett's NBCL, with its more respectable image, was nevertheless fighting for a more thoroughgoing legislative reform—a bill simply removing birth control from any definition of obscenity.

Margaret Sanger's leadership was particularly responsible for making birth control a medical issue in the United States. In the 1920s she also courted recognition and support from another group of professionals—the demographers, geneticists, and other academics who led the eugenics movement. But in promoting professionals to increasing importance in the birth-control movement, Sanger just helped along a trend that would have happened without her. She was not responsible for the decline of the feminist movement, although her individualist and dominating style of working did not help to build solidarity with surviving feminist groups. She was not responsible for the repression, division, and shrinking of the socialist movement; her opportunist alliances with antisocialists and conservatives for the cause of birth control were partly necessitated by the refusal of maledominated socialism to incorporate birth-control and women's liberation issues into their programs. All these factors plus the economic weakening of the working class created a political power vacuum where the socialists had been. Sanger did not wish to give up her birth-control campaign, nor could she fill that vacuum by herself; she had to find support. Sanger has often been criticized for her urge to dominate and her liking for power, weaknesses she clearly had. But not even she had the personal influence to substitute for a movement, or to articulate the needs of masses of American women when the masses were silent and depoliticized.

DOCTORS

Despite the efforts made by pro-birth-control doctors in attacking sexual continence, most physicians remained opposed to contraception in the early 1920s. The predominant position among prestigious doctors was not merely disapproval but revulsion so hysterical that it prevented them from accepting facts. As late as 1925 Morris Fishbein, editor of the *Journal of the American Medical Association,* asserted that there were no safe and effective birth-control methods.[5] In 1926 Frederick McCann wrote that birth control had an insidious influence on the female, causing many ailments; and that although "biology teaches" that the primary purpose of the sexual act is to reproduce, the seminal fluid also has a necessary and healthful effect on the female.[6] Many doctors believed that they had a social and moral responsibility to fight the social degeneration that birth control represented. The social values underlying their opposition were often extremely conservative. ". . . fear of conception has been an important factor in the virtue of many unmarried girls, and . . . many boys are likewise kept straight by this means. . . . the freedom with which this matter is now discussed . . . must have an unfortunate effect on the morals of our young people. It is particularly important . . . to keep such knowledge from our girls and boys, whose minds and bodies are not in a receptive frame for such information."[7] George Kosmak, a prominent gynecologist, attacked the birth controllers for their affiliations with anarchism and quackery. Although he acknowledged that physicians should have the right to prescribe contraception in those extraordinary cases in which it was necessary to save life, he reasserted that sexual abstinence ought to be the means of avoiding not only unwanted children but also deleterious sexual excess.

Physicians arguing for a higher valuation of human sexuality as an activity in itself had gained support by 1920, not only among radicals. A leading spokesman for this point of view among prestigious physicians was gynecologist Robert Latou Dickinson. He had used his medical expertise to comment on social problems for several decades previously. In 1902 he had written on masturbation, urging a less hysterical view of its dangers;[8] in 1895 he had defended women's bicycling against those who argued that it might foster the masturbation habit.[9] He believed that mutual sexual satisfaction was essential to happy marriage. As early as 1908 he was giving instruction in contraception as premarital advice to his private patients.[10]

Dickinson encouraged his Ob/Gyn colleagues to take greater initiatives as marriage and sex counselors. In his 1920 address as president of the American Gynecological Society he recommended that the group take an interest in sociological problems. He too disliked the radical and unscientific associations of the birth-control movement. But unlike Kosmak he preferred to respond not by ignoring the movement but by taking it over, and he urged his colleagues to that strategy as early as 1916.[11] At first Dickinson and his physician supporters were hostile to the Sanger clinic. They tried to get Sanger and Dr. Dorothy Bocker, head of the Clinical Research Bureau, to accept the supervision of a panel of medical men, but failed. In 1925 Dickinson wrote a report scathingly critical of the value of Bocker's scientific work.[12] But several factors intervened to lessen this hostility and even bridge the gap between Sanger and the Committee on Maternal Health. One was the fact that the CMH clinic found it difficult to get enough patients with medical indications for contraception. The CMH insistence on avoiding publicity and open endorsement of birth control made women reluctant to try the clinic, anticipating rejection and/or moralistic condemnation of their desire for birth control. Furthermore, it was still extremely difficult to obtain diaphragms, which had to be smuggled into the country. By 1926 three years of work had produced only 124 incomplete case histories. Meanwhile Sanger's clinic saw 1655 patients in 1925 alone, with an average of three visits each.[13]

Another factor leading toward unity between the two clinics was Sanger's conciliatory, even humble, attitude toward Dickinson and other influential doctors. Her organization, the American Birth Control League, had been courting medical endorsement since its establishment in 1921. The League accumulated massive medical mailing lists, for example, and sent out reprints of pro-birth-control articles from medical journals.[14] Sanger's wealthy second husband paid a $10,000 yearly salary to a doctor, James F. Cooper, to tour the country speaking to medical groups for the ABCL.[15] Although even he was not immune from attacks as a quack,[16] he commanded the attention of male physicians as no woman agitator could ever have done. And Cooper's prestige was enhanced by his sharing the speakers' platform with prestigious European physicians at the International Birth Control Conference held in New York in 1925 under ABCL auspices. Indeed, the prestige of the Europeans—whose medical establishment was far more enlightened on the birth-control question than the American—was sufficient to entice the president of the AMA, William A. Pusey, to offer a lukewarm endorsement of birth control at that conference.[17] The ABCL kept exhaustive files, not only of letters but also from their clipping service, on every physician who appeared even mildly favorable to birth control. By 1927 they had 5,484 names.[18] These were collected from the thousands all over the country who wrote asking the ABCL for help. The writers were asked for the names of doctors near them; the ABCL then wrote the doctors asking whether "it is your custom to give contraceptive advice in your regular course of practice, to those patients who in your judgment need it." The names of those who responded positively were then sent to applicants from their vicinity.[19]

In response to criticism of her clinic from the Dickinson group in 1925, Sanger, avoiding any defensive reaction, asked the Committee on Maternal Health to take over and run the clinic, hoping in return to be able to get licensing from the State Board of Charities. Dickinson demanded in return the removal of all propagandistic literature and posters, to which Sanger agreed. The scheme failed anyway, because Sanger's radical reputation and opposition from the Catholic Church led the State Board to refuse a license.[20] Dickinson, on the other hand, made his professional influence clear and useful to Sanger by procuring for her a $10,000 grant from the Rockefeller-backed Bureau of Social Hygiene.

Undoubtedly, the largest single factor drawing doctors into the birth-control movement, however, was Sanger's support for a "doctors-only" type of birth-control legislation. Sanger had apparently been strongly influenced by Judge Crane's 1918 decision in her trial for the Brownsville clinic. In it he had upheld her conviction under the New York State law on obscenity but suggested the possibility of a broad interpretation of section 1145 of the act which made an exception for physicians prescribing contraception for the cure or prevention of disease, by defining disease broadly, as any pathological bodily change. Since then Sanger and her ABCL had worked, both on a state and a federal level, for legislation that would simply strike out all restrictions on doctors' rights to prescribe contraception, giving them unlimited discretion. The ABCL also proposed an amendment to section 211 of the U.S. Penal Code exemption from Post Office restriction on all medical and scientific journals, all items prescribed by physicians, and all items imported by manufacturers, wholesalers, or retail druggists doing business with licensed physicians.[21]

Mary Ware Dennett and her colleagues in the Voluntary Parenthood League, meanwhile, continued to campaign for an open bill, exempting discussion of contraception from all restrictions for anyone. VPL arguments against the doctors-only bill were substantial. "Yes, of course we believe in medical advice for the individual, but again how about the large mass of women who cannot reach even a clinic? . . . Mrs. Sanger's own pamphlet on methods finds its way through the American mails . . . and *it is not a physician's compilation.* . . . Mrs. Sanger herself testified 'that the Clinical Research Department of the American Birth Control League teaches methods so simple that once learned, any mother who is intelligent enough to keep a nursing bottle clean, can use them."[22] Furthermore, Dennett argued, the doctors-only bill left "the whole subject . . . still in the category of crime and indecency."[23] Not only did it accept the definition of sexuality without reproduction as obscene, but it also removed the technique of birth control from a woman's own control. If women could not have direct access to birth-control information, they would have to get their information from doctors along with censorship at worst and moral guidance at best. . . .

Many doctors, of course, believed that they had an ethical duty to oppose an "open bill." Sharing the views expressed by Kosmak in 1917, their sense of professional responsibility and importance led them to anticipate all sorts of moral and physiological disasters should contraceptive information and devices be generally available. Strategically, Dickinson feared that an open bill would increase religious opposition to birth-control legalization.[24] Sanger's opposition to Dennett's bill combined condescension, conservatism, and compromising practicality. "I have come to realize," she wrote to Dennett supporter James Field in 1923, "that the more ignorant classes, with whom we are chiefly concerned, are so liable to misunderstand any written instruction that the Cause of Birth Control would be harmed rather than helped, by spreading abroad unauthoritative literature." To Dennett Sanger wrote that "clean repeal" was impossible because it would have to mean removing abortion from the obscenity category as well, something which Sanger knew could never win and which she probably did not personally accept. "You," she wrote to Dennett, . . . are interested in an abstract idea . . . I am interested in women, in their lives. . . ."[25]

Doctors-only bills were defeated in every state in which they were proposed, even in states without large Catholic populations.[26] Indeed, the pattern of development of the Birth Control League of Massachusetts (BCLM) was echoed in many local birth-control leagues. After the radical originators of the movements left for other causes that seemed to them more pressing (or in a few instances were pushed out by professionals and conservatives), the birthcontrol leagues sunk into lower levels of activity and energy. The impact of professionals—particularly doctors—on birth control as a social movement was to depress it, to take it out of the mass consciousness as a social issue, even as contraceptive information continued to be disseminated. Furthermore, the doctors did not prove successful in the 1920s in winning even the legislative and legal gains they had defined as their goals. Although some birth-control organizers, such as Cerise Jack of the BCLM, felt that they were torn between radical demands and effectiveness, in fact there is reason to question whether the surrender of radical demands produced any greater effectiveness. . . .

By 1930 there were fifty-five clinics in twenty-three cities in twelve states.[27] In Chicago a birth-control clinic was denied a license by the City Health Commissioner, but the League secured a court order overruling him and granting a license. Judge Fisher's 1924 decision in this case marked out important legal precedents. His opinion held that the project was a clinic under the meaning of the law; that there existed contraceptive methods not injurious to health; that the actions of the Health Commissioner (who had cited biblical passages in his letter of refusal to license!) amounted to enforcing religious doctrines, an illegal use of power; that the obscenity statutes only sought to repress "promiscuous" distribution of contraceptive information; that "where reasonable minds differ courts should hesitate to condemn."[28]

As the clinic movement mushroomed around the country, however, conflict continued about how and by whom the clinics should be controlled. In New York Sanger still resisted relinquishing personal control of her clinic to the medical profession. No doubt part of her resistance came from a desire to control things herself, especially since she had lost control of the ABCL and the *Birth Control Review* by 1929.[29] But part of her resistance, too, came from disagreement with the doctors' insistence on requiring medical indications for the prescription of contraceptive devices. Her Clinical Research Bureau had consistently stretched the definition of appropriate indications; and if an appropriate medical problem that justified contraception could not be found, a patient was often referred to private doctors, for whom prescribing contraceptives would be less dangerous.[30] Sanger was willing to avoid an open challenge to the law on the question of indications, but she was not willing to allow close medical supervision to deprive physically healthy women of access to contraception. Sanger always retained a critical view of medical control. As late as 1940 she wrote to Dr. Clarence Gamble, "I am absolutely against our educational or propaganda or organizational work being in the hands of the medicos. . . . Being a medico yourself you will know exactly what I mean because you are not strictly medical."[31] Yet nationally her work had the objective impact of supporting medical control. The only birth-control help the ABCL ever offered individuals was directing them to sympathetic physicians. At ABCL-sponsored birth-control conferences nonmedical people were excluded from the sessions that discussed contraceptive technique.[32] The VPL protested against this policy; but the VPL was also excluded from these conference programs.[33] There was resistance to these policies in some local birth-control groups. Caroline Nelson, for example, the IWW birth controller of the prewar period, still active in California, complained in 1930 of

nothing more nor less than an effort to get the laymen out of the field to leave it to the doctors. Now we have this Conference called by Margaret Sanger, who wants the dissemination of the information limited to doctors, which means that every doctor can demand the arrest and prosecution of every layman who hands it on. Fine! The whole proposition has been evolved outside the medical profession. They have tried with all their professional sneers to hold it back, and refused to include it in their medical curriculum. Now when they find that they can't hold it back, they want to appropriate it and police the layman.[34]

But Sanger's control over the national conferences, lobbying efforts, and publicity was complete, and the increasing medical control was not checked.

Sanger faced a serious problem: without medical approval her clinics were illegal and vulnerable. In New York she continued to seek a license to guarantee the safety and stability of her clinic. When she withdrew the clinic from the auspices of the ABCL in 1928, Sanger once again approached Dickinson requesting that he find her a medical director whose prestige might help obtain a license. Dickinson in reply demanded that the clinic be entirely turned over to a medical authority, suggesting New York Hospital. Sanger was convinced that such an affiliation would hamstring her work and refused it. Then, in April 1929, the clinic was raided by the police. As at Brownsville thirteen years before, a plainclothes policewoman asked for and was supplied with contraceptives. She even came for her second checkup to make sure her diaphragm was fitting her well—then returned five days later with a detachment of police, arrested three nurses and two physicians, and confiscated the medical records. The last action was a mistake on the part of the police, for it united the medical profession behind Sanger and in defense of confidential medical records. Furthermore, the policewoman had been a poor choice because the clinic doctors had indeed found that she had pelvic abnormalities that provided a proper medical indication for giving her a diaphragm. The case was thrown out of court. (Some time later the policewoman returned to the clinic, off duty, to seek treatment for her pelvic disorders!)[35]

. . . Increasingly, the clinics were operated by groups of professional and well-to-do people for the poor. They were charities, not self-help organizations. Eugenic logic had convinced many of these educated people that this particular charity was very much in their own interest; that without population limitation the poor and the unwashed could become a political threat. The members of the ABCL were not the main clients of the clinics they had sparked, but went to private doctors. The attitude of many doctors toward their private patients continued, well into the mid-twentieth century, to parallel that of many elite nineteenth-century doctors: although they opposed the "promiscuous," "indiscriminate" dissemination of contraception, they did not question their own discrimination and even thought it important that private doctors should be able to make exceptions to the policies they supported as general rules. Well-to-do women were able to secure diaphragms without medical indications from doctors who may themselves have opposed making it possible for clinics to use the same principles. The discretionary right of the individual doctor was a privilege as cherished by the profession as that of privacy—and the latter, of course, protected the former.

The new respectability of the birth-control movement shaped the constituency of the ABCL. In 1927 questionnaires were mailed to a random fifth (7,800) of ABCL members and of these 964 were completed.[36] This sample may have tended to raise the apparent class level of the members as more educated people were more likely to reply, but even allowing for some degree of distortion the results are significant. Politically the membership was slightly more Republican than the whole country, the men more inclined to be Republican than the women. (Fifty-five percent of men were Republicans, 19 percent Democrats; the women's figures were 46 percent and 25 percent.) One-third of the members were from cities of more than fifty thousand people; 43 percent of the members were within five hundred miles of New York City, although this proportion had declined from 60 percent in 1922, suggesting increasing penetration of the whole country with birth-control interest and knowledge. The organization seemed not to be dominated by big cities, with half the membership from population centers of less than twenty-five hundred. ABCL techniques in procuring members, however, require a reinterpretation of this phenomenon. Throughout the 1920s ABCL responses to letters of inquiry about birth control either explicitly or implicitly told writers that they could not receive information unless they joined the League. "The information that you desire can only be given to League members," said a form letter signed by Sanger.[37] Thus big-city dwellers, more likely to have access to clinics or local birth-control organizations, had less incentive to join the national organization; ABCL membership could not, therefore, be said to be representative of the overall distribution of people interested in birth control as a cause.

The only check on professional influence would have been a broader-based, popular birth-control movement. No social group of equal size could contest the power of the professionals; only a much larger group could have done that, either a working-class movement or a feminist one. The former was unimaginable by 1920. Even the union movement lost ground in the 1920s; working-class movements demanding larger social change had been severely beaten in the repressive period that followed World War I. Furthermore, the men who dominated all forms of working-class organization at that time were hostile to and/or uninterested in birth control.

The source of the feminist failure in birth control is complex. In addition to many external factors, a contradiction within the feminist movement itself was sharply debilitating; that is, the vision of a new sexual order which this feminism contained was threatening to many of its advocates. . . . In the nineteenth century contraception—the severing of sex from reproduction and hence from family control—was not in the interest of the majority of women. In the 1920s that situation had changed. Sex outside of marriage had been incorporated into a relatively stabilized new family structure, and contraception itself was accepted by most women. But the potential volatility of a continued social movement frightened the relatively privileged women who became reformers in the 1920s. Whether themselves "career women" or, more commonly, leisured wives able to do volunteer work, they were a generation reaping the benefits of a relative social emancipation, one that applied only to their class. . . .

The problem was that their very estrangement from the less privileged majority of women cost them their own coherence as feminists. The essence of feminism has always been a view of all women as united by certain problems and strengths. . . . When class distinctions make this vision of a common womanhood impossible, they dissolve the basis for any feminist analysis or strategy. Taking advantage of their class privileges for their own personal advancement, the prosperous reformers of the 1920s lost the mass base that could have made them a powerful influence. Without a constituency demanding change, they became merely a group of individuals, whereas their male professional rivals in the birth-control organizations had the power of the capitalist class behind them. Their inability to spark a mass movement made them simultaneously unable to create even a coherent militance among a small group, for they had no larger goals that distinguished them from their male colleagues.

Notes

1. Frederick Blossom to Rose Pastor Stokes, November 11, 1916. Stokes mss., Tamiment Library.
2. Henry Fruchter to Elizabeth Gurley Flynn, report on Blossom, September 16, 1922; Margaret Sanger to Flynn, November 3, 1922, both in Sanger, Library of Congress (hereafter LC).
3. Margaret Sanger, *Autobiography* (New York: W. W. Norton, 1938), pp. 211–12, and *My Fight for Birth Control* (New York: Farrar & Rinehart, 1931), p. 110; Mary Ware Dennett, *Birth Control Laws* (New York: F. H. Hitchcock, 1926), p. 11.
4. Letter to members of NBCL from its Executive Committee, January 11, 1917, Stokes mss.; statement by Dennett, November 18, 1921, Sanger, LC.
5. Morris Fishbein, *Medical Follies* (New York: Boni & Liveright, 1925), p. 142.
6. Frederick McCann, Presidential Address to League of National Life, printed in *Medical Press and Circular,* November 3, 1926, p. 359.
7. See George Kosmak in *Bulletin, Lying-in Hospital of the City of New York,* August 1917, pp. 181–92. For similar views among other doctors, see, for example, Edward C. Podvin, "Birth Control," *New York Medical Journal,* February 10, 1917, pp. 258–60; C. Henry Davis, "Birth Control and Sterility," *Surgery, Gynecology and Obstetrics,* March 1923, pp. 435–39; B. S. Talmey, in *New York Medical Journal,* June 23, 1917, pp. 1187–91.

8. Robert L. Dickinson, "Hypertrophies of the Labia Minora and Their Significance," *American Gynecology* 1 (1902): 225–54, quoted in James Reed, "Birth Control and the Americans," Harvard dissertation, 1974.

9. Robert L. Dickinson, "Bicycling for Women from the Standpoint of the Gynecologist," *American Journal of Obstetrics* 31 (1895): 24–37, quoted in Reed thesis, pp. 51–52.

10. Robert L. Dickinson, "Marital Maladjustment: The Business of Preventive Gynecology," *Long Island Medical Journal* (1908): 1–5, quoted in Reed thesis, p. 58.

11. David M. Kennedy, *Birth Control in America: The Career of Margaret Sanger* (New Haven: Yale University Press, 1970), p. 179.

12. Kennedy, *Birth Control in America,* p. 191.

13. James W. Reed, "Birth Control and the Americans, 1830–1970," Ph.D. dissertation, Harvard University, 1974, pp. 77–82; Kennedy, *Birth Control in America,* p. 190; Lawrence Lader, *The Margaret Sanger Story and the Fight for Birth Control* (Garden City, NY: Doubleday, 1955), p. 216.

14. ABCL files, quoted in F. M. Vreeland, "The Process of Reform Groups in the Field of Population," Ph.D. dissertation, University of Michigan, 1929, p. 280.

15. Sanger to J. Noah Slee, February 22, 1925, Sanger, LC; see also ABCL Papers, Boxes 4, 5, 6, Houghton Library, Harvard University.

16. W. N. Wishard, Sr., "Contraception. Are Our County Societies Being Used for the American Birth Control League Propaganda?" *Journal of the Indiana Medical Association,* May 1929, pp. 187–89.

17. *Proceedings, Sixth International Birth Control Conference,* 3:19–30, 49–60.

18. Vreeland, "Process of Reform," p. 280.

19. Form letters in ABCL.

20. Kennedy, *Birth Control in America,* p. 196.

21. ABCL, *An Amendment to the Federal Law Dealing with Contraception,* pamphlet, n.d., in ABCL.

22. Mimeographed letter to VPL members from President Myra P. Gallert, December 2, 1925, Alice Park mss., Stanford University.

23. Dennett, *Birth Control Laws,* p. 88.

24. Kennedy, *Birth Control in America,* pp. 222–23.

25. Sanger to James Field, June 5, 1923, ABCL, Box 2; Sanger to Dennett, March 4, 1930, and unmailed draft of same February 25, 1930, in Sanger mss., Sophia Smith Collection, Smith College [hereinafter given as Sanger, Smith]; see also *Journal of the American Medical Association* 85 (1925): 1153–54; and Sanger to Dennett, [1929], Park mss.

26. Dennett, *Birth Control Laws,* pp. 72–93.

27. There were six in New York, seven in Los Angeles, three in San Francisco, four in Alameda County in California, three in Chicago, and others in Baltimore, Detroit, Cleveland, Buffalo, Philadelphia, Denver, Atlanta, Minneapolis, Newark, Cincinnati, San Antonio, and Charlottesville. See Lader, *Margaret Sanger Story,* p. 219; and Appendix B, pp. 358–59.

28. *Birth Control and Public Policy, Decision of Judge Harry M. Fisher of the Circuit Court of Cook County, November 1923,* pamphlet, Illinois Birth Control League, 1924.

29. Sanger was undoubtedly a difficult person who did not thrive on cooperative work. Her personal struggles within the birth-control movement are well described in Kennedy's *Birth Control in America.*

30. For example, see minutes of advisory council, Harlem Clinical Research Bureau, May 20, 1931, in Sanger, Smith.

31. Sanger to Dr. Clarence Gamble, February 4, 1940, in Sanger, Smith.

32. Conference program, Sanger, LC.

33. Letter to VPL from Gallert; for Sanger's justification of this exclusion, see, for example, Sanger to Prof. James Field, August 13, 1923, BCLM.

34. Caroline Nelson to Alice Park, February 3, 1930, Park mss.

35. Sanger, *Autobiography,* pp. 402–408.

36. The findings of this survey are presented in Vreeland, "Process of Reform," pp. 154 ff., and all the following information is taken from that source.

37. Sanger form letter and many responses are in ABCL.

Chapter 19

Why Were Most Politically Active Women Opposed to the ERA in the 1920s?

Kathryn Kish Sklar

The dispute over whether to pursue strategies for women's advancement based on women's difference from men or on women's similarities to men, accentuated by the Equal Rights Amendment proposed in 1922, debilitated the "women's movement" during the interwar years. Reflecting its nineteenth-century origins, the suffrage movement's mainstream continued to support notions of difference to justify women's political goals and unique contributions to the nation's welfare. Expressing new notions of sexual equality that emerged shortly before the 1920s, however, the National Woman's Party threatened a wide range of legislation that had been carefully constructed on gender differences, including a path-breaking 1921 statute benefiting infant and maternal health. Thus, the strategy whereby "social feminists" had emphasized gender differences as a means of obtaining legislation to enhance the lives of poor people generally conflicted with the strategy of ERA proponents to advance the interests of professional women. Fueled by this fundamental class distinction in their goals, these groups formed two warring camps until the 1970s, one advocating the interests of working women through such institutions as the U.S. Women's Bureau, the other advocating the interests of professional women.

Students of the history of American women are often surprised to discover that the vast majority of suffrage supporters were opposed to the Equal Rights Amendment when it was first proposed in the 1920s. Why were groups as diverse as the National Women's Trade Union League, the General Federation of Women's Clubs, and the League of Women Voters initially hostile to the ERA? Why did some of them remain hostile for decades thereafter? Why did most women reformers view the amendment's proponents as traitors to the cause of "organized womanhood?" Answers to these questions are important to a complete understanding of the history of the Equal Rights Amendment. They help explain not only why most politically active women opposed the ERA in the 1920s, but why they continued to do so until the 1970s, long after the conditions that generated their initial hostility had ceased to exist. As a strategy for understanding that hostility, this essay focuses on Florence Kelley, the amendment's chief opponent.

Opposition to the amendment had many sources within the ranks of those who supported woman suffrage. Some championed a more conservative approach to the advancement of women's rights, preferring piecemeal or gradual changes to the "blanket" approach of a constitutional amendment. Others objected to the cult of personality that developed within the National Woman's Party around the amendment's originator, Alice Paul. But by far the chief origin of resistance to the early

This article is adapted from "Why Were Most Politically Active Women Opposed to the ERA in the 1920s?" by Kathryn Kish Sklar, in Joan Hoff-Wilson, ed., *Rights of Passage: The Past and Future of the ERA.* Copyright © 1986 by Indiana University Press. Reprinted by permission.

ERA was the fear generated among opponents that the amendment would invalidate a wide range of labor and health legislation that women reformers during the past thirty years had struggled to obtain for American working and poor women.[1]

Such legislative efforts peaked in 1921 with the passage of the Sheppard-Towner Maternity and Infancy Protection Act, which sought to reduce the nation's high rates of infant and maternal mortality through the allocation of federal funds for health education at the county level. The Sheppard-Towner Act exemplified a four stage pattern of action that was well established within women's political culture by 1920: "investigate, educate, legislate, and enforce."

The U.S. Children's Bureau—itself the creation of women reformers in 1911, and staffed by them thereafter—undertook rigorous and extensive investigations of infant mortality rates. They found that the United States ranked seventeenth in maternal and eleventh in infant mortality. Poor babies were at greater risk. One baby in six died in families with annual incomes of less than $450; one in ten died among those earning $650–$850; while only one in sixteen died in families enjoying incomes of $1,250. Meanwhile, nations like New Zealand with public clinics for infant health achieved an infant death rate of one in twenty-one. Many women's organizations, including the National Consumers' League and the newly founded League of Women Voters, joined the Children's Bureau in educating the public about the need for a program of nationally funded clinics to stem the tide of unnecessary infant deaths. Mass-circulation magazines like *Good Housekeeping* and *Woman's Home Companion* fueled the publicity campaign. Bowing to the effectiveness of this campaign, Congress passed the Act and placed the Children's Bureau in charge of the allocation of its funds. In Sheppard-Towner women not only obtained the passage of path-breaking legislation, they also oversaw its enforcement.[2]

Nowhere else in the western world did women's political culture exercise such power. Their achievement was partly due to the success of the Women's Joint Congressional Committee, a coalition of nearly two dozen national women's organizations, in claiming to speak for 20,000,000 members. Partly it was due to the desperate need for infant and maternal health care, which was not forthcoming from any other source. Other industrial nations provided for infant and maternal health through governmental programs run by male doctors and bureaucrats. The absence of such programs in the United States opened unprecedented opportunities for women's political culture. In this as in many other examples, women's political culture used gender-specific legislation as a means of meeting the needs of poor people.[3]

The American Medical Association strenuously opposed the Sheppard-Towner Act, calling it an "imported socialistic scheme."[4] The American Public Health Association opposed it on the grounds that it empowered women bureaucrats rather than (male) professionals. The supporters of the ERA seemed to play into the hands of the enemies of the most popular legislation ever advanced by American women. The amendment was doomed from the start, since only a tiny minority of women activists (primarily from elite backgrounds) were willing to jeopardize what most women saw as essential protections for female workers and for mothers.[5]

Although scholars have only begun to study the history of early opposition to the Equal Rights Amendment, it seems clear that many active opponents viewed themselves as participants in a class struggle to alleviate the oppression of poor women and children. Florence Kelley (1859–1932) typified and led this source of ERA opposition. Whereas most hostility toward the ERA in the 1980s tended to come from the political right, in the 1920s it was located primarily on the political left. Kelley herself was a lifelong socialist. As secretary general of the National Consumers' League from its founding in 1899 until her death in 1932, she was the single most powerful force behind the passage of child-labor legislation and hours and wages laws for working women.[6]

In 1953, U.S. Supreme Court Justice Felix Frankfurter wrote that Kelley "had probably the largest single share in shaping the social history of the United States during the first thirty years of this century," owing to her powerful role "in securing legislation for the removal of the most glaring abuses of our hectic industrialization following the Civil War." Even more important than the legislation itself, Frankfurter thought, was "the continuing process she so largely helped to initiate, by which social legislation is promoted and eventually gets on the statute books."[7]

The passage of social legislation was more difficult in the United States than in Great Britain and elsewhere. That was in part because of the power invested in the judicial branch of government, especially the U.S. Supreme Court, which in the late nineteenth and early twentieth centuries was very conservative. A fateful court decision in 1905 defined the vexatious terms under which American reformers had to lobby for social legislation in ensuing decades. In *Lochner v. New York*, the court ruled unconstitutional a state law limiting to ten hours the working day for those employed in bakeries. The rationale behind the law was that longer hours were unhealthy, tending to promote tuberculosis and other diseases, which were then passed on to customers. The court's opinion held, however, that hours could be regulated only when the worker himself was exposed to unhealthy conditions, such as in mines. Otherwise the terms of the contract between employers and employees could not be regulated.[8]

Eventually the court reversed this stand, ruling in *Bunting v. Oregon* in 1917 that state laws limiting working hours in manufacturing to ten a day were constitutional. The precedent for the court's 1917 ruling came in 1908, when in response to the *Lochner* decision, Florence Kelley and her allies successfully argued in *Muller v. Oregon* that the hours of women working in manufacturing could constitutionally be limited to ten a day, since sociological evidence demonstrated that women's health was injured when they labored longer than ten hours daily.[9]

Historians of labor legislation in the United States have noted that men tended to "fight the battle from behind the women's petticoats," since men benefited from laws passed to protect women, and since men's laws tended to follow the legal precedent set by women's.[10] That was true in other countries, as well, but nowhere so emphatically as in the United States, since in no other Western nation was it so difficult to obtain such regulations. In the 1920s, one-half of those employed in the steel industry worked twelve hours a day—longer than in any other nation except Japan.[11] Even though the eight-hour day was the single most popular goal of the labor movement in the United States as early as the 1880s, it was not established for all workers by federal legislation until the Fair Labor Standards Act of 1938—an act upheld by the U.S. Supreme Court in 1941. Thus, in response to the 1905 *Lochner* decision, Kelley and her associates in the National Consumers' League pursued a strategy of obtaining court approval of minimum-hour legislation for women and then extending that approval to cover men. She and her allies were almost as instrumental in the 1917 *Bunting* decision as in the 1908 *Muller* decision.[12] They used gender-specific legislation as a means of advancing class-specific goals.

Florence Kelley was extremely effective in organizing middle-class women consumers into groups that undertook political action on behalf of what they saw as the rights and interests of working women and children. By 1912 some sixty local chapters of the National Consumers' League had successfully agitated for legislation governing the labor of children in almost every state, and that of women in most states.[13]

Kelley's personal charisma and moral indignation over the oppression of women and children workers fueled much of this activity. During a 1908 visit to the United States, the German sociologist Max Weber found Kelley "by far the most outstanding figure" he and his wife had met; he learned from her "a great deal more about the radically evil things in this world."[14] In part Kelley's moral fervor came from her Quaker family background. As early as 1882, the year she graduated from

Cornell, she published an article on the oppression of women workers, "Need Our Working Women Despair?"[15] In part her fervor was due to her knowledge of the "scientific materialistic" writings of Karl Marx and Friedrich Engels, which she translated in the 1880s. She developed a lifelong commitment to socialism in the 1880s and saw class struggle behind the exploitative practices of the sweatshop conditions in which women and children toiled long hours for pitifully small wages.

As a socialist, Kelley saw the power of the state as the logical means of ending such oppression. And as the daughter of one of the most influential congressmen in the nineteenth century (William "Pig Iron" Kelley, who was elected to fifteen consecutive terms in the U.S. House of Representatives between 1860 and 1890), Florence Kelley knew that government was responsive to organized groups, especially those that represented the interests of capital. As she saw it, her contribution to the political process was to make government more responsive to the interests of laboring women and children.

Florence Kelley's success was based on more than her own personal charisma and background, however, for she was born into a generation of middle- and upper-middle-class women who constituted the first generation of college-educated women, many of whom did not marry and instead devoted their lives to much-needed social reforms. In the 1890s, a significant number of these college graduates joined forces in the social settlement movement. Living together in houses in the midst of urban slums, these reformers formed lifelong communities, providing one another with mutual support and supplying their society with an ongoing critique of the causes and consequences of urban poverty. In 1891 there were only six settlements in the United States; by 1900 over a hundred had been founded, and by 1910 were more than four hundred. Thereby talented women were recruited into social reform in every American city.[16]

Jane Addams, cofounder in 1889 of America's most famous social settlement, Hull House of Chicago, was the best known of this group of college-educated women, but it also included many other activists who organized themselves and others to advance enlightened public policy. Hull House residents included, for example, Julia Lathrop, first director of the U.S. Children's Bureau from 1911 to 1920; Dr. Alice Hamilton, founder of the field of industrial medicine; and Grace Abbott, founder in 1907 of the Immigrants Protective League. In New York at the Henry Street Settlement, which she founded in 1895, Lillian Wald pioneered in the organization of public-health nursing. Florence Kelley was a bridge between the settlements of Chicago and New York, since she lived with Addams in the 1890s and with the Henry Street group from 1899 until 1926. More than at any time before or since, settlements made possible the consolidation of the energies of women activists, vastly increasing their social and political effectiveness.[17]

Thus, when the suffrage movement modernized its tactics under the direction of Carrie Chapman Catt in 1910 and embarked on the last stage of its protracted struggle to bring women into the mainstream of American political life, other women were already well established in that mainstream. Viewing their causes as mutually beneficial, social reformers and suffragists joined forces during the decade before the passage of the Nineteenth Amendment in 1920. Votes for women would enhance the power of social reformers, while the reformers' social agenda strengthened the suffrage cause by providing concrete examples of the good that would flow from women's votes.[18]

Nevertheless, any coalition as diverse as the one supporting woman suffrage in 1920 was likely to break up when the single issue that tied it together was accomplished. Thus, even more surprising than the divergence of the National Woman's Party from the rest of the suffrage movement in 1921 was the solidarity that persisted among other elements of the suffrage coalition after the vote was won.

That solidarity was nowhere more visible than in the movement's opposition to what they called the "blanket amendment." By January 1923, the *New York Times* listed the following organizations in the amendment's "counterlobby": "the League of Women Voters, the National Consumers' League, the Women's Trade Union League, the Charity Organization Society, the Girls' Friendly Society, the National Council of Catholic Women, the Council of Jewish Women, the National Association for Labor Legislation, the Woman's Christian Temperance Union, the American Association for Organizing Family Social Work, the National League of Girls' Clubs, the Parent Teachers' Association, the National Federation of Federal Employees, and the National Congress of Mothers."[19] Also opposed were the American Association of University Women, the YWCA, and the General Federation of Women's Clubs. Only the National Federation of Business and Professional Women's Clubs did not openly oppose the proposed amendment.[20]

This remarkable unanimity among women's groups was partly due to their reluctance to venture into new and more radical solutions to women's inequality. To a considerable degree, however, it was also due to the momentum of social reform within the suffrage movement that supported the enactment of special protective legislation for working and for poor women. The Sheppard-Towner Act was passed in 1921 as a result of effective lobbying efforts of some twenty women's organizations combined under the umbrella organization of the Women's Joint Congressional Committee. Many believed that such special legislation, as well as state mothers' pension laws and other protective measures, would be invalidated by the Equal Rights Amendment.

A solution to this dilemma was tried in the state of Wisconsin,[21] where in 1921 a version of the ERA was passed with a clause that exempted all legislation designed to protect women. The Wisconsin example failed to resolve the debate, however, because the Wisconsin judiciary was noted for its political liberalism and thus could not provide an adequate test of how the amendment might be interpreted by the more conservative federal judiciary.[22]

Meanwhile, the antagonism to the amendment by reform leaders such as Florence Kelley was vastly increased in the early 1920s by the U.S. Supreme Court's consideration of the constitutionality of minimum-wage laws for women. By 1923, fifteen states and territories, beginning with Massachusetts in 1912, had passed minimum-wage statutes for women. Florence Kelley and the National Consumers' League were the chief proponents of this reform. In *Adkins v. Children's Hospital*, the U.S. Supreme Court ruled the Washington, D.C. minimum-wage law unconstitutional, saying that the Nineteenth Amendment demonstrated that men and women were equal, and therefore women did not need special legislation. Revealing the antilabor and procapital bias of the decision, the court wrote that "it should be remembered that of the three fundamental principles which underlie government, and for which government exists—life, liberty, and property—the chief of these is property."[23] Minimum-wage laws were crippled by this decision until the Supreme Court began to face an avalanche of New Deal labor legislation in the 1930s. In 1937 it reversed itself on minimum wages for women in *West Coast Hotel v. Parrish*, and in 1941 it finally unambiguously approved minimum wages for all workers producing goods intended for interstate commerce in *United States v. Darby*, thus upholding the constitutionality of the 1938 Fair Labor Standards Act.

The struggle over the ERA in the 1920s took place in a context in which women's organizations endorsed special legislation for women as part of a general reform effort to improve working conditions for women and men alike. The strategy worked with hours legislation, but it failed with wage legislation. In 1923 the National Woman's Party heralded the Supreme Court's decision in the Adkins case, allying itself with what the National Consumers' League considered reactionary political forces. The politics of gender and the politics of class were inextricably combined. At issue was not only what was best for women but what was best for American society as a whole. This clash of social visions was intensified in the late 1920s, when, reflecting the more conservative temper of the times, the Sheppard-Towner Act was allowed to die for lack of funding. The forces of progressive reform no longer could command legislative majorities at the state or federal level, but there was one thing they could and did continue to do long after the conditions that initially had generated their animosity had passed—oppose the Equal Rights Amendment. Support for the amendment on the political left and within the ranks of organized labor came in the 1970s from a new generation that had not experienced "the women's war" of the 1920s.

Notes

1. The best study of ERA opposition is J. Stanley Lemons's chapter "Feminists against Feminists" in his book *The Woman Citizen: Social Feminism in the 1920's* (Urbana: University of Illinois Press, 1973), pp. 181–208.
2. See Lemons, *Woman Citizen*, pp. 153–80.
3. Lemons, *Woman Citizen*, p. 157. For a comparative perspective on infant health care, see Alisa C. Klaus, "Babies All the Rage: The Movement to Prevent Infant Mortality in the United States and France, 1890–1920," (Ph.D. diss., University of Pennsylvania, 1986).
4. Lemons, "The Sheppard-Towner Act: Progressivism in the 1920s," *Journal of American History*, 55 (1969), 776–86.
5. See Lemons, *Woman Citizen*, pp. 153–80.
6. For biographical information on Florence Kelley, see Louise Wade on Kelley in *Notable American Women*, 3 vols., ed. Edward T. James, Janet Wilson James, and Paul S. Boyer (Cambridge: Harvard University Press, 1971).
7. Felix Frankfurter's "Foreword," in Josephine Goldmark, *Impatient Crusader: Florence Kelley's Life Story* (Urbana: University of Illinois Press, 1953).
8. See Stanley Kutler, ed., *The Supreme Court and the Constitution, Readings in American Constitutional History* (New York: W. W. Norton, 1977, 2d ed.), pp. 282–89.
9. *Ibid.*, pp. 291–92.
10. Elizabeth Brandeis, "Labor Legislation," in John R. Commons, *History of Labor in the United States, 1896–1932*, 4 vols. (New York: Macmillan Co., 1935), vol. 3, p. 462. See also Anne Corinne Hill, "Protection of Women Workers and the Courts: A Legal History," *Feminist Studies* 5, no. 2 (Summer 1979): 247–73.
11. David Brody, *Steelworkers in America: The Nonunion Era* (Cambridge: Harvard University Press, 1960), pp. 271–73.
12. See Louis L. Athey, "The Consumer's Leagues and Social Reform, 1890–1923" (Ph.D. diss., University of Delaware, 1965), p. 221.
13. *Ibid.*, p. 270.
14. Marianne Weber, *Max Weber: A Biography* (New York: Wiley and Sons 1975), p. 302.
15. Florence Kelley, "Need Our Working Women Despair?" *International Review* (Nov. 1882), pp. 517–26.
16. See Allen F. Davis, *Spearheads for Reform: The Social Settlements and the Progressive Movement, 1890–1914* (New York: Oxford University Press, 1967), p. 12 and passim.
17. For a list of eighteen women reform leaders in the social settlement movement, see "Settlement House Leaders" in the "Classified Index," vol. 3 of *Notable American Women*.
18. See William O'Neill, *Everyone Was Brave: A History of Feminism in America* (New York: Quadrangle, 1969). This title was taken from a eulogy of Kelley at her memorial service, where Newton Baker said, "Everybody was brave from the moment she came into the room."
19. "The Woman's War," *New York Times*, Jan. 14, 1922. Clipping from Mary Van Kleek Collection, box 96, folder 1519, Sophia Smith Collection, Smith College.
20. See Lemons, *Woman Citizen*, p. 190.
21. *Ibid.*, pp. 181–208.
22. *Ibid.*, pp. 187–189.
23. See Athey, "Consumer's Leagues," pp. 171–204; quote from Lemons, *The Woman Citizen*, p. 239.

Chapter 20

Companionate Marriage and the Lesbian Threat

Christina Simmons

With the advent of woman suffrage and a more forthright acceptance of women in the public sphere, the 1920s saw a new emphasis on "companionate marriage" in contrast to the Victorian view of the separation of women's and men's responsibilities within marriage. Increasingly, commentators acknowledged women's sexuality and the importance of mutual sexual satisfaction. The price for this new view of marital relations was a marked denigration of homosocial or homosexual relations among women. What once was viewed as a natural expression of affection among women was now viewed as deviant. Christina Simmons makes clear the interrelationship between these two developments and the implications of the "lesbian threat" in terms of power considerations between the sexes.

> Back in the dim ages when I was a schoolgirl we were not so well informed about the proper names for things. . . . If, now, Miss Barnes' school is representative at all, we have indications of a growth in half-knowledge which makes all girlish fondnesses suspect, so that the door is shut on these minor "innocent" outlets which have done so much to preserve woman's purity, or else it is opened wide on the horrendous and fascinating.
>
> —Lorine Pruette, "The Flapper"[1]

Citing Carman Barnes' story about a girls' boarding school, psychologist Lorine Pruette reflected in 1930 that sharpened public awareness of sexuality was creating a new kind of moral rigidity in American culture. Affection and friendship between young women which had seemed innocent in the nineteenth century might arouse disapproval in the twentieth.[2] A girl might either be pushed ever earlier into "the frankness of a heterosexual relation" or be exposed to homosexual possibilities newly made "horrendous and fascinating" by the flapper's modish but superficial sexual knowledge.[3] Pruette commented that the older women in Katharine B. Davis' famous study had moved easily "between homosexual and heterosexual relations without necessarily evil consequences," but they had been raised "before our present era of frankness was well under way."[4] Pruette's reflection raises an important historical question—why fear of lesbianism constituted such a significant problem in the dominant heterosexual ideology of the 1920's and 1930's.

As much of the "sexual revolution" of the 1920's took place in words as in actions.[5] A spate of literature outlining the new "companionate" marriage, one based on friendship and sexual satisfaction, appeared in the 1920's, followed by more technical marriage manuals and popular medical advice in the next decade.[6] These works represented the cultural definition of changes in gender relations which had been stirring in social life since the late nineteenth century.[7] Those who wrote

"Companionate Marriage and the Lesbian Threat," by Christina Simmons, from *Frontiers*, IV:3 (1979): 54–59. Reprinted by permission.

Molly Dewson and Polly Porter on the dairy farm where they lived together in western Massachusetts, c. 1912. Virginia S. Bourne.

books and articles on sex were educators, social workers, psychologists, physicians, and others in a rising class of trained professional people, mostly male. In the 1910's and 1920's radical voices among them spoke for feminism and/or for sexual liberation.[8] Many more, however, acknowledged social changes but feared conflict between the sexes might result. They sought harmony between the sexes by reforming what seemed the most oppressive elements of Victorian marriage. This latter group articulated a new sexual ideology which achieved cultural hegemony by the 1930's and which represented a morality more suited to the social needs of the corporate liberal state than its Victorian predecessor.[9]

Proponents of the new companionate marriage gave great attention to women because they attributed the need for sexual reform primarily to historical changes in women's lives. The nineteenth-century sex-segregation of leisure among the respectable classes began dissolving in the 1890's; by the 1910's a small but noticeable group of elite urban women were going to restaurants and cabarets in male company. Middle-class couples joined working-class men and women at the new movie theaters. Already in the 1910's a few women adopted boyish "flapper" clothing and male habits like smoking and drinking in public. They turned against styles which emphasized women's distance and differentiation from men.[10] The expansion of women's education and of their paid employment in the higher social classes by 1900 generated a less exclusively domestic image of women in the culture. The professional work of some college women, the political activity of the suffrage movement, even the social and charitable activity of club women gave women a more salient presence outside the home.[11] Women of the upper-middle and upper classes were the implicit concern because they were the most immediate subjects of the dominant sexual morality and were expected to exemplify it to the women of other classes.[12]

As women discarded Victorian delicacy they seemed more like men, that is, as individuals with a right to personal fulfillment rather than a duty to sacrifice self for men and children. For example, in one 1919 novel an aspiring young social researcher exclaims, when asked if she would disobey her father, "Certainly! First of all I am a human being. That is what Ibsen's Nora said."[13] Being drawn into the public sphere made them more sexual, too: "By the very act of working, something has happened to her . . . she has become in important psychological elements, a man . . . more significantly they absorb, with their jobs, the masculine attitude toward sex."[14] Recognition of women's individuality and sexuality was a way of acknowledging a new kind of energy and social power, which pertained to more than reproduction and the domestic sphere. Companionate marriage represented the attempt of mainstream marriage ideology to adapt to women's perceived new social and sexual power.

This power was manifested, as one man observed, in "the increasing subordination of . . . maternity to sexuality . . . of love to passion, or procreation to recreation." The "vast reservoirs of erotic energy resident in women," freed from purely domestic and reproductive activities, were overflowing.[15] Many sexual reformers cited Freudian concepts to justify belief in the strength and universality of sexual drives. They argued that suppressing sexual desire was psychologically and even physically unhealthy.

Companionate marriage directed female sexual energies toward men and marriage. Judge Ben Lindsey popularized the essential elements in his 1927 book *Companionate Marriage:* 1) easier divorce, especially for childless marriages; 2) legalization of birth control; 3) provision of sex education for youth. These concrete reforms relied on two assumptions: that intense psychological companionship, or friendship, should characterize relations between husband and wife and that the sexual aspect of this intimacy was particularly important.[16] This form of marriage was said to provide the equality women deserved and to be a bond of "creative companionship and interdependent cooperation." "Does the husband really want a mere permanent housekeeper, a faithful drudge, an unpaid servant, or does he desire a real life companion and a friend . . . ?"[17] The wife was to be included in the budget planning and was to have access to money without asking for it; the husband might help a little with dishes and housework. Women were to receive their rights to sexual pleasure as well; sexual literature warned men to abandon the stereotypical Victorian sexual aggression in favor of sensitivity, gentleness, and a slower pace.[18] Divorce, birth control, and sex education all helped women to exercise greater control over the conditions of the marital bond.

The new model compared favorably with reformers' exaggerated image of Victorian marriage—its duty-bound separate male and female spheres and its emotional and sexual repression. One sociologist concluded "there is every reason to suppose that asceticism has received in this generation a death blow from which it can never recover. It has passed forever from the category of ideals into that of mental abnormalities, and its morbid significance is being generally recognized."[19] By deprecating nineteenth-century marriage, advocates of companionate marriage in effect showed how enlightened and fair the new form was.

But what happened if women did not wholly reject Victorian gender relations but rather kept their distance from men and preferred each other's company? The ponderous traditions and social structures separating and differentiating the sexes now appeared as obstacles to heterosexual comradeship and romance. And conversely, women's segregation and solidarity with each other took on a menacing aspect unknown in earlier generations.[20] If women's sexual desires exhibited the urgency long attributed to men's, and if an intense love relationship seemed vital for personal happiness, then lesbian relationships were the logical result of the absence or failure of heterosexuality. "We do not blame anyone for seeking normal affection and love; we all need it to be happy. How can we blame a woman, who, through no fault of her own, has been deprived of such affection from a man, and turns to another woman for it?"[21] In these writings the specter of lesbianism arose in association with perceptions of the persisting differences and distance between men and women. But as is so clear in racial segregation, such separation meant inequality as well and consequently resistance from the oppressed group. Whether female resistance to heterosexual relationships actually occurred or not, the recognition of sexual inequality engendered in the culture a male *fear* of resistance, often expressed as a fear of lesbianism.

Within the voluminous literature of this new sexual ideology a conception of homosexuality was developing which made it into a very significant, if not the major, "deviation" from the dominant heterosexual pattern, especially for women. Historian Carroll Smith-Rosenberg has argued that early nineteenth-century American culture did not define lesbianism as a distinct sexual pattern.[22] Such innocence was gone by 1920. Accompanying the reformulation of heterosexual ideology during this period was a surprisingly extensive commentary on female homosexuality. The critical point about this literature is that it treated homosexuality as a condition which developed in specific relation to heterosexuality, namely through the failure or deprivation or rejection of the latter. Consequently, such writings denigrated not only exclusive lesbians but also women who might once have moved easily between homosexuality and heterosexuality and women experiencing conflict in relationships with men.[23]

By the 1920's discussion of homosexuality was expanding a little beyond strictly medical and scientific circles and was using popular Freudian concepts.

Older theories of homosexuality as a congenital abnormality still appeared, and some researchers pursued hormone theories, but environmental explanations were taking precedence.[24] The ascendancy of psychodynamic explanations focused attention on the process whereby young people "acquired" homosexuality and strengthened efforts to control it by changing the predisposing environmental factors. Both lay and medical writers loosely included factors from social as well as from family life among possible causes.

Whether homosexuality was actually increasing or not, some commentators said that it was, owing to the disruptions of the Great War and the changing sexual morality of the 1920's. "The rhythm of the jazz age has infected our sex life. . . . The modern mad quest for stimulation is driving men and women into the arms of abnormality."[25] Such beliefs can be understood as expressions of cultural anxiety about the supposed social sources of homosexuality, as discussions of the "social" causes of homosexuality were a constituent element of the dominant heterosexual ideology. Often, homosexuality was turned into a threatening, oppositional alternative to the heterosexual pattern, especially in the case of women, thus presenting a cultural meaning that homosexuality had not carried in the nineteenth century.

Inherited rules governing social interaction between the sexes were premised on a fear of heterosexual contact for respectable women outside of marriage. But some marriage reformers began to feel that the spirit of the rules was so directed against heterosexuality that to some women romantic involvement with other women appeared socially safer than involvement with men: "Paradoxically many women believe, long after they have grown up, that an emotional relationship with a member of their own sex is no such breach of the conventions as an intimate relationship with a man."[26] Several authors noted that the hazards of adolescent heterosexual adventures were much exaggerated compared to the failure of heterosexuality altogether: "The anxious parental and social attempts to insure against such accidents, by repression and segregation, can produce homosexuality, perversions of all sorts, and sexual and emotional incapacities which can in the long run produce more individual unhappiness and more social ills than a boy's gonorrhea or a girl's illegitimate baby."[27]

Sex-segregated institutions, particularly schools, were said to be keeping young women and men from learning to know and live with each other. Sexual theorists' emphasis on individual fulfillment and romantic intimacy made marriage an arena for compromise and adjustment between two personalities. As the marriage manifestoes of the 1920's faded into the more technical advice works of the 1930's, problems of psychological adjustment within marriage received much attention.[28] Concerned about sources of marital instability, reformers scrutinized single-sex education: "The unwholesome fashionable practice of sex-segregated schools brings young people into a homosexual atmosphere." Deprived of male contact, young girls might not learn to love men. They would develop an "unconscious homosexuality" which would operate "to make mating so difficult as to be almost impossible, and to make matings unsatisfactory and unstable when they . . . [were] formally achieved."[29]

Failure to "achieve" heterosexual union was labeled immaturity. Critical of women's "emotional debauchery," one pair of researchers said of a lesbian college student: "she was so much of a child that she needed the complete understanding which only a person of her own sex could give her."[30] From another perspective, one might say the defenders of marriage were afraid that if psychological compatibility had become a major criterion for good relationships, then two women might sometimes find happiness more easily than a woman and a man.

The many single graduates of the women's colleges as well as independent young reformers and professional women, made notorious when Theodore Roosevelt accused them of causing race suicide, were widely known to live with other women when they did not live with their families.[31] Suspicion accumulated that these relationships were "unhealthy" at least. The mother of a young statistician portrayed in one novel asked, " 'Have you never met a man you fancied?' . . . 'I shall never love romantically,' was the forcible answer. 'What time have I for love?' " Yet the daughter "spoke with more enthusiasm" of her roommate: " 'She is studying to be a librarian. We met each other last year and we've been rooming together since this fall; she means everything to me, mummy.' " The novelist judges the daughter's bohemian existence unnatural, the result of feminist disdain for domesticity and absorption in work and social causes.[32]

Despite overwhelming male economic advantages and social and political power, some women, especially in the higher social classes, were better able than their mothers and grandmothers had been to decline marriage if they chose.[33] One psychologist attributed female homosexuality in part to a feminist desire for life work besides motherhood and an unwillingness to marry the average man.[34] Another author speculated, not unreasonably, that women's ability not to marry had raised public awareness of lesbianism: "For thousands of years moralists and legalists have denounced homosexuality between men, but no code has ever forbidden physical relationship between women . . . since it did not necessarily prevent child-bearing, or cause children to be born illegitimately. . . . When feminism . . . increased, and women began to be increasingly celibate, the question of 'mannish' women began finding its way into popular novels (*The Well of Loneliness*) into plays (*The Children's Hour*) and into parlor conversations."[35]

Suspicions of lesbianism often centered on women of higher status because they were perceived to have significant power. One critic noted that employment made all women more sexually receptive but that working-class women became heterosexually promiscuous while professional women became lesbians.[36] Upper-middle-class and upper-class women were the ones who worked for suffrage and Progressive reforms and lived in social settlements, but they were still needed to support, comfort, and provide children for men of their class. Roosevelt had criticized their childlessness, but dominant-class ideologues of the 1920's and 1930's showed fear and disapproval of these women's independence by insinuating their lesbianism.[37] What marriage reformers were doing in effect was to perceive women's autonomy and resistance to male domination in sexual terms and to deprecate the legitimacy of their social and economic aspirations.

Remnants of Victorian gender relations, then, acted as social causes of homosexuality according to many architects of the new marriage. Influenced by rules of propriety and sex-segregated institutions, women with education and financial resources established domestic arrangements that were free of male support or control and which were possibly lesbian.[38] Some critics found lesbianism an unfortunate but understandable result of such conditions, to be pitied, even tolerated. As companionate marriage gained legitimacy, however, others began to see a "psychologically sick" lesbianism as the cause rather than the effect of women's resistance to heterosexuality. They became defensive, trying to reduce women's protests to narrowly sexual motivation: "The driving force in many agitators and militant women who are always after their rights, is often an unsatisfied sex impulse, with a homosexual aim. Married women with a completely satisfied libido rarely take an active interest in militant movements."[39] Such a reversal occurred among reformers concerned about the persistence of sexual conflict even in the new marriage. Claiming that companionate marriage had ended Victorian inequities, they found in lesbianism an "irrational" psychological cause for behavior which subtly challenged male sexual dominance within marriage.

Lesbianism was blamed for both aggressive and inhibited female sexuality. Despite the alleged equality of partners in companionate marriage, male sexual leadership remained the norm. Women who flouted feminine decorum in intercourse drew harsh disapproval. The male superior position in coitus, for example, symbolized the man's dominance in the relationship, and a women who wished to usurp it risked censure. One physician claimed, "A homosexual woman often wants to possess the male and not to be possessed by him. . . . With them orgasm is often only possible in the superior position."[40] He associated lesbianism with a rejection of women's natural, subordinate role within heterosexual activity.

The complete absence of female sexual participation, however, also indicated lesbianism to these modern defenders of marriage. Women had to walk a fine line between appropriate modesty and neurotic prudery. The latter became problematic when women internalized sexual conventions so thoroughly as to resist heterosexuality in disgust or fear. Because sexual harmony was so sought after in companionate marriage, too much female naivete or embarrassment was counterproductive and seemed old-fashioned by the 1920's.[41] Purity, too, began to arouse suspicions of lesbianism. An upbringing of "excessive repressions" or "morbid or silly warnings against the opposite sex" might encourage lesbian tendencies. Alternatively, a person characterized by " 'prudishness' and 'stiffness,' or more favorably . . . 'unapproachable purity' or 'high ideals,' " might be influenced by "unconscious homosexuality."[42]

More specifically, prudery caused frigidity, the leading female problem in marital adjustment according to most proponents of companionate marriage. Many writers expressed sympathy for women with the problem and saw them as victims of a sexually repressive socialization. In that sense frigidity provided an argument for sex education and women's sexual rights in companionate marriage.[43] At the same time, certain reformers, including some who also expressed sympathy, feared or resented female frigidity. They interpreted it as a sign of "man-hating," or rejection of the female role.

Mixed with words of encouragement to women to accept and express their sexuality were warnings of what might happen if they did not: "women will have to be bluntly reminded that one main source of prostitution and unfaithfulness is the selfish and unsurrendered wife."[44] Losing a husband was what women risked when they failed in heterosexual "adjustment."

As the cultural definition of marriage shifted to include greater emphasis on mutual sexual pleasure, women's dissatisfaction grew proportionately more alarming. "The woman who gets no pleasure at all in coitus cannot truly love her husband. Love demands more than respect or admiration." Respect or admiration might have been sufficient for the Victorians, but no more. Defensive sexual advisers turned to attack. "Some married women thought to dislike coitus only because of a superior modesty, in reality are deceiving themselves and others. Their frigidity is on a homosexual basis, all their real interests being feminine."[45] Another man described the "nightmare" of marriage to a lesbian: After intercourse, "they feel cold, and do not experience the normal glow; they talk *as though nothing important had happened*. These women often despise their husbands in various ways" (my italics).[46] In normal heterosexual intercourse "something important" did happen—when a woman expressed or feigned love and desire for a man in spite of the socially determined inequality between them, she symbolized some acceptance of her position, whether from having achieved an individually satisfactory relationship or from the need to please him. Overt sexual coldness destroyed the illusion of harmony.

Thus in cultural terms lesbianism represented women's autonomy in various forms— feminism, careers, refusal to marry, failure to adjust to marital sexuality.[47] It became a symbol in a cultural context of increased expectation and evaluation of sexual activity for women as well as for men in the new form of companionate marriage. How well this new ideology of marriage described the typical patterns of people's sexual lives requires investigation, but no one could have remained totally isolated from its power. Directives about gender relations were expressed not only in articles and books of advice but directly by health care and social work professionals, clergy, radio, movies, advertising, and government policies.[48] We cannot know how many people were influenced by arguments for co-education, earlier dating and marriage, and breaking up friendships between adolescent girls. The intention was clear—"to train young people for—we need not hesitate to use the phrase—living happily ever after in heterosexual matehood."[49]

The ebullient atmosphere of sexual liberation which characterized the 1910's and 1920's allowed room for more open discussion of lesbianism than had ever existed in the United States before. Trying to explain what most of them could not accept as legitimate, sexual theorists found social causes of lesbianism in clashes between an anachronistic morality and a perceived new female power in social and sexual life. As the ideology of companionate marriage became established, however, attitudes toward female resistance, and thus toward lesbianism, hardened among many marriage theorists and counselors. Creators of the new ideology had hoped to modify some extreme features of male dominance but were far from ready to institute what feminists would have defined as equality. The decline of organized feminism after 1920 must certainly have been one factor allowing dissemination of such an intensely heterosexual vision of personal life. In the absence of a powerful feminist voice, exponents of companionate marriage tempered the liberating potential of new sexual ideas and judged women's sexuality acceptable only insofar as its energy was channeled into marriage and the service of men.

Notes

1. Lorine Pruette, "The Flapper," in V. F. Calverton and S. D. Schmalhausen, *The New Generation: The Intimate Problems of Modern Parents and Children* (New York: Macaulay, 1930), pp. 574–75.
2. Diana Frederics [pseud.], *Diana: A Strange Autobiography* (1939; rpt. New York: Arno, 1975), p. 222.
3. Pruette, p. 577.
4. *Ibid.,* p. 585. Katharine B. Davis did one of the earliest sociological studies of sexual behavior. She used written questionnaires to survey college graduates and club women in the early 1920's and published the results in 1929 in *Factors in the Sex Life of Twenty-Two Hundred Women* (New York: Harper & Bros.).
5. Maurice A. Bigelow, *Sex-Education: A Series of Lectures Concerning Knowledge of Sex in Its Relation to Human Life* (New York: Macmillan, 1916), p. 254; Ernest R. Groves, *The Marriage Crisis* (New York: Longmans, Green, 1928), pp. 165–68.
6. For example, Ben Lindsey and Wainwright Evans, *The Companionate Marriage* (New York: Boni and Liveright, 1927); Floyd Dell, *Love in the Machine Age: A Psychological Study of the Transition from Patriarchal Society* (New York: Farrar, 1930); LeMon Clark, *Emotional Adjustment in Marriage* (St. Louis: C. V. Mosby, 1937); *Sexology,* 1933+; *Popular Medicine,* 1934+.
7. Christopher Lasch, *Haven in the Heartless World: The Family Beseiged* (New York: Basic Books, 1977), p. 9; V. F. Calverton, *The Bankruptcy of Marriage* (New York: Macaulay, 1928), p. 146.
8. Grete Meisel-Hess, *The Sexual Crisis: A Critique of Our Sex Life,* trans. Eden and Cedar Paul (New York: Critic and Guide, 1917), pp. 20–24, 74; V. F. Calverton, "Sex and Social Struggle," in *Sex in Civilization,* ed. V. F. Calverton and S. D. Schmalhausen (New York: Macauley, 1929), p. 271; J. William Lloyd, "Sex Jealousy and Civilization," in *Sex in Civilization,* pp. 233–46; Calverton, *Bankruptcy,* p. 215.
9. Dell, p. 68; Stuart Ewen, *Captains of Consciousness: Advertising and the Social Roots of the Consumer Culture* (New York: McGraw-Hill, 1976), especially Part III, chapters 1, 5, 6.
10. Lewis Allan Erenberg, "Urban Night Life and the Decline of Victorianism: New York City's Restaurants and Cabarets, 1890–1918," Diss, University of Michigan, 1974, p. 131; Lary Linden May, "Reforming Leisure: The Birth of Mass Culture and the Motion Picture Industry, 1896–1920," Diss. University of California, Los Angeles, 1977, p. 110; James R. McGovern, "The American Woman's Pre-World War I Freedom in Manners and Morals," *Journal of American History,* 55 (1968), 322; Floyd Dell, *Looking at Life* (New York: Knopf, 1924), pp. 23–24.
11. Phyllis Blanchard and Carlyn Manasses, *New Girls for Old* (New York: Macaulay, 1930), pp. 231, 235, 241–46; C. Gasquoine Hartley, *Women's Wild Oats: Essays on the Re-Fixing of Moral Standards* (New York: Stokes, 1920), pp. 38, 43; S. D. Schmalhausen, "The Sexual Revolution," in *Sex in Civilization,* pp. 359–60.
12. Daniel Scott Smith has argued that working-class sexual behavior was beginning to leave behind Victorian styles after 1875 and that the "sexual revolution" of the 1920's was middle-class, "The Dating of the American Sexual Revolution: Evidence and Interpretation," in *The American Family in Social-Historical Perspective,* ed. Michael Gordon (New York: St. Martin's, 1973), pp. 321–35. Floyd Dell also explicitly proclaims sexual changes as a "middle-class revolution," *Love in the Machine Age,* p. 201.
13. Nalbro Bartley, *A Woman's Woman* (Boston: Small, Maynard, 1919), p. 46.
14. Horace Coon, *Coquetry for Men* (New York: Amour Press, 1932), pp. 110–11; Clark, p. 51.
15. Schmalhausen, "The Sexual Revolution," pp. 379, 402. Younger feminists of the period differed from their predecessors in embracing sexuality more enthusiastically. See Elaine Showalter, ed., *These Modern Women: Autobiographical Essays from the Twenties* (Old Westbury, N.Y.: Feminist Press, 1978), p. 15.

16. Lindsey and Evans, pp. 175–76; Coon, pp. 184–88; Ira S. Wile and Mary Day Winn, *Marriages in the Modern Manner* (New York: Century, 1929), pp. 12–13, 263–64.

17. Sherwood Eddy, *Sex and Youth* (Garden City, N.Y.: Doubleday, Doran, 1929), pp. 140, 149; Wile and Winn, p. 178; Beatrice Forbes-Robertson Hale, "Women in Transition," in *Sex in Civilization,* p. 75.

18. Eddy, pp. 151, 154; Margaret Sanger, *Happiness in Marriage* (New York: Blue Ribbon, 1926), pp. 122–24, 225; Groves, p. 100.

19. Groves, p. 214.

20. Carroll Smith-Rosenberg, "The Female World of Love and Ritual: Relations between Women in Nineteenth-Century America," *Signs,* 1, 1 (Autumn 1975), 27.

21. Ralph Hay, "Mannish Women or Old Maids?" *Know Yourself,* 1 (July 1938), 78; also, Lindsey and Evans, p. 187; Eleanor Bertine, M.D., "Health and Morality in the Light of the New Psychology," *Proceedings of the International Conference of Women Physicians* (New York: The Woman's Press, 1919), IV, pp. 10, 11.

22. Smith-Rosenberg, 8, 27; Jonathan Katz, *Gay American History* (New York: Thomas Y. Crowell, 1976), p. 449.

23. Katz includes a good example of such doubt in excerpts from the diary of Dorothy Thompson, 1932, p. 558.

24. Arno Karlen, *Sexuality and Homosexuality: A New View* (New York: Norton, 1971), pp. 324, 330; John F. W. Meagher, M.D., "Homosexuality: Its Psychobiological and Psychopathological Significance," *The Urologic and Cutaneous Review* 33, (1929), 510.

25. S. D. Schmalhausen, "The Freudian Emphasis on Sex," in *The Sex Problem in Modern Society,* ed. John Francis McDermott (New York: Modern Library, 1931), p. 64; also, Olga Knopf, *Women on Their Own* (Boston: Little, Brown, 1935), p. 157.

26. Dorothy Dunbar Bromley and Florence Haxton Britten, *Youth and Sex: A Study of 1300 College Students* (New York: Harper, 1938), p. 129; also Hay, 77; Noah E. Aronstam, M.D., "*The Well of Loneliness*—An Impression," *The Urologic and Cutaneous Review,* 33 (1929), 543.

27. Floyd Dell, "Sex in Adolescence," in *Sex Education: Facts and Attitudes* (New York: Child Study Association of America, 1934), p. 49; Norman Himes, *Your Marriage: A Guide to Happiness* (New York: Farrar & Rinehart, 1940), p. 24. One of the authors more tolerant of homosexuality argued that homosexuality was indeed less serious than illegitimacy or venereal disease and that people should not be so upset about it. Aaron J. Rosanoff, M.D., "Human Sexuality, Normal and Abnormal, From a Psychiatric Standpoint," *Urologic and Cutaneous Review,* 33 (1929), 530. The novel *A Woman's Woman* (above, note 13) contrasts a celibate sister who lives with another woman and the other sister in the family, a flirtatious girl who falls for a worthless man. The latter's failings are much better accepted by the family.

28. For example, Blanchard and Manasses, pp. 186–87; Clark, p. 7.

29. Dell, *Love in the Machine Age,* pp. 238, 308; also Bromley and Britten, p. 118. The proportion of American colleges confined to one sex or the other declined continuously from 1870 on, mostly because the majority of new schools were co-educational. Very few women's colleges opened after 1930; I have not discovered whether fears of lesbianism played any direct role in this phenomenon. See Mabel Newcomer, *A Century of Higher Education for American Women* (New York: Harper, 1959), pp. 37–40.

30. Bromley and Britten, p. 129; also, Himes, p. 22.

31. Linda Gordon, *Woman's Body, Woman's Right* (New York: Grossman, 1976), p. 136; Eleanor Rowland Wembridge, "The Professional Education of Women and the Family Problem," *Social Hygiene,* 6, (1920), 183.

32. Bartley, pp. 27–29.

33. Peter Filene, *Him/Her/Self: Sex Roles in Modern America* (New York: Harcourt, Brace, Jovanovich, 1974), pp. 29–30. Filene cites figures showing that in 1915, for instance, only 39 percent of all living alumnae of eight women's colleges and Cornell were married, p. 27. Actually the proportion of ever-married people in the population was rising, and the age of marriage was declining, from 1890 on. Because the reality differed from reformers' impressions, it seems even more likely that the more visible single women of higher classes were the primary concern. See Donald J. Bogue, *The Population of the United States* (Glencoe, Ill.: The Free Press, 1959), p. 216.

34. Phyllis Blanchard, *The Adolescent Girl: A Study From the Psychoanalytic Viewpoint* (New York: Moffat, Yard, 1920), pp. 170–71.

35. Hay, 77.

36. Coon, pp. 112–15; also Maurice Chideckel, M.D., *Female Sex Perversion* (New York: Eugenics, 1935), p. vii. In practice, accusations were not restricted by class. In the film, *With Babies and Banners: Story of the Women's Emergency Brigade,* Women's Labor History Film Project, 1978, about women's participation in the 1937 autoworkers' strike in Flint, Michigan, one participant recalls that male unionists called women "queers" when they wanted to do more than traditional support work for the union.

37. Blanche Wiesen Cook has described these women's relationships with each other and with men in "Female Support Networks and Political Activism: Lillian Wald, Crystal Eastman, Emma Goldman," *Chrysalis,* No. 3 (1977), pp. 43–61.

38. Katz, p. 449. Katz notes the historical change from the assumption of asexual friendships to "vulgarizations of Freudianism," which found sex everywhere.

39. Meagher, 511.

40. Meagher, 513; see also George K. Pratt, M.D., "Accepting One's Sexual Role," in *Sex Education: Facts and Attitudes,* p. 39; Ernest R. Groves, Gladys Hoagland Groves, and Catherine Groves, *Sex Fulfillment in Marriage* (New York: Emerson, 1942) suggested for instance, that other positions were useful in exceptional circumstances such as when the man was weak or lacking in sexual control, pp. 163, 179–80.

41. Eddy, p. 127; Dell, *Love in the Machine Age,* p. 311; Sanger, p. 100.

42. In order, Meagher, 508; Edward Podolsky, M.D., " 'Homosexual Love' in Women," *Popular Medicine,* 1 (February 1935), 375; Dell, *Love in the Machine Age,* p. 308. See also Blanchard, p. 169.

43. Groves, *Marriage Crisis,* p. 100; Wile and Winn, p. 54; Clark, p. 96; Joseph Collins, M.D., *The Doctor Looks at Love and Life* (Garden City, N.Y.: Doubleday, Doran, 1926), pp. 36, 43.

44. Eddy, p. 316; also Clark, pp. 31, 97; Lindsey and Evans, pp. 119, 199; Groves et al., *Sex Fulfillment,* p. 186.

45. Meagher, 512.

46. Podolsky, 375.

47. Blanche Wiesen Cook has argued similarly in her essay, " 'Women Alone Stir My Imagination': Lesbianism and the Cultural Tradition," *Signs,* 4, 4 (Summer 1979), 739.

48. Robert S. Lynd and Helen Merrell Lynd, *Middletown: A Study in Modern American Culture* (New York: Harcourt, Brace, and World, 1929), pp. 266–71; May, pp. 212–31; Ewen; Lasch, pp. 20–21; U.S. Public Health Service, *Sex Education: A Symposium for Educators* (Washington, D.C.: 1927), pp. v–vi.

49. Dell, *Love in the Machine Age,* p. 364; also Himes, p. 26; Lindsey and Evans, p. 134; Edwood L. Fantis, M.D., "Homosexuality in Growing Girls," *Sexology,* 2 (February 1935), 349.

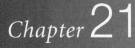
Redefining "Women's Work": The Sexual Division of Labor in the Auto Industry During World War II

Ruth Milkman

An overly rosy view of "Rosie the Riveter" is the object of Ruth Milkman's revisionist analysis of women's work in the automobile industry during World War II. She marshals an impressive array of evidence to argue for a short-term, wartime shift in the boundaries between men's and women's work. Ultimately, she shows, women's wartime experience included the persistence of job segregation by sex even in the face of dramatic economic growth and change. The emergence in the postwar years of what Betty Friedan called the "Feminine Mystique" provides further evidence that the wartime experience of women did not pose any enduring challenge to power relations across the gender divide.

Feminist have deliberately idealized the experience of women workers during World War II, challenging the ideology of "woman's place" which obliterated women's wartime contribution to industrial production from public memory. The stunning imagery of female strength and versatility captured in photographs of women industrial workers in the 1940s has become a mainstay of contemporary "feminist realism." Ultimately, our vision of social change encompasses more than securing equal access for women to alienating jobs in capitalist industry: work itself must be fundamentally transformed—for both women and men. But in the meantime, so long as women workers are excluded from basic industry and ghettoized in low-status, poorly paid jobs, the woman war worker will remain a resonant symbol.

A closer look at the actual experience of women industrial workers during the war years, however, suggests that the retrospective feminist construction of their place in history is apocryphal. Women were hired to do "men's jobs" during the war on a scale unparalleled before or since, but this was in no way the result of a feminist campaign. In basic industries like auto, employers were initially quite resistant to the idea of hiring women for war work. They did so only when the supply of male labor had been completely exhausted because of military conscription on the one hand and the rapid expansion of demand for labor to produce military hardware on the other. It was not a change in management beliefs about women's capabilities in industry that led to their incorporation into jobs previously considered suitable only for men, but rather the male labor shortage during the war years which led to the change in management's beliefs.

This article is excerpted from FEMINIST STUDIES, Volume 8 (1982): 336–72, by permission of the publisher, FEMINIST STUDIES, Inc., c/o Women's Studies Program, University of Maryland, College Park, MD 20742.

Cover of UAW publication, *Ammunition*, August, 1944. The Archives of Labor and Urban Affairs, Wayne State University.

Once women were drawn upon to meet the need for labor in war- bloated "heavy" industries, moreover, they were not randomly incorporated into "men's jobs" as vacancies occurred. Instead, *new* patterns of occupational segregation by sex were established "for the duration" within sectors of the economy previously monopolized by men. So Rosie the Riveter did a "man's job," but more often than not she worked in a predominantly female department or job classification.[1]

The wartime experience of women in industry is a fruitful object of feminist analysis, then, but for reasons opposite to those generally presumed. The economic mobilization led to a shift in the location of the boundaries between "men's" and "women's" work, not the elimination of those boundaries. The persistence of segregation during the war, in the face of a massive influx of women into the labor force and a dramatic upheaval in the previously established sexual division of labor, poses quite starkly the fundamental problem of explaining how and why job segregation by sex is maintained and reproduced over and over again throughout the history of capitalist development.[2]

The underlying forces that continually reproduce segregation within the supposedly "impersonal" wage labor market remain obscure if the problem is approached at the level of the individual employer or firm. Once women have been introduced into the paid labor force at a lower cost than men, one would expect that the relentless efforts of capital to maximize profits would lead employers to substitute women for men whenever possible, at least until the costs of female and male labor power are equalized. It appears quite irrational for management to differentiate rigidly between women and men workers, as if they were truly noninterchangeable sources of labor power. But the ideology of sex typing and the job segregation it legitimates do serve the *class* interest of capital, despite the countervailing pressures impinging on individual capital.

Collectively, capital benefits from the existence of gender divisions within the working class in that they—like racial and other intraclass cleavages—foster political disunity within what might otherwise be a stronger source of opposition to capital.[3] In addition, and crucially, segregation by sex within the wage labor market helps to secure the daily and generational reproduction of the working class through the unpaid household labor of women, by denying female workers a living wage and maintaining their economic dependence on men and on families. At the same time, the sexual division of labor in the household is exactly what constitutes women as a source of "cheap" and expendable labor to begin with.[4]

Of course, not only collective capital but also male workers benefit from job segregation by sex, at least in the short term. Not only do men receive higher wages than women within the wage labor market, but the concentration of women in poorly paid, insecure jobs ensures that women will perform personal services for men in the household even if they also work for pay. While capital, not the male work force, generally controls the process of job definition and allocation, insofar as men mobilize themselves to maintain the subordination of women within the wage labor market, the interest of collective capital in a gender-segregated labor market is reinforced.[5]

But if male workers pursued their *class* interest, rather than seek to maintain their position as a privileged gender, they would mobilize *against* job segregation by sex. Male workers have a class interest in working-class unity. Job segregation by sex, even as it reinforces male power over women, threatens at the same time to undercut the bargaining power of male labor vis-à-vis capital, precisely because of the "cheapness" of female labor. In short, the class interest and what might be called the gender interest of male workers directly conflict with one another. Historically, the apparent domination of men's gender interest over their class interest in shaping their relationship to job segregation by sex must be explained, not presumed from the outset as inevitable or "given." It is crucial for feminists to understand the specific historical conditions under which male workers' class interests might predominate over their gender interests, if we are to have any hope of successfully eliminating job segregation.

Unions, which historically have been disproportionately controlled by men, have often served to maintain the gender privileges of their male members. But there are also historical instances in which the class interest of male workers instead has prevailed in the policy and practice of unions. For example, fear of female substitution, jeopardizing the labor market position of male workers, may lead male-dominated unions to struggle for equality between women and men in the labor market, in spite of the immediate benefits the male gender enjoys as a result of job segregation.

For the class interest of male workers to prevail over their gender interest in a sustained way, however, an oppositional ideology must be generated which challenges the legitimacy of the elaborate and deeply rooted ideology of gender division. The most thoroughgoing such oppositional ideology, namely, feminism, has had remarkably *little* influence on the American labor movement.

But there have been moments in the history of industrial unionism when an ideological commitment to nondiscrimination and class unity has galvanized male workers and their organizations to struggle against rather than for job segregation.

Failing this, the interest of collective capital is reinforced by the gender interest of male workers in job segregation by sex and its rationalizing ideology of occupational sex typing. Both these interests are served by the maintenance of the family as an institution of social reproduction based on unpaid female labor. Women's participation in wage labor on equal terms with men would ultimately undermine the unequal sexual division of labor in the household. Access to an individual wage, even on terms unequal to men, erodes the structure of women's economic dependence on men and on families. This is precisely why, rather than disappearing as women's labor force participation increases, occupational sex typing persists and indeed becomes ever more important: it constructs women's "primary" commitment as devotion to home and family, whether or not they also work for pay.

This interdependence between the circumscribed roles of women in the family and in the labor market, which has been observed in a wide range of circumstances by feminist scholars, helps explain the particular case of the reconstruction of job segregation by sex within the mobilized economy of the early 1940s. During the World War II years, married women and mothers poured into the labor force in massive numbers for the first time, posing an unprecedented threat to family stability.[6] Thus, far from being rendered unnecessary by the exigencies of the war emergency, job segregation was more crucial than ever before at this juncture. The sex typing of the jobs newly opened to women "for the duration" reconciled women's new economic situation with their traditional position as guardians of the hearth. This was manifested in the pervasive wartime propaganda image of "woman's place" on the nation's production lines, which portrayed women's war work in industry as a temporary extension of domesticity.

The World War II experience not only reveals the resilience of the structure of job segregation by sex and of the *general* ideology of sexual division which legitimates it, but it also renders completely transparent the specific *idiom* of sex typing, which is flexibly applied to whatever jobs women and men happen to be doing. Jobs which had previously been cast in terms suggestive of the very quintessence of masculinity were suddenly endowed with femininity and glamour "for the duration." The propaganda newsreel *Glamour Girls of '43*, for example, suggested:

> Instead of cutting the lines of a dress, this woman cuts the pattern of aircraft parts. Instead of baking cakes, this woman is cooking gears to reduce the tension in the gears after use. . . . They are taking to welding as if the rod were a needle and the metal a length of cloth to be sewn. After a short apprenticeship, this woman can operate a drill press just as easily as a juice extractor in her own kitchen. And a lathe will hold no more terrors for her than an electric washing machine.[7]

Virtually any job could be labeled as "woman's work" in this way.

Idioms of sex typing are unified in the global presumption that "men's work" and "women's work" are fundamentally distinct, but they also vary among sectors of the economy, specific industries, and even individual firms. In "pink collar" service and clerical sector jobs, the skills and capacities presumed to be developed by wives and mothers, such as nurturance, solicitousness to emotional and sexual needs, and skill in providing personal services, are the central reference point of the idiom of sex typing. Sex segregation in the manufacturing sector speaks a different language, rooted less in women's family role than in their real or imagined biological characteristics. No one pretends that being nurturant or knowing how to make a good cup of coffee are important qualifications for "female" factory jobs. Here the idiom centers on such qualities as manual dexterity, attention to detail, ability to tolerate monotony, and, of course, women's relative lack of physical strength. Analogies to domestic labor are present in both the pink collar and blue collar idioms, but the physical tasks comprising housework are paramount in descriptions of women's manual labor outside the home, rather than the psychological tasks stressed in relation to women's paid "mental" work.

If the underlying logic of job segregation by sex is rooted in the collective interest of capital, reinforced by the gender interest of male workers, in preserving the sexual division of labor within the family, this still does not adequately explain the *specific* location of women in the wage labor force at a given point in time. Once established, idioms linking women's paid and unpaid work tend to acquire a certain ideological stability, in the form of "tradition." In practice, such "traditions" often guide the actual hiring and placement policies pursued by management. Yet, as suggested by the flexibility with which the idiom was readjusted during the war, the ideological construction of the sexual division of labor obscures the economic and political forces that help shape the particular configurations of sex-specific employment.

Employers must take account of a range of economic considerations in their hiring decisions: not only the available supplies of female and male labor and their relative costs, but also such factors as the proportion of a firm's capital outlays made up by wages, and the ease with which labor costs can be passed on to consumers. There are also political constraints which limit, or potentially limit, management's freedom in allocating jobs to women and men. For example, the greater the actual or anticipated male resistance to feminization, the less likely an employer may be to attempt it. Managerial initiatives affecting the sexual division of labor may become objects of political struggle for women and/or men workers, especially when the sex-specific supply-and-demand equilibrium in a labor market is disrupted—which occurs quite regularly in a dynamic capitalist economy. Usually these struggles are over marginal changes in the sexual division of labor, but there are times when more dramatic shifts in the structure of the labor market take place, presenting political opportunities for a broader challenge to the sexual division of wage labor as a whole. The large-scale economic dislocations associated with the mobilization for World War II and the subsequent postwar reconversion presented one such historical opportunity. . . .

"WOMEN'S WORK" IN THE PREWAR AUTO INDUSTRY

Automotive manufacturing relied on an overwhelmingly male work force in the years before World War II, with women accounting for less than one-tenth of its labor force throughout that period. The revolutionary organization of production around the moving assembly line laid the basis for auto's development as a high-wage, capital-intensive industry, in which employers had relatively little incentive to substitute female labor for its more expensive male equivalent. While the representation of women in the industry was abnormally low, women auto workers were concentrated in a relatively small number of jobs and in particular branches of the industry, consistent with the broader pattern of job segregation by sex found throughout the nation's economy. Although small numbers of women could be found scattered through many departments of the plants, they were clustered primarily in the upholstery or "cut-and-sew" divisions of body plants, and in small parts assembly.[8]

Although women auto workers earned wages higher than those available in most other fields of female employment, throughout the industry women's wages were far below men's. In 1925, the average hourly earnings of female workers in the auto industry were forty-seven cents, compared with a seventy-three cent average for men.[9] . . .

The idiom in which the sexual division of labor in the prewar auto industry was cast stressed the suitability of women for "light" or "delicate" work in accounting for their concentration in particular job classifications. "In finishing, polishing, and upholstery, where much hand work is required," wrote one observer in 1929, "they [women] are considered fast workers." In another typical rendition, it was suggested that women were especially well represented in the parts branch of this industry "since they are adept at assembly of light units."[10] These were the characteristics associated with "women's work" in the manufacturing sector generally, in the prevailing idiom of sex typing: "light," "repetitive" work, demanding manual "dexterity."

Yet the actual sexual division of labor in the prewar auto industry bore at best a limited relationship to such factors. The majority of jobs done by both women and men in the industry were repetitive operations, and most required some degree of manual "dexterity." There were also some "women's jobs" which required substantial physical exertion. . . .

Once firmly established, the sexual division of labor in the auto industry remained remarkably stable during the years before the war. Even during the economic depression of the 1930s, when the auto industry underwent a severe profitability crisis, there was surprisingly little change in the sexual division of labor. . . .

During the 1930s, then, the auto industry remained predominantly male with a clearly demarcated "women's place" in its various divisions, essentially unchanged in this respect from the nonunion era. It was not the political forces unleashed with unionization, but the economic impact of World War II that exploded the traditional sexual division of labor in the auto industry.

REDEFINING "WOMEN'S WORK" IN THE WARTIME AUTO INDUSTRY

The immediate impact of U.S. entry into World War II on the auto industry was a complete shutdown of production. Consumer production of cars and trucks was banned shortly after Pearl Harbor, and in February 1942 the last car rolled off the assembly line. There followed massive layoffs of auto workers, as the industry retooled for war production, and "conversion unemployment" was particularly pronounced among women auto workers. The number and proportion of women in the industry therefore dropped in the first part of 1942, but this was followed by a sudden rise in the representation of women as demand for labor outstripped the available supply of men. In April 1942, only one of every twenty auto production workers was a woman; eighteen months later, one out of four workers in the industry's plants was female.[11]

Initially, women war workers in the auto industry were employed only in jobs that had long before been established within the industry as "women's work." Although a U.S. Employment Service survey of war work in early 1942 found that women could capably perform the tasks required in 80 percent of job classifications, UAW woman-employing plants showed women in only 28 percent of the classifications, on average, in July of that year. "The chief classifications on which they were employed," the UAW reported, "were assembly, inspection, drill press, punch press, sewing machines, filing, and packing."[12] Such positions had long before been associated with women. . . .

The government pressured the auto firms to hire women, but made no effort whatsoever to influence their placement within the industry once management let them into the factory gates. The U.S. Employment Service routinely filled employer job openings which called for specific numbers of women and men, and while ceilings were imposed on the number of men who could be allocated to each plant, employers had a free hand in placing women and men in particular jobs within this constraint.[13] Although the UAW sometimes contested the sexual division of labor after the fact, the initial decisions about where to place women within the plant job structure were left entirely to management.

Women were not evenly distributed through the various jobs available in the war plants, but were hired into specific classifications which management deemed "suitable" for women and were excluded from other kinds of jobs. . . . A 1943 government survey of the industry's Detroit plants, for example, found over one-half of the women workers clustered in only five of seventy-two job classifications. Only 11 percent of the men were employed in these five occupations.[14]

Job segregation by sex was explicitly acknowledged in many automotive plants during the war. . . . Management was quick to offer a rationale for the concentration of women in certain kinds of jobs and their exclusion from others, just as it had done in the prewar period. "Womanpower differs from manpower as oil fuel differs from coal," proclaimed the trade journal *Automotive War Production* in October 1943, "and an understanding of the characteristics of the energy involved was needed for obtaining best results." . . .

Repeatedly stressed was the lesser physical strength of the average woman worker. . . . This emphasis on the physical limitations of women workers had a dual character. Not only did it provide a justification for the sexual division of labor, but it also served as the basis for increased mechanization and work simplification. "To adjust women's jobs to such [physical] differences, automotive plants have added more mechanical aids such as conveyors, chain hoists and load lifters." Although production technology was already quite advanced in auto relative to other industries, the pace of change accelerated during the war period. This was due at least as much to the combined impact of the labor shortage and the opportunity to introduce new technology at government expense as to the desire to make jobs easier for female workers, but the latter was particularly stressed by the industry's spokespersons.[15]

There was a contradiction in the management literature on women's war work. It simultaneously stressed the fact that "women are being trained in skills that were considered exclusively in man's domain" and their special suitability for "delicate war jobs."[16] The link between these two seemingly conflicting kinds of statements was made primarily through analogies between "women's work" in the home and in the war plants. "Why should men, who from childhood on never so much as sewed on buttons," inquired one manager, "be expected to handle delicate instruments better than women who have plied embroidery needles, knitting needles and darning needles all their lives?"[17]

Glamour was a related theme in the idiom through which women's war work was demarcated as female. As if calculated to assure women—and men—that war work need not involve a loss of femininity, depictions of women's new work roles were constantly overlaid with allusions to their stylish dress and attractive appearance. . . .

Ultimately, what lay behind the mixed message that war jobs were at once "men's" and "women's" jobs was an unambiguous point: women *could* do "men's work," but they were only expected to do it temporarily. . . .

The wartime idiom of job segregation by sex combined such familiar prewar themes as women's dexterity and lack of physical strength with a new emphasis on the value of women's multivaried experience doing housework and an unrelenting glamourization of their new work roles. That the construction of a "women's place" in the wartime auto industry was achieved so quickly and effectively owed much to the power of this elaborate ideology of occupational sex labeling. Although the initiative came from management, neither unions nor rank-and-file workers—of either gender—offered much resistance to the *general* principle of differentiation of jobs into "female" and "male" categories. Nor was the idiom of "woman's place" in the war effort ever frontally challenged. There was a great deal of conflict, however, over the location of the boundaries between the female and male labor markets within the wartime auto industry, and over wage differentials between these newly constituted markets.

AMBIGUITY AND LABOR-MANAGEMENT CONFLICT OVER "WOMEN'S WORK"

. . . A dilemma pervaded the auto industry, and other war industries as well, in the aftermath of conversion. How to go about classifying the new sets of jobs which had come into existence "for the duration" was ambiguous not only for management, but also for workers themselves—both female and male. There was of course some resemblance between many of the new war jobs and their predecessors in the peacetime auto industry, but the conversion process with its attendant technological changes and the dramatic shifts in the composition of the labor force combined to create tremendous disarray in what had before the war been a relatively stable system of job organization. Although in this example the issue of gender was not explicitly broached, distinctions like "heavy" and "light," or "major" and "minor" more often than not coincided with the sexual division of labor in this period. The problem of ambiguity in job classifications was not limited to the dilemma of where to assign sex labels, but this issue was central to the more general case illustrated here. . . .

It was the union's official policy to leave initial decisions on such matters to management, and then to negotiate any necessary adjustments. None of the women at the [United Automobile Workers (UAW) Women's Conference in 1942] objected to the idea of using some system of job classification arrived at in this way—on the contrary, they hoped it might protect them from assignment to overly strenuous jobs. Evidence that such abuses had occurred in the prewar period only served to reinforce the women's support for a more systematic classification of jobs.

This view, however, was soon proven naive. The union historically had developed other principles of job assignment which conflicted with the notion that women should be placed on the lighter jobs. There were numerous charges that management was manipulating the sexual division of labor in the mobilization period in ways calculated to undermine the seniority-based job preference rights of the prewar (that is, predominantly male) labor force. . . .

There were also numerous grievances . . . filed by the UAW against General Motors (GM) in late 1943 and early 1944. "When female employees were brought into the plant and assigned to various jobs," according to the Umpire's summary of one set of such grievances concerning the Chevrolet Gear and Axle Plant,

> complaints arose from the male employees who were on the so-called "waiting lists" pending possible promotion to higher rated classifications. These male employees complained that the placing of women in the jobs above them in rate prevented the male employees from gaining the promotions to which they would ordinarily have been entitled.[18]

What provoked these union challenges was not a belief that the idiom of sex typing (on which all parties seemed to agree) had been incorrectly applied. Rather, the central concern was that management was undercutting the seniority principle as a factor in job placement. Thus the evolution of the sexual division of labor in the war years became entangled with political and economic conflicts which involved a range of other issues. The ways in which management, the union, and rank-and-file workers defined and sought to advance their respective interests in relation to the sexual division of labor were determined in the larger context of labor relations and shop floor politics.

What was the role in these struggles of the women workers whose position in the auto industry was directly affected by their outcomes? Many of the key wartime conflicts over the sexual division of labor took place before many women had even entered the auto industry and were essentially fought out between male workers and management. The new women workers, most of whom had no factory or union experience, scarcely had time to get their bearings, much less develop the political resources they needed to participate effectively in struggles over job classification, during the short period when the wartime sexual division of labor was established. . . .

For the majority of the new women auto workers, the chance to work in a unionized basic industry, in virtually any job category, meant an enormous improvement in their economic circumstances. . . . Under such circumstances, it is not surprising that most women were relatively indifferent to their placement within what was in any case a completely new and unfamiliar system of job classification. . . .

The explicit struggles waged by the UAW (generally on behalf of its prewar, predominantly male, membership), in opposition to managerial initiatives affecting the sexual division of labor, effectively incorporated the interests of men into the process of defining boundaries between "women's work" and "men's work." In addition, the way in which management initially constructed the wartime sexual division of labor reflected the differential in political power between the sexes, and the anticipation that any opposition to the specific pattern of job placement by sex would come from men rather than from women. Thus, beneath the idiomatic construction of the sexual division of labor in terms of "heavy" and "light" jobs, and so forth, a set of political principles can be discerned according to which the allocation of jobs by gender was organized. In the wartime auto industry, women were excluded from positions where they supervised men or directly preceded them in the flow of work. Indeed, this was the case throughout the economy, and not only during the war: *job segregation* coincides with a *gender hierarchy* within the labor market.[19] . . .

CONCLUSION

The changes in the sexual division of labor in the auto industry during the mobilization for World War II illustrate the way in which job segregation by sex can be reproduced in the face of dramatic changes in the economic setting. Although neither the war period nor the auto experience is typical in women's labor history, that job segregation was reconstituted under such extreme circumstances—in a high-wage industry and in a situation in which women's incorporation into basic industry's work force was construed as temporary—suggests the resilience of the ideology of sex typing and the job segregation it enforces. The auto experience during this period reveals the way in which that ideology, as constrained by a particular set of economic exigencies and political forces, provided the basis for automotive management to construct a new sexual division of labor "for the duration."

In the absence of an organized feminist movement or consciousness, the only vehicle for political struggle over the sexual division of labor in this period was the labor movement. The UAW did challenge managerial initiatives in this area during the mobilization, most importantly in the form of demands for "equal pay for equal work." Here the conflict was essentially between male auto workers and management, as women were new to both the industry and the union and were not yet a politically effective force. In addition, just securing access to "men's jobs" in the auto plants brought such a dramatic improvement in women workers' status and pay that the sexual division of labor *within* the wartime industry understandably did not preoccupy them.

During the postwar reconversion, when these gains were threatened and when women had accumulated some political experience, they would mobilize in opposition to management's effort to return to the prewar sexual division of labor in the auto industry. In the mobilization period, however, women and men alike generally accepted as legitimate the overall idiom of the sexual division of labor in that industry. The struggles which took place focused on where the boundaries between women's and men's work should be drawn, without questioning the existence of such boundaries, as the equal pay example well illustrates. Ultimately, then, despite the dramatic upheaval in women's position in the work force during the war, the ideology of sex typing retained its power for both workers and management in the auto industry. In the absence of either a more fully developed class consciousness or a feminist movement, there was really no political basis for a sustained challenge to job segregation and the ideology of gender division which underpins it. Rather than romanticizing the wartime experience of women workers, we need to specify the kind of consciousness, of both class and gender, that might make it possible to dismantle the sexual division of paid labor and to transform work itself.

Notes

1. Karen Skold, "The Job He Left Behind: Women and Shipyard Workers in Portland, Oregon During World War II," in *Women, War, and Revolution*, ed. Carol R. Berkin and Clara M. Lovett (New York: Holmes, Meier, 1980). For a more detailed account of the situation in the auto industry, see Ruth Milkman, *Gender at Work: The Dynamics of Job Segregation by Sex during World War II* (Urbana: University of Illinois Press, 1987).

2. To be sure, the existence of a clearly defined sexual division of labor is not peculiar to capitalist societies—quite the contrary. Yet the persistence and reproduction of job segregation within capitalist relations of production presents a distinct theoretical problem—and an especially paradoxical one. . . . An adequate theoretical account of the continuous reproduction of job segregation by sex in capitalist societies has yet to be developed. The perspective frequently put forward by Marxist feminist theorists—that male domination exists as a "system," usually called "patriarchy," which is separate from and preceded capitalism, and is theoretically irreducible to it—while a possible starting point for such a theory, by itself offers no way out. This simply *presumes* the persistence of gender inequality within capitalism in general, and the capitalist labor market in particular, rather than *explaining why* it persists, which is hardly self-evident.

3. This consideration is stressed in the literature on "labor market segmentation" developed by Marxist economists. See, for example, Richard Edwards, Michael Reich, and David Gordon, eds., *Labor Market Segmentation* (Lexington, Mass.: D.C. Health and Co., 1975), especially the Introduction. However, this literature fails to distinguish between the class interests of capital and the interests of individual capital, missing a critical aspect of the problem altogether.

4. This dynamic has been discussed extensively in Marxist feminist literature. See especially Veronica Beechey, "Some Notes on Female Wage Labour in Capitalist Production," *Capital and Class*, no. 3 (Autumn 1977), pp. 45–66; and Heidi Hartmann, "Capitalism, Patriarchy, and Job Segregation by Sex" in *Women and the Workplace: The Implications of Occupational Segregation*, eds. Martha Blaxall and Barbara Reagan (Chicago: University of Chicago Press, 1976).

5. This is the main emphasis in Hartmann, "Capitalism, Patriarchy, and Job Segregation."

6. The war years produced a "family crisis" with many parallels to that of our own time and aroused many of the same concerns among contemporaries. This is discussed indirectly in Karen Anderson, *Wartime Women: Sex Roles, Family Relations and the Status of Women in World War II* (Westport, Conn.: Greenwood Press, 1981), chap. 3.

7. The transcript of this newsreel was made available to me by the Rosie the Riveter Film Project, Emeryville, California. Additional examples of the wartime idiom are cited below.

8. Statistics on the representation of women in the auto industry for this period are scattered and not entirely consistent. The 1930 Census reported that women were 7 percent of all workers employed by the industry, and the 1940 Census enumeration produced a figure of 9 percent. U.S. Department of Commerce, Bureau of the Census, *Fifteenth Census of the United States, 1930: Population*, 5:468; and *Sixteenth Census of the United States, 1940; Population*, 3:180. William McPherson reported in 1940 that women made up about 5 percent of the wage earners in auto assembly plants, about 10 percent of those in body plants, and about 20 percent of those in parts plants. See his *Labor Relations in the Automobile Industry* (Washington, D.C.: Brookings Institute, 1940), pp. 8–9.

9. U.S. Department of Labor, Bureau of Labor Statistics, *Wages and Hours of Labor in the Motor Vehicle Industry: 1925*, Bulletin No. 438 (1927), pp. 2–3.

10. Robert W. Dunn, *Labor and Automobiles* (New York: International Publishers, 1929), p. 74; William McPherson, "Automobiles," in *How Collective Bargaining Works*, ed. Harry A. Millis (New York: Twentieth Century Fund, 1942), p. 576.

11. On conversion, see Barton J. Bernstein, "The Automobile Industry and the Coming of the Second World War," *Southwestern Social Science Quarterly* 47 (June 1966): 22–33; and Alan Clive, *State of War: Michigan in World War II* (Ann Arbor: University of Michigan Press, 1979), pp. 18–42.

12. "Women in War Industries," *UAW Research Report*, 2 (September 1942), p. 1.

13. U.S. Congress, Senate, *Manpower Problems in Detroit*, Hearings before a Special Committee Investigating the National Defense Program, 79th Cong., 1st Session, March 9–13, 1945, pp. 13534, 13638.

14. Computed from data in U.S. Department of Labor, Bureau of Labor Statistics, Division of Wage Analysis, Regional Office No. 8-A, Detroit, Michigan, 3 December 1943, Serial No. 8-A-16, "Metalworking Establishments, Detroit, Michigan, Labor Market Area, Straight-Time Average Hourly Earnings, Selected Occupations, July 1943," Mimeographed copy in UAW Research Department Collection, WSUA, Box 28, Folder: "Wage Rates (Detroit) Bureau of Labor Statistics, 1943–5." Women were 22 percent of the labor force surveyed here. If these data are compared to those in the 1940 Bureau of Labor Statistics survey cited in note 8, the degree of segregation by sex in the auto industry during the war is put into better perspective. In 1940, women were only 2.5 percent of the labor force, and two occupational groups accounted for one-half of the women in the industry. In 1943, five groups accounted for 51 percent of the women, which, given the much greater representation of women in the auto work force, does not indicate a significant decline in the degree of segregation.

15. "Provisions in Plants for Physical Differences Enable Women to Handle Variety of War Jobs," *Automotive War Production* 2 (September 1943): 7. Also see "Technological Advances in Automotive Plants Help to Combat Growing Manpower Crisis," *Automotive War Production* 2 (September 1943): 3; and "Automotive Industry Reducing War Costs Through Improved Production Techniques," *Automotive War Production* 2 (March 1943): 3.

16. "Women Work for Victory," *Automotive War Production* 1 (November 1942): 4; "Engineers of Womanpower," *Automotive War Production* 2 (October 1943): 4–5.

17. "Engineers of Womanpower," p. 4.

18. Umpire Decision No. C-139, 29 November 1943, "Hiring of Women," *Decisions of the Impartial Umpire Under the October 19, 1942 Agreement between General Motors Corporation and the International Union, United Automobile, Aircraft and Agricultural Implement Workers of America—Congress of Industrial Organizations*, vol. 1 (privately published, Detroit: General Motors Corporation and United Automobile Workers), pp. 465–67.

19. I have not uncovered evidence of this specific to the auto industry, but the wartime literature on managerial policy toward women war workers generally is replete with insistences that women make "poor supervisors" and the like. See, for example, American Management Association, *Supervision of Women on Production Jobs: A Study of Management's Problems and Practices in Handling Female Personnel*, Special Research Report No. 2 (New York: AMA, 1943). For a general discussion of this issue, see also Joan Acker and Donald R. Van Houten, "Differential Recruitment and Control: The Sex Structuring of Organizations," *Administrative Science Quarterly* 19 (June 1974): 152–63.

Chapter 22

When Women Arrived: The Transformation of New York's Chinatown

Xiaolan Bao

The exclusion of Chinese immigrants between 1882 and 1943 and the overwhelmingly male character of earlier Chinese immigration to the United States meant that for sixty years the Chinese community in New York City consisted predominantly of married men separated from their families or male bachelors. The post-World War II years, when female immigration predominated, were, in the view of Xiaolan Bao, a period of family reunion and family formation. Bao explores the changing work and family lives of Chinese women in the postwar decades as a mother-centered, dual wage-earner family became the typical form of family organization in New York's Chinatown.

World War II affected the lives of all Americans, but it had a particularly profound impact on Asian Americans. The end of the war marked an especially important turning point in the history of New York's Chinatown. From a relatively homogeneous, highly segregated, and small, service-oriented bachelor society, New York's Chinatown was transformed into a relatively diverse and family-oriented community with manufacturing industries. Although the extent of change was evident only after the passage of the amendment of the U.S. immigration law in 1965, the changes originated in the immediate postwar era.

The entry of Chinese women immigrants into the United States, a key factor in this transformation, resulted from changes in federal law during and after World War II. The 1943 repeal of the Chinese Exclusion Acts made Chinese, but not other Asians, eligible for naturalization and provided Chinese with an immigration quota. Among the new laws that lifted restrictions on Chinese, some specifically fostered the entry of Chinese women: The 1945 War Brides Act allowed men who had served in the U.S. military to bring spouses to the United States as nonquota immigrants, and the 1946 Alien Fiancees and Fiances Act allowed the Chinese wives of U.S. citizens, both native-born and naturalized, to immigrate on a nonquota basis. The 1953 Refugee Relief Act further provided women with opportunities for immigration by reserving a number of visas for Chinese refugees and their families . . .

As a result, Chinese women began to enter the United States in significant numbers,[1] initiating profound changes in family pattern, economic structure, and culture of major Chinese settlements in the United States. Focusing on New York's Chinatown, this essay examines the impact of these changes and traces the important role of women, working-class women in particular, in bringing about the transformation.

NEW YORK'S CHINATOWN BEFORE 1945

As John Kuo Wei Tchen states, New York's Chinatown was not simply "an extension of San Francisco's and [the] Pacific Coast's," its foundation having "been laid long before the surge of the anti-Chinese sentiment on the West Coast."[2] The regional particularities of the early Chinese population were shaped by the more cosmopolitan nature of New York City as an important national and international port.

With respect to the scarcity of Chinese women, New York was exceptional. Although the sex-ratio imbalance was a common phenomenon among Chinese settlements in this country for most of the nineteenth century, by 1870 the Chinese female population had reached 3,873 in California, but "no Chinese women seemed to have actually settled in New York."[3] The small number of Chinese women who entered the city in the following years were predominantly the wives of Chinese merchants, women who were kept strictly indoors and hardly ventured beyond. The sight of Chinese women was such a rarity that they were said to be treasured as "pearls" in the bachelors' eyes . . . Even at the end of World War II, when the national sex-ratio imbalance of the Chinese population had dropped significantly, New York City's remained at almost six males to one female.[4]

One obvious consequence of this imbalance was intercultural marriage in New York, which was clearly recorded in state census records of the second half of the nineteenth century. In 1855, of the thirty-eight Chinese men found by the census takers in the third, fourth, and fifth wards of old Lower Manhattan, eleven were married to Irish women.[5] In 1870, the census taken in the fourth and sixth wards of the same area showed that eighteen of the sixty-four Chinese male residents were married to European American women, with a total of twenty-one bicultural children.[6] The rate of Chinese-Irish intercultural marriage began to decline only when anti-Chinese sentiment began to sweep through the city in the late nineteenth century.

The rate of Chinese intercultural marriage in New York in this era never surpassed one-third of the entire population,[7] largely for financial reasons. Census records show that the Chinese who married Irish women were financially secure; Chinese men without means had little opportunity for intercultural marriage.[8] The ethnocentric nature of traditional Chinese culture probably discouraged many other Chinese men from out-marriage. If the early settlers had few opportunities, forced bachelorhood became nearly universal for Chinese by the end of the nineteenth century, with the passage of the Chinese Exclusion Act of 1882, which strictly prohibited the immigration of the wives of Chinese laborers, and the mounting anti-Chinese sentiment. Many men were members of what sociologist Evelyn Nakano Glenn terms the "split household," characterized by the separation of the breadwinner from his family; this family pattern was common in the first seventy years of Chinese settlements in the United States.[9] Family life did not become a dominant living arrangement in New York's Chinatown until the postwar period.

This pattern of "split households" and forced bachelorhood tended to undermine the patriarchal nature of traditional Chinese culture and its family system. Traditional Chinese culture emphasized the importance of family-line continuity, with its ideal of extended multigenerational family. Centering on the male's role as *wai zi*, the only breadwinner of the family and the sole dealer with the outside world,[10] Chinese tradition invested the male patriarch with absolute authority over women and the younger generation in the family.

The immigration experience deprived Chinese male laborers of their male prerogatives in several spheres. From the beginning of their experience in this country, most Chinese laborers were forced to resign themselves to a life of bachelorhood. Although it was the common assumption that married and single Chinese men would go back to China, to visit their families or to marry, few could afford to do so. Consequently, most married men were severed from their families, the traditional domain of their power, and bachelors with no options for marriage were unable to carry on their family lines.

In this period, married Chinese men did try to maintain their traditional position in the family by sending remittances to their male kin and relying on them to oversee their wives; but they had little control over their families. Their absence particularly affected their roles as fathers. In traditional Chinese families, children tended to have a formal and distant relationship with their fathers . . . It was from this awesome image as discipliners that men derived their authority over their children. In the Chinese American "split household," [this] image was undermined by the father's lack of daily contact with his children because of his prolonged absence from the family. . . .

A strengthened mother-child relationship filled the vacuum in the Chinese American "split household." As the anthropologist Margery Wolf aptly pointed out, an informal mother-centered . . . family operates in the formally male-dominated Chinese extended family. Since the mothers conducted the sons' early socialization in the traditional Chinese family, close emotional ties could be formed between them; this bond was reinforced by filial piety, a central value of Confucianism, and in many cases led the son to act as the mother's spokesman in domestic and public affairs. Thus married women were able to wield a degree of power in the male-dominated world,[11] and women whose husbands were in America had fewer obstacles to acquiring such power.

Moreover, the prolonged absence undermined the Chinese fathers' dominant position in the family, and their traditional masculine roles were further reduced by the feminization of their occupations in this country after anti-Chinese agitation began to grow. By the 1870s, Chinese men in New York City no longer engaged in the wide range of occupations they had previously held.[12] The Chinese laborers who had come to this country in search of gold found jobs on railroads, mines, and farms; when anti-Chinese sentiment mounted across the nation, they were relegated to the service sector, especially in small ethnic enterprises. The hand laundry business, along with restaurants, grocery stores, and gift shops, became major occupations in New York's Chinatown.[13] Unlike trades that required a large amount of capital, a familiarity with tradesmen elsewhere, and a degree of English-language skill, the laundry business originally required only soap, scrubbing boards, and physical labor.[14] Limited by their capital, many former laborers went into this trade in partnership. One or two-man Chinese hand laundries proliferated; by the 1930s, an estimated seven to eight thousand Chinese hand laundry shops involved almost half of the adult population in New York's Chinese community.[15] Commonly working from twelve to sixteen (and some reported twenty) hours a day, wielding an eight-pound iron in a hot, cramped environment, the Chinese men called their work "the blood and tears eight-pound livelihood."[16]

In China, as in other parts of the world, women traditionally did laundry.[17] Driven into a labor sector that they would have shunned in China . . . the Chinese laundry men probably experienced profound psychological injury as a result of this restriction to what they regarded as women's work. Holding on to their dream of returning to China . . . some men in New York's Chinese enclave sought emotional escapes in gambling, opium, tong wars, and prostitution, outlets common to many male-dominated societies. What made the vice-plagued bachelor society of New York's Chinatown unique among the major Chinese settlements in the United States was the presence of prostitutes from many ethnic groups, another consequence of the scarcity of Chinese women in the community.[18]

If the wives left behind in China were . . . able to gain some additional influence, they paid a high price.[19] Toiling day and night for the families left behind by their husbands, taking care not only of their children but also members of their husbands' families, they shouldered tasks that were culturally allocated both to themselves and to their husbands.[20] Their drudgery was not appreciated. While they labored for their husbands' families, their conduct and chastity were constantly under the strict surveillance of their husbands' kin. The suffering of Chinese women during this period was enormous. The loneliness, frustration, and unfairness could hardly be compensated for by the possible strengthening of their relations with their children as a result of their husbands' prolonged absence.

Not until the end of World War II did family life become the norm in New York's Chinatown. As immigration restrictions were lifted, Chinese women came to the United States in large numbers. In fact, women constituted almost 90 percent of the Chinese immigrants between 1947 and 1952. The national sex ratio of the Chinese population nearly balanced in forty years, dropping from 285:100 in 1940 to 110:100 in 1979.[21]

This influx of women in the postwar era significantly changed the Chinese community in New York City. Of the 7,956 Chinese women who entered the United States between 1945 and the end of 1950, it is estimated that half settled in New York's Chinatown.[22] The sex-ratio imbalance in the city dropped from almost 6:1 in 1940 to 3:1 in 1950.[23] As many families entered small-capital and labor-intensive trades—grocery and restaurant and, mainly, the laundry business—a new form of family economy emerged, the "small producer household." Glenn has asserted that this pattern had become dominant in other major Chinese settlements by the 1920s,[24] but it appeared in New York City almost three decades later.

In New York City and elsewhere in the country, the Chinese "small producer household" blurred the demarcation between family and work life. This was especially true in the Chinese laundry enterprise.[25] The family living quarters, situated behind or above the shop . . . were where women and children worked, providing housekeeping and other kinds of assistance to the family business. Men worked in the shop, taking care of customers and dealing with the outside world. By pooling together the labor of all members of the family, Chinese working-class families in New York City managed to survive. . . .

Some Chinese immigrant women who arrived in the postwar era from urban China and with some formal education found it easier to adapt to their new environment. They learned English, dressed themselves in Western apparel, and tried to make friends with their American neighbors. But even they often experienced discrimination. Mrs. Yu, for instance, whose experience was reported in 1951 in the *China Daily News*, came in 1948 with English-language skills and a previous experience of serving in a Red Cross organization in Kunming City, China. She wholeheartedly embraced the values of democracy, which she believed could be found only in the United States. After her husband retired from the army, however, the couple had a difficult time finding a home to rent because of the racial bias of white homeowners. Dismayed, she knew she had been unfairly treated by people who did not acknowledge her predicament. "I knew people had different feelings, but I did not expect I would be discriminated just because of the color of my skin. People said we did not want to move out. In fact, it is not that we do not want to move out, but that we are restricted by our conditions."[26]

The majority of Chinese immigrant women of this period were from rural China and had little education. The language barrier and difficulties in adapting to an entirely alien culture were aggravated by the hostility to the Chinese in New York City. Coverage of their difficult lives appeared frequently in Chinese community newspapers. . . .

Many more suffered not only from household chores and loneliness but also from tensions with their husbands. Strained marital relations were commonplace among the newly formed or recently reunited families in this period, with couples citing the lack of sufficient understanding and affection as a major cause. Most Chinese women who came to the United States in the immediate postwar period were wives who had long been separated from their husbands or new war brides who had recently married ex-servicemen of Chinese origin. These two groups differed in terms of age, level of education, cultural adaptability, and life experience. The reunited wives tended to be much older and had suffered long periods of separation from their husbands. The younger war brides were slightly better educated but were under more pressure for cultural adaptation as the young men they married were more Americanized than their fathers. . . .

These already strained marital relations were commonly aggravated by economic problems. Unable to shoulder their family responsibilities, men tended to vent their frustrations and anger on their wives. As many articles in the Chinese newspapers of the period show, women were frequently battered, abused, and even forced to divorce their husbands.[27] Zhonghai Chen, president of the pro-Taiwan Chinese Consolidated Benevolent Association (CCBA), the most influential political organization in the community at that time, was revealed to have battered, abused and abandoned his wife. Interestingly, this case was covered by the pro-Beijing *China Daily News* (or *Huagiao Ribao*) to attack his political loyalty,[28] but the coverage ignored the widespread problem of wife abuse in the community. The fact that Zhonghai Chen, a public figure, had recklessly abused his wife in a community where one's reputation was treasured most suggests that wife battering transcended any political interpretation.

The difficulties in their lives drove some immigrant women to commit suicide. According to one estimate, up to the late 1970s the suicide rate among Chinese women in New York remained twice that of women of other groups in the city.[29] Many other Chinese women were reportedly on the verge of a nervous breakdown.[30] High suicide rates and high divorce rates among newly reunited or married couples were recognized as major problems in the community.[31] . . .

The rise of the garment factories in Chinatown in the late 1940s and early 1950s offered a solution to some of these problems. The help-wanted advertisements of the garment shops first appeared in the *China Daily News* on June 27, 1952. After that, a slowly increasing number of Chinese American women began to enter the garment industry. Work in these shops carried different meanings for women of different social status. For the very small number of women who were from relatively well-off families, garment factories provided important channels to socialize and make use of their talents.

For the majority of women, however, the garment factories offered an important supplement to their family income. Their employment helped ease the anxiety and tension in their lives. For some, the need for wageearning labor was only temporary. This was true for many of the wives of the "stranded" Chinese students who chose to stay in the United States when the communists took over China in 1949. To help finance the education of their husbands, who were no longer supported by funds from China, some women chose to work in garment shops. Their numbers were small, and they often were isolated from the rest of the workers because of their dialect and cultural and class differences.[32] Many of these workers moved out of the industry to become "uptown" Chinese after their husbands completed their education and obtained professional jobs.[33]

For many garment workers, however, their incomes remained crucial to their families. A dialogue recorded in a local newspaper of the time vividly illustrated this aspect of wage work.

"Old Aunt Mark, where are you going, why are you in such a hurry and out in such an early hour?"

"I am rushing to work."

"Then what about the kids? Who takes care of them?"

"Well, to tell you the truth, with two kids needing to be taken care of, I do wish I could stay home. But things are not always as good as you wish. You know that, in the past, Old Mark could get three to four days' work a week. The thirty something dollars he earned each week was barely enough to pay our rent and board. Now, as our luck would have it, Old Mark has been sick for months and we could only live on money borrowed from friends and relatives . . . How could we live on like this? I cannot but come out to work."

"Isn't it too hard on you?"

"Well, I ask a woman to take care of the kids and pay her fifteen dollars a week. I myself work in the shop and earn more than thirty dollars a week. After paying the babysitter, I still have some money left for family expenses. I feel much better now."[34]

The employment opportunities provided by the garment industry were . . . crucial to some families. . . .

Garment shops first appeared in the Chinese community around 1948.[35] By 1952, there were three Chinese-owned garment shops in the Chinatown area, hiring approximately fifty workers. Women workers were relatively young; even the finishers, who now tend to be much older, were only in their thirties. This was mainly because the laundry business continued to remain the major source of income for the community. Older women tended to help their husbands with the laundry business at home. Furthermore, garment shop owners did not hire older women because they believed they could not work as rapidly as younger women. Also, husbands of the younger women were not yet able to have businesses of their own, and their wives worked in the shops.[36]

The number of Chinese-owned garment shops grew slowly from three in 1952 to eight in 1960 and thirty-five in 1965.[37] By 1965, they hired approximately 10 percent of the Chinese female adult population of the city.[38] Although the impact of the garment industry was limited, it brought tangible changes to the community and foreshadowed the future transformation of New York's Chinatown. First, it gave rise to the "double wage-earner family" in New York's Chinatown. This family pattern, characterized by the labor force participation and economic contribution of both husband and wife, challenged traditional Chinese family values. The story of Mary Yan is a case in point.

Like many Chinese women who came to the United States after the passage of the War Brides Act, Yan had a rosy dream of life in the "Golden Mountain." The dream was crushed after she arrived. Her husband was in poor health and could not guarantee a regular income. After giving birth to two children, Yan started a career as a seamstress. Her husband worked out of town, where there was less competition than in the city. Yan, who was now the main breadwinner and sole parent at home, saw her children as her only hope. Like many working mothers in Chinatown, she devoted most attention to her children's education; she was stern when they did not do well at school and a most loving mother when they performed excellently.[39] . . .

Second, the growth of Chinatown's garment industry and its unionization integrated Chinese workers into the larger American society. The International Ladies' Garment Workers' Union (ILGWU) began to unionize Chinatown garment shops in the 1950s, and in 1957 information about union benefits first appeared in the *China Daily News*. Since then, the garment industry has become the only unionized industry in the community. Although the white, male-dominated leadership of the ILGWU was indifferent to the particular interests of its Chinese members, especially before the 1982 Chinese garment workers' strike, unionization carried tremendous meaning for Chinese women workers. It provided them with benefits and services and exposed them to the world outside Chinatown.[40] . . .

The modern dual wage-earner family did not become the dominant family pattern in New York's Chinatown until the late 1960s, when the garment industry began to grow dramatically and the laundry business was almost entirely wiped out by modern washing machines, dryers, and laundromats. The number of Chinese-owned laundry shops in the New York metropolitan area dropped from about five thousand in 1946 to one thousand in 1970.[41] With the decline of the laundry business, men looked for employment in the larger community, many of them working in restaurants.

Because of the men's limited incomes and the unstable nature of their employment, working-class Chinese American families badly needed a second income. It was at this juncture that the garment industry stepped into the economic center of the community.

Three major factors contributed to the growth of the Chinatown garment industry: the availability of inexpensive loft space and housing in the area; the entry of a group of Chinese entrepreneurs eager to make a fortune in their new land and ready to take advantage of changing market opportunities; and, most important, the 1965 amendment to the Immigration and Nationality Act, which phased out the discriminatory national-origins quotas and allowed Chinese immigrant women to enter in large numbers and supply the labor force needed by the garment industry.[42]

From 1966 to 1970, more than 19,500 Chinese immigrants came to the United States annually. The number soared to almost 23,000 in the 1970s and reached over 42,000 in the 1980s.[43] From 1966 to 1989, a total of 734,521 Chinese immigrants came to the United States, making the Chinese the largest Asian group and the second-largest immigrant group in the United States.[44] New York City became a mecca for Chinese immigrants. From 1965 to 1977, 22 percent of all Chinese selected New York City as their destination before their arrival; seven out of twelve Chinese who landed in San Francisco ended up in New York City; and few Chinese left New York once they had settled there.[45] Between 1960 and 1980, the Chinese population in New York City increased fourfold. By 1970, New York had replaced San Francisco as the city with the largest concentration of Chinese residents in the United States.[46]

The jobs available in New York City, easily learned and requiring little English, influenced the type of immigrant. Many of the best-educated and highly skilled Chinese settled in California; many of the relatively poor, less-educated, and low-skilled Chinese settled in New York City.[47] Although an increasing proportion of Chinese Americans were middle-class professionals, Chinese immigrants in New York City were predominantly working class.

Like other newcomers after 1965, more than half of the Chinese immigrants were women, effectively lowering the sex-ratio imbalance of the Chinese population in the city.[48] Most of the new Chinese immigrant women did not speak English and had lower-level skills; most were married, and their families were in straitened economic circumstances.[49] Fortunately, most were also in the prime of their working years.[50] Under the pressure of economic need, they were eager to work at any wages and at any time. One-third to one-half of the Chinese women who immigrated to the city with their families changed their occupation from full-time housewife to garment worker.[51]

The Chinese women workers were in many ways similar to the women who came to the Lower East Side from Europe in the late nineteenth and early twentieth centuries. Clustering in the same area as the earlier immigrants, these Chinese workers had few alternatives to poorly paid work in the garment industry, which at the time was threatened by a shortage of labor. Confined to the highly competitive low-priced lines, the garment industry in Chinatown managed to grow by hiring these women at low pay.

The number of Chinese-owned shops grew from 34 to 247 between 1965 and 1975 and reached a peak of 430 in 1980.[52] As the number of jobs in the traditional midtown garment center dropped from 40,000 to 22,000, the number of jobs in Chinatown's garment industry grew from 8,000 to 13,400, and the number of union-affiliated shops more than tripled.[53] By 1980, Chinatown held 40 percent of the recorded production jobs in the women's outerwear industry in the city.[54] It became the largest center for garment production in the United States.

The rise of the Chinatown garment industry had a tremendous impact on the Chinese community. Garment shops employed one-third of Chinatown's labor force in 1969.[55] By 1983, it provided incomes for 60 percent of Chinatown families and 40 percent of the Chinese American families in the city.[56] The garment industry rejuvenated the restaurant business in the area, which had begun to decline in the 1960s. Catering to the needs of workers whose long hours forced them to eat two meals in the shop, small restaurants, offering fast and reasonably priced food, grew quickly in the area.[57] The garment industry also offered many Chinese immigrants a path to proprietorship. Many restaurant owners, heads of import-export companies, and realtors originally made their money in the garment shops.[58]

The garment industry also transformed the family life of working-class Chinese Americans in the city. By 1980, almost 60 percent of the Chinese female working population was employed in the industry, which significantly challenged the male-dominated nature of the Chinese American family.[59] The mother-centered Chinese working-class family, which emerged in the postwar era, became more evident for several reasons. First, women's labor participation was indispensable to their families' well-being. The garment industry was the only one to offer family health insurance to its members . . . Also, because of the increased competition and declining wages for men's employment, women's economic contribution was no longer secondary to men's. Second, many men spent long hours away from home. Chinese restaurant workers had irregular work hours; most male employees worked from ten or eleven in the morning to eleven or later in the evening if business was good. For most of the week, home for them was merely a place to sleep . . . Chinese male restaurant workers who worked outside the city visited their families only two days every other week. Exhausted by their long workdays, they played no significant role when they were home. This failure to play a substantial role in the life of their families, coupled with their decreased economic role, made them virtually invisible in their families. The entire household responsibilities fell on the shoulders of the women garment workers, whose work hours were more regular and flexible. . . .

Although this mother-centered, dual wage-earner family imposed a heavy burden on women workers, it also provided them self-confidence. This confidence in turn stimulated their political awakening. In 1982, a large-scale garment workers' strike took place in New York's Chinatown. Facing the Chinese shop owners' resistance to signing a new labor contract, twenty thousand women workers turned out to join the union rally, which remains the largest one in the history of New York's Chinatown.

How far will this new family pattern develop among the Chinese working class of New York City? Time will tell. Meanwhile, we know that its origin can be traced to the immediate postwar era, when the Chinese community was transformed.

Notes

1. The best accounts of these new laws can be found in Roger Daniels, *Asian Americans: Chinese and Japanese in the United States Since 1850* (Seattle: University of Washington Press, 1988), 186–98, 299–316; and David M. Reimers, *Still the Golden Door: The Third World Comes to America* (New York: Columbia University Press, 1985), 11–29.
2. Both quotes are from John Kuo Wei Tchen, "New York Chinese: The Nineteenth-Century Pre-Chinatown Settlement," in *Chinese America: History and Perspectives 1990*, (San Francisco: Chinese Historical Society of America/Asian American Studies, San Francisco State University Press, 1990), 183–184.
3. *Ibid.*, 173; see also Judy Yung, *Chinese Women of America: A Pictorial History* (Seattle: University of Washington Press, 1986), 119.
4. Bernard P. Wong, *Chinatown: Economic Adaptation and Ethnic Identity of the Chinese* (New York: Holt, Rinehart and Winston, 1982), 59.
5. Tchen, "New York Chinese," 161–162.
6. *Ibid.*, 173.

7. *Ibid.*, 162, 173.

8. As pointed out by Tchen, eleven Chinese men who married Irish women in 1855 included boarding-house operators and merchant mariners. None of the peddlers, who constituted one-third of the Chinese population found by the census takers in the area, was among them. *Ibid.*, 161–162.

9. Evelyn Nakano Glenn, "Split Household, Small Producer and Dual Earner: An Analysis of Chinese-American Family Strategies," *Journal of Marriage and the Family*, February 1983, 35–46.

10. *Wai zi*, the culturally constructed name for the husband, means the person who deals with the outside world (external affairs). It was used versus *nei zi*, the wife, meaning the person who deals with the inside world (internal, or domestic, affairs).

11. For a detailed discussion of this particular feature of the traditional Chinese family, see the discussion of the informal mother-centered uterine family in Margery Wolf, *Chinese Families in Rural Taiwan* (Stanford: Stanford University Press, 1975); and Kay Ann Johnson, *Women, Family and Peasant Revolution in China* (Chicago: University of Chicago Press, 1983), 10, 18–20.

12. Tchen, "New York Chinese," 161.

13. Wong, *Chinatown*, 37.

14. For a detailed discussion of the early trades in New York's Chinatown. see *ibid.*, 41–42.

15. Renqiu Yu, *To Save China, to Save Ourselves: A History of the Chinese Hand Laundry Alliance of New York* (Philadelphia: Temple University Press, 1992), 9.

16. Chen Hsiang-shui and John Kuo Wei Tchen, "Towards a History of Chinese in Queens," working paper, Asian American Center/CUNY Queens College, 4.

17. Wong, *Chinatown*, 37.

18. Guo, *Huafu Cangsang*, 214.

19. See also Glenn, "Split Household," 39.

20. Due to the patrilocal nature of the traditional Chinese family, once married, women had to move into their husbands' families. They were expected to take care not only of their own family but also of all members of their husbands' families.

21. Daniels, *Asian Americans*, table 6.3, p. 199; and Yung, *Chinese Women of America*, 118.

22. The number 7,956 was arrived at from Daniels, *Asian Americans*, table 6.3, p. 199. The estimate that half the Chinese women who came to the United States settled in New York's Chinatown was suggested by Xia Zhu (Chu, Y. K.), *Meiguo Huaqiao Gaishi* (A General History of the Chinese in America) (New York: China Times, 1973), 135. This is a very rough estimate, subject to dispute.

23. Abeles, Schwartz, Haeckel, and Silverblatt, Inc., *The Chinatown Garment Industry Study* (hereafter cited as *Study*), a study commissioned by Local 23–25, International Ladies' Garment Workers Union, and the New York Skirt and Sportswear Association, 1983, 95; and Wong, *Chinatown*, 59.

24. Glenn, "Split Household," 39.

25. Wong, *Chinatown*, 60; Chen, "Towards a History," 4; and Glenn, "Split Household," 40.

26. *China Daily News* (hereafter cited as *CDN*), November 26, 1948.

27. *CDN*, May 27, June 22, and November 24, 1950.

28. *Ibid.*, May 5, 1950.

29. *Ibid.*, September 22 and 24, 1979.

30. *Ibid.*

31. *Ibid.*, November 24, 1950, Lee, *Chinese in the United States of America*, 200–201; Guo, *Huafu Cangsang*, 62–64; Xia Zhu, *Meiguo Huaqiao Gaisi*, 179–182.

32. These workers spoke Mandarin, and most of them came from urban sections of northern China, while the majority of workers spoke Taishan dialect and were from rural Guangdong Province.

33. A discussion of the "uptown" Chinese in this period can be found in Peter Kwong, *The New Chinatown* (New York: Hill and Wang, 1987), 59–60.

34. *CDN*, May 29, 1952, translated by the author. A good discussion of the Chinese immigrant families in this period can be found in *ibid.*, May 14, 1952.

35. The exact date of the first appearance of garment shops in New York's Chinatown remains in dispute. The year 1948 is based on Peter Kwong's assessment in *The New Chinatown*, 32, and the transcripts of the

workshops on the garment industry organized by the New York Chinatown History Project in 1984. The transcripts are located at the New York Chinatown History Museum (formerly New York Chinatown History Project) at 70 Mulberry Street, New York City.

36. This discussion is based on Guo, *Huafu Cangshang*, 88–89.

37. *Study*, 42.

38. *Ibid.*, 94.

39. As she recalled regretfully, once she was so angry with her son because of his poor school work that she ordered him to kneel on the floor with his book on his head for more than half a day.

40. The most important union benefit was family health insurance. . . .

41. The 1946 figure is from Ruzhou Chen, ed., *Meiguo Huajiao Nianjian* (Handbook of Chinese in America) (New York: Office of China People's Foreign Affairs Association in New York, 1946), 381; the 1970 figure is from Wong, *Chinatown*, 40; and Kwong, *The New Chinatown*, 28.

42. These three major factors are discussed in *Study*, 44–72.

43. U.S. Immigration and Naturalization Service, *Annual Reports*, 1966–1989.

44. *Study*, 45; and Kwong, *The New Chinatown*, 4, 22.

45. Kwong, *The New Chinatown*, 25. The net immigration of 45,846 Chinese to New York between 1970 and 1980 is the number remaining from the 48,364 overseas Chinese immigrants who came to the city during that period. *Study*, 94.

46. *Ibid.*, 45.

47. The 1979 data show that 70 percent of the New York arrivals with prior occupational experience had worked in blue-collar or service occupations. Only 3.2 percent of the Chinese professional and technical immigrants intended to stay in New York. *Study*, 45, 98.

48. *Ibid.*, 95; and Wong, *Chinatown*, 11.

49. Many of the women workers were originally agricultural workers in China or urban women engaged in homework in Hong Kong. The preponderance of low-skilled workers was so pronounced that in 1979 only 20 percent of the adult female newcomers reported any previous work experience; of these, only 5 percent had been employed in white-collar positions, and only 30 percent had engaged in factory production. *Study*, 45, 97–98. In addition, most of them were married. The 1979 data show that 71 percent of the Chinese women arrivals over nineteen were married. *Ibid.*, 95.

50. Almost 75 percent were between the ages of sixteen and sixty-four, and 37 percent were twenty to forty years old. *Ibid.*

51. Betty Lee Sung, *Survey of Chinese American Manpower and Employment* (New York: Praeger, 1976), 91.

52. *Study*, 44.

53. They grew from 73 to 247. *Ibid.*, 41.

54. *Ibid.*, 84.

55. Chinatown Study Group, "Chinatown Report: 1969," Columbia University East Asian Studies Center, 1969.

56. *Study*, 64.

57. Kwong, *The New Chinatown*, 32–33.

58. *Ibid.*, 32.

59. Zhou Min, *Chinatown: The Socioeconomic Potential of an Urban Enclave* (Philadelphia: Temple University Press, 1992), 170.

Chapter 23

Nina Simone, Culture, and Black Activism in the 1960s

Ruth Feldstein

The transition from the integrationist stance of the classic civil rights movement in the United States to the more ambiguous perspective of Black Power has traditionally been viewed in male-centered terms, with Martin Luther King, Jr. and Malcolm X serving as the central figures in historical treatments. However, Ruth Feldstein brings an illuminating perspective to the history of black activism in the 1960s with her focus on the popular black singer Nina Simone. Her analysis of Simone's changing place in the civil rights struggle shows the emergence of black power through the eyes and actions of an entertainer who both reflected and shaped grassroots changes in attitudes in the 1960s and 1970s.

On September 15, 1963, Nina Simone learned that four young African American girls had been killed in the bombing of the Sixteenth Street Baptist Church in Birmingham, Alabama. Prior to that point, Simone, an African American singer, pianist, and songwriter, had an eclectic repertoire that blended jazz with blues, gospel, and classical music. Immediately after hearing about the events in Birmingham, however, Simone wrote the song "Mississippi Goddam." It came to her in a "rush of fury, hatred and determination" as she "suddenly realized what it was to be black in America in 1963." It was, she said, "my first civil rights song."[1]

Unlike Simone's earlier work (one critic had dubbed her a "supper club songstress for the elite"), "Mississippi Goddam" was a political anthem.[2] The lyrics were filled with anger and despair and stood in stark contrast to the fast-paced and rollicking rhythm. Over the course of several verses Simone vehemently rejected the notions that race relations could change gradually, that the South was unique in terms of discrimination, and that African Americans could or would patiently seek political rights. "Me and my people are just about due," she declared. Simone also challenged principles that are still strongly associated with liberal civil rights activism in that period, especially the viability of a beloved community of whites and blacks. As she sang toward the end of "Mississippi Goddam":

> All I want is equality
> For my sister, my brother, my people, and me.
> Yes, you lied to me all these years
>
> You told me to wash and clean my ears
> And talk real fine, just like a lady
> And you'd stop calling me Sister Sadie.
> But this whole country is full of lies
> You're all gonna die and die like flies
> I don't trust you anymore
> You keep on saying "Go Slow."

Advertisement for June 1963 civil rights benefit in Harlem featuring Nina Simone and sponsored by the New York State NAACP. Notice the linking of African identity and the struggle against segregation and police brutality. Credit: *New York Amsterdam News*, May 25, 1963, p. 14.

"Mississippi Goddam" expressed on a cultural terrain pain and rage. It also offered one of the many political perspectives that people in and out of movements were developing in the early 1960s, well beyond the emphasis on interracial activism that predominated among liberal supporters of civil rights. It suggests themes this essay engages at greater length: the political work a song could do and the multiple ways in which cultural production mattered to black activism—far more than as merely the background sound track to the movement, and not simply as a reflection of the pre-existing aspirations of political activities.

Despite the swirling range of ways African Americans envisioned freedom in the early 1960s, activism that had little to do with integration or federal legislation has, until recently, been marginal to civil rights scholarship. Instead, historical accounts have largely focused on, and reproduced, a narrative that characterizes black nationalism, and in fact all demands other than integration, as something problematic that emerged in the late 1960s. . . .

This particular historiographical trend has led to significant, and symptomatic, absences in accounts of the 1960s. Simone's political activism and fiery denunciations of the well-mannered politics of "going slow" were well noted at the time. Indeed, "Mississippi Goddam" was the first of many songs that Nina Simone performed in which she dramatically commented on and participated in—and thereby helped to recast—black activism in the 1960s. In the decade that followed, she was known to have supported the struggle for black freedom in the United States earlier, more directly, and in a more outspoken manner around the world than had many other African American entertainers. She recorded nearly twenty albums and received critical and commercial acclaim within and outside the United States; by the late 1960s, Simone had a global audience for wide-ranging recordings that included Beatles songs and those that considered segregation's effects on children, the assassination of Martin Luther King Jr., gender discrimination and color consciousness among African Americans, and black pride. Many critics from around the world concluded that she was "the best singer of jazz of these last years," who had a particularly "extraordinary presence" in live performances and a magical ability to connect to her audiences.[3]

Nevertheless, beyond brief references to "Mississippi Goddam," she has largely fallen through the cracks of scholarship—on music, on civil rights, and on women's activism. . . . this essay explores the nature and implications of Nina Simone's activism in the 1960s *and* the sources for the subsequent invisibility of that activism. It argues that gender and sexuality were central to Simone's reception from the outset of her career in the late 1950s onward and to her racial politics in the early 1960s. . . . More specifically, I argue that with her music and her self-presentation Simone offered a vision of black cultural nationalism within and outside the United States that insisted on female power—well before the apparent ascendance of black power or second-wave feminism in the late 1960s and 1970s. Drawing on reactions to Simone, to the lyrics from songs on her first overtly political album, and to her self-representations in the United States and abroad, this essay demonstrates that events and issues from the 1960s that are often treated as separate were in fact deeply intertwined: These are the development of black cultural nationalism, the role of women in black activism more generally, and the emergence of second-wave feminism. These were connected and widespread well before the "official" rise of black power or second-wave feminism.

Moreover, Simone was not alone—in her assessments of liberal activism or in her gendered racial politics. She was connected to many cultural producers and activists, men and women. Musically, socially, and politically, she came of age in the late 1950s and early 1960s as part of an interracial avant-garde in Greenwich Village and Harlem that included Langston Hughes, Lorraine Hansberry, Leroi Jones (later Amiri Baraka), Abbey Lincoln, Miriam Makeba, and James Baldwin, among others.[4] Her political education began as a result of her friendship with the playwright Lorraine Hansberry; she chose to write explicitly political songs shortly after influential jazz critics censured the vocalist Abbey Lincoln for making a similar move. Certainly, Nina Simone's music and politics stood out in 1963 when she wrote "Mississippi Goddam"; coming just one month after the record-setting March on Washington for Jobs and Freedom and Martin Luther King's famous "I Have a Dream" speech, she provocatively departed from conventional wisdom in a moment often remembered as the heyday of liberal interracial activism. Yet she was emphatically not a solitary figure or a voice out of nowhere. Simone is a window into a world beyond dominant liberal civil rights organizations and leaders and into networks of activist cultural producers in particular. She matters not necessarily because she definitively caused a specific number of fans to change their behavior, but because the perspectives on black freedom and gender that she among others articulated circulated as widely as they did in the early 1960s.

The historian Evelyn Brooks Higginbotham has referred to an "emergent revisionism" in civil rights scholarship that has focused attention on the *coexistence* of nonviolence and armed self-defense, of activism in the North and in the South, of local organizing and an internationalist perspective. Invaluable work on women and gender and civil rights, culture and civil rights, and the transnational dimensions to civil rights activism has increased in recent years.[5] With Nina Simone, these fields of knowledge come together, and we see that cultural commodities, activist women entertainers, and changing meanings of femininity and masculinity were part of what enabled ideas about African American political activism to circulate around the world.

"NOT EXACTLY A JAZZ PERFORMER . . . A LOT MORE THAN JUST A JAZZ PERFORMER": PRODUCING A BIOGRAPHY OF DEFIANCE

Nina Simone, whose birth name was Eunice Waymon, was born in 1933 in the small town of Tryon, North Carolina. Her mother was a housekeeper by day and a Methodist minister at night; her father worked mostly as a handyman. Simone started tapping piano keys when she was three years old and was soon playing hymns and gospel music at her mother's church. By the time she was five, and as a result of local fundraising efforts on the part of whites and blacks in her town, she was studying classical music with a white teacher. After high school, Simone continued her studies at the Juilliard School in New York City. She planned to go from Juilliard to the Curtis Institute of Music in Philadelphia and hoped to be the first African American classical pianist. She was dismayed when the Curtis Institute rejected her in 1951.[6]

Several years later, tired of giving piano lessons and in need of money (in part so that she could continue her own classical training), Simone started to play popular music at an Atlantic City nightclub. Under pressure from her boss, she also started to sing and then to write her own music and lyrics. Simone's first popular hit came in 1958 with a ballad-like recording of the George Gershwin song "I Loves You, Porgy." The song received considerable airtime on the radio; it reached number 2 on the rhythm and blues (R&B) charts and the top 20 in the summer of 1959. Simone moved to Manhattan, performing and recording regularly. In 1959, one critic suggested that she might be "the greatest singer to evolve in the last decade and perhaps the greatest singer today. . . . the greatest compliments could only be understatements of her talent." Within the world of jazz vocals, a critically acclaimed star was born. Or, as Simone later put it, "I was a sensation. An overnight success, like in the movies. . . . Suddenly I was the hot new thing."[7]

At that point, press coverage of the "hot new thing" increased. Simone was the subject of discussion in publications that crossed racial, political, and cultural divides; she received reviews in the premier jazz journal of the day, *Down Beat*, and in the entertainment industry's bible, *Variety;* critics discussed her in black newspapers and magazines such as the *New York Amsterdam News* and *Ebony* as well as in the *New York Times* and *Time*. Even before her first performances in Europe in 1965, jazz magazines abroad had praised her extensively. In discussions of Simone from around the world, fans and critics gave up on efforts to define the type of music she played. "She is, of course, not exactly a jazz performer—or possibly one should say that she is a lot more than just a jazz performer," wrote a reviewer for *Down Beat*.[8]

If critics could not define her music, they agreed that Simone's upbringing mattered to the kind of performer she had become. In a proliferating discourse, Simone's "origins story" was told and consistently retold. A profile in *Metronome* was typical:

> Born Eunice Waymon in Tryon, North Carolina (population 1,985), the sixth of eight children, her father was a handyman, her mother a housekeeper who was an ordained Methodist minister. At four Eunice was able to play piano; at seven she was playing piano and organ. . . . The story itself is exciting, revealing, an American one.[9]

In the repetition of this story about a poor black girl who had received training in classical music and became a popular vocalist whose style defied musical categories, more was going on than the recycling of promotional materials. In key aspects of her life and in numerous *accounts of* that life—that is, in her own self-representations and as the object of representation—Simone departed from then-dominant depictions of African American entertainers, and of African American women entertainers specifically. As she later described this period, "Unlike most artists, I didn't care that much about a career as a popular singer. I was different—I was going to be a classical musician." The story of Simone's origins in the rural South and the classical musical training she had received inserted African American women into debates about jazz and high culture, venues that had historically excluded them and had favored a certain model of masculinity.[10]

When Simone first caught the attention of jazz critics and fans and this biographical narrative became more common, the jazz world was undergoing dramatic changes. This was a period of musical innovation when musicians, producers, consumers, and critics of jazz engaged in sometimes acrimonious debates: about the "appropriate" role of politics in jazz, about discrimination in the industry, and about the relationship between jazz and high culture, on the one hand, and a seemingly ever-encroaching mass culture, on the other. Scholars of jazz studies have noted that since the early twentieth century, but especially in the post–World War II decades, jazz had stood at a crossroads between perceptions of it as an organic art form rooted in black communities—and therefore "authentic"; as a commodified mode of mass entertainment; and as an elite aesthetic expression. Simone was by no means the only jazz musician whose music and performance styles fans and critics discussed in contradictory ways or who blended jazz, classical, and other music genres.[11]

Nevertheless, it was relatively rare for African American women musicians, many of whom were singers, to be part of a critical discourse about jazz as art. Consequently, the biographical narrative that accompanied Simone's early years as a performer was doubly subversive. Her "origins story" countered a racial essentialism that had historically rendered all black artists "natural" entertainers. The emphasis on Simone's years of classical piano training and hard work challenged the myth, still common in the 1960s, that African Americans were inherently inclined only to entertain. At the same time, stories about Simone undermined a gender exclusivity that assumed that African American virtuosity was gendered male. In the 1920s, for instance, women blues singers had been extremely successful, but many people had regarded them simple as popular entertainers and had associated them with sexuality and working-class urban vices more than with technical skill or acquired artistry. Twenty years later, as the scholar Farah Jasmine Griffin has noted, "even" when a white-dominated musical establishment conceded that African American musicians might be "geniuses," there was still an assumption that this genius in someone such as Charlie Parker had come "naturally" or, in the case of a woman such as Billie Holiday especially, was "undisciplined."[12]

African American musicians had long sought to counter this racial essentialism. They did so most effectively, perhaps, in the 1940s, when Parker, Dizzie Gillespie, Thelonious Monk, and others associated with the development of bebop positioned themselves as highly skilled modernist artists who scorned popular entertainment. But they forged a gendered ethos of African American musical virtuosity that implicitly equated cultural creativity with masculinity. The ethnomusicologist Ingrid Monson has explained how, despite the actual presence of women jazz musicians, the " 'subcultural' image of bebop was nourished by a conflation of the music with a style of black masculinity." White audiences especially regarded this as a countercultural or oppositional masculinity. Gendered meanings of jazz infused the music with an avant-garde radicalism *and* with associations to a modernist universal high culture in ways that seemed to preclude women.[13]

The Simone who emerged in this critical discourse, however, straddled the worlds of high art and mass culture, of so-called authentic blackness and a universal genius that transcended race and gender. . . . And yet, because this biographical narrative emphasized region and class, the classically trained Simone retained her status as an authentic African American singer who represented her race. Fans and critics repeatedly noted that she was a child prodigy who had grown up in the rural South and had played church music even before classical music. "Undoubtedly, her early training in the church and her years of singing in her father's choir, contributed strongly to the gospel patterns" in Simone's music, according to one portrait.[14] Simone, with her rural southern background, was regarded as "authentic"; paradoxically, this was the case whether or not she played music associated with racial specificity or blackness, which frequently she did not.

While critics commonly depicted Simone in terms of both musical virtuosity and racial authenticity, few did so as vividly or evocatively as did Langston Hughes. Hughes was expansive in his praise of Simone's technical skill: "She plays piano FLUIDLY well, SIMPLY well, COMPLICATEDLY well, THEATRICALLY well, DRAMATICALLY well, INDIVIDUALLY well, and MADLY well. Not just WELL." Yet, he noted reassuringly, "She is far-out, and at the same time common. . . . She has a flair, but no air." Her skill, he added, did not distance her from black people or blackness. "She is a club member, a colored girl, an Afro-American, a homey from Down Home." Nina Simone, he concluded, was as different as "beer is from champagne, crackers from crepes suzettes . . . Houston from Paris—each real in their way, but Oh! How different—and how fake it is if it is not Houston you want but the 'city of light.' "[15] For Hughes as for others, Simone simultaneously embodied racial authenticity and yet could not be pigeonholed. . . .

Ultimately, the status that Simone's biography conferred countered but could not dislodge the gendered meanings of jazz that were becoming increasingly dominant. From the outset of her career, professional music critics and fans, advocates and detractors, referred frequently to the fact that she was "difficult to work with" and hostile to audiences, across lines of race, if they were not "sufficiently respectful." At the Apollo, in Harlem, Simone "found out how rude the place could be when I started to introduce a song and people laughed at me." She declared that she would never play the Apollo again. Early on, critics associated this behavior too with her origins. They linked Simone's "high standards" to her training in classical music and disregard for mass consumer culture. She might yell at noisy audiences or even walk off a stage mid-show if fans were too "boisterous," but observers explained that because the "stormy petrel of the piano" had a "deep-felt desire to be heard with the respect due an artist," she emphasized the " 'social graces' "; Simone insisted that music should not be interrupted and that whether she was in a club or a concert hall "one must be neatly dressed and observe the proper decorum."[16]

*   *   *

But if rudeness in male jazz musicians confirmed their genius, similar behavior confirmed something else about Simone. The point is not to debate Simone's behavior—which by all accounts was unpredictable and difficult—but to consider the gender-specific meanings it assumed. Over time, she was far more likely to be depicted as "a witch" than as an artist with high standards. " 'Temperamental' is one word that is applied to her frequently; 'insulting' and 'arrogant' are also favorites." Critics and fans characterized her as notoriously "mean," "angry," and "unstable" or as eccentric and beset by "inner fires."[17] This refrain was almost as common as references to her classical training. On the one hand, these references placed Simone more in a long line of unstable women celebrities than as a member of an exclusive club of innovative black male artists. As a black woman, however, her status as a demanding diva evoked racially specific kinds of fear.

The repetition of Simone's biography highlighted gender's significance to the racial and cultural politics of jazz in the late 1950s and early 1960s. Her origins story distanced her from the so-called sleazy blues woman and countered essentialist assumptions about race and musical skill by insisting on the presence of women and hard work. It included African American women in the black modernist critique of mass culture that was part of jazz in this period—a world in which "musical achievement had also become a symbol of racial achievement," as Ingrid Monson has explained.[18] Even as an ever-recycled biographical narrative cast Simone as difficult or unstable, it rendered her a defiant figure in two important respects: Her music defied categorization, and she was defiant toward her fans. These qualities were not incidental to Simone's racial politics but were integral to her participation in black activism. In part because of the ways in which this biography of defiance took shape in the early years of her career and the role that gender played in that narrative, Simone was poised, by the early 1960s, to expand the parameters of her activism.

"HER MUSIC COMES FROM A PARTICULAR POINT OF VIEW": PERFORMING BLACK ACTIVISM

By 1963, Simone was maintaining a relentless schedule of recording and performing, but she was also accelerating her involvement in black freedom struggles. Well before she wrote "Mississippi Goddam," she supported national civil rights organizations such as the Student Nonviolent Coordinating Committee (SNCC), the Congress of Racial Equality (CORE), and the National Association for the Advancement of Colored People (NAACP) and such local organizations as the Harlem Young Men's Christian Association (YMCA) by offering her name as a sponsor and performing at numerous benefit concerts. At that point, she did not think of herself as "involved," because she was only "spurring them [activists] on as best I could from where I sat—on stage, an artist, separate somehow." That feeling of detachment did not last, however, as Simone became "driven by civil rights and the hope of black revolution."[19] In 1964, she headlined for SNCC several times in just a few months, including an event at Carnegie Hall that added to her reputation as a musician worthy of that location and as committed to the movement. The following year, Simone's husband and manager, Andrew Stroud, volunteered her "services" to CORE, agreeing to a deal in which Simone would perform at CORE-sponsored fund raisers around the country at a minimal cost. These benefit concerts were very important to the treasuries of civil rights organizations. According to one estimate, CORE planned to raise close to two thousand dollars per Simone concert, considerably more than many other musicians and entertainers raised in benefit performances.[20]

Simone also traveled south to the site of many civil rights battles. The "ever-arresting Simone," as a journalist for the *New York Amsterdam News* described her, was on the roster of stars scheduled to perform at an "unprecedented show" in Birmingham, Alabama, in the summer of 1963. In Birmingham, the American Guild of Variety Artists together with the Southern Christian Leadership Conference (SCLC), SNCC, CORE, the NAACP, the National Urban League, and the Negro American Labor Council cosponsored a "Salute to Freedom '63" concert. Designed in part to raise money for the upcoming March on Washington, the concert was originally planned for an integrated audience at Birmingham's city auditorium. When organizers faced opposition from local whites, they moved the show to a local all-black college. According to one estimate, the controversial concert raised nine thousand dollars. Simone also performed in Atlanta and for marchers during the Selma-to-Montgomery march in 1965.[21]

The historian Brian Ward has argued that this kind of visible political engagement on the part of African American popular musicians—those with mass appeal among African American and white audiences—was relatively rare in the early to mid-1960s and that going to the South as Simone did was especially noteworthy. Entertainers risked alienating white fans as well as the deejays who chose what music got airtime.[22] . . . While showing up was clearly a risky political choice that Simone made, she did more than perform her standard "supper club" music at political events. The lyrics to the songs she wrote also changed and became more explicitly political. As one reviewer would later note, approvingly, "Her music comes from a particular point of view." The album that marked this transition was *In Concert* (1964). Because it was relatively rare for musicians outside of the world of folk music to bring culture and politics together so directly in this period in their lyrics, it is worth considering how Simone made this move.[23] *In Concert* offers a framework for understanding the intersections of gender and music, art and activism in Simone's career both before and after the album's release.

Gender and Racial Politics on *In Concert*

In Concert, like other albums by Simone, blended moods, styles, and genres. Over the course of seven songs, recorded from a live performance in New York, Simone moved from tender love songs to more classic blues to folk songs. Simone's skillful transitions between styles and her engagement with the live audience all added to the album's power and confirmed the challenge she posed to conventional cultural categories. Three songs on the album indicate with particular clarity how gendered strategies of protest were consistent parts of Simone's repertoire. Indeed, rejecting any singular definition of African American womanhood was part of the album's racial politics and remained central to Simone's participation in black activism beyond *In Concert*.[24]

In the song "Pirate Jenny," Simone transformed a song about class relations in London from Kurt Weill and Bertholt Brecht's *The Threepenny Opera* into a song about race, class, and gender relations in the American South. By maintaining ties to the original version, Simone associated her own antiracism with Brecht's antifascism and evoked a historical alliance between African American musicians and an interwar political Left—one that, according to the scholar Michael Denning, "permanently altered the shape of American music.[25] But there were unique aspects to Simone's version of a song about a poor and abused woman's fantasies of revenge. After the ominous beating drum in the opening bars, the lyrics introduced a black woman scrubbing a floor:

> You people can watch while I'm scrubbing these floors
> And I'm scrubbing the floors while you're gawking.
> Maybe once you'll tip me and it makes you feel swell
> In this crummy southern town in this crummy old hotel.
> But you'll never guess to who you're talking.

In the verses that followed, the woman envisioned violence and her own empowerment. She witnessed a "ship, the black freighter" come into the town "shooting guns from her bow" and leaving every building in the town but the hotel "flattened." The woman then determined the fate of the abusive town members, deciding whether they should be killed "now or later." In a powerful whisper, devoid of any musical accompaniment, Simone offered her protagonist's answer: "right now."

From the opening bars until the final drum, the song conveyed a woman's rage with the rhythm, instrumentals, and Simone's rich contralto voice—together with the lyrics. African American women and their labor were Simone's point of entry in "Pirate Jenny." They were the means through which she exposed the socioeconomic and gendered dimensions of racism and expressed a fantasy about vengeance. In singing about this fictional woman in a Brecht-Weill song that had classical undertones and links to the Left in an era known for "We Shall Overcome," Simone also rejected expectations of what protest music might be. "Perhaps it is a masterpiece; certainly it is a warning," suggested the liner notes.[26]

*   *   *

Beyond *In Concert*: Gender, Liberalism, and Black Cultural Nationalism

Overall, *In Concert* questioned patient nonviolence, Christianity, the interracial folk revival and the related celebration of freedom songs, and white-defined images of blacks; it celebrated a more racially politicized culture. But Simone's focus on sexuality and gender allowed her to put women at the center of multiple struggles for civil rights. In . . . "Mississippi Goddam," when Simone rejected the impulse to "talk like a lady," she effectively claimed that doing so would not halt such discriminatory practices as calling black women "Sister Sadie." Simone undermined a historically potent gendered politics of respectability that persisted in African American activism of the late 1950s and early 1960s. In a critique of both whites and blacks, she challenged the notion that certain kinds of gender roles were a route toward improved race relations. Her lyrics unleashed a liberation of another sort—the liberation from doing the right thing in the hopes of being recognized as deserving. In both songs, elements that potentially repressed black activism (nonviolence) and elements that potentially repressed female sexuality were linked in ways that challenged liberalism itself. In her performance of rage—and "Mississippi Goddam" and "Pirate Jenny" were just two early examples—Simone further defied expectations of respectable black womanhood. In addition to the specific if brief reference to "Sister Sadie," Simone's delivery and performance of "Mississippi Goddam" was nothing short of a declaration of independence for "Sadies" everywhere—including in the civil rights movement.[27]

The challenges to liberalism that Simone posed in her songs about race relations led many fans to associate her with black power and black cultural nationalism. Associations between Simone and a racial militancy that was more highly publicized in the late 1960s heightened her notoriety in those years but obscured the fact that Simone's perspective predated the end of the decade. It differed significantly, moreover, from that of many African American men with whom this militancy was equated.

Black power and black cultural nationalism were fluid and broad phenomena with long histories and multiple manifestations. Both found expression in diverse arenas—ranging from Maulana Karenga's US Organization, which stressed the importance of African traditions among African Americans, to the Deacons for Defense and Justice, a Louisiana-based armed organization for self-defense formed in 1964, and to the black arts movement, with its belief that politicized black cultural producers and cultural products were essential preconditions to black liberation. James Brown popularized (and commodified) these very different impulses when he sang "Say It Loud—I'm Black and I'm Proud" in 1968.[28] Political histories of the civil rights movement tend to associate the phrase black power with Stokely Carmichael, a SNCC activist who issued a formal call for black power in 1966, months after organizing a third party in Alabama (the Lowndes County Freedom Organization) with a black panther as its symbol.[29] Despite this diversity, black power and black cultural nationalism were often conflated—with each other and with the Black Panther party, formed in Oakland, California, under the leadership of Bobby Seale and Huey Newton in 1966—and associated with the late 1960s.

African American women participated significantly in movements and expressions of black cultural nationalism and black power. A growing body of scholarship and memoirs suggests that women were leaders, grass-roots activists, and cultural producers. Yet many organizations remained, for the most part, male-dominated; further, in the late 1960s, assertions of black *male* pride remained at the center of calls for black power that were implicitly and explicitly gendered male.[30]

Not surprisingly, then, few Americans, white or black, were likely to associate African American women with the perceived shift from nonviolent civil rights activism to black power. In 1967, one critic suggested that part of what made such songs as "Mississippi Goddam" so powerful was that they sounded as if they *should* have been written by "some black power disciple of the caliber of Leroi Jones or Stokely Carmichael," while in fact they were the words of a "woman who has become one of the show world's most popular and controversial entertainers." A journalist at the *New York Post* cemented the link between Simone and a male racial militancy publicized in the late 1960s; alluding to the Black Panther Eldridge Cleaver's prison memoir, *Soul on Ice*, which in 1967 had shocked readers with its visions of violence by blacks, the *Post* headlined its profile of the singer "Nina Simone: Soul on Voice." From the time of its initial release, rumors had circulated that

"Mississippi Goddam," known for its "bold lyrics and profane tide," was banned from radio stations in the South and from national television; at least one observer suggested, however, that it "was banned by radio stations because a woman dared put her feelings into song. . . . the principal objection raised by most critics to the Mississippi song was apparently not so much its militant lyrics, but the fact that an entertainer, and a woman entertainer at that, had dared to put them to music."[31]

* * *

"Mississippi Goddam" and the genealogy of that song also suggest that Simone was among those who helped to create a version of black cultural nationalism as early as 1963 in ways that did not devalue women. According to Simone, "Mississippi Goddam" "erupted out of me" right after she had heard about the church bombing. As she explained it, she had first used materials that her husband, an ex–police officer, had around the house to try to build a gun. Then she realized, "I knew nothing about killing, and I did know about music. I sat down at my piano. An hour later I came out of my apartment with the sheet music for 'Mississippi Goddam' in my hand." The song thus anticipated the arguments that Amiri Baraka would make about the political purposes of culture when he organized the black arts movement in 1965. Baraka and others, however, forged links between black culture and revolutionary politics with associations among militant poems, militant men, violence, and sex: "Poems that shoot guns," for example, were those "that come at you, love what you are, breathe like wrestlers, or shudder strangely after pissing."[32] Simone's creative contributions to black cultural nationalism are important because they indicate that this type of masculinism, and even misogyny in some instances, was not a given, nor was it inherent to black cultural nationalism and black power.

Simone was not alone in this regard. As scholars have shown, black women writers such as Alice Childress, Claudia Jones, and Lorraine Hansberry were among those who "developed a model of feminism" in the late 1950s, in the words of Mary Helen Washington. Beyond the realm of cultural production, in the mid-1960s women in SNCC addressed the intersections of racism and sexism within and beyond the civil rights movement. By 1968, members of the Third World Women's Alliance were just some of the women who criticized black men for defining "the role of black women in the movement. They stated that our role was a supportive one; others stated that we must become breeders and provide an army; still others stated that we had kotex power or pussy power." The publication of *The Black Woman: An Anthology* in 1970 was a landmark, not because the ideas were brand new, but because the editor and activist Toni Cade Bambara captured in this single-volume collective manifesto competing strands of black feminism that had been developing for years.[33] Simone contributed to this discourse early in the decade and on the cultural front where she was literally center stage.

"I'd Arrived Somewhere Important": Africa and Black Cultural Nationalism

While Simone had many influences, Africa was one important resource for her articulation of a black cultural nationalism that emphasized female power and that found clear expression on the album *In Concert*. In December 1961, just days after her second marriage (to Stroud), Simone joined a group of thirty-three black artists, musicians, and intellectuals for her first trip to Africa; the group was going to Lagos, Nigeria, on behalf of the American Society of African Culture (AMSAC). AMSAC, an organization founded in the late 1950s by the activist John A. Davis, was committed to promoting African culture as "high" culture in the United States and to encouraging collaboration between African and African American artists and intellectuals in particular.

* * *

Simone continued thereafter to emphasize the importance of Africa to African Americans. She embraced physical markers of black cultural nationalism in ways that joined the struggle of African Americans to a more transnational vision of African freedom, making both visible through her female body. She dressed more frequently in what critics called African garb and performed African music at the Dinizulu African Festival. In promotional photos that circulated in 1961 and onward, Simone appeared with her hair "natural"—an Afro. These styles persisted, if inconsistently, and elicited strong reactions throughout the decade. In a performance at New York's Philharmonic Hall in 1966, Simone "stirred up excitement in her audience," according to one critic, "by walking on stage in a stunning African motif hat and gown ensemble."[34]

Simone was direct about her desire both to educate and to entertain in Europe. As she put it to the French journalists Michel Dellorme and Maurice Cullaz toward the end of her first European tour, she considered herself an ambassador of sorts for her race: "because of the lack of respect that has lasted for hundreds of years, each time I go to a new country, I feel obliged to include in my repertoire songs that proudly affirm my race." In this context, as a female entertainer who produced and performed certain kinds of music—and who was an object of consumption herself—Simone helped to export American civil rights activism, and black nationalism in particular. Her politics and her performances were deeply and self-consciously intertwined.[35]

Yet Simone was not simply one in a long line of African American entertainers who achieved greater success among audiences in Europe than in the United States; nor did she merely compare non-American race relations favorably to those in the United States and position Europe as an oasis. Instead, she conceived of racism as an international problem. As she observed to European journalists, she had "found prejudice in Britain, in Holland, and even Morocco. . . . Now I love being in London—it has its own personality and character and I love the way the people talk; but I don't really feel any more welcome in London than I do at home."[36] Simone was able to infuse her eclectic repertoire—including African chants—with meanings that were not solely national. Farah Jasmine Griffin has argued that, when Billie Holiday sang "Strange Fruit" in Europe, audiences could indict racial violence in the United States such as lynching without having to consider histories of colonialism and race relations in their own countries. By contrast, Simone was popular and performing at a time of rising student and anticolonialist activism in Europe; that temporal overlap combined with her own outspokenness and appearance made such distancing more difficult. For example, at one concert in England, she declared that the performance was "for all the black people in the audience." Whites were shocked, including ardent fans, and were well aware that at this British club Simone was talking to, naming as black—and identifying with—her many black fans of West Indian and African descent and not African Americans. Or, as she told one British reporter, "The Negro revolution is only one aspect of increasing violence and unrest in the world." In 1969, she questioned assumptions that the civil rights movement had improved the lives of African Americans, but she also suggested that her recording of the song "Revolution" was significant because it was about far more than "the racial problem."[37]

* * *

Black Activism and Feminism, or Movements in Motion

It is worth emphasizing that Nina Simone was making these interventions and claiming these styles early in the 1960s. She was part of a larger group that Robin Kelley has identified in the late 1950s and early 1960s as "black poets, writers, musicians . . . for whom the emancipation of their own artistic form coincided with the African freedom movement." As has become clear, women cultural producers played a significant part in this turn-of-the-decade subculture; the jazz singer Abbey Lincoln, the folk singer Odetta, the actress Cicely Tyson, and the fictional Beneatha, heroine of Lorraine Hansberry's landmark play *A Raisin in the Sun*, were just some of the other women who wore their hair in Afros in the late 1950s and early 1960s. Simone's shift from a glamorous performer to a singer with a militant physical presentation associated with black power and Africa became more consistent after 1965, but it was not new to that period. What was relatively new was that the Afro and other styles became widespread among black male militants—sufficiently so to make it seem that anyone who had done so prior to that point was "early." Individually, each woman might seem to have been ahead of the times. Taken together, we can begin to see how much our sense of the times and the ways in which we narrate black activism and black cultural nationalism have tended not to include women.[38]

This point has historical and historiographical implications. Scholars have become more aware that black cultural nationalism was ascendant well before the late 1960s—that the liberal political activism and the beloved community of the early 1960s did not simply give way to the more radical cultural nationalism of the late 1960s. Simone highlights the centrality of African American women to this reperiodization and the relevance of black feminism to black activism more generally.[39] Songs from *In Concert* and Simone's subsequent performance strategies suggest how women forged black cultural nationalism through the prism of gender and did not just critique the assumptions about masculinity in black power and black cultural nationalism after the fact, important as those later critiques were.[40]

The ways in which Simone played with gender roles and cultural categories—how she could be said to have been "improvising womanhood," as the historian Sherrie Tucker has formulated that idea—indicate, too, that a concern with gender politics did not necessarily develop out of or after concerns with civil rights and racial politics. In other words, black women's role in black activism has implications for analyses of second-wave feminism. In her autobiography, Simone located "sisterhood" as the central catalyst to her politicization around race. It was her friend Lorraine Hansberry, she wrote, who launched her "political education" in 1961 and "first took me out of myself and allowed me to see the bigger picture." As a result of Hansberry's influence, "I started to think about myself as a black person in a country run by white people and a woman in a world run by men." In the 1960s and subsequently, Simone emphasized how constitutive gender solidarity was to her "political education." When she introduced "To Be Young, Gifted, and Black," a song that became an anthem of black pride and reached the top 10 on the R&B charts in 1969, Simone repeatedly paid tribute to Hansberry, who had died in 1965. At a concert in Berkeley, she exhorted her audience to sing the chorus of the upcoming song with her and then explained, "this song is dedicated to the memory of my dear, dear friend whom I miss very much, and if I don't control myself, I could talk about all night. Lorraine Hansberry, who wrote 'Raisin in the Sun' and died before her time." Here and elsewhere, Simone made relationships between women central to the very idea of black pride. She later noted that in the early 1960s she and her more politically informed friend had "never talked about men or clothes or other such inconsequential things when we got together. It was always Marx, Lenin, and revolution—real girls' talk."[41] As in her songs, Simone reversed the usual model in which women first joined civil rights organizations only to have issues of gender inequities dawn on them.

*   *   *

"NOT LUXURY, NOT LEISURE, NOT ENTERTAINMENT, BUT THE LIFEBLOOD OF A COMMUNITY": CULTURE AND CIVIL RIGHTS SCHOLARSHIP

Over the course of the 1960s, Nina Simone stood out in several respects. Her music defied categorization, blurring the lines between jazz, classical, folk, blues, and soul music; representations of her as a performer with classical training who blended many styles made it impossible to fit her into any one musical genre. With her explicitly political lyrics as early as 1963, Simone defied a liberal civil rights ethos. Finally, by making gender central to her radical racial politics, she unlinked what some radical men had linked: racial progress, racial power, and masculine sexual power. Because she was a performer whose fans cut across lines of race, class, gender, and nation, these multiple levels of defiance set Simone apart, reinforcing both her celebrity and her notoriety in the 1960s.

*   *   *

In the 1970s, Nina Simone suffered a series of setbacks. Her second marriage ended, she had numerous financial difficulties and legal conflicts with the Internal Revenue Service (IRS), and, with the decline in African American activism and the repression of black radicalism by the U.S. government, she grew increasingly pessimistic, if not despairing. In the face of considerable personal, legal, and political difficulties, she performed and recorded infrequently. Simone led a peripatetic if not nomadic life, living in Barbados, Liberia, France, and Switzerland over the course of the 1970s and 1980s, returning to the United States only briefly.[42]

When Simone died in April 2003, obituary writers from around the world affirmed her relationships to civil rights activism, and some referred to her internationalism. At the funeral service in France, Miriam Makeba offered the "condolences of the whole South Africa," and according to some accounts Simone's cremated body was to be scattered across several African countries. Many reports, however, depicted Simone as a historical relic from a bygone era or as an entertainer who had supplied background music for the civil rights movement more than as an activist in her own right. Even in acknowledging her contributions, then, this coverage implicitly reinforced a dichotomy between culture and politics.[43]

Today, it is all too easy to document the ways in which politics is shaped, if not supplanted, by entertainment and popular culture. One might forget that creative and productive meshings of progressive political movements and cultural commodities seemed possible in the 1960s; further, many people concluded that to do so would invigorate and transform both arenas. As Simone explained to a *Time* reporter in 1969, " 'When I'm on that stage . . . I don't think I'm just out there to entertain.' " The journalist then elaborated, "Nina is a Negro and proud of it: she is out there to share with audience what Soul Singer Ray Charles calls her 'message things.' "[44]

It is worthwhile for historians of politics as well as historians of culture to take these assertions seriously. Simone, on and off stage and in and out of the United States, was a political subject. She points to the importance of getting past cultural and political hierarchies that took shape in the 1960s and subdisciplinary divides that have persisted subsequently. Nina Simone's stardom over the course of the 1960s—her music, her activism, her reception and self-presentation, and the intersection of all of these in her highly visible public persona—helps us to render black activism in all of its richness.

Notes

1. Nina Simone, "Mississippi Goddam," performed by Nina Simone, [1964], *In Concert—I Put a Spell on You* (compact disk; Polygram Records 846543; 1990); Simone referred to Alabama in the first line but emphasized with the song's title the state known for the most violence against African Americans. Nina Simone with Stephen Cleary, *I Put a Spell on You: The Autobiography of Nina Simone* (New York, 1992), 89–90.
2. Phyl Garland, *The Sound of Soul* (Chicago, 1969), 176.
3. "Best singer": "la meilleure chanteuse de jazz de ces dernières années" in Maurice Cullaz, "Une Divine Nina," *Jazz Hot* (May 1969), 7; "extraordinaire présence" in F. Hofstein, "Nina; Back to Black," *Jazz Magazine* (May 1969), 13; quotations from French sources were translated into English by Eren Murat

Tasar. For her powerful effects on crowds, see, for example, John S. Wilson, "Recital Victory for Nina Simone," *New York Times*, Dec. 30, 1968, clipping, Nina Simone file, Schomburg Center for Research in Black Culture Clipping File, 1925–1974 (Widener Library, Cambridge, Mass.). For a more critical assessment, see Alan Walsh and Jack Hutton, "Antibes Jazz Festival Report: Miles, Peterson, and Nina on Form," *Melody Maker*, Aug. 2, 1969, p. 6. . . .

4. For this subculture, see especially Robin D. G. Kelley, "Nap Time: Historicizing the Afro," *Fashion Theory*, 1 (Dec. 1997), 330–51; Simone with Cleary, *I Put a Spell on You*, 66–72; and Judith Smith, *Visions of Belonging; Ordinary Families, Popular Culture, and Postwar Democracy, 1940–1960* (New York, 2004). For civil rights activism in New York City, see Biondi, *To Stand and Fight.*

5. Evelyn Brooks Higginbotham, "Foreword," in *Freedom North: Black Freedom Struggles outside the South, 1940–1980*, ed. Jeanne F. Theoharis and Komozi Woodard (New York, 2003), xiii. In addition to work cited, for gender and civil rights, see Barbara Ransby, *Ella Baker and the Black Freedom Movement: A Radical Democratic Vision* (Chapel Hill, 2003); for culture and civil rights, see Adolph Reed Jr., ed., *Race, Politics, and Culture: Critical Essays on the Radicalism of the 1960s* (New York, 1986); for domestic civil rights in an international perspective, see Mary L. Dudziak, *Cold War, Civil Rights: Race and the Image of American Democracy* (Princeton, 2000). For discussions of gender, culture, and the transnational dimensions of civil rights in relation to each other, see Mary L. Dudziak, "Josephine Baker, Racial Protest, and the Cold War," *Journal of American History*, 81 (Sept. 1994), 543–70; Kevin Gaines, "From Center to Margin: Internationalism and the Origins of Black Feminism," in *Materializing Democracy: Toward a Revitalized Cultural Politics*, ed. Russ Castronovo and Dana D. Nelson (Durham, 2002), 294–313; Paul Gilroy, *The Black Atlantic: Modernity and Double Consciousness* (Cambridge, Mass., 1993); Ingrid Monson, *Freedom Sounds: Jazz, Civil Rights, and Africa, 1950–1967* (New York, forthcoming); and Penny M. Von Eschen, *Satchmo Blows Up the World: Jazz Ambassadors Play the Cold War* (Cambridge, Mass., 2004).

6. According to Simone she was rejected because she was black, but she noted that "the wonderful thing about this type of discrimination is that you can never know for sure if it is true": Simone with Cleary, *I Put a Spell on You*, 42. Simone did not apparently feel connected to a long history of classically trained black women. See, for example, Kathryn Talalay, *Composition in Black and White: The Life of Philippa Schuyler* (New York, 1995); and Allan Keiler, *Marian Anderson; A Singer's Journey* (Champaign, 2002).

7. Ira Gershwin, DuBose Heyward, and George Gershwin, "I Loves You, Porgy," [1935], performed by Nina Simone, [1957], *Little Girl Blue* (compact disk; Neon B000055Y5G; 1994). See Joel Whitburn, *Top R&B Singles, 1942–1995* (Menomonee Falls, Wisc., 1996), 402; and David Nathan, liner notes, *Very Best of Nina Simone, 1967–1972.* The critic Sidney Lazard, *Chicago Sun-Times*, quoted in Garland, *Sound of Soul*, 175. Simone with Cleary, *I Put a Spell on You*, 66–67. Biographical information is based on consistent accounts in memoirs, secondary sources, and sources from the 1960s, including, for example, Simone with Cleary, *I Put a Spell on You*, David Nathan, *The Soulful Divas: Personal Portraits of over a Dozen Divas from Nina Simone, Aretha Franklin, and Diana Ross to Patti Labelle, Whitney Houston, and Janes Jackson* (New York, 1999), 42–65; Philippe Carles, "Antibes 65: Entretien avec Nina Simone," *Jazz Magazine* (Sept. 1965), 46–48; and Jennifer Gilmore, "Nina Simone," *Salon.com.* June 20, 2000 <http://www.salon.com/people/bc/2000/06/20/simone/index.html> (Nov. 8, 2001). "I Loves You, Porgy" was one of several songs associated with Billie Holiday that Simone recorded. For Holiday's complex legacy, see especially Farah Jasmine Griffin, *If You Can't Be Free, Be a Mystery: In Search of Billie Holiday* (New York, 2001).

8. John S. Wilson, "Newport, the Music," *Down Beat*, Aug. 18, 1960, p. 18.

9. "The Rareness of Nina Simone," *Metronome* (June 1960), 30.

10. Simone with Cleary, *I Put a Spell on You*, 65. For gender, women, and jazz, see especially Sherrie Tucker, *Swing Shift: "All-Girl" Bands of the 1940s* (Durham, 2000); Sherrie Tucker, "Improvising Womanhood, or a Conundrum Is a Woman: Race, Gender, and Representation in Black Women's Jazz," in *Black Culture, Industry, and Everyday Life*, ed. S. Craig Watkins (New York, forthcoming); and Monson, "Problem with White Hipness."

11. For an influential articulation of blues as the authentic black culture, see Leroi Jones, *Blues People* (New York, 1963); for debates about jazz and race, see Ira Gitler et al., "Racial Prejudice in Jazz, Part I," *Down Beat*, March 20, 1962, pp. 20–26; and Ira Gitler et al., "Racial Prejudice to Jazz, Part II," *ibid.*, March 29,

1962, pp. 22–25. For a rich intellectual and cultural history of African American jazz musicians, see Eric Porter, *What Is This Thing Called Jazz? African American Musicians as Artists, Critics, and Activists* (Berkeley, 2002); see also Guthrie P. Ramsey Jr., *Race Music: Black Cultures from Bebop to Hip-Hop* (Berkeley, 2003); Nichole Rustin, "Mingus Fingers: Charles Mingus, Black Masculinity, and Postwar Jazz Culture" (Ph.D. diss., New York University, 1999); and Scott Saul, *Freedom Is, Freedom Ain't: Jazz and the Making of the Sixties* (Cambridge, Mass., 2003). Other African American musicians who blended jazz and classical music included Charlie Parker, Charles Mingus, and Mary Lou Williams.

12. For women singers having their "jazz credentials called into question," see Porter, *What Is This Thing Called Jazz,* 155; for women blues singers, see Angela Davis, *Blues Legacies and Black Feminism: Gertrude "Ma" Rainey, Bessie Smith, and Billie Holiday* (New York, 1998); and Hazel Carby, " 'It Jus Be's Dat Way Sometime': The Sexual Politics of Women's Blues," in *Unequal Sisters: A Multicultural Reader in U.S. Women's History,* ed. Vicki Ruiz and Ellen Dubois (1986; New York, 1994), 330–42. Griffin, *If You Can't Be Free, Be a Mystery,* 15.

13. Monson, "Problem with White Hipness," 402.

14. "Nina Simone: Angry Woman of Jazz," *Sepia,* 16 (March 1967), 64. See also Maurice Cullaz, "Nina Simone," *Jazz Hot* (Sept. 1965), 27–31; and Maurice Cullaz, "Antibes," *ibid.* (Sept. 1969), 41. For the rural South and the church as repositories for African American music, see Marybeth Hamilton, "Sexuality, Authenticity, and the Making of the Blues Tradition," *Past and Present* (no. 169, Nov. 2000), 132–60.

15. Langston Hughes, "Nina Simone," *New York Post,* June 29, 1962, clipping, Simone file, Schomburg Center for Research in Black Culture Clipping File, 1925–1974, emphasis in original. For this description by Hughes as a way to promote Simone, see *Chicago Defender,* March 21, 1964, clipping, *ibid.*; and the compilation of reviews that the International Talent Associates, Inc., assembled to represent Simone, *ibid.*

16. "Nina Simone Pregnant: Settles Suit Secretly," *New York Amsterdam News,* March 17, 1962, p. 1; Smith, "Other (More Serious) Side of Nina," 7. Simone with Cleary, *I Put a Spell on You,* 74. "Nina Simone Pregnant," 1. Robert Lucas, "Nina Simone: A Grid with Guts," *Negro Digest* (Feb. 1962), 23–24; "Nina Simone Pregnant"; final three quotations in Lucas, "Nina Simone," 23–24. For a similar emphasis on Simone's hostility to fans and to mass culture in accounts of her opposition to bootlegging, see "Trend May Be Set by Nina's Suit," *New York Amsterdam News,* Feb. 20, 1965, p. 13.

17. Nat Shapiro, liner notes, *In Concert—I Put a Spell on You,* "Simmering Down," Sept. 30, 1963, p. 82, clipping, Simone file, Schomburg Center for Research in Black Culture Clipping File, 1925–1974. "Mean" in "Simmering Down"; "angry" in "Nina Simone: Angry Woman of Jazz"; "unstable" in Raymond Robinson, "Nina Simone Thrills, Oscar Brown Chills," *New York Amsterdam News,* Dec. 3, 1966, p. 10; "inner fires" in John S. Wilson, "Nina Simone Sings Stirring Program," *New York Times,* April 17, 1965, clipping, Simone file, Schomburg Center for Research in Black Culture Clipping File, 1925–1974. See also "Snarls at Apollo Audience," *New York Citizen-Call,* Feb. 18, 1961, p. 15.

18. Monson, "Problem with White Hipness," 410.

19. For the Student Nonviolent Coordinating Committee (SNCC), see "SNCC Backers," *New York Amsterdam News,* July 6, 1963, p. 5; and "Sponsors of Carnegie Hall, February 1st [1963] Benefit for SNCC," n.d., microfilm reel 45; B-I-13, #1094, Student Nonviolent Coordinating Committee (SNCC) Papers, 1959–1972 (Widener Library). For the Congress on Racial Equality (CORE), see Jesse H. Walker, "Theatricals," *New York Amsterdam News,* July 20, 1963, p. 15. For the National Association for the Advancement of Colored People (NAACP), see "Mammoth Benefit to Fight Segregation and Brutality: New York State Conference of NAACP Presents the Amazing Nina Simone," advertisement, *New York Amsterdam News,* May 25, 1963, p. 14. For the Young Men's Christian Association (YMCA), see "Nina Sings for YMCA on Sunday," *ibid.,* Feb. 27, 1965, p. 16. Simone with Cleary, *I Put a Spell on You,* 90–91.

20. For Carnegie Hall, see Julia Prettyman to Nina Simone, May 5, 1964, microfilm reel 45: B-I-12, #1053. SNCC Papers, 1959–1972; Prettyman to Andrew Stroud, June 17, 1964, microfilm reel 45: B-I-12, #1058, *ibid.* For CORE, see Stroud to Jim McDonald, April 26, 1965, microfilm reel 12: E-II-44, #0892, Papers of the Congress on Racial Equality (CORE)—Addendum, 1944–1968 (Widener Library); Alan Gartner to Stroud, Aug. 20, 1965, microfilm reel 12: E-II-44, #0892, *ibid.*; Jesse Smallwood to Allen Gardner [*sic*], telegram, Aug. 23, 1965, microfilm reel 12: E-II-44, #0895, *ibid.*; and Simone with Cleary, *I Put a Spell on*

You, 108. For $2,000, see "Fund Raising Department Report," Oct. 1965, microfilm reel 8: B-I-13, #0735, CORE Papers—Addendum, 1944–1968. Other concerts at which jazz musicians played in 1963 and 1964 to support the civil rights movement raised $984.10 and $1,354.65: see "Caught in the Act," *Down Beat*, Aug. 1, 1963, p. 37; and "Hollywood Benefit Raises $1,354 for Civil-Rights Campaign," *ibid.*, Nov. 5, 1964, p. 9. For the relationship between jazz and benefit concerts for civil rights organizations, see Ingrid Monson, "Monk Meets SNCC," *Black Music Research Journal*, 19 (Autumn 1999), 187–200.

21. *New York Amsterdam News*, Aug. 10, 1963, p. 42; "Fund Raisers for Freedom; Celebrities Rally to Civil Rights Call by Helping to Raise Thousands in Cash," *Ebony* (Oct. 1963), 120–26. $9,000 estimate in Ward, *Just My Soul Responding*, 302. See also Simone with Cleary. *I Put a Spell on You*, 101–3; and Bob Hunter, "Singer Gloria Lynne in Her Glory," *Chicago Defender*, Feb. 16–22, 1963, p. 22.

22. Ward, *Just My Soul Responding*, 289–93.

23. Bill Mclarney, "Caught in the Act," *Down Beat*, Jan. 23, 1969, p. 34. For the reluctance of other musicians, see Ward, *Just My Soul Responding*. Lincoln's *Straight Ahead* is one exception in its mix of culture and politics, as is Max Roach and Oscar Brown, *We Insist! The Freedom Now Suits*, performed by Max Roach, Oscar Brown, et al., [1960] (compact disk; Candid CCD 9002; 1987). Both of those albums are solidly entrenched in a postwar Jazz canon in ways that Simone's music is not. See Saul, *Freedom Is, Freedom Ain't*; and Porter, *What Is This Thing Called Jazz?* For more coded references to racial politics in popular music, see Suzanne Smith, *Dancing in the Street: Motown and the Cultural Politics of Detroit* (Cambridge, Mass., 1999).

24. Due to constraints of space, I focus on three songs in which the relevance of gender to racial politics is particularly apparent, but, as noted, Simone made related moves in other songs and on other albums. The focus is lyrics more than music because it was Simone's style of lyrics that changed on this album.

25. Kurt Weill and Bertholt Brecht, "Pirate Jenny," performed by Nina Simone, [1964], *In Concert—I Put a Spell on You*; Kurt Weill and Bertholt Brecht, *The Threepenny Opera*, [1928], English adaptation by Marc Blitzstein, [1954] (compact disk; Deca B00004X09T; 2000). Michael Denning, *The Cultural Front: The Laboring of American Culture in the Twentieth Century* (New York, 1996), 324. For the relationship between German left-wing modernism and American protest music, see Russell Berman, "Sounds Familiar? Nina Simone's Performances of Brecht/Weill Songs," in *Sound Matters: Essays on the Acoustics of German Culture*, ed. Nora M. Alter and Lutz Koepnick (New York, 2004).

26. Shapiro, liner notes, *In Concert—I Put a Spell on You*. Simone did hold one long high note for her final reference to the "ship, the black freighter"; see Berman, "Sounds Familiar?"

27. For gender and the politics of respectability, see Evelyn Brooks Higginbotham, *Righteous Discontent: The Woman's Movement in the Black Beaptist Church, 1880–1920* (Cambridge, Mass., 1993). For respectability and the civil rights movement, see William Chafe, *Civilities and Civil Rights: Greensboro, North Carolina, and the Black Struggle for Freedom* (New York, 1980); and Marisa Chappell, Jenny Hutchinson, and Brian Ward, " 'Dress modestly, neatly . . . as if you were going to church': Respectability, Class, and Gender in the Montgomery Bus Boycott and the Early Civil Rights Movement," in *Gender in the Civil Rights Movement*, ed. Peter J. Ling (New York, 1999), 69–100. For Abbey Lincoln's musical expressions of rage, see Porter, *What Is This Thing Called Jazz?*; and Griffin, *If You Can't Be Free, Be a Mystery*.

28. For diverse arenas in which black power and black cultural nationalism took shape, see, for example, Manning Marable, *Black American Politics: From the Washington Marches to Jesse Jackson* (New York, 1985); Nikhil Pal Singh, "The Black Panthers and the 'Undeveloped Country' of the Left," in *The Black Panther Party Reconsidered*, ed. Charles Jones (Baltimore, 1998), 63; William Van Deburg, ed., *Modern Black Nationalism: From Marcus Garvey to Louis Farrakhan* (New York, 1997); Tyson, *Radio Free Dixie*; James Smethurst, "Poetry and Sympathy: New York, the Left, and the Rise of Black Arts," in *Left of the Color Line*, ed. Mullen and Smethurst, 259–78; and Leroi Jones and Larry Neal, eds., *Black Fire: An Anthology of Afro-American Writing* (1965; New York, 1968), 303. James Brown, "Say It Loud—I'm Black and I'm Proud," performed by James Brown, [1968], *Say It Live and Loud: Live in Dallas 08.26.68* (compact disk; Polydor 31455-7668-2; 1998).

29. See Henry Hampton and Steve Fayer, *Voices of Freedom: An Oral History of the Civil Rights Movement from the 1950s through the 1980s* (New York, 1990), 276, 291; and Robert Weisbrot, *Freedom Bound: A History of America's Civil Rights Movement* (New York, 1990), 195.

30. For memoirs, poetry, and scholarship documenting women's participation in black power and black cultural nationalism, see, for example, Elaine Brown, *A Taste of Power: A Black Woman's Story* (New York, 1992); Nikki Giovanni, *The Selected Poems of Nikki Giovanni* (New York, 1995); Sharon Harley, " 'Chronicle of a Death Foretold': Gloria Richardson, the Cambridge Movement, and the Radical Black Activist Tradition," in *Sisters in the Struggle: African American Women in the Civil Rights–Black Power Movement*, ed. Bettye Collier-Thomas and V. P. Franklin (New York, 2001), 174–96; Regina Jennings, "Why I Joined the Party: An African Womanist Reflection," in *Black Panther Party Reconsidered*, ed. Jones, 257–65; Angela D. LeBlanc-Ernest, " 'The Most Qualified Person to Handle the Job': Black Panther Party Women, 1966–1982," *ibid.*, 305–34; and Sonia Sanchez, *We a BadddDD People* (Detroit, 1970). For how masculinity constituted expressions of black power and black cultural nationalism, see, for example, Phillip Brian Harper, *Are We Not Men? Masculine Anxiety and the Problem of African-American Identity* (New York, 1996); Kelley, *Freedom Dreams*; Ward, *Just My Soul Responding*, 388–415; and Jerry Gafio Watts, *Amiri Baraka: The Politics and Art of a Black Intellectual* (New York, 2001), 325–47.

31. "Nina Simone: Angry Woman of Jazz," 60. Lee Dembart, "Nina Simone: Soul on Voice," *New York Post*, March 15, 1969, sec. 3, p. 1, clipping, Simone file, Schomburg Center for Research in Black Culture Clipping File, 1925–1974; Eldridge Cleaver, *Soul on Ice* (New York, 1968). "Nina Simone: Angry Woman of Jazz," 61–62; for Simone and censorship, see also, for example, Cordell Thompson, "Young, Gifted, and Black Tune May Have Nixed Nina's TV Showing," *Jet*, May 14, 1970, pp. 60–61. For more on the impact of "Mississippi Goddam," see Wilson, "Recital Victory for Nina Simone."

32. Simone with Cleary, *I Put a Spell on You*, 89–90. Amiri Baraka, "Black Art" (1969), in *Leroi jones/Amiri Baraka Reader*, ed. Harris, 219.

33. Mary Helen Washington, "Alice Childress, Lorraine Hansberry, and Claudia Jones: Black Women Write the Popular Front," in *Left of the Color Line*, ed. Mullen and Smethurst, 185. For women in SNCC, see Frances Beale, "Double Jeopardy: To Be Black and Female," in *The Black Woman: An Anthology*, ed. Toni Cade Bambara (New York, 1970), 95–98. Third World Women's Alliance, "Statement" (1968), in *Dear Sisters: Dispatches from the Women's Liberation Movement*, ed. Rosalyn Fraad Baxandall and Linda Gordon (New York, 2000), 65. For black women and feminism, see also Rosalyn Baxandall, "Re-Visioning the Women's Liberation Movement's Narrative: Early Second Wave African American Feminists." *Feminist Studies*, 27 (Spring 2001), 225–45.

34. See "Mammoth Benefit to Fight Segregation and Brutality," 14; and "Rareness of Nina Simone," 30. Robinson, "Nina Simone Thrills, Oscar Brown Chills," 10. See also Philharmonic Hall Concert Program, Nov. 22, 1966, Simone file, Schomburg Center for Research in Black Culture Clipping File, 1925–1974.

35. "Because of": "A cause de ce manque de respect qui dure depuis des centaines d'années, chaque fois que je vais dans un nouveau pays, je me sens obligée d'inclure dans mon répertoire des chants qui affirment orgueilleusement ma race" in Michel Delorme and Maurice Cullaz, "Nina Simone: Affirmer orgueilleusement ma race," *Jazz Hot* (Sept. 1965), 7. In this regard, she was quite different from Josephine Baker and others whose offstage critiques of American race relations were not as central to onstage performances; see Dudziak, "Josephine Baker, Racial Protest, and the Cold War."

36. Smith, "Other (More Serious) Side of Nina," 7. On the "ever-increasing number of jazzmen making their homes in Europe," see "Americans in Europe, a Discussion," *Down Beat*, July 2, 1964, pp. 64–73, esp. 64; Joachim Berendt. "Americans in Europe, a Dissident View," *ibid.*, Sept. 10, 1965, p. 19; and Tyler Stovall, *Paris Noir; African Americans in the City of Light* (Boston, 1996).

37. See Griffin, *If You Can't Be Free, Be a Mystery*, 106. Nathan interview. Smith, "Other (More Serious) Side of Nina," 7. Royston Eldridge, "Nina's the Medium for the Message," *Melody Maker*, April 19, 1969, p. 5; to Eldridge, Simone offered more positive assessments of race relations in Europe. Nina Simone, "Revolution," performed by Nina Simone, [1969], *To Love Somebody—Here Comes the Sun* (compact disk; BMG Entertainment 74321 924792; 2002).

38. Kelley, "Nap Time," 344; for other women and for the role of the fashion industry in this process, see *ibid.*, 330–51; see also Smith, *Visions of Belonging*. Lorraine Hansberry, *A Raisin in the Sun* (1959; New York, 1961); For an emphasis on the late 1960s, see, for example, William Van Deburg, *New Day in Babylon: The Black Power Movement and American Culture, 1965–1975* (Chicago, 1992), esp. 192–204.

For the dominance of white male new leftists in scholarship on the 1960s, see Alice Echols, " 'We Gotta Get Out of This Place': Notes toward a Remapping of the Sixties," *Socialist Review*, 92 (no. 2, 1992), 9–33.

39. In addition to works cited, for reperiodizing the sixties, see also, for example, James C. Hall, *Mercy, Mercy Me: African American Culture and the American Sixties* (New York, 2001); for the centrality of African American women to such a reperiodization, see Gaines, "From Center to Margin"; and E. Frances White, "Africa on My Mind: Gender, Counterdiscourse, and African American Nationalism," in *Dark Continent of Our Bodies: Black Feminism and the Politics of Respectability*, ed. E. Frances White (1990; Philadelphia, 2001), 117–50.

40. For examples of black feminist critiques, see Bambara, ed., *Black Woman*; and "Combahee River Collective, a Black Feminist Statement" (1977), in *The Black Feminist Reader*, ed. Joy James and T. Denean Sharpley-Whiting (Malden, 2000), 261–70. While many of the ideas in the anthology *Black Woman* took shape earlier in the 1960s, other selections were reactions to events in the mid- to late 1960s—to the (in)famous Moynihan report (Daniel Patrick Moynihan, "The Negro Family: The Case for National Action," 1965), among others.

41. Tucker, "Improvising Womanhood, or a Conundrum Is a Woman." Simone with Cleary, *I Put a Spell on You*, 86–87. Nina Simone and Weldon Irvine Jr., "To Be Young, Gifted, and Black," performed by Nina Simone, [1969], *Nina Simone, Platinum Series*; Nathan, liner notes, *Very Best of Nina Simone, 1967–1972*. Simone with Cleary, *I Put a Spell on You*, 86–87. For a now-classic analysis of feminism developing out of and after a commitment to civil rights, see Sara Evans, *Personal Politics: The Roots of Women's Liberation in the Civil Rights Movement and the New Left* (New York, 1979).

42. See Nathan, *Soulful Divas*, 60–63; and "Nina Simone Ends Voluntary Exile from U.S.," *Jet*, April 22, 1985, pp. 54–55.

43. See, for example, Richard Harrington, "Nina Simone, a Voice to Be Reckoned With," *Washington Post*, April 22, 2003, sec. C, p. 1: and John Fordham, "Nina Simone: Soul-Jazz Diva Whose Music Spoke of Love, Respect, and Their Opposites—Particularly in Relation to Race," *Guardian Review*, April 22, 2003, p. 23. Miriam Makeba quoted in Susan Bell, "Friends and Family Pay Their Tributes to Jazz Legend's Political Courage at Packed Funeral," *Scotsman*, April 26, 2003, p. 17. Exceptions include Craig Seymour, "An Appreciation: Nina Simone's Voice Fused Art, Politics," *Atlanta Journal and Constitution*, April 23, 2003, p. 1E.

44. "More than an Entertainer," *Time*, Feb. 21, 1969, clipping, Simone file, Schomburg Center for Research in Black Culture Clipping File, 1925–1974.

Chapter 24

A New Women's Movement: The Emergence of the National Organization for Women

Cynthia Harrison

The second wave of feminism in the United States emerged in the decade of the 1960s from activism on two fronts— lobbying at the state and federal levels for an expansion of women's rights and the growth of consciousness raising in women's personal lives. Cynthia Harrison, in this excerpt from her book, On Account of Sex, *traces the emergence of the National Organization for Women out of organizing efforts within the federal government in this period. She shows how resistance within federal circles led women to organize independently, in this way becoming a more effective pressure group advocating women's interests.*

In October 1966, three years to the month after the President's Commission on the Status of Women [PCSW] presented its report to John Kennedy, the first avowedly feminist organization to emerge since suffrage held its inaugural conference. With the appearance of the National Organization for Women, women leaders outside of government, building upon the President's Commission's report, took over the creation of the policy agenda for women from those in government who had served as "midwives of the Women's Movement."[1] The new movement adopted the objectives of the activists who had laid the groundwork, but it went beyond their work in a signal way. The women's movement of the 1960s forged a new, coherent, feminist philosophy that would enable women finally to make a claim for complete equality both in and outside the home.

THE CREATION OF THE NATIONAL ORGANIZATION FOR WOMEN

Martha Griffiths was not alone in her indignation at the behavior of the [Equal Employment Opportunity Commission]. Although initially disturbed by the threat to protective labor laws Title VII represented, by 1966 virtually every women's organization protested the EEOC's cavalier attitude toward sex discrimination. By June, a "proto-feminist" nucleus in Washington ([Esther] Peterson, Catherine East, Mary Eastwood, and EEOC commissioner Richard Graham) had come to believe that the EEOC would not improve unless outside pressure from organized women served to heighten the commissioners' interest in enforcing the sex provision of Title VII. This cadre had begun to work toward the formation of a new outside group devoted exclusively to sex discimination, starting with the traditional women's associations of the Women's Bureau coalition.[2] These groups were reluctant, however, to establish an activist group that would fight exclusively for women's rights;[3] as council

Excerpted from Cynthia Harrison, *On Account of Sex: The Politics of Women's Issues, 1945–1968* (Berkeley: University of California Press, 1988), pp. 192–209, 300–06. Used by permission of the publisher and the author.

member Viola Hymes had earlier explained, women's organizations hesitated to take the lead in the fight "for fear it would be interpreted that they were favoring women instead of looking upon everyone as having equal opportunity."[4]

But other, less familiar, avenues were being explored. Betty Friedan, author of *The Feminine Mystique*, who had begun work on a book concerning the new law on sex discrimination, was now in close touch with Catherine East, Sonia Pressman, Pauli Murray, and Martha Griffiths—part of what Friedan later described as the "feminist underground" in Washington. Pressman, an attorney at the EEOC, told Friedan that only she could start a national organization to fight for women as the civil rights movement had for blacks. Richard Graham, too, urged Friedan on, telling her that he had asked the mainstream women's associations, such as the League of Women Voters and the American Association of University Women, to develop such an organization, but they had declined. Friedan nevertheless delayed. Although East and Eastwood supplied her with lists of women likely to be sympathetic, Friedan suggested that the state commissions on the status of women take the lead. East protested that women on the state commissions were too dependent on state governors and had too little power of their own. . . . East invited Friedan to attend the Washington gathering of the state commissions in June.[5]

. . . Shortly before the meeting Friedan, to her dismay, had learned through her Washington friends that Lyndon Johnson did not intend to reappoint Richard Graham to the EEOC after his initial term expired in July. . . . Mindful of East's words, Friedan invited a group of interested women participating in the state commission conference to come to her hotel room and discuss what could be done about Graham's reappointment and about the recent EEOC ruling regarding sex-segregated advertising. The women who caucused in Friedan's room agreed that a civil rights organization for women was not necessary but proposed that a resolution be offered at the conference supporting Graham and insisting on better enforcement efforts by the EEOC. . . .

Administration officials had anticipated some expression of irritation at the conference. Esther Peterson confided to John Macy that "95 percent" of the delegates believed that the EEOC was lax about enforcing the sex provision of Title VII. Moreover, she said, a grapevine made up of "women active in women's groups, unions, civil rights groups and political parties" was communicating dissatisfaction because Lyndon Johnson's campaign to bring more women into government had lapsed.[6]

. . . However, when [Kathryn] Clarenbach conferred with [Margaret] Hickey, [Mary] Keyserling, and Peterson about offering resolutions on the subject, all three told her it could not be done because the conference participants were not official delegates and because conference organizers did not want resolutions critical of the administration emerging from a federally supported gathering. . . . Having had their request for action denied, the fifteen women who had met in Friedan's room the night before took over two tables at the conference luncheon. Within sight of the conference directors, Friedan, Clarenbach, and their colleagues planned an inaugural meeting for a new women's association. Friedan scribbled the name on a paper napkin: NOW—the National Organization for Women.[7]

In addition, disregarding the official decree, eighty representatives in the Title VII workshop voted for a resolution asking Lyndon Johnson to reappoint Richard Graham. . . . Mary Keyserling ignored the disputes and the ire of conference participants. She reported to Secretary Wirtz that the conference had been "very successful," mentioning no disagreement of any kind.[8]

Keyserling tried to pretend that nothing had happened, but the June conference constituted a crucial point in the history of women in the 1960s. Until then, both influential individuals and official government bodies had created a federal agenda for women and moved with caution and deference to traditional views about women, carefully couching requests for specific improvements in the language of liberal ideals and obeisance to women's "natural" roles as wife and mother. The formation of NOW indicated that many women were no longer satisfied working within the constraints imposed by being official members of governments. From that time forward, the federal government would no longer control or restrain the agenda of the women's movement; NOW could take action, as official groups could not, without executive sanction. At the conclusion of the June conference, NOW officers sent telegrams to Lyndon Johnson asking him to reappoint Richard Graham to the commission and requesting the EEOC to revise its ruling on sex-segregated want ads.[9]. . .

The situation [at the EEOC] continued to decline. . . . In September [Aileen] Hernandez sent a memorandum to the commission and its staff expressing her dismay at the long time lag in responding to complaints and at the neglect of sex discrimination. This grievance had no effect, however, and in October Hernandez submitted her resignation in disgust, effective November 10.[10]. . .

AN OUTSIDE PRESSURE GROUP

The new women's rights organization convened its inaugural conference in October 1966, the first formal expression of the new wave of feminism. At the meeting, the membership elected Friedan president and Clarenbach, in absentia, chairman of the board; former EEOC commissioners Aileen Hernandez and Richard Graham both became vice-presidents. The composition of the board of directors disclosed NOW's origins in the discontent of elite women and their male supporters. The board included seven university professors or administrators, five state or national labor union officials, four federal or local government officials, four business executives, four members with some affiliation to a state commission on women, one physician, and three members of religious orders. Thanks to the media experience of the professionals in the organization, the October conference elicited a surprising amount of press attention, which greatly enhanced NOW's impact from its birth.[11]

Although NOW appeared because its founders grew impatient with the timid posture of [government groups] in relation to the Equal Employment Opportunity Commission, the formation of NOW did not imply a renunciation of the President's Commission on the Status of Women or of the ongoing groups created at the commission's request to implement its recommendations. Rather, the originators of the new organization were motivated by an understanding of the intrinsic limitations of federal bodies. . . . The architects of NOW established the organization in order to commence "a civil rights movement for women" that would confront law and custom "to win for women the final right to be fully free and equal human beings."[12] Although upset by the decision of Peterson, Keyserling, and Hickey not to permit a resolution at the conference, NOW's founders held no grudge against the administration officials concerned with women. Friedan later referred to Esther Peterson and Eleanor Roosevelt as the "two towering figures of recent history," who had first brought together many of the new organizations' founders in the President's Commission on the Status of Women.[13]

Likewise, Peterson bore no ill will toward the organization that was preparing to wrest control of women's policy from the administration groups. In a memorandum to Civil Service Commission chairman John Macy, she described the membership list of the new organization as "very distinguished," although she found its positions "rather militant." Their governing principle, she wrote, was that sex and race discrimination were intertwined (many had been active in the civil rights movement) and that the EEOC had proved consistently inadequate in righting these injustices. Moreover, . . . Peterson said, "An organization is needed to focus the underlying resentment and frustration into constructive channels. If NOW does not succeed, some other organization will take its place."[14]

Although Peterson characterized NOW's positions as "militant," in its first months NOW's program closely paralleled the program of the president's commission. In subsequent years NOW continued to owe to the president's commission its penchant for seeking federal action to ameliorate women's problems, its emphasis on employment issues, and its attractiveness for middle-class women who had first been sensitized to women's issues by the reports of the national and state commissions. As "targets for action" in the first year, NOW highlighted equal employment opportunity and the actions the federal government could take toward that end, including amendment of Executive Order 11246, which prohibited federal contractors from discriminating on the basis of race. It also focused on full deductability of childcare expenses, greater enforcement powers for the EEOC, the appointment of the full number of commissioners, revision of the regulations concerning advertising, and equal attention to the needs of minority women in federal poverty programs. The agenda was very broad and included economic rights for homemakers, training programs for mothers reentering the labor force, projects to address discrimination in educational institutions, prohibition of distinctions based on sex in jury service, and equal protection for women under the Constitution. The people who founded NOW were friends or colleagues of members of the presidential commission, or members themselves, and they agreed generally with the commission on many of the most pressing problems and their solutions.[15]

As with the president's commission, NOW's founders did not raise questions concerning sexual freedom. In 1966 NOW did not mention homosexuality, and a statement that women should control their own reproduction was excised from the statement of purpose as being "too controversial." NOW's creators assumed that women would continue to live in traditional families, and they did not envision or endorse a radical restructuring of most institutions.[16]

Similarly, in its founding year NOW approved the presidential commission's proposal regarding constitutional equality. Upon hearing of NOW's formation, the National Woman's Party, hoping for an ally, wrote immediately asking for the organization's statement in favor of the Equal Rights Amendment. Mary Eastwood . . . wrote on NOW's behalf to the NWP that the ERA amendment was superfluous because the Constitution, properly interpreted, would guarantee equality without disturbing state labor laws.[17]

But if NOW considered the PCSW a model in many ways, it also differed from the governmental bodies that preceded it in two significant respects. First, unlike the presidential commission, NOW was independent of traditional political structures and owed no allegiance to a party or politician. . . . Since membership in NOW did not depend on the good favor of president or governor, NOW's freedom of action had few limits. It could afford to be, to use Peterson's term, "militant."

Second, and more important, NOW declined to share the presidential commission's view that sex roles were immutable. In its statement of purpose, the organization's founders declared: "We reject the current assumptions that a man must carry the sole burden of supporting himself, his wife and family . . . or that marriage, home and family are primarily woman's world and responsibility—hers, to dominate—his to support. We believe that a true partnership between the sexes demands a different concept of marriage, an equitable sharing of the responsibilities of home and children and of the economic burdens of their support."[18]

This renunciation of biological destiny ultimately permitted NOW to demand a kind of equality for women that neither the president's commission nor any other women's group preceding NOW could have claimed. For the first time, women seeking equal rights for women could offer a coherent and logical program, founded on an internally consistent philosophy. Women could insist on equal treatment in the workplace because fathers, too, had the responsibility to take care of children. With this theoretical leap of great consequence, the feminists in NOW anticipated, rather than reflected, the prevailing viewpoint.

*   *   *

Administration officials recognized immediately the significance of a new organization dedicated to fighting for women's rights. In November, Civil Service Commission chief John Macy and three EEOC commissioners met with NOW officials to discuss the points NOW raised in its letter. EEOC chair Stephen Shulman indicated to correspondents that he was aware of NOW's position on the matters under discussion.[19] . . . Esther Peterson promised her support: "Your organization will be very useful at this moment and I am sure you know I am following it with great interest and will be helpful in any way I can."[20]

The White House reacted more guardedly. The letter to the president went to Peterson with a request that she handle it, and Shulman counseled the president not to meet with NOW's officers, advising him that the EEOC commissioners had already done so. He suggested that the president wait a year to see "whether or not they have achieved a status worthy of Presidential attention."[21]

*   *   *

Presidential acknowledgment came quickly, in fact. In March 1967 an aide advised the organization's officers that the President found their recommendations "most welcome" and that in keeping with one of their proposals he was willing to amend the executive order prohibiting racial discrimination in federal employment and contractors to include sex discrimination.[22]

Johnson's letter reflected the culmination of a series of developments. The President had issued EO 11246, which required affirmative action programs to ensure equal opportunity for all races, in September 1965. By that time, Congress had already passed the Civil Rights Act, which prohibited sex discrimination in employment, and Esther Peterson had warned that the omission of sex in the executive order "might prove embarrassing to the President." Furthermore, she argued, if left out then, it would create serious problems with women's organizations; it would have to be added eventually. . . . (As support for the change grew, Peterson turned out to be right; Johnson asked the Interdepartmental Committee on the Status of Women ICSW to recommend the form of the new executive order. With relatively little discussion, the ICSW advised the president simply to amend the original order to add the word *sex* wherever the phrase "race, creed, color or national origin" appeared. This he did in October 1967. The dispute over whether sex discrimination should be treated like racial bias had ended.[23] . . . NOW president Betty Friedan claimed credit for the new amendment. The discussion of sex discrimination, Friedan declared, was "out in the clear light of day."[24]

The cordial relationship between the new organization and the federal bodies concerned with women's status quickly became problematical with the continued equivocation of the EEOC on protective labor legislation. Initially, NOW's founders themselves had no unified position. Pauli Murray and Mary Eastwood had come to the conclusion, argued in their landmark article, "Jane Crow and the Law," in the December 1965 issue of the *George Washington Law Review*, that laws for women alone had "waning utility." Kathryn Clarenbach, in contrast, continued to support the position espoused by Mary Keyserling and the Women's Bureau coalition that the EEOC should not overrule protective labor laws. But when a California woman filed a complaint with the EEOC against a firm that refused to promote her because of the state's maximum hours laws, and the commission declined to rule, NOW offered the woman its assistance in getting the California law nullified. Peterson suggested that the Department of Labor take a public position in favor of the plaintiff, as NOW requested; Keyserling, backed by the National Consumers League and the other members of the Women's Bureau coalition, urged the secretary not to intervene. Secretary Wirtz sided once again with Keyserling.[25]

But the administration position on the issue of protective labor legislation could no longer be addressed and decided only "in house." NOW's membership grew rapidly—one year after its creation it counted twelve hundred members, with chapters in several states—but its influence continuously outstripped its actual numbers.

*   *   *

NOW testified at the EEOC hearings in 1967 against protective labor legislation, in company with Representative Martha Griffiths and representatives of the National Federation of Business and Professional Women's Clubs (BPW) and the United Automobile Workers, and together they succeeded in bringing about a change unwelcome to die-hard advocates of differential treatment for women. . . . In February 1968, the commission overturned its 1966 decision to leave the judgment entirely to the courts or to states for reconciliation, and it announced it would consider the arguments on a case-by-case basis.[26] Labor unions objected again; the Amalgamated Clothing Workers called this application of Title VII "a modern version of the effort years ago to use the so-called Equal Rights Amendment . . . to deprive women workers of the protection of this legislation."[27] Yet as more and more groups, from NOW to state commissions to labor unions, began to endorse the position that state labor laws applying only to women did more harm than good, the advocates of special treatment became increasingly isolated, outside the mainstream.

*   *   *

Forcing a change in the want ads position proved more difficult. In December 1967 the EEOC became the target of the first feminist demonstration in five decades when NOW set up picket lines in front of EEOC offices in five cities. . . . Finally, in August, the EEOC promulgated the sought-after regulation that barred employers from advertising in sex-segregated newspaper columns.[28] Fortas's prediction notwithstanding, the Supreme Court upheld the regulation in a 1973 decision, ruling that the First Amendment does not extend fully to commercial speech.

The issues raised by the EEOC's enforcement of Title VII of the 1964 Civil Rights Act dominated NOW's earliest days but did not consume them entirely. Once a clear position on protective labor legislation had been arrived at within the organization, NOW's endorsement of the Equal Rights Amendment followed quickly. . . . At the 1967 national conference, NOW decided to back the ERA by a vote of eighty-two to three, with twelve abstentions. . . . Carl Hayden and Emanuel Celler, unimpressed by the new movement, continued to stymie congressional action. Feminists did not succeed in freeing the ERA from the House Judiciary Committee until 1970.[29]

Despite its conversion to the amendment, NOW's insistence on a broad program of women's rights distinguished its method of operation from the one-issue approach of the National Woman's Party. Alice Paul's pleasure with NOW's advocacy of the ERA was therefore restrained. She took particular exception to NOW's 1967 endorsement of the movement to repeal abortion laws in recognition of women's right to control their own bodies.[30] Paul contended that taking positions on such issues as abortion "gets the men all mixed up."[31] NOW, interested in achieving equality and autonomy for women in every area of American life, as well as in drawing large numbers of women and men into the movement, saw no purpose to narrowing its focus. Still, it considered the ERA to be of major importance. . . .

The 1968 presidential campaign took place in the midst of turmoil over racism, urban riots, the war in Vietnam, and paralyzing student demonstrations. The assassinations that year of Martin Luther King, Jr., in April and Robert Kennedy in June, the "Poor People's Campaign" in Washington in the spring, and the violent clashes between peace marchers and the police at the Democratic National Convention in Chicago all highlighted and focused the impulse toward social reform. The just-emerging women's movement was a small part of that tableau, but even so, women's issues were achieving a new salience.

In the 1968 campaign, both NOW and the National Woman's Party urged all the candidates to speak on behalf of the ERA, and most did. During the New Hampshire primary Eugene McCarthy, the amendment's chief sponsor and challenger of Lyndon Johnson for the Democratic party's nomination, highlighted his support for the amendment in his campaign literature. . . . Hubert Humphrey, calling the ERA a "vital issue," reminded amendment advocates of his allegiance while in the Senate. American party candidate George Wallace favored the ERA, as many conservatives always had, and held up his wife, Lurleen, as one who contributed to women's advancement in her role as governor of Alabama. Richard Nixon again affirmed his long-standing approval. Senator Robert Kennedy was less enthusiastic; he promised support only if other measures proved inadequate. Unlike the National Woman's Party, however, the National Organization for Women asked the candidates to express themselves as well on a whole variety of women's issues.[32] For the first time in four decades, a genuine national women's movement was bringing a wide array of issues to the attention of a national audience.

A chain of events accounted for the appearance of the first new feminist organization of the 1960s. The civil rights movement served as the vanguard, its philosophy, tactics, and successes priming the political and social environment and providing models for action. The changing configuration of women's work lives and their now-established place in the workforce produced a disjuncture between women's lives as they were living them and the social setting that offered few supports, either ideological or material. The formation of the President's Commission on the Status of Women in 1961, in recognition of this disjuncture, had resulted in the creation of a national network of knowledgeable women concerned about their status. In 1964, the proponents of the ERA accomplished a legislative coup with the enactment of a federal law that barred sex discrimination in employment. The statute had problematical implications for the Women's Bureau coalition, but the derision exhibited by the Equal Employment Opportunity Commission, the agency responsible for enforcing the law, angered the national network of women newly sensitized to inequities confronting women. Indeed, the commission's behavior spurred the women into establishing a new association committed to fighting for women's rights. Inaugurated by women affiliated with the president's commission and the resulting state commissions, the National Organization for Women reflected both the commission's successes in bringing the status of women to the fore and their limitations in taking effective action to improve it. NOW's creation bespoke as well the short reach of the narrowly focused, ingrown movement for the Equal Rights Amendment and expressed the frustration of politically sensitive women relegated to token appointments.

After the formation of NOW, federal policy makers had to start responding to demands sustained by a high degree of public awareness rather than initiating moderate actions in the relative calm of general disinterest. . . . Unquestionably, by the end of Lyndon Johnson's term the federal government faced demands and expectations concerning women undreamt of at the time of John Kennedy's inauguration.

Moreover, yet another strain of active feminism emerged at the end of the decade, with the appearance of women's groups on the community level growing out of the antiwar struggle and the movement for social justice. In the fall of 1967 local women's liberation groups began to appear in several cities, as radical women recognized the futility of reform within New Left civil rights and community action organizations. Younger than the women who had formed NOW and committed to local, rather than national, activity, these small, autonomous groups developed a technique of uncovering the political nature of the oppression of women through candid discussion of women's personal lives.[33]

"Consciousness raising" became the initiation rite of the women's movement; locally focused groups went from there to organizing day-care centers, rape crisis committees, women's health collectives, and a plethora of movement publications.[34] By the mid seventies, women involved in these groups had begun to seek state and federal support for local programs, forming coalitions with staid feminist organizations such as NOW. And NOW, which had started life as a top-heavy lobbying group, itself encouraged the emergence of local chapters. The branches of the women's movement, in their essential parts, had merged. With forty thousand members in 1974, NOW offered a highly visible and respectable link to a national movement, but the diversity of smaller groups provided comfortable alternatives for almost any woman to join.[35]

The women's movement ultimately forced federal policy makers to consider action to ameliorate the disadvantages women suffered in virtually every part of their lives. But the federal initiatives taken *before* the movement's rebirth played a crucial role in forming that movement; they broke a critical stalemate among women's organizations, set much of the early agenda, legitimated the idea of women fighting for their rights, provided legislative tools, and helped to establish a network of women nationwide who could be easily mobilized for the cause of women.[36]

Notes

1. Betty Friedan, *It Changed My Life: Writings on the Women's Movement* (New York: Random House, 1976), 77.
2. Esther Peterson to the Secretary, 26 January 1966, folder PE-4-2, "Peterson, Esther, 1966," box 400, RG 174 (Wirtz), NA; Citizens' Advisory Council on the Status of Women, transcript of the meeting of 31 May 1966, pp. 93–96, box 13, CACSW papers, National Archives (hereafter NA).
3. "How NOW Began, Background Memorandum on NOW from Betty Friedan," n.d. [1967], in folder "NOW," box "Women's Organizations," Catherine East papers (Arlington, Va.); Interview with Catherine East, 6 July 1978 (Arlington, Va.); Frances Kolb, "The National Organization for Women: A History of the First Ten Years," chap. 1 (unpublished manuscript); Friedan, *It Changed My Life*, 77–84.
4. Citizens' Advisory Council on the Status of Women, transcript of the meeting of 12 October 1964, pp. 30–35, box 13, CACSW papers, NA.
5. Friedan, *It Changed My Life*, 77–84; East interview, 6 July 1978 (Arlington, Va); Friedan, "How NOW Began," in folder "NOW," box "Women's Organizations," Catherine East papers (Arlington, Va.).
6. Esther Peterson to John Macy, n.d., in folder "NOW," box "Women's Organizations," Catherine East papers (Arlington, Va.).
7. According to Clarenbach, Esther Peterson was more receptive to the idea of permitting resolutions than the others, but Peterson later explained that she could not side with Clarenbach because Keyserling opposed the plan and insisted that Peterson not usurp her authority at the conference (Interview with Esther Peterson, 17 June 1980 [Washington, D.C.]; Telephone interview with Kathryn Clarenbach, 22 June 1981 [Madison, Wis.]). Friedan, "How NOW Began," in folder "NOW," box "Women's Organizations," Catherine East papers (Arlington, Va.); Friedan, *It Changed My Life*, 77–84; *Washington Post* and *Washington Evening Star*, 1 July 1966, clippings, in folder "Publicity," drawer "1966 Conference," PCSW papers (Washington, D.C.); *U.S. News and World Report*, 4 July 1966, 61–62, clipping in folder "NOW," Esther Peterson papers (in Peterson's possession).
8. Mary Keyserling, "Report to the Secretary on the Third National Conference of Commissions on the Status of Women, June 28–29–30," 12 July 1966, in folder "1996—Committee—ICSW (June–July)," box 349, RG 174 (Wirtz), NA; Olya Margolin to Andrew Biemiller, 5 August 1966, folder 22, box 55, Legislative Reference Files, Meany Archives.
9. Kolb, "National Organization for Women," chap. 1.
10. *Detroit News*, 13 November 1966, clipping, in folder "General 1964–66," box "Title VII," Catherine East papers (Arlington, Va.); Toni Carabillo, "A Passion for the Possible," *Do It NOW* 9, no. 9 (October 1976): 5–8.

11. Carabillo, "A Passion for the Possible"; Friedan, *It Changed My Life*, 83–85; Kolb, "National Organization for Women," 4, 23, 39–44; Judith Hole and Ellen Levine, *Rebirth of Feminism* (New York: Quadrangle Books, 1971), 84.

12. Carabillo, "A Passion for the Possible," 5–8; National Organization for Women, "An Invitation to Join," September 1966, reel 110, NWP papers (microfilm ed.); National Organization for Women, "Statement of Purpose," in *Up From the Pedestal: Selected Writings in the History of American Feminism*, ed. Aileen S. Kraditor (Chicago: Quadrangle Books, 1968), 363–69.

13. Friedan, "How NOW Began," in folder "NOW," box "Women's Organizations," Catherine East papers (Arlington, Va.).

14. Esther Peterson to John Macy, attached to untitled memorandum beginning, "The specific events I have set forth . . . ," n.d., in folder "NOW," Esther Peterson papers (in Peterson's possession); Esther Peterson to John Macy, n.d., in folder "NOW," box "Women's Organizations," Catherine East papers (Arlington, Va.).

15. Kolb, "National Organization for Women," 19–33; National Organization for Women, "Targets for Action, 1966–67" (draft), 26 October 1966, in folder "NOW," box "Women's Organizations," Catherine East papers (Arlington, Va.).

16. Kolb, "National Organization for Women," 25, 30–31; Friedan, *It Changed My Life*, 34.

17. Kolb, "National Organization for Women," 20–21.

18. NOW, "Statement of Purpose," in Kraditor (ed.), *Up From the Pedestal*, 363–369.

19. Betty Friedan to John Macy, 24 January 1967, in folder "NOW," Esther Peterson papers (in Peterson's possession); Stephen Shulman to Edith Green, 27 February 1967, in folder "EEOC," box 67-12, Edith Green papers, OHS.

20. Esther Peterson to the officers of NOW, 15 December 1966, in Betty Friedan papers, cited in Kolb, "National Organization for Women," 112.

21. Betty Friedan to Marvin Watson, 5 December 1966 (plus attachments) folder HU3 (General), box 58, LBJL Library (hereafter LBJL).

22. Harry McPherson, Jr., to Kathryn Clarenbach, 20 March 1967, folder S2-3/1967/HU2/Pro/A–Z, box 90, LBJL.

23. Penelope H. Thunberg to Willard Wirtz, 14 April 1967, in folder "H.R. 643(2)," box "Women," Esther Peterson papers, Schlesinger Library (hereafter SL); Attachment 2 to FPM letter 713–7, 13 October 1967, "Catherine East to Esther Peterson, 17 February 1967," in folder "Government—Federal Woman's Award, 1963, 1966–67," box "Correspondence Files," Esther Peterson papers, SL; Joseph Goldberg to Esther Peterson, 30 September 1966, in folder "NOW," Esther Peterson to the Secretary, 24 March 1967, [no folder], Esther Peterson papers (in Peterson's possession); Willard Wirtz to the President, 2 June 1967, attached to Wilfred Rommel to Mr. Levinson, 21 June 1967, folder HU2-1 (Exec.), box 43, LBJL; Harry McPherson, Jr., to Kathryn Clarenbach, 20 March 1967, folder SP2-3/1967/HU2/Pro/A–Z, box 90, LBJL; Francena Miller to the President, 19 October 1967, folder HU3 (General), box 58, LBJL; White House press release, 28 February 1966, folder MA1/F, box 2, LBJL; White House press release, 10 October 1967, in folder "1967—Committee—ICSW (Oct.–Dec.)," box 53, RG 174 (Wirtz), NA; Betty Friedan, Report of the President, NOW Second National Conference, 18 November 1967, reel 110, NWP papers (microfilm ed.); U.S. Congress, House, 90th Cong., 1st sess., 16 and 17 October 1967, *Congressional Record* 113: 28948–28949, 29098–29099; Federal Woman's Award Study Group on Careers for Women, Progress Report to the President, 3 March 1967, in notebook "ICSW meeting, 18 April 1967," box 23, CACSW papers, NA.

24. Betty Friedan, Report of the President, NOW Second National Conference, 18 November 1967, reel 110, NWP papers (microfilm ed.).

25. Wisconsin Commission Resolution, 20 April 1966, in folder "1966—Committee—ICSW (Jan.–Apr.)," box 349, RG 174 (Wirtz), NA; Dorothy Height to Luther Holcomb, 28 July 1966, in folder "Women's Bureau, Interdepartmental Committee on the Status of Women," reel 25, DOL microfilm, LBJL; "Statement adopted by the Commissioners at meeting #123 of August 19, 1963," in folder "1967—Committee—ICSW (Feb.)," box 53, RG 174 (Wirtz), NA; Esther Peterson to Willard Wirtz, 9 December 1966, in folder "ICSW meeting, 17 January 1967," box 23, CACSW papers, NA; Summary of meeting

with representatives of Consumers League, 4 January 1967, in folder "1967—Committee—ICSW (March)," box 53, RG 174 (Wirtz), NA; Mary Keyserling to Esther Peterson, 23 January 1967, in folder "Title VII," reel 17, DOL microfilm LBJL; Draft working paper, Title VII and State Protective Laws, in folder "Equal Opportunity (1)," reel 20, DOL microfilm, LBJL; Proposed Department of Labor position on state labor standards relating to the employment of women and their relationship to Title VII of the Civil Rights Act of 1964, 14 March 1967, in folder "Title VII," reel 17, DOL microfilm, LBJL; Department of Labor position on state labor standards laws relating to the employment of women and their relationship to Title VII of the Civil Rights Act of 1964, 16 March 1967, in folder "Labor Standards," reel 16, DOL microfilm, LBJL; Draft position paper on inter-relationship of state labor legislation and Title VII of the Civil Rights Act of 1964, 2 February 1967, attached to Title VII and State Protective Laws, draft working paper, n.d., attached to Briefing for meeting with representatives of the National Consumers League, 8 March 1967, in folder "1967—Committee—ICSW (March)," box 53, RG 174 (Wirtz), NA.

26. Despite the new policy, the issue was finally decided by the courts. Litigation, supported by NOW and other feminist groups organizing in its wake, raised the matter repeatedly, and by 1971 federal courts ruled consistently that hours laws and weight-lifting laws that applied only to women were invalidated by Title VII. . . . [See, e.g.,] *Rosenfeld v. Southern Pacific*, 293 F. Supp. 1219 (C.D. Cal. 1968), Aff'd, 444 F.2d. 1219 (9th Cir. 1971).

27. CACSW, "Summary of Equal Employment Opportunity Commission Hearings."

28. Carabillo, "A Passion for the Possible," 5–8; Hole and Levine, *Rebirth of Feminism*, 40–44; Equal Employment Opportunity Commission press release, 6 August 1968, in folder "Equal Employment Opportunity, President's Commission on," box 68–4, Edith Green papers, OHS; *Federal Register* 33 (14 August 1968): 11539; Freeman, *Politics of Women's Liberation*, 76–79; Jacob Potofsky to Willard Wirtz, 7 March 1968, and Willard Wirtz to Jacob Potofsky, 29 April 1968, in folder "WA-3 Employment Advancement 1968," box 95, RG 174 (Wirtz), NA.

29. Freeman, *Politics of Women's Liberation*, 80–81; Jean Witter to Alice Paul, 15 April 1968, reel 111, NWP papers (microfilm ed.). Congress submitted the ERA to the states in March 1972. In 1982, when the ratification period expired, the ERA went down, having won approval from only 35 of the 38 states needed. . . .

30. National Organization for Women press release, 20 November 1967, in folder "NOW" box 92, Martha Griffiths papers, BHL; Miriam Holden to Miss Newall, 1 February 1967, and Ernestine Powell to Alice Paul, 25 January 1968, reel 110, NWP papers (microfilm ed.).

31. Alice Paul oral history, pp. 530–535.

32. Margery Leonard, "The Equal Rights Amendment in the New Hampshire Primary," telegram sent to all presidential candidates by Betty Friedan, 15 May 1968, National Organization for Women press release, 6 May 1968, George Wallace to Alice Paul, 20 July 1968, Statement by former Vice-President Richard M. Nixon on the Equal Rights Amendment, [July 1968], reel 111, NWP papers (microfilm ed.); *New York Times*, 7 May 1968; National Organization for Women press release, 6 May 1968, reel 111, NWP papers (microfilm ed.).

33. See Sara Evans, *Personal Politics: The Roots of Women's Liberation in the Civil Rights Movement and the New Left* (New York: Knopf, 1979).

34. See Cynthia Harrison, *Women's Movement Media* (New York: Bowker, 1975), for a contemporaneous compilation of the publications of the women's movement.

35. Freeman, *Politics of Women's Liberation*, 83–92, 145–151.

36. For discussions of the policy impact of the women's movement, see Freeman, *Politics of Women's Liberation;* Hole and Levine, *Rebirth of Feminism;* Irene L. Murphy, *Public Policy on the Status of Women: Agenda and Strategy for the 70s* (Lexington, Mass.: Lexington Books, 1973); and Joyce Gelb and Marian Leif Palley, *Women and Public Policies* (Princeton: N.J.: Princeton University Press, 1982).

Chapter 25

State Building, Health Policy, and the Persistence of the American Abortion Debate

Helene Silverberg

Why are American policies about abortion the focus of such political conflict? Political scientist and lawyer Helene Silverberg employs a cross-national perspective to address this question. Examining twentieth-century American health policy and abortion law, she looks at the effects of traditions of limited government in the United States that have undercut health care provision generally. In most European countries, even Catholic nations like Italy, traditions of positive government provide health care to working people and health professionals rather than politicians shape health care provisions, thereby removing abortion from popular contention and debate. She might have added that low birthrates in most European countries motivate health care professionals to promote women's reproductive health. Because the criminalization of abortion puts women's lives and future reproductive capabilities at risk, it is not considered a means of promoting higher birthrates. In the United States, however, high rates of immigration and higher birthrates among immigrants mean that the nation's birthrate is not a source of concern to politicians or health care professionals.

> When we talk compromise on this issue, what we are asked to compromise is a human life. . . . That is not much of a compromise.

—Congressman Henry Hyde (1979)[1]

In the years since the Supreme Court handed down its ruling in *Roe v. Wade* (1973), the abortion controversy has raged across America with increasing vigor. . . . The continuing battle over abortion in the United States contrasts quite sharply with the relatively stable compromises worked out in Western Europe. Over the last twenty years, all but two countries (Ireland and Switzerland) abandoned strict abortion laws in favor of a more permissive stance. Since 1967, when England became the first country to relax its legal restrictions on abortion, the regulations governing when and under what conditions a woman may voluntarily terminate an unwanted pregnancy have changed rapidly and radically[2] As in the United States, the reform of restrictive abortion laws generated divisive national debates. But unlike the United States, Western European countries (with the partial exception of Germany) reached a relatively stable political compromise that helped end the acrimony.[3] In no country has the backlash been so intense, the erosion of the initial decision so rapid, or the question remained so vexed as in the United States.

Excerpted from Helene Silverberg, "State Building, Health Policy, and the Persistence of the American Abortion Debate," *Journal of Policy History* 9:3 (1997): 311–38. Copyright 1997 by The Pennsylvania State University. Used by permission of The Pennsylvania State University Press and the author.

Why has the debate in the United States been so protracted and apparently irresolvable? Why has our political system, usually so adept at forging compromises and making incremental change, been unable to foster an agreement between the combatants? Three explanations dominate the current literature. One common explanation suggests that the American abortion debate persists because abortion as a social practice implicates fundamental moral values on which Americans are deeply divided. Early formulations of this approach tended to focus on gender-related issues, emphasizing Americans' disagreements over changes since the 1960s in women's roles and in attitudes toward sexuality (especially women's) outside marriage; more recent studies have stressed contending views of the sanctity of life and the importance of liberty. In this explanation, the American abortion conflict has endured because compromise on these issues is, by definition, impossible.[4] . . .

A[nother] explanation points to the American system of interest representation. In this view, America's weak political parties and its highly fragmented and diverse interest-group system have hindered efforts to resolve the conflict. American parties (especially since the wave of reforms in the late 1960s) lack the resources and mechanisms for identifying a compromise and then enforcing cooperation among . . . congressional members and between Congress and the executive branch. This cooperation has been made all the more difficult in light of the numerous interest groups active in the abortion debate and their increasing influence in electoral politics. Western Europe's stronger and more programmatic parties, it is argued, possessed the tools to forge a compromise and then to impose discipline on their party members. They also enjoyed sufficient organizational autonomy from abortion-related groups to assume—and maintain—a position independent of, and, in some cases, contrary to, the preferences of these organizations.[5]

Plausible as these arguments sound, however, they cannot fully explain the failure of the United States to resolve its abortion debate. Explanations pointing to some intrinsic attribute of abortion seem especially problematic. If these arguments were correct, we would expect debates over abortion to be equally divisive and morally charged both over time and across countries. But this is clearly not the case. Historically, the *meaning* of abortion as a social practice, as well as the extent of controversy it generated, has varied quite dramatically. Until the mid-nineteenth century, abortion was viewed as an aspect of a woman's menstrual cycle and abortifacients were sold over the counter (and used) as a simple means of "unblocking the menses." The successful campaign in the late nineteenth century by American physicians to boost their professional status by criminalizing abortion recast abortion as a medical issue that provided the conceptual underpinnings for what Kristin Luker has called "the century of silence."[6] Cross-national comparisons raise similar problems, for as Mary Ann Glendon has noted, the Western European experience concerning abortion suggests that "political compromise is not only possible but typical."[7] Countries once as deeply divided as our own, including nations with large Catholic populations such as Italy, have found grounds for compromise *despite* conflicting points of view on abortion. The explanation for the American case cannot, therefore, rest solely on the notion that abortion is an *intrinsically* irresolvable social dilemma. Rather, we must ask, *how* and *why* the American debate over abortion came to be constructed in such terms. . . .

In this article, I offer an alternative explanation for the persistence of the American abortion debate. In doing so, I alter the conventional angle of vision on the American abortion in two ways: first, by extending the time horizon back to the postwar period and, second, by placing the current conflict in the context of the historical development of the U.S. state in the domain of health policy.

In Western Europe, administratively autonomous and politically powerful national health ministries, with authority over national health insurance systems, ensured that the "problem" of legal abortion remained defined as a health issue, and was therefore amenable to national compromise.

Searching for the terms of a national settlement in the context of a preexisting public health-care system, European legislators negotiated over the timing, tempo, and terms on which abortion would be incorporated into the national health-care system. Although right-to-life groups forcefully and regularly challenged these settlements, the inclusion of abortion within universal health insurance systems helped to insulate abortion (both conceptually and politically) from the ensuing backlash. Defined as a health (rather than a rights) issue, compromise on legal abortion in Europe has been both possible and relatively stable.[8]

In the United States, I argue, the political viability of the health perspective was greatly diminished by the structure of American health-policymaking institutions inherited from the 1940s. The fragmentation and decentralization of these institutions and the federal government's limited capacity for formulating and overseeing health policy fractured reproductive health issues and left abortion both conceptually isolated and politically vulnerable. During the 1970s, the Supreme Court's willingness to involve itself in the abortion controversy provided members of Congress with a politically attractive alternative to the potentially costly option of using health policy. Whereas Europeans were compelled to fit abortion into a system of universal public health provision, American policymakers could—and did—bypass health policy and embrace a rights-based strategy to abortion policy.

The structure of health-policymaking institutions also frustrated the development of compromise proposals that might have helped to end the controversy.

U.S. STATE CAPACITY IN HEALTH

America's late start in launching its welfare state set powerful limitations on the emergence of federal administrative capacities in the domain of health. Prior to the New Deal, the primary federal health agencies were the U.S. Public Health Service (USPHS), created in 1789 and reorganized by the Public Health Services Act of 1944 to oversee foreign quarantine activities, and the Children's Bureau, created in 1912 in the Department of Labor, which briefly administered the Sheppard-Towner Act, a maternal and child health-care program from 1921 to 1929.[9] In the first years of the New Deal, the federal government seemed poised on the verge of a very substantial expansion of its role in the provision of health care. But President Franklin Roosevelt was compelled to drop national health insurance from the Social Security Bill in 1935, for fear that opposition from the AMA would sink the entire legislative package. . . . The chief health policy accomplishment of the post-war period was the extension of comprehensive health care to veterans through the G.I. bill of 1944. The Veterans Administration, located outside HEW, would administer its own network of hospitals, outpatient clinics, and nursing homes in America's only program of direct delivery of health care.[10]

In the place of a public health-care system, administered and financed by the federal government, the United States developed an extensive system of *private* health insurance and medical institutions, underwritten by federal funds. . . . Thus after the war, when both national health insurance was defeated and the unions gained the right to bargain over health benefits, fringe-benefit packages, including health insurance, became a centerpiece of the American collective-bargaining framework. They quickly spread from unionized to nonunionized occupations and industries to cover the majority of working-class and middle-class families. Administered by private insurance companies and other private health service providers, these arrangements enabled many Americans to enjoy very generous health benefits even in the absence of national health insurance.[11] Governmental authority and federal funds also built and strengthened private health providers during these years.

The Hospital Survey and Construction Act of 1946 (popularly known as Hill-Burton), for example, provided government funds that helped build an extensive network of private hospital and allied institutions.[12]

This framework of private health institutions and insurance systems had two important political consequences for the future of American health provision in general and abortion politics in particular. First, the DHEW never developed the corps of health experts and reservoir of information and analysis that would later be necessary for policy innovation in the area of reproductive health. Federal health capacities did expand during this period—the USPHS's Division of Medical Facilities, the Veterans Administration, and the National Institutes for Health all grew dramatically—but these agencies had little to contribute to the formulation or administration of reproductive health policy.[13] Such learning about reproductive health at this time was taking place within private organizations such as the Ford Foundation, Planned Parenthood of America, and the Population Council, all of which were concerned with the emerging "population problem." Their support for demographic and medical research on reproductive behavior created a new corps of policy-oriented demographers, located at universities and foundations around the country, who were developing new nonmedical, social scienceoriented concepts for analyzing reproductive behavior. But this expertise would not be easily accessible to DHEW policymakers in the 1960s, when a window of opportunity for innovation in these areas briefly opened.[14]

Second, the growth of the private health insurance system removed large sections of the middle and working classes from a potential coalition for national health insurance. With their health costs covered through private subscription plans offered through their place of employment, most middle- and working-class Americans no longer worried about the financial risks associated with serious illness, and the demand for governmental action greatly weakened. For similar reasons, middle-class women's need for public funding of reproductive health services also evaporated. Most major private health insurance carriers, including Blue Cross and Blue Shield, covered family planning and abortion services in their commercial group contracts even before *Roe* expanded the grounds on which women could request an abortion. As the politics of abortion unfolded, the chief concern of most working- and middle-class women would be confined to the legalization of abortion.[15]

The burst of health policy innovation enacted during the Johnson administration did not substantially alter the fundamental structure of health- policymaking institutions inherited from the 1940s. Although Medicare and Medicaid dramatically expanded the federal government's role in health provision (in ways that would lead to a huge rise in U.S. health expenditures), they only minimally expanded the institutional foundations for federal involvement in reproductive health. Rather than substantially expanding and strengthening the federal health bureaucracy, the federal government chose instead to rely upon a wide variety of private and quasi-public third parties— insurance companies, hospitals, physicians—to administer the programs. The result was only a limited expansion of the federal government's capacity for policy innovation and implementation in the area of reproductive health. . . .

These features of the American governmental framework in the realm of health policy, in turn, both delayed and circumscribed federal involvement in family planning when the issue emerged on the national agenda in the early 1960s. As early as 1942, the Children's Bureau had quietly provided small grants to state and local health departments for family planning services through its maternal and child health program (Title V of the Social Security Act). The bureau's emphasis on family planning as an aspect of maternal health gave the program a distinct identity and, importantly, shielded it from controversy, but the bureau never sought to expand its small program. In the late 1950s and early 1960s, as concern about the world's population explosion increased, several top DHEW officials also became interested in family planning. But opposition by Presidents Eisenhower and Kennedy to any federal role in family planning precluded department involvement.[16]

President Johnson's more liberal view of the federal role in family planning provided new opportunities to extend health agencies' responsibilities in the area. Beginning in January 1966, Secretaries of HEW John Gardner and then Robert Finch took several steps to heighten DHEW's capacity for policy-oriented research and centrally coordinated policy implementation. A new Office of Population Affairs was created, to be directed by a new Deputy Assistant for Population Affairs directly responsible to the Assistant Secretary for Health. Dr. Louis M. Hellman, a well-known gynecologist and obstetrician who had openly (and with much publicity) challenged the Catholic Church's influence in the New York City public hospital system in 1958, was appointed to be the new Deputy Assistant.[17] A new National Center for Family Planning Services was established in the Health [formerly Medical] Services Administration, and the NIH's Center for Population Research was reorganized. The department also loosened its regulations to permit the Children's Bureau, the USPHS, and the Health Services Administration to provide grants to states for family planning services. Congress also took action to expand DHEW's role in the provision of family planning. Concerned with AFDC's expanding roles and rising costs (and persuaded by new research by demographers showing the relationship between family size and poverty), in 1967 the House Ways and Means Committee amended the Social Security Act's Titles V (maternal and child health) and XX (Medicaid) to require the provision of family planning services.[18]

These efforts, however, produced limited results. First, DHEW's health agencies failed to provide (or ensure that the states provided) the required new services. Established health-interest groups, working through their longtime allies on the House health and appropriations committees, succeeded in blocking the redistribution of staff and money in the health agencies to the family planning services. In the absence of a major increase in appropriations for health programs, family planning consistently lost out to health concerns with more established constituencies. Second, and equally important, was the strong opposition to family planning by Representative John Fogarty (D-R.I.). As chairman of the House Appropriations' subcommittee on DHEW, he was strategically positioned to frustrate efforts to expand the federal role in family planning by refusing to appropriate funds for this purpose.

*   *   *

On the eve of *Roe v. Wade*, then, the federal government's ability to guide and shape the politics and policy of reproductive health was quite limited. A decade of health and family-planning policy innovation had left a surprisingly meager legacy. Although new programs had been created, little in the way of institution building or even substantial institutional reform had been accomplished. DHEW's administrative and intellectual capacities remained nearly as limited in the area of reproductive health as they had been twenty years before. The federal government's reliance on private actors to provide family planning solved in the short term the problems posed by the recalcitrant health agencies, and it helped attract broad support for the program by distributing funds across numerous congressional districts. But it created new obstacles to the development of federal capacities by strengthening and multiplying the private actors who had a stake in reproductive health policy. Perhaps most important, the institutional and programmatic framework created during these years worked over time to fracture the concept of reproductive health along the administrative and political cleavages that constrained health policy more generally. These arrangements fostered new conceptual boundaries separating health policy, family planning, and abortion that would leave abortion politically vulnerable.

DEFINING THE PROBLEM: RIGHTS VERSUS HEALTH

The initial terms of the contemporary American conflict over abortion reflected the legacies of the nineteenth-century abortion controversy. Between 1850 and 1890, American physicians waged a successful campaign for passage of state laws prohibiting all abortions except those performed on the advice of (and by) a physician, and usually only to save the life of the mother. When concern over abortion reappeared in the early 1960s, the terms of these laws shaped the language and participants of the new debate. Doctors (who sought to bring the laws into conformity with changing professional practice), state public health personnel (concerned about the public health effects of illegal abortion), and district attorneys (who were responsible for prosecuting the state laws) were the first to raise questions about the laws and to agitate for their liberalization. These early participants in the reform campaign viewed abortion in public health and medical terms; they sought only to codify a broader interpretation of the meaning of the laws.[19] They were joined in the late 1960s by groups of middle-class women who increasingly sought repeal (rather than liberalization) of the laws. Although these women (and men) rejected physicians' control of abortion, believing instead the decision belonged solely in the hands of women, most feminists initially viewed abortion as a women's health issue—even if they also increasingly embraced the language of rights to articulate women's demand for sexual and reproductive self-determination.[20]

When efforts to repeal the laws through the state legislature encountered opposition, advocates of legal abortion took the issue to court. In 1967, Colorado, North Carolina, and California passed new laws on abortion and, by the end of 1972, almost a third of the states had "liberalized" their laws. By 1970, five states (Oregon, Alabama, Hawaii, New York, and Washington) had fully legalized abortion. These successes provoked a vigorous countermobilization by the Catholic Church, which increasingly blocked legalization through this route. After 1969, advocates of legal abortion began to shift strategy, taking their campaign to the federal courts, where their legal expertise more than counterbalanced their smaller numbers. The Warren Court had already signaled its willingness to enter this area of social policy in *Griswold v. Connecticut* (1965) and *Baird v. Massachusetts* (1965), and several federal courts had begun to grapple with challenges to state abortion statutes as early as 1969.[21] . . .

The Supreme Court's decision in *Roe* on January 23, 1973, interjected an additional perspective on the meaning of abortion into the growing debate. Working with the Supreme Court's own distinct conceptual tools, Justice Harry Blackmun recast the abortion controversy as a problem of women's constitutional right to privacy. *Roe* maintained that the Fourteeth Amendment's concept of personal liberty was broad enough to encompass a woman's decision about whether to terminate her pregnancy, although the right to privacy was not unqualified. The Supreme Court clearly saw *Roe* as consistent with the long-standing view of abortion as a health issue, and *Roe* openly deferred to medical authority by rooting a woman's access to abortion on the privacy of her relationship with her doctor. The trimester framework also turned on considerations of a woman's health as it changed over the course of her pregnancy. But the Supreme Court's central view of abortion was that it was a privacy right. In its view, the proper role for government was rights enforcement.[22]

The ensuing uproar in Congress revealed the power of the contending perspectives. The legalization of abortion through constitutional interpretation rather than enactment of new legislation led opponents of *Roe* to turn initially to constitutional amendments guaranteeing the "right to life" to the unborn. By November, more than two dozen resolutions to overturn *Roe* by constitutional amendment were before the House and Senate Judiciary committees.[23] After delaying more than a year, the Senate Judiciary Committee's Subcommittee on Constitutional Amendments, chaired by presidential hopeful Birch Bayh (D-Ind.), held Congress's first full-scale hearings on abortion, lasting from March 1974 through May 1975. In extensive testimony before the committee, health and medical experts from the family planning issue network emphasized the ways in which legal abortion furthered important public health goals and enhanced women's personal health. Christopher Tietze, a physician, demographer, and senior consultant at the Population Council, testified that from "a medical and public health perspective . . . legal abortion is a necessary component of a complete system of voluntary fertility control."[24] Although DHEW did not take a position on the amendments, Dr. Carl Tyler, chief of the Family Planning Evaluation Division of DHEW's Centers for Disease Control, also testified to the favorable health effects of legal abortion.[25] But the hearings also revealed the growing appeal of the language of rights to both supporters and opponents of *Roe*. Cardinal John Krol, archbishop of Philadelphia and president of the U.S. Catholic Conference, speaking in favor of a constitutional amendment, argued that "the right to life is not an invention of the Catholic Church . . . [but] a basic human right which must undergird any civilized society."[26] The subcommittee failed to approve any constitutional amendment and efforts to bypass the Judiciary Committee also failed.[27] Nevertheless, within a few years, the language of rights raced through Congress and quickly marginalized the health perspective on abortion.

*   *   *

The Supreme Court's perspective prevailed for three reasons. First, it possessed several institutional advantages not shared by DHEW. In particular, its institutional authority and the intellectual coherence of its jurisprudence strengthened the appeal of the rights approach. The Court's prestige was at its peak in the early 1970s, bolstered by wide respect for its decisions in civil rights cases, and its opinion carried great weight among members of Congress. Congress's many lawyers assured the Court's perspective an audience familiar with, and supportive of, its approach to social problems. The Supreme Court's formal independence from the political process strengthened the view that its approach was based on neutral, impartial principles rather than informed by departmental or partisan bias. Finally, the intellectual force of the Court's approach was enhanced by the fact that the language of rights, including a "woman's right" to access to an abortion, operated within an established tradition of argument.

By contrast, DHEW remained a weak and much maligned federal department, widely regarded in Congress as incompetent and poorly managed. Its views carried little weight in Congress, particularly during this period of divided government. The health perspective was further disadvantaged by the department's inability to make a comparably powerful or coherent case. Its long-standing organizational weaknesses were compounded by the reorganization accomplished under the banner of Nixon's "New Federalism," in which the department had . . . drastically cut its specialized family planning staff.[28] The department's limited administrative resources thus hampered its ability to construct new (and strengthen old) rationales for the health perspective. Finally, DHEW's extreme vulnerability to charges of partisan or agency bias, as well as to retribution from opponents of abortion on the House Appropriations Committee, further disadvantaged the health perspective. The department consistently declined to promote a health-oriented understanding of abortion, and the weakness of its case when it did invited charges that its views were political rather than based on its expertise in health policy.

Second, the rights approach fit far better with the federal government's existing administrative capacities and policy commitments in the domain of health policy. From the perspective of liberal Democrats and other supporters of *Roe*, rights-based policymaking was attractive because it did not require any institution building in DHEW or new health programs that might disturb interest groups attached to existing health institutions and policies. Nor did it require expanding the federal government's limited capacity for delivering health care. Indeed, as Catherine McKinnon and others have noted, *Roe's* formulation of abortion as a *privacy* right relieved the federal government of any obligation to take positive action in this area.[29]

The triumph of the rights-based strategy had important consequences for subsequent intellectual and programmatic approaches to abortion by helping to weaken the political coalitions and institutions needed to sustain the health approach to abortion. Unable to directly challenge *Roe* through passage of a constitutional amendment, opponents of legal abortion turned the language of rights on federal health programs, hoping to chip away at the financial support, moral legitimacy, and political shelter abortion received through them. The vulnerability of these programs, a direct legacy of the structure of postwar health-policymaking institutions, both encouraged and facilitated this campaign. Over the next three years, opponents of legal abortion amended a wide variety of bills, including the omnibus Health Program Extension Act of 1973, the Nurses Training Act of 1975, the Legal Services Corporation Act of 1974, the Health Revenue Sharing and Health Services Act of 1975, and the National Science Foundation reauthorization bill to exclude all abortion-related activities.[30]

* * *

The emergence of Medicaid funding as the central battleground of the American abortion conflict directly reflected these developments. As one of the federal government's largest health programs, and the one that provided health care primarily to young women, Medicaid provided substantial (between $45 to $50 million in 1973) funding for abortion.[31] Medicaid was an easy target for conservatives, who had failed to win passage of a constitutional amendment overturning *Roe:* unlike Medicare (or the public health insurance programs in Europe), it was funded through the annual appropriations process and its public support was relatively narrow, since it subsidized health care only for the poor. ... Democratic acquiescence to the [Hyde Amendment] marked a key turning point, as American abortion politics broke along the central political fault line created by American health policy. Four years later, in *Harris v. MacRoe* (1980), the Supreme Court upheld the Hyde Amendment by declaring that *Roe* did not require the federal government to fund abortion. In writing for the majority, Justice Potter Stewart argued that "it simply does not follow that a woman's freedom of choice carries with it a constitutional entitlement to the financial resources to avail herself of the full range of protected choices."[32]

By 1977, then, Congress had firmly embraced the rights-based approach to abortion policy. Rights-based policymaking had proved politically attractive to both sides of the abortion debate, but it had negative consequences for the future shape of the conflict. The successful effort to sever abortion from its already limited institutional and conceptual moorings in federal health policy left abortion without the conceptual cover and political support health policy provided. It also weakened the institutional positions from which supporters of the health perspective could operate. Moreover, once abortionrelated activities were banned from health programs, the non-negotiability of rights locked Congress in a stalemate for which it could not devise a solution.

Clinton's election in November 1992 initially seemed to promise still further conflict within the old, divisive framework of American abortion politics. As the first pro-choice president since *Roe*, Clinton moved swiftly to reverse the restrictive policies of previous administrations. He appointed Donna Shalala, a strong supporter of abortion rights, to the key position of Secretary of Health and Human Services, and he lifted the executive order banning abortion counseling in federally funded family planning clinics. Most important, he omitted from the DHHS budget the ban on Medicaid funding of abortion for the first time in twelve years, permitting the states to decide whether to fund abortion. This approach conformed more to Clinton's own federalist sympathies; it also promised to relieve him of a big political headache by shifting the Medicaid funding debate to the states.[33] Clinton also endorsed several abortion-related measures emerging from the Democratic Congress. Clinton supported the Freedom of Choice Act, which would have codified *Roe* and overturned most restrictions passed by the states since *Webster*, and he signed the Clinic Access bill when it arrived on his desk.[34] Beyond these relatively limited policy initiatives, however, Clinton did not seem disposed to launch a direct challenge to the existing framework of abortion politics.

Central to Clinton's strategy for consolidating his election coalition, however, was health-care reform. Clinton made health-care reform one of the centerpieces of his campaign in an effort to capitalize on the concern of middle-class Americans about the affordability of health care. In January 1993, Clinton appointed Hillary Rodham Clinton to head the National Health Care Reform Task Force to draw up plans for a massive overhaul of the health-care system. The task force brought together Clinton political advisers with more than three hundred health care experts drawn from academia, as well as both the public and the private health-care systems, who were prepared to rethink fundamentally the federal government's role in health-care provision. This assemblage of policy intellectuals provided the executive branch with precisely the wide-ranging policy-oriented technical expertise, analytical tools, and holistic vision of health care that DHHS had long lacked. When Clinton's bill was finally presented to Congress in September 1993, the Task Force's proposal exploded the old boundaries that had come to separate health policy, family planning, and abortion, and it promised to the lay the groundwork for a new politics of abortion.[35]

The Health Security Act outlined a new framework for the purchase and regulation of health insurance and the delivery of health care. It created a new National Health Board to set quality standards and to approve the state benefit packages authorized by the act, and it gave both DHEW and the Department of Labor responsibility for overseeing the system. It required all Americans to enroll in a health plan and mandated a standard package of health benefits that included abortion services. (The Clinton bill did not use the word "abortion," but administration officials said it was included in coverage for "pregnancy related services.") The new health system was to be financed primarily by employers, who were required to pay at least 80 percent of the average local cost. Together, these features of the bill promised dramatically to expand access to abortion services by compelling employers to subsidize abortions for low-income women, which the federal government itself had refused to do since the Hyde Amendment. Moreover, this reconfigured delivery system promised to end the extreme political vulnerability of health-care provision (including access to abortion services) for low-income women. The new health alliance system, into which Medicaid was to be subsumed, established a single health system for both middle-class and poor women. Together, this new set of institutions and mechanisms had the potential to transform the conceptual underpinnings of the American abortion debate by treating abortion as a health service like any other.[36]

The demise of Clinton's plan has been analyzed elsewhere and need not be repeated here.[37] Disagreement over abortion was only one of many conflicts that helped doom national health reform. It is sufficient for purposes of the argument presented here to note the ways in which the new institutional framework promised by the bill (temporarily) redefined the strategic environment for members of Congress and interest groups. The evolution of the bill passed by the Senate Finance Committee, the committee viewed as the most representative of the Senate and which had never dealt with abortion policy before, is especially illustrative. Initially, abortion opponents on the committee tried and failed to exclude abortion explicitly from the list of covered services. The urgent need for some agreement encouraged John Danforth (R-Mo.), a moderate Republican who had not previously been active in the abortion debate, to offer a compromise in the form of an expanded "conscience clause." According to the terms of Danforth's proposal, an employer who opposed abortion could refuse to buy a health insurance plan that included it. In addition, providers would not have to perform services, and insurance companies would not have to cover services, to which they objected on moral or religious grounds. In each of these respects, the Senate Finance Committee's compromise was not unlike the one that emerged in Europe, and it won the support of a majority of the committee's members. The bill passed the full committee 11 to 6.[38]

To be sure, the Senate Finance Committee's capacious "conscience clause" threatened to undercut the principle of a universal health-care package that included abortion, as feminist groups were quick to note.[39] But the emergence of a compromise that reinserted abortion back into health policy and won the support of congressional moderates of both parties offered a glimpse of the new abortion politics that might have taken hold had national health-care reform passed.

CONCLUSION: AMERICAN STATE CAPACITIES AND THE ABORTION DEBATE

In the analysis presented here, the particularly tenacious American abortion debate emerges fundamentally as a problem in American state building in the domain of health policy. In the United States, the Department of Health, Education, and Welfare never possessed the capacity to elaborate a coherent and persuasive intellectual framework that defined abortion in health terms. Nor did the federal government possess the organizational capacities that would have been necessary to implement this vision. Instead, DHEW's limited intellectual and organizational capacities in the decades prior to *Roe* opened the way for the Supreme Court's rights-oriented perspective to set the terms of Congress (and, subsequently, national) debate. Once the American abortion debate had taken shape in these terms, and once both politicians and interest groups developed a strong stake in this view, it became very difficult to reorient the debate in ways more amenable to compromise. Conventional views of the American abortion debate have thus clearly captured a key element of the explanation for the tenacity of the American abortion conflict; the current rights-oriented terms of the debate *have* clearly hampered the search for a compromise all Americans can live with. But these terms, I have suggested, reflect the prior historical development of the U.S. state in the domain of health care rather than the intrinsic character of the issue, the problem of judicial review, or the interest representation system.

The argument presented here also raises important questions about the implications *specifically for women* of the trade-offs involved in national settlements on abortion. From one perspective, European political compromises may seem to have been achieved at the expense of women. In many respects, European laws regulating access to abortion appear to be more restrictive than the terms set out in *Roe.* Moreover, and perhaps more important, European women's access to abortion has not been secured through the creation of a specific individual right and so appears more vulnerable to shifting political winds than the legal guarantee American women possess in *Roe.*[40] But the analysis presented here challenges the conventional view. The most important factor in determining women's access to abortion is not the formal terms of the law, but the availability of health facilities providing abortion services within a distance women can reasonably reach and at a cost they can afford. From this perspective, American women's access to abortion is quite limited. The concentration of abortion providers in major cities and their near absence in rural areas, combined with a system of private financing of health care, have severely restricted American women's access to abortion *in practice*—despite the rights secured in *Roe.*[41] . . . Indeed, European women's right to abortion may prove to be even more secure than American women's precisely because it has been embedded—institutionally and conceptually—in a national health-care system with broad, cross-class political support.

Notes

1. U.S. House of Representatives, *Congressional Record*, 9 October 1979, 27536.
2. Rebecca Cook and Bernard Dickens, "A Decade of International Change in Abortion Laws: 1967–1977," *American Journal of Public Health* 68 (July 1978): 637–44; idem, "International Developments in Abortion Laws: 1977–1988," *American Journal of Public Health* 78 (October 1988): 1305–11; Stanley K. Henshaw, "Induced Abortion: A Worldwide Review, 1990," *Family Planning Perspectives* 22 (March-April 1990): 76–89.
3. For an evaluation of recent abortion politics in Western Europe see Joni Lovenduski and Joyce Outshoorn, eds., *The New Politics of Abortion* (London: Sage, 1986); and Drude Dahlerup, ed., *The New Women's Movement: Feminism and Political Power in Europe and the USA* (London, 1986), part 1.
4. See, for example, Laurence Tribe, *The Clash of Absolutes* (New York, 1990); Ronald Dworkin, *Life's Dominion: An Argument About Abortion, Euthanasia, and Individual Freedom* (New York, 1993); Roger Rosenblatt, *Life Itself: Abortion in the American Mind* (New York, 1992). Earlier formulations that emphasize gender-related issues include Kristin Luker, *Abortion and the Politics of Motherhood* (Berkeley, 1984), and Faye Ginsburg, *Contested Lives* (Berkeley, 1989).
5. See, for example, Gilbert Y. Steiner *et al.*, eds., *The Abortion Dispute and the American System* (Washington, D.C., 1983).
6. Luker, *Abortion and the Politics of Motherhood*, chap. 3; James C. Mohr, *Abortion in America: The Origins and Evolution of National Policy* (New York, 1978); and Carroll Smith-Rosenberg, "The Abortion Movement and the AMA, 1850–1880," in Carroll Smith-Rosenberg, ed., *Disorderly Conduct* (New York, 1985), 217–44.
7. Glendon, *Abortion and Divorce in Western Law* (Cambridge, Mass., 1987), 40.
8. See, for example, Lovenduski and Outshoorn, eds., *The New Politics of Abortion;* Keith Hindell and Madeleine Simms, *Abortion Law Reformed* (London, 1971); David Marsh and Joanna Chambers, *Abortion Politics* (London, 1981); Paul Sachdev, ed., *International Handbook on Abortion* (New York, 1988); Eva Maleck-Lewy, "Between Self-Determination and State Supervision: Women and the Abortion Law in Post-Unification Germany," *Social Politics* 2 (Spring 1995): 62–75.
9. Steven Jonas, David Banta, and Michael Enright, "Government in the Health Care Delivery System," in Steven Jonas, ed., *Health Care Delivery in the United States* (New York, 1977), 297–98. On the Children's Bureau and the Sheppard-Towner Act, see Theda Skocpol, *Protecting Soldiers and Mothers* (Cambridge, Mass., 1992).
10. Frank J. Thompson, *Health Policy and the Bureaucracy: Politics and Implementation* (Cambridge, Mass., 1981), chap. 6.
11. Paul Starr, *The Social Transformation of American Medicine* (New York, 1982), book 2, chap. 2; Beth Steven, "Blurring the Boundaries: How the Federal Government Has Influenced Welfare Benefits in the Private Sector," in Margaret Weir, Ann Shola Orloff, and Theda Skocpol, eds., *The Politics of Social Policy in the United States* (Princeton, 1988).
12. Thompson, *Health Policy and the Bureaucracy*, chap 2; Starr, *The Social Transformation of American Medicine*, 348–51; 375–77.
13. Thompson, *Health Policy and the Bureaucracy*, 30–38, 187–97; Starr, *The Social Transformation of American Medicine*, 338–47.
14. Donald T. Critchlow, "Birth Control, Population Control, and Family Planning: An Overview," *Journal of Policy History* 7, no. 1 (1995): 8–9.
15. David Rothman, "A Century of Failure: Health Care Reform in America," *Journal of Health Policy, Politics, and Law* 18 (Summer 1993): 273–77; Charlotte F. Muller, "Health Insurance for Abortion Costs: A Survey," *Family Planning Perspectives* 2 (October 1970): 12–20. In many cases, abortion coverage was broader than state law since most group policies did not restrict their benefit to in-hospital procedures.
16. Phyllis Tilson Piotrow, *World Population Crisis: The United States Responds* (New York, 1973), chap. 6; Critchlow, "Birth Control, Population Control, and Family Planning," 10–11. Kennedy did, however, quietly endorse federally sponsored basic research in the area of human reproduction.
17. On Hellman, see "A Tribute: Louis M. Hellman (1980–1990)," *Family Planning Perspectives* 12 (January–February 1991): 36–37.

18. Piotrow, *World Population Crisis*, 141–42.

19. Luker, *Abortion and the Politics of Motherhood*, chaps. 2, 4.

20. *Ibid.*, chap. 4; Claudia Dreifus, ed., *Seizing Our Bodies: The Politics of Women's Health* (New York, 1977).

21. By the fall of 1970, there were five cases before the Supreme Court, more than twenty cases in the lower federal courts, and many more in the courts of eleven states. Raymond Tatalovich and Byron Daynes, *The Politics of Abortion* (New York, 1981), 24–28. For the best history of *Roe*, see David J. Garrow, *Liberty and Sexuality: The Right to Privacy and the Making of Roe* (New York, 1994).

22. The text of *Roe* can be found in Leslie Friedman Goldstein, ed., *The Constitutional Rights of Women*, rev. ed. (Madison, Wisc., 1988), 336–47. See also Rhonda Copelon, "From Privacy to Autonomy," in *From Abortion to Reproductive Freedom* (Boston, 1990), 35.

23. "Abortion: Campaign to Upset Supreme Court Ruling," *Congressional Quarterly*, 10 November 1973, 2974.

24. U.S. Senate, Committee on the Judiciary, Subcommittee on Constitutional Amendments, *Abortion*, Part 2, 93d Cong., 2d sess. (Washington, D.C., 1976), 4.

25. *Ibid.*, 125–34.

26. "Hearings Air Abortion Controversy," *Congressional Quarterly Almanac, 1974*, 430.

27. "Abortion: Campaign to Upset Supreme Court Ruling," *Congressional Quarterly*, 10 November 1973, 2973–76; "Abortion: Should Constitution Be Amended?" *Congressional Quarterly*, 3 May 1975, 917–22; "Constitutional Convention Sought on Abortion Ban," *Congressional Quarterly*, 1 July 1978, 1677–79; Frederick Jaffe, Barbara Lindheim, and Philip Lee, *Abortion Politics: Private Morality and Public Policy* (New York: McGraw-Hill, 1981), chap. 9.

28. David Weinberg, "Family Planning and the American States," in Elihu Bergman, ed., *Population Policymaking in the American States* (Lexington, Mass., 1974), 75–99.

29. This has become one of the most prominent feminist criticisms of *Roe v. Wade*. See, for example, Catharine MacKinnon, "Privacy v. Equality: Beyond Roe v. Wade," in Catharine MacKinnon, *Feminism Unmodified: Discourses on Life and Law* (Cambridge, Mass., 1987), 93–102.

30. Barbara Hinkson Craig and David M. O'Brien, *Abortion and American Politics* (Chatham, N.J.: Chatham House, 1993), 112–113; *Congressional Almanac, 1973*, 489–90.

31. Craig and O'Brien, 110.

32. The text of *Harris v. McRae* (1980) is reprinted in Goldstein, *The Constitutional Rights of Women*, 439–40.

33. Alissa J. Rubin, "Searching for the Middle," *Congressional Quarterly*, 3 July 1993, 1737. Clinton's position on Medicaid funding was somewhat less than liberals hoped. To avoid forcing the states to pay for Medicaid abortions, the Clinton administration planned to classify abortion as an "optional" rather than "medically necessary" service. Alissa Rubin, "Clinton's Funding Ban Repeal May Leave States in Charge," *Congressional Quarterly*, 3 April 1993, 839–40.

34. "Clinton Reverses Directives; Battle Begins Anew," *Congressional Quarterly*, 23 January 1993, 182; "For Family Planning Program, New Funding and New Day," *Congressional Quarterly*, 6 February 1993, 270; Alissa Rubin, "Clinton's Funding Ban Repeal May Leave States in Charge," 839; idem, "Freedom of Choice Bill Returns: Too Early to Predict Outcome," *Congressional Quarterly Weekly*, 20 March 1993, 675; Alissa J. Rubin, "Deep Divisions over Specifics Could Be Bill's Undoing," *Congressional Quarterly*, 27 March 1993, 755–56; "Issue: Abortion," *Congressional Quarterly*, 11 December 1993, 3389–90.

35. Julie Kosterlitz, "Is Hillary's Team Ready to Play?" *National Journal*, 6 February 1993, 368.

36. *Congressional Quarterly Almanac, 1994*, 321–23. The two leading alternatives to the Clinton bill, introduced by Senator John Chafee (R-R.I.) and Representative Jim Cooper (D-Tenn), also required health insurance plans to offer all "medically necessary and appropriate services," a phrase usually interpreted by the courts to include abortion. Alissa J. Rublin, "Lobbying Focuses on Abortion," *Congressional Quarterly*, 14 May 1994, 12220.

37. See, for example, the excellent articles in *Journal of Health Politics, Policy and Law* 20 (Summer 1995).

38. Alissa J. Rubin, "Mixed Signals," *Congressional Quarterly*, 9 July 1994, 1871; *Congressional Quarterly Almanac, 1994*, 336.

39. Rubin, "Mixed Signals," 1871.

40. As Canadian feminist D. Gail Kellough has put it, "In the United States, women won the symbolic right to choice without the corresponding right of access to medical services. In Canada, women won the symbolic right of access but without the corresponding right to choose." See D. Gail Kellough, "Pro-Choice Politics and Postmodern Theory," in William Carroll, ed., *Organizing Dissent: Contemporary Social Movements in Theory and Practice* (Toronto, 1992), 83.

41. Recent studies show that 93 percent of all counties outside the major cities are without an abortion provider; the lack of access in nonmetropolitan areas has been intensified by a 13 percent reduction since 1985 in the number of hospitals that offer abortion services (a particularly key aspect of availability, since the poor rely heavily on public hospitals for health care). In 1989, the average abortion clinic charged $245 for a first-trimester abortion. Stanley K. Henshaw and Jennifer Van Vort, "Abortion Services in the United States, 1987 and 1988," *Family Planning Perspectives* 22 (May–June 1990): 102–8, 142; Stanley K. Henshaw, "The Availability of Abortion Services in the United States," *Family Planning Perspectives* 23 (November–December 1991): 246–52, 263; J. D. Shelton, E. A. Brann, and K. F. Schulz, "Abortion Utilization: Does Travel Distance Matter?" *Family Planning Perspectives* 8 (November–December 1976). For an explicit comparison of the United States and a Scandinavian country on reproductive health services, see Henry David, Janine Morgall, Mogens Osler, Niels Rasmussen, and Birgette Jensen, "United States and Denmark: Different Approaches to Health Care and Family Planning," *Studies in Family Planning* 21 (January–February 1990): 1–19.

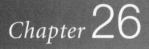

Buscando La Vida: Mexican Immigrant Women's Memories of Home, Yearning, and Border Crossings

María de la Luz Ibarra

With the passage of the Immigration Reform Act of 1965, the framework for new immigration changed dramatically. For the first time since 1882, Asian immigration was treated identically to that from other regions. Moreover, Latin American immigration came under numerical limits for the first time in the nation's history. In the four decades since these changes, Mexico has become the leading sending nation with women comprising more than 40 percent of the migrant flow. Maria de la Luz Ibarra interviewed women domestics in Santa Barbara and captured their feelings about and experiences in the immigration process.

Mexican women are increasingly migrating north, leaving their homes and families behind and looking for private domestic work in U.S. cities. The journey, fraught with danger for those lacking legal entry documents, involves moving across social and cultural divides as well as an international political border. Women bear this dislocation and danger not through unencumbered choice, but within a context of structural constraint. The contemporary movement of Mexican women across borders is rooted in globalization processes—the economic restructuring and crises brought about by unequal relations of power between nations in a capitalist world system.[1] Undocumented Mexican women form part of a labor migration directly tied to changing patterns of capital accumulation that have produced an exodus of at least seven million people from Mexico during the past thirty years.[2]

In the United States . . . Mexican migration has sparked outrage among nativists and some public officials who fear becoming an "alien nation," both culturally and demographically.[3] Mexican migration is perceived as an incursion into a space imagined as sovereign and "American," and immigrants are seen as a threat to the cultural, racial, and economic make-up of that space. Women are viewed as particularly dangerous because of their reproductive potential.[4] For some, the presence of Mexican immigrants represents the possibility of a "reconquest of the American Southwest," and support measures aimed not only at controlling Mexican entry into the United States, but also in controlling access to social benefits such as health care and education.[5] Here, clearly, demographic change brought about by transnationalism is not celebrated, but rather actively resisted to the detriment of migrants.

And yet, despite these negative repercussions to Mexican migrants, even U.S.-centered scholars interested in the local effects of physical movement across borders tend to portray transnationalism as something overwhelmingly positive. In particular, scholars point to transformatory, oppositional, or transnational identity formation as an example of "resistance," and thus an example of the formation of a "valiant subject."[6]

Less discussed are the "narratives of disillusionment," the accounts of negative changes or effects of transnationalism on individuals.[7] In particular, the effects of moving itself—the clandestine crossings as planned and experienced by individual Mexicanas from a broad range of backgrounds and regions—have been glossed over.[8] This is surprising, considering the recognition that "journeys are rich anthropological veins to be mined and interpreted."[9] It is individual crossings, after all, that leave marks on landscape, bodies, and minds, a circumstance that has long informed Chicano/a poetics.[10] For good reason, a Mexican migrant to Santa Barbara described this journey as "*buscando la vida*" (searching for life).

In this paper I focus on undocumented, single women whose experiences have been little explored in the academic literature. Single women are here defined as those who at the time of the study had never been married, or were widowed or divorced—with or without children. I examine these Mexicanas' narratives of crossing and explore the borderlands that lie somewhere between leaving and arriving. I address memories of home—those places that held women's yearnings to go north. I also address memories of the border—that space where violence shatters illusions and reconstitutes women's sense of themselves. Neither transnationalism nor resistance necessarily results in a more just life or a more positive identity. Women's crossing narratives expose the dark underside of an economic regime that increasingly relies on cheap, flexible, and "illegal" bodies to ensure profits for corporations and comfort for U.S. families who, in the restructured, global economy, hire Mexican women as housecleaners and care providers.[11]

MEMORIES OF HOME

For the Mexicanas who were part of my long-term anthropological study on domestic employment in Santa Barbara, California, "home" meant many different places.[12] The restructuring of Mexico's industry and the consequent economic crisis that have taken place in the last thirty years have had a negative impact on a broad spectrum of people—members of the working and middle classes, living in both rural and urban areas. Likewise, migrants derive from both "traditional" and "new" sending areas and—unlike the previous era of bracero migration between 1942 and 1964—include large numbers of women and children.[13] Consequently, there is now a more complex Mexican migrant profile in the United States. . . .

In this article I draw from interviews with thirty single Mexican women who migrated to the United States between 1985 and 2000. This group is heterogeneous and, as E. Valentine Daniel found among Tamils in Great Britain, their "nostalgia for their home country differed qualitatively," as did their reasons for making the trip to the United States.[14] Most Mexicanas' memories were of rural areas, where they felt that their gendered opportunities were more limited than those of urban dwellers. Thirty-two-year-old Anabel, for example, had grown up in a small agricultural town of fifteen hundred people in Chihuahua, where the majority of women married and had children. While she fondly remembered her tightly-knit female-headed, middle-class family and the importance that her mother and grandmother placed on becoming a mother and wife, she knew from an early age that it was not enough for her. She wanted to be able to choose a life outside of marriage, and that meant "earning her own way." It meant finding a life outside of her village "where everyone knew everybody else's business." Work outside of the home was important to her, and going to the United States would be the only way to fulfill this desire, because even Mexico's urban centers no longer offered the opportunities they once did.

Women from rural areas felt that failed romances not only negatively marked them in their small communities, but also created difficult, long-term repercussions. Thirty-six-year-old Lupe, for example, who came from a working-class farming family, spoke of having fallen madly in love with a "handsome liar," who had given her an "illusion" of a better life. Her erstwhile lover, however, did not come through with his promises of marriage, and instead left her with the responsibility of caring for their two young daughters and with a reputation in her hometown of Jalisco as a woman with few morals. She remembers the judgments placed on her and the "unwelcome advances" on her person. In such a small place, it was impossible to escape. And so she decided to become hard "like a man" and begin to think of herself as someone who would need to be employed in order to meet her obligations. For this, she needed to go someplace where there were opportunities. The United States offered this possibility.

Other women felt that limited social options in rural areas exacerbated the effects of sexual violence. Thirty-five-year-old Cecilia, from a small town outside of Acapulco, Guerrero, recalls that "life was always work" in her working-poor family, and she never conceived of marriage as expanding her possibilities. In fact, her parents' experience "taught" her that marriage meant having to bear large numbers of children, and it meant men were not to be trusted, since her father often drank the family's earnings. At the age of seventeen these already-clear images of life were burned into her person: she was kidnapped and raped by a soldier, who then forced her to become his "wife." In his rural village, a place where she had no support or connections, she was a prisoner for four years, and during that time she gave birth to two children and took care of her kidnapper's elderly mother. She was finally able to execute her escape, a process that implied certain death should she be caught. Until she arrived in the state of Jalisco, where she had family, she sat on the bus in a state of terror. Two years later her husband was spotted in her neighborhood, and she knew then that only by going to the United States could she escape "that man forever."

For women in urban areas, memories of home also centered on gender and its relation to roles and careers, sexuality, and violence. However, among middle-class urban women, reminiscences were less about a lack of opportunity and more about financial losses. For these women, memories dwell on the shattering effects of economic crisis on their families, and on the consequences of crisis on their class position. Dora–twenty-one years old and one of the youngest women in the group–had memories of home that revolved around a "nice" apartment in the city where she lived with two siblings, her parents, and her grandmother. Dora remembers many family meals and celebrations, good friends coming over prior to attending sporting events, and going to parties, movies, or shopping malls. For Dora, the most immediate and visible sign of financial strife following the country's 1982 economic crisis was her dissolving consumer lifestyle—the lack of luxuries such as shopping and traveling, and later the inability to find temporary life-enriching work. Crossing into the United States—what she described as "travel"—represented her yearnings of holding on to a piece of her disappearing middle-class life.

For other middle-class Mexicanas from cities, memories of home centered on the negative consequences of the economic crisis on their employment and gendered identities. Thirty-one-year-old Teresa, for example, remembered the initial joy of finding a position as a car salesperson at a Nissan plant during the early 1980s in Mexico City. This was a "good," high-paying job with considerable responsibility that allowed her to construct an identity of herself as a self-sufficient, strong, and upwardly-mobile woman. She remembers paying for her own apartment and helping support her boyfriend, who was often unemployed. Memories of home, however, are also clouded by having been laid off when car sales began to decline, and then working in a string of low-paid jobs, experiences that shattered her sense of strong womanhood and of possibility. It also shattered her sense of "reality," and for more than a year after she lost her job, she felt numb and cut off from the world. She yearned to cross the border in order to recompose herself.

For working-class women in cities, reminiscences are different from those of their middle-class counterparts: memories of home are not only about the period of economic crisis, but about long-term material insufficiency. Jacklyn, a twenty-one-year-old Mayan, lovingly remembered her parents' small house in Merida. There, her grandparents, parents, and siblings lived in four small rooms, a fact that brought tears to her eyes, as she described their poverty and, alongside it, her family's support and kindness to each other. Jacklyn clearly longed for her home, but she also remembered the constant lack of money and, later, her father's failing health and his inability to find a job after being laid off as a municipal street sweeper. These dual images of love and hardship, she said, tugged at her, leaving her unable to sleep some nights as she worried about so many needs in their lives. The United States held the possibility of her being able to help support her family.

The previous vignettes illustrate that Mexicanas' memories of home and nostalgia for it track different places and social possibilities. They also trace intimate details of family life that are not uniform, but rather hold distinct patterns of support, understandings of love, deception, and heartache. The vignettes also sketch yearnings, yearnings to provide material comforts and sustenance in a way that had become familiar, or yearnings to escape conditions, create something new, and find safety for themselves and their families. These diverse yearnings, in the context of structural constraint, are the basis for understanding why so many Mexicanas seek work as domestics in the United States.

CULTURE OF MIGRATION

When describing their different reasons for wanting to leave their homes, of going "in search of a life," Mexicanas clearly spoke about the constraining structural context of limited economic resources and opportunities, and about the constraints of gender and gender relations as potent elements in their memories of home. But women's narratives also make it clear that their yearnings were shaped by a culture of migration present in many communities. Mexicanas who grew up during the 1970s and 1980s heard about others who made the trip to the United States and also saw both men and women migrate. In some cases, women came from families or communities whose members had engaged in international labor migration to the United States for several generations. [15] In other cases, migration was less entrenched but was nonetheless an important part of the experiences of people known to these women. And yet, this culture of migration as perceived by Mexicanas has been ignored in the literature, with one scholar arguing that single Mexican women did not grow up "immersed in a culture that oriented them toward northward migration. [16]

But a culture of migration does include women and subsequently has helped shape their desire to migrate. This "culture" is most evident among migrants from central-western states, because from the late nineteenth century to the present, the majority of Mexican migrants to the United States has come from this region. [17] Not surprisingly, communities in these states have developed rituals to mark both the absence and return of community members, rituals that in turn help recreate the importance of migration to the people who live there. One ritual of absence in the Zamora Valley of Michoacan is the "*ausente* hour" on the radio. In this public service for the benefit of U.S. migrants and their families, letters and messages sent from migrants in the United States are read on the air, and special song requests and dedications are played for wives and sweethearts. [18] This keeps not only the memory, but also the voice and will of the migrant alive. In other rituals, migrants themselves not only mark their absence but their travails and sufferings through votive offerings such as *retablos*, paintings on tin that are left in churches. *Retablos* document the dangers that migrants face away from home, but also point to religious beliefs that help tie migrants to particular places in Mexico and, in fact, from the point of view of believers, help save their lives.[19]

While these public rituals of absence are important, so are those found in private homes. Mexicans most often remember the absent loved ones with photographs placed on family altars and in places of daily living, such as dining and sleeping areas. The women I interviewed described themselves and other family members looking at these photographs on a regular basis. Their gaze was sometimes accompanied by a fleeting touch of the person's photographic image, including making the religious sign of the cross over them as a protective action. Likewise, Mexicanas remember the collection of photographs that over time record changes in the life cycle of those absent. Mexicanas poignantly describe moments of catharsis in front of these pictures—moments in which tears marked the passing of time. Other markers of absence were the gifts that remained after a migrant's visit—blankets, radios, beds, or a room addition. Twenty-eight-year-old Luz described the boxes of chocolates that her grandmother would hoard—never eating them—because these were a tangible symbol of her son's hard work and love. Others recalled the bittersweet weekly or monthly wait for the phone call that for a few minutes brought them closer to their loved one and then left a deep resonance.

Alongside rituals of absence, which help to reproduce the importance of migration in a community or in a household, there are also public rituals of return that do the same thing. In many communities the celebration of the town's patron saint is one such ritual of return. Douglas Massey and his colleagues write: "On this date, migrants join together to pay the costs of music, church decorations, fireworks, and other diversions. Those who have been able to return participate in the processions and liturgical acts, and in his sermon the priest reaffirms the 'great family' with a patron saint who looks over all."[20] Other rituals are planned and paid for by city residents. In a small city in Jalisco, Lupe remembers the yearly Christmas season's *Noche Mexicana* at the Lion's Club. At this event, male migrants back home on vacation are the guests of honor and are treated to all those "Mexican" things—food, hospitality, entertainment, goods—that are perceived to be missing in the United States. Lupe also describes the clandestine flirting and formal courting by these male migrants, activities that promoted for many young women a sense of the United States as a place not only of economic possibility but of romantic entanglements. As Lupe said, "When I saw him I thought he was very handsome, and I wondered what would it be like to go to the United States with him." This ritual of return for men becomes an opportunity to imagine a life away from home for women.

Rituals of return, like rituals of absence, are likewise not limited to public displays. There are more personal events, such as family gatherings, where banquets of *tamales, barbacoa*, or *asado* are prepared in honor of a migrant relative's visit. Likewise, migrants may return to take part in others' important rites of passage, such as a marriage or baptism, and thus reinforce the ties to a place and to people who matter. Other practices that serve to maintain ties between U.S. and Mexican communities are migrants' participation in community improvement projects and politics.[21] In sum, rituals of return solidify the importance of migrants and migration to a community.

In places where a local tradition of migration was less prevalent, personal experiences were important to women who chose migration as an option to improve their lives. In some cases, Mexicanas had migrated to or taken pleasure trips to the United States as younger persons and had good memories of that experience. Margarita, for example, grew up in Mexico City, and as a young woman had attended a three-month art seminar in Los Angles as part of an educational exchange program. When she went back to Mexico, she did so reluctantly, as she liked the American city and the possibilities it held for her. In other cases, women had a girlfriend or a female relative who had gone to the United States. Tere grew up in a rural area of Oaxaca and did not have family members in the United States, but she had a girlfriend who had made the trip. Thus, the United States was at some level a known entity—a real possibility.

The influence of Western culture through the media cannot be underestimated as a source for familiarizing potential migrants with the United States and subsequently making it easier for them to consider moving there.[22] Mexicans are exposed to movies that depict life in the United States, to magazines that favor Western fashions and tastes, and to music that infiltrates the popular imagination. However, Mexicanas do not hold only positive images of the United States. Mexican popular culture in movies, books, and songs also depict life in the north in a more threatening light. Movies like *La India Maria* satirize the dangers faced by undocumented immigrants, while books by writers like Luis Spota call attention to the harsh treatment of Mexicans. In one grating line from a best-seller, Spota writes: "*En Texas ser mexicano no es nacionalidad, sino un oficio. El peor y mas despreciable de todos*" ("In Texas, being Mexican is not a nationality but a job—the worst and most despicable of all").[23] *Ranchera* and *norteño* music tell stories of common people detained and deported, and of the unending search for and daily practice of work in the United States. One of many popular songs by the Tigres del Norte, for example, characterizes the United States as a "*jaula de oro*" ("a golden cage")—a country that simultaneously offers some opportunity for material improvement through work, but also maintains Mexicans in an unequal social position.[24]

Thus, Mexicanas are immersed in a culture of migration that shapes the way they see their world and their possibilities within it. Migration means suffering, but it also means the possibility of personal and family advancement. This fact is one "web of meaning" in a larger complexity of webs that contributes to local Mexican cultures. For men and women, migration is not beyond the bounds of imagination or experience. Imagining crossing the border and imagining being on the "other side," however, are several steps removed from the actual physical process of doing it.

PLANNING TO CROSS THE BORDER

Crossing the border for most women is a pivotal act, one that Leo Chavez considers a rite of passage that marks the transition from one social status to another.[25] He argues that, among other things, this rite involves a process of separation from the country of origin. One neglected aspect of this separation, however, is the everyday practices engaged in by women, which in turn play a role in shaping a culture of migration. To get to the other side of the border requires considerable forethought, effort, and planning. In my sample group, single women most often did not act opportunistically after an invitation to go north; rather, planning was the norm.

Specifically, Mexicanas persuade parents, husbands, or lovers to support their migration; they seek financial help or build up their savings through employment; and they make connections and undertake negotiations with different people (relatives, friends, acquaintances, and ex-employers in the United States) who can help them once they are on the other side. Social networks are crucial for most women, and as others have shown, female networks are essential for Mexicana migrants.[26]

For young single women, one of the most important elements of the planning involves convincing their parents to support their decision to migrate. It is not "seeking permission" to migrate exactly, because in many cases Mexicanas have made up their mind to go regardless of their parents' perspectives. But for women with close family ties, it is important to get their family members to agree and provide emotional support. Twenty-six-year-old Maria, for example, began planning to leave for the United States after protracted conversations with a neighbor who described the income-earning potential in the United States. This meant convincing her father, a task that required a period of more than six months, and then contacting a paternal uncle who lived in Santa Barbara. Maria's father "agreed" to her trip on the condition that she travel with her brother and, once arriving in Santa Barbara, live with her uncle, for whom she would provide domestic assistance. This uncle would also provide an initial loan to pay for the costs of a coyote, or human smuggler. From the time she originally conceptualized the idea to go north to the time she began the journey, eight months had gone by.

Thirty-three-year-old Lulu also sought the blessing of her parents, but would have left even if they had not provided it in a "reasonable" amount of time. Ever since she was a little girl, Lulu had a desire to go to the United States, like her father did six months out of every year. To this end, she saved the income from a job she took for this purpose for a period of two years. Once she had enough money to pay for her transportation and a little extra for living expenses, she worked at convincing her parents. After two months, her parents grudgingly agreed, and she made plans to cross the border clandestinely with her father during the spring. They had both decided spring was safer because neither the cold nor heat would be unbearable. The plan she had worked out through phone conversations was to join a friend's family and begin work as a hotel maid. Her father would then return to Mexico by himself.

Jacklyn, on the other hand, did not have parents who initially and actively opposed her trip when she announced plans to go to Santa Barbara and join her sister. When she told her father that she had been thinking and talking about leaving for over a year, he counseled her to reflect and think about it carefully a little longer, because "the United States changes people." Because she respected her father, Jacklyn did continue to reflect, but eventually came to the conclusion that it was necessary for her to undertake the journey so that she could help provide for her family. She had never been outside of Merida, and so through phone conversations had her sister describe the bus trip to Tijuana and the types of things she might expect on the way. She also sought information about clandestine crossings so that she could arm herself psychologically. She did not want to be a burden, so she asked her sister to help her find a job as child care provider, so that she could be assured employment upon arrival.

Of course, not all women are able to exactly plan the journey north. This is particularly the case for women with weak social networks in the United States prior to their arrival. After saving or borrowing money, some women left Mexico only with the possibility that an estranged parent or sibling might help them once they got to the other side. Ernestina, for example, carefully planned for her trip north—saving money, arranging for care of her children while she was in the United States, and buying goods she thought necessary for her children. Once this was done, she planned the bus trip north to Tijuana. Not until she was safely across the border in the United States, however, did she plan to call three of her brothers whom she had not seen for longer than ten years. Waiting to call, I learned, was a common tactic. When I asked Maria why she had not called estranged relatives prior to leaving for the United States, she said it was too much of a risk. It was easier for these relatives to say no, if the petitioning relative was still in Mexico. But if they were already at the border, it was much more difficult to refuse. Thus, even apparently last-minute actions reveal forethought by Mexicanas crossing the border.

Margarita made the decision to leave Guadalajara with her son, even without a concrete invitation from a relative or friend. She hoped that once she arrived in Tijuana, her father, whom she had not seen in fifteen years, would help her. She had no idea whether the phone number she had been given would still be good when she arrived, whether he would be there, and even whether her father would accept her. This type of waiting strategy is a gamble that does not always work, and some women end up homeless, sleeping under freeway underpasses, and gratefully taking the first live-in domestic job that becomes available. Most often these jobs are the lowest paid and most exploitative, as it is obvious that these Mexicanas have limited options.

A central part of women's journeys north is the planning that takes place before they leave. These everyday separation practices, in turn, become part of the broader system of meaning that shapes local Mexican cultures.

CROSSING THE BORDER

For undocumented women who cross the border on foot, the trip is a test of their bodies, their character, ingenuity, and desperation. Crossing the border is no easy feat. And yet, if we look at the literature on transnationalism, this very crucial part of the trip for Mexicanas is for the most part absent. This absence serves to negate the trauma of crossing experienced by growing numbers of women who seek jobs as private household workers in the United States. This absence, as well, gives the mistaken impression that Mexicanas who go in search of work in a transnational space are like any other job seeker, but they are not. They are criminalized by their crossing, and the southern U.S. border zone is militarized to guard against their entrance.

The historical process of border militarization began in 1848 after the U.S.Mexican War and the American conquest of half of Mexico's former territory. In the last three decades, however, militarization has been spurred to new levels. The U.S. recession of the 1970s was the context within which Leonard Chapman, head of the Immigration and Naturalization Service (INS) and a former general, first conceptualized Mexican immigrants as a "national security threat." In subsequent decades, the United States invested unprecedented amounts of money, men, and machines to keep the United States safe, not only from Mexicans reconfigured as criminals intent on stealing U.S. jobs and social services, but also from the "communist menace" in Central America and drug runners from Latin America."[27]

By 1992, when President Clinton took office, the INS budget had swelled, and much of the infrastructure of deterrence had been laid: night scopes, ground sensors, barriers, armed tanks, and agents were in place along the border. Under the Clinton administration, Congress continued to approve evergrowing budgets for border control, totaling more than four billion dollars for the 2001 fiscal year.[28] Policy in dealing with potential "illegal" border crossers has also changed since 1993. One of the most deadly of these policies, proposed by military intelligence, is to reroute migrants from crossing in populated areas to physically difficult terrain. "Operation Gatekeeper" in California and "Operation Hold the Line" in Arizona are two examples of these policies, both involving more fencing and more agents in populated areas.[29] Since 1993, more than sixteen hundred migrant deaths have been documented, with numbers mounting in the last two years. These deaths are primarily a result of dehydration, hypothermia, and drowning in extreme terrain and weather conditions.[30]

Extreme conditions found in the deserts and mountains are by no means the only danger lurking in the night, however. Human rights organizations also regularly document "abuses" of power at the hands of the border patrol, including sexual violations, beatings, and shootings.[31] Additionally, thieves, drug smugglers, and vigilantes, as well as coyotes themselves, prey on vulnerable people who often carry the money they need to cross the border. The sums are not inconsequential because the increasing difficulty of crossing has raised the amount that migrants need for an "illegal" entry. During the 1980s and early 1990s, the cost of a guide was approximately three hundred dollars, but now it is more in the range of eight hundred to thirteen hundred dollars.[32]

The crossing is often a traumatic event, one with the very real probability of harm or death, and women who survive the experience can have psychological and physical scars. As is the case with victims of torture, Mexican women's narratives about their crossing vacillate between wanting to share the details and then wanting to guard the memories from anyone who, however well meaning, could trivialize their experiences.[33] Initially, Mexicanas I interviewed glossed over events and provided me with a broad and vague description. I respected this boundary, but in each case, the Mexicana would come back to her memories and later verbally guide me to the border, to a fateful day that had altered her in a deep and meaningful way. For example, when first recollecting her memories of crossing, Lupe said, "I have no words to describe what I felt when I saw my children scared, dirty, and tired. What I can tell you is that under no circumstances would I do it again." Her sentence was final, her eyes averted, and I did not press. Only later, Lupe's memories began to slowly unwind and details began to spot her narratives. "Do you remember," she asked me, "when I told you that I crossed?" "Yes," I answered. "You know, that I crossed without papers?" she asked me. "Yes, Lupe," I answered, "You didn't tell me, but I guessed—there's a lot of people who cross that way." "Yes," she answered, "lots of people, right?" I nodded. She went on, "I don't know—one is always left with the memory, and one thinks that one is unique." Then without prompting, and again without looking at my eyes, she said, "It's awful. One feels like a trapped animal—maybe worse because you never imagined it would happen to you." She began her crossing narrative by formally saying, "We made our way to the border, and it was very cold that night." In between long pauses, she continued:

> I was really worried because Joaquin was only one, and with so much cold children can get very ill. And also, I had my other children [ages five and eight], and really all I could think about was them—they were too little. Imagine a child of five walking across the hills? No, it is not just, and I knew it was not just, but one has to eat their rage so that it does not stop you. What gave me strength was that my cousins were there with me, and they each took one of the children—and, well, I had invested so much time, and I had left my life behind, and I really had no other choice but to go forward. And so the coyote . . . there were two ... took us across and we walked a while—I don't know how long. One becomes disoriented with so much worry, but I think very soon . . . The people started shouting, because the lights [border patrol helicopter] were coming toward us. And one of the coyotes told us to get down, but obviously everyone was scared, and I just remember that I couldn't move. Fear paralyzed me, because I was afraid that if I ran they would kill my child. And the worst part was that I couldn't immediately see the other two [cousins and children], and I just shouted out, "Francisco, don't run, they'll kill us." And thank God, he heard me. He shouted back to me, "Here I am cousin." And, I didn't hear anymore because there was a lot of shouting—I don't remember how many men [border patrol] there were, at that time it seemed a lot. I don't think I moved, but the baby's crying and everything else, I was very nervous, and I don't know, one of the agents hit me as he tried to hold someone else, and I fell, and all I could think of was to hold on to my baby. But he fell out of my hands anyway, and that's when I just could not [stand it.] I began to cry out of fear, yes, but also rage. There I was a grown woman with a child, where could I have gone? But the only thing that mattered to them was to get us. I swear to you, I am a good person, but in that moment I wanted to do something to him [border patrol agent]. There I was like an animal, worse, a nothing. I get so angry [she began to cry] . . . but I did nothing. I stayed there and waited for them to load us on the van."

Guadalupe was transported back to Tijuana, and it took her two days to build up the "courage" to try crossing again. The second time, they made it across without being chased by the border patrol.

Once in the safety of her cousin's home in Los Angeles, Guadalupe realized that something in her had "changed." The crossing had marked her in a way that others could not visibly see, but which she could feel. "From that day," she said, "I became harder and more aggressive."

This realization of change was one that other women also described. However, they did not always become harder, but rather just the opposite—they became "damaged," more "nervous," and psychologically vulnerable. Elvia, for example, a small, thin woman with radiant hazel eyes and a pale complexion was thirty-two years old when I first met her. She was constantly moving, getting up from our conversations to undertake small chores, or cutting off the conversation and beginning a new topic. One afternoon as I sat on her bed, and she organized her closet while talking about her small son Horacio, she surprised me by slowing down. She sat beside me and asked if I wanted to know about how she came to the United States. I said yes, and she began to tell me her story in a detached, matter-of-fact voice, as if relating the plot of a movie. She looked at me until she got to the part relating the beatings and the rape. Then she began to cry softly, self-consciously, looking down at her hands, and only occasionally up into my eyes. She began her narrative with, "I came over the mountains with three coyotes. I didn't know there were going to be three, but they just passed us along to each other." She continued:

When we got to the last coyote, we were put in a house, and there were six of them—all wearing guns. Here we were supposed to call the people responsible for paying our way. . . . One of the women who couldn't reach her relatives was really pretty, and I could tell the coyote liked her. He told her, "If you can't find your relative, I can help you get a job and then you can pay me." She said she would like to do this, and he told her to follow him. I had my money with me, but I didn't want to tell them, because I was afraid they would take it without taking me across. [Meanwhile,] a man called his relatives, but the number was no longer in service. The coyotes told him he better find someone soon, or he was going to be sorry. I could tell he was really scared, so I went over to sit by him. He asked me if I thought they would really hurt him, and I said, "No—no one can be that bad." A few hours later, the pretty woman came back, and I could tell she was not well, but, she didn't say anything. . . . [By now a day had gone by] and other people had also not been able to contact their relatives. The coyotes yelled at them, and threatened. I got really scared then, because if I didn't tell them I had the money with me, they would do to me what they were threatening to do to the other people, and if I did tell them, I ran the risk of having the money taken from me. I took the risk and told them. The man who couldn't reach his relative came over again, and asked me for a favor: If anything should happen to him, please call his wife in Tepic, so she would know. I said, yes, and wrote her number down, as well as that of his relative in Los Angeles. . . . Then they took out some of the men who had not been able to reach their relatives. The rest of us were inside the house. Pretty soon we started to hear screams, and my son was at the window—I went to pull him away, and then I saw the blood all over the ground, and bodies being kicked. I couldn't turn away, and I saw my friend run to the bathroom, but they got him. We were all crying inside the house, and the pretty woman told us the coyote had lied to her. He had taken her in his truck and then raped her. The other woman who had not been able to reach her relatives became hysterical, and all of us were hysterical with her. Then those of us with money decided to try to help her, and we collected what we could, but it wasn't enough. We needed four hundred dollars. Then another woman who had a gold bracelet and some rings took them off and put it in with the money. Then the screaming stopped and the coyotes came back in to take our money. We gave it to them, and also the money and jewelry for the woman. But he wouldn't take it. He asked us, "What I am going to do with a bracelet?" Then he told the pretty woman to follow him again. He came back a long time afterwards, but she was not with him. He told us it was time for us to get in the truck, because it was almost dark. He told the woman who had no money to just stay in the house. We didn't know what to do, we were so scared. We walked outside and there was blood everywhere, and we had to step in the blood to get to the truck. We didn't see any bodies. Even the men—who are stronger than women—told us to not say a word, to just stay quiet. We got in the truck, and no words were said.

When she finished her story, she shook her head and closed her eyes for a long time. Finally, she looked up again and asked me, "Why is it so difficult to work?" Why, indeed. Five years after she asked me, the question is still in my mind.

In the context of structural constraints produced by globalization, increasing numbers of single Mexicanas of diverse social class, backgrounds, age, family types, and region yearn for a life that is different from that which economic crisis produced or made worse in their home country. As they dream about a new life, the United States looms large. A pattern and culture of migration in central western Mexican states, as well as evolving networks in new sending areas of Mexico, help support this yearning. Migration is conceptualized as feasible for growing numbers of people, including single women. Yearning is then followed by active planning to find the support and means necessary for making the trip and having some type of security once they reach their destination. But prior to getting to their destination, Mexicanas who must cross the border clandestinely face fear, dislocation, and sometimes injury. These experiences alter the women's sense of themselves, and not always positively, as is often suggested by the bulk of the transnational literature. It is therefore necessary to address transnational migration as a nuanced process and to document the diversity of experiences faced by both men and women.

In the excerpts of narratives I have provided, Mexicana's words shed light on experiences that generally remain "invisible, unknown, and unimagined" as U.S. employers consume the labor that is women's lives.[34] But through these narratives we are able to perceive the tensions inherent in physical movement across political borders—power-laden spaces that at once hold women's hopes for the future as well as a violence that explode their imaginings. This violence, this individual suffering—when multiplied by the many women who form part of the increasing south to north migration—becomes a story of social suffering on the borderlands. To ignore the pain that marks women's narratives of crossing is to sanitize history and not fully understand the meaning of Mexican labor migration in the New World Order.

Notes

1. Saskia Sassen, *The Mobility of Labor and Capital: A Study in International Investment and Labor Flow* (New York: Cambridge University Press, 1988), 55–84.
2. Susan González Baker, Frank D. Bean, Agustin Escobar Latapi, and Sidney Weintraub, "U.S. Immigration Policies and Trends: The Growing Importance of Migration from Mexico," in *Crossings: Mexican Immigration in Interdisciplinary Perspectives*, ed. Marcelo Suárez-Orozco (Cambridge, Mass.: Harvard University, David Rockefeller Center for Latin American Studies, 1998), 79–112.
3. Leo Chavez, "Immigration Reform and Nativism," in *Immigrants Out!: The New Nativism and the Anti-Immigrant Impulse in the United States*, ed. Juan Perea (New York: New York University Press, 1997), 67.
4. Dorothy Roberts, "Who May Give Birth to Children?" in Perea, *Immigrants Out!*, 205–22.
5. Chavez, "Immigration Reform and Nativism," 68; and Pierrette Hondagneu Sotelo, *Gendered Transitions: Mexican Experience of Migration* (Berkeley: University of California Press, 1994).

6. Ong argues that the subaltern migratory subject is reified as an unidimensional "valiant resistor." She notes that poor "immigrants are thus converted from being minorities to be assimilated into the host society into being some kind of universalized lower-class subjects who attain subaltern vindication" (Ong, *Flexible Citizenship*, 9). Michael Peter Smith and Luis Guarnizo also argue that identities forged from "below" are not inherently subversive or counterhegemonic *(Transnationalism from Below* [New Brunswick, N.J.: Transaction Publishers, 1998], 23). For a broader discussion about this reification trend in anthropology, see Sherry Ortner, "Beginning," in *Life and Death on Mt. Everest: Sherpas Himalayan Mountaineering* (Princeton, N.J.: Oxford University Press, 1999, 17–25).

7. Sarah Mahler, *American Dreaming: Immigrant Life on the Margins* (Princeton, N.J.: Princeton University Press, 1995), 75.

8. Leo Chavez, *Shadowed Lives: Undocumented Immigrants In American Society* (New York: Harcourt Brace, 1998). For critique of lack of focus on women, see Juan Gomez-Quiñones, "Outside Inside–The Immigrant Workers: Creating Popular Myths, Cultural Expressions, and Personal Politics in Borderlands Southern California 1986–1996," in *Chicano Renaissance: Contemporary Cultural Trends*, ed. David Maciel, Isidro Ortiz, and Maria Herrera-Sobek (Tucson: University of Arizona Press, 2000), 49–92.

9. Mahler, *American Dreaming*, 75.

10. Some examples include Americo Paredes, *Folktales of Mexico* (Chicago: University of Chicago Press, 1970); Enersto Galarza, *Barrio Boy* (Notre Dame, Indiana: Notre Dame University Press, 1971); Yolanda López, *Who's the Illegal Alien, Pilgrim?* (Offset lithograph, 1978); Gloria Anzaldúa, *Borderlands/ La Frontera: The New Mestiza* (San Francisco: Spinsters/Aunt Lute Books, 1987); Sandra Cisneros, *Woman Hollering Creek and Other Stories* (New York: Random House, 1991); and Carlos Vélez-Ibañez, *Border Visions: Mexican Cultures of the Southwest United States* (Tucson: University of Arizona Press, 1999).

11. Various scholars have observed that there is both a new and increasing demand for Mexican immigrant women to labor as domestics. In particular, see Ruth Milkman, "The Macrosociology of Paid Domestic Work," *Work and Occupations* 25:4 (1998): 483–510; Maria Ibarra, "Mexican Immigrant Women and the New Domestic Labor," *Human Organization* 59:4 (2000): 452-67; and Pierrette Hondagneu-Sotelo, *Dómestica: Immigrant Workers Cleaning and Caring in the Shadows of Affluence* (Berkeley: University of California Press, 2001).

12. I undertook two phases of fieldwork among sixty-five Mexican immigrant women in Santa Barbara— the first phase between 1994 and 1996 and the second between 1998 and 2000. The term *Mexicana* is the self-referent most commonly used by the women I interviewed.

13. Wayne Cornelius, "From Sojourners to Settlers: The Changing Profile of Mexican Immigration to the United States," in *U.S.-Mexico Relations: Labor Market Interdependence*, ed. Jorge A. Bustamante, Clark W. Reynolds, and Raul A. Hinojosa Ojeda (Stanford, Calif.: Stanford University Press, 1992), 155–93.

14. E. Valentine Daniel, "Suffering Nation and Alienation," in *Social Suffering*, ed. Arthur Kleinman, Veena Das, and Margaret Lock (Berkeley: University of California Press, 1997), 309–58.

15. Douglas Massey et al., *Return to Aztlán: The Social Process of International Migration from Western Mexico* (Berkeley: University of California Press, 1987); and Wayne Cornelius, "Ejido Reform: Stimulus or Alternative to Immigration?" in *The Transformation of Rural Mexico, Reforming the Ejido Sector*, ed. Wayne Cornelius and David Myhre (La Jolla, Calif.: Center for U.S.-Mexican Studies, University of California, San Diego, 1998), 229–46.

16. Hondagneu-Sotelo, *Gendered Transitions*, 87.

17. Massey et al., *Return to Aztlán*.

18. Massey et al., *Return to Aztlán*, 144–45.

19. Douglas Massey and Jorge Durand, *Miracles on the Border: Retablos of Mexican Migrants to the United States* (Tucson: University of Arizona Press, 1995).

20. Massey et al., *Return to Aztlán*, 143–44.

21. David Fitzgerald, *Negotiating Extra-Territorial Citizenship: Mexican Migration and the Transnational Politics of Community*, Monograph 2 (La Jolla, Calif.: Center for Comparative Immigration Studies, University of California, San Diego, 2000).

22. Sassen, *The Mobility and Labor of Capitol*.

23. Alberto Ledesma, "Narratives of Mexican Immigration to the United States," in *Culture Across Borders: Mexican Immigration and Popular Culture*, ed. David R. Maciel and Maria Herrera-Sobek (Tucson: University of Arizona Press, 1998), 76.

24. Ledesma, "Narratives of Mexican Immigration," 67–98.

25. Chavez, *Shadowed Lives*, 25–43.

26. Mary O'Connor, "Women's Networks and the Social Needs of Mexican Immigrants," *Urban Anthropology and Studies of Cultural Systems and World Economic Development* 19:1 (1990): 81-98; and Hondagneu-Sotelo, *Gendered Transitions*, 72–75.

27. Timothy Dunn, *The Militarization of the U.S.-Mexico Border, 1978–1992: Low Intensity Conflict Doctrine Comes Home* (Austin: CMAS Books, University of Texas at Austin, 1996), 18.

28. Wayne Cornelius, *"Muerte en la Frontera, La Eficacia y las Consecuencias 'Involuntarias' de la Politica Estadounidense de Control de la Inmigración, 1993–2000,"* Este Pais 119:6 (2001), 2–18.

29. Peter Andreas, *Border Games: Policing the U.S.-Mexico Divide* (Ithaca: Cornell University Press, 2000), 15–50.

30. Michael Huspek, Roberto Martinez, and Leticia Jimenez, "Violations of Human and Civil Rights on the U.S.-Mexico Border, 1995–1997: A Report," *Social Justice* 25:2 (1998): 110–30.

31. Karl Esbach et al., "Death at the Border," *International Migration Review* 33:2 (1999): 430–54.

32. Cornelius, *"Muerte en la Frontera,"* 3.

33. E. Valentine Daniel, *Charred Lullabies: Chapters in an Anthropography of Violence* (Princeton, N.J.: Princeton University Press, 1996), 139–43.

34. William Cronon, *Nature's Metropolis: Chicago and the Great West* (New York: W.W. Norton, 1991), 384.

Chapter 27

Christians for Biblical Equality and the Fight for the Middle Ground

Julie Ingersoll

With the rise of second-wave feminism, women's issues came to play an increasing role in politics beginning in the mid-1960s. Conservative opposition mounted, particularly that organized by evangelical Christian networks. But even within these groups, new activist women contested traditional expectations for women, as Julie Ingersoll traces in the following chapter from her recent book, Evangelical Christian Women.

I interviewed Nikki, a professor at a well-known conservative seminary, at a Christians for Biblical Equality conference. She told me of the problems she had encountered in her position at the seminary and also shared stories about coworkers and students. She then described how CBE functioned as the core of women's support networks, helping them adapt their theology to make sense of what they believed to be true in a manner that allowed them to maintain their faith commitments.

> The CBE becomes their place to go where they are going to be loved. They are accepted. They are with it scripturally, not a heretic. And this is where the strength comes from here and why we have to be here. For those of us who are really in the fundamentalist thing there is tremendous fear of losing our scriptural foundations because we are so afraid of what will happen to us spiritually. . . . There is still [at CBE] this sense that the Scripture is the whole counsel of God. You don't ignore any part of it because you don't happen to agree with it but you look at it in the wholeness of it rather than in bits and pieces. . . . It's the one place I know where I can express my heart toward God and my desire for what I would like to do and what I would like to see the church look like and not be laughed at or have a Bible verse thrown in my face. It's a place where I can come and affirm the femininity as well as the masculinity of God and not be told I am a heretic.

She explained how CBE strengthened her and gave her a vision of how she could stay within the conservative Christian world and make a difference.

* * *

During the 1970s and 1980s, a significant feminist movement developed among conservative American Protestants and at a number of organizations that promoted "biblical feminism"; related viewpoints gained support in many key institutions. The growing belief that the Bible commands gender equality produced a generation of conservative Christian women who expected opportunities they ultimately did not find. Christians for Biblical Equality (CBE) was one of the groups in the forefront of promoting biblical feminism, challenging a key point in the dominant ideology of the evangelical subculture and at the same time working to retain its position within that subculture.[1] The fact that CBE members are educated (graduate degrees are common), white, and middle class significantly influenced the form and activities of this movement, which consist almost exclusively of publications and conferences.[2] CBE has two primary goals: to educate conservative Christians about the "truth" concerning women and women's equality according to the Bible and to maintain the legitimacy of its place within the larger evangelical subculture so that it can effectively pursue the first goal.[3]

BIBLICAL FEMINISM: IS CBE REALLY FEMINIST?

Evangelical Christians who call themselves feminists are not readily accepted by the larger feminist movement as ideological kin. Since there is no single definition of "feminist," assessing the legitimacy of CBE's use of the term is more difficult than it might seem. In defense of its use of the label, CBE cites *Webster's New Collegiate* Dictionary: "Feminism is the theory of the political, economic, and social equality of the sexes [or] organized activity on behalf of women's rights and interests."[4]

CBE describes itself as "an organization of Christians who believe that the Bible, properly interpreted, teaches the fundamental equality of men and women." It thus sees itself as rightful heir to the nineteenth-century women's rights movement.[5]

Biblical feminists believe that church leadership and pastoral roles should not be denied to women, that the ideal for a marriage relationship is "mutual submission," and that a just society will not use gender as a reason for limiting the roles a person may play: "any limitation or denial of the human rights of women cannot be reconciled with Christ's clear call to take up our cross and follow him."[6] For the most part, CBE promotes the use of inclusive language in the church, although there is still some reluctance to change "God language."[7]

But some secular and religious feminists outside this evangelical movement take issue with the limited, narrow dictionary definition of feminism embraced by CBE. Many of them believe that a commitment to feminism includes more than support for functional equality between men and women; for these feminists, feminism is a deeper critique that seeks reform of underlying patriarchal structures that shape perspectives and attitudes about women.

CATHERINE KROEGER AND THE FOUNDING OF CBE

Catherine Kroeger believes that she has a mission from God. At more than seventy years of age, she still gets up before daybreak to make the two-hour drive from her home in Brewster, Massachusetts, to Gordon Seminary, where she teaches Greek. Kroeger has felt called to some kind of professional Christian service at least since she was a seventeen-year-old college student. She described those years as ones in which she struggled to discern what God would have her do with her life: "I tried to pass over the difficult biblical passages for a time, but they eventually caught up with me," she said.

She continued, "As a student at Bryn Mawr College during World War II, I asked A. J. Gordon's daughter Harriet[8] about women in the Bible, and she gave me a copy of Katherine Bushnell's *God's Word to Women*."[9] Kroeger had studied some Greek and believed it was enough to "check on Bushnell's argument." "I found it a bit extreme," she told me, "so I put it away, but every year or so something would happen and I'd bring it out." Paraphrasing Bushnell, Kroeger said,

> Until we get people to deal with all of this [the 'difficult' passages], women will be given
> over to fashion and folly. "Where are our women interpreters?" I asked. But I'm going to
> be a missionary to Saudi Arabia, I sure hope God works it out.

But, due to health problems, Kroeger never made it to the foreign mission field. Her concern about
women and what God wants for them led her to find her own mission field among women in conservative churches here in the United States.

Like many of the women I interviewed, for years Kroeger believed that she was alone in her
views. When she attended the Washington meeting of the Evangelical Women's Caucus (EWC), in
1975, she was "thrilled to find so many women with these same ideas." My respondents each echoed
this sentiment. They compared their discovery of the biblical feminist movement to finding home
after being lost for years; the terms they use are quite like terms used to describe a conversion experience. Feeling alienated from the rest of Christendom, many of those involved found a surrogate
church and family among their evangelical feminist sisters.

Kroeger's vision, which was shared by many from the beginning, was for the biblical feminist
movement to serve as a feminist outreach to women in conservative churches. Many of the early
supporters had come from such churches and knew firsthand the anguish experienced by evangelical/
fundamentalist women who had made "nontraditional" choices (or who longed to do so). According
to Kroeger and to the women I interviewed at the CBE conference, many of them needed "solid biblical exegesis" to reconcile their conservative faith with their feminist sensibilities, and they recognized that they were unlikely to find a home in more secular feminism.

Kroeger was heavily involved in the EWC from that 1975 meeting on. She believes, in hind-
sight, that there were divisions from the beginning (particularly over the issue of homosexuality)
that would eventually prove to be insurmountable. Kroeger told me, "people kept asking me what
did I really think [about the lesbian presence]. I was increasingly troubled, but kept telling myself,
'you can't have everything.'"

In 1986, the question of homosexuality was brought to a head when the Evangelical Women's
Caucus voted in favor of the following resolution supporting civil rights for homosexuals:

> Whereas homosexual people are children of God, and because of the biblical mandate of
> Jesus Christ that we are all created equal in God's sight, and in recognition of the lesbian
> minority in the Evangelical Women's Caucus International, EWC takes a firm stand in
> favor of civil rights protection for homosexual persons.[10]

Opposition from many of the more conservative feminists stemmed, at least in part, from a
genuine concern for the implications of embracing this particular civil rights issue for the mission of
the organization. Many believed that identification with gay and lesbian rights would decimate any
hope of influencing evangelicalism on the question of the roles of women. Furthermore, many of
the women in EWC were in delicate positions as leaders in conservative churches or as teachers at
evangelical colleges. They were painfully aware of the precariousness of their positions, and many
had already faced difficulties because of their embrace of feminism. They feared that for them to
identify with an organization that was perceived as endorsing lesbianism might be tantamount to
committing professional suicide.[11] One interviewee said it most clearly:

> I did not want the group taking this on as a major issue because I felt like then it would
> weaken our defense of biblical feminism. And so that's the point that really upset me.

I thought it was a major political mistake. I thought it meant the death of EWC, and it has. I mean the organization still survives, but it's not the same organization. . . . People to whom the organization could speak just discredit it.[12]

Many of those conservatives felt the need to distance themselves from EWC and met to discuss the possibility of forming a new organization. Initially the group established itself under the umbrella of a London-based group, Men, Women, and God (MWG). MWG had some instant credibility in evangelical circles because of its association with the London Institute for Contemporary Christianity and with the well-known evangelical theologian John Stott. The international ties, however, proved to be cumbersome, and shortly thereafter, the North American group established its independence and renamed itself Christians for Biblical Equality.[13]

By 1989, CBE had joined the National Association of Evangelicals and boasted a circulation of 1,540 for its quarterly journal, *The Priscilla Papers*. Since its founding, CBE has sponsored a major conference on biblical feminism every other year. The organization produces two regular periodicals, *The Priscilla Papers* and *Mutuality*, publishes and distributes biblical feminist books, and supports various local chapter activities.

HOLDING THE MIDDLE GROUND

Since its founding, CBE has walked a thin line between embracing what is seen by many in the subculture as a liberal cause and maintaining the solidity of its position within the evangelical subculture. It has worked to mitigate criticisms that biblical feminism cannot "really be Christian," largely by offering repeated reassurances that permitting women to exercise greater authority, and even to achieve equality with men, will not ultimately alter the foundations of the evangelical worldview.

From the beginning, CBE has relied on the credibility and endorsement of sympathetic "big names" to allay the fears of suspicious evangelicals. In 1990, when CBE took a full-page ad in *Christianity Today* that included a list of illustrious signatories, you could almost hear readers asking, "How bad could it be? I mean, Richard Mouw thinks it's okay." As early as 1986, the support of John Stott was seen as crucial to the survival of the fledgling organization. Through the years, Kroeger actively cultivated a list of well-known supporters (which, according to Kroeger, now has well in excess of two hundred names), knowing the ability of these "stars" to confer credibility. At least one interviewee, who participated in CBE conferences, saw in this tactic the persistence of patriarchal hierarchicalism.

I think the structure [of CBE] is very male-hierarchical. I think they've just replaced one hierarchical structure with another. . . . I think a feminist organization has to propose an alternative. The board [of CBE] should be consciously nonhierarchical. The speakers and leaders should be presented as everyday people.[14]

This same respondent explained that she thought that CBE's understanding of feminism was different from hers on this point. What she was looking for was a "worldview change—a more women-friendly environment—less focused on celebrities." She argued that "you're not going to be able to include women in general, or empower them, until you change the rules." CBE, on the other hand, had staked out a position that minimized the significance of the changes that would be necessary for women to achieve equality. . . .

Biblical feminists are insistent on their credentials as evangelicals by virtue of their "endorsement of, and submission to, biblical authority." The thoughts of a CBE member who pastors a small church in California were representative of many in her answer to my question "What is your view of the Bible?" She said, "I believe the Bible is infallible. I believe everything in the Bible is the revealed word of God. And I believe the Bible includes everything we need to know to understand God and our salvation."[15]

When asked "What about your doctrine of salvation? Must people accept Jesus to be saved?" she answered yes and continued that she believed that Jesus was literally God in human form and that the virgin birth literally happened.

Most biblical feminist books begin with some sort of disclaimer to this effect. Even the most outspoken opponents of biblical feminism, John Piper and Wayne Grudem, acknowledge biblical feminists' claim to this most important of evangelical credentials:

> These authors differ from secular feminists because they do not reject the Bible's authority or truthfulness, but rather give *new interpretations* of the Bible to support their claims. We may call them "evangelical feminists" because by personal commitment to Jesus Christ and by profession of belief in the total truthfulness of Scripture they still identify themselves clearly with evangelicalism.[16] (italics in original)

The style of exegesis employed by evangelical feminists is also in keeping with the style approved in the larger community of evangelical believers. Arguments over the best translation of the Greek and Hebrew texts are ongoing. . . . Entire books are devoted to debates over the interpretation of certain texts.[17]

Biblical feminists work diligently to reclaim the history of the evangelical movement and even the history of Christianity itself. They argue that antifeminism is recent and, in fact, itself an accommodation to the culture of the 1950s.[18] In the face of talk about "traditional family values," biblical feminists point to Margaret Fell's 1667 argument for women's right to speak in public[19]; to the involvement of nineteenth-century evangelical women in the movements for abolition, temperance, and women suffrage; to the activities of women evangelists and missionaries; and to Katherine Bushnell's work in 1912. The fall 1992 issue of *The Priscilla Papers* included an article on the degree to which turn-of-the-century fundamentalists and holiness churches supported, trained, and encouraged women missionaries. A later issue contained an article on nineteenth-century women hymn writers.[20] CBE's 1995 catalog includes several books about women mentioned in the Bible (which they see as the historical record, including women's history); an entire section is headed "Women in the History of the Church." CBE even sells photocopies of Janette Hassey's out-of-print *No Time for Silence*, which, as the promotional note for the book illustrates, fosters this goal of reclaiming history. The note describes Hassey's book as

> An historical examination of the ministry of women in evangelical groups and denominations between 1880 and 1930. Shows that groups formerly welcoming and affirming women in the ministry often now oppose them, not understanding their own history.[21]

Through the promotion and distribution of these works, evangelical feminists endeavor to show that so-called traditional evangelical attitudes toward women and women's leadership are actually relatively new and that women have always served God in public roles. They are thus calling the church back to what they see as the truth and away from its imposition of more limited roles for women, which they view as a modern innovation.

Biblical feminists also attempt to safeguard their position as evangelicals by supporting the behavioral codes and notions of purity that predominate in the larger evangelical world, aligning themselves with socially conservative evangelicals. An interview with a pastor, a member of CBE, drove home the importance of this alignment for maintaining this moral legitimacy:

> Some people [in a church considering hiring her as their pastor] were afraid that if I was a pastor I would be against marriage and kids and having a family. But they knew I had a good marriage. I had great kids. So even though some people said that, they already knew it wasn't true.[22]

In another example of this endorsement of traditional Christian morality, an issue of *The Priscilla Papers* that was devoted to singleness included an article entitled "Sexual Infidelity as Exploitation," which equated premarital sex with infidelity.[23] Perhaps the clearest example of this assent to traditional evangelical morality is CBE's statement of faith, which begins by acknowledging the authority of the Bible and concludes with the following statement, which grew out of the earlier conflict over gay and lesbian rights: "We believe in the family, celibate singleness, and faithful heterosexual marriage as the patterns God has designed for us."[24] In one fell swoop, CBE shows that, with the exception of the submission of women to men, it is basically supportive of the "pro-family" views of evangelicals.

One CBE conference package contained a listing of the conference speakers and provided biographical information for each. Showing that biblical feminists are not a threat to the family, most of the introductions concluded with the name of the speaker's spouse and the number of children the couple had; none said that the speaker was single or divorced. Being married and having children is clearly still a badge of honor in this world. . . .

Antifeminist evangelicals have charged that feminists are in league with those who would promote moral laxity and sexual license. Biblical feminists have set out to differentiate themselves from the larger culture on these issues and to align themselves with other conservative Christians. This is nowhere more clear than it is concerning the issue of homosexuality. It was the apparent endorsement of lesbianism by the EWC that prompted the formation of CBE. Kroeger told me that there were many points on which she disagreed with other EWC leaders but that the resolution in favor of civil rights for homosexuals was the one that couldn't be ignored.

*   *   *

CBE members are emphatic that, while homosexuals are deserving of Christian love, the practice of homosexuality is unequivocally sinful. One biblical feminist respondent who has remained a member of EWC and supported the gay and lesbian rights resolution articulated the position clearly:

> I don't want to judge people, women who choose to live together, and I would like to be their friend. I like to just not have a judgmental spirit toward them even though I don't believe that's the way human kind was intended to function. . . . I guess you could say I'm heterosexist. I have good friends who are lesbians and I don't feel like it's my place to judge. I can't get around what it seems to be Scripture clearly teaches about same-sex relationships. I don't think you can get around it without really twisting Scripture a lot.[25]

Homosexuality is unrivaled as a hot-button issue among conservative evangelicals and fundamentalists.[26] It is particularly problematic for biblical feminists who wish to retain a claim to evangelical orthodoxy. In the larger feminist movement, gay rights and women's rights have been inextricably linked. And, even in the evangelical world, the interpretation of texts used by biblical feminists is often also used to defend homosexuality.

This point has not been missed by the "traditionalist" opponents of biblical feminism. Evangelical opponents of biblical feminism charge that biblical feminists believe that, aside from biological differences, men and women are exactly the same and that nonbiological gendered differences are all cultural.[27] Like secular feminists, biblical feminists disagree over this question, but the fact remains that there is a pervasive concern that equality for women (as defined by feminists) will result in an increased incidence of homosexuality and will leave no grounds from which to oppose homosexuality. This concern is apparent in the most significant recent antifeminist work, Piper and Grudem's *Recovering Biblical Manhood and Womanhood: A Response to Evangelical Feminism:*

> To us it is increasingly and painfully clear that biblical feminism is an unwitting partner in unraveling the fabric of complementary manhood and womanhood that provides the foundation for biblical marriage and biblical church order, but also for heterosexuality as well.[28] The effort of contemporary society to eradicate the differences between the sexes has spawned an increase in strident lesbianism and open homosexuality, a quantum leap in divorces, an increase in rapes and sexual crimes of all sorts—and families smaller in size than ever before.[29]

*   *   *

Those who formed CBE believed that they had to distance themselves from any endorsement of homosexuality if they were to maintain their middle ground between feminism and conservative Protestantism. They believed that there were many evangelicals who might be open to differing views on the roles of women but who would never accept even the hint of support for homosexuality. If evangelicals were to accept their argument that Christianity requires equality for women, biblical feminists themselves had to be above reproach with regard to issues of "purity and morality." They clearly see, though, that their hold on this middle ground is precarious, and they continue to offer constant reassurance that biblical feminism need not undermine the family, heterosexuality, marriage, children, and the like. They pledge their evangelical orthodoxy by maintaining a high view of the authority of the Bible and by claiming the support of evangelical leaders, both past and present. By siding with the larger evangelical subculture on these issues, biblical feminists not only set up their version of feminism as morally acceptable but also created a situation in which they could claim common enemies in the larger culture (although they have never attacked those enemies the way some in the larger evangelical subculture have). In doing so, they have preserved the evangelical demarcation between "us" and "them" and thereby solidified biblical feminists' position on the "us" side with evangelicals. With their loyalty, they buy the power to participate in the production of the dimension of culture they most care about: gender ideology.

LIVING IN THE MIDDLE

Maintaining the middle ground is not easy. Many in this movement have lived through experiences that they might describe as being torn limb from limb. One early supporter was dismissed from his position with a major evangelical publisher because of to his support for, and his wife's publication defending, biblical feminism. Men and women have left seminary teaching positions over the issue of women's place in ministry. A woman who taught at another conservative evangelical seminary told me she was agonizing over whether she could remain there, given her views. The situation in which she found herself was so stressful and difficult that she was in therapy and on antidepressants. I interviewed women pastors who keep their CBE membership secret for fear of repercussions in their churches or denominations. One woman told me,

> When I come to CBE I'm home spiritually. It is the one place I'm at home. For years I was just a closet member; I couldn't tell anybody I was part of it. I lived for *The Priscilla Papers*, because four times a year I could read something that would confirm in me that I was not a heretic and I was not headed straight for eternal damnation, that I was still well within the confines of evangelical belief. And yet, where was I going to get my understanding that women are created in the image of God confirmed by scholars? And I really needed it because I couldn't find it anywhere [else].

Another woman, an author of a recent book that puts forth a moderate version of biblical feminism, struggled over whether to use her real name on the cover out of concern for the implications for her husband's career in the subculture.[30]

In interviews with students on several evangelical college campuses, I found that many of them call feminism "the f-word." In surveys at one West Coast and one East Coast school, I found only an insignificant number who had heard of biblical feminism, evangelical feminism, Christian feminism, CBE, or EWC. The few students in the "middle ground" on these campuses reported that they had been berated by fellow students after being seen reading biblical feminist books.[31]

This tension with the larger subculture contributes to the overwhelming joy described by biblical feminists when they find a group like CBE that serves as a surrogate family, an alternative church community, a professional network, and a locus for group therapy. One woman I interviewed at a CBE conference told me,

> Here at the CBE conference there is enormous hurt in the air. I mean, I am sensing it, you look at people's faces and there is a lot of anguish on them. This is not one of those conferences where people are coming to it because they are excited about what they are doing. They are coming for healing here because they're fighting so many battles where they are coming from—many of them are seminary graduates and their heart is in serving their churches, and they can't be ordained, they can't serve communion, they can't even usher, they can't find a church that welcomes them.

Interviewing nearly a decade after the split between the Evangelical Women's Caucus and the Christians for Biblical Equality, I found women still so pained by the event that they had difficulty talking about it. This response makes sense only when we take into account the centrality of this community to these women. Whether they maintained their association with one or both of the factions, the women viewed these groups as refuges from the larger subculture, which they felt undermined their value as human beings.

Prior to the split between EWC and CBE, at least two divergent feminisms were developing. Conservative members saw feminism as a fight for equality between men and women and for justice (narrowly defined) on specific issues such as what opportunities would be open to women in the church and in society at large. At the same time, other members were developing an understanding of sexism as a pervasive social problem (related to racism, militarism, and other forms of oppression) that had to be addressed by a challenge to the patriarchal system that undergirds society.

Incorporating the fight for lesbian and gay rights, therefore, was, for them, integral, rather than peripheral.[32] Conservatives held fast to their more narrow focus, avoiding what they saw as detractions from their fight to secure functional equality for women in the church and in the family; a significant part of the traditionalist opposition to women's equality is based on their fear that to accept women as equals would set them on a slippery slope that would ultimately lead to acceptance of homosexuality. Leaders of CBE chose to address this challenge by attempting to extricate their corner of the women's movement from the broader movement against the litany of social evils that are of concern to the subculture. As they did so, the two visions of feminism were increasingly at odds with each other.

Despite divisions within the biblical feminist movement, CBE was relatively successful in promoting its agenda regarding the roles of women in the larger conservative Christian world. It has been particularly successful in influencing major fundamentalist and evangelical institutions. In the 1980s, I was a student at Fuller Theological Seminary, where there was broad-based support for women's equality. Fuller had hosted a conference of the biblical feminist organization Evangelical Women's Caucus (before its split into two factions). There was an active chapter of EWC on campus, all faculty supported women's ordination, and there was an institutional policy requiring that students use gender-inclusive language in their coursework. Fuller was one of many seminaries influenced in this way. *Christianity Today* also regularly presents biblical feminist views and issues and has done so for some time. Even the "Christian Men's Movement" group Promise Keepers has been described as promoting "soft patriarchy" in that it argues for male headship but does so in a way that seems to reflect the softening influence of biblical feminist views and arguments.

* * *

Notes

1. For a brief history of evangelical feminism as a movement, see Margaret Lamberts Bendroth, *Fundamentalism and Gender, 1875 to the Present* (New Haven: Yale University Press, 1993), 118 ff.
2. In 1991, Christians for Biblical Equality commissioned a survey of its membership to be conducted by C. J. Olsen Marketing Research, Inc., in Minneapolis, Minnesota. The survey was made available to me by Catherine Kroeger during my field research and indicated that CBE's membership is 75 percent female, 69 percent married, and 95 percent white; 58 percent of its members hold graduate degrees of some sort.
3. The data for this chapter are drawn from several sources. I have made use of a collection of books, tapes, articles, newsletters, and other documents produced and/or distributed by CBE. I spent nearly a week with the CBE founder Catherine Kroeger at her home in Cape Cod in February 1995 and attended the CBE conference held at Gordon College in Wenham, Mass. in the summer of 1995. Kroeger graciously gave me access to her private collection of biblical feminist materials as well as free run of the archives of CBE. During those two research trips, plus additional trips to Los Angeles and San Francisco in the spring of 1995 and trips to Massachusetts, Pennsylvania, and Kentucky during the summer of 1995, I conducted twelve formal interviews lasting from forty-five minutes to several hours, as well as innumerable informal interviews, that have informed my field notes. A research grant from the Society for the Scientific Study of Religion underwrote the cost of having these interview tapes transcribed.
4. Gretchen Gaebelein Hull, "Biblical Feminism," *Priscilla Papers* 5, no. 3 (summer 1991): 1.
5. For an example of this point, see Mary Stewart Van Leeuwen, ed., *After Eden: Facing the Challenge of Gender Reconciliation* (Grand Rapids, Mich.: William B. Eerdmans, 1993), 31–36.
6. Hull, "Biblical Feminism," 2.
7. Gretchen Gaebelein Hull, "Inclusive Language," lecture given at the CBE conference, Wenham, Massachusetts, Gordon College, July 1995.

8. Gordon was a well-known fundamentalist and one of the founders of the seminary where Kroeger later taught.

9. Katherine Bushnell, *God's Word to Women*.

10. *Update* 10, no. 3 (fall 1986): 5–6.

11. This concern was expressed to me repeatedly in interviews and appeared in the discussion of the Fresno conference published in *Update* 10, no. 3 (fall 1986).

12. Kaye Cook, interview by author, 9 February 1995, Wenham Mass., tape recording.

13. While its remaining ties with EWC are strained, CBE maintains very friendly ties with MWG. In fact, MWG and CBE exchange speakers internationally from time to time.

14. This respondent requested anonymity.

15. Patricia Litton, interview by author, 24 January 1995, Ventura, Calif., tape recording.

16. John Piper and Wayne Grudem, *Recovering Biblical Manhood and Womanhood* (Wheaton, Ill.: Crossway Books, 1991), xiii.

17. For examples of these works see Paul K. Jewett, *MAN as Male and Female* (Grand Rapids, Mich.: William B. Eerdmans, 1975); Jewett, *The Ordination of Women* (Grand Rapids, Mich.: William B. Eerdmans, 1980); Charles Trombley, *Who Said Women Can't Teach?* (South Plainfield, N.J.: Bridge, 1985); and Shirley Stephens, *A New Testament View of Women* (Nashville: Broadman Press, 1980).

18. For an example of this argument see Rebecca Merrill Groothuis, *Women Caught in Conflict: The Culture War between Traditionalism and Feminism* (Grand Rapids, Mich.: Baker Book House, 1994), 152 ff.

19. Margaret Fell was a Quaker and the wife of George Fox. Her seventeenth-century essay "Women Speaking Justified" put forth many of the arguments against scriptural interpretations that would keep women silent in churches that are still used by evangelical feminists.

20. Kari Torjesen Malcolm, "The Golden Age for Women Preachers," *Priscilla Papers* 6, no. 4 (fall 1992): 12; Julie Ann Flora, "Nineteenth-Century Women Hymn Writers," *Priscilla Papers* 8, no. 1 (winter 1994): 8.

21. CBE Resource Ministry, September 1995 catalog (St. Paul, Minn.: Christians for Biblical Equality), 5.

22. Marie Wiebe, interview by author, 23 January 1995, Camarillo Calif., tape recording.

23. Craig S. Keener, "Sexual Infidelity as Exploitation," *Priscilla Papers* 7, no. 4 (fall 1993): 15.

24. This statement appears in every issue of the *The Priscilla Papers* and every issue of *Mutuality*. Both are available from CBE.

25. Interview with Ginny Hearn, Berkeley, California, March 11, 1995.

26. I have argued elsewhere that homosexuality has actually replaced abortion as the cornerstone of the political agenda of the Christian Right. "From Right to Life to Anti-Gay Rights: Shifting Traditional Family Values," paper presented at the annual meeting of the Society for the Scientific Study of Religion, Raleigh, North Carolina, November 1993.

27. See Piper and Grudem, *Recovering Biblical and Womanhood*. The charge is made repeatedly throughout this work

28. Piper and Grudem, *Recovering Biblical Manhood and Womanhood*, 84.

29. Ibid., 376.

30. Although I've cited names where possible, for obvious reasons many of these stories have been included without names.

31. These interviews were conducted between January and June 1995. While some were in-depth taped interviews, others were informal conversations. I also distributed a one-page written questionnaire to fifty randomly selected students on two different campuses.

32. For examples of the developing idea that a sweeping critique of patriarchy was necessary, see "A Conversation with Virginia Mollenkott," *The Other Side* (May–June 1976): 21–75; Kathleen E. Corley and Karen J. Torjesen, "Sexuality, Hierarchy, and Evangelicalism," *TSF Bulletin* 10, no. 4 (March–April 1987): 23–27; Anne Eggebroten, "Handling Power: Unchristian, Unfeminine, Unkind?" *The Other Side* (December 1986): 20–25.

SELECTED LINKS TO U.S. WOMEN'S HISTORY RESOURCE MATERIALS ON THE WORLD WIDE WEB

In recent years a wide array of primary documents and secondary accounts in American women's history has been mounted on the World Wide Web, readily accessible for use by teachers and students. What follows is a selective listing of materials chosen because of their relevance to issues raised in the readings in *Women and Power in American History*. Items on the "Women and Social Movements" website, also edited by Kathryn Kish Sklar and Thomas Dublin, include discussion questions. You can go beyond what is recommended here by using search engines to locate additional materials related to the readings in this book. To access the materials listed below, go to the web address noted with the description of each website. In addition, we are maintaining a World Wide Web site, http://chswg. binghamton.edu/womenandpower.htm, where you will be able to link to a regularly updated version of this list of related websites. If URLs for sites change after the publication of this edition, the correct URLs will be found at this website. If new web-based materials appear that relate closely to this reader, descriptions of those materials and URLs will be added to this website. Using the website is the best way for you to access the most current web materials relating to the articles in this reader.

Pocahontas and Powhatan Links
URL: http://members.tripod.com/~AlanCheshire/index-15.html

This website offers a large number of links of varying quality and reliability. Examine the first group of links associated with Pocahontas and Powhatan in light of the analysis offered by Kathleen M. Brown in the article, "The Anglo-Algonquian Gender Frontier." This particular group of links permits readers to consider the interplay of history and memory and to think about how views of the interrelations between Euro-Americans and Algonquins of the Powhatan Confederacy have changed over the centuries and how those views reflect the vantage points of subsequent artists and writers. Particularly worth considering are the perspectives offered on the Pocahontas myth as expressed by representatives of the Renape Powhatan Nation (today's New Jersey descendants of the Virginia Algonquin nation) and the analysis of the Disney treatment offered by David Morenus in "The Real Pocahontas."

"Africans in America," a PBS Website Accompanying a Six-Hour Documentary Film of the Same Title.
URL: http://www.pbs.org/wgbh/aia/home.html

This extensive website includes historical documents and historians' commentaries on African-American history between 1450 and 1865. The first of its four sections, "The Terrible Transformation, 1450–1750," explores the origins and institutionalization of slavery in the British southern mainland colonies, and offers numerous connections to the analysis offered by Allan Kulikoff in his article, "The Beginnings of the Afro-American Family in Maryland."

The Elizabeth Murray Project
URL: http://salticid.nmc.csulb.edu/cgi-bin/WebObjects/eMurray.woa/wa/select/

As both Deborah Rosen and Barbara Clark Smith have demonstrated, women were active and integral participants in the colonial economy. This resourceful site examines Elizabeth Murray, a Boston retailer and importer, whose life illustrates many of the complexities of life in eighteenth-century America. Site developer, Professor Patricia Cleary, tells the story of Murray through letters, portraits, newspaper articles, and maps, and also includes teaching resources.

Women in the American Revolution
URL: http://asp6new.alexanderstreet.com/wasm/wasmrestricted/amrev/doclist.htm

This site depicts the vigorous support given to the Revolutionary cause by the members of the Ladies Association of Philadelphia. It demonstrates the ways that American women drew on their traditional activities to contribute to opposition to Great Britain. Library subscription required.

Martha Ballard, the Maine Midwife, at the DoHistory Website
URL: http://dohistory.org/diary/index.html

This website reproduces the diary kept by Maine midwife Martha Ballard between 1785 and 1812 and numerous other historical documents that Laurel Thatcher Ulrich used to write her Pulitzer-Prize-winning history, *The Midwife's Tale.* The sources highlight issues related to childbirth and midwifery and relations between men and women in northern New England in the early national period. Case studies of particular incidents permit users to follow Ulrich's keen detective work with the documents to arrive at understandings that are not self-evident at the outset.

Women Working, 1800–1930
URL: http://ocp.hul.harvard.edu/ww/

This extensive collection, drawn from Harvard University's library and museum collections, features over 500,000 digital pages and images related to the history of women and work in the United States. Resources on this freely accessible website relate to articles in the reader by Dublin, Lasser, and Peiss.

Lowell Mill Women: "Uses of Liberty Rhetoric among Lowell Mill Girls"
URL: http://www.library.csi.cuny.edu/dept/americanstudies/lavender/start.html

Professor Catherine Lavender, at the College of Staten Island, has assembled an interesting group of images and primary documents focusing on the "ways nineteenth-century women used 'liberty rhetoric' to argue for changes in their worlds." The resources at this website explore, in turn, the Revolutionary tradition, women in Lowell, and the 1848 Declaration of Sentiments adopted at Seneca Falls. From the site's home page, click on the Lowell section and examine the primary sources assembled there in relation to the argument made by Thomas Dublin in the article, "Women, Work, and Protest in the Early Lowell Mills."

The Digital Scriptorium, Rare Book, Manuscript, and Special Collections Library, Duke University: African-American Women
URL: http://scriptorium.lib.duke.edu/collections/african-american-women.html

This site provides scanned images and transcriptions of writings by three African-American women during the nineteenth century, as well as background essays. Materials include an 85-page memoir and other published writings by Elizabeth Johnson Harris (1867–1923), a letter written in 1857 by a North Carolina slave named Vilet Lester; and four letters written between 1837 and 1838 by Hannah Valentine and Lethe Jackson, slaves on an Abingdon, Virginia, plantation. The themes illustrated by these primary sources reinforce the argument offered by Virginia Meacham Gould in her exploration of slave women in antebellum New Orleans.

Harriet A. Jacobs: *Incidents in the Life of a Slave Girl Written by Herself*, 1861
URL: http://xroads.virginia.edu/~HYPER/JACOBS/hjhome.htm

This website provides an online edition of a notable slave memoir written by the escaped slave Harriet Jacobs, edited by the abolitionist Lydia Maria Child and published in 1861. Like the New Orleans slave women discussed by Virginia Meacham Gould in this collection, Jacobs was an urban house slave whose first mistress was the half-sister of her slave grandmother. Until the death of her mistress the young Jacobs had been sheltered from the harshest elements of slavery. Her life as a house slave, however, soon exposed her to some of the worst abuses of slavery and she became the mistress of a white neighbor rather than submit to being the concubine of her master. Jacobs's narrative confirms Gould's argument concerning the importance of family to slave women and shows a slave woman's agency even under the constraints of unfreedom.

Angelina Grimké: Speech at Pennsylvania Hall, Philadelphia, May 1838
URL: http://www.pbs.org/wgbh/aia/part4/4h2939t.html

After the Massachusetts tour in the spring and summer of 1837 on behalf of abolition, Angelina Grimké spoke in public for the last time in May 1838 at Pennsylvania Hall in Philadelphia. While she spoke, the hall was attacked by a hostile mob estimated at about 10,000 men who threw stones, broke windows, and disrupted the proceedings inside. That night the mob burned the Hall to the ground. This online document provides the text of Angelina's speech transcribed by a person in the audience at the time and printed shortly afterward. Interruptions by the mob are noted in the transcription. For an account of the women's exit from the Hall before the mob torched the building, see Kathryn Kish Sklar, *Florence Kelley and the Nation's Work*, pp. 18–19. This speech provides a rich example of the rhetoric that Angelina Grimké probably employed in the Massachusetts campaign treated by Kathryn Kish Sklar in "Women's Rights Emerges within the Antislavery Movement."

Catharine Beecher: A Letter to Mary Lyon, 17 November 1844
URL: http://clio.fivecolleges.edu/mhc/lyon/a/2/ff22/441117/02.htm

The archives and special collections of the University of Massachusetts, Amherst College, Smith College, Hampshire College, and Mount Holyoke College have joined together to sponsor the Five College Archives Digital Access Project. The project has digitized significant portions of numerous manuscript collections from their respective holdings. Included in these online resources is the Mary Lyon Collection at Mount Holyoke College, with letters from the educational reformer Catharine Beecher. In one letter Beecher outlined her plans to draw on Protestant women as teachers in the West.

Harriet Beecher Stowe: Her Work, Her Life
URL: http://xroads.virginia.edu/~MA97/riedy/hbs.html#HER

This brief examination of the life and work of Harriet Beecher Stowe is part of an online project of the American Studies Department at the University of Virginia entitled "Mothers in Uncle Tom's

America." After reading the brief quote at the outset from one of Harriet Beecher Stowe's letters, read the three additional letters that appear in the section "Her Life" further down on the page. How do the letters underscore the argument that Kathryn Sklar makes about Stowe's efforts at birth control in her article, "Victorian Women and Domestic Life"?

How Did White Women Aid Former Slaves during and after the Civil War, 1863–1891?
URL: http://asp6new.alexanderstreet.com/wasm/wasmrestricted/aid/doclist.htm (subscription website)

Carol Faulkner has collected documents that explore gender conflict within the Freedman's Aid movement during the Civil War and Reconstruction. In these years, northern white women volunteered to assist freedmen and women and sought to mobilize the federal government in support of these efforts. With private assistance and through the Freedmen's Bureau, these women taught in schools, dispensed charity, ran employment bureaus, and assisted migration. This project tells the story of their efforts and the conflicts that arose with male reformers whose chief priority was to end freedpeople's dependence on others. Library subscription required.

Helen Lefkowitz Horowitz, "Victoria Woodhull, Anthony Comstock, and Conflict over Sex in the United States in the 1870s"
URL: http://www.historycooperative.org/journals/jah/87.2/horowitz.html

This online article appeared in the September 2000 issue of the *Journal of American History* and offers a thoughtful complement to the article, "Reproductive Control and Conflict in the Nineteenth Century," by Janet Farrell Brodie. Horowitz explores the conflict between sex reformer Victoria Woodhull and the federal morals agent, Anthony Comstock. She places the 1872 trial of Woodhull and other legal cases during the 1870s within a broader set of cultural frameworks that she argues shaped representations of sexuality in the United States in the nineteenth century. The article offers concrete examples of the changing legal treatment of abortion and contraception that Brodie delineates.

Angel Island Poetry
URL: http://www.english.uiuc.edu/maps/poets/a_f/angel/angel.htm

This site, published by the University of Illinois at Urbana-Champaign English Department, offers an excellent compilation of primary and secondary information related to Angel Island Immigration Station, the point of entry for most Chinese immigrants. Resources include poems, essays, photographs, a timeline, and the text of the 1882 Chinese Exclusion Act, and offer an excellent complement to Sucheng Chan's essay on the experiences of Chinese women during the exclusion period.

African-American Women in the Woman's Christian Temperance Union (WCTU), 1880–1900
URL: http://asp6new.alexanderstreet.com/wasm/wasmrestricted/wctu2/doclist.htm (subscription website)

This document project from the "Women and Social Movements" website illuminates the participation of African-American women in the WCTU between 1880 and 1900. Documents include annual reports made by the three superintendents of colored work in the WCTU in these years, Frances E. W. Harper, Sarah J. Early, and Lucy Thurman. It also treats a controversy that erupted between black activist Ida B. Wells and long-time WCTU President Frances Willard over the Union's stance toward lynching and its tolerance of segregation in its Southern locals. These documents provide a national framework within which to place the North Carolina study presented by Glenda Gilmore in "Race and Womanhood."

Jane Addams, *Twenty Years at Hull-House,* 1912
URL: http://xroads.virginia.edu/~HYPER/ADDAMS/title.html

This online edition of Jane Addams's autobiography offers a first-person memoir of the life and early settlement house work of the noted reformer Jane Addams at Chicago's Hull-House. Her account complements Kathryn Sklar's analysis of the first decade at Hull-House in her article, "Hull House in the 1890s: A Community of Women Reformers."

The Early Years of the National Association of Colored Women
URL: http://asp6new.alexanderstreet.com/wasm/wasmrestricted/nacw/doclist.htm (subscription
    website)
and

The National Woman's Party and the Enfranchisement of Black Women, 1919–1924
URL: http://asp6new.alexanderstreet.com/wasm/wasmrestricted/nwp/list.htm (subscription
    website)

Rosalyn Terborg-Penn examines the place of African-American women in the woman suffrage movement. These two web projects provide useful images and documents to complement that essay. The project on the National Association of Colored Women documents the efforts of middle-class African-American women to organize for racial uplift and to secure for themselves a respected place among women reformers between 1890 and 1920. The project on the National Woman's Party, in turn, reveals obstacles that African-American women faced as late as the early 1920s in their effort to secure the right to vote. These two document projects require library subscription.

Margaret Sanger and *The Woman Rebel*: A Mini-Edition
URL: http://mep.cla.sc.edu/ms/ms-table.html

The Margaret Sanger Papers offer a group of documents about the founding in 1914 of the feminist journal, *The Woman Rebel,* and the emergence of Margaret Sanger as the foremost leader of the birth control movement in the United States. The documents address Sanger's early radical years, setting the scene for "The Professionalization of Birth Control" described by historian Linda Gordon.

The Emma Goldman Papers
URL: http://sunsite.berkeley.edu/Goldman/

The Emma Goldman Papers, edited at the University of California, Berkeley, provide one of the premier websites in U.S. women's history. The site's home page describes Goldman in these terms: "An influential and well-known anarchist of her day, Goldman was an early advocate of free speech, birth control, women's equality and independence, organization, and the eight-hour work day. Her criticism of mandatory conscription of young men into the military during World War I led to a two-year imprisonment, followed by her deportation in 1919. For the rest of her life until her death in 1940, she continued to participate in the social and political movements of her age, from the Russian Revolution to the Spanish Civil War." The site includes sample documents, an online exhibition, and curriculum materials for student use.

The Debate over the Equal Rights Amendment in the 1920s
URL: http://asp6new.alexanderstreet.com/wasm/wasmrestricted/era/doclist.htm (subscription website)

This collection of documents expresses both sides of the lively debate between proponents and opponents of the ERA in the 1920s. Introduced with a brief essay by Kathryn Sklar on the history of the ERA, it complements Sklar's essay on why most politically active women opposed the ERA in the 1920s. Library subscription required.

Civil Rights in Mississippi Digital Archive
URL: www.lib.usm.edu/%7Espcol/crda/index.html

While Ruth Feldstein's article focuses on the ways in which one individual—Nina Simone—participated in the black freedom struggle through her music, this digital archive provides access to local documents that provide rare views of this struggle on the ground. The University of Southern Mississippi (USM) has assembled these materials and describes the project in these terms: "Mississippi was a focal point in the struggle for civil rights in America, and Hattiesburg, where USM is located, had the largest and most successful Freedom Summer project in 1964. The original sources collected in the state represent local collections with truly national significance."

Women at War: Redstone's WWII Female "Production Soldiers"
URL: http://www.redstone.army.mil/history/women/welcome.html

This web project provides an interesting account of women's wartime employment at the Huntsville (Ala.) Arsenal during World War II. The text and accompanying photos show how the facility came to rely increasingly on women workers as the war went on, accounting for fully 37 percent of the arsenal's 6,700 workers in September 1944. The site complements well Ruth Milkman's article on women workers in the automobile industry during World War II.

VOAHA: The Virtual Oral/Aural History Archive: Women's History
URL:http://salticid.nmc.csulb.edu/cgi-bin/WebObjects/OralAural.woa/wa/series?ww=1024&wh=608&pt=109&bi=1&col=a1000

This site offers extensive oral history collections related to twentieth century women's history. Collections include recordings relevant to the history of suffrage, women workers and professionals, Chicana and Asian-American feminist activists, welfare rights, and women during WWII.

Mujeres Latinas Digital Collection
URL: http://cdm.lib.uiowa.edu/cdm4/index_latinas.php?CISOROOT=/latinas

This project by the Iowa Women's Archives provides oral histories, clippings, postcards, text, and photographs related to the history of Latinas in Iowa, providing interesting possibilities for comparison and contrast with María de la Luz Ibarra's treatment of Mexican migrant domestic workers in Santa Barbara.

Making Face, Making Soul . . .
URL: http://www.chicanas.com/

This site contains numerous resources for Chicana history, including biographies, cultural resources, literature and poetry. It offers an excellent complement to the essay by Ibarra.

Documents from the Women's Liberation Movement
URL: http://scriptorium.lib.duke.edu/wlm/

The guide to this online collection describes it well: "The materials in this on-line archival collection document various aspects of the Women's Liberation Movement in the United States, and focus specifically on the radical origins of this movement during the late 1960s and early 1970s. Items range from radical theoretical writings to humorous plays to the minutes of an actual grassroots group." Coupled with Cynthia Harrison's treatment of the origins of NOW in her article, "A New Women's Movement: The Emergence of the National Organization for Women," these documents will help readers understand the rebirth of feminism in the 1960s and 1970s.

The 1977 Houston National Women's Conference
URL: http://asp6new.alexanderstreet.com/wasm/wasmrestricted/dp59/doclist.htm (subscription website)

The National Women's Conference at Houston in November 1977 marked a high point in the influence of second-wave feminist ideas on policy formulation. This document project presents audio selections from speeches at the conference, transcripts of speeches, the conference program, newspapers published during the conference, all the individual planks considered at Houston, and follow-up evaluations of progress on those planks in 1988 and 1997. Library subscription required.

SUGGESTIONS FOR FURTHER READING

Allen, Paula Gunn. *Pocahontas: Medicine Woman, Spy, Entrepreneur, Diplomat.* San Francisco, CA: HarperSanFrancisco, 2003.

Allgor, Catherine. *Parlor Politics: In Which the Ladies of Washington Help Build a City and a Government.* Charlottesville: University Press of Virginia, 2000.

Anderson, Bonnie S. *Joyous Greetings: The First International Women's Movement, 1830–1860.* New York: Oxford University Press, 2000.

Anderson, Karen. *Changing Woman: A History of Racial Ethnic Women in Modern America.* New York: Oxford University Press, 1996.

Armitage, Susan, and Elizabeth Jameson, eds. *The Women's West.* Norman: University of Oklahoma Press, 1987.

Baker, Jean H. *Sisters: The Lives of America's Suffragists.* NY: Hill & Wang, 2005.

————, ed. *Votes for Women: The Struggle for Suffrage Revisited.* Oxford: Oxford University Press, 2002.

Baker, Paula. "The Domestication of Politics: Women in American Political Society, 1780–1920." *American Historical Review* 89 (June 1984): 620–47.

Barakso, Maryann. *Governing NOW: Grassroots Activism in the National Organization for Women.* Ithaca, N.Y.: Cornell University Press, 2004.

Bendroth, Margaret Lamberts, and Virginia Lieson Brereton. *Women and Twentieth-Century Protestantism.* Urbana: University of Illinois Press, 2002.

Benson, Susan Porter. *Counter Cultures: Saleswomen, Managers, and Customers in American Department Stores, 1890–1940.* Urbana: University of Illinois Press, 1986.

Bergmann, Barbara R. *The Economic Emergence of Women.* New York: Basic Books, 1986.

Berkin, Carol. *Revolutionary Mothers: Women in the Struggle for America's Independence.* New York: Knopf, 2005.

Berkovitch, Nitza. *From Motherhood to Citizenship: Women's Rights and International Organizations.* Baltimore: Johns Hopkins University Press, 1999.

Berry, Mary Frances. *My Face is Black is True: Callie House and the Struggle for Ex-Slave Reparations.* New York: Knopf, 2005.

Blair, Karen. *The Clubwoman as Feminist: True Womanhood Redefined, 1868–1914.* New York: Holmes and Meier, 1979.

Blewett, Mary. *Men, Women, and Work: Class, Gender, and Protest in the New England Shoe Industry, 1789–1910.* Urbana: University of Illinois Press, 1988.

Bloch, Ruth. *Gender and Morality: in Anglo-American Culture, 1650–1800.* Berkeley: University of California Press, 2003.

————. "The Gendered Meanings of Virtue in Revolutionary America." *Signs* 13 (1987): 37–58.

Bolt, Christine. *Sisterhood Questioned? Race, Class and Internationalism in the America and British Women's Movements, c. 1880s–1970s.* London: Routledge, 2004.

Bordin, Ruth. *Frances Willard: A Biography.* Chapel Hill: University of North Carolina Press, 1986.

————. *Women and Temperance: The Quest for Power and Liberty, 1873–1900.* Philadelphia: Temple University Press, 1981.

Boylan, Anne M. *The Origins of Women's Activism: New York and Boston, 1797–1840.* Chapel Hill: University of North Carolina Press, 2002.

Braude, Ann, ed. *Transforming the Faiths of Our Fathers: Women Who Changed American Religion.* New York: Palgrave Macmillan, 2004.

Brekus, Catherine A. *Female Preaching in America: Strangers and Pilgrims, 1740–1845.* Chapel Hill: University of North Carolina Press, 1998.

Brodie, Janet Farrell. *Contraception and Abortion in Nineteenth-Century America.* Ithaca, N.Y.: Cornell University Press, 1994.

Brown, Dorothy M., and Elizabeth McKeown. *The Poor Belong to Us: Catholic Charities and American Welfare.* Cambridge, Mass.: Harvard University Press, 1997.

Brown, Kathleen M. *Good Wives, Nasty Wenches and Anxious Patriarchs: Gender, Race, and Power in Colonial Virginia.* Chapel Hill: University of North Carolina Press, 1996.

Buechler, Steven. *The Transformation of the Women's Suffrage Movement: The Case of Illinois, 1850–1920.* New Brunswick, N.J.: Rutgers University Press, 1986.

Buhle, Mari Jo. *Women and American Socialism, 1870–1920.* Urbana: University of Illinois Press, 1983.

Butler, Anne M. *Daughters of Joy, Sisters of Mercy: Prostitution in the American West, 1865–1890*. Urbana: University of Illinois Press, 1985.

Bynum, Victoria E. *Unruly Women: The Politics of Social and Sexual Control in the Old South*. Chapel Hill: University of North Carolina Press, 1992.

Cahn, Susan K. *Coming on Strong: Gender and Sexuality in Twentieth-Century Women's Sport*. Cambridge: Harvard University Press, 1994.

Camp, Stephanie M. H. *Closer to Freedom: Enslaved Women & Everyday Resistance in the Plantation South*. Chapel Hill: University of North Carolina Press, 2004.

Caughfield, Adrienne. *True Women and Westward Expansion*. College Station, Tex.: Texas A&M University Press, 2005.

Censer, Jane Turner. *The Reconstruction of White Southern Womanhood, 1865–1895*. Baton Rouge: Louisiana State University Press, 2003.

Chambers-Schiller, Lee Virginia. *Liberty, A Better Husband: Single Women in America, the Generations of 1780–1840*. New Haven, Conn.: Yale University Press, 1984.

Clark-Lewis, Elizabeth. *Living In, Living Out: African American Domestics in Washington D.C., 1910–1940*. Washington D.C.: Smithsonian Institution Press, 1994.

Cleary, Patricia. *Elizabeth Murray: A Woman's Pursuit of Independence in Eighteenth-Century America*. Amherst: University of Massachusetts Press, 2000.

Cobble, Dorothy Sue. *Dishing It Out: Waitresses and Their Unions in the Twentieth Century*. Urbana: University of Illinois Press, 1991.

———. *The Other Women's Movement: Workplace Justice and Social Rights in Modern America*. Princeton: Princeton University Press, 2004.

Cole, Johnnetta Betsch, and Beverly Guy-Sheftall. *Gender Talk: The Struggle for Women's Equality in African American Communities*. New York: One World/Ballantine, 2003

Collier-Thomas, Bettye, and V. P. Franklin, eds. *The Reconstruction of White Southern Womanhood, 1865–1895*. Baton Rouge: Louisiana State University Press, 2003.

Cott, Nancy F. *The Bonds of Womanhood: "Woman's Sphere" in New England, 1780–1835*. New Haven, Conn.: Yale University Press, 1977.

———. "Eighteenth-Century Family and Social Life Revealed in Massachusetts Divorce Records." *Journal of Social History* 10 (Fall 1976): 20–43.

———. *The Grounding of Modern Feminism*. New Haven, Conn.: Yale University Press, 1987.

———. "Passionlessness: An Interpretation of Victorian Sexual Ideology, 1790–1850." *Signs* 4 (1978): 219–36.

———. *Public Vows: A History of Marriage and the Nation*. Cambridge, Mass.: Harvard University Press, 2000.

Critchlow, Donald T. *Phyllis Schlafly and Grassroots Conservatism: A Woman's Crusade*. Princeton: Princeton University Press, 2005.

D'Emilio, John, and Estelle Freedman. *Intimate Matters: A History of Sexuality in America*. New York: Harper and Row, 1988.

Davis, Allen F. *Spearheads of Reform: The Social Settlements and the Progressive Movement, 1890–1914*. New York: Oxford University Press, 1967.

DeBerg, Betty A. *Ungodly Women: Gender and the First Wave of American Fundamentalism*. Minneapolis: Fortress Press, 1990.

Degler, Carl. *At Odds: Women and the Family in America from the Revolution to the Present*. New York: Oxford University Press, 1980.

Demos, John. *A Little Commonwealth: Family Life in Plymouth Colony*. New York: Oxford University Press, 1970.

Des Jardins, Julie. *Women and the Historical Enterprise in America: Gender, Race, and the Politics of Memory, 1880–1945*. Chapel Hill: University of North Carolina Press, 2003.

Deutsch, Sarah. *Women and the City: Gender, Space, and Power in Boston, 1870–1940*. New York: Oxford University Press, 2000.

Diner, Hasia. *Erin's Daughters in America: Irish Immigrant Women in the Late Nineteenth Century*. Baltimore: Johns Hopkins University Press, 1983.

Diner, Hasia R., and Beryl Lieff Benderly. *Her Works Praise Her: A History of Jewish Women in America from Colonial Times to the Present*. New York: Basic Books, 2002.

D'Itri, Patricia Ward. *Cross Currents in the International Women's Movement, 1848–1948*. Bowling Green: Bowling Green State University Popular Press, 1999.

Drachman, Virginia C. *Enterprising Women: 250 Years of American Business*. Chapel Hill: University of North Carolina Press, 2002.

Dublin, Thomas. *Farm to Factory: Women's Letters, 1830–1860*. second ed. New York: Columbia University Press, 1993.

———. *Transforming Women's Work: New England Lives in the Industrial Revolution*. Ithaca, N.Y.: Cornell University Press, 1994.

————. *Women at Work: The Transformation of Work and Community in Lowell, Massachusetts, 1826–1860.* New York: Columbia University Press, 1979.

DuBois, Ellen Carol. *Feminism and Suffrage: The Emergence of an Independent Women's Movement in America, 1848–1869.* Ithaca, N.Y.: Cornell University Press, 1978.

————. *Harriot Stanton Blatch and the Winning of Woman Suffrage.* New Haven, Conn.: Yale University Press, 1997.

Dudden, Fay. *Serving Women: Household Service in 19th Century America.* Middletown, Conn: Wesleyan University Press, 1983.

Dunn, Mary Maples, "Women of Light." in *Women of America: A History.* Edited by Carol Berkin and Mary Beth Norton, 114–38. Boston: Houghton Mifflin, 1979.

Dye, Nancy Schrom. *As Equals and As Sisters: Feminism, the Labor Movement, and the Women's Trade Union League of New York.* Columbia: University of Missouri Press, 1980.

Edwards, Wendy J. Deitchman, and Carolyn De Swarte Gifford, eds. *Gender and the Social Gospel.* Urbana: University of Illinois Press, 2003.

Enloe, Cynthia. *The Curious Feminist: Searching for Women in a New Age of Empire.* Berkeley: University of California Press, 2004.

Evans, Sara. *Personal Politics: The Roots of Women's Liberation in the Civil Rights Movement and the New Left.* New York: Vintage, 1979.

————. *Tidal Wave: How Women Changed America at Century's End.* New York: The Free Press, 2003.

Ewen, Elizabeth. *Immigrant Women in the Land of Dollars: Life and Culture on the Lower East Side.* New York: Monthly Review Press, 1985.

Ezekiel, Judith. *Feminism in the Heartland.* Columbus: Ohio State University Press, 2002.

Faderman, Lillian. *To Believe in Women: What Lesbians Have Done for America—A History.* Boston: Houghton Mifflin, 1999.

Faulkner, Carol. *Women's Radical Reconstruction: The Freedmen's Aid Movement.* Philadelphia: University of Pennsylvania Press, 2004.

Faragher, John. *Women and Men on the Overland Trail.* New Haven, Conn.: Yale University Press, 1981.

Faust, Drew Gilpin. *Mothers of Invention: Women of the Slaveholding South in the American Civil War.* Chapel Hill: University of North Carolina Press, 1996.

Feldstein, Ruth. *Motherhood in Black and White: Race and Sex in American Liberalism, 1930–1965.* Ithaca, N.Y.: Cornell University Press, 2000.

Fine, Lisa. *The Souls of the Skyscraper: Female Clerical Workers in Chicago, 1870–1930.* Philadelphia: Temple University Press, 1990.

Flanagan, Maureen A. *Seeing With Their Hearts: Chicago Women and the Vision of the Good City.* Princeton: Princeton University Press, 2002.

Flexner, Eleanor and Ellen Fitzpatrick. *Century of Struggle: The Woman's Rights Movement in the United States,* enlarged ed. Cambridge: Harvard University Press, 1996; originally published in 1959.

Fox-Genovese, Elizabeth. *Within the Plantation Household: Black and White Women of the Old South.* Chapel Hill: University of North Carolina Press, 1988.

Frankfort, Roberta. *Collegiate Women: Domesticity and Career in Turn-of-the Century America.* New York: New York University Press, 1977.

Freedman, Estelle B. *Maternal Justice: Miriam Van Waters and the Female Reform Tradition.* Chicago: University of Chicago Press, 1996.

————. *No Turning Back: The History of Feminism and the Future of Women.* Ballantine Books, 2002.

Gamber, Wendy. *The Female Economy: The Millinery and Dressmaking Trades, 1860–1930.* Urbana: University of Illinois Press, 1997.

Gerhard, Jane. *Desiring Revolution: Second-Wave Feminism and the Rewriting of American Sexual Thought 1920 to 1982.* New York: Columbia University Press, 2001.

Giesberg, Judith Ann. *Civil War Sisterhood: The U.S. Sanitary Commission and Women's Politics in Transition.* Boston: Northeastern University Press, 2000.

Gilmore, Glenda Elizabeth. *Gender and Jim Crow: Women and the Politics of White Supremacy in North Carolina, 1896–1920.* Chapel Hill: University of North Carolina Press, 1996

Ginzberg, Lori D. *Untidy Origins: A Story of Woman's Rights in Antebellum New York.* Chapel Hill: University of North Carolina Press, 2005.

Glazer, Penina and Miriam Slater. *Unequal Colleagues: The Entrance of Women into the Professions, 1890–1940.* New Brunswick, N.J.: Rutgers University Press, 1987.

Glenn, Evelyn Nakano. *Issei, Nisei, War Bride.* Philadelphia: Temple University Press, 1986.

————. *Unequal Freedom: How Race and Gender Shaped American Freedom and Labor.* Cambridge: Harvard University Press, 2002.

Glenn, Susan. *Daughters of the Shtetl: Life and Labor in the Immigrant Generation.* Ithaca: Cornell University Press, 1990.

————. *Female Spectacle: The Theatrical Roots of Modern Feminism.* Cambridge: Harvard University Press, 2000.

Goldman, Karla. *Beyond the Synagogue Gallery: Finding a Place for Women in American Judaism.* Cambridge: Harvard University Press, 2000.

Goodwin, Joanne L. *Gender and the Politics of Welfare Reform: Mothers' Pensions in Chicago, 1911–1929.* Chicago: University of Chicago Press, 1997.

Gordon, Ann D. et al., eds. *The Selected Papers of Elizabeth Cady Stanton and Susan B. Anthony,* Vols. 1–4. New Brunswick, N.J.: Rutgers University Press, 1997–2006.

Gordon, Felice. *After Winning: The Legacy of New Jersey Suffrage, 1920–1947.* New Brunswick, N.J.: Rutgers University Press, 1987.

Gordon, Linda. *Heroes of Their Own Lives: The Politics and History of Family Violence, 1880–1980.* New York: Viking, 1988.

————. *Pitied but Not Entitled: Single Mothers and the History of Welfare.* New York: Free Press, 1994.

————. *Woman's Body, Woman's Right: Birth Control in America.* New York: Viking, 1976.

Green, Elna. *Southern Strategies: Southern Women and the Woman Suffrage Question.* Chapel Hill: University of North Carolina Press, 1997.

Gutman, Herbert. *The Black Family in Slavery and Freedom, 1750–1925.* New York: Pantheon, 1976.

Hall, Jacquelyn Dowd et al. *Like a Family: The Making of a Southern Cotton Mill World.* Chapel Hill: University of North Carolina Press, 1987.

Hall, Jacquelyn Dowd. *The Revolt Against Chivalry: Jessie Daniel Ames and the Women's Campaign Against Lynching.* New York: Columbia University Press, 1979.

Hardesty, Nancy A. *Your Daughters Shall Prophesy: Revivalism and Feminism in the Age of Finney.* Brooklyn, N.Y.: Carlson, 1991.

Harrison, Cynthia. *On Account of Sex: The Politics of Women's Issues, 1945–1968.* Berkeley: University of California Press, 1988

Harrison, Patricia Greenwood. *Connecting Links: The British and American Woman Suffrage Movements, 1900–1914.* Westport, Conn.: Greenwood, 2000.

Hart, Vivien. *Bound by Our Constitution: Women, Workers, and the Minimum Wage.* Princeton, N.J.: Princeton University Press, 1994.

Hartmann, Susan. *The Homefront and Beyond: American Women in the 1940s.* Boston: G.K. Hall, 1982.

————. *The Other Feminists: Activists in the Liberal Establishment.* New Haven, Conn. Yale University Press, 1998.

Hayden, Dolores. *The Grand Domestic Revolution: A History of Feminist Designs for American Homes, Neighborhoods, and Cities.* Cambridge, Mass.: M.I.T. Press, 1981.

Hewitt, Nancy. *Southern Discomfort: Women's Activism in Tampa, Florida, 1880s–1920s.* University of Illinois Press, 2001.

————. *Women's Activism and Social Change: Rochester, New York, 1820–1870.* Ithaca, N.Y.: Cornell University Press, 1984.

Higginbotham, Elizabeth. *Too Much to Ask For: Black Women in the Era of Integration.* Chapel Hill: University of North Carolina Press, 2001.

Hill, Mary A. *Charlotte Perkins Gilman: The Making of a Radical Feminist, 1860–1896.* Philadelphia: Temple University Press, 1979.

Hobson, Barbara Meil. *Uneasy Virtue: The Politics of Prostitution and the American Reform Tradition.* New York: Basic Books, 1987.

Hodes, Nancy. *White Women, Black Men: Illicit Sex in the Nineteenth-Century South.* New Haven, Conn.: Yale University Press, 1997.

Horowitz, Helen. *Rereading Sex: Battles over Sexual Knowledge and Suppression in Nineteenth Century America.* New York: Alfred A. Knopf, 2002.

Hune, Shirley, and Gail M. Nomura, eds. *Asian/Pacific Islander American Women: A Historical Anthology.* New York: New York University Press, 2003.

Hunter, Jane. *The Gospel of Gentility: American Women Missionaries in Turn-of-the-Century China.* New Haven, Conn.: Yale University Press, 1984.

————. *How Young Ladies Became Girls: The Victorian Origins of American Girlhood.* New Haven: Yale University Press, 2002.

Isenberg, Nancy. *Sex and Citizenship in Antebellum America.* Chapel Hill: University of North Carolina Press, 1998.

James, Janet Wilson, ed. *Women in American Religion.* Philadelphia: University of Pennsylvania Press, 1980.

Janiewski, Dolores. *Sisterhood Denied: Race, Gender, and Class in a New South Community.* Philadelphia: Temple University Press, 1985.

Jeffrey, Julie Roy. *Frontier Women: The Trans-Mississippi West.* New York: Hill and Wang, 1979.

Jensen, Joan M. *Calling This Place Home: Women on the Wisconsin Frontier, 1850–1925.* Minneapolis: Minnesota Historical Society Press, 2006.

————. *Loosening the Bonds: Mid-Atlantic Farm Women, 1750–1850.* New Haven, Conn.: Yale University Press, 1986.

————. *With These Hands: Women Working on the Land.* New York: Feminist Press, 1981.

———— and Lois Scharf, eds. *Decades of Discontent: The Women's Movement, 1920–1940.* Westport, Conn.: Greenwood, 1983.

———— and Sue Davidson, eds. *A Needle, A Bobbin, A Strike: Women Needle Workers in America.* Philadelphia: Temple University Press, 1984.

Jones, Jacquelyn. *Labor of Love, Labor of Sorrow: Black Women, Work, and the Family from Slavery to the Present*. New York: Vintage, 1985.

————. *Soldiers of Light and Love: Northern Teachers and Georgia Blacks, 1865–1873*. Chapel Hill: University of North Carolina Press, 1980.

Kaplan, Amy. *The Anarchy of Empire in the Making of U.S. Culture*. Cambridge: Harvard University Press, 2002.

Karlsen, Carol. *The Devil in the Shape of a Woman: Witchcraft in Colonial New England*. New York: W.W. Norton, 1987.

Katzman, David. *Seven Days a Week: Women and Domestic Service in Industrial America*. Urbana: University of Illinois Press, 1978.

Kerber, Linda. *No Constitutional Right to Be Ladies: Women and the Obligations of Citizenship*. New York: Hill and Wang, 1998.

————. *Women of the Republic: Intellect and Ideology in Revolutionary America*. Chapel Hill: University of North Carolina Press, 1980.

Kessler-Harris, Alice. *Out to Work: A History of Wage-Earning Women in the United States*. New York: Oxford University Press, 1982.

————. *In Pursuit of Equity: Women, Men, and the Quest for Economic Citizenship in 20th Century America*. Oxford University Press, 2001.

Kirkby, Diane. *Alice Henry: The Power of Pen and Voice: The Life of an Australian-American Labor Reformer*. Cambridge: Cambridge University Press, 1991.

Koehler, Lyle. *A Search for Power: The "Weaker Sex" in 17th Century New England*. Urbana: University of Illinois Press, 1980.

Kulikoff, Allan. *Tobacco and Slaves: The Development of Southern Cultures in the Chesapeake, 1680–1800*. Chapel Hill: University of North Carolina Press, 1986.

Kwolek-Folland, Angel. *Incorporating Women: A History of Women and Business in the United States*. New York: Twayne, 1998.

Larson, Rebecca. *Daughters of Light: Quaker Women Preaching and Prophesying in the Colonies and Abroad, 1700–1775*. Chapel Hill: University of North Carolina Press, 1999.

Laughlin, Kathleen A. *Women's Work and Public Policy: A History of the Women's Bureau, U.S. Department of Labor, 1945–1970*. Boston: Northeastern University Press, 2000.

Leach, William. *True Love and Perfect Union: The Feminist Reform of Sex and Society*. New York: Basic Books, 1980.

Leavitt, Judith W., ed. *Women and Health in America: Historical Readings*. Madison: University of Wisconsin Press, 1984.

Leavitt, Sarah A. *From Catharine Beecher to Martha Stewart: A Cultural History of Domestic Advice*. Chapel Hill: University of North Carolina Press, 2002.

Lebsock, Suzanne. *The Free Women of Petersburg: Status and Culture in a Southern Town, 1784–1860*. New York: W.W. Norton, 1984.

Lemons, J. Stanley. *The Woman Citizen: Social Feminism in the 1920s*. Urbana: University of Illinois Press, 1975.

Leonard, Elizabeth D. *Yankee Women: Gender Battles in the Civil War*. New York: W.W. Norton, 1994.

Lerner, Gerda. *The Creation of Patriarchy*. New York: Oxford University Press, 1986.

————. *The Grimké Sisters from South Carolina*. New York: Schocken, 1967.

Love, Barbara J., ed. *Feminists Who Changed America, 1963–1975*. Urbana: University of Illinois Press, 2006.

Matthews, Jean V. *The Rise of the New Woman: The Women's Movement in America, 1875–1930*. Chicago: Ivan R. Dee, 2003.

May, Elaine Tyler. *Great Expectations: Marriage and Divorce in Post-Victorian America*. Chicago: University of Chicago Press, 1980.

McCurry, Stephanie. *Masters of Small Worlds: Yeoman Households, Gender Relations, and the Political Culture of the Antebellum South Carolina Low Country*. New York: Oxford University Press, 1997.

McFadden, Margaret H. *Golden Cables of Sympathy: The Transatlantic Sources of Nineteenth-Century Feminism*. Lexington: University Press of Kentucky, 1999.

McGirr, Lisa. *Suburban Warriors: The Origins of the New American Right*. Princeton, N.J.: Princeton University Press, 2001.

MacLean, Nancy. *Freedom is Not Enough: The Opening of the American Workplace*. New York: Russell Sage, 2006

Mead, Rebecca J. *How the Vote Was Won: Woman Suffrage in the Western United States, 1868–1914*. New York: New York University Press, 2004.

Melder, Keith. *Beginnings of Sisterhood: The American Woman's Rights Movement, 1800–1850*. New York: Schocken, 1977.

Melosh, Barbara. *The Physician's Hand: Work Culture and Conflict in American Nursing*. Philadelphia: Temple University Press, 1982.

Meyerowitz, Joanne. *How Sex Changed: A History of Transsexuality in the United States*. Cambridge: Harvard University Press, 2002.

————. *Women Adrift: Industrial Wage Earners in Chicago, 1880–1930*. Chicago: University of Chicago Press, 1988.

Michel, Sonya. *Children's Interests/Mothers' Rights: The Shaping of America's Child Care Policy*. New Haven, Conn.: Yale University Press, 1999.

Milkman, Ruth, ed. *Women, Work and Protest: A Century of United States Women's Labor Activism*. Boston: Routledge and Kegan Paul, 1985.

————. *Gender at Work: The Dynamics of Job Segregation by Sex During World War II.* Urbana: University of Illinois Press, 1987.

Mohr, James. *Abortion in America: The Origins and Evolution of National Policy, 1800–1900.* New York: Oxford University Press, 1979.

Morantz-Sanchez, Regina. *Sympathy and Science: Women Physicians in American Medicine.* New York: Oxford University Press, 1985.

Morgan, Francesca. *Women and Patriotism in Jim Crow America.* Chapel Hill: University of North Carolina Press, 2005.

Morgan, Jennifer I. *Laboring Women: Reproduction and Gender in New World Slavery.* Philadelphia: University of Pennsylvania Press, 2004.

Morgen, Sandra. *Into Our Own Hands: The Women's Health Movement in the United States, 1969–1990.* New Brunswick, N.J.: Rutgers University Press, 2002.

Murray, Sylvie. *The Progressive Housewife: Community Activism in Suburban Queens, 1945–1965.* Philadelphia: University of Pennsylvania Press, 2003.

Nelson, Jennifer. *Women of Color and the Reproductive Rights Movement.* New York: New York University Press, 2003.

Nielsen, Kim E. *Un-American Womanhood: Antiradicalism, Antifeminism, and the First Red Scare.* Columbus: Ohio State University Press, 2001.

Norton, Mary Beth. *Founding Mothers and Fathers: Gendered Power and the Forming of American Society.* New York: Knopf, 1996.

————. *In the Devil's Snare: The Salem Witchcraft Crisis of 1692.* New York: Alfred Knopf, 2002.

————. *Liberty's Daughters: The Revolutionary Experience of American Women, 1750–1800.* Boston: Little, Brown, 1980.

Opdycke, Sandra. *The Routledge Historical Atlas of Women in America.* New York: Routledge, 2000.

O'Reilly, Jean, and Susan K. Cahn, eds. *Women and Sports in the United States: A Documentary Reader.* Boston: Northeastern University Press, 2007.

Orleck, Annelise. *Common Sense and a Little Fire: Women and Working-Class Politics in the United States, 1900–1965.* Chapel Hill: University of North Carolina Press, 1995.

————. *Storming Caesars Palace: How Black Mothers Fought Their Own War on Poverty.* Boston: Beacon Press, 2005.

Paton-Walsh, Margaret. *Our War Too: American Women Against the Axis.* Lawrence: University of Kansas Press, 2002.

Peiss, Kathy. *Cheap Amusements: Working Women and Leisure in Turn-of-the-Century New York.* Philadelphia: Temple University Press, 1986.

————. *Hope in a Jar: The Making of America's Beauty Culture.* New York: Henry Holt, 1998.

Plane, Ann Marie. *Colonial Intimacies: Indian Marriage in Early New England.* Ithaca, N.Y.: Cornell University Press, 2000.

Ransby, Barbara. *Ella Baker & the Black Freedom Movement: A Radical Democratic Vision.* Chapel Hill: University of North Carolina Press, 2003.

Reger, Jo. *Different Wavelengths: Studies of the Contemporary Women's Movement.* New York: Routledge, 2005.

Riley, Glenda Gates. *Women and Indians on the Frontier, 1825–1915.* Albuquerque: University of New Mexico Press, 1984.

Ritter, Gretchen. *The Constitution as Social Design: Gender and Civic Membership in the American Constitutional Order.* Stanford: Stanford University Press, 2006.

Robertson, Stacey M. *Parker Pillsbury: Radical Abolitionist, Male Feminist.* Ithaca, N.Y.: Cornell University Press, 2000.

Rosen, Robyn L. *Reproductive Health, Reproductive Rights: Reformers and the Politics of Maternal Welfare, 1917–1940.* Columbus: Ohio State University Press, 2003.

Rosen, Ruth. *The Lost Sisterhood: Prostitution in America, 1900–1918.* Baltimore: Johns Hopkins University Press, 1982.

————. *The World Split Open: How the Modern Women's Movement Changed America.* New York: Viking, 2000.

Rosenberg, Rosalind. *Beyond Separate Spheres: The Intellectual Roots of Modern Feminism.* New Haven, Conn.: Yale University Press, 1982.

Roth, Benita. *Separate Roads to Feminism: Black, Chicana, and White Feminist Movements in America's Second Wave.* Cambridge: Cambridge University Press, 2004.

Rouse, Jacqueline Anne. *Lugenia Burns Hope: Black Southern Reformer.* Athens: University of Georgia Press, 1989.

Ruiz, Vicki. *From Out of the Shadows: Mexican Women in Twentieth-Century America.* New York: Oxford University Press, 1998.

Rupp, Leila J. *A Desired Past: A Short History of Same-Sex Love In America.* Chicago: University of Chicago Press, 1999.

Ryan, Mary P. *Cradle of the Middle Class: The Family in Oneida County, New York, 1790–1865.* Cambridge: Cambridge University Press, 1981.

————. *Women in Public: Between Banners and Ballots, 1825–1880.* Baltimore: Johns Hopkins University Press, 1990.

Salerno, Beth. *Sister Societies: Women's Antislavery Organizations in Antebellum America.* DeKalb: Northern Illinois University Press, 2005.

Salmon, Marylynn. *Women and the Law of Property in Early America.* Chapel Hill: University of North Carolina Press, 1986.

Saxton, Martha. *Being Good: Women's Moral Values in Early America.* New York: Hill and Wang, 2003.

Scharf, Lois. *To Work and to Wed: Female Employment, Feminism, and the Great Depression.* Westport, Conn.: Greenwood Press, 1980.

Scharff, Virginia. *Twenty Thousand Roads: Women, Movement, and the West.* Berkeley: University of California Press, 2003.

Schechter, Patricia A. *Ida B. Wells-Barnett and American Reform, 1880–1930.* Chapel Hill: University of North Carolina Press, 2001.

Schlissel, Lillian. *Women's Diaries of the Westward Journey.* New York: Schocken, 1982.

Schneider, Elizabeth M. *Battered Women and Feminist Lawmaking.* New Haven: Yale University Press, 2000.

Schwalm, Leslie A. *A Hard Fight for We: Women's Transition from Slavery to Freedom in South Carolina.* Urbana: University of Illinois Press, 1997.

Scott, Anne Firor, and Andrew MacKay Scott. *One Half of the People: The Fight for Woman Suffrage.* Urbana: University of Illinois Press, 1982.

Scully, Pamela, and Diana Paton, eds. *Gender and Slave Emancipation in the Atlantic World.* Durham, N.C.: Duke University Press, 2006.

Seller, Maxine Schwartz. *Immigrant Women,* second ed. Philadelphia: Temple University Press, 1994; originally published in 1981.

Shammas, Carole. "Black Women's Work and the Evolution of Plantation Society in Virginia." *Labor History* 26 (1985): 5–28.

Sims, Anastasia. *The Power of Femininity in the New South: Women's Organizations and Politics in North Carolina, 1880–1930.* Columbia: University of South Carolina Press, 1997.

Sizer, Lyde Cullen. *The Political Work of Northern Women Writers and the Civil War, 1850–1872.* Chapel Hill: University of North Carolina Press, 2000.

Sklar, Kathryn Kish. *Catharine Beecher: A Study in American Domesticity.* New York: W.W. Norton, 1973.

————. *Florence Kelley and the Nation's Work: The Rise of Women's Political Culture, 1830–1900.* New Haven, Conn.: Yale University Press, 1995.

————. "The Historical Foundations of Women's Power in the Creation of the American Welfare State, 1830–1930." in *Mothers of a New World: Maternalist Politics and the Origins of Welfare States.* Edited by Seth Koven and Sonya Michel, 43–93. New York: Routledge, 1993.

————. *Women's Rights Emerges within the Antislavery Movement, 1830–1870.* Boston: Bedford Books, 2000.

————, Anja Schüler, and Susan Strasser. *Social Justice Feminists in the United States and Germany: A Dialogue in Documents, 1885–1933.* Ithaca, N.Y.: Cornell University Press, 1998.

Sleeper-Smith, Susan. *Indian Women and French Men: Rethinking Cultural Encounter in the Western Great Lakes.* Amherst: University of Massachusetts Press, 2001.

Smith, Daniel Scott. "Family Limitation, Sexual Control, and Domestic Feminism in Victorian America." *Feminist Studies* 1 (Winter–Spring 1973): 40–57.

Smith-Rosenberg, Carroll. "The Female World of Love and Ritual: Relations Between Women in Nineteenth-Century America." *Signs* 1 (1975): 1–29.

Solinger, Rickie. *Pregnancy and Power: A Short History of Reproductive Politics in America.* New York: New York University Press, 2005.

Solomon, Barbara Miller. *In the Company of Educated Women: A History of Women and Higher Education in America.* New Haven, Conn.: Yale University Press, 1985.

Spruill, Julia Cherry. *Women's Life and Work in the Southern Colonies.* New York: W.W. Norton, 1983; originally published in 1938.

Stanley, Amy Dru. *From Bondage to Contract: Wage Labor, Marriage, and the Market in the Age of Slave Emancipation.* New York: Cambridge University Press, 1998.

Stansell, Christine. *City of Women: Sex and Class in New York, 1789–1860.* New York: Knopf, 1986.

Sterling, Dorothy, ed. *We Are Your Sisters: Black Women in the 19th Century.* New York: W.W. Norton, 1984.

Stevenson, Brenda E. *Life in Black and White: Family and Community in the Slave South.* New York: Oxford University Press, 1996.

Storrs, Landon R. Y. *Civilizing Capitalism: The National Consumers' League, Women's Activism, and Labor Standards in the New Deal Era.* Chapel Hill: University of North Carolina Press, 2000.

Strasser, Susan. *Never Done: A History of American Housework.* New York: Pantheon Books, 1982.

Tate, Gayle. *Unknown Tongues: Black Women's Political Activism in the Antebellum Era, 1830–1860.* East Lansing: Michigan State University Press, 2003.

Taylor, Ula. *The Veiled Garvey: The Life & Times of Amy Jacques Garvey.* Chapel Hill: University of North Carolina Press, 2002.

Tentler, Leslie Woodcock. *Catholics and Contraception: An American History.* Ithaca, N.Y.: Cornell University Press, 2004.

Terborg-Penn, Rosalyn. *African American Women in the Struggle for the Vote, 1850–1920.* Bloomington: Indiana University Press, 1998.

Turk, Diana B. *Bound by a Mighty Vow: Sisterhood and Women's Fraternities, 1870–1920.* New York: New York University Press, 2004.

Ulrich, Laurel Thatcher. *Good Wives: Image and Reality in the Lives of Women in Northern New England, 1650–1750.* New York: Oxford University Press, 1982.

———. *A Midwife's Tale: The Life of Martha Ballard, Based on Her Diary, 1785–1812.* New York: Knopf, 1990.

Ware, Susan. *Beyond Suffrage: Women in the New Deal.* Cambridge, Mass.: Harvard University Press, 1981.

———. *Partner and I: Molly Dewson, Feminism, and New Deal Politics.* New Haven, Conn.: Yale University Press, 1987.

Weigand, Kate. *Red Feminism: American Communism and the Making of Women's Liberation.* Baltimore: Johns Hopins University Press, 2000.

Weiner, Lynn. *From Working Girl to Working Mother: The Female Labor Force in the United States, 1820–1980.* Chapel Hill: University of North Carolina Press, 1985.

Wellman, Judith. *The Road to Seneca Falls: Elizabeth Cady Stanton and the First Woman's Rights Convention.* Urbana: University of Illinois Press, 2004.

Wheeler, Marjoire Spruill, ed. *Votes for Women!: The Woman Suffrage Movement in Tennessee, the South, and the Nation.* Knoxville: University of Tennessee Press, 1995.

White, Deborah Gray. *Ar'n't I a Woman?: Female Slaves in the Plantation South.* New York: W.W. Norton, 1985.

———. *Too Heavy a Load: Black Women in Defense of Themselves, 1894–1994.* New York: W.W. Norton, 1999.

Winship, Michael P. *The Times and Trials of Anne Hutchinson: Puritans Divided.* Lawrence: University of Kansas Press, 2005.

Yasutake, Rumi. *Transnational Women's Activism: The United States, Japan, and Japanese Immigrant Communities in California, 1859–1920.* New York: New York University Press, 2004.

Yellin, Jean Fagan. *Harriet Jacobs: A Life.* New York: Basic Civitas Books, 2004.

Zeitz, Joshua. *Flapper: A Madcap Story of Sex, Style, Celebrity, and the Women Who Made America Modern.* New York: Crown Publishing Group, 2006.

PHOTO CREDITS